I0815800

← Aech Fish Trap of the Yapese, Yap.

Lo—TEK
/lō'tek/

A DESIGN MOVEMENT TO REBUILD AN UNDERSTANDING OF INDIGENOUS PHILOSOPHY AND VERNACULAR DESIGN THAT GENERATES SUSTAINABLE, CLIMATE-RESILIENT TECHNOLOGIES.

JULIA WATSON

Lo—TEK WATER

A Field Guide for TEKnology

FOREWORD
DR. LYLA JUNE JOHNSTON

TASCHEN

This book is dedicated to my children,
Ocean Sy and Cyprian Blue,
born on the island edge of the western Atlantic,
and to their next seven generations.

"When you are in your mother's womb, the whole history of your ancestors comes together there; your grandmother's womb, your great-grandmother's womb, and the wombs of all the generations are there. [...] In the cosmovision of some Indigenous peoples, the sea is the mother's amniotic fluid. So, when something affects the sea, it also affects the mother's womb. And despite all the damage that has been done to it, the sea still continues to produce food with much love. So we can say that energy is love, because the Earth is all love, the Sun is all love, planets, the stars, the Moon, [...] and everything that we have on Earth—placenta, oil, coal—is pure love, because they are bodies of Mother Earth. We Indigenous peoples have taken advantage of this, but in a harmonious way. The knowledge of our peoples allows us to have a relationship of coexistence with energy."

From the Guna-Dule People of Panama and Colombia, poised to become some of the Americas' first climate change refugees.

CONTENTS

3 FRESH

FRESH

TEKnology
/tek'näləjē/

TEKNOLOGY IS THE APPLICATION OF TRADITIONAL ECOLOGICAL KNOWLEDGE (TEK) TO DESIGN AND IMPLEMENT SOLUTIONS TO ENVIRONMENTAL, AGRICULTURAL, ARCHITECTURAL, AND SOCIAL CHALLENGES. IT EMBODIES PRACTICES, TOOLS, AND PRINCIPLES THAT ENABLE RESPECTFUL AND RECIPROCAL ENGAGEMENT WITH INDIGENOUS KNOWLEDGE SYSTEMS, HONORING THEIR UNDERLYING INTENTIONS, VALUES, AND ECOLOGICAL LOGIC. TEKNOLOGY SHIFTS SOCIETY FROM EXTRACTIVE APPROACHES TOWARD REGENERATIVE RELATIONSHIPS, CONNECTING PEOPLE TO BOTH PLACE AND PLANETARY SYSTEMS.[1]

[1] Nathalie Kelley Mallqui, Dr. Lyla June Johnston, Julia Watson, and Timo Granzotti coined the term *TEKnology*™ and formed a group called *The TEKnologists*™, discussing its principles during a conversation on January 24, 2025.

INTERCULTURALITY BY DR. LYLA JUNE JOHNSTON

As a half Diné—half European woman raised in what is now called the Southwest United States, I have seen the issue of colonization from different angles. As an Indigenous woman, I know the pain of having everything under your feet ransacked and your people nearly annihilated. As a settler European, I know the shame of carrying this colonial blood in my veins, the feeling of loss of identity, the disconnection from ancestral roots, and the yearning to be close to the earth again.

Depending on our positionality, we all have important roles to play in the healing of the fabric of the earth and of society. Indeed, we are all Indigenous to place(s), but we are not all Indigenous to the place we stand—an important distinction. My grandfather once told me that the way to maintain peace on earth is to follow the lead of the Indigenous peoples wherever you are. While his words can't be held in our hands like a hammer or a phone, they are still a kind of technology in their own right. They comprise a conceptual tool and device that procures functional human societies. He suggested that we always follow the lead of local people with institutional knowledge that spans millennia; those who have tried, failed, and thereby honed and passed on the science and the art of living in that specific place, for generations upon generations.

The colonial and implausible myth that a random and new incoming culture could somehow better live and thrive in foreign land can finally be declared dead. Investments in this myth over the centuries have only left the world more and more bankrupt, and in more ways than one. Even I, as an Indigenous woman with brown skin, brown eyes, and brown hair, must walk humbly around North and South America (hereafter referred to as Turtle Island[1] and Abya Yala[2]). As a desert woman, if I go to the Pacific Northwest, I must follow the lead of the Salmon Nations. If I go to the Plains, I must follow the lead of the Buffalo Nations. If I go to the west, I must follow the lead of the Acorn Nations. If I go to the east, I must follow the lead of the Chestnut Nations. Of the thousands of Native civilizations and languages that have roamed Turtle Island and Abya Yala, not all walked so picture perfectly. Indeed, we dabbled in warfare and hierarchy at times. But many, after feeling the burn of war, decided that peace was the way to go and adopted these peacekeeping measures, as my grandfather had.

Thus, descendants of settlers like me have an exciting opportunity to reverse the perverse and incompetent legacies of our forefathers by humbly standing behind the Indigenous peoples of whatever land we find ourselves on. I believe this is how an immigrant person can finally come to *belong* on a land not their own: through fierce, beautiful, and powerful solidarity with the local peoples—standing not beside them, nor in front of them, but squarely behind them. We come to belong by supporting a path they outline for their own liberation. We cannot come in saying "we know what you need" as missionaries, NGOs, and corporations have said in the past to local people. Indigenous Nations know what they need and it is our decision to follow that path, and provide ideas and resources only as requested.

I have seen this solidarity play out time and time again and it is breathtaking, as if the whole earth finally exhales and cries pent up tears as humanity rejoins itself in right relations. I have never seen this solidarity as a burden or a chore. Quite the contrary; I see it as a grand adventure. For what is more exciting than to spend our time being a loving balm on the injured heart of humanity, the injured heart of life? Isn't that all we could ever hope to be? And what more ripe opportunity to do that than to bravely acknowledge the past and commit ourselves to a better intercultural dynamic for the present and the future? It's not that we as newcomers "have" to be in solidarity with Indigenous Nations. Indeed, *we get* to be in solidarity with Indigenous Nations, fighting alongside them to pick up the pieces of unimaginable colonial destruction. What a joy and an honor to be a part of this team! I have always known that, even though we are children of war, we can choose to become people of peace. I can think of no more exciting and fulfilling task than this!

With that said, we are now about to ingest a lot of information about various Indigenous Nations and their technologies. These are not just physical technologies; they are also technologies of the heart and mind, with philosophical and moral codes that guide, underpin, and sustain our physical tools. I have come to believe that our most precious gifts to the world as Indigenous peoples are not physical things at all, but showing how the *intention* of a system is far more consequential than the system itself. I have seen how vitally important it is that we prime and prepare ourselves to receive this knowledge. The forefathers of colonial society (and many of their descendants today) saw everything as a business opportunity. They saw Native Nations using willow bark and turned it into marketable aspirin. They took our sacred and nourishing corn and transformed it into a death syrup cash crop. They took the syringes we invented to heal, and they now use them to inject medicines that keep them sick and dependent. They saw the oyster gardens we carefully stewarded for thousands of years, and dredged them for short-term profit; for example, Chesapeake Bay now has less than 1 percent of its original oyster population. They saw the ancient shell mounds of the Bundjalung Nation in Byron Bay, Australia and demolished them to make their roads. They saw the sacred Welsh oak groves and gobbled them up to build warplanes and warships. They took the gift of the acai berry and marketed it as a hip superfood with little return to the Native communities that brought this berry into being through generations of genetic selection and cultivation. They saw the rubber our ancestors used in precolonial times for waterproof containers, canoes, game balls, and shoes, and enslaved those same ancestors to tap all the rubber we use for the tires of motorcars. They took the physical treasures but they failed to retrieve the most important treasure of all: the moral code by which we relate to and interact with Creation. *Why* we build an oyster habitat is as equally important as *how* we build it. Is it for profit? Or is it in service to all life? Today, roughly 60 percent of the types of foods eaten across the world were gifts from Turtle Island and Abya Yala. But what percentage of these foods, birthed from reverent and biodiverse practices, are now monocropped for the bank accounts of Big Ag? Thus, it is the task of the world to break from this legacy of theft and appropriation of Indigenous intellectual property (IIP).

We must come in a new way. We must come in a good way. We must come as humble learners who seek to contribute more to Native Nations than we seek to receive. It is our choice now to comport ourselves as good relatives to others and to all life forms. It is our choice now to lay down this fear of scarcity, which drives our hoarding behavior, and take up the mantle of trust and faith—in ourselves, in others, and in the beautiful earth's ability to care for us all. We are in an exciting time where, instead of continuing this bitter legacy of capitalizing on Indigenous knowledge, we can make up for the past by relating to Indigenous Nations with reverence, respect, responsibility, and reciprocity.

We must not learn from these technologies just to run away with them and make a buck, as so many have done before. We must learn to use this knowledge in ways—and only in these ways—that local nations give us permission to use it. My Indigenous foremothers have stated that this knowledge is to be used, and only to be used, in the selfless service of Life. Moreover, this knowledge is here to remind us that the land is in good care when we allow Indigenous peoples to lead the way in their own countries and homelands. Yes, we can be inspired by these technologies and apply them to our personal worlds as much as possible. But we must also see this book as a rationale for restoring leadership and decision-making power to Indigenous peoples (and especially Indigenous women, as requested by Indigenous grassroots communities). As the UN has recently reported, Indigenous Nations, though they represent only 5 percent of the world's population, now oversee 80 percent of the world's biodiversity.

It is not our decision to be the "entrepreneur" of Indigenous knowledge, which in French literally means "the taker." It is our choice to step back into our true purpose and behave as "entredonneurs," or those who innovate more ways to give and contribute. If we are of settler society, either by choice or by force, how can we come to stand behind these champions of biodiverse cultivation? It is time now for the complete overhaul of colonial society in the name of planet earth and future generations. We have had a long run with hierarchy and domination as core values, and it isn't working. No one can ever again argue that capitalism is "efficient" and "useful" as it drives us to the precipice of global collapse. It has incentivized humanity into the insanity of destroying our own water sources, our own life sources, our own food sources. It has pushed our behavior toward and beyond cannibalism, as we not only sacrifice our fellow man but even eat our own Mother.

So before we peruse these pages, we must prime ourselves to ingest this knowledge with the goal of being in deep solidarity with Native Nations, and a concurrent quest to understand our own personal Indigenous roots wherever those may be. In other words, it is not enough to be inspired by this book. We must concurrently fight in tangible ways for the liberation of the very communities who lend this inspiration. Indeed, it is vital that we integrate these values and strategies into global society as soon as possible. These gifts are what our elders have been trying to share with the world for centuries. But the knowledge in these pages should never be re-created at the expense, extraction, or continued suppression of Indigenous peoples.

The improvement of Native Nations must be in lockstep with that of colonial society. For every acre we apply these ideas to the landholdings of colonial culture, four acres must concurrently be returned to those who have been violently dispossessed (a process also known as "Land Back"). For every dollar that these strategies provide to a colonial business, four dollars must be returned to those Indigenous civilizations who are fighting for their lives in the wake of brutal colonization. For too long my mother's people have lived in the chains of poverty, wrought by resource extraction that fuels the miserable and unsustainable colonial world. For too long my mother's people have lived in the shadows of the monuments that glorify those who attempted our genocide. For too long my mother's people have been eclipsed from history books and lived invisible in their own homelands. My mother's people eat, sleep, and breathe our own oppression in what is now called the United States and enough is enough. We need the world to understand the urgency of living rightly in relationship with the same Native Nations positioned in this book to rescue us from failing systems.

Therefore, I exuberantly invite you to join myself, Julia, and all the coauthors of this beautiful book on a journey of intercultural healing. I excitedly beckon you all onto a path—paved by forgiveness, love, accountability, unity, and creativity—that will lead us to a place of beauty, equality, dignity for our descendants, and the deep joy of building a righteous, pluralistic, functioning society. As the clam gardeners of the Pacific Northwest have taught us—the same nations who augment the clam habitat with the careful positioning of intertidal rock walls—just one small adjustment can trigger waves of positive cascading effects that ripple outward to feed all life. Imagine what could happen if we make many of these small adjustments: moving from hoarding to giving, numbness to feeling, begrudging to forgiving, dividing to uniting, shame to responsibility and action, self-hate to self-celebration, leeching to keystone species-ing, fear to faith, apathy to warriorhood, and mediocrity to excellence.

Imagine if we began to see all life as our equal, not as our "resource." Imagine if we remembered that our cognitive gifts are not some divinely ordained license to dominate all life, but are a divinely endowed responsibility to care for all life. Indeed, parents do not have greater power than their children because they are there to enslave them. On the contrary, that power endows them with the ability to care for them. So, too, are our God-given gifts of opposable thumbs and prefrontal cortexes not some divine license to dominate other life forms. They are signs of our divine responsibility to care for other life forms and for each other. In the Yoruba language of West Africa, the word for human being translates as "chosen one"—not because we are chosen by the Almighty to dominate the earth, but because we are designated by the Almighty to steward the earth. This is our role. This is our calling. This is our purpose. Indeed, this is our design.

And so, before I conclude, I want to share one more message from my heart and it is this:

On my doctoral journey, I studied many Indigenous Regenerative Ecosystem Designs (IREDs). I devoured hundreds of scientific articles that detailed the scale and function of these breathtaking anthropogenic landscapes. I was left awestruck by the magnitude and ingenuity of these ancient systems time and time again. I found that they are all thousands of years old. I found that they support perennial and predictable food supplies that outpace commercial food system production by a landslide. I saw how these human hands can paint exquisite worlds in deep and reverent collaboration with the forces of nature. I saw how we have coauthored stories with Mother Earth so beautiful that they would restore even the staunchest cynic's faith in the goodness and beauty of humanity. But about three years into my doctoral research, and after thoroughly pouring over the literature, becoming obsessed with the size, age, materials, and species makeup of these systems, I realized that by only focusing on what I could outwardly measure, I was missing the whole point.

I realized that the invisible value systems that underlie those human creations are far more important than their visible manifestations. When you look at the 3,500-year-old clam gardens of the Kwakwaka'wakw Nation in the Pacific Northwest, what you will see are kilometers and kilometers of ancient rock walls, but what you won't see are the songs that were sung as the people built these walls, which speak of the importance of being in service to the earth. What you will see are dozens of different clam species supported by this system, but what you won't see is how Kwakwaka'wakw elders teach their children that these clams have a "nation" of their own, and we must honor their dignity on a nation-to-nation basis. We don't see the worldview that Kwakwaka'wakw Peoples hold that all life is equal to us. What you can empirically measure is the warmer pools of water that these intertidal rock walls contain and create, which ingeniously augment the conditions clams need to thrive; what is harder to measure is the self-image this community has as guardians, protectors, and stewards of a living earth.

These intangible worlds of our hearts and minds constitute what I call the software of the human being, which drives the hardware of the human body. These invisible inner dimensions of IRED systems are the real magic that we as objectifying and quantifying scientists often fail to recognize, comprehend, and appreciate. Our material-focused culture often fails to see that the real treasure of the world cannot be held in our hands, but is held in our hearts and known in the microscopic synapses of our minds. The heart of IRED technology, then, is not how these systems are made and with what materials—rather, it is the ancient, "soft" technology of reverence, respect, reciprocity, and responsibility for and to all our relations as our equals. This deep and, I dare say, sacred outlook on the world and on ourselves is what will truly save humanity—not some set of best practices, a new material, or some strategy. Until we again take up our honor and our responsibility as warriors, who nourish and protect the sacredness of the earth, we will not enjoy the sheer abundance that IRED systems have afforded many human societies.

On the other hand, one could argue that the "software" of capitalist culture is based on human centrism, profit maximization, self aggrandizement, patriarchy, and system output without regard for system sustainability. For example, you could give the very same clam garden technology to a capitalist culture, and I can guarantee it would not last 3,500 years. It would have a brief but profitable lifespan that benefits a few, until the system collapses and even those few profiteers and their families are eventually left bankrupt. If we make these systems to maximize profits, establish dominance, entrench hierarchy, and build our reputation, then it doesn't matter how good our design is, we will keep running into the same walls, and collapse beneath the weight of our hubris.

Conversely, so long as the *intention* of our system is to maximize generosity, support and nourish life, give more than we receive, and live as stewards of sacred life, then our design will naturally fall into place in a successful and beautiful way. It can be likened to the difference between a vacuum cleaner and a warm wood stove: One sucks up anything in its path, and one radiates nourishing warmth all around it. Until we step back into that mode of positive outflow and giving, rather than the mode of grasping extraction, we will not be happy or create holistic environments. Ironically, we must be givers, not takers, to truly experience the wealth and abundance IRED has to offer.

This is all to say that what is more important than how we design the shoreline is *why* we step to the shoreline in the first place. These IRED nations go to the shoreline because they want to feed all life around them and serve species outside of their own. Like St. Francis of Assisi, who achieved his sainthood through his service to plants and animals, we, too, are spiritually and morally elevated when we bend down to care for the life of clams and otters, minks and waterbirds, and when we take all the power vested in our humanhood, and place it in service of the world around us. We will finally become "civilized" when we adopt that "nation-to-nation" protocol and cease trespassing on their rights as sacred beings—recognizing they are equal to us. This is the worldview, the invisible software, that drives the hardware of the clam garden system.

For my mother's people, the Diné, we noticed that all life on earth owes its existence to the love story between Father Sky and Mother Earth. We saw how the sun and the rain of the sky impregnates the soul and the soil of the earth and gives birth to all life. We saw how we all share the same father, and the same mother, and therefore we are all siblings on this planet. When we love and serve other creatures and children of Father Sky and Mother Earth, we merge with the love they have for all creation and we become closer to this love. This illustration of my people may sound romanticized, but one look into the everyday language and creation stories of Diné People will illuminate that I am not exaggerating at all. Our world is a place of kinship and love with creation. When we view ourselves not as reapers of natural bounty, but as warriors in service to others, we step more deeply into our true nature and our true purpose, as countless Indigenous societies have modeled and continue to model today.

On my doctoral journey I learned that we must focus on and reprogram our software if we ever hope to once again manifest these sustainable societies. We could have all the answers and all the technologies in the world but we will still end up in the same place, until we debug this corrupted colonial software of its program of fear. Conversely, if we simply restore our societies to operate on the software of reverence, respect, reciprocity, and responsibility, these rudders would naturally steer the human ship toward sustainability and calmer waters. This is because the software—the inner values and intentions of a society—define what our goals as a society are. Our goals then dictate what our strategies are to achieve them. These strategies then become our daily practices. Our daily practices then shape the world around us. If our value is profit maximization, then our goal as a society will be to get as much as we can as fast as we can from the earth. If our value is reverence, then our goal will be to create wealth for *all* nations, human and more-than-human. It all begins with the values and intentions, reflecting what we, as a community, deem important. Until that value switches from taking to giving, capitalizing to serving, fear to trust, we will not fundamentally change anything, nor will we find ourselves in a better situation. We see this in the world of carbon credits, where we are trying to apply capitalistic values to the climate problem. Instead of creating a more sustainable world, we are simply monetizing life, and creating a mosaic of sacrifice zones and areas of privilege. The system is thus reentrenched and not transformed anywhere close to the degree its architects had promised.

On Quadra Island, British Columbia, 35 percent of the coastline has become clam habitat because of their ancestors, and they do this to feed not only themselves but the otters, minks, and waterbirds that come to enjoy this abundance. They build these walls in the spirit of love for all life. At the risk of sounding unscientific, I do believe this love is the secret sauce, the key to success, of IRED systems. Love is the software we must reinstall into all our societies to get the hardware up and running smoothly again. We can get so caught up in the outward manifestation of IRED systems that we forget that the invisible and internal engine of the human heart is what makes it all tick. In other words, the size, age, species makeup, and materials used to make these Lo—TEK systems, are not as important as the love these architects have for their Mother Earth and the life forms they share their home with. Indeed, the beautiful physical manifestations of IRED systems in this book are made possible by the intangible world of human thought, which drives the nature of human deed.

Like air, sometimes the unseen gives breath and life to what is seen. As an invisible substance, air is hard to measure, hold, and feel, yet the very existence of terrestrial biota depends upon it. The physical worlds we create can similarly depend profoundly on the invisible winds of our beliefs, morals, principles, creation stories, and their meanings. Though unable to be held or easily measured, they are the powerful drivers of the physical worlds we create. For example, if Kwakwaka'wakw People believe that something as small as a clam is equal to them, and is deserving of dignity and respect, then their human-made clam gardens will be designed to benefit both humans and clams equally. They will be designed in gratitude for these small beings that in part give life to human nations. In this way our stories drive our behavior, which in turn powerfully sculpts the world around us. This is why the work of the artist and the philosopher is so important; they garden the realm of the mind, which in turn creates our built environments. I believe that when a society can see something as small and different as a clam, and deem them as our equal, we will finally be civilized again. Until then, we will stew in the mediocrity, immaturity, and boredom of anthropocentrism and human supremacism.

The invisible roots of a tree nourish the trunk, branches, and leaves we see above ground. Similarly, our symbols, stories, and their underlying value systems are the unseen, underground cultural roots that anchor and sustain the visible, physical worlds around us. The intangible languages, songs, priorities, and worldviews of Indigenous Nations are blueprints and compasses for how to live and create. Generally speaking, they were refined over time through trial and error, to teach us how to honor and protect the sacred. Based on this large collection of millennial-scale food systems, this angle on life has proven successful. Grounded in the truth of the sacredness of the earth, and how she is deserving of our respect and care, many Indigenous Nations became prosperous both physically and spiritually.

My final message is to take note of the intangible worldviews that sustain, shape, and drive the outward manifestation of Indigenous food and land management systems. Let us dedicate ourselves first and foremost to the invisible, and garden the inner landscape of our heart, so that we can become better landscapers of the world around us. We have the power to transform this world from a place of despair to a place of abundance by loving ourselves, each other, and this beautiful Mother Earth.

ENDNOTES

1. Turtle Island is an Indigenous term for North America and comes from a creation narrative shared by the Haudenosaunee, Anishinaabeg, and other Indigenous Nations. This story honors women, honors the smallest animals, and depicts humans and animals working together symbiotically. The word "America" comes from a historical figure—Amerigo Vespucci—a European explorer commissioned to look for people to enslave and gold to extract. I and many others do not feel it is appropriate to name these lands for a man whose life was dedicated to and symbolized atrocity and avarice.
2. Abya Yala is an Indigenous term for Central and South America. It comes from the Dule People of Panama and Colombia and means "land in its full maturity." This has come to be a more accepted term in Native communities for the same reasons Turtle Island has become more frequently used.

PREFACE

THE DAY THE WATER DIED

One of the most vivid memories from my childhood was sitting glued to the television, watching the horrifying events of the first televised oceanic environmental disaster. On an early spring morning in 1989, a supertanker ran aground in Alaska's Prince William Sound, tearing the ship's hull and spilling over 10 million gallons of crude oil into a pristine marine ecosystem.[1] The aftermath was devastating—two thousand kilometers of coastline covered in thick tar, marine life found suffocating or poisoned, and oil-slicked seabirds washed with dish soap to desperately decontaminate their sick, feathered bodies. Yet, as the world watched the Exxon Valdez oil spill, mourning the loss of hundreds of thousands of animals, one fact remained unreported—the water itself had died.[2]

Indigenous Alaskan communities, who had cared for these waters for millennia, understood this loss in ways that the world that was watching along did not. Chief Walter Meganack of Port Graham's Unangax̂ village, when explaining what had happened, said simply: "Oil in the water, lots of oil killing lots of water. Never in the millennium of our tradition have we thought it possible for the water to die, but it's true."[3]

That memory shaped my understanding of water—not as a commodity, or merely as a resource, but as something alive, endowed with memory, an entity that Indigenous peoples have long recognized as kin.[4]

Today, the warning that the Exxon Valdez sounded has only grown louder. Across the globe, we regularly witness mass marine life die-offs, sometimes in the hundreds of thousands, as waterborne animals flee unseen subsurface threats. The waters of our oceans, rivers, and lakes are dying en masse, carrying the cumulative weight of pollution, warming, and acidification. Yet the lesson that Indigenous communities have long taught—and that guides Lo—TEK Water—remains vital: water is not a resource to be extracted or managed, but a living relative, a system of memory, intelligence, and reciprocity. To understand water in this way is to recognize our role within its flows, and to design, steward, and act in ways that revive its lifeforce and nurture the life it sustains.

A JOURNEY TOWARD LO—TEK

Years later, as a young architecture student in Australia, I enrolled in a course called Aboriginal Environments, led by Dr. Paul Memmott. It was in that classroom that I experienced an unlearning—of colonial geographies, histories, and systems that I'd been convinced were the objective truth. I discovered a different

1

2

1 Exxon Valdez cleanup workers skimmed oil from the water's surface, sprayed oil-dispersant chemicals in the water and onshore, washed oiled beaches with hot water, and rescued and cleaned animals trapped in oil.
2 During rescue efforts, birds and other animals covered in oil were stabilized and washed in Dove dish soap, to remove the toxic pollutant.

way of viewing the world—*Etuaptmumk* or Two-Eyed Seeing—combining Western science and Indigenous knowledge systems that had shaped landscapes and sustained settlements in harmony with their environments for millennia to obtain a holistic understanding that I previously couldn't conceive.[5] That semester rewired my thinking, offered me a holistic understanding of the world that I previously couldn't conceive, and ultimately led me to compose the *Lo—TEK* series.

Lo—TEK is more than a compendium of Indigenous technologies—it is a manifesto, a framework, and a call to action. It challenges the dominant narratives of technological progress, which have so often dismissed the generational intelligence embedded in local, nature-based solutions. With this book series, I hope to offer readers the same revelation I had in that classroom—to shift their perspectives, to recalibrate their understanding of what constitutes innovation, and to recognize that some of the most state-of-the-art water technologies are not industrial but ancestral.

WHY A FIELD GUIDE?

With some of the most imminent threats to civilization arising from water—rising seas, droughts, floods—this volume expands *Lo—TEK*'s mission by documenting water-based ancestral TEKnologies.[6] These are systems designed for aquaculture, agriculture, and habitation—rooted in principles of adaptation, resilience, and reciprocity.

But this book is not just historical nonfiction. It is a tool kit for the future. By cataloging both ancestral and contemporary water-based TEKnologies, this guide aims to equip architects, engineers, planners, and innovators with practical knowledge and guiding principles to reintegrate these solutions into the systems of today. This field guide is written for anyone who wants to transition from extractive to regenerative practices, connecting with people, place and planet through TEKnology.[7]

ENDNOTES

1. Duane A. Gill and Steven J. Picou, "The Day the Water Died: The Exxon Valdez Disaster and Indigenous Culture," in *American Disasters*, ed. Steven Biel (New York: New York University Press, 2001), 277.
2. Gill and Picou, "The Day the Water Died," 278.
3. Gill and Picou, "The Day the Water Died," 277.
4. Oren Lyons, "Fall 2005 Commencement Address" (speech, UC Berkeley College of Natural Resources, Berkeley, CA, December 2005).
5. Cheryl Bartlett, Murdena Marshall, and Albert Marshall, "Two-Eyed Seeing and Other Lessons Learned within a Co-Learning Journey of Bringing Together Indigenous and Mainstream Knowledges and Ways of Knowing," *Journal of Environmental Studies and Sciences 2, no. 4* (2012): 331–340.
6. Dr. Lyla June Johnston coined the term *TEKnology*™ in an essay draft, which I coauthored, for the *Venice Architecture Biennale 2025 Catalogue*, on January 21, 2025.
7. Nathalie Kelley Mallqui, Dr. Lyla June Johnston, Julia Watson, and Timo Granzotti coined the term *TEKnology*™ and formed a group called *The TEKnologists*™, discussing its principles during a conversation on January 24, 2025.

INTRODUCTION

WATER REMEMBERS WHAT HUMANS FORGET

"How inappropriate to call this planet Earth, when it is quite clearly Ocean."
Arthur Clarke, science-fiction writer and futurist

In many traditions, water is kin.[1] The Guna-Dule people of Panama and Colombia, whose ancestral lands are now threatened by rising seas, speak of the ocean as the mother's amniotic fluid, carrying the essence of previous generations. When the sea is harmed, they say, it is as if the womb itself is wounded.[2] This teaching is not merely metaphorical—it is a profound acknowledgment of interconnection, a worldview that understands water as an extension of life itself.

Western scientists and Indigenous knowledge keepers agree that water is where life began. Over eons of earthly rotations, the water submerging the earth's surface was the medium for creation. In an emergent symphony of survival, it orchestrated the exchange of energies that connected the elements, species, and systems that sustain life to this day. Water has memory, having shaped the history of life on earth, sculpted landscapes, and sustained civilizations, and having bound human survival to the natural world.[3] Indigenous cultures have long recognized water as a sentient entity—one that instructs, warns, and remembers.[4]

Western urbanism and industrialization have fractured this amniotic ancestry. Where once cities like Tenochtitlán were built to flow with water woven into the fabric of urban life, modern metropolises treat it as an obstacle. Can a city learn to live again by remembering how to work with water? The thriving Aztec capital, built in harmony with its lake system, was supported by a vast aquatic agricultural system of *chinampas* that produced food, filtered water, and supported biodiversity. The rivers that fed the ancient lake civilization—now buried beneath asphalt, diverted into concrete canals, or polluted beyond recognition—are dead. Today's Mexico City, which was built by colonial conquistadors atop the drained ruins of Tenochtitlán, is sinking.[5] By ignoring the fundamental principles of water's movement and memory, what was once a blueprint for coexistence has almost been erased. In the words of one Indigenous leader, the waterways that run through modern cities are characterized as "places of death that smell bad, full of primitive people who defecate in clean water."[6] The sacredness of water has been forgotten. Yet water endures—both a keeper of memory and an untamed force, holding the knowledge forgotten while remaining one of the greatest existential threats.

For millennia, Indigenous cultures have understood water not as a passive element, but as a living intelligence, communicating through its cycles, currents, and rhythms. Water signals through patterns—rising daily with the tides, filling monthly with the moon's orbit, flooding seasonally to nourish the land, retreating in drought, and, when ignored, reclaiming lost relationships. Reading these patterns requires deep observation, a practice cultivated over generations.

As Tyson Yunkaporta of the Apalech clan explains, Indigenous knowledge functions as a vast, interconnected web—a system of verification built on generations of observation and exchange.[7] Unlike Western science, which often isolates phenomena into discrete categories, Indigenous ways of knowing recognize the interwoven relationships between water, land, and life. The rivers that feed forests, the wetlands that cleanse and replenish seas, the floodwaters that regenerate soils—each is part of a continuous dialogue informed by millions of conversations over thousands of generations between ecosystems and entities.

ENTITY
A thing with distinct and independent existence.

Yet, as urbanism and industrialization accelerate, this dialogue is being silenced. Where Indigenous communities hear the warnings carried by water—rivers running dry, aquifers collapsing, ancestral fisheries disappearing—Western science counts the losses in data points and extinction rates. But when water dies, it does not die alone. It takes entire worlds with it.

The intelligence of water has always been there, embedded in landscapes, encoded in the knowledge systems of those who listen. The question is whether humanity will revive its relationship with water in time to adapt, or continue designing while denying a millennia of shared memory.

THE CRISIS OF WATER WITHOUT WISDOM

Across time and territories, civilizations have risen and fallen based on their relationship with water, and today we find ourselves in an era where water crises shape the human condition. Rising sea levels endanger entire nations, and droughts devastate food systems, forcing mass migrations. Aging urban infrastructures designed for conditions that no longer exist are increasingly overwhelmed by floodwaters, while pollution transforms rivers into toxic runways, destroying ecosystems and contaminating vital sources of drinking water.

More than 50 years after Syukuro Manabe and Richard T. Wetherald developed the first accurate climate model, their warnings remain ignored.[8] We now witness their predictions materializing—atmospheric warming, ice sheets melting, weather patterns destabilizing, and entire communities displaced by water's increasing force. Yet Western science is still grappling with what Indigenous cultures have long understood—the fate of humanity is inseparable from the fate of water.

But climate scientists were not the first to sound the alarm. Long before the modern climate crisis, ancestral knowledge keepers watched the waters and foretold the consequences of imbalance. In many Indigenous traditions, water is a messenger, revealing the health of the world through its rhythms and cycles. The Hopi prophecies speak of the Fifth World, a time when rivers and lakes would turn against humanity, signaling the end of abundance and the arrival of great upheaval.[9] For the Anishinaabe, who honor water as the lifeblood of Mother Earth, the Seventh Fire Prophecy speaks of a time when humanity stands at a crossroads, faced with a choice—one path leading to renewal and the other to destruction.[10] The Yup'ik people of Alaska, skilled in reading the subtlest shifts in seawater, ice, and currents, warned generations ago: "When the world changes, the weather will change along with the people."[11] Water, they understood, is the first to respond—a warning when the balance is lost.

As these prophecies remind us, water is reflective—it mirrors the choices humanity makes. The floods, droughts, and poisoned rivers are not random events but consequences of a lost coexistence. We can regenerate that relationship, guided by the wisdom of those who have always listened, or remain ignorant to water's warnings while surrounded by surmounting ruin.

As the broker of tensions between the atmosphere and the earth's ecosystems, water still carries the memories of a time when it enveloped the earth. It shaped the histories of vanished civilizations and holds the plans for future survival. When it rises onto the land, it does not come to ruin but to remind us that we're distracted from our role as its custodians. As the bearer of life, water too wants to live, but, just like us, water too can die.

While governments and industries debate how to control water, Indigenous and traditional communities have spent millennia understanding how to live with it. The technologies they have perfected—farming with floods, designing floating settlements, cleansing through nature-based systems—are not relics of the past. They are solutions for the future. The question is not whether humanity has the tools to adapt. The question is who will listen.

THE AGE OF TEKNOLOGY

We are living through an era that is being defined by its relationship to technology. Some call it the Fourth Industrial Revolution; others, the Age of AI or the Anthropocene Tech Epoch.[12] Yet an alternative, parallel paradigm is emerging—one that does not separate technology from ecology, nor digital from ancestral knowledge. This is the rise of a TEKnological renaissance, where traditional ecological knowledge (TEK) is interwoven with contemporary solutions, creating regenerative water systems that sustain both human and ecological communities.

This age is not just about reviving ancient practices but reimagining a future where water is recognized as a living intelligence—a force that shapes design, governance, and urban resilience. Instead of resisting water through rigid infrastructure, TEKnological urbanism embraces its natural rhythms, allowing cities and settlements to coevolve with tides, rivers, and rainfall. *Lo—TEK, Water* serves as a field guide for those pioneering this shift, offering blueprints for a world where water is no longer an obstacle to be controlled but a cocreator in design.

A TEKnologist is a practitioner who applies traditional ecological knowledge to water-based challenges in environmental management, architecture, and urban planning.[13] Their role is to shift society from extractive water systems toward regenerative hydrological networks that sustain life for generations to come. This book serves as a field guide for TEKnologists by

- documenting Indigenous water technologies that have sustained civilizations for millennia—such as flood-responsive agriculture, aquifer recharge systems, and floating settlements;
- exploring contemporary architectural and ecological projects that integrate TEK into modern climate-adaptation strategies, ensuring cities work with, rather than against, water; and
- providing structured frameworks for integrating TEK into policy, planning, design and education—demonstrating how Indigenous hydrological knowledge can inform international climate-resilience efforts.

By embracing water as a central force in TEKnological urbanism, we open the door to a future where cities, landscapes, and communities flourish in symbiosis with the very element that sustains all life.

NAVIGATING THIS FIELD GUIDE

This book is not just a historical account of Indigenous water systems—it is a blueprint for the future. It challenges the dominant narrative that technology must be high-tech, expensive, and industrial. Instead, it reveals that some of the most advanced aquatic technologies already exist, embedded in the knowledge systems of those who have lived with water rather than against it.

Lo—TEK, Design by Radical Indigenism redefined technology—not as the extractive, high-tech solutions of the industrialized world, but as the sophisticated, place-based systems Indigenous and local communities have innovated over millennia.[14] It revealed that the most resilient infrastructures—those that thrive in the face of climate extremes—are deeply rooted in ecological intelligence. These systems are not superior to nature, nor are they trying to save it; instead, they are designed in symbiosis with it.

This second volume, *Lo—TEK, Water*, builds on the foundation of *Lo—TEK, Design by Radical Indigenism*, expanding the discourse on ancestral technologies by focusing on water infrastructures. Structured as a compendium of Indigenous water technologies, the book bridges past and future, showcasing both TEK systems and contemporary architectural projects inspired by them. These systems illustrate how Indigenous communities have worked with water for millennia, developing infrastructures that are becoming increasingly relevant in today's intensifying climate crises.

Organized by water type—salty, brackish, and fresh—each TEK system is coauthored with Indigenous knowledge keepers to ensure accuracy and cultural integrity. The book details each system's elevation, water level fluctuations, and ecological role, mapping them within three significant climate adaptation and development frameworks to provide a comparative foundation for integrating TEK into institutional climate-adaptation strategies. These strategies include the water–energy–food nexus by the Food and Agriculture Organization (FAO), highlighting how these systems sustain ecological and human communities;

the adaptation responses to sea level rise by the Intergovernmental Panel on Climate Change (IPCC), demonstrating their role in flood management and coastal resilience; and the World Bank's nature-based solutions (NBS) framework, classifying these technologies based on their ecological functions and benefits.[15,16] By positioning ancestral aquatic technologies within contemporary resilience frameworks, *Lo—TEK: Water* demonstrates how these time-tested innovations offer sustainable, adaptive solutions for a world increasingly defined by water instability.

These ancestral infrastructures—like the *chinampa* floating islands of the Nahua Xochimilca people—demonstrate that Indigenous communities have long designed in concert with tidal flows, monsoon cycles, and freshwater ecosystems. These systems operate without industrial technology, relying instead on passive, nature-based strategies that regenerate landscapes, sustain biodiversity, and ensure food and water security. Floating agricultural systems, such as the *baira* of Bangladesh, transform waterlogged landscapes into highly productive farmlands. Wetland filtration systems, like the *sangjiyutang* dike-ponds of China, integrate aquaculture with natural water purification, demonstrating a sustainable approach to nutrient cycling. Indigenous communities have also developed tidal aquaculture structures that harness oceanic rhythms, such as the V-shaped *aech* fish weirs of the Yapese in Micronesia, which guide migrating fish into sustainable catchment areas.

Similarly, adaptive irrigation systems like the *ngais pasir* terracing of Indonesia respond to fluctuating water levels, maximizing agricultural yield while preserving soil integrity. Along coastlines, resilience strategies like the *asi* coral islands of the Solomon Islands use reef-building techniques to buffer against rising seas and coastal erosion. From the *ngúmā* weir fishing of the Baka in Cameroon, which temporarily redirects river flows for sustainable fishing, to the *atob* fish weirs of the Visayans in the Philippines, built from basalt stone to capture migrating fish, creating living breakwaters that support marine biodiversity, these infrastructures demonstrate the diversity of water-based ingenuity. The *mithache agor* solar salt-production pans of the Goans in India transition to aquaculture ponds during monsoon seasons, while the *yakhchāl* ice pits of Persia become passive cooling systems that store freshwater ice year-round. The examples catalogued in the first half of the book all exemplify how human civilizations have long harnessed water's intelligence.

The second half of this book shifts the focus from ancestral water technologies to contemporary architectural projects that infuse TEK for modern climate adaptation. These projects demonstrate that Indigenous and nature-based solutions are not relics of the past but essential blueprints for the future. Systems like Kongjian Yu's Sponge Cities have been celebrated for their climate resilience, but their lineage—grounded in aquatic Indigenous knowledge—has remained unrecognized. A curated selection of 22 contemporary design projects is presented, showcasing a global movement toward hybrid TEK-led design. *Lo—TEK, Water* reframes these innovations through a TEK lens, highlighting how they work with water, rather than against it. These projects span material innovation, ecological restoration, landscape-scale interventions, and regenerative urban planning. Whether activated by tidal rhythms, solar heating, radiant cooling, microbial ecosystems, or material decay, these water infrastructures function through passive, dynamic flows rather than rigid industrial controls.

Some of the projects profiled in this section embrace traditional materials, reintroducing Indigenous aquatic construction techniques to modern building practices. At Pontificia Universidad Católica del Perú, researchers have collaborated with Indigenous communities around Lake Titicaca to develop totora reed insulation for earthquake-resistant housing, reviving a practice deeply embedded in the region's architecture. In Denmark, Kathryn Larsen's Seaweed Thatch Reimagined draws on centuries-old eelgrass construction to offer a nontoxic, fire-resistant, and regenerative building material for contemporary structures. In Colorado's San Luis Valley, architects Ronald Rael and Virginia San Fratello of Emerging Objects merge Indigenous earth-based construction with digital fabrication in their project Mud Frontiers, a series of habitable structures created from 3D-printed adobe.

In the field of aquatic ecological restoration, contemporary projects take inspiration from Indigenous floating wetlands and wetland filtration systems to address urban water crises. The National Institute for Biotechnology and Genetic Engineering in Pakistan has developed floating treatment wetlands that mimic natural aquatic ecosystems to cleanse wastewater while providing habitat for wildlife. In the United States, the University of Washington's Green Futures Lab has deployed floating wetlands along the Duwamish River, an initiative designed to restore degraded ecosystems while supporting the migratory patterns of juvenile salmon.

Other projects presented in this section apply TEK-based strategies on an architectural scale, rethinking climate adaptation, disaster relief, and food security through Indigenous wisdom. In Bangladesh, where monsoon flooding disrupts access to education, Mohammed Rezwan's floating Nouka Schools provide an adaptive solution by transforming school infrastructure into floating classrooms. In Canada, the Star Blanket Cree Nation has partnered with MacPherson Engineering to develop the Blanket of Warmth, a passive heating system designed to bring cost-effective thermal comfort to First Nation homes. In Thailand, Chat Architects' Angsila Oyster Scaffolding Pavilion integrates bamboo scaffolds historically used in oyster farming into an ecotourism and climate-adaptation model.

Across the globe, designers are turning to TEK to guide large-scale urban-resilience projects. Bangkok's first major green infrastructure project, Chulalongkorn University Centenary Park, integrates strategies from the Yakrong Indigenous flood garden system to manage stormwater. In China, landscape architect Kongjian Yu has pioneered the Sponge City model, an urban flood-control strategy inspired by ancient Chinese water management and farming techniques. These projects challenge conventional urban planning paradigms, demonstrating that climate resilience can be achieved by working with water's natural rhythms rather than resisting them.

A comparative visual essay connects the two bookends, pairing ancestral systems with contemporary interventions based on their shared performances. Each pairing highlights how TEK-infused principles continue to shape resilient, adaptive solutions to environmental challenges. Aquatic plants and mollusks function as biofilters, purifying water while supporting biodiversity and local economies. Intertidal rock walls and floating islands create protective habitats, buffering storm surges and enhancing marine ecosystems. Amphibious and earthen constructions regulate moisture, insulate against temperature extremes, and adapt to seasonal inundation. Cut-and-fill polder dikes and terraced agriculture optimize water retention, mitigate erosion, and sustain food production in fluctuating climates. Across diverse landscapes, these systems perform as climate-responsive, self-regenerating infrastructures that balance human habitation with ecological resilience. Together, the stories told in the visual essay highlight the enduring relevance of TEK, proving that ancestral wisdom, when integrated with modern innovation, can offer sustainable and resilient solutions for a rapidly changing climate.

Following the conclusion, the section titled "Future Directions" presents two transformative frameworks: the Lo—TEK City Model and the Smart Oath of Understanding (SOU). The Lo—TEK City Model provides a scalable and adaptable blueprint for integrating Indigenous ecological knowledge, regenerative infrastructure, and community-led governance into contemporary urbanism. This model offers a flexible, place-based approach that fosters biocultural resilience, biodiversity, and cultural continuity, ensuring that cities evolve in reciprocity with their environments. The Lo—TEK City Model is informed by Indigenous-Led Urban Frameworks rooted in land rematriation, legal recognition of sacred geographies, and Indigenous-led governance. The Lo—TEK City Model offers a practical pathway for cities to uphold local, traditional and Indigenous rights while advancing ecological stewardship and long-term urban resilience. The second framework, known as the SOU, provides an ethical and practical protocol for respectfully engaging with Indigenous knowledge in design, planning, and policy. It safeguards traditional ecological practices, ensuring that they are honored, applied equitably, and contribute to both Indigenous self-determination and urban sustainability. Together, these frameworks serve as essential tools for architects, planners, policymakers, and communities to design cities that are not only sustainable but truly alive—coevolving with the landscapes, waters, and cultural narratives that sustain them.

THE POWER OF ANCESTRAL ENERGY

One of the *Lo—TEK* series' most enduring arguments dismantles the myth that communities in the Global South are the most vulnerable to climate change simply due to a lack of expensive high-tech infrastructure. Instead, it asserts that these communities are the keepers of critical, enduring knowledge systems and water solutions—deeply regenerative, intergenerational, and reciprocal. Rather than being replaced, these Indigenous and traditional technologies should be recognized, invested in, and expanded as blueprints for climate-adaptive water infrastructures worldwide. The survival of cities, coastlines, and ecosystems will not be secured by concrete dams and concrete seawalls, but by restoring our ability to listen—to water, to land, and to the original architects of resilient design. *Lo—TEK, Water* calls for a radical shift—from viewing TEK as a relic of the past to understanding it as a vital strategy for the future. The solutions to our climate crisis have been here all along.

Lo—TEK are not only original infrastructures but also the world's first renewable energy technologies, shifting the narrative from high-tech dependence to ancestral resilience. Long before the fossil fuel era, Indigenous and traditional societies engineered hydraulic systems that sustained civilizations with energy-efficient, regenerative water management. These innovations—such as China's *sangjiyutang* ponds, Bangladesh's *baira* floating islands, and Mexico's *chinampas*—demonstrate that sustainable energy solutions are not only industrial inventions but can also be ancestral knowledge systems that continue to operate today. In some cases, they are even being retrofitted for modern bioenergy production, proving their relevance in contemporary climate-adaptation strategies.

Unlike costly, centralized fossil fuel infrastructures, ancestral renewable systems offer low-cost, high-yield solutions that enhance economic resilience. Traditional hydraulic systems require minimal external inputs, relying instead on nature's regenerative cycles to sustain productivity. They reduce dependence on fossil fuels by harnessing naturally occurring energy sources like water flow, tidal forces, and organic decomposition for power and food production. These systems support local economies by empowering communities to manage their own energy and water infrastructures, reducing reliance on imported resources. They also encourage job creation in restoration, resilience infrastructure, and sustainable management, offering employment opportunities in regenerative agriculture, aquaculture, and bioenergy innovation. By working with nature rather than against it, they provide long-term financial savings through reduced maintenance costs and mitigation of disaster-related expenses.

Unlike industrial energy systems that extract and deplete, ancestral renewables function as living, regenerative infrastructures that support biodiversity, carbon sequestration, and ecosystem stability. They prevent land degradation and erosion by aligning with natural hydrology, maintaining fertile soils and wetlands. These systems enhance carbon capture through aquatic plant life, peat formation, and organic material cycling, contributing to climate change mitigation efforts. They also reduce waste and pollution by integrating waste-to-energy loops, such as using organic matter from floating farms for natural biofuel. Additionally, they improve water management by reducing flood risks, purifying water, and replenishing groundwater reserves, making them essential for climate resilience and complementary to high-tech renewable-energy systems.

Ancestral renewable systems are deeply intergenerational, equitable, and community-driven, reinforcing social resilience in the face of climate change. They ensure energy sovereignty by reducing vulnerability to geopolitical energy crises through localized energy production. These systems provide food security through agroecological methods that combine energy generation with sustainable food cultivation. They also strengthen cultural resilience, as they are embedded in Indigenous knowledge traditions that reinforce community identity and governance. Perhaps most importantly, they increase disaster resilience, having been designed over centuries to withstand climate extremes, from monsoons to droughts.

Protecting cities, coastlines, and ecosystems demands more than the rigid industrial solutions that have long defined urban resilience—concrete dams, steel seawalls, and high-tech interventions that often disrupt the very landscapes they aim to defend. Instead, true resilience lies in reengaging with ancestral renewables—living, adaptive systems that have sustained human and ecological communities for millennia. These systems are not relics of the past but blueprints for the future, offering regenerative approaches to water, energy, and food security that work in harmony with the land. By restoring and evolving these infrastructures, we are not merely reviving ancestral knowledge but unlocking a new paradigm of urbanism—one that is dynamic, just, and deeply attuned to the rhythms of nature.

A Lo—TEK Living emerges from this paradigm shift, reimagining urban life through ancestral water wisdom, Indigenous ecological knowledge, and regenerative design to create cities that evolve with, rather than against, their environments. Rather than relying on extractive and rigid industrial models, this approach prioritizes hyperlocal water management, material sustainability, and communal stewardship, ensuring that resilience is not imposed but cultivated. Rooted in TEKnological urbanism, it recognizes that sustainability is not a one-size-fits-all solution but must be informed by biocultural resilience, intergenerational knowledge exchange, and community-led governance. The 10 guiding principles of a Lo—TEK City—spanning water-centered urban planning, ancestral technologies, multispecies urbanism, and circular economies—offer a framework for cities that do not just endure but thrive, adapting and regenerating alongside the ecosystems that sustain them. These principles, elaborated in "Future Directions," present a nuanced framework for rethinking urbanism through the integrated wisdom of Indigenous knowledge and ecological design.

THE URGENCY OF REMEMBERING

Water holds memory—but in a time of crisis it is up to humans to remember. For centuries, colonialism, industrialization, and extractive economies have erased the original instructions—the teachings of how to live in balance with water. Yet the blueprints remain, carried forward by Indigenous knowledge keepers, embedded in landscapes, waiting to be recognized.

We stand at a crossroads. Do we continue to build in defiance of water, or do we learn to build with it? The solutions are not hypothetical. They already exist. We need only listen.

Lo—TEK is not authored by any single person; it is an ongoing conversation between landscapes, knowledge keepers, and the generations who have observed, adapted, and innovated with nature's systems. It is orated by innumerable voices, translating millions of conversations that have taken place over thousands of years—between people and rivers, between forests and rain, between tides and the shorelines they shape. This volume emerges from a profound need to question the ways of thinking that no longer serve us and to challenge a system that dismisses Indigenous knowledge as unscientific. Decolonizing design means recognizing that the intelligence of water is already embedded in the world's oldest infrastructures, that technology does not need to be invented anew, but rather remembered and reactivated.

Decolonizing design also asks us to reframe the foundations of our discipline—not by rejecting form, but by reimagining its relationship to life. Instead of the modernist dictum form follows function, we return to a more ancestral logic: form follows flux. This principle acknowledges that design must move with the rhythms of living systems, not against them—centering reciprocity, adaptability, and cultural continuity as pathways to resilience.

The shift—toward a deeper, more reciprocal relationship with our planetary systems—will be fraught with failures and frictions. It will require an unlearning and a rewriting of colonial narratives. But, as documented in the pages of this volume, the process has already begun. The memory of water is calling. The question is whether we are ready to respond.

ENDNOTES

1. Oren Lyons, "Fall 2005 Commencement Address" (speech, UC Berkeley College of Natural Resources, Berkeley, CA, December 2005).
2. United Nations Economic and Social Council, *The Rights of Indigenous Peoples in Relation to the Global Energy Mix* (New York: UN Headquarters, 2022).
3. Ailton Krenak, *Ancestral Future*, trans. Jamille Pinheiro Dias and Alex Brostoff (Cambridge: Polity Press, 2024).
4. Oren Lyons, "Our Responsibility to the Seventh Generation," in *The Rights of Nature: A Legal Revolution That Could Save the World*, ed. Cormac Cullinan (Cape Town: Siber Ink, 2007), 25.
5. Fabiola Sosa-Rodriguez, "Impacts of Water-Management Decisions on the Survival of a City: From Ancient Tenochtitlán to Modern Mexico City," *International Journal of Water Resources Development 33, no. 2* (2017): 220, https://doi.org/10.1080/07900627.2016.1238344.
6. Delcy Morelos (artist), in discussion with the author, August 2022.
7. Stephanie Hazel, "Indigenous Plant Wisdom of Time and Place: Tyson Yunkaporta on Sacred Herbalism," November 27, 2023, in *The Elder Tree Podcast*, presented and produced by the Elder Tree, podcast, MP3 audio, 13:08, https://podcasts.apple.com/us/podcast/55-indigenous-plant-wisdom-of-time-and-place/id1646328719?i=1000632942464.
8. Ethan Siegel, "The First Climate Model Turns 50, and Predicted Global Warming Almost Perfectly," *Forbes*, March 15, 2017, https://www.forbes.com/sites/startswithabang/2017/03/15/the-first-climate-model-turns-50-and-predicted-global-warming-almost-perfectly/.
9. Richard O. Clemmer, "Then Will You Rise and Strike My Head from My Neck: Hopi Prophecy and the Discourse of Empowerment," *American Indian Quarterly 24, no. 4* (2000): 534–58.
10. Robin Wall Kimmerer, *Braiding Sweetgrass* (Minneapolis: Milkweed Editions, 2013), 365–73.
11. Paul Hawken, *Regeneration: Ending the Climate Crisis in One Generation* (New York: Penguin, 2021), 115.
12. Gissel Velarde, "Artificial Intelligence and Its Impact on the Fourth Industrial Revolution: A Review," *International Journal of Artificial Intelligence & Applications 10, no. 6* (2019): 41–48, https://arxiv.org/pdf/2011.03044.pdf.
13. Nathalie Kelley Mallqui, Dr. Lyla June Johnston, Julia Watson, and Timo Granzotti coined the term *TEKnology*™ and formed a group called *The TEKnologists*™, discussing its principles during a conversation on January 24, 2025.
14. Julia Watson, *Lo—TEK, Design by Radical Indigenism* (New York: TASCHEN, 2019), Introduction.
15. Fatima Denton et al., "Climate-Resilient Pathways: Adaptation, Mitigation, and Sustainable Development," in *Climate Change 2014: Impacts, Adaptation, and Vulnerability. Part A: Global and Sectoral Aspects. Contribution of Working Group II to the Fifth Assessment Report of the Intergovernmental Panel on Climate Change*, ed. C. B. Field et al. (Cambridge: Cambridge University Press, 2014), 1101–31.
16. World Bank, *A Catalogue of Nature-Based Solutions for Urban Resilience* (Washington, DC: World Bank Group, 2021).

1 SALTY BRACKISH FRESH

ATOB FISH WEIRS *of* THE VISAYANS *Philippines*

ATOB FISH WEIRS *of* THE VISAYANS *Philippines*

Coauthored with
Dr. Cynthia Neri Zayas and Margie Francisco

PEOPLE Visayans LOCATION Visayan Archipelago, Philippines TECHNOLOGY stone fish weir
ELEVATION 0 m ORIGIN 1668 CE
DISTANCE ABOVE OR BELOW WATERLINE −1.5 to +1 m
WATER LEVEL FLUCTUATION, TIDAL OR SEASONAL −0.1 to +1.5 m

FAO Nexus
WATER salt ENERGY tidal FOOD fish

IPCC Adaptation Pathway
protect

World Bank NBS
CATEGORY sandy shores
FUNCTIONS coastal erosion regulation, biodiversity, coastal flood regulation, sea level rise adaptation
BENEFITS coastal flood risk reduction, resource production, carbon storage and sequestration, biodiversity, cultural, social interaction

Submerged in the warm coastal waters of the central Philippine Visayan Archipelago, curved stone walls stand as echoes of a megalithic culture. Occasionally used today, though not as frequently as in the past, these infrastructures intricately connect the Visayan people to the sea's abundance. The ancient curving fish weirs—supplementing produce grown on the coralline islands—ingeniously work with the ebb and flow of tides. They do so by trapping marine species as they enter while navigating the warm coastal waters. Known as *atob* in the Bisaya language, which is also the name for a pile of stones forming a breakwater, these weirs serve as aquaculture technologies and tidal barriers, working with receding waters to catch a variety of marine species.[1]

1

1 A curved stone wall of a fish weir exposed by the ebb and flow of the tide.

2

2 The Visayan Archipelago consists of seven larger and hundreds of smaller islands.

3 Heart-shaped fish weirs are constructed on the reef shelf surrounding an island.

The Visayan Archipelago comprises islands separated by a vast inland sea, which stands as one of the region's largest fishing grounds. Derived from the word *bato*, meaning "stone," *atob* structures proliferated across the Philippines, adopting diverse names and construction methods depending on the local context.[2] While the practice of *atob* aquaculture around the Visayan Archipelago is not as common today, some locals still maintain these structures to catch fish; the weirs also function as barriers that control the flow of water and are valued for their spiritual and historical significance.

The Visayan *atob* has many similarities to other stone fish weirs from across the Pacific Ocean, influencing the design of Penghu weirs in Taiwan and Nagasaki weirs in Japan.[3] Archaeologists suggest this region was an ancient

3

migration route between Australia and Oceania.[4] While the earliest reference to *atob* can be traced to the 17th century, when the Spanish surveyed the region, it's likely this technology was built in the Visayan Archipelago prior to these records.[5]

The scarcity of farmland due to soils with high salinity, low nutrients, aluminum, iron, and hydrogen sulfide toxicity led Visayan communities to seek sustenance from the sea—an ecosystem that has shaped the livelihoods of local communities for generations.[6] Historically, *atob* aligned communities, as activities revolved around their construction, maintenance, repair, catches, and the subsequent distribution of fish. The traditional knowledge of tides, currents, and marine life is reflected in the craftsmanship and placement of the stone structures.[7] They fostered a communal culture, in symbiosis with surrounding ecosystems and embedded with profound spiritual importance.

Ownership of each *atob*, which can be communal or individual, is accompanied by customary relationships that are established during weir construction and maintenance.[8] If the *atob* is communally owned, it is built and maintained by the community, as it is *bayanihan* (for the community's benefit). During fishing activities, community members often rearrange communally owned *atob* stones to uncover fish hiding beneath, though sometimes failing to restore them to their original positions, characteristic of communal ownership.

Atob are passed generationally through *pamana* (parental inheritance).[9] However, increasing disinterest and urban youth migration has resulted in dwindling ownership and upkeep. Today, some *atob* have become fish sanctuaries, with the Marine Protected Area designation allowing them to maintain their structural and cultural identity.[10] Accompanying this formal system of protection, an informal system protects *atob* sites through *anito*—spirits related to nature and ancestry who are the guardians of these locations. Local taboo also forbids misuse or control of the sea, which is believed to belong to supernatural beings. To appease these entities, ritual offerings are made before and after the fishing seasons to seek favor for success.[11]

4

4 Little is known of the antiquity of these fishing innovations, which are owned by the descendants of Visayan fish-trap builders.

Along the coastlines of many islands in the Visayan Archipelago, shallow areas extend into the sea for several hundred meters. These gradually sloping, submerged landscapes, located between the open sea and rocky coasts, are home to *atob* fish weirs of various shapes, including horseshoe and heart-like configurations. Ranging from 50 to 150 meters in length, *atob* resembling an arch are strategically located in deeper waters, serving a dual purpose: as barriers against waves and typhoons and as a source of sustenance for local communities.

Along the southwestern edge of North Gigante Island and located closer to the shore than their arch-shaped counterparts, heart-shaped *atob* are constructed over seven hundred meters into the sea. These *atob* are labyrinthine in nature, gradually guiding fish toward a small opening located at the apex, where the two rounded edges meet. Heart-shaped *atob* typically feature a *sanga*—a straight wall positioned in the middle weir, which directs fish toward its entrance. The walls of this heart-shaped typology range from half a meter to one meter wide. Accompanying *atob* weirs are smaller stone holding cells known as *atob-atob*, which form circular walled enclosures at the end of the *sanga*. *Atob-atob* are used to store and preserve fish for easy retrieval from the ocean.

Different Types of *Atob* Weirs Are Located in Relation to the *Shoreline*

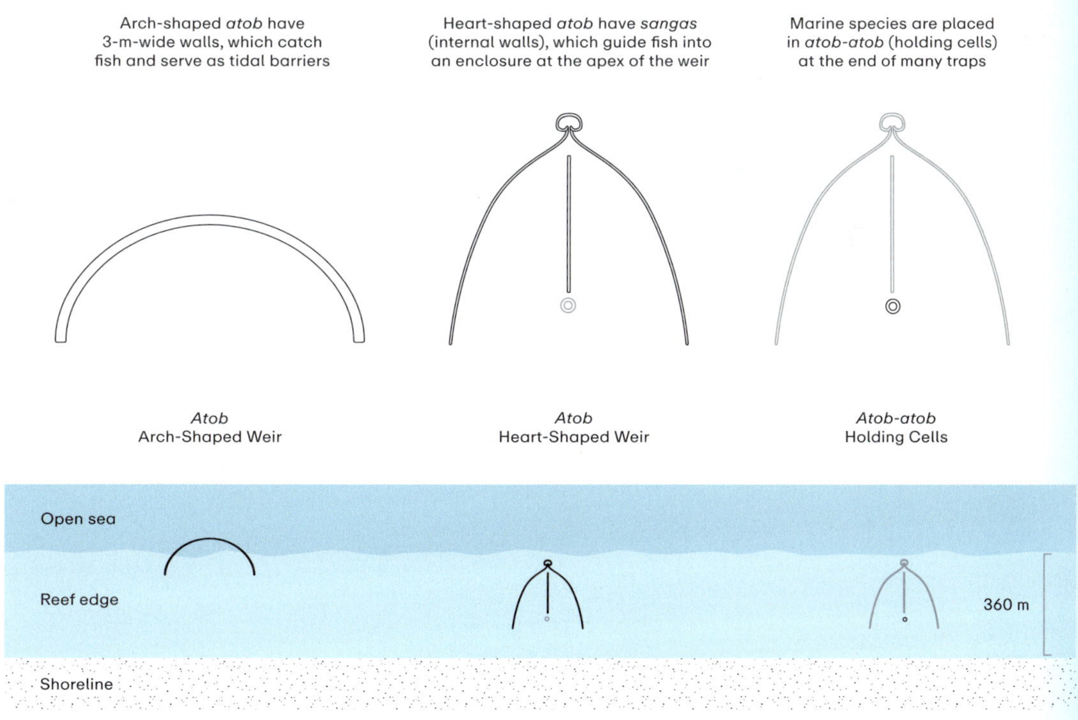

Fish Are Guided into a Small Opening at the Apex of a Heart-Shaped *Atob*

Coral stones are moved to form a *sawang* (pathway) in the water, allowing people and boats to access *atob* weirs

Fish are preserved in circular *atob-atob* holding cells

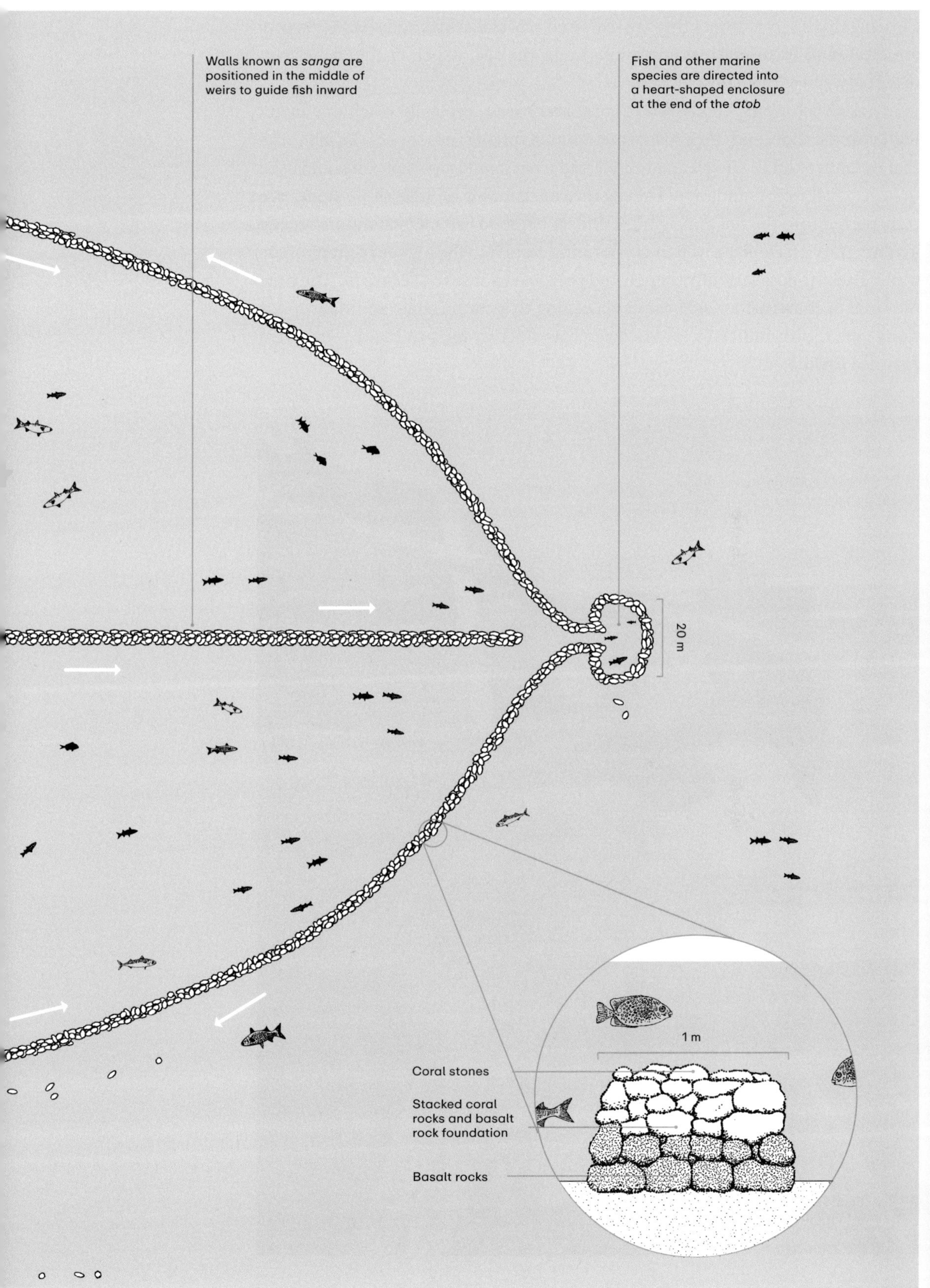
Walls known as *sanga* are positioned in the middle of weirs to guide fish inward
Fish and other marine species are directed into a heart-shaped enclosure at the end of the *atob*
20 m
1 m
Coral stones
Stacked coral rocks and basalt rock foundation
Basalt rocks

Clearings in the coral stones that are scattered across beaches and shallow waters are created to form *sawangs* (pathways) into the sea, which enable fishermen to access weirs without obstruction.

Atob fish weirs, composed of coral and basalt, typically reach one meter high near the shore and three to five meters high further into the sea. Basalt rocks that weigh around 10 kilograms are collected from inland riparian zones and used to form a fish weir foundation. During the construction of *atob*, these stones are transported into the sea during high tide on bamboo rafts. Once waters recede, a community assembles a weir, incorporating coral into the higher sections of the wall.[12] Each stone is carefully shaped and polished to ensure a secure fit. The time required to construct an *atob* varies according to location, size, and tidal conditions; one record indicates it took two years for two men to build a weir that spanned 109 meters.[13]

5

5 The fish weirs support ecologically sustainable methods of capture, while also playing a vital role in safeguarding marine ecosystems.

6

6 While capturing a diversity of sea creatures including eels, squids, soft-shelled crabs, sea cucumber, and stingrays, the fishermen prefer mullet, mojarra, scorpion fish, needlefish, catfish, and other small fish species.

Atob weirs play a vital role in the marine ecosystem of the Visayan Sea, safeguarding fish from predators and providing a stable habitat for maturation. The weir walls offer a surface on which spat, the larva of bivalves like oysters, can grow, while also serving as the ideal location for algae proliferation, the nutritional foundation of all marine life that lives in and around each *atob*.[14] The design of each *atob*, built in relation to the natural fluctuations of coastal water, creates a temporary enclosure during high tide and mimics the natural seafloor once the tide recedes, when fish are often caught by hand or net—a task commonly undertaken by women and children.[15] Typically, the harvest from an *atob* is divided among the laborers and the owner of the weir, fostering a sense of shared responsibility and communal benefit.[16] Despite the labor-intensive process involved in the construction of an *atob*, once built, the weir is a relatively passive and ecologically sustainable means of catching fish and other marine species.

Aware of overexploitation and armed with an innate understanding of monsoon seasons, productive locations, and suitable fishing methods, the Visayan people adopted a seasonal approach to sustenance, akin to a maritime "slash-and-burn" strategy. This approach materialized through *pangayaw*, or seasonal journeys, when resources in their homes dwindled.[17] Divided into two distinct seasons, which are marked by the monsoon winds: *habagat* (southwesterly winds) and *amihan* (northeasterly winds), significantly impact local fishing community activities. In May, the western Visayan Sea experiences heavy rainfall, while significant waves appear in the east. Fishermen from the west travel eastward in seasonal expeditions known as *pangayaw*. The *habagat* season usually lasts until October, when strong winds and high waves render fishing activities impossible. This is especially prevalent in December and January, when the winds are at their strongest—a period referred to as *kusog*.[18]

Although some *atob* fish weirs are still in use today, there's been a decline in their reconstruction. This decline is attributed to the scarcity of labor and

7

8

stones, dwindling populations of migratory fish exacerbated by the loss of coastal mangroves, as well as overfishing and resource mismanagement.[19,20] Today, resources such as basalt stone and mangrove timber, once used in the production and maintenance of *atob* fish weirs, are appropriated for the construction of homes and other uses. As yields become smaller—particularly during the off-season—the cost of maintaining weirs becomes a greater burden, with little to no return on investment.[21] In some cases, the returns on investment may be as insignificant as a mere kilogram of fish or none at all. Though the catch from these stone barriers is usually insufficient for commercial sale nowadays, it can still support the subsistence of fishermen's families. Despite the current state of many weirs, a renewed focus has initiated revitalization efforts, as the *atob* continues to be a vital asset to local communities, contributing to their livelihood and sustaining the delicate balance of the marine ecosystem.[22]

Due to their strategic placement along shorelines, traditional *atob* fishing structures have the potential to function as wave energy converters. While *atob* fishing weirs can become tourist destinations, adapting abandoned weirs to sustainably generate tidal energy could establish their cultural and historical significance through the provision of new services.

Seen as "living fossils of fixed fishing gear," the *atob* fish weirs are ingenious tidal technologies that hold historical and cultural significance.[23] Rooted in the rich diversity of the Austronesian language family, they are considered early precursors to a diverse family of Pacific fish weirs. For the Visayan people, these weirs remain vital to local livelihoods, while supporting diverse aquatic communities. Despite the challenges posed by declining mangrove forests, overfishing, and land reclamation, these stone structures continue to be treasured by local communities, not for commercial use, but as connections to history and spirituality.

7 *Bangkas* are a traditional type of wooden outrigger boat used by Filipino artisanal fishermen to catch a variety of fish.

8 The harvest from an *atob* is typically divided among the laborers and the owner of the weir.

ENDNOTES

1. Cynthia Neri Zayas, "Describing Stewardship of the Common Sea among Atob Fishers of the Pacific Rim Islands: Cases from the Philippines, Taiwan and Japan" *South Pacific Studies* 31, no. 2 (2011): 72–73.
2. Cynthia Neri Zayas, "Stone Tidal Weirs Rising from the Ruins," *Journal of Ocean & Culture* 2 (2019): 1.
3. Cynthia Neri Zayas, "Pangayaw and Tumandok in the Maritime World of the Visayan Islanders," in *Fishers of the Visayas*, ed. Iwao Ushijima and Cynthia Neri Zayas (Quezon City: University of the Philippines Press, 1994), 77.
4. Peter Bellwood et al., "Archaeological and Palaeoenvironmental Research in the Batanes and Ilocos Norte Provinces, Northern Philippines," *Indo-Pacific Prehistory Association Bulletin* 23 (2003): 141.
5. Cynthia Neri Zayas, "Importance of Stone-Weir Heritage in the Arch of Instability" (paper presented at workshop on Indigenous People, Traditional Ecological Knowledge, and Climate Change: The Iconic Underwater Cultural Heritage of Stone Tidal Weirs, June 11–17, 2023, sponsored by the National Central University, Taoyuan, Taiwan and the Bureau of Cultural Heritage, Government of Taiwan), 3.
6. Rodelio B. Carating, Raymundo G. Galanta, and Clarita D. Bacatio, "Soils and the Philippine Economy," in *The Soils of the Philippines* (Amsterdam: Springer, 2014): 5.
7. Zayas, "Stone Tidal Weirs Rising," 91–92.
8. Zayas, "Describing Stewardship of the Common Sea," 3.
9. Zayas, "Importance of Stone-Weir Heritage," 5–6.
10. Margie Francisco (South Gigantes Island fisher), in discussion with the author, January 2024.
11. Zayas, "Importance of Stone-Weir Heritage" 5–6.
12. Zayas, "Stone Tidal Weirs Rising," 99.
13. Zayas, "Describing Stewardship of the Common Sea," 73.
14. Cynthia Neri Zayas and Cornelio Selorio, "Innovation of Stationary Fishing Gear in Guimaras Island, Central Philippines," *Philippine Quarterly of Culture and Society* 37, no. 1 (2009): 20.
15. Zayas, "Describing Stewardship of the Common Sea," 72.
16. Zayas and Selorio, "Innovation of Stationary Fishing Gear," 21.
17. Zayas, "Pangayaw and Tumandok in the Maritime World," 126.
18. Zayas, "Pangayaw and Tumandok in the Maritime World," 86.
19. Zayas and Selorio, "Innovation of Stationary Fishing Gear," 23–24.
20. Zayas, "Pangayaw and Tumandok in the Maritime World," 92.
21. Cynthia Neri Zayas, "Atob and Bato: Two Sides of Philippine Lithic Heritage," *Pilipinas* 43 (2004): 64.
22. Zayas, "Stone Tidal Weirs Rising," 90–91.
23. Zayas, "Stone Tidal Weirs Rising from the Ruins," 90.

COAUTHOR

MARGIE FRANCISCO

South Gigantes Island Fisher

Margie Francisco, the chairwoman for the Barangay Power Association (BAPA), is a resident of Charles, Iloilo City. She attended Lantangan Elementary School before pursuing her high school education at Northern Iloilo Polytechnic State College of Fisheries (NIPSCF), formerly the Western Visayas College of Fisheries in Estancia, Iloilo.

Following her secondary education, Francisco enrolled in a two-year secretarial course at NIPSCF. While living in Iloilo City, Francisco worked as a secretary at Fred Tayo Enterprises, where she embraced the dynamic energy of urban life in the Philippines.

Francisco relocated to South Gigantes Island in 1970 with her husband, Herson Francisco, a fisherman. Together, they raised their son, Jay, now 31 years old, who recently graduated in maritime navigation from John B. Lacson Foundation Maritime Academy in Villa Arevalo, Iloilo City. In her community, Francisco has been actively involved in various roles. She served as a councilwoman for Barangay Gabi, where she chaired the committee on violence against women and children. Before this, she was chair of the committee on budget and infrastructure matters in the same *barangay*, a term referring to the smallest administrative division in the Philippines, akin to a village or neighborhood.

Currently, Francisco holds the position of chair for BAPA, an electric company serving the community. Through her dedicated service and leadership, Francisco continues to make significant contributions to the development and welfare of her *barangay*.

COAUTHOR

CYNTHIA NERI ZAYAS, PHD

Maritime Anthropologist

Dr. Cynthia Neri Zayas is a maritime anthropologist with a specialization in the Philippines and Japan. Formerly the director of the University of the Philippines Diliman Center for International Studies from 2011 to 2017, she has also chaired the board of the Philippine Social Science Council and served as a member of the board for the Anthropological Association of the Philippines.

Born on the northern island of Mindanao in the Philippines, Zayas was raised in Manila and spent her summer breaks in her hometown. Her family ties to the Sultanate of Lanao and her mother's storytelling influenced her interest in anthropology. Family members, including a Jesuit priest and a cousin who is an anthropologist and former curator of the Philippine National Museum, further nurtured her passion for the field.

Zayas earned her MA in Asian studies and BA in anthropology from the University of the Philippines before pursuing further studies in Japan. She completed her PhD in cultural anthropology at the University of Tsukuba in Japan, focusing on the anthropology and history of fishing communities. Collaborating with Japanese anthropologists, she led the Visayas Maritime Anthropological Studies research team for over a decade, exploring family-based fisheries, local markets, and cultural life around the Visayan inland sea.

In recognition of her contributions, particularly in pioneering maritime anthropological studies, Zayas was awarded the Order of the Rising Sun Gold Rays with Rosette by the Japanese emperor in 2023. Despite retiring as a full professor from the University of the Philippines in 2018, she remains active in teaching, research, and extension work, particularly among Indigenous peoples and fishers.

AECH FISH WEIRS
of THE YAPESE
Micronesia

AECH FISH WEIRS *of* THE YAPESE *Micronesia*

Coauthored with
Aloysius Guchbuw and Thomas Ganang

PEOPLE Yapese LOCATION Yap State, Micronesia
TECHNOLOGY aquaculture
ELEVATION 0 m ORIGIN 1000 CE
DISTANCE ABOVE OR BELOW WATERLINE −2 to +1 m
WATER LEVEL FLUCTUATION, TIDAL OR SEASONAL +0.4 to +3 m

FAO Nexus
WATER salt ENERGY tidal FOOD fish

IPCC Adaptation Pathway
protect

World Bank NBS
CATEGORY sandy shores
FUNCTIONS coastal erosion regulation, biodiversity, coastal flood regulation, sea level rise adaptation
BENEFITS coastal flood risk reduction, resource production, carbon storage and sequestration, biodiversity, cultural, social interaction

In the vast expanse of the Pacific, Yap is one of the four Federated States of Micronesia, located 15 hundred kilometers west of the islands of Chuuk, Pohnpei, and Kosrae. Guam hovers above, 840 kilometers to the northeast.[1] Before the 20th century, Yap consisted of three volcanic islands: Marbaa, Rumung, and Maap, until a German-built canal split Yap proper and the newly formed Gagil-Tamil in two. Submerged in a shallow cerulean blue lagoon surrounding the island are arrow-shaped fish weirs pointing toward the open sea, so immense they can be seen from space. Measuring up to two hundred meters long and made from stacked coral, *aech* fish weirs form a unique sea-facing aquaculture technology. Their staggering size attracts schools of fish to swim deep into

WEIR
An enclosure set in a waterway to capture fish.

1

2

1 Arrow-shaped *aech* fish weirs of the Yapese point out to sea.
2 The island of Yap is ringed by a coral reef and covered in subtropical forest.
3 When the tide is low, the fish traps are active.
4 Fishermen gather together in a meeting house called a *faluw* before and after a catch.

3

4

their labyrinthine walls, where they're caught. Hundreds of *aech* fish weirs surround the shallow shoreline of the island, converting the lagoon landscape into a human-made artificial reef.[2, 3] Though largely unused, the *aech* now forms an extensive breakwater system that has survived successive waves of catastrophic climate events and colonization by the Spanish, Germans, and Japanese.[4] As with many island communities whose energy needs are limited, these ancestral scaffoldings could also one day offer refuge for a form of tidal energy infrastructures as they once did for fish, powered by the same tidal forces.

Different stories describe the origin of the *aech*, which were conceived by spirits; the first three were arrow-shaped weirs built in the Delipeebinaew, Weloy, and Gagil regions of the island.[5] In Delipeebinaew, a spirit named Long

5

5 An arrow-shaped weir featuring a secondary chamber.

appeared in human form to build the first *aech*, which was completed by villagers. This *aech* had a shaft so long it continued up to the shore and several meters across the land.[6, 7] Taking the form of a freshwater eel, Long ventured to Weloy, where he formed the second *aech* in the village Keng. In Gagil, he took the form of a man named Mer to build the third *aech*.[8]

Passed down through families, the *aech* reinforce relationships while offering food security and even protecting villages during times of war by obstructing canoes.[9] Each weir is owned by a family with a governing role in the community, like ambassador or warrior. The 134 villages that span Yap's 95 square kilometers are populated by 20,000 Yapese people, who follow a caste system of nine classifications ruled by three chiefs in the municipalities of Gagil, Tomil, and Rull.[10, 11] The *aech* require regular maintenance to ensure structural integrity against powerful waves, with a well-constructed and -maintained weir signifying a family's status.[12] Fishing groups of men will gather in a meeting house called a *faluw* before and after an expedition to an *aech*. Larger catches are shared among families by a chief, while smaller catches are distributed by the owning families.[13, 14, 15] On Yap, fishing in deeper ocean waters beyond the lagoon is taboo; *barum* fishing—a form of fly fishing using a torch and basket—is the only reason to travel further.[16]

Construction techniques vary from island to island, influenced by coastal waters, topography of the seabed, strength of the tide, direction of the current, and diversity of fish species.[17] Rather than descending continuously into the ocean, the bottom of the lagoon forms a shallow reef flat, poked by sinkholes up to 22 meters deep, which moves into a steep reef front before sloping away into the sea.[18] The reef flat is a rocky mixture of coral stone and sediment from the shoreline mangroves that help cultivate pastures of seagrass. While exposed and almost dry at low tide, during high tide the flat averages a depth of two to three meters. Despite being situated in the middle of the Pacific, Yap rarely receives typhoons—a phenomenon that the Yapese historically attributed to magic.[19]

Each *aech*, named after the owner, the estate, or the village it belongs to, is designed in response to its local shoreline and reef flat condition.[20] The most prominent weir in Yap is the *aech* arrow-shaped weir, while two other types are the single- and multiple-V-shaped weirs, which form a zigzag configuration.[21, 22] Constructed of stacked coral rocks and limestone sourced from shoreline outcrops and floated to their locations on timber rafts, an *aech* measures 30 to 50 meters in length.[23, 24] Large limestone slabs form the base of walls of varying heights, from 40 to 150 centimeters.[25, 26] These broad stones are placed and compacted at a 45-degree angle. Smaller rocks are strategically inserted into gaps to "lock" the structure together, while still permeable enough to allow fish to enter.[27] The placement and configuration of a weir is based on shoreline conditions; for example, if the current is strong, stones will be stacked in particular angles and directions.[28] The wall heights within a single *aech* also vary, with the tallest walls being located at the seaward tip of the arrow.[29] When the tide recedes, this wall section at the rear end is the first to be exposed.[30] If damaged by a typhoon, the pale limestone assembly of the *aech* is repaired using charcoal-colored basalt rock, adding an ashy gradient to the mostly white walls.

Position of Typical Weirs in Relation to the Shoreline

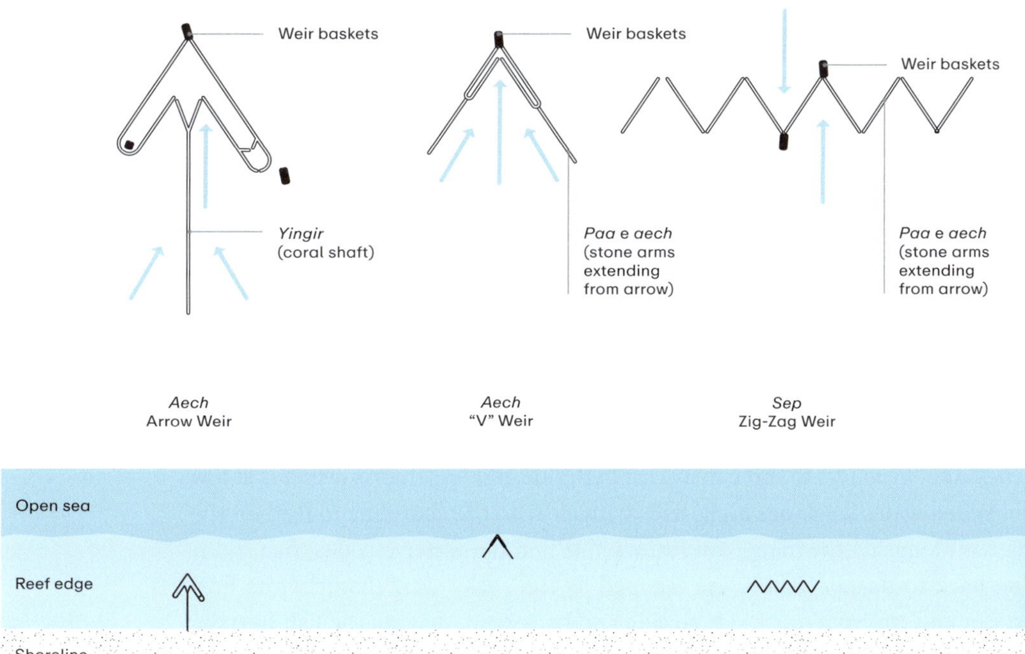

6

7

8

6 Traps capture a variety of sea creatures, including turtles.
7 Limestone rocks are used to construct the base, while coral rocks are stacked above to build up the weir.
8 Calcium carbonate from crustaceans forms a solid mortar between the rocky elements of the weir construction.

The labor-intensive construction of an *aech* begins with placing large limestone rocks in a tight line across a shallow portion of the lagoon. The force of the tide wedges these foundational rocks together.[31] Each weir is composed of a *yingir*—a long straight coral shaft—that extends from the shore into the sea and two entrances located at the end of the shaft, where it meets the base of the arrow. Some *aech* may position as many as three arrows in succession, while other weirs are positioned with their tip at a blue hole to capture fish from the deeper waters.[32, 33]

Weirs work with the receding tide on a diurnal cycle, where water levels fluctuate between two to three meters at high tide and less than one meter at low tide. When water levels are high, fish swim close to the shoreline to feed on the seagrass alongside the mangrove forests.[34] When the water recedes, fish swimming back to deeper waters are trapped as the rocky weir disturbs the flow of water and currents move side to side and backward, driving the fish into the weir.[35] When the high tide returns, fish can easily escape over the top of the *aech*, but some prefer to stay and feed near the bottom of the weir walls.[36]

Guided along the rocky walls, fish swim into the first chamber of the *aech* through two small entrances. Here, larger fish are trapped while smaller fish

9

swim to a secondary chamber protecting them from predators, through a narrow entrance between coral walls and a bamboo barricade called a *may*.[37, 38] Lateral currents also direct fish into other chambers and weir baskets.

An *aech* weir can be thought of as an icebox where fish can be caught without overexploitation or escape—in the past, this was a regular aspect of everyday food gathering.[39] Fish are harvested with either *k'ef* (butterfly nets) or baskets hidden by layered *nuyu* (coconut fronds), which are located inside the weirs or attached to the outside through openings in the coral wall.[40, 41] Built of split green bamboo tied with coconut cords and soaked for several days in seawater to increase durability, weir baskets are called *yanup*, *omat*, *sonom*, *ual*, or *levinau*, depending on their design and use.[42] The bamboo weave of a weir basket is porous enough to let water in, but tight enough to capture algae, coconut shells, leaves, and other marine nutrients when the tide recedes. These plants and

10

9 Rafts ferrying coral rocks are floated out to new weir construction sites.
10 Active weir fishing photographed in 1910.

Larger Fish Are Contained in the Primary Chamber While Smaller Fish Are Channelled to the Secondary Chamber

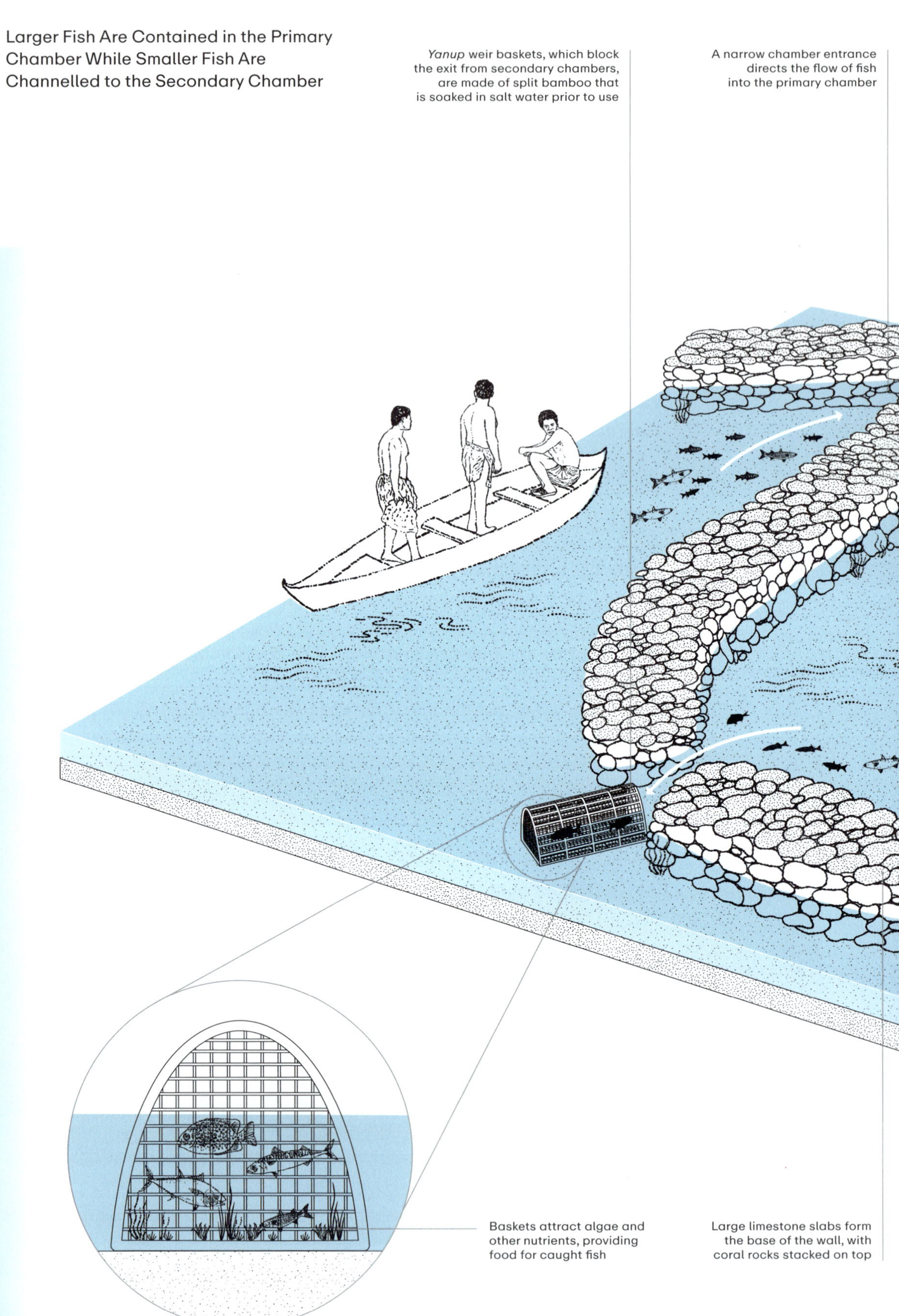

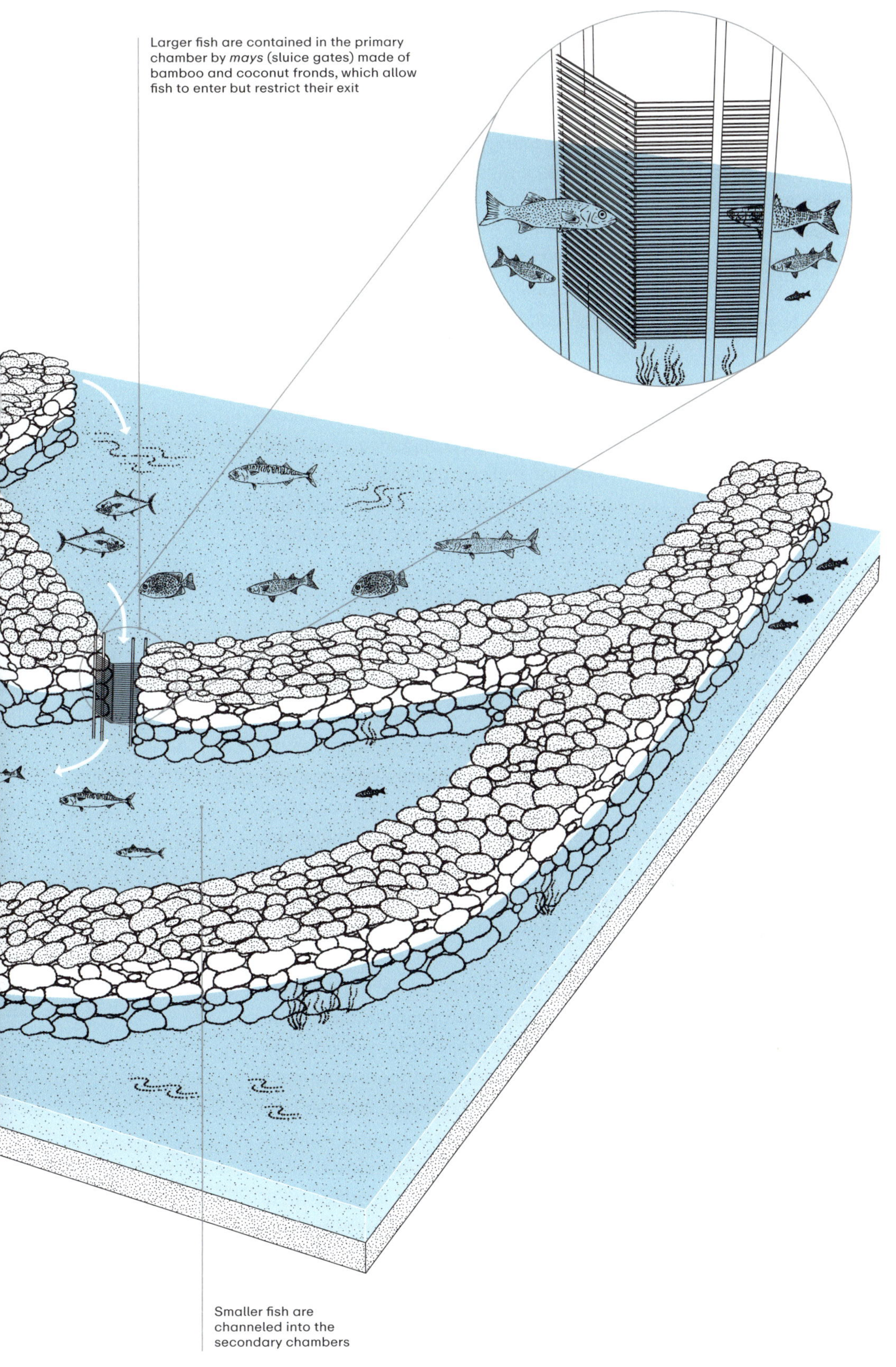
Larger fish are contained in the primary chamber by *mays* (sluice gates) made of bamboo and coconut fronds, which allow fish to enter but restrict their exit
Smaller fish are channeled into the secondary chambers

organisms decay inside the basket, becoming food for trapped fish.[43] To harvest fish, baskets are enveloped in a large net, then brought to shore and emptied with a hand net.[44] One arrow weir can fill a cargo canoe.[45] The amount and species of fish caught depends on the "fish season." For example, mackerel migrate near the shore from September to December and can be captured during those months.[46]

Before colonization and the introduction of pigs and cows, fish were the Yapese community's major food source. Today, fish is still considered a significant part of the island's cuisine, with particular fish species belonging to different communities based upon the ruling law.[47] For example, fish designated for the three higher-ranking villages include *wahu wahu*, yellowfin tuna, and bluefin tuna, while lower-ranking villages are allocated barracudas, puffer fish, and sharks.[48]

Though Yap's coastal waters are inhabited by as many as seven hundred *aech*, to avoid overexploiting marine species, they are never used simultaneously.[49] This vast number of weirs coexisted, as they could be ingeniously opened when unused or closed and converted into seaside reefs for aquatic species, such as *qurich* (swimming crab), *quloch* (mullet), *dayit* (rabbitfish), *saadiin* (baitfish), and *qey* (sea turtle).[50, 51] With over four hundred species of fish, 99 species of algae, and 168 species of coral, the Yapese fish weir's ability to capture such a diverse range of species demonstrates a deep intuition of the land, the sea, and the complexity of this coastline ecosystem.[52]

This intuition not only influenced the system's ability to catch but also release, protect, regulate, and cleanse. While *aech* form permeable, biodiverse habitats for a variety of species, they also help control the amount of fish harvested by giving the option to release those that are not needed, differentiating this technique from net fishing.[53, 54] Composed of a combination of limestone pavement and outcrops with a sediment cover, the reef flat is home to seven species of seagrass.[55] The fish weirs drive the current to deeper areas, moving runoff to the seagrass, which cleanses the water.[56] *Aech* also lessen the effects of typhoons by slowing waves like a breakwater.[57] Some of the larger weirs have reshaped the coastline by trapping sand and fortifying the shoreline and seagrass beds, while minimizing coastal erosion.[58]

Though these fish weirs have supported human and aquatic populations for millennia, fewer *aech* have been constructed since European contact in the 19th century. Colonization brought significant changes to Yapese communities and their infrastructures. There was a notable increase in coral stone mining from reefs for construction, which led to a high demand for male labor, causing conflicts with fishing schedules and resulting in the degradation of natural habitats for reef fish.[59] Today, Yapese people fish with nets, lines, spears, and weirs.[60, 61] Despite falling into disuse, the continued existence of the weirs signifies their centuries-long durability in the face of extreme climate events. Many still provide habitat for the reef fish that sustain Yap communities.[62] However, sea level rise has affected the height of fish weirs, requiring them to be raised.[63] As the direction of currents begins to shift, the optimal location for weir construction is changing as well.[64]

In recent years, historic preservationists have spoken out in support of the *aech*, and provided funding for the restoration of abandoned infrastructures.[65] Five Yap fish weirs have been restored, but their use has remained limited as they require time, labor, and further funding.[66] While there is a significant demand for Yapese fish in Guam, this market is supported by spearfishing.[67] Most owners of fish weirs work in town, while attending to the weirs early in the morning or on free days.[68] However, the essence of *aech* is still deeply tied to community.[69, 70] Using the tidal forces that capture fish, these ancient aquaculture infrastructures could one day be retrofitted with tidal technology, such as tidal-range exploitation, producing renewable energy for the Yap island community.[71] Such a hybridization could revitalize this powerful symbol of Yapese coastal culture and offer a reliable source of power to an underserved island community.

The *aech* of the Yapese are a fishing system activated by tidal fluctuations that also form an artificial reef habitat for many aquatic species. By allowing fish to live in the weir with water at low tide, the technology respects the limits of the ecosystem by not exercising overexploitation. These weirs have great potential to inform flood-adaptation infrastructure in the face of climate change by protecting the coastline, promoting biodiversity, storing water and carbon, producing resources, and adapting to rising sea levels. Beyond this, the cultural structure associated with particular fish species among certain villages, and the traditional practices behind fishing expeditions, signify the local value of the *aech*. While *aech* have become scarcely used, with funding knowledge, this original infrastructure can be further regenerated in Yap, and inform similar intelligent systems in other aquatic environments.

11

11 Restoration of abandoned infrastructures, funded by historic preservationists, has begun in recent years.

ENDNOTES

1. Bill Jeffery and William Pitmag, *The Aech of Yap: A Survey of Sites and Their Histories* (Yap: Yap State Historic Preservation Office, 2010): 3.
2. Jeffery and Pitmag, *The Aech of Yap*, 111.
3. Jeffery and Pitmag, *The Aech of Yap*, 119.
4. Jeffery and Pitmag, *The Aech of Yap*, 12.
5. Jeffery and Pitmag, *The Aech of Yap*, 12.
6. Jeffery and Pitmag, *The Aech of Yap*, 115–16.
7. Jeffery and Pitmag, *The Aech of Yap*, 115–16.
8. Jeffery and Pitmag, *The Aech of Yap*, 115–16.
9. Jeffery and Pitmag, *The Aech of Yap*, 45.
10. Rosalind L. Hunter-Anderson, "Yapese Stone Fish Traps," *Asian Perspectives* 24, no. 1 (1981): 88.
11. Jeffery and Pitmag, *The Aech of Yap*, 5.
12. Hunter-Anderson, "Yapese Stone Fish Traps," 85.
13. Jeffery and Pitmag, *The Aech of Yap*, 7.
14. Thomas Ganang (*aech* owner and construction expert) and Aloysius Guchbuw (restoration coordinator, Yap State Historic Preservation Office), in discussion with the author, January 2023.
15. Hunter-Anderson, "Yapese Stone Fish Traps," 85.
16. Ganang and Guchbuw, discussion.
17. Jeffery and Pitmag, *The Aech of Yap*, 119.
18. Jeffery and Pitmag, *The Aech of Yap*, 4.
19. Jay Dobbin and Francis X. Hezel, "The Old Religion of Yap," in *Summoning the Powers Beyond: Traditional Religions in Micronesia* (Honolulu: University of Hawai'i Press, 2011), 140.
20. Bill Jeffery, "Reviving Community Spirit: Furthering the Sustainable, Historical and Economic Role of Fish Weirs and Traps," *Journal of Maritime Archaeology* 8, no. 1 (2013): 40.
21. Jeffery and Pitmag, *The Aech of Yap*, 1.
22. Jeffery and Pitmag, *The Aech of Yap*, 138.
23. Jeffery and Pitmag, *The Aech of Yap*, 11–15.
24. Hunter-Anderson, "Yapese Stone Fish Traps," 85.
25. Jeffery and Pitmag, *The Aech of Yap*, 63.
26. Hunter-Anderson, "Yapese Stone Fish Traps," 81.
27. Ganang and Guchbuw, discussion.
28. Ganang and Guchbuw, discussion.
29. Jeffery and Pitmag, *The Aech of Yap*, 119.
30. Jeffery, "Reviving Community Spirit," 42.
31. Margie C. Falanruw and Lubuw Falanruw, "Stone Fish Weirs of Yap," *Traditional Marine Resource Management and Knowledge*, special edition (2003): 16.
32. Jeffery and Pitmag, *The Aech of Yap*, 16.
33. Falanruw and Falanruw, "Stone Fish Weirs of Yap," 17.
34. Jeffery, "Reviving Community Spirit," 45.
35. Jeffery and Pitmag, *The Aech of Yap*, 13.
36. Jeffery and Pitmag, *The Aech of Yap*, 12–13.
37. Jeffery and Pitmag, *The Aech of Yap*, 13.
38. Jeffery and Pitmag, *The Aech of Yap*, 15.
39. Ganang and Guchbuw, discussion.
40. Kata Karáth, "The Genius of Fishing with Tidal Weirs," *Nautilus*, April 7, 2022, https://nautil.us/the-genius-of-fishing-with-tidal-weirs-238455/.
41. Jeffery and Pitmag, *The Aech of Yap*, 13.
42. Jeffery and Pitmag, *The Aech of Yap*, 14.
43. Jeffery and Pitmag, *The Aech of Yap*, 12–13.
44. Jeffery and Pitmag, *The Aech of Yap*, 13.
45. Hunter-Anderson, "Yapese Stone Fish Traps," 85.
46. Ganang and Guchbuw, discussion.
47. Ganang and Guchbuw, discussion.
48. Ganang and Guchbuw, discussion.
49. Jeffery and Pitmag, *The Aech of Yap*, 19.
50. Ganang and Guchbuw, discussion.
51. Jeffery and Pitmag, *The Aech of Yap*, 18.
52. Jeffery and Pitmag, *The Aech of Yap*, 4.
53. Ganang and Guchbuw, discussion.
54. Ganang and Guchbuw, discussion.
55. Jeffery and Pitmag, *The Aech of Yap*, 4.
56. Ganang and Guchbuw, discussion.
57. Ganang and Guchbuw, discussion.
58. Jeffery and Pitmag, *The Aech of Yap*, 120.
59. Hunter-Anderson, "Yapese Stone Fish Traps," 88–89.
60. Jeffery and Pitmag, *The Aech of Yap*, 7.
61. Jeffery and Pitmag, *The Aech of Yap*, 113.
62. Falanruw and Falanruw, "Stone Fish Weirs of Yap," 17.
63. Ganang and Guchbuw, discussion.
64. Ganang and Guchbuw, discussion.
65. Jeffery, "Reviving Community Spirit," 38.
66. Ganang and Guchbuw, discussion.
67. Ganang and Guchbuw, discussion.
68. Ganang and Guchbuw, discussion.
69. Ganang and Guchbuw, discussion.
70. Jeffery and Pitmag, *The Aech of Yap*, 9–10.
71. Simon P. Neill et al., "Tidal Range Energy Resource and Optimization—Past Perspectives and Future Challenges," *Renewable Energy* 127 (2018): 764, https://doi.org/10.1016/j.renene.2018.05.007.

COAUTHOR

THOMAS GANANG

Aech Construction Expert

Thomas Ganang, a specialist in *aech* construction and aquaculture, comes from the village of Gachpar on the island of Gagil in the Micronesian state of Yap. At seven years old, he began frequently helping community elders maintain local weirs. Ganang ventually received an *aech* from his father to collect is own fish. He attended a local high school before elocating to Koror, Republic of Palau, where he earned is associate's degree in education from the College f Micronesia.

Today, Ganang actively works to impart the nowledge he inherited from his family to the next eneration in Gachpar. In recent years, he has helped ead a number of initiatives centered around commu-ity resilience and local ecology, including the onstruction of men's houses in two towns, the estab-shment of a seawall along Gachpar's coastline, and he development of the Gachpar marine protected reas program. Ganang is known to teach community nembers how to restore and maintain their *aech*— practice that is returning weirs to their original con-ition after years of disuse.

Ganang plays an active role in his community, erving as a leader and teaching young boys the art f constructing fish weirs. Ganang enjoys fishing and ardening; he has cleared much of his property o grow native plants like yam and taro which are sta-les in local Yapese cuisine. He and his wife still live n Gachpar. Together they have a son and a daughter, vho have moved to the United States.

COAUTHOR

ALOYSIUS GUCHBUW

Restoration Coordinator for Yap State's Historic Preservation Office

Aloysius Guchbuw, the restoration coordinator of Yap State's Historic Preservation Office (YSHPO), was born in the village of Gachpar in Gagil Municipality. His father serves as the chief of Gagil, which contributed to a strong sense of community and leadership throughout his upbringing. During his childhood, he often went fishing, tended to his family garden, and learned about taro patch agriculture.

During his early childhood, Guchbuw attended Gagil Community School from first to eighth grade, before attending Yap High School. Eager to pursue further education after receiving his high school diploma in 2012, Guchbuw enrolled at Palau Community College for a year before traveling to Northeast Normal University in 2013 to study Chinese. Guchbuw then enrolled at Dalian University of Technology and Engineering in 2014, majoring in civil engineering and graduating in 2018.

After receiving his degree, Guchbuw returned to his hometown in Yap. As restoration coordinator of YSHPO, he oversees the revitalization and preservation of cultural sites, managing paperwork and ensuring projects are completed successfully. His passion for his work at YSHPO is evident in his accomplishments, including the completion of 21 projects on historic sites since 2018.

Outside of work, he enjoys connecting to his roots through fishing and gardening. Guchbuw is actively involved in his community, attending to the needs of the village. He is currently working on new restoration initiatives, collecting oral history in his community, and a canoe building project.

BOUCHOT MUSSEL TRESTLES *of* THE BRETONS *and* NORMANS *France*

BOUCHOT MUSSEL TRESTLES *of* THE BRETONS *and* NORMANS *France*

Coauthored with Ian Wood

PEOPLE Bretons and Normans LOCATION Bay of Mont Saint-Michel, France TECHNOLOGY mussel trestles ELEVATION 5–80 m ORIGIN 123 CE DISTANCE ABOVE OR BELOW WATERLINE +2.7 to −2.7 m WATER LEVEL FLUCTUATION, TIDAL OR SEASONAL 0 to +14 m

FAO Nexus
WATER salt ENERGY tidal FOOD mussels

IPCC Adaptation Pathway
protect

World Bank NBS
CATEGORY sandy shores, salt marshes, natural inland wetlands
FUNCTIONS water pollution regulation, biodiversity, soil pollution regulation
BENEFITS resource production, carbon storage and sequestration, biodiversity, cultural, stimulate local economies and job creation, education, tourism and recreation

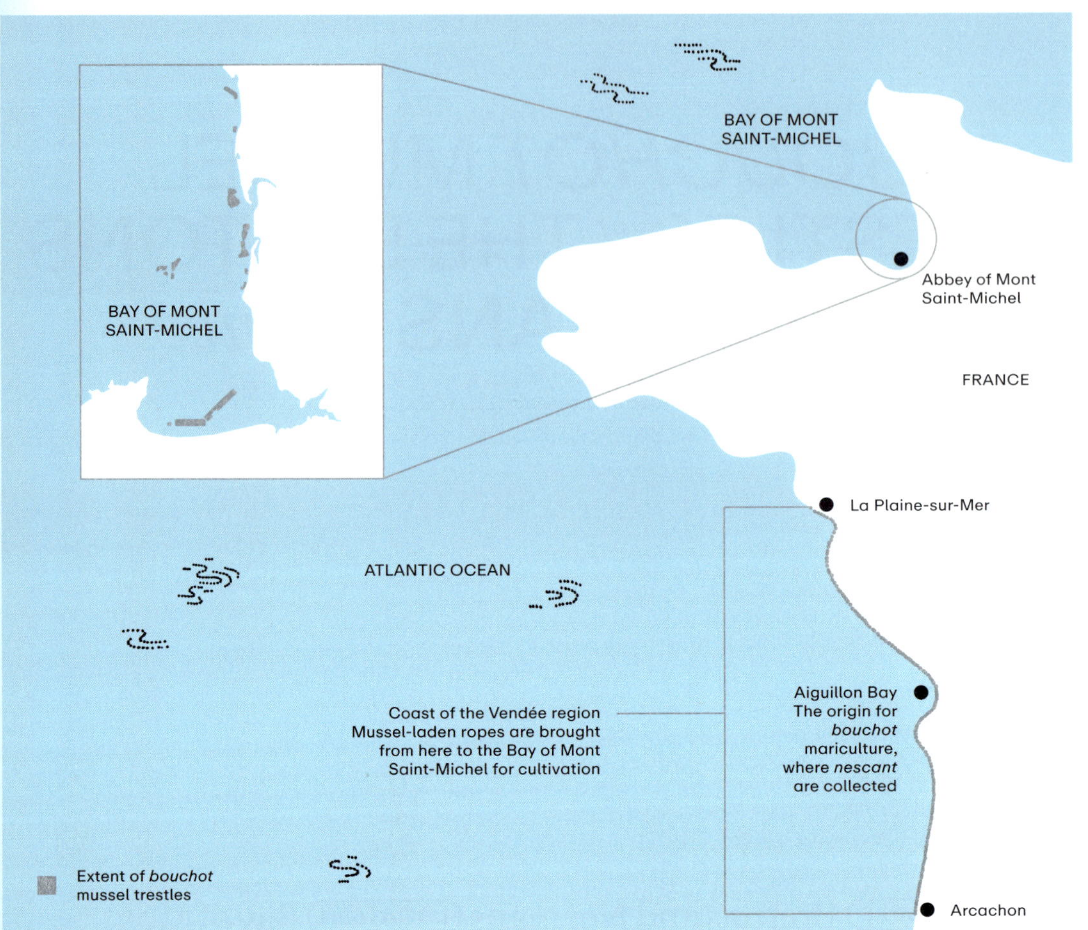

The five-hundred-square-kilometer Bay of Mont Saint-Michel, where the sea flows across a 14-meter fluctuation, is home to the largest tidal range in Europe.[1] If timed with the ebb and flow of the tides, visitors can walk through a three-hundred-square-kilometer forest of wood pylons, or *pieux*, used as scaffoldings for mussel farming, with the mystical medieval Mont-Saint-Michel Abbey in the distance.[2, 3] Indigenous to the French Atlantic coast, *bouchot* mussel trestles use pilings sunk deep into the sand and wrapped in rope. These rope-covered *pieux* then become home to the seeds of young mussels (*Mytilus edulis*).[4, 5] The word *bouchot* refers to the traditional technique of mussel aquaculture whereby a single farm is composed of a row of square timber *pieux* that rise twice the height of a human.[6, 7] Dwarfed by comparison, the miniature mussels, en masse, work to enrich and maintain the equilibrium of the bay ecosystem.[8, 9]

It is the unique tidal phenomenon in the bay that makes it possible to sustain *bouchot* aquaculture, among the most esteemed and protected practices of mussel cultivation in the world. This phenomenal tidal range also highlights the potential for the bay to produce a renewable energy source that could coexist with the *bouchot* to create a revolutionary nature-based mariculture infrastructure that could clean water, generate energy, and produce food.

1 Algae-covered bouchot mussels cluster along ropes laid horizontally across wooden frames known as *chantiers*.
2 A mussel farmer wrapping mussel-filled ropes surrounded by netting around *bouchot* posts

For centuries, *bouchot* aquaculture was practiced exclusively on the French Atlantic coast. While the word *bouchot* itself is used to refer to an area where mussels are bred, it is attributed to several origins—some understand it as a contraction of the English *bout* (fence) and *chot* (of wood), while others consider it to be derived from the French *bouche* (mouth). Tracing back to a 17th-century story by writer Louise Swanton, the *bouchot* was invented by an Irishman named Patrick Walton, who shipwrecked in the Aiguillon Bay in 1235. Upon settling, he began to hunt seabirds by stretching nets between wooden poles staked along the coastline.[10] To his surprise, masses of mussels attached to the pylons, and the tradition of mussel growing began.[11] Although the 13th-century origin of this technology was in the distant Aiguillon Bay, the Bay of Mont Saint-Michel has become known for its *bouchot* aquaculture. Mussel farming began here in 1954 in the village of Vivier-sur-Mer.[12, 13] Perfectly suited to the drastic tidal fluctuations, the technology quickly flourished, producing healthy, mineral-rich mussels.[14]

The palm-sized common blue mussel (*Mytilus edulis*) is the main *bouchot* species. Growing in dense populations, mussels breathe and feed through their gills, while contributing to the health of their ecosystems by filtering pollutants from the water, increasing the content of carbon and nitrogen in sediments, and

1

2

modifying substrates to support communities of algae.[15, 16, 17] Their orange-yellow bodies are encased in smooth, round, flattened, hinged shells made of calcium carbonate and adorned with blue and brown rays, which develop a purple hue as they age.[18] Today, *bouchot* accounts for 65 percent of the country's aquaculture production and 25 percent of all mussels grown in France.[19, 20] The same form of cultivation is found in Brittany and Normandy, on the Atlantic Ocean, and also along the North Sea coast.[21]

While the intertidal basin of the Bay of Mont Saint-Michel is ideal for the cultivation of the mussels, the water isn't warm enough for the natural reproduction and collection of the non-native *Mytilus edulis* mussel in its juvenile state, known as *nescant*.[22, 23, 24] Few mussel seeds will naturally attach themselves to the pilings, so the one- to two-millimeter-long *nescant* are captured elsewhere using ropes, which are eventually coiled around the *bouchot*.[25, 26]

In March, *nescant* collection begins in the Vendée region of the French Atlantic coast, about three hundred kilometers from Bordeaux.[27] For two months, hundreds of meters of biodegradable hemp or coconut-fiber ropes are strung horizontally on offshore platforms to collect thousands of mussel larvae, which stick to the hairy texture of the ropes to develop and produce shells.[28]

3 Biodegradable hemp or coconut-fiber ropes collect thousands of mussel larvae, which stick to the hairy texture of the ropes while developing.
4 From June until late summer the mussel-covered ropes are arranged on *chantiers*.

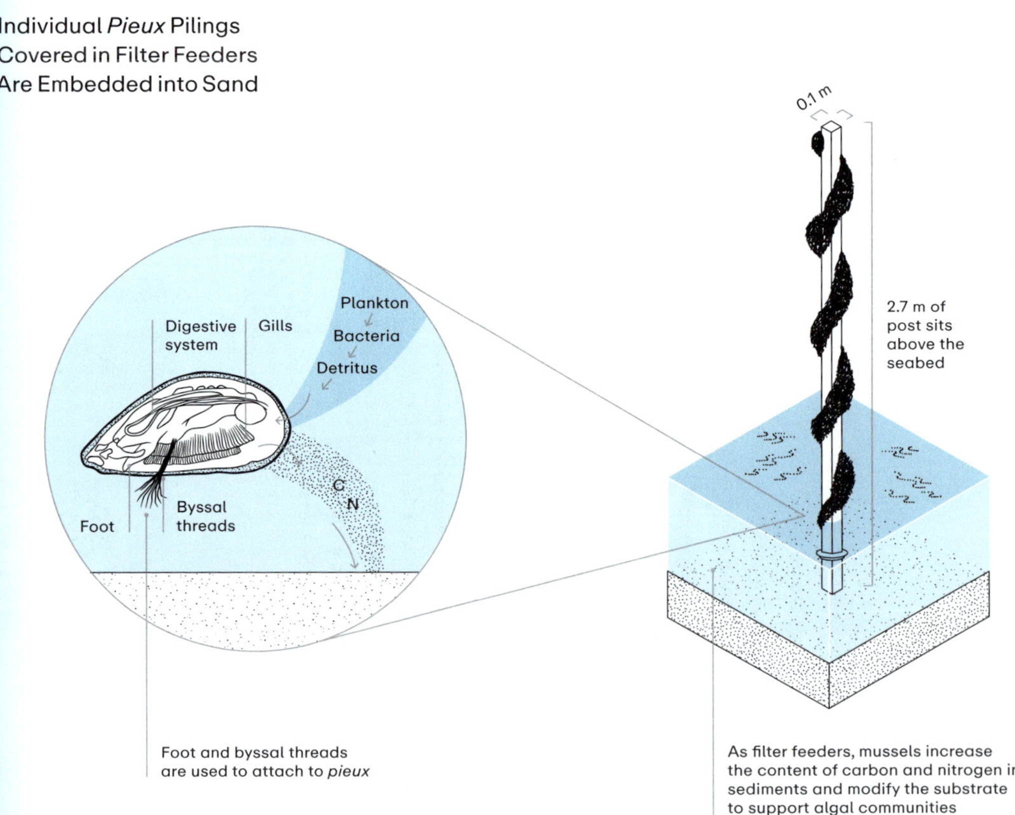

3

4

One-hundred-meter-long ropes covered in *nescant* are then coiled into a plastic, basketlike container to be driven to the Bay of Mont Saint-Michel.[29]

At the beginning of April, the ropes are placed on table-like wooden structures called *chantiers*, where they continue to grow before they're coiled around *pieux*.[30, 31] *Chantiers* can be placed between lines of *bouchot* farms, or up to 20 kilometers away. The mussel-covered ropes remain on the *chantiers* from April to May, awaiting the previous season's harvest. Once the *pieux* becomes available, the new ropes, laden with young mussels, are coiled around them.[32] These mussels eventually grow to cover the entire length of the piling, 10 centimeters wide,

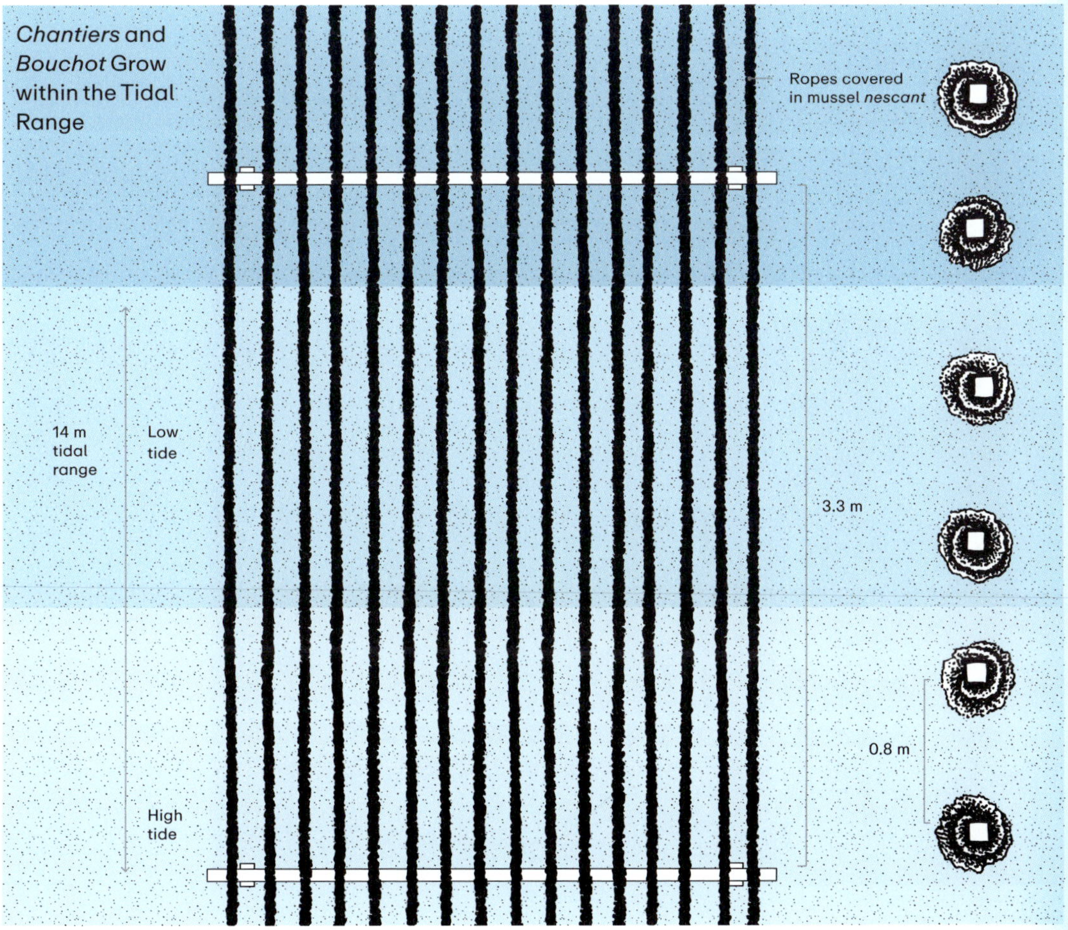

Chantiers and *Bouchot* Grow within the Tidal Range

Ropes covered in mussel *nescant*

14 m tidal range

Low tide

High tide

3.3 m

0.8 m

Seasonal Life Cycle of *Bouchot* Mariculture

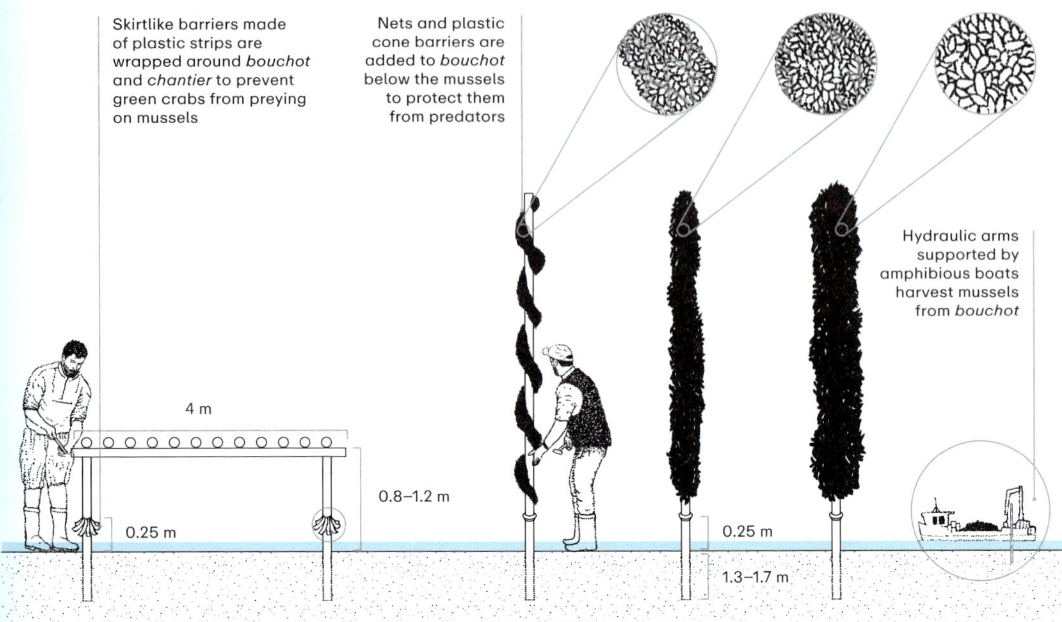

5

5 Between 25 and 50 *nescant*-covered ropes are placed on 100-meter-long *chantiers* to grow mussels.

four to five meters in length, though embedded to stand only 2.7 centimeters high.[33] By the end of July, next year's ropes have been cut into intervals of 3.3 meters, the ideal length to be evenly wrapped around the wooden pilings at least 25 centimeters from the bottom, to keep mussels safe from the muddy seabed and predators.[34, 35] Made of pine and oak in the past, today's pylons in the Bay of Mont Saint-Michel are commonly made from *Lophira alata* and *Dinizia excelsa* timber, sourced from South America and West Africa.[36]

Positioned one hundred meters perpendicular from the shore, a *bouchot* farm is composed of one line of individual pilings, stretching 110 to 130 meters from the shore to the sea. Placed side by side in lines 25 meters apart, a group of farms will typically cover 20 hectares.[37, 38, 39] Exposure to the sun and changing sea levels fortify their shells and produce well-developed flesh; mussels located farther out tend to grow faster.[40, 41]

As the mussels grow, ducks, fish, oyster drills, seagulls, and spider crabs prey on the farms. *Bouchot* farmers use protective barriers, including nets of different stiffnesses, which mitigate weather conditions; cone-shaped plastic barriers directly at the base of the ropes; and "hula skirts" made of plastic strips. The location of the *bouchot* farm and the local predators determine what type of protective barrier is used for the *chaintier* and *bouchot* pilings, such as hula

One-Hundred-Meter Line
of *Bouchot* Is One Farm

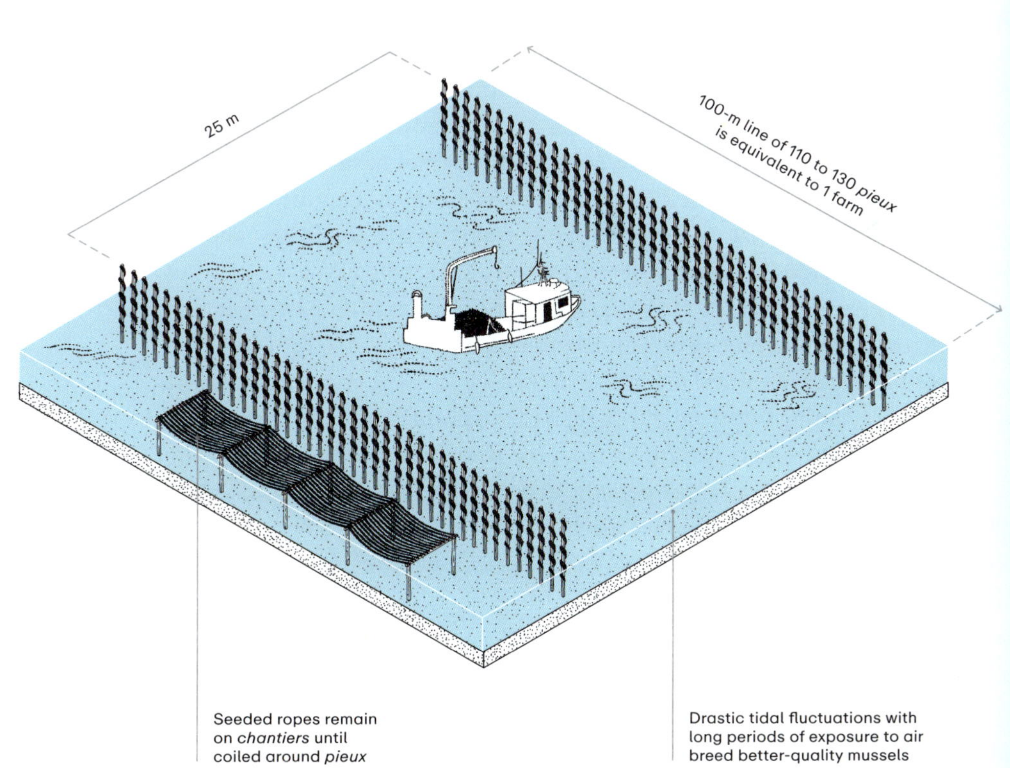

6

7

skirts, which protect the mussels from dog whelks (*Nucella lapillus*) and green shore crabs (*Carcinus maenas*). Farmers also remove excess algae to protect the mussels from predators in the algae and to remove a natural ladder for predators to climb.[42, 43]

Every year in August, a mussel festival held in Vivier-sur-Mer serves freshly gathered *bouchot* mussels from the bay.[44] Between July and September, mature mussels greater than four centimeters long are harvested by hydraulic arms supported on amphibious boats.[45, 46, 47] The mussels are placed in an oxygenated purification pool of pumped bay water, then sorted, cleaned, and distributed.[48]

Bouchot mussels in the Bay of Mont Saint-Michel have been protected, since 2006, by the Appellation d'Origine Contrôlée, which identifies products from a specific area that are grown using traditional knowledge, and by a European Protected Designation of Origin, since 2011.[49] However, they are not considered "organic" because of the agricultural pollution from pesticides that flows into the bay from three rivers: the Couesnon, the Sélune, and the Sée.[50] The bay experiences a rare natural phenomenon known as *le mascaret* (tidal bores), in which the incoming tide from the English Channel enters the bay in the opposite direction of the waters flowing in from the three rivers.[51] This exposes the mussels to the open air for longer periods, and, in response, they remain tightly closed outside of water and produce hardier mussels.[52] Nearby ecosystems also benefit, such as the submerged seagrass (*Zostera marina*) in the Chausey Archipelago, which thrives off the silt produced by mussels.

Due to the size and slope of the bay, which causes significant fluctuations in water temperature, it is known as "the nursery." Hedgerows and polders; marine environments, like mudflats; and transitional environments between land and sea like marine and freshwater marshes, estuaries, and rivers flowing into the bay all coexist here, fostering the beginning of life for a large number

POLDER
A tract of lowland reclaimed from a body of water by the construction of dikes parallel to the shoreline.

ESTUARY
Where a river meets the sea, creating a mix of salt water and fresh water.

8

9

6 Predators such as crabs attack newly wrapped ropes laden with young mussels.
7 Mussels are removed from the *pieux* with the fisher and placed on the tray of the tractor trailer.
8 Mussel farming in the bay in 2013 generated more than 20 million euros and employed 315 people.
9 Mussel boats attached with hydraulic arms for extraction.

of animals.[53] These conditions of the bay also affect the movement of matter, microorganisms, and nutrients, which provide an abundant food supply for the filter feeders, while preventing diseases and parasites among *bouchot* farms.[54, 55, 56]

While a thriving ecosystem and market economy are a rare coexistence, in 2013 it was reported that mussel production in the Bay of Mont Saint-Michel generated more than 20 million euros and employed over 315 people.[57] In the late 1950s, commercial-scale mussel mariculture was introduced, bringing plastics such as nets and a parasite called *mytilicol*. In response, growers limited the quantity, density, location, and seeding rate of *bouchot* in the bay, which resulted in the growth of healthier, more resilient mussels. With a low carbon footprint compared to land breeding systems, carbon-sequestration and eutrophication-mitigation rates fluctuate in response to the management of discarded shells, fuel consumption for transport, and the use of more durable, imported exotic woods.[58, 59]

In the background of the bay's *bouchot* looms the medieval Gothic structure of the Abbey of Mont Saint-Michel, which was declared a historic monument in 1862 by the Benedictines. Built in the 11th and 16th centuries, the abbey became a site for Christian pilgrimage throughout the Middle Ages.[60] Crucially tied to the cultural value of the abbey, the bay was later protected through coastal law and the Ramsar Convention; however, processes like tidal flush to remove sediment have had a negative impact on the health of the aquaculture.[61]

While aquaculture and tourism are the strongest economies of the bay, the impressive tidal dynamics, which are ideal for growing *bouchot*, also offer an untapped source of renewable tidal energy. Shaped like a funnel, with a narrow entrance that creates a tidal bore up to 14 meters in height, renewable energy could coexist alongside the *bouchot*, or be integrated in the physical infrastructure of the *pieux*. Both this significant tidal range and the strong tidal currents could be exploited by retrofitting this traditional low carbon footprint coastal infrastructure, using technologies like tidal stream generators, tidal barrage, or tidal range turbines to create a new hybrid system or ancestral renewables. A hybrid system would have multifunctional benefits—food production and water cleansing; support of critical surrounding ecosystems and their marine wildlife populations, which buffer coasts from flooding and storm surge; carbon sequestration and eutrophication mitigation through wooden pilings and in mussel shells—while also producing local, clean energy.[62, 63, 64] In turn, this transition would mitigate carbon emissions, which is the greatest threat to the system itself and to the entire oceanic landscape.

Bouchot mussel Trestles in the Bay of Mont Saint-Michel are an ancestral architecture for food production that also sustains and protects its surrounding ecosystem. As filter feeders, the cultivated *Mytilus edulis* mussels improve water quality, stabilize the bay's ecosystem, support habitat diversity, and accelerate the migration of important chemical elements.[65] In many ways, the attention associated with mussel production in this particular bay has stemmed from the cultural value associated with the medieval Abbey of Mont Saint-Michel. As cultural values change in the wake of the climate crisis, these aquaculture infrastructures could also evolve to generate clean, renewable energy, which reduces fossil fuel dependence and greenhouse gas emissions. Akin to Walton's discovery of spontaneous mussel architecture along this stretch of the French Atlantic coast, the future of this protected ecosystem could foster a new frontier in tidal energy and aquaculture production.

EUTROPHICATION
When a body of water becomes overly enriched with nutrients, causing excessive harmful growth of algae and plants.

RAMSAR CONVENTION
A global treaty that seeks to conserve, recognize, and sustainably manage wetlands.

CARBON SEQUESTRATION
The process of capturing and storing carbon dioxide to reduce its presence in the atmosphere.

10 Lines of *bouchot* posts range across the tidal landscape of the bay.

10

1. Antoine Mury et al., "High Resolution Shoreline and Shelly Ridge Monitoring over Stormy Winter Events: A Case Study in the Megatidal Bay of Mont-Saint-Michel (France)," *Journal of Marine Science and Engineering* 7 (2019): 4, https://doi.org/10.3390/jmse7040097.
2. "Mont-Saint-Michel and Its Bay," UNESCO World Heritage Convention, accessed February 17, 2024, https://whc.unesco.org/en/list/80.
3. Marilyn Brouwer, "Mussels from the Bay of Mont Saint-Michel," France Today, October 19, 2016, https://francetoday.com/culture/made_in_france/mussels-from-the-bay-of-mont-saint-michel/.
4. Joël Aubin and Caroline Fontaine, "Environmental Impacts of Producing Bouchot Mussels in Mont-Saint-Michel Bay (France) using LCA with Emphasis on Potential Climate Change and Eutrophication," in *Proceedings of the 9th International Conference on Life Cycle Assessment in the Agri-Food Sector*, ed. R. Schenck and D. Huizenga (Vashon, WA: ACLCA, 2014), 64.
5. Ian Wood (*bouchot* and shellfish farmer), in discussion with the author, November 2022.
6. Wood, discussion.
7. Lisa Gauvrit and Burkhard Schaer, "PDO Saint-Michel's Bay Bouchot Mussels in France," in *Sustainability of European Food Quality Schemes*, ed. Filippo Arfini and Valentin Bellassen (Cham: Springer Nature, 2019), 487, https://doi.org/10.1007/978-3-030-27508-2_25.
8. Pia Norling, "Importance of Blue Mussels for Biodiversity and Ecosystem Functioning in Subtidal Habitats" (PhD dissertation, Stockholm University, 2009).
9. Aubin and Fontaine, "Environmental Impacts of Producing Bouchot," 67–68.
10. Marie-Jose Dardignac-Corbeil, "La Culture des Moules sur Bouchots," *Science de la Pêche, Bulletin de l'Institut des Pêches Maritimes* 244 (1975): 1.
11. "Moule de Bouchot," Pleine Mer, accessed February 17, 2024, https://www.pleinemer.com/bouchot.htm.
12. Gauvrit and Schaer, "PDO Saint-Michel's Bay Bouchot," 488.
13. "Bouchot Mussels from Mont-Saint-Michel Bay," France-Voyage, accessed February 18, 2024, https://www.france-voyage.com/gastronomy/bouchot-mussels-from-mont-saint-michel-bay-486.htm.
14. Kat Craddock, "These Disappearing Mussels Are Grown in the Shadow of a Medieval Floating Castle," Saveur, June 29, 2018, https://www.saveur.com/mussels-in-saint-michel-bay/.
15. Vicki Bonham and David Roberts, "Mytilus Edulis (Common Blue Mussel)," *CABI Compendium* (2022): 3, https://doi.org/10.1079/cabicompendium.73755.
16. Bonham and Roberts, "Mytilus Edulis (Common Blue Mussel)," 19.
17. Norling, "Importance of Blue Mussels for Biodiversity."
18. Bonham and Roberts, "Mytilus Edulis (Common Blue Mussel)," 4.
19. Elizabeth Gosling, *Marine Mussels: Ecology, Physiology, Genetics and Culture* (Hoboken: Wiley, 2012), 637, https://doi.org/10.1002/9781119293927.
20. Brouwer, "Mussels from the Bay of Mont Saint-Michel."
21. Gauvrit and Schaer, "PDO Saint-Michel's Bay Bouchot," 487.
22. Aubin and Fontaine, "Environmental Impacts of Producing Bouchot," 65.
23. Gosling, *Marine Mussels*, 637.
24. Wood, discussion.
25. Prou Jean and Goulletquer Philippe, "The French Mussel Industry: Present Status and Perspectives," *Bulletin of the Aquaculture Association of Canada* 102, no. 3 (2002): 18.
26. Gauvrit and Schaer, "PDO Saint-Michel's Bay Bouchot," 487.
27. Dardignac-Corbeil, "La Culture des Moules sur Bouchots," 5.
28. Jean and Philippe, "The French Mussel Industry," 18.
29. Wood, discussion.
30. Jean and Philippe, "The French Mussel Industry," 18.
31. Dardignac-Corbeil, "La Culture des Moules sur Bouchots," 3.
32. Wood, discussion.
33. Gosling, *Marine Mussels*, 637.
34. Wood, discussion.
35. "Bouchot Mussels," *Taste France*, February 18, 2024, https://www.tastefrance.com/us/french-products/seafood/bouchot-mussels.
36. Aubin and Fontaine, "Environmental Impacts of Producing Bouchot," 65.
37. Aubin and Fontaine, "Environmental Impacts of Producing Bouchot," 65.
38. Wood, discussion.
39. Gosling, *Marine Mussels*, 637.
40. Gauvrit and Schaer, "PDO Saint-Michel's Bay Bouchot," 487.
41. Craddock, "These Disappearing Mussels."
42. Gosling, *Marine Mussels*, 637.
43. Wood, discussion.
44. "Bouchot Mussels from Mont-Saint-Michel Bay."
45. Wood, discussion.
46. "Working on the Mussels," accessed April 17, 2024, http://laperlefine.fr/perlemouleng.html.
47. Brouwer, "Mussels from the Bay of Mont Saint-Michel."
48. Aubin and Fontaine, "Environmental Impacts of Producing Bouchot," 65–66.
49. Gauvrit and Schaer, "PDO Saint-Michel's Bay Bouchot," 489.
50. Wood, discussion.
51. Philippe Deneufve, "The Tides around the Mont-Saint-Michel," Normandy Tourism, February 13, 2023, https://en.normandie-tourisme.fr/the-tides-of-the-mont-saint-michel/.
52. Craddock, "These Disappearing Mussels."
53. Wood, discussion.
54. Craddock, "These Disappearing Mussels."
55. Gauvrit and Schaer, "PDO Saint-Michel's Bay Bouchot," 492.
56. Wood, discussion.
57. Gauvrit and Schaer, "PDO Saint-Michel's Bay Bouchot," 494.
58. Wood, discussion.
59. Aubin and Fontaine, "Environmental Impacts of Producing Bouchot," 67–68.
60. Brouwer, "Mussels from the Bay of Mont Saint-Michel."
61. Wood, discussion.
62. Gauvrit and Schaer, "PDO Saint-Michel's Bay Bouchot Mussels in France," 492.
63. Aubin and Fontaine, "Environmental Impacts of Producing Bouchot," 67–68.
64. Wood, discussion.
65. Norling, "Importance of Blue Mussels for Biodiversity."

COAUTHOR

IAN WOOD

Bouchot and Shellfish Farmer

Born in the United Kingdom, Ian Wood has resided in France for the past 28 years, currently calling a small village in the south of Normandy home. Wood oversees the production of *bouchot* mussels, oysters, clams, and cockles at the Huîtrier du Marae farm situated on the Chausey Archipelago in the Bay of Mont Saint-Michel. Eleven years ago, he joined forces with three other Normans to begin the shellfish farm—a project that involved revitalizing a neglected property into a successful aquaculture operation. His years of experience led him to become an expert in the unique practice of *bouchot* cultivation.

Throughout his childhood, Wood aspired to become a marine biologist. He pursued higher education in the United Kingdom, but transitioned into a career in outdoor sports coaching. Subsequently, he embarked on a four-year military education and eventually relocated to France. Upon settling in Normandy, he found that the winter climate was not conducive to the outdoor sports he specialized in. This prompted his exploration into oyster farming, eventually branching into other forms of shellfish cultivation, including *bouchot* mussels.

Today, he and his team manage the production of a variety of shellfish around the Bay of Mont Saint-Michel. This involves receiving baby mussels, placing them on *chantier*, coiling mussel ropes around *bouchot* posts, protecting mussels from predators such as seabirds and crabs, assessing when mussels are ready for harvest, and clearing the mussels beginning in mid-August. Throughout these processes, mussel farmers like Wood must be mindful of the large tidal range of the bay, where high to low tides range across 14 meters in five hours.

Wood's role involves navigating constant change. While his primary focus is on shellfish production, success hinges on numerous dynamic factors, including the behavior of the shellfish themselves, interactions with other bay inhabitants, tidal patterns, and weather conditions. Over the past three years, seagulls and crabs have posed a greater threat to mariculture practices, as mishandled human waste, fishing restrictions, and global warming have affected populations of natural predators. This led Wood and his team to experiment with different protection systems, including nets and plastic barriers, to dissuade predators from eating mussels. The effectiveness of these measures is evaluated during harvest, when teams decide whether strategies are worthwhile investments.

The time and energy required for Wood's job can be expansive, as a round of mussel cultivation can last from three to four years. Understanding the environment and its uncertainties are crucial to the development of his work, and will continue to be its leading force.

When not engaged in mussel farming, Wood leads people on pilgrimages across the Bay of Mont Saint-Michel, navigates sea kayaks along the French coast, and is currently undertaking the construction of a wooden house.

ASI CORAL ISLANDS *of* THE WALE I ASI *Solomon Islands*

ASI CORAL ISLANDS *of* THE WALE I ASI *Solomon Islands*

Coauthored by
Tsatsa Seimarlie and Gideon Bouro

PEOPLE Wale I Asi LOCATION Langa Langa Lagoon on Malaita, Solomon Islands TECHNOLOGY *asi* artificial coral rock islands ELEVATION 0 m ORIGIN 1700 CE DISTANCE ABOVE OR BELOW WATERLINE +1 to +2 m WATER LEVEL FLUCTUATION, TIDAL OR SEASONAL +0.7 to +9 m

FAO Nexus
WATER salt ENERGY tidal + passive
FOOD coconut + lettuce + fish

IPCC Adaptation Pathway
advance

World Bank NBS
CATEGORY sandy shores, mangrove forests
FUNCTIONS sea level rise adaptation, heat regulation, biodiversity
BENEFITS coastal flood risk reduction, resource production, carbon storage and sequestration, biodiversity, cultural, human health, social interaction

1

2

3

1 Aerial view of the artifical islands of Funafou and Niuleni.
2 Aerial view of Funafou Island shows the diversity of built and natural programs in response to microclimatic conditions.
3 A dock for boats on an island where residents spend most of their time on the water.

Among the shallow-watered seagrass meadows of the ocean-side Akwalaafu Lagoon on the northwest side of the Solomon Islands' Malaita Province, clusters of Wale I Asi homes are built on islands of stacked coral rock.[1] These saltwater people, whose lineage is steeped in folklore linking them to ancient sharks, are thought to have traveled to the lagoon from other territories 15 to 20 generations ago.[2] Constructed from local materials, the *asi* (sea) islands are a unique form of aquatic land expansion.[3] Materials collected from coral reefs, combined with shallow waters and a sheltered lagoon, create the perfect conditions for their construction. Generally small, these artificial islands are scaled to fit only a few families, maintaining a balance with the environment and ensuring that materials are used sustainably and that oceanic flows remain unrestricted.

The Wale I Asi (people of the sea), also referred to as Wane Asi and the saltwater people of Malaita, are a Melanesian community that live on islands of coral rock in the Langa Langa Lagoon.[4, 5] They are a community of fishers who have historically bartered fish for root crops and vegetables with the Wane Tolo (bush people), who inhabit the interior of the Malaita forest and practice shifting cultivation. Today, this distinction is less absolute, as Wale I Asi and Wane Tolo interchangeably practice fishing and cultivation; however, the names for their communities remain.[6] The Wale I Asi produce *tafuli'ae* (shell wealth), which are strings of the polished shells used as currency throughout the Solomon

Archipelago.[7] They travel along the west coast of Malaita to trade shells and harvest natural marine resources. The exchange of shell money has also contributed to the vibrant transformation of Malaita and the Solomon Islands into a hub for skilled shipbuilding.

One of the main ethnic subgroups of the Wale I Asi are the Langalanga, a six-thousand-person community inhabiting the *asi* artificial islands of the lagoon, making it one of the most populated areas in the region.[8] The Langalanga people are deeply connected to the environment, as evidenced by their language's many bodily metaphors for landscape—for example, *gwaula kwai* refers to "head of a river," *abalola kwai* means "body of a river," and the the notion of human change to the environment is expressed as *fuli aela* (footprint).[9] The Langalanga distinguish inhabited artificial islands, called *falaua tolea*, from once-inhabited but now abandoned islands, *fau rara* (rock shore).[10] As families grow, more rocks are collected during low tides and new ground for extra housing is built. Dwellings are located around the island's perimeter, forming a central public space for communal activities.

The Langa Langa Lagoon stretches 22 kilometers north to south along the coast, reaching two kilometers wide.[11] Two theories explain the existence of the *asi* islands in this lagoon environment: as protection from enemies on land or to reduce the spread of malaria in coastal communities.[12] Some of the islands are entirely artificial, while others are artificial expansions of natural islands, ranging in size from one thousand square meters to approximately 120,000 square meters, which is the size of the largest known *asi*, Laulasi Island.[13] Usually,

Strategic Siting of *Asi* Artificial Coral Islands

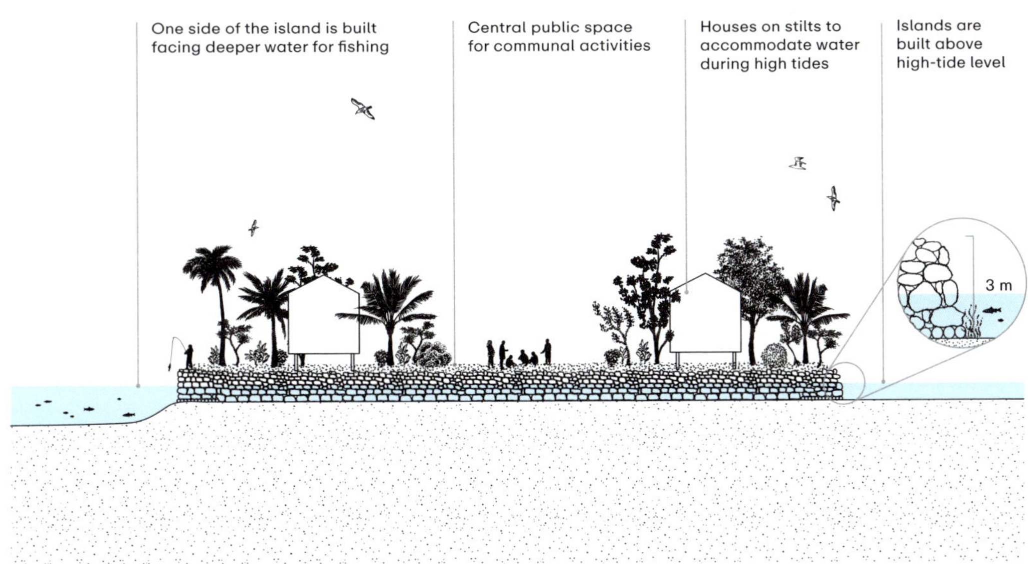

4

4 Some islands are entirely artifical, while others are expansions of existing natural islands.

the islands rise just above the high-water mark, and houses are further raised above the water level on stilts.[14]

To begin construction of an *asi*, the Langalanga paddle to the mainland, where stones and gravel are gathered and carried to a desired location using a log raft.[15] Rafts are positioned at the island perimeter to designate its construction zone, then they are weighted and submerged with local coral stone. Stones are continuously stacked until the island's surface reaches above the high-water mark, which is often more than three meters. Fine coral rubble and soil gathered from the river, beach, or reef are then added to level the island, followed by a layer of seagrass (*Halophila ovalis*) to smooth and soften the island's surface, making it easier to traverse.[16]

To ensure an island's durability, the first rock is placed by the *kastom* (custom) priest to secure the power of the shark, believed to be a reincarnation of ancestors who protect their descendants.[17] The Langalanga participate in a weekly communal effort to maintain these permanent landmasses, carrying gravel and stones to the islands to ensure their resilience against waves and tidal impact, in a continuous process of maintenance.[18]

While one side of an island is uniquely positioned in deeper water to accommodate fishing, atop the islands, the Langalanga plant trees such as *Excoecaria*, developing a strong, intricate root system that grows to bind the coral rocks and soil together.[19] *Alu* (banyan trees or *Ficus benghalensis*) are planted on every island to provide shade, alongside fish poison trees (*Barringtonia asiatica*).[20, 21] Coconut and lettuce trees (*Pisonia*) are also planted for food production on the *asi* and have diversified the livelihoods of the Wale I Asi.

Stages of *Asi* Island Construction

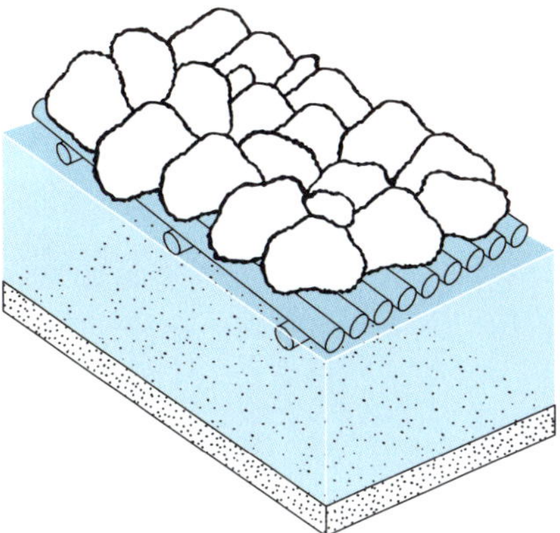

1. Stones are carried to new island site using a log raft, positioned at the perimeter to designate the construction zone

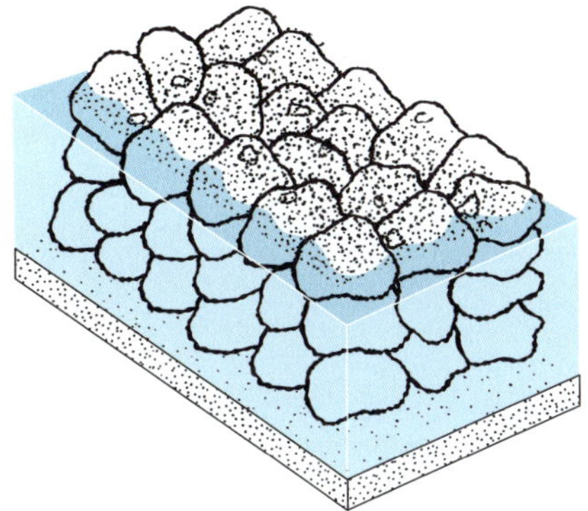

3. Fine coral rubble and soil, gathered from riverbeds, beaches, and reefs, are added to fill holes and level new land

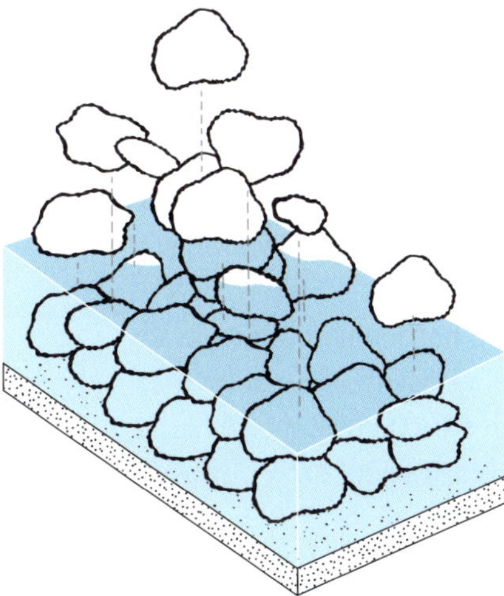

2. Coral stones are sunk, then layered until their stacked surface rises above the high-water mark

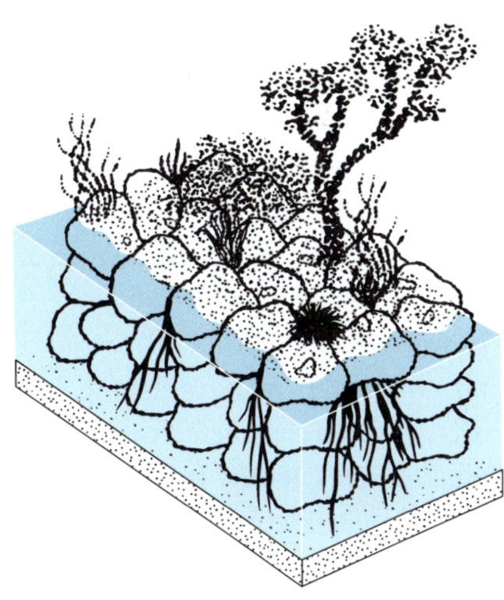

4. Plants like *alu* are planted, binding the coral stones together, before *asi* are inhabited

5

5 Stones are continuously stacked until the island's surface reaches above the high-water mark.
6 Houses are constructed on stilts to accommodate high tides.

Powder-puff trees (*Barringtonia racemosa*), known locally as *fala'adai*, are used as living fence posts for pig enclosures that keep growing and require minimal repair. Historically, marauding tribes were warded off by two- to three-meter-high stone walls built around the *asi* coral islands. To this day, *fera* (sacred shrines) are raised on a coral platform in a central area for meetings and worship.[22]

The Wale I Asi are naturally resourceful, necessitated by a lack of easy access to materials; the reuse of the local commodities is commonplace. Local tree species *mamafua* (*Flueggea flexuosa*) serves as housing posts that last for over 50 years, and its leaves, used to thatch roofs, which are continuously replaced. Wood used for the rafters, floor joists, cross beams, purlins, and studs of houses come from mangrove species like *Rhizophora apiculata, Ceriops tagal, Lumnitzera littorea,* and *Bruguiera paviflora*.[23]

As population density and infrastructure grows, houses are built to straddle the land and water, making fishing and canoeing easily accessible. The wooden posts are also constructed using timber from various tree species such as *U'ula* (*Intsia bijuga*), locally known as *ifit*, New Guinea teak (*Vitex coffasus*), beach cordia (*Cordia subcordata*), and mangrove species such as *Rhizophora apiculata*, *Bruguiera gymnorrhiza*, or *Lumnitzera littorea*.[24]

While the islands were not originally built in response to climate change, the *asi* of the Langalanga are uniquely intelligent constructions of organic, local materials that create landmasses in place of water. Along with the materials used to construct an island's base, the reefs and mangrove forests offer the lagoon protection from strong waves. Gathered predominantly from mangroves on the mainland, firewood sustains life on the *asi*. However, in the face of deforestation,

Islands Range in Size from 1,000 to 120,000 Square Meters

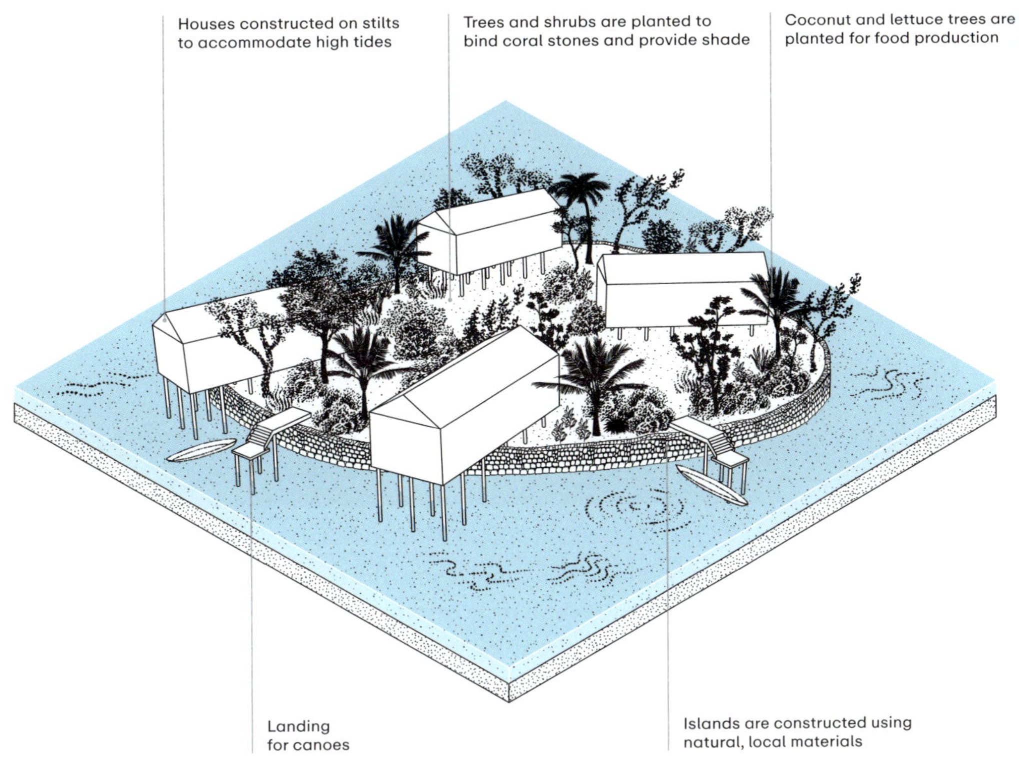

a sustainable quantity and a specific type of wood is gathered.[25] Over time, the design of the *asi* has evolved to accommodate extremes in tides, with islands built above high-water mark and plantings positioned on the ocean side, creating further layers of shoreline to lessen the impact of storms. Houses have been elevated to protect from inundation during extreme events, while, during low tides, residents are able to walk to the islands.

6

The Wale I Asi people also institute conservation practices to protect their sea and forest resources. For the saltwater people, an area of the coast is declared a "conservation area" by placing a coconut frond tied to a cross pole in the sea. The purpose of conservation is twofold. Firstly, it protects an area depleted of coral or other marine resources. Secondly, this practice declares an area for conservation for the purpose of a *maoma* (feast), which takes place every five years.[26] *Maoma* is a time for recommitment with the spiritual beings

7

who are guardians of the tribal community. Those related to the tribe and residing elsewhere may come to participate, often with certain decorations only related to the tribe. Within the confines of the stone walls, the administration of the *maoma* is conducted with instruction from the central governing body, located in the *fera*.[27]

Recent shifts in Langa Langa Lagoon's environment are the result of complex social factors, beginning with European contact and colonization in the 1900s. Europeans introduced products like steel axes, fishhooks, and guns, which opposed the traditional way of life and caused violence, limited the mobility of saltwater people, and brought about land-related conflicts by attracting populations to the coast.[28] Starting in the 1920s, *asi* have been increasingly abandoned following a gradual relocation of many Wale I Asi to the mainland, closer to missions, schools, hospitals, and roads. Contrary to the media portrayal of *asi* as highly vulnerable to sea level rise, abandonment is the main cause for their erosion, as they require constant maintenance. Paper and electronics, which are vulnerable to water damage, have also shifted people's relationship with water exposure, which historically was accepted on these islands.[29] New buildings on *asi* are often constructed with concrete and timber instead of traditional sago stalks.

8

Extreme weather events like tropical cyclones have also affected the artificial *asi* islands of Langa Langa Lagoon. In 1966, Cyclone Angela produced a nine-meter-high storm surge, flooding the islands. Rarata Island was permanently abandoned following Cyclone Namu in 1986. Such weather events have been part of Langalanga life for centuries though, and have helped inform design iterations for natural land expansion like *asi*. Today, king tides, common from December to January, are the most threatening occurrence attributed to climate change, alongside soil compaction and mangrove deforestation.[30]

The *asi* are an adaptive infrastructure in their ability to be expanded and accommodate agricultural and fishing practices. This small-scale, low-impact land-reclamation system designed for tidal fluctuations uses only local material for construction, reducing overexploitation of the ecosystem and allowing lagoon waters to continue to flow naturally. The living systems of the *asi* are extraordinarily intelligent in that the living fences and the root systems of plantings act as mortar that knits all the structural elements of an island together, while also feeding, shading, and cooling its inhabitants. The *asi* offer an example of a unique sustainable and biodegradable land-reclamation strategy for aquatic habitation that addresses the pressure of rising sea levels and the need for new settlements—potentially serving purposes beyond habitation, farming, and fishing. Informed by their natural environments, both in material choices and environmental conditions, the *asi* offer protection for those human and more-than-human species on and around the islands.

9

7 One side of the houses is positioned over the water for easy access by boat or for fishing.
8 Wale I Asi are also known as the saltwater people.
9 Islands are constructed using natural local materials.

ENDNOTES

1. Jan van der Ploeg et al., "Sinking Islands, Drowned Logic: Climate Change and Community-Based Adaptation Discourses in Solomon Islands," *Sustainability* 12, no. 17 (2020): 1, http://doi:10.3390/su12177225.
2. Akira Goto, "Lagoon Life among the Langalanga, Malaita Island, Solomon Islands," *Senri Ethnological Studies* 42 (1996): 13, http://doi.org/10.15021/00002976.
3. George Ivens Walter, *The Island Builders of the Pacific* (London: Seeley, Service and Company, 1930), 199.
4. Van der Ploeg et al., "Sinking Islands, Drowned Logic," 3.
5. Pei-yi Guo, "Island Builders: Landscape and Historicity among the Langalanga, Solomon Islands," in *Landscape, Memory and History: Anthropological Perspectives*, ed. Pamela J. Stewart and Andrew Strathern (London: Pluto Press, 2003), 194.
6. Van der Ploeg et al., "Sinking Islands, Drowned Logic," 3.
7. Van der Ploeg et al., "Sinking Islands, Drowned Logic," 5.
8. Van der Ploeg et al., "Sinking Islands, Drowned Logic," 5.
9. Guo, "Island Builders," 202.
10. Guo, "Island Builders," 195.
11. Van der Ploeg et al., "Sinking Islands, Drowned Logic," 5.
12. Van der Ploeg et al., "Sinking Islands, Drowned Logic," 10.
13. "Langalanga, Solomon Islands," Google Earth, accessed March 8, 2024, https://earth.google.com/web/search/Langalanga,+Solomon+Islands/@-8.87794648,160.73662473,2.78664836a,1059.14536729d,35y,0h,0t,0r/data=CigiJgokCfAZ3YVD1QnAEYzOJmdFYSnAGQsSZ7kc9WRAITBD1fASJmNAOgMKATA.
14. Van der Ploeg et al., "Sinking Islands, Drowned Logic," 4.
15. Tsatsa Seimarlie (adaptation officer, Climate Change Division, Solomon Islands Government), in discussion with the author, April 2023.
16. Gideon Bouro (forest consultant, Australian Center for International Agriculture Research, Solomon Islands), in discussion with the author, April 2023.
17. Guo, "Island Builders," 195.
18. Seimarlie, discussion.
19. Bouro, discussion, April 2023.
20. Walter, *The Island Builders of the Pacific*, 52.
21. Bouro, discussion, April 2023.
22. Gideon Bouro (forest consultant, Australian Center for International Agriculture Research, Solomon Islands), in discussion with the author, October 2023.
23. Bouro, discussion, April 2023.
24. Bouro, discussion, April 2023.
25. Seimarlie, discussion.
26. Bouro, discussion, October 2023.
27. Bouro, discussion, October 2023.
28. Van der Ploeg et al., "Sinking Islands, Drowned Logic," 5.
29. Van der Ploeg et al., "Sinking Islands, Drowned Logic," 10.
30. Van der Ploeg et al., "Sinking Islands, Drowned Logic," 10–11.

COAUTHOR

GIDEON BOURO

Community Forestry Specialist

Gideon Bouro is a forestry specialist, silviculturist and agronomist from Saliau village, located on an artificial island nestled in the Langa Langa Lagoon. Alongside his brother, Bouro has contributed his expertise to forestry roles in the Solomon Islands government. He lives in the town of Auki in Malaita Province, where he serves as a community forestry specialist. His research includes soil dynamics, forestry programs, nutrient management, and the preservation of mangroves. With his expertise in performing carbon calculations, he is the only local auditor of forestry stewardship council certification in the Solomon Islands.

Logging operations, often exploitative in pursuit of profit, have led to the destruction of numerous forests across Malaita and the broader Solomon Islands. Bouro's strategy for protecting local forests revolves around community-based resource management, offering viable alternatives to logging. Bouro also assists tribal leaders with self-governance, community groups with capacity building such as receiving payments for carbon trading, and ecosystem services through forest conservation.

Though he was brought up speaking Lau, he has learned 20 languages throughout his life. Bouro holds a Master of Forestry degree from the Australian National University, with a Bachelor of Science degree in forestry from Papua New Guinea, and a diploma in Tropical Forestry Science in Papua New Guinea, a diploma on Design of Community Forestry from Wageningen University in the Netherlands. He has worked as the Commissioner of Forest for the Government of Solomon Islands, which led him to work with various international organizations, including the Secretariat of the Pacific Community and the European Union. He has authored a book called *Na Fiuna Maedani* (The Seventh Day).

COAUTHOR

TSATSA SEIMARLIE

Environmental Scientist and Vulnerability Assessment Specialist

Tsatsa Seimarlie has worked closely with communities in the Solomon Islands who build and inhabit *asi* artificial islands. As an environmental scientist and vulnerability assessment specialist, Seimarlie worked on a province-specific road map for achieving the national adaptation plans for climate change. She currently works at Plan International, an NGO focused on children's rights.

Seimarlie comes from the Western and Choiseul Provinces of the Solomon Islands. While she initially planned to become a doctor, a scholarship opportunity redirected her path toward studying environmental science in Papua New Guinea. Her studies in environmental science, biology, and chemistry at Pacific Adventist University sparked her interest in the ocean. Tasked with evaluating the vulnerability of *asi* island communities, Seimarlie has primarily worked with groups in Lau Lagoon, though she has also spent time working in Langa Langa Lagoon. Her work involves looking at energy security, food, income security, water security, community health, security of place, and, relatedly, the state of ecosystems like forests and watersheds. As *asi* islands are affected by tides, they must be maintained—a time-consuming process requiring the collection of materials and extensive rebuilding.

Seimarlie believes that in order for an NGO to be successful it must engage people, respecting and learning from their unique specialties. She shares that the people she works with have sparked her passion for her job. In her free time, Seimarlie loves to travel and take photographs. Today, she also spends her time assisting members of her community in selling fresh reef fish in the city.

2 SALTY BRACKISH FRESH

3

4

3 Dotted among wetlands on Tunisia's coast, a patchwork of tiny human-made islands stretches out toward the Mediterranean.
4 Ploughed in neat furrows and shored up by sandbanks inside a lagoon, *ramli* are home to a centuries-old system of agriculture.

The *ramli* farms require continual maintenance, as farmers cultivate a system that requires a balance between tidal movements, parcel height, and the layered composition of sand and manure stabilized by surrounding rocks. Familiar with the root depth of each crop, including a variety of vegetable species and some fruit trees, farmers alter the soil's access to fresh water by adding or removing sand and manure.[4] The rectangular plots are situated along the shorelines of the lagoons, also forming islets within them.[5] This system's ingenious design ensures the well-being of *fellaheen* and their families, simultaneously generating sufficient food for nearby communities.[6]

Today, nearly two-thirds of Tunisia's 12 million residents live on dry coasts that pose a challenge to conventional agriculture because of a lack of arable land, poor soil, and water scarcity. In the 17th century, a diasporic group of Andalusians settled along the Gulf of Tunis, where they began to cultivate crops by terracing the foothills of Ennadhour Mountain.[7] While some of this terracing remains today, most Andalusians migrated to a thin belt of land wedged between the steep slopes of Ennadhour and the Mediterranean coast, to meet the needs of a growing population. It was here that many members of this diaspora forged new farmland from the shorelines of two lagoons—Ghar El Melh and Sidi Ali El Mekki. Fed by natural freshwater irrigation, the *ramli* saltwater lagoon farms were born.

Ramli can be found in four areas around the wetland of Ghar El Melh, which is located north of the Gulf of Tunis. On the coastal strips between Sidi Ali El Mekki Lagoon and the Mediterranean Sea, where they are called *hay*; on the edge of Sidi Ali El Mekki Lagoon, where they are called *dhrii*; on the marsh of Ghar El Melh Lagoon, where they are called *mlellah*; and in the middle of Sidi Ali El Mekki Lagoon, where they are called *guettayas*. While all four are built using the same construction method, they can be distinguished by how they engage with surrounding land. For example, the *guettayas* are completely surrounded by water, while the *hay* and *dhrii* are situated next to land and the *mlellah* in marshland.

Derived from the Arabic word for "sand," *ramli* refers to its transportation to reclaim land along lagoon shorelines to create this unique system of constructed sand beds.[8] The lagoons are continuously constructed and reshaped using a sandy substrate that is excavated from the shoreline. A mix of seasonal,

Three Types of *Ramli*, Named by Location

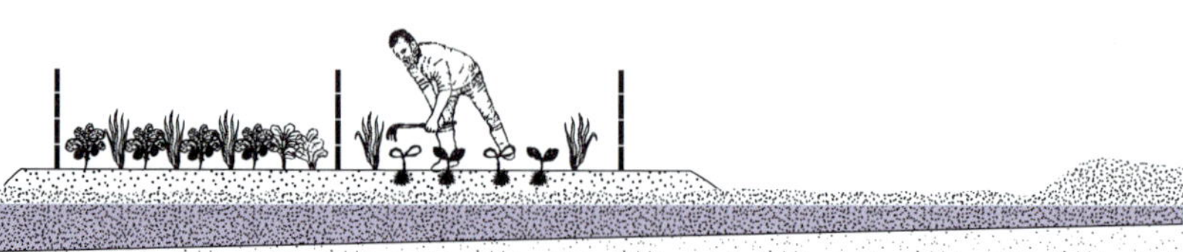

Mellah ramli, constructed on marshland

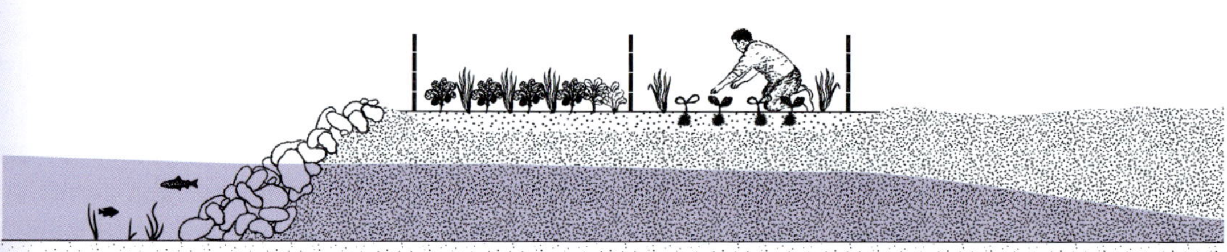

Dhrii, Hay ramli, constructed partially on land and partially on water

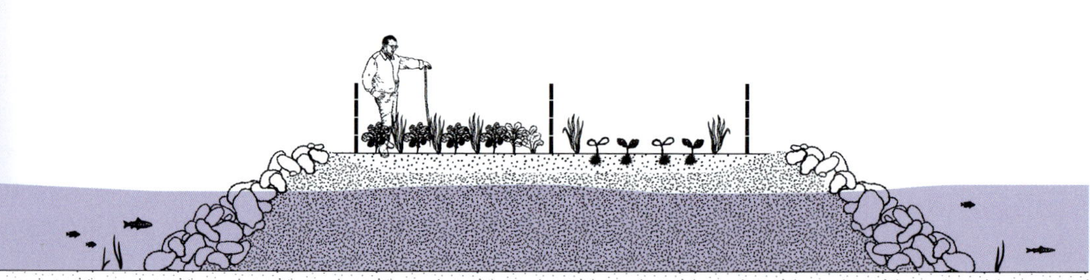

Guettayas ramli, constructed on water

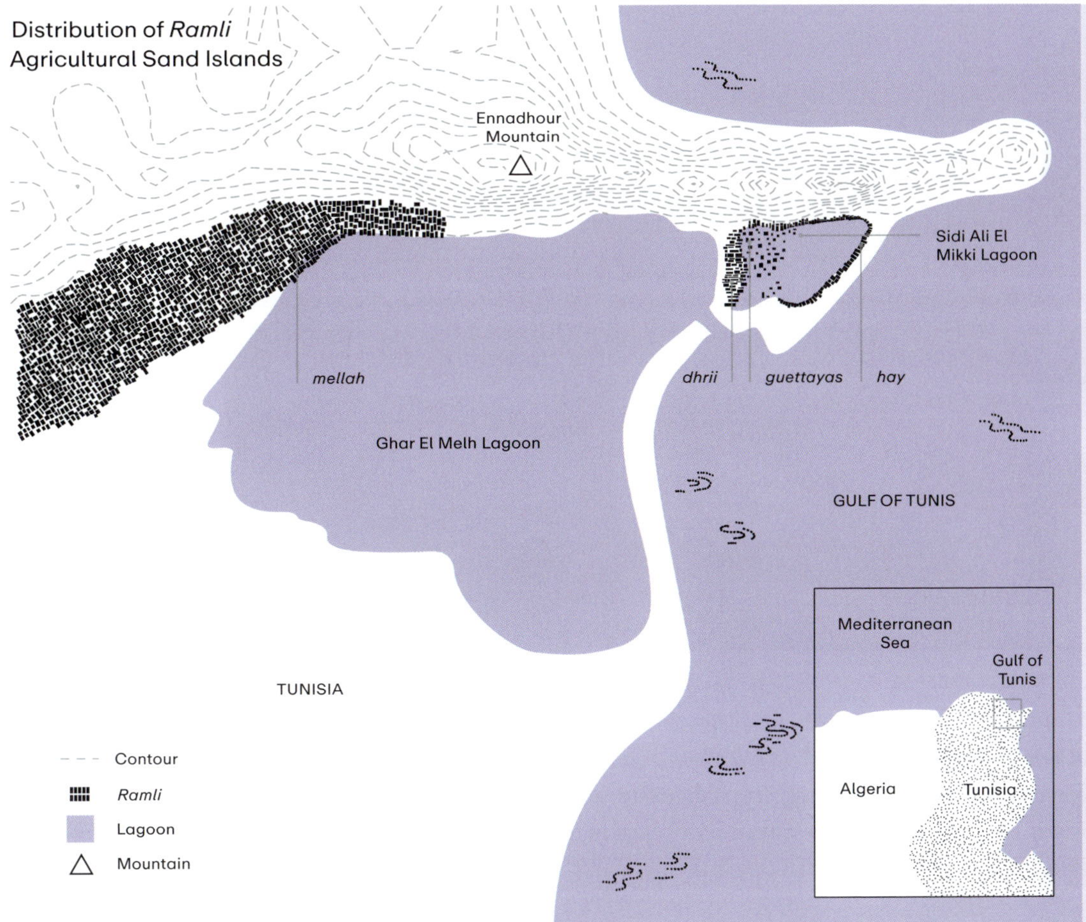

shallow-rooted crops like potatoes, onions, beans, watermelons, tomatoes, pepper, and fennel are grown on the *ramli*, which yield two annual crop cycles using natural freshwater irrigation from a fine layer of fresh water formed above the lagoons' salty base, in an otherwise saline ecosystem.[9, 10]

Ramli parcels are usually divided into several *qallah* (sand beds) of varying sizes. Each sand bed is constructed 30 centimeters high and between five and one hundred meters in length and width. In some cases, the parcels are constructed by transporting and placing heavy stones around their perimeters, to stabilize the beds. In other cases, *fellaheen* add more sand to beds until they are raised above water level, before a final layer of sand and manure are added where crop seeds are planted.[11] Hedges and fruit trees are cultivated peripherally while a curtain of cane-branch fencing is added every four meters between *qallah* to protect them from sea spray, slow the evaporation process, and stabilize the sand beds.

Facing significant challenges arising from water scarcity, *fellaheen* have devised an ingenious year-round passive irrigation system that leverages freshwater tidal fluctuations in the lagoon.[12] During the rainy season, the *fellaheen* rely on a thin layer of freshwater formed on the saltwater in the lagoon to irrigate crops.[13]

5

From natural tidal movements, this thin layer of fresh water, less dense than seawater, floats above it. The *fellaheen* construct the ramli to capture this thin freshwater layer, nourishing crop roots through the soil's dampness in the saltwater environment.[14] This naturally occurring thin freshwater layer fluctuates two times over the span of a day, moving about 10 centimeters every six hours

6

5 Ali Garsi has farmed a 0.8-hectare plot in the Ghar El Melh wetlands, which lie some 60 kilometers north of Tunis, for 20 years.
6 Relying on a layer of fresh water that feeds his plants above a salt water base, he grows mainly potatoes, onions, and tomatoes.

Construction of *Ramli* Agricultural Sand Islands

1. Farmers transport sand from the shore to build the base of the plot in the lagoon

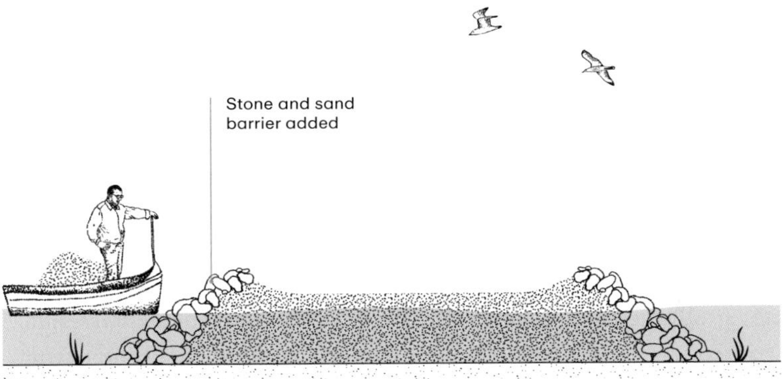

2. When 30 cm high, stones and a sand barrier are built to protect and support the island

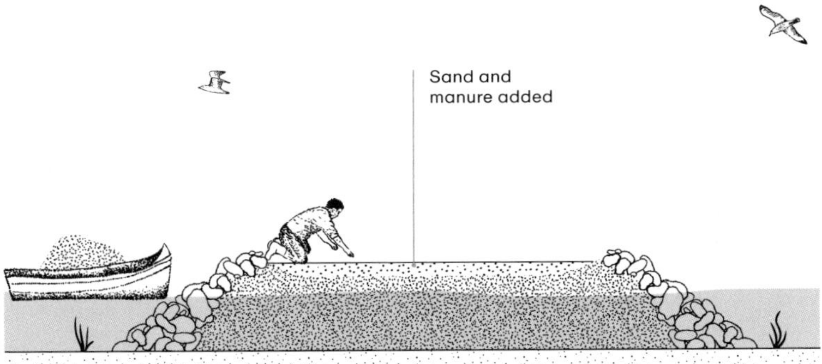

3. A layer of sand and manure is added to supply the crop with nutrients throughout the year

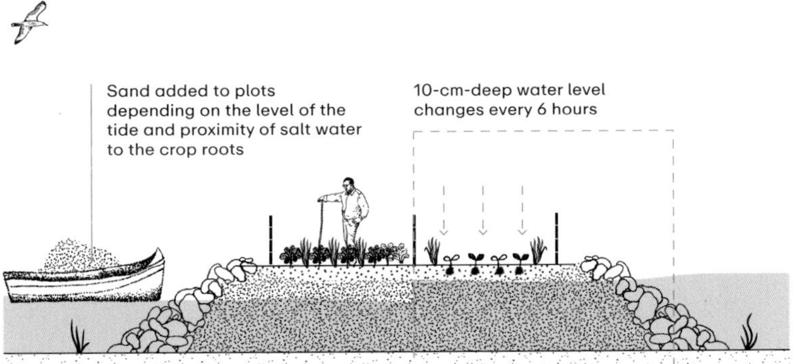

4. Sugarcane fences spaced 400 cm apart are anchored into the island to protect crops from sea spray and wind

at high and low tide. The thin freshwater layer is reconstituted each year by run-off from the mountains as well as rainwater that falls directly into the lagoon, mainly in winter, still allowing two crop cycles per year. The crops will fail if their roots either extend below the freshwater level and touch salt water or if they don't grow to reach water.[15] Because of this, soil heights of a bed are constantly adapted by *fellaheen*, who add a layer of sand and manure to fertilize crops and ensure root contact with natural fresh water.[16] A hole is constructed in the substrate of the plots to precisely observe water levels.

The *ramli* farms are uniquely constructed to support freshwater agriculture in a saltwater environment. While adaptable to a variety of water levels, the act of consistently adding sand and manure to manage tidal fluctuations also stabilizes the coastal edges of the lagoons themselves. This agricultural system also supports biodiversity by providing a habitat for almost 230 plant species, as well as migrating birds such as cormorants, pochards, greylag geese, mallard ducks, and northern shoveler ducks.[17] With half of the village populations along the coastlines dependent on *ramli* crops and fishing for their daily livelihood, the balancing act of this system plays an incredibly vital role for every community, both human and more-than-human. As a system that locates itself at the interface between salt and fresh water, there exists the potential for colocation with osmotic energy, produced by a semipermeable, double-sided membrane— in contact with fresh water on one side and seawater on the other—that lets water

7 Sand is added to plots depending on the level of the tide and proximity of salt water to the crop root.
8 Meaning "sandy" in Arabic, the *ramli* agricultural system irrigates crops entrenched in a mix of sand and manure via their roots.

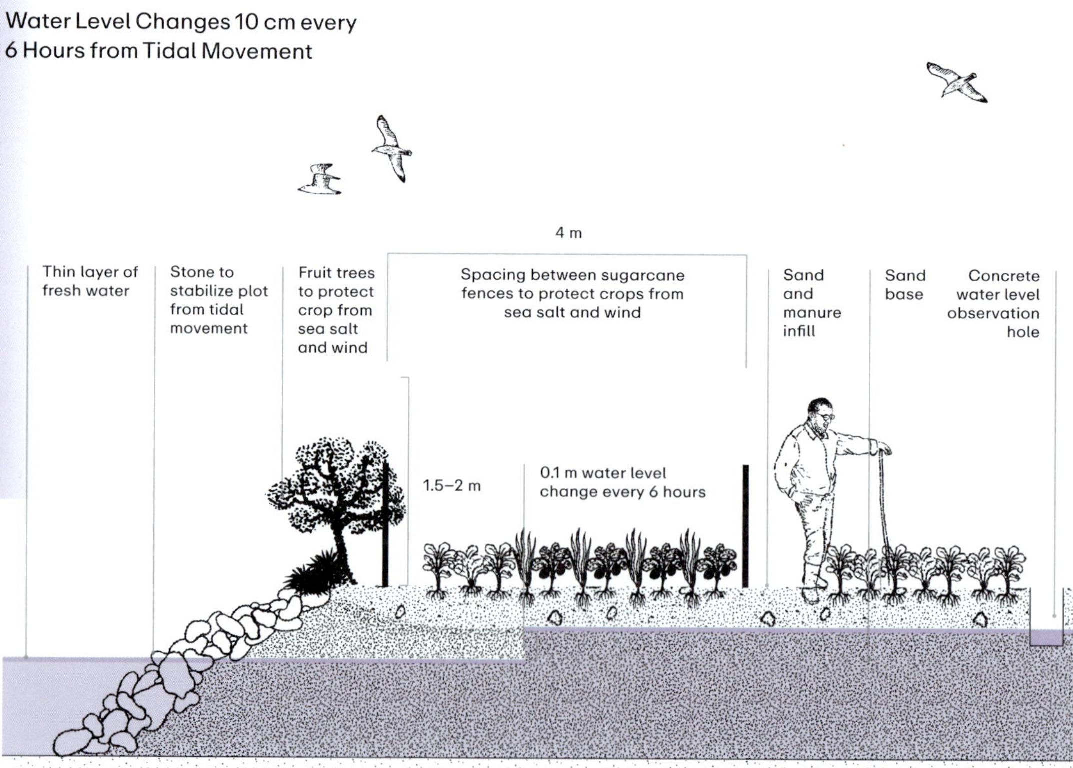

7

8

9 This water-shortage-resistant method gained global renown in 2020 when the Food and Agriculture Organization of the United Nations added Ghar El Melh to its list of Globally Important Agricultural Heritage Systems.

through but captures mineral salts. While still in its infancy, this form of energy generation produces immense volumes with small amounts of surface area. Even though its application in this scenario is only theoretical, the interface between salt and fresh water that triggers this technology could one day host a holistic water–energy–food technology.

Today, the *ramli* system is facing challenges from drought and falling groundwater levels, which reduce the amount of fresh water that can be sourced directly from the rain and by the springs from Ennadhour Mountain. Climate change and sea level rise have also become major threats to the *ramli* system—vulnerable to flooding, as the coastal lagoon system that protects farms from high tidal fluctuations gradually submerges. Furthermore, a survey of the

9

fellaheen conducted by Professor Hamouda Samaâli from the University of Tunis revealed an aging population, with nearly 90 percent aged over 40 and only 10 percent under 20. This demographic composition poses challenges for the future of the system.[18]

Given the vulnerability of Tunisia's densely populated coast in the face of climate forecasts, the *ramli* become vitally important agricultural systems that work with subtle tidal fluctuations to capture scarce freshwater supplies in a hostile saline environment. Half of the village populations along the coastlines of Ghar El Melh are dependent on *ramli* and fishing for their daily livelihood, offering food security and a means of land protection.[19] As a land-reclamation strategy, this system has been extraordinarily successful in providing essential habitat for hundreds of species, rather than typically playing a role in their erasure. This balancing act of symbiosis is most notably displayed in the ingenious method of naturally captured freshwater irrigation, which works with local water cycles and responds to the water regimes of the crops in the high saline environment, allowing year-round cultivation. The migration and hybridization of technologies like the *ramli* will be vital to resuscitating global coastlines facing freshwater scarcity, and where salt water threatens agriculture and livelihoods.[20]

10

10 The system's reliance on a fragile balance of rain and sea tides means it is facing unprecedented challenges.

ENDNOTES

1. Abdelhakim Aissaoui, "Sowing Seeds in Tunisian Sands," FAO, June 17, 2020, https://www.fao.org/neareast/news/details/Sowing-seeds-in-Tunisian-sands/.
2. FAO, *Dossier de candidature au Programme des Systèmes Ingénieux du Patrimoine Agricole Mondial* (n.p.: n.p., 2020), 1–36.
3. Abdelhakim Issaoui (general engineer in agronomy and ecology), in discussion with the author, December 2020.
4. FAO, *Dossier de candidature*, 8.
5. Hamouda Samaâli and Ibtissem Tounsi-Guerin, "Les 'Ramli', Jardins de culture du littoral nord-est tunisien : cartographie de l'évolution récente d'un système original d'irrigation," *Mappemonde* 125 (2019): 1–21, https://doi.org/10.4000/mappemonde.751.
6. FAO, *Dossier de candidature*, 9.
7. FAO, *Dossier de candidature*, 30.
8. Aissaoui, "Sowing Seeds in Tunisian Sands."
9. Issaoui, discussion.
10. FAO, *Dossier de candidature*, 12.
11. Issaoui, discussion.
12. Seed World Europe, "Tunisia's Unique Farming Systems Win Recognition as Part of the Global Agricultural Heritage," Seed World, June 22, 2020, https://www.seedworld.com/europe/2020/06/22/tunisias-unique-farming-systems-win-recognition-as-part-of-the-global-agricultural-heritage/.
13. Aissaoui, "Sowing Seeds in Tunisian Sands."
14. FAO, *Dossier de candidature*, 4.
15. Aissaoui, "Sowing Seeds in Tunisian Sands."
16. FAO, *Dossier de candidature*, 4.
17. Richard V. Lansdown et al., *Characterisation and Conservation Assessment of Terrestrial Biodiversity in the Ghar El Melh Area* (Malaga: IUCN Centre for Mediterranean Cooperation and World Wide Fund for Nature North Africa, 2021).
18. Samaâli and Tounsi-Guerin, "Les 'Ramli'," 20.
19. FAO, *Dossier de candidature*, 9.
20. Issaoui, discussion.

COAUTHOR

ABDELHAKIM ISSAOUI

General Engineer in Agronomy and Ecology

Abdelhakim "Hakim" Issaoui was born in Saddaguia Saddaguia, a rural area near the central Tunisian town of Sidi Bouzid. Today, Issaoui is based in the capital city of Tunis, where he works as an engineering expert in agroecology with a focus in biodiversity, desertification, and drought. Collaborating with NGOs and government agencies in Tunisia and abroad, Issaoui develops strategic programs and projects that address critical environmental issues in the region. Issaoui credits his career in sustainability to his upbringing in a largely agricultural, rural area of the country.

Issaoui received his degree in agronomy engineering from the Tunisian Institute of Agronomy in 1989. After earning a diploma in Advanced Studies in Plant Ecology from the Faculty of Sciences in Tunisia in 1993, he joined Tunisia's National Institute for Research in Rural Engineering, Water, and Forestry as a researcher. From 1990 to 1994, he conducted ecological research on vegetation in protected areas of the country.

Issaoui later joined the Tunisian Ministry of the Environment as an engineer, where he led programs aimed to combat desertification and promote biodiversity. His appointed role at the ministry strategized solutions for climate-related stressors in Tunisia, in addition to the management of natural and agricultural heritage sites. Leveraging this expertise, he contributed to national focal points for several multilateral agreements, including for the Cartagena Protocol, the Nagoya Protocol, and, more recently, the United Nations Convention to Combat Desertification, FAO's Globally Important Agricultural Heritage Systems (GIAHS), and UNESCO's Man and Biosphere Program. Issaoui has participated in more than 10 conferences at these international conventions.

Issaoui has overseen a number of projects at the Ministry of Environment's Department of Nature Conservation and Rural Environment, with a particular emphasis on natural resources and biological diversity. These projects include the conservation of natural plant heritage and study of vegetation in Tunisia's national parks (1997–1999) and the coordination of the National Gene Bank project (2002–2007) and the Botanic Gardens program (1995–2007). Issaoui was an executive board member of Arid Land Institute Tunisia until 2019. He has also been on the executive board of Gene Bank Tunisia since 2008.

Outside his work as an engineering expert for government agencies, Issaoui has worked as an environmental educator, with previous teaching appointments at Heritage Institute of Tunisia, the National Agronomic Institute of Tunisia, and the Silvopastoral Institute of Tabarka. He has lectured on the management of protected areas, the production of local, natural resources, and forest product value chains. When he isn't working at the Ministry of Environment or teaching, Issaoui can be found tending to his vegetable garden at his home in Tunis.

LOKO I'A FISHPONDS
of THE NATIVE HAWAIIANS
United States

From the barren volcanic mountaintops and highland forests of the Hawaiian Islands to river valleys flowing into farmlands and *loko iʻa* (fishponds), each *ahupuaʻa* (land division) contained all the resources for subsistence, including agriculture, water, aquaculture, fisheries, and coastal protection.[1] Divided by the *aliʻi* (high chief), the royal system based on the division of watersheds was held in trust and controlled by the *konohiki* (land manager).[2] Trade happened upslope between the coastal or inland fishponds, fertile lowlands, and higher farmlands. Here, taro, sweet potato, breadfruit, and other upland crops were exchanged for fish and salt. At the land-sea interface lay *loko iʻa*, which are typically enclosed bodies of fresh or brackish water. These Indigenous innovations are constructed from local materials, basalt, and coral.[3] While mostly built four to six hundred years ago, the fishponds are thought to have originated in the 14th century.[4] Many types of ponds evolved over time, responding to resources, population size, topographies, and ecosystems. Serving as nurseries for fish and reflecting the importance of brackish-water ecosystems, *loko iʻa* create *puʻuhonua*, which are safe places bestowed with a magical attraction for fish.[5]

AHUPUAʻA
A traditional subdivision of land extending from the mountains to the sea.

1 Composed of a slice of an island, an *ahupuaʻa* stretched from a mountaintop to a shoreline following the boundary of a stream.
2 Each *ahupuaʻa* included a lowland cultivated area and an upland forested region.
3 *Loko iʻa* were extensive operating systems that produced an average of 400–600 pounds of fish per acre per year.

1

2

Before 1848, most Hawaiian lands, fishponds, and spiritual centers were "owned" by the *ali'i*, and "contracted" to *konohiki*.[6] Permanent and temporary land divisions were clearly marked and allocated by community members knowledgeable in local histories and land boundaries. For example, sections of land, *'ili* and *mo'o'āina*, were granted to individual families, or *'ohana*, and *loko i'a* to *kia'i loko*, or pond guardians, to cultivate.[7] In exchange for fish, inland villages exchanged agricultural foods and wood to build canoes with coastal communities.[8] Fishponds were one of two major food systems established in Hawai'i—the other being taro cultivation.[9] More food production reflected peace and stability on the island. A well-maintained *loko i'a* and water system was a signifier of a healthy *ahupua'a*.[10,11]

3

The maintenance of *loko iʻa* involves a well-rounded system of knowledge and spiritual practice. Human and more-than-human guardians, both known as *kiaʻi loko*, keep the fishpond, fish, and stewards safe.[12] *Kilo* is informed observation practiced by those present in a particular space. Keen observation informs the conservation, restoration, and management of fishponds.[13] A common form of *kiaʻi loko* are large, dragon-like creatures known as *moʻo*. *Moʻo* are often associated with a specific fishpond and accompanied by a unique story, such as *Meheanu*, the *moʻo* of Heʻeia Fishpond on the coast of Oʻahu. Many guardian figures are women depicted as nurturing and caring, while also exuding strength and power.[14] Another form of *kiaʻi loko* is *manō* (sharks), who would move through underground lava tubes to protect fishponds. A series of underground cave systems, which still exist today, are said to be the subterranean pathways of the *manō* and *moʻo*.[15]

4

During the height of fishpond use, historical accounts describe stability and prosperity. There was ample time dedicated to building, strengthening, and maintaining the structures of *loko iʻa*.[16] Heʻeia Fishpond on Oʻahu was built by thousands of Hawaiians who collectively passed down rocks from the Koʻolau mountains over several years.[17]

Loko iʻa range in size from two thousand square meters to two square kilometers. They were built near natural sources of freshwater—be they stream, spring, or groundwater—and were found both inland and along the coast. *Waihapakai*, meaning "brackish water," is the blend of fresh and saltwater that is preferred by herbivorous fish and typically desirable in ponds—a condition easily established through the placement and construction of *loko iʻa*.[18]

4 Kalauhaʻihaʻi Fishpond was the site of King Kamehameha and Queen Kaʻahumanu's royal kalo patch and former summer home.

5 Constructed sometime between the early 1200s and early 1400s, Heʻeia Fishpond, located at Heʻeia on the island of Oahu, is the only Hawaiian fishpond fully encircled by a wall.

5

While names relate to function, the different fishpond types show an evolution of the technology over time.[19] The first two *loko iʻa* types were naturally occurring and included the *loko kaheka* (tidal ponds), followed by *loko puʻuone*, with *puʻuone* meaning sand dune.[20] These coastal, brackish-water ponds were created where tidal movement had built up wide permeable, irregular walls of rubble, dirt, sand, and coral.[21] *Loko wai*, with *wai* meaning freshwater, made use of a spring or stream as their water source. An ancient form of aquaponics, *loko iʻa kalo* were irrigated ponds that allowed for the simultaneous cultivation of taro and fish.

Loko *ʻumeiki* were fish traps necessitating a more hands-on approach for fish harvest, involving the use of nets and other common fishing gear.[22] The walls of loko *ʻumeiki* were constructed primarily of basalt and operated tidally. Canal-like openings allowed for ocean water to flow in and out of the *loko ʻumeiki*. On high tides, fish would come into the *ʻumeiki* to graze on algae; fishers would take advantage of the daily and seasonal fish patterns. Each fishpond had a human *kiaʻi loko* who lived nearby to oversee maintenance and management.

Loko kuapā, with *kua* meaning backbone or spine and *pā* meaning flat surface, were the last iteration of fishponds that included walls constructed

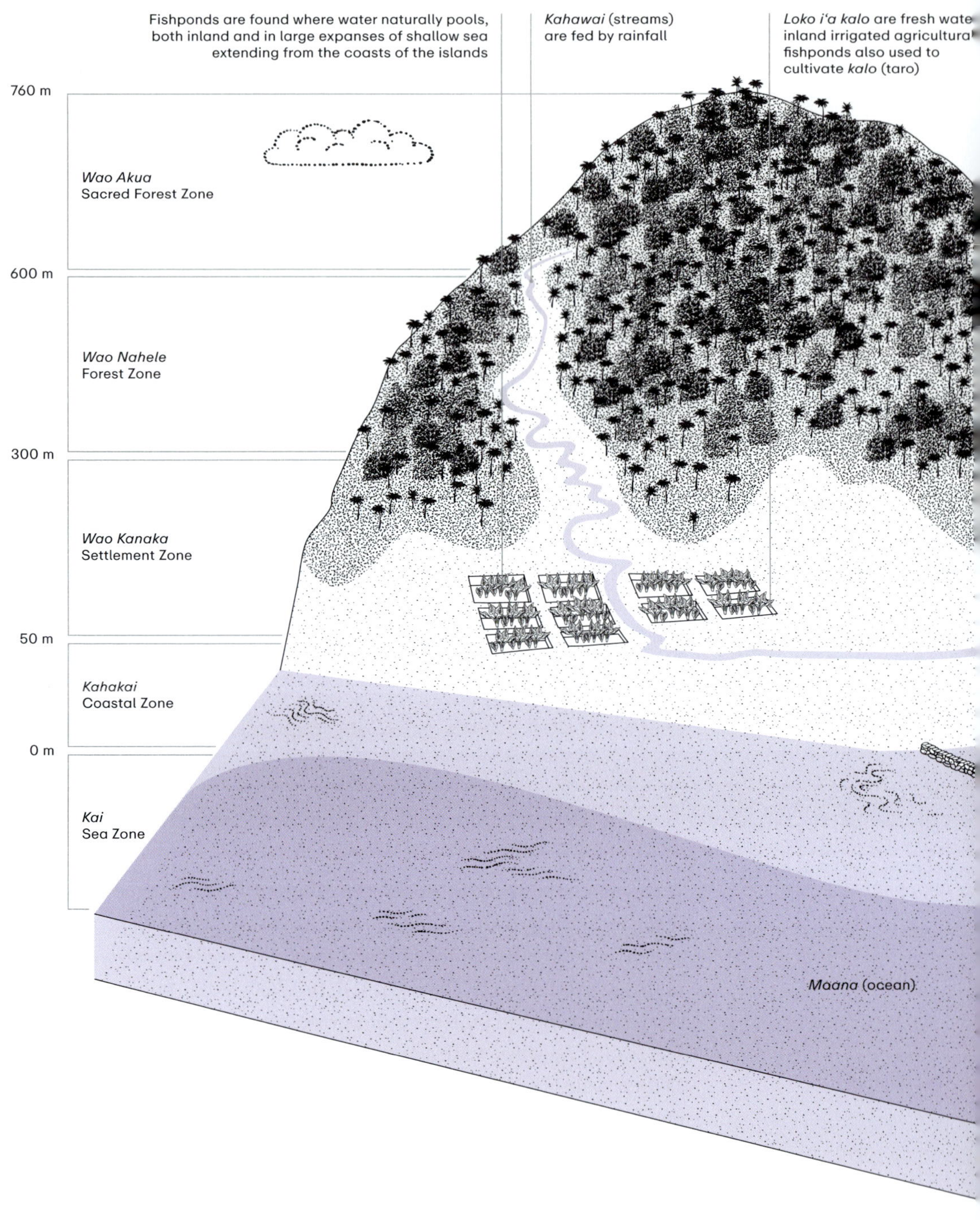

Loko i'a Created in *Ahupua'a* for Subsistence Living and Coastal Protection

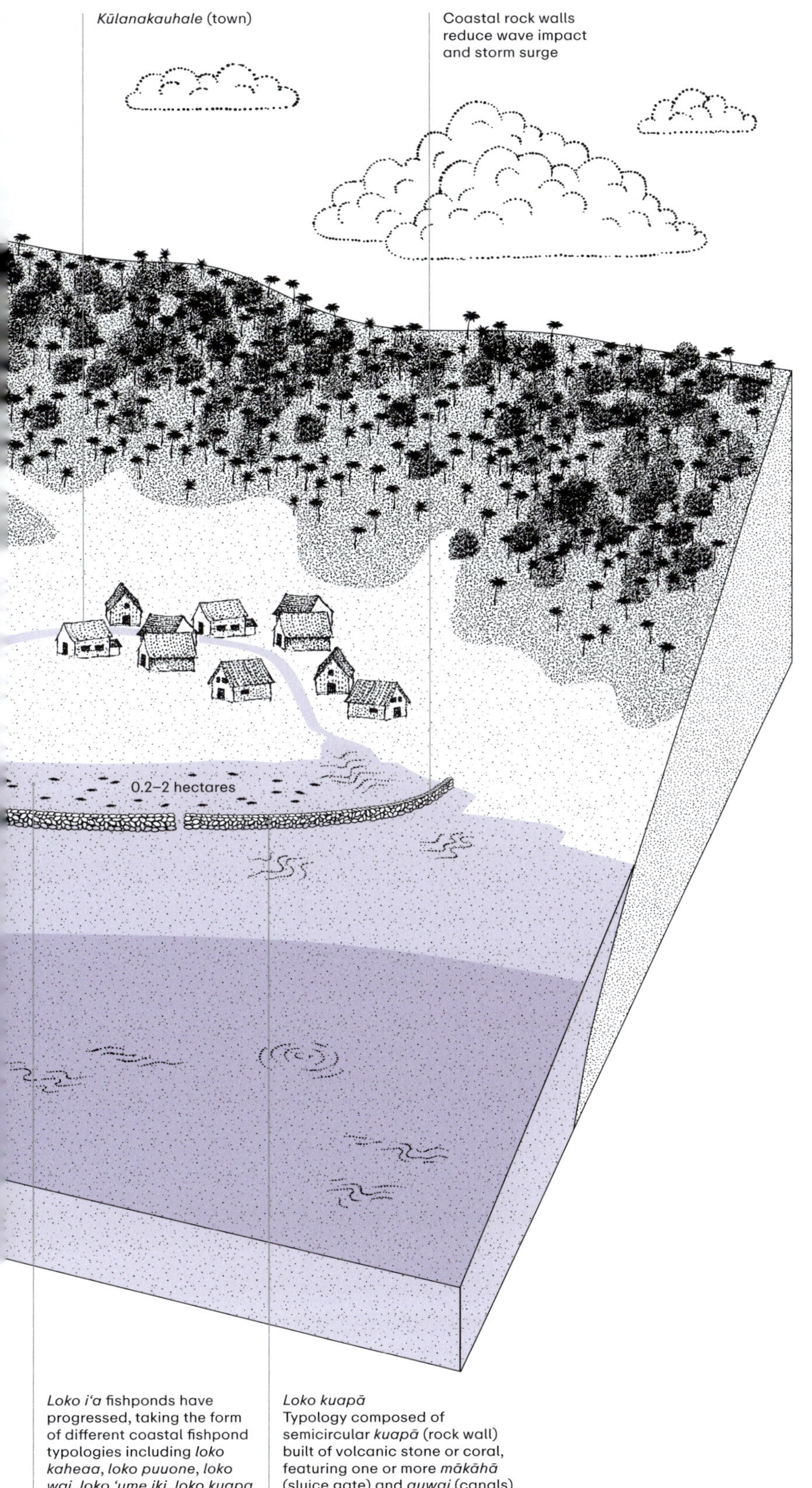
Kūlanakauhale (town)
Coastal rock walls reduce wave impact and storm surge
0.2–2 hectares
Loko iʻa fishponds have progressed, taking the form of different coastal fishpond typologies including *loko kaheaa*, *loko puuone*, *loko wai*, *loko ʻume iki*, *loko kuapa*
Loko kuapā
Typology composed of semicircular *kuapā* (rock wall) built of volcanic stone or coral, featuring one or more *mākāhā* (sluice gate) and *auwai* (canals)

6

7

6 Prior to its reconstruction, rocks used to build Waiaʻōpae Fishpond on Lānaʻi's eastern coast 800 years ago lay in the sand where wind, waves, and ocean tides had toppled them over the centuries.

7 The compact style of wall in Heʻeia Fishpond slows water flow, which allows the pond to maintain a base water level even at the lowest tides, and forces more water to the *mākāhā*, or sluice gates.

of volcanic (basalt) stone passed, hand by hand, down to the sea.[23] *Loko kuapā* fishponds are located in shallow coastal areas, in some cases with extensive semicircular walls. These *kuapā* (seawalls) were built using volcanic rock, coral, or a combination of the two. They also consisted of *ʻauwai*, or canals, and *mākāhā*, or sluice gates. *Kuapā* ranged from 46 to 1,920 meters long. In most cases, coralline algae, barnacles, and oysters naturally grew on and over the stones, functioning like a natural cement, further strengthening them.[24] *ʻAuwai* were built into the walls of the *kuapā* and outfitted with a *mākāhā* (fishpond gate), connecting the enclosure to the sea in order to circulate, clean, stock, and harvest ponds with minimal human effort.[25] The narrow grates of the *mākāhā* allow young fish to enter the pond to feed on seaweed and phytoplankton. These gates are made of *lama*, *ʻōhiʻa*, or *ʻōhiʻaʻai* (types of native timber), lashed together vertically to create one-and-a-half- to two-centimeter gaps, always allowing small fish to enter the pond. When fish have grown and reached maturity, they attempt to return to the sea on the rising tide for spawning, but their size prevents them from passing through the *mākāhā* openings. It was at this time that fish could be harvested. The pond keepers would deliberately release larger fish into the sea to spawn so that they did not overexploit the coastal ecosystem.[26]

These fishpond typologies are constructed and managed in harmony with the local ecology and watershed dynamics of the *ahupuaʻa* where they are situated. *Loko iʻa* have exemplified sustainable resource management through pond keepers' selective harvesting and release of fish. This careful approach involves a nuanced understanding of local fish populations, ensuring that some mature individuals are harvested while others are released into the sea to achieve a balanced marine ecosystem.

Loko kuapā Are a Type of *Loko iʻa* Located in Shallow Coastal Areas

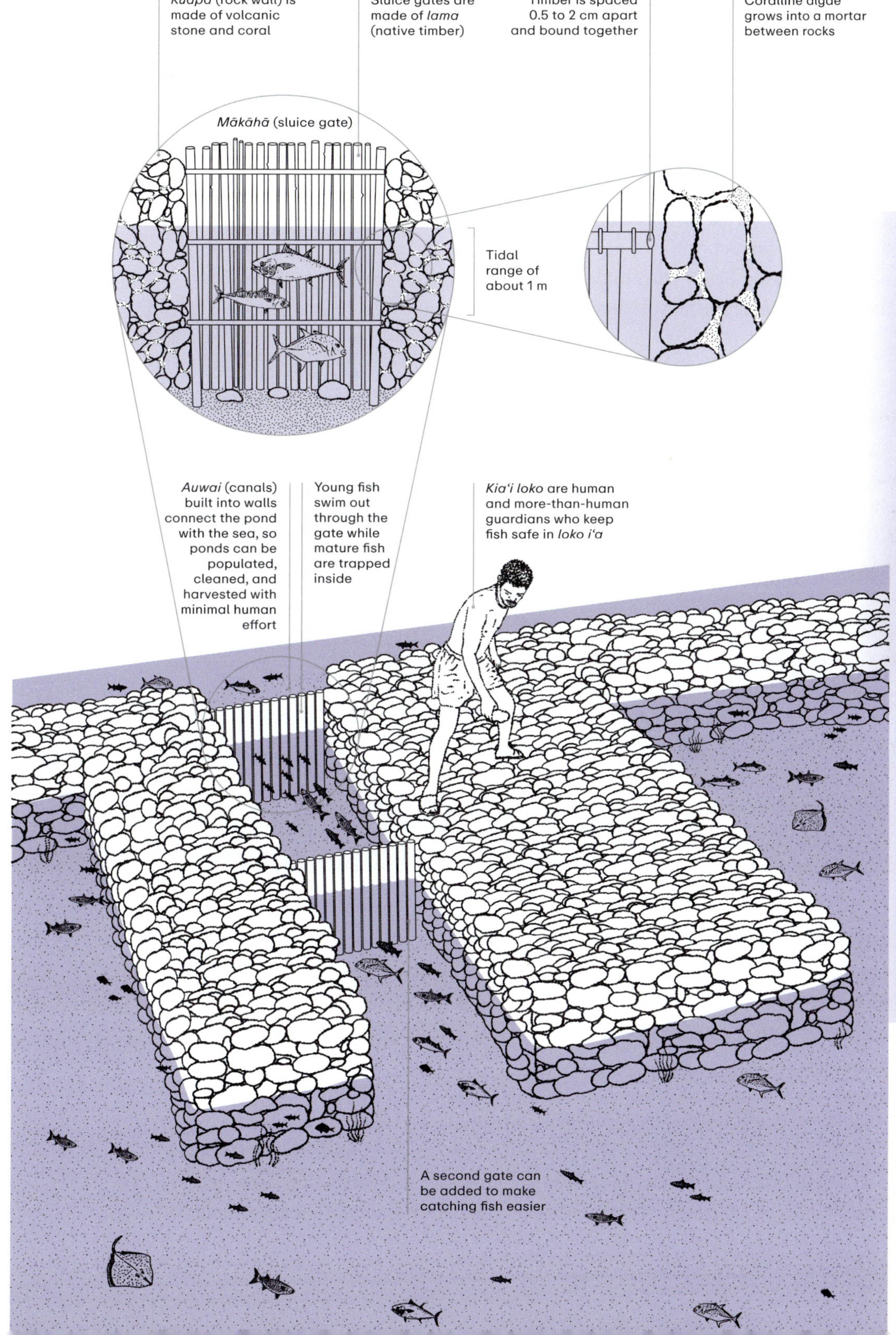

Permitting the entry of both fresh and salt water into the pond establishes a brackish-water environment, creating an optimal habitat for the proliferation of *limu*, or algae. This algal growth serves as a nutrient source for species in the pond, enabling pond keepers to efficiently rear fish without additional feeding. The popular fatty mullet fish (*Mugil cephalus*) is the main species cultivated in these systems.[27] Various species of *pāpaʻi* (crab), *ʻōpae* (shrimp), and *puhi* (eel) inhabit *loko iʻa* in symbiosis with herbivorous fish.

The construction and upkeep of walled fishponds makes use of natural and biodegradable materials, reducing contamination to coastal waters. Mulching, composting, and amending soil using grass cuttings, invasive seaweed, crab and oyster shells, and other agricultural waste from neighboring ecosystems offers a sustainable alternative to chemical fertilizers.[28] Coastal fishponds offer buffers to lessen the impact of waves and storm surges, hinting at their hybridization potential as wave break-surrounded aquaculture systems for coastal cities, serving as both production and protection.

8

When European colonizers made contact with native Hawaiians in 1778, there were 360 fishponds recorded across the Hawaiian Islands, providing food for thousands of people.[29] After colonization, traditional Hawaiian ruling systems broke down, the barter economy of the *ahupuaʻa* was replaced, and foreign epidemics decimated the Hawaiian population.[30] The Great Mahele in 1848, a land division that resulted in Hawaiian land being purchased by Hawaiians and foreigners, led to a rapid decline of fishponds and integrated farming systems.[31]

By the early 1900s, as the population of native Hawaiians decreased, fewer than one hundred ponds and traps remained, still producing seven hundred pounds of fish yearly. This number dropped to four operational fishponds

8 Below the Molokai sea cliffs are traditional fishponds that were part of the *ahupuaʻa* system.

9 Built nearly 1,000 years ago, ʻAlekoko Menehune Fishpond, located a half mile inland from Nāwiliwili Harbor, is separated from Hulēʻia Stream by a 900-foot-long and five-foot-high wall of meticulously assembled lava rock.

across the islands by 2003. Many factors contributed to the loss of this practice, including warfare among chiefs, who destroyed the fishponds of enemies; the sandalwood trade depleting mountain forests, causing erosion while diverting labor from the shoreline; natural disasters; disease; land development; and the shift from a subsistence to market economy.[32] Mangrove, an invasive species introduced in 1902, hindered the growth of algae and transformed the ponds into mudflats. Today, some ponds on Molokaʻi use mangroves to protect the walls from larger tidal influxes and waves stemming from climate change.[33]

9

Despite the destruction of numerous *loko iʻa* and the suppression of Indigenous knowledge following colonization, recent progress has been made in the restoration of fishponds. Established in 2001, Paepae o Heʻeia is a community-led organization based on Oʻahu that has played a crucial role in restoring Heʻeia Fishpond. Situated on the northeastern coast of the island, this fishpond, boasting an extensive *kuapā* spanning over 2,100 meters, has a history dating back six to eight hundred years. Though the site was damaged by natural disaster and fell into disrepair due to colonial influence in the 20th century, Heʻeia Fishpond stands as a thriving and fully functioning *loko iʻa* today—a testament to the community-driven restoration efforts led by Paepae o Heʻeia.

Unlike contemporary infrastructures and materials, such as reinforced concrete used to construct seawalls, these Indigenous structures use local materials, support oceanic ecosystems, and offer habitats for symbiotic species such as oysters and algae, which support the health of the broader ecosystem.[34, 35] While there are far less *loko iʻa* present in Hawaiʻi today, they still exist as an example of a conscientious approach to aquaculture, capable of sustaining a major population while supporting the health of the natural environment.[36] Today, native birds and fish living in and around *loko iʻa* are considered modern *kiaʻi loko* guardians, reminding us of the importance of maintaining and recuperating these ingenious infrastructures.[37] *Loko iʻa* technology can inform the design of coastal infrastructure to address flooding, biodiversity depletion, food scarcity, and more. Having emerged from the *ahupuaʻa* land-division system designed for subsistence living, and evolved into a gravity-fed, elevational densification strategy for agriculture and coastal protection, the *loko iʻa* inspire crucial thinking for global coastal challenges.

ENDNOTES

1. Barry Costa-Pierce, "Aquaculture in Ancient Hawaii," *BioScience* 37, no. 5 (1987): 322, https://doi.org/10.2307/1310688.
2. Costa-Pierce, "Aquaculture in Ancient Hawaii," 322.
3. Kinohi Fukumitsu (Lohe Pono Fellow, Kuaʻaina Ulu ʻAuamo), in discussion with the author, November 2022.
4. Catherine C. Summers, *Hawaiian Archaeology: Hawaiian Fishponds* (Honolulu: Bishop Museum Press, 1964), 12.
5. Fukumitsu, discussion.
6. Costa-Pierce, "Aquaculture in Ancient Hawaii," 322.
7. Costa-Pierce, "Aquaculture in Ancient Hawaii," 323.
8. Jason K. Levy and Joseph Chernisky, "Sustainable Water Resources Management in Hawaii," *Water Resources IMPACT* 7, no. 2 (2005): 20–22.
9. Fukumitsu, discussion.
10. "Restoring the Loko Iʻa," ʻAoʻao O Nā Loko Iʻa O Maui, http://mauifishpond.com/no-ka-oi-magazine-article/.
11. Fukumitsu, discussion.
12. Fukumitsu, discussion.
13. Fukumitsu, discussion.
14. Fukumitsu, discussion.
15. Fukumitsu, discussion.
16. Fukumitsu, discussion.
17. Costa-Pierce, "Aquaculture in Ancient Hawaii," 322.
18. Costa-Pierce, "Aquaculture in Ancient Hawaii," 325.
19. Costa-Pierce, "Aquaculture in Ancient Hawaii," 326.
20. Costa-Pierce, "Aquaculture in Ancient Hawaii," 326.
21. Costa-Pierce, "Aquaculture in Ancient Hawaii," 326.
22. Fukumitsu, discussion.
23. Fukumitsu, discussion.
24. Costa-Pierce, "Aquaculture in Ancient Hawaii," 326.
25. Costa-Pierce, "Aquaculture in Ancient Hawaii," 326.
26. Fukumitsu, discussion.
27. Fukumitsu, discussion.
28. Costa-Pierce, "Aquaculture in Ancient Hawaii," 320.
29. Costa-Pierce, "Aquaculture in Ancient Hawaii," 324.
30. Costa-Pierce, "Aquaculture in Ancient Hawaii," 324.
31. Costa-Pierce, "Aquaculture in Ancient Hawaii," 324.
32. "Restoring the Loko Iʻa." ʻAoʻao O Nā Loko Iʻa O Maui.
33. "Restoring the Loko Iʻa." ʻAoʻao O Nā Loko Iʻa O Maui.
34. Fukumitsu, discussion.
35. Fukumitsu, discussion.
36. Fukumitsu, discussion.
37. Fukumitsu, discussion.

COAUTHOR

HI'ILEI KAWELO

Executive Director of Paepae o He'eia

A *wahine lawai'a* (fisherwoman) who draws from the traditions of the Kāne'ohe Bay, Hi'ilei Kawelo is the executive director of Paepae o He'eia, a nonprofit organization dedicated to the restoration and sustainable management of He'eia ishpond, located on the island of O'ahu.

Kawelo attended the University of Hawai'i t Mānoa, where she earned her Bachelor of Arts egree in zoology and a certificate in the Marine ptions Program. Throughout her undergraduate tudies, Kawelo held internships with the Hawai'i lature Center, the Hawai'i Youth Conservation Corps, he Department of Land and Natural Resources' 'orestry and Wildlife, the Kaho'olawe Island Reserve :ommission, and the Hawai'i Institute of Marine iology. Upon graduating, Kawelo joined the Oceanic nstitute (OI) as a research technician, where she vorked in the Fisheries and Environmental Sciences rogram/Stock Enhancement Program. A desire to ngage in more hands-on work led her to volunteer vork and part-time employment at He'eia Fishpond— *loko i'a* dating back six to eight hundred years and uilt by the community to feed people throughout the *hupua'a* of He'eia.

After her five-year tenure at OI, Kawelo was rawn to the promising momentum and community ngagement opportunities at He'eia Fishpond. This ecision culminated in the establishment of the non-rofit organization Paepae o He'eia in 2001. Kawelo ecame Paepae o He'eia's executive director in 2007 fter having served as an educator, facilities manager, nd *kū hou kuapā* coordinator for the organization for ix years. She has gained recognition for her dedica-ion to safeguarding and restoring traditional aqua-ulture practices and resource management. Through er endeavors, Kawelo has played a foundational role n revitalizing He'eia Fishpond, an invaluable cultural nd educational asset for the surrounding community.

KINOHI FUKUMITSU

Lohe Pono Fellow, KUA

Kinohi Fukumitsu, an advocate for Hawaiian cultural and environmental preservation, was born and raised in Waimānalo, O'ahu, where she currently resides with her *'ohana* (family) of eight. She holds a bachelor's degree in Hawaiian studies from the University of Hawai'i at Mānoa.

Her journey in cultural and environmental preservation began in 2008, when she joined the nonprofit organization Paepae o He'eia as an intern, subsequently taking on the roles of internship coordinator and restoration manager. Today, she shares the knowledge from her time at He'eia Fishpond with her hometown community in Waimānalo.

With over a decade of experience at Paepae o He'eia, Fukumitsu transitioned to KUA in January 2021 as a Lohe Pono Fellow. KUA is a community-based initiative that protects, restores, and cares for *'āina* (land) across Hawai'i. The organization collaborates with government agencies and local organizations to advance community-based natural resources management and revive the traditional stewardship role of Hawai'i's communities over their lands and waters. In addition to her fellowship role at KUA, she is actively involved with Ke Kula Nui o Waimānalo and Hoala'āina Kūpono in Hakipu'u. Beyond her responsibilities at KUA, Fukumitsu is a skilled dry-stack stone wall mason, writer, weaver, and mother to six *keiki* (children). In her role as a cultural practitioner, she has acquired various valuable skills, including the art of rope making. A strong advocate for using natural resources, she crafts lengths of rope from natural fibers, employing them for traditional purposes like lashing, as well as for modern applications, such as organizing cords around the house.

MITHACHE AGOR
SALT PANS *of* THE GOANS
India

MITHACHE AGOR SALT PANS *of* THE GOANS *India*

Coauthored by
Joachim Cabral

PEOPLE Mithgaudas, Gauddos, Bhandaris, Agris, and Agers (salt-producing communities)
LOCATION Goa, India TECHNOLOGY salt pans
ELEVATION 0 m ORIGIN 500 CE
DISTANCE ABOVE OR BELOW WATERLINE −1 to +2.5 m
WATER LEVEL FLUCTUATION, TIDAL OR SEASONAL 0 to +4 m

FAO Nexus
WATER brackish ENERGY solar evaporation
FOOD salt + rice + fish

IPCC Adaptation Pathway
accommodate

World Bank NBS
CATEGORY sandy shores, salt marshes, river floodplains, bioretention areas, river and stream renaturation
FUNCTIONS coastal flood regulation, pluvial flood regulation, riverine flood regulation, biodiversity
BENEFITS coastal flood risk reduction, pluvial flood risk reduction, riverine flood risk reduction, resource production, carbon storage and sequestration, biodiversity, cultural, stimulate local economies and job creation

The wild salt of Goa, known as *gaunthi mith*, is described as a flaky, earthen delight that lingers in the mouth.[1] On a hot summer day, the *mittkaars* (salt makers) swirl this salt in their mouths, poking and prodding it with tongues that are trained to determine its quality, while they balance on narrow bunds bordering the shallow, gridded system of pools encrusted with salt. The *mithache agor* (salt pans) of Goa, also referred to as *mithagar*, are a traditional irrigation system for solar salt production by chemical reaction, requiring only a steady influx of salt water and sunlight.[2]

In these coastal pools, salty residues are coaxed from saline waters through a delicate passage from one shallow pan to the next, until the seawater has completely evaporated.[3] Climatic conditions, coupled with the state's low-lying landscape, contribute to Goa's reputation as a salt-producing epicenter. Practiced for millennia, this traditional method of producing salt provides an essential culinary ingredient, crops and fish during the monsoon, fertilizer for soils, and a cleaning agent for sanitation. Together, the salt pans provide a seasonal habitat for animals during the monsoon, and protect the coastal communities of Goa by maintaining a managed absorption field.

Bordering the Arabian Sea in India, Goa is a watery state with a humid, tropical climate and a long monsoon, lasting from June to October.[4] The sea slices Goa's shoreline, which stretches 110 kilometers along this southwestern coast of India, with six river estuaries: Terekhol, Chapora, Baga, Mandovi, Zuari, and Sal.[5] River salinity fluctuates with the seasons—the rivers have a high salt

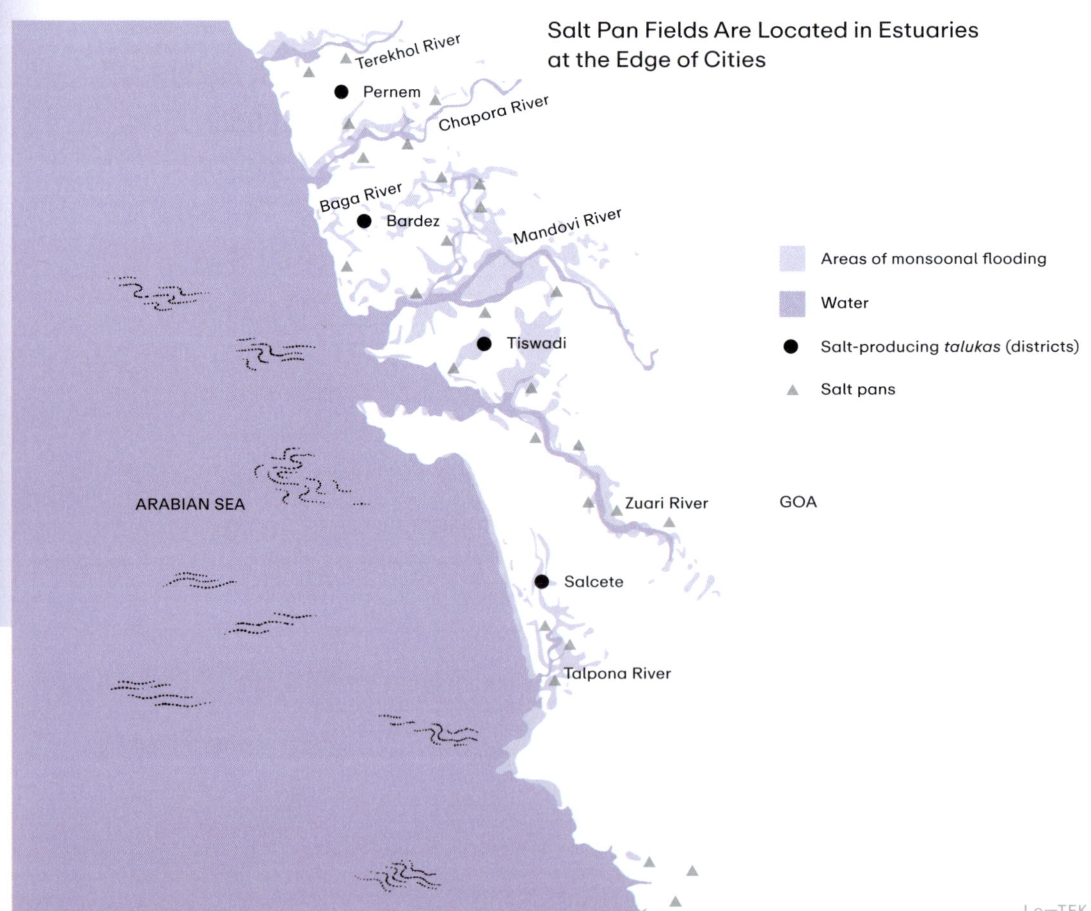

1 For three months each year, March to May, *mittkaars* spends hours every evening harvesting *mitt*, or salt, a Goan tradition that dates back 1,500 years.

1

concentration in the summer, which dilutes during the monsoon when rainwater infiltrates, making them ideal locations for local salt production. Along these rivers lie 36 villages in the talukas (district subdivisions) of Pernem, Bardez, Tiswadi, and Salcete, where *gaunthi mith* (wild salt) is produced.[6]

Fifteen hundred years ago, Goa's salt pans were molded from a waterlogged, marshy landscape known as *khazan*. These lands were reclaimed by the *gaonponn*, the name given to an agriculture or aquaculture village community.[7, 8] Though the term is widely used to describe collective land ownership among the Goans, the *gaonponn* serve multiple functions. Thriving for millennia, they are collective farming societies; regulators of religious, cultural, and economic activity; infrastructure commissions; and village councils.[9] Communal agricultural activity is regulated through the village council, which assigns individual families tracts of land. The income from salt production, agriculture, and aquaculture is collected by the *gaonponn* and used to fund community-development activities.

2

While most of India was colonized by the British from 1757 onward, Goa was established as a province under Portuguese rule in 1510, with salt production soon after becoming paramount to the Portuguese economy. Salt collected from the pans of Goa was shuttled to Portugal, the Middle East, and other regions of the global Portuguese Empire.[10] The local Goan economy relied on the trade of salt, coconuts, and areca nuts to offset the cost of imported rice, clothing, and other goods.[11] Today, there is no tax on salt in India—a result of the 1930 Salt March led by Mohandas Karamchand Gandhi (or Mahatma Gandhi) from Ahmedabad to the Arabian Sea coast. The Salt March was instigated to protest British rule, which had previously prohibited Indians from collecting and selling salt.[12] With salt being a staple in the Indian diet, Gandhi and his supporters defied the existing law by producing their own salt through seawater.[13]

Among Goans, the use of salt has deep cultural connections to food preparation, as well as practical, spiritual, and medicinal practices. Ayurveda, an Indigenous Indian system of medicine, makes use of salt for its healing properties.[14, 15] Some rituals incorporate salt to protect against evil spirits, such as the burning of salt and lime around homes.[16] *Gaunthi mith* is also used for the construction of wood-fired ovens when combined with sand.[17] Salt-infused brine pickling is common in Goan cuisine, including raw mango pickling. During monsoon season—a period when fishing is inhibited by rough seas and high tides—Goan diets rely on fish preserved through salting and pickling.[18]

2 Salt pans are part of a 3,500-year-old network of reclaimed wetlands called *khazans*. Unique to Goa, these wetlands are the saline floodplains along Goa's estuaries anchored by mangrove forests.

3 Salt production was carried out across various *talukas*, each with its own unique set of villages where this traditional occupation persists.

The seasonal salt-producing *mithache agor* system is composed of a cross-hatching of interlinked pans where water moves through a cycle of evaporation and salt production. While salt pans are located slightly lower than sea level, two-and-a-half-meter-high dikes are built around the land-facing edges of the system. These dikes, also called bunds, block seawater during the dry season and offer dry, raised land for *mittkaar* houses.[19] Carved into the landscape, the pans and surrounding bunds form a large-scale floodable foreshore infrastructure. Acting as retention basins and containing the movement of water, the system protects nearby agricultural fields and roads from flooding.[20]

3

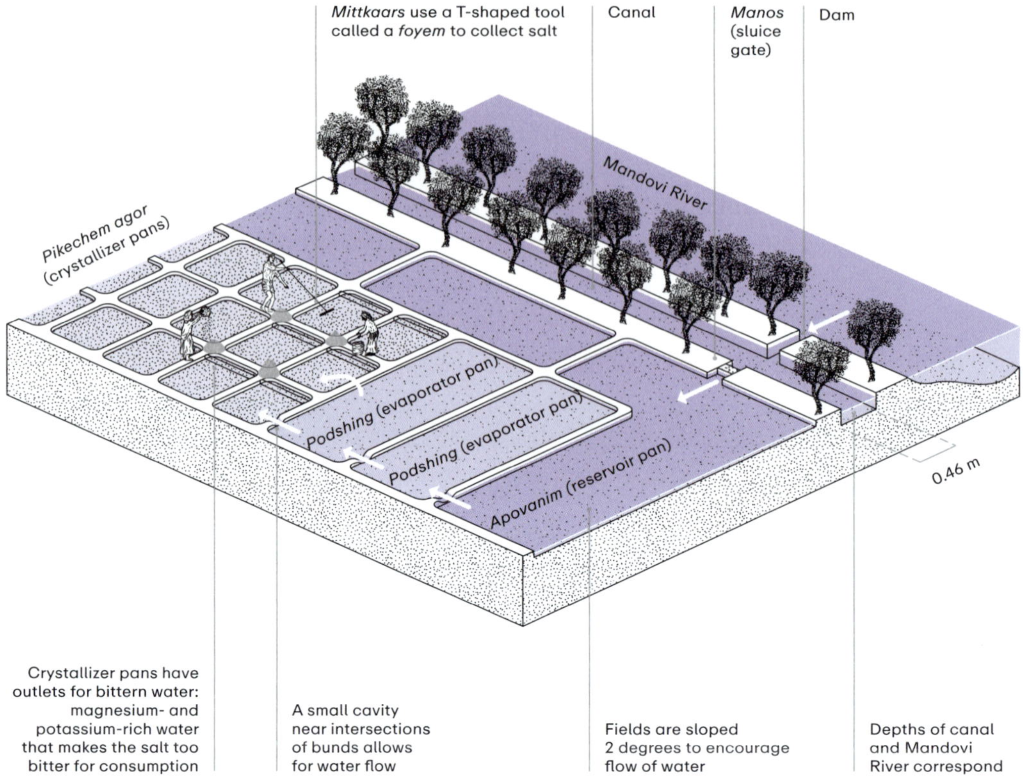

Mittkaars use a T-shaped tool called a *foyem* to collect salt

Canal

Manos (sluice gate)

Dam

Mandovi River

Pikechem agor (crystallizer pans)

Podshing (evaporator pan)

Podshing (evaporator pan)

Apovanim (reservoir pan)

0.46 m

Crystallizer pans have outlets for bittern water: magnesium- and potassium-rich water that makes the salt too bitter for consumption

A small cavity near intersections of bunds allows for water flow

Fields are sloped 2 degrees to encourage flow of water

Depths of canal and Mandovi River correspond

The year-round production cycle of this seasonally adaptive system can be divided into two phases: salt production during the dry season and cultivation of rice and fish in the wet. When the solar salt is baking in the dry months, the infrastructure is composed of three different pan typologies: a reservoir pan known as *tapovanim*, an evaporator pan referred to as *podshing*, and a crystallizer pan called *pikechem agor*.[21] Forming 15- to 30-centimeter-wide pathways for mittkaars, bunds constructed from *chikol* (clay) separate each pan. Small openings are dug into the corners of bunds to allow water to pass through.[22]

4

4 Salt is produced by collecting seawater in shallow ponds or basins, and allowing it to evaporate under the sun's heat, leading to salt crystals forming.
5 During the summer, these crystals are harvested, washed, and dried to create wild sea salt.
6 Small openings are dug into the corners of bunds to allow water to pass between pans.

Incoming salt water from the river flows through a canal before reaching a *manos* (sluice gate), which controls the inlet of water to the reservoir pan, especially during tidal influxes. Reservoir pans line the perimeter of the salt pans, containing the largest volume of water as they are almost always entirely full. These pans range from 18 to 20 meters in length, 10 to 12 meters in width, and are half a meter in depth.[23] Following the reservoir pan, water enters a series of two shallower evaporator pans, both measuring 18 to 20 meters in length, six to eight meters in width, and 25 centimeters in depth.[24] In the final stage, the water moves to the smaller crystallizer pan, which is the same depth as the evaporator pan, but only six to eight meters in length, and four to five meters in width. Here, the water completely evaporates, leaving behind salt crystals. Exact pan dimensions are based upon a *mittkaars'* preference and established during the preparation phase, which causes pan depth to vary seasonally.[25]

5

6

7

8

Many of the salt pans lie submerged during the monsoon season, when waters can reach four meters above sea level.[26] Relying on tidal influx, the sluice gate, and evaporation, excess water is drained from the *mithache ago*r at the end of the monsoon season. Salt ponds are prepared in December and January, before *mittkaars* begin salt production in February and May. Prior to the production stage, bunds between pans are rebuilt into hard, long impermeable mounds.[27, 28] A tool called a *ghor* or *neyo* is used to remove excess mud from the

9

10

7 The walls of the bunds that surround the salt pans are compacted using a clublike tool called a *petne*.
8 A *ghor* or *neyo* is used to remove excess mud from the base of pans.
9 In the preparation phase, seawater, which sits in the evaporator and crystallizer pans for 20 to 25 days, is stirred with a four-meter-long tool with toothlike protrusions called a *danto*.
10 The brine is then released to crystallizer pans, where the salt crystallizes out and is then harvested.

base of pans. With nothing wasted, the mud is added to fortify the sides of the bunds, while the walls of the bunds are compacted using a club-like tool called a *petne*.[29] Mittkaars also stamp the crystallizer pans to harden their clay base, repeating the process every few days until the crystallizer pans are flat and level.[30] During this preparatory phase, seawater sits in the evaporator and crystallizer pans for 20 to 25 days, and is stirred with a *danto*, which is a four-meter-long tool with toothlike protrusions.[31]

Rotating between Agriculture and Aquaculture throughout a Three-Season Year Composed of Premonsoon, Monsoon, and Postmonsoon

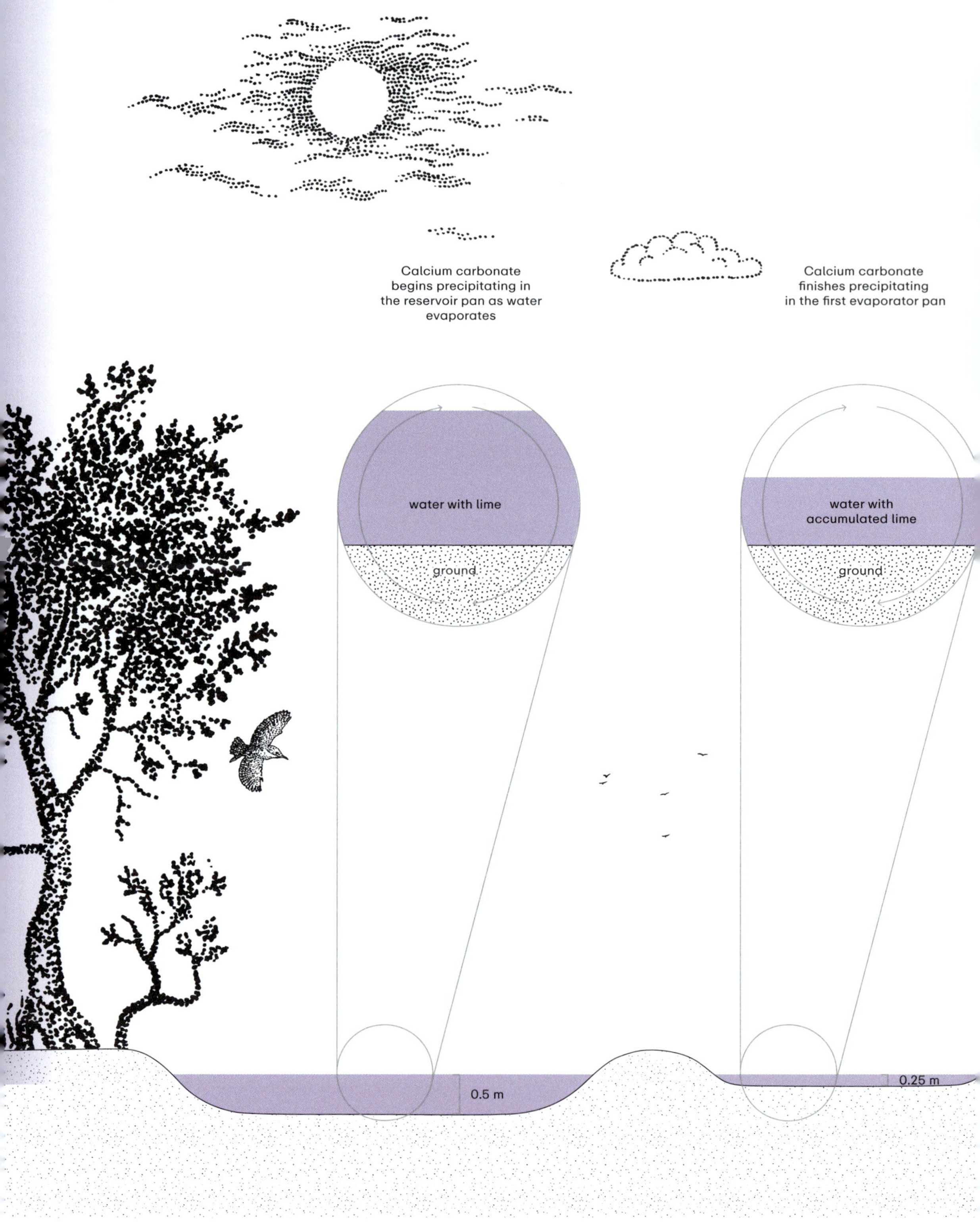

Calcium carbonate begins precipitating in the reservoir pan as water evaporates

Calcium carbonate finishes precipitating in the first evaporator pan

water with lime

ground

water with accumulated lime

ground

0.5 m

0.25 m

Tapovanim (reservoir pan)
0.45 m water depth

← Open this fold to reveal full illustration.

Once the system is prepared, salt harvesting begins in mid-February and lasts until May or early June, when high-intensity sunlight, strong winds, and high tides bring an influx of salt water from the rivers.[32] Water is released into the crystallizer pan every morning and harvested every evening. As the water evaporates, shallower pans become more concentrated with salt, until only the sodium chloride (NaCl) remains.[33] In the reservoir pans, calcium carbonate (CaCO3) precipitates as water evaporates, providing nourishment for the algae that floats along the surface.[34] Once the salinity achieves 5°Bé, or a 5 percent concentration, it is moved to the first evaporator pan, where calcium carbonate continues to precipitate until the water achieves a salinity of 13–15°Bé, or 13 to 15 percent concentration.[35] When the water is released into the second evaporator pan, calcium sulfate (CaSO3) begins to precipitate in a hard layer of gypsum that lines the bottom of the pan, until the water reaches 25°Bé, or 25 percent salinity, when it is then released to the crystallizer pan. The salt reaches its desired state, sodium chloride, at 27°Bé or 27 percent salinity.[36]

The first batches of salt made atop the mud are generally full of pathogens and are unfit for consumption.[37] The process is usually repeated two or three times to form a salt floor, remove excess mud, and ensure a clean surface for the production of edible salt.[38] Each layer of salt takes up to 10 days to produce, and the process is repeated two to three times.[39] If salt water is left for too long, magnesium and potassium begin to precipitate, forming a bitter taste; this water is moved to the edges of the crystallizer pan, where a microtopography of bunds funnel water to an outlet channel.[40] *Mittkaars* use a T-shaped tool, called a *foyem*, with a four-meter-long stem and rectangular wooden base to collect salt.[41] Harvested salt is further purified with a concentrated brine solution, allowed to drain along the intersections of bunds, collected with bamboo baskets into heaps, then transferred to a storing house.[42] Both fertilizer-grade salt, which is the initial harvest containing impurities like mud and clay, and consumption-grade salt, which follows, are produced in Goan salt pans.[43]

The success of each season depends upon the *mittkaars'* ability to read the climatic conditions of the area and the molecular composition of the salt. They rely on taste, traditional knowledge, and a process of trial and error to determine the readiness of salt water and its concentration levels. *Mittkaars* know the concentration of the pan is correct when salt crystallizes on the surface of the water. If no salt appears on the surface, the water is too diluted, and less water is released from the reservoir the following day. The slightest variation in the water volume of the pan can result in a lack of salt precipitation, so *mittkaars* manage a daily balance between water level, temperature, and sunlight.

From June to October, salt pans are converted into grassy aquaculture ponds as the monsoon season brings an influx of rainwater and reduced sunlight—ideal conditions for growing rice.[44, 45] During this period, the excess water also transforms the reservoir pans into an aquaculture system to raise shrimp, catfish, *goshi*, *chonak* (red snapper), and *maankyo* (squid). The fish and rice from these biodiverse cultivation ponds—harvested from October to December, following the end of the monsoon season—also serve as a food

A Symbiosis between the Crop Cycle of Rice and the Migration of Fish from the Sea to the Rivers

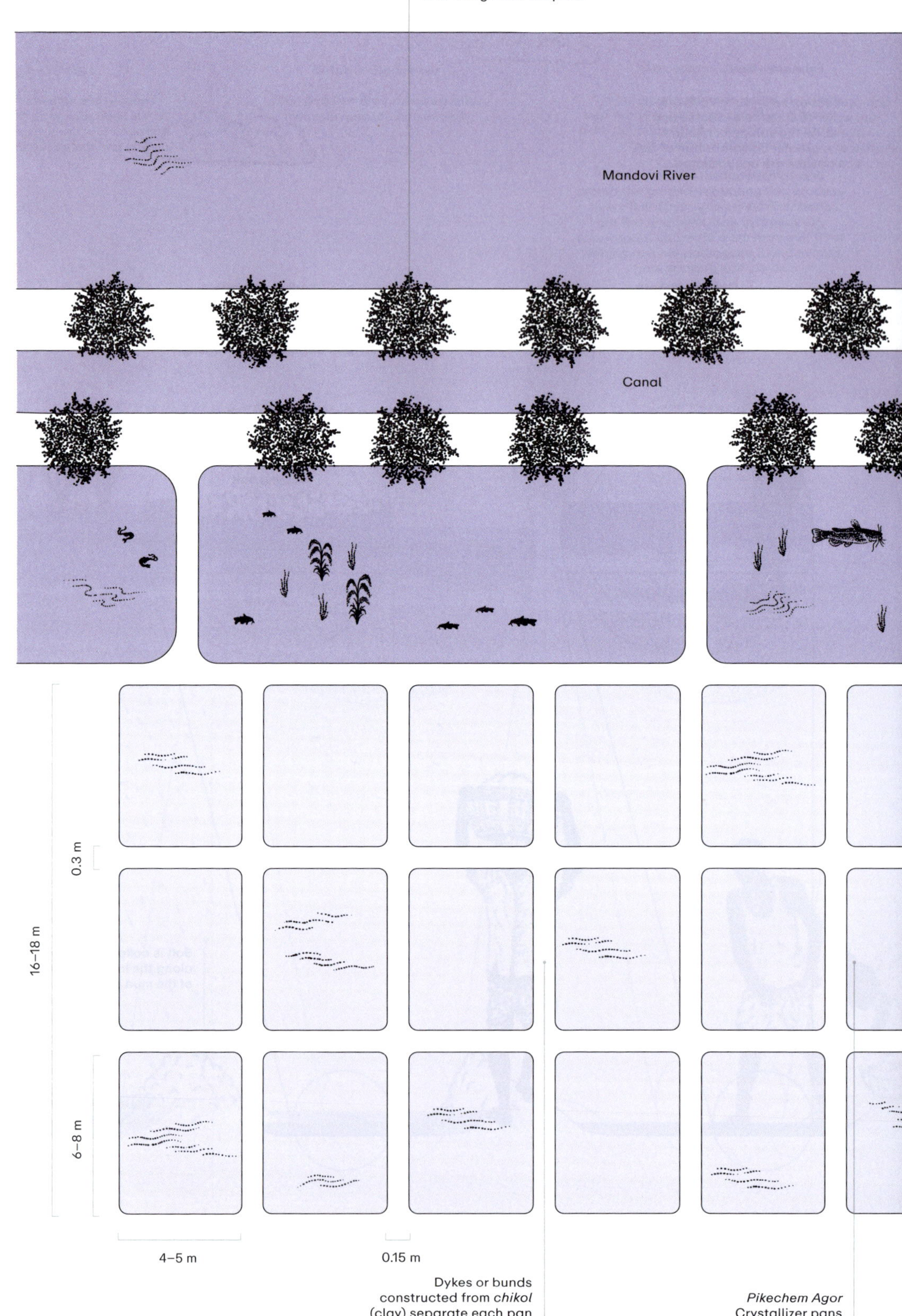

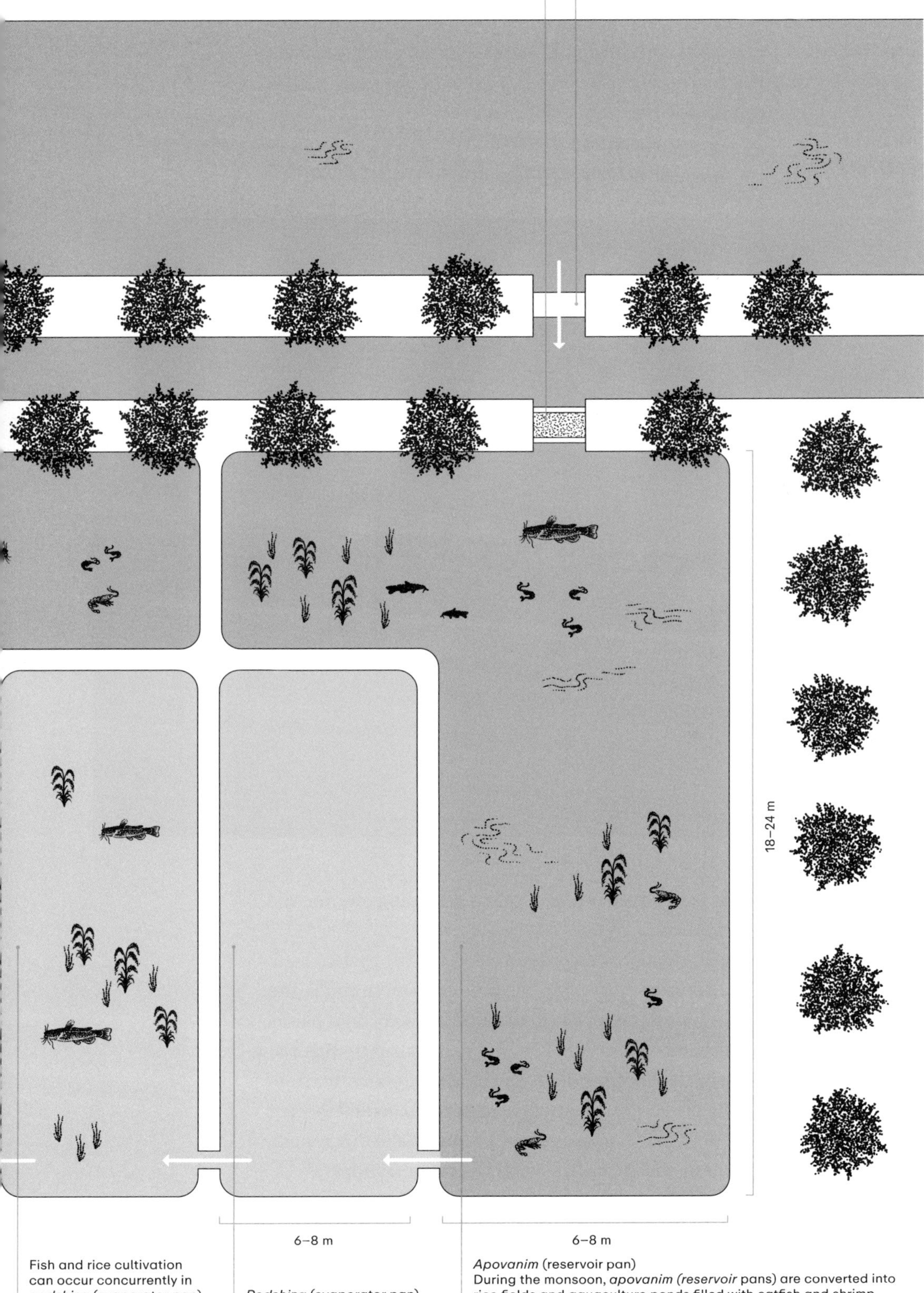
Manos (sluice gates) are filled with mud to stop the flow of water
Dam
18–24 m
6–8 m
6–8 m
Fish and rice cultivation can occur concurrently in *podshing* (evaporator pan)
Podshing (evaporator pan)
Apovanim (reservoir pan)
During the monsoon, *apovanim (reservoir* pans) are converted into rice fields and aquaculture ponds filled with catfish and shrimp

source for waterfowl.[46] This fallow period of heavy saturation ensures the land rests on an annual basis, contributing to its long-term sustainability.

The success of the salt pan system stems from its year-round production cycle and seasonal adaptability, producing salt in the dry months and propagating rice and fish in the wet months. Originally converted from the marshy *khazan* land, the pans are returned to a swamp-like landscape during the rainy season, when conditions are favorable for rice cultivation, and the pans can be found brimming with fish. Solar salt ponds create a dynamic habitat for many organisms due to their extensive variances in temperature, salinity, oxygen levels, and

11 During the monsoon, salt pans flood with marine life—shrimp, mullet, pearlspot—while salt-resistant rice strains are grown in the pans.

11

nutrient content.[47] The seasonal conversion also offers a feeding site for the waterfowl that nest in the mangroves.

In this symbiotic system, waste is a resource used in the life cycles of surrounding soil, vegetation, and animal species. In the premonsoon summer, the muddy batches of salt unfit for human consumption are fed to the coconut palms and mangrove trees as fertilizer and termite repellent.[48] Organisms including bacteria, archaea, and fungi assist by recycling nutrients and removing pollutants from within the system.[49] Occupying the murky waters of the reservoir pans and the first evaporator pans, algae is an important source of energy production in this system: It traps sunlight, feeds crustaceans and birds, and is harvested for fertilizer.[50]

ARCHAEA Single-celled prokaryotic organisms with distinct molecular characteristics separating them from bacteria and eukaryotes.

Today's *mithache agor* differ significantly from those of the past, experiencing a notable decline due to the impact of climate change and a lack of financial support.[51] Historically, over four hundred functional salt pans dotted the region, compared to the 30 that exist today.[52] Unlike earlier reliance on natural tidal fluctuation, a motorized pump is now used to remove excess water from the aquaculture system in December, after the monsoon season ends and prior to starting preparation for salt production.[53] Since 2020, year-round rains have disrupted salt production, leading to challenges in generating profits.[54] Moreover, competition from larger industrial salt producers has triggered a decline, rendering salt pans no longer profitable to operate.[55] Subsequently, most salt pan workers are now migrant laborers from the neighboring state of Gokarna, which also has a salt-making practice.[56] These workers return annually from May to October, spreading word of Goa's seasonal economic opportunities once they return home.[57] Although the *khazan* committee is responsible for the maintenance

12

13

12 Salt production is an environmentally clean, nonpolluting, low-capital, labor-intensive, and employment-generating rural economic activity.

13 The pans support a vast array of bird life, with algae in the reservoir pans attracting brine shrimp, which attract fish that feed the birds.

of agricultural land, including the salt pans, the decision to continue operations varies from plot to plot, because they are family owned.

Over the past decade, a drastic rise in sea levels during the monsoon season has also allowed crocodiles to swim upstream—particularly in the Mandovi River—and eat fish that are grown in the aquaculture ponds.[58] River otters also pose a threat to aquaculture and rice cultivation in the pans. *Mittkaars* have been prompted to divest from aquaculture practices due to growing challenges associated with predatory animals.[59] Currently, *mittkaars* only cultivate what flows into the pans with the tides, and distribute the fish among community members for sustenance.[60] However, there has been increasing interest in exploring renewable passive solar and hydropower production in the salt pans using the same techniques that produce the wild salt. Abundant sunlight, strong winds, and significant tidal shifts increase the potential for colocation of solar, wind, and tidal energy, while microturbines hybridized within the system could assist with local energy generation.

As a traditional system for solar salt production, the gridded *mithache agor* of Goa are reliant on the seasonal saline fluctuations of the area's rivers; the salt pans function through passive solar and hydropower, accompanied by minerals and nutrients. The unique process achieved through evaporation produces the key cultural resource of salt—a fertilizer for crops and an agent for cleaning. Simultaneously, the pans are a seasonal cultivation system for rice and fish, and a retention basin for water during monsoon seasons.

14

14 The salt pans of Goa form a complex ecological system providing sustenance to villagers each season.

The *mithache agor* provide a floodable infrastructure for seasonal, productive adaptation. Panaji, Goa's capital city built on reclaimed land threaded with internal rivers, is vulnerable to flooding, and benefits from infrastructure like this.[61] These architectures also represent opportunities for hybridization and adaptation within and beyond Goa in the context of seasonal landscape shifts and coastal, riverine, and pluvial flooding. Beyond their cultural relevance, the Goan salt pans should be restored and supported given the system's dynamic potential for food production, job creation, flood mitigation, energy production, and biodiversity promotion to help address contemporary and future climate-related challenges.

ENDNOTES

1. Arti Das, "Salt of the Earth," *Whetstone Magazine*, June 24, 2021, https://www.whetstonemagazine.com/south-asia-journal/salt-of-the-earth.
2. Kabilan Mani et al., "Community Solar Salt Production in Goa, India," *Aquatic Biosystems 8*, no. 1 (2012): 1, https://doi.org/10.1186/2046-9063-8-30.
3. Harischandra Tucaram Nagvenkar, "Salt and the Goan Economy (A Study of Goa's Salt Industry and Salt Trade in the 19th and 20th Centuries during the Portuguese Rule)" (master's thesis, Goa University, 1999), 3.
4. Mani et al., "Community Solar Salt Production," 2.
5. Mani et al., "Community Solar Salt Production," 2.
6. Mani et al., "Community Solar Salt Production," 2.
7. Nagvenkar, "Salt and the Goan Economy."
8. Mani et al., "Community Solar Salt Production," 3.
9. Nagvenkar, "Salt and the Goan Economy," 48.
10. Mani et al., "Community Solar Salt Production," 2.
11. Nagvenkar, "Salt and the Goan Economy," 1.
12. History.com editors, "Salt March," History.com, June 10, 2010, https://www.history.com/topics/asian-history/salt-march.
13. History.com editors, "Salt March."
14. Avantika Velho (biodesigner), in discussion with the author, August 2022.
15. Velho, discussion.
16. Velho, discussion.
17. Pravin Kamble, "The Dying Salt Pans in Goa," Make It Happen, March 15, 2023, https://makeithappen.co.in/the-dying-salt-pans-of-goa/.
18. Velho, discussion.
19. Joachim Cabral *(mittkaar)*, in discussion with the author, December 2022.
20. Cabral, discussion.
21. Mani et al., "Community Solar Salt Production," 3.
22. Cabral, discussion.
23. Mani et al., "Community Solar Salt Production," 4.
24. Mani et al., "Comtmunity Solar Salt Production," 4.
25. Velho, discussion.
26. Gauree Malkarnekar, "Goa: All 12 Talukas Have 'Safe' Groundwater Levels," *The Times of India*, October 28, 2021, https://timesofindia.indiatimes.com/city/goa/all-12-talukas-have-safe-ground-water-levels-central-body/articleshow/87319400.cms.
27. Nagvenkar, "Salt and the Goan Economy," 56.
28. Cabral, discussion.
29. Nagvenkar, "Salt and the Goan Economy."
30. Nagvenkar, "Salt and the Goan Economy."
31. Mani et al., "Community Solar Salt Production," 4.
32. Mani et al., "Community Solar Salt Production," 5.
33. Mani et al., "Community Solar Salt Production," 4.
34. Mani et al., "Community Solar Salt Production," 4–5.
35. Mani et al., "Community Solar Salt Production," 4.
36. Mani et al., "Community Solar Salt Production," 4.
37. Velho, discussion.
38. Mani et al., "Community Solar Salt Production," 5.
39. Mani et al., "Community Solar Salt Production," 5.
40. Mani et al., "Community Solar Salt Production," 5.
41. Mani et al., "Community Solar Salt Production," 5.
42. Mani et al., "Community Solar Salt Production," 5.
43. Mani et al., "Community Solar Salt Production," 5.
44. Mani et al., "Community Solar Salt Production," 1.
45. Velho, discussion.
46. Cabral, discussion.
47. Mani et al., "Community Solar Salt Production," 5.
48. Mani et al., "Community Solar Salt Production," 5.
49. Mani et al., "Community Solar Salt Production," 5.
50. Mani et al., "Community Solar Salt Production," 5.
51. Cabral, discussion.
52. Das, "Salt of the Earth."
53. Nagvenkar, "Salt and the Goan Economy," 56.
54. Cabral, discussion.
55. Mani et al., "Community Solar Salt Production," 1.
56. Cabral, discussion.
57. Cabral, discussion.
58. Cabral, discussion.
59. Cabral, discussion.
60. Cabral, discussion.
61. Velho, discussion.

COAUTHOR

JOACHIM CABRAL

Head Mittkaar of the Cabral Family

ɔrn and raised in Mercês, Goa, Joachim Cabral a skilled *mittkaar* who has devoted his life to water anagement and salt pan cultivation. He works the salt pans in Ribandar along the Mandovi iver, in a region known for its unique environmen- l conditions ideal for salt production. With over) years of experience in the salt fields, Cabral has come a master of his craft and is widely respected his community for his expertise.

Cabral was first introduced to salt farming y his father, who worked in the salt pans for over) years. He grew up watching his father design and uild the intricate system of channels, uice gates, and walls that allowed for e controlled flow of salt water into the ans. From an early age, he was capti- ted by the complex and fascinating orld of water management.

Over the years, Cabral has devel- ped his own unique techniques for nsuring that the salt pans remain pro- uctive year after year. One of his key cills is his ability to create channels f water during high tide, which he then aps and diverts into the pans. This requires constant aintenance and repair work, as the walls and sluice ates need to be checked and reinforced regularly prevent leaks or breaches.

Cabral is also known for his innovative use f plastic mesh in the sluice gates, which helps filter aste like algae and other debris. The dried algae nd moss are then used as fertilizer for coconut trees, roviding an additional source of income for him and is family. During the monsoon season, Cabral also reeds fish and prawns in his *khazan*, adding another yer of productivity to the land.

Despite the many challenges that Cabral and ther *mittkaars* face, including a lack of labor and the ccasional loss of yield, they remain committed to their work, understanding that the delicate balance between salt water, fresh water, tradition, and innovation must be maintained to ensure the continued productivity of the salt pans in the future.

The *khazan* lands where Cabral is employed belong to the Velho family and other community members, who have granted them to the *mittkaars* without charge. This marks a significant departure from the practice of levying taxes on such lands for *mittkaars*, underscoring the vital role of this trade in sustaining the local economy and preserving the ecology.

Perhaps Cabral's greatest achievement, however, is that his six-year-old son is already showing an interest in the trade. Cabral is proud to have the opportunity to pass on his skills and knowledge to the next generation and hopes that his son will one day take up the mantle of *mittkaar*. Through tireless efforts and innovative techniques, his family has helped ensure the sustainability of the *khazan* lands for generations and will do so for generations to come.

HORO I'A FISH WEIRS *of* THE MĀ'OHI
French Polynesia

HORO I'A FISH WEIRS *of* THE MĀ'OHI *French Polynesia*

Coauthored by
Dorothy Peggy Lubin-Lévy

(PEOPLE) Mā'ohi (LOCATION) Huahine Nui, Society Islands, French Polynesia (TECHNOLOGY) fish weirs (ELEVATION) 0–2.5 m (ORIGIN) 1600 CE (DISTANCE ABOVE OR BELOW WATERLINE) −2.5 to +0.6 m (WATER LEVEL FLUCTUATION, TIDAL OR SEASONAL) +0.1 to +0.3 m

FAO Nexus
(WATER) brackish (ENERGY) tidal (FOOD) fish

IPCC Adaptation Pathway
protect

World Bank NBS
(CATEGORY) sandy shores, bioretention areas
(FUNCTIONS) coastal erosion regulation, biodiversity, coastal flood regulation, sea level rise adaptation
(BENEFITS) coastal flood risk reduction, resource production, carbon storage and sequestration, biodiversity, cultural

Wading by moonlight with a bundled reed torch in one hand and a spear in the other, a Māʻohi fisherman traverses the shallow, sandy lagoon, illuminating a long line of sunken coral stones. The moon and easterly winds govern the ebb and flow of the tides, channeling seawater into the lake and ushering in large fish in search of prey. On the island of Huahine, this long narrow lagoon links the open waters of the South Pacific and the expansive, shallow saltwater lake called Fauna Nui.[1, 2] Here, a *parc à poissons*, meaning "fish park," is characterized by a series of V-shaped fish weirs that culminate in circular enclosures called *haapua*—an ingenious intertidal aquaculture technology.[3, 4] Submerged in the coastal waters that envelop the jungles of the Society Islands, these ancient stone weirs known as *horo iʻa* (fish runs) are the ancestral technology of the Māʻohi. With origins tracing back centuries, they could one day bring renewable energy for those island communities faced with an unpredictable climate future.

1 The long, narrow lagoon linking the South Pacific to the saltwater lake of Fauna Nui.
2 The lagoon is known as the *parc à poissons*, meaning "fish park."

1

2

The Society Islands constitute a group of five islands amid the larger expanse of the 118 islands and atolls that make up French Polynesia. Referred to by the Māʻohi people as "The Wild Island," Huahine is situated to the northwest of Tahiti and is split into two parts: Huahine Nui, or "Big Huahine," and Huahine Iti, meaning "Little Huahine." With a total population of 6,075 inhabitants, the island has been preserved as a sanctum for sacred temples and archaeological artifacts.[5]

The culture of the Māʻohi people Indigenous to this archipelago is deeply intertwined with the natural world. This profound connection finds expression through various forms, including *haka*, songs, stories, dances, tattooing, and traditional aquaculture practices. *Horo iʻa* have been built in various locations among the Society Islands, including Tetiaʻroa, Bora Bora, Tahaʻa, Maupiti, Huahine, and Tahiti.[6] Along Huahine's northeast coast, a receding tide will reveal an array of traditional *horo iʻa* fish weirs. Located between the mainland Maeva village and the Haʻamitti barrier reef, these formations are strategically designed to channel fish through stone-walled labyrinths and into circular basins, guided by the prevailing currents and winds.

The earliest recorded history of Maeva village can be traced to an archaeological ceremonial site located at Mataʻireʻa Hill on the eastern side of the island, dating to 700–1000 CE.[7] Here stood the marae, revered gathering spaces where ariʻi (chiefs) assembled to pay homage to their ancestors; these sacred spaces lined the island's narrow lagoon and the saltwater lake of Faʻuna Nui.[8] For centuries, Māʻohi chiefdoms implemented a sophisticated system of resource management that guided land and sea harvests, with restrictions known as *rahui*.[9] This guaranteed that resources were never overharvested, and ensured the livelihoods

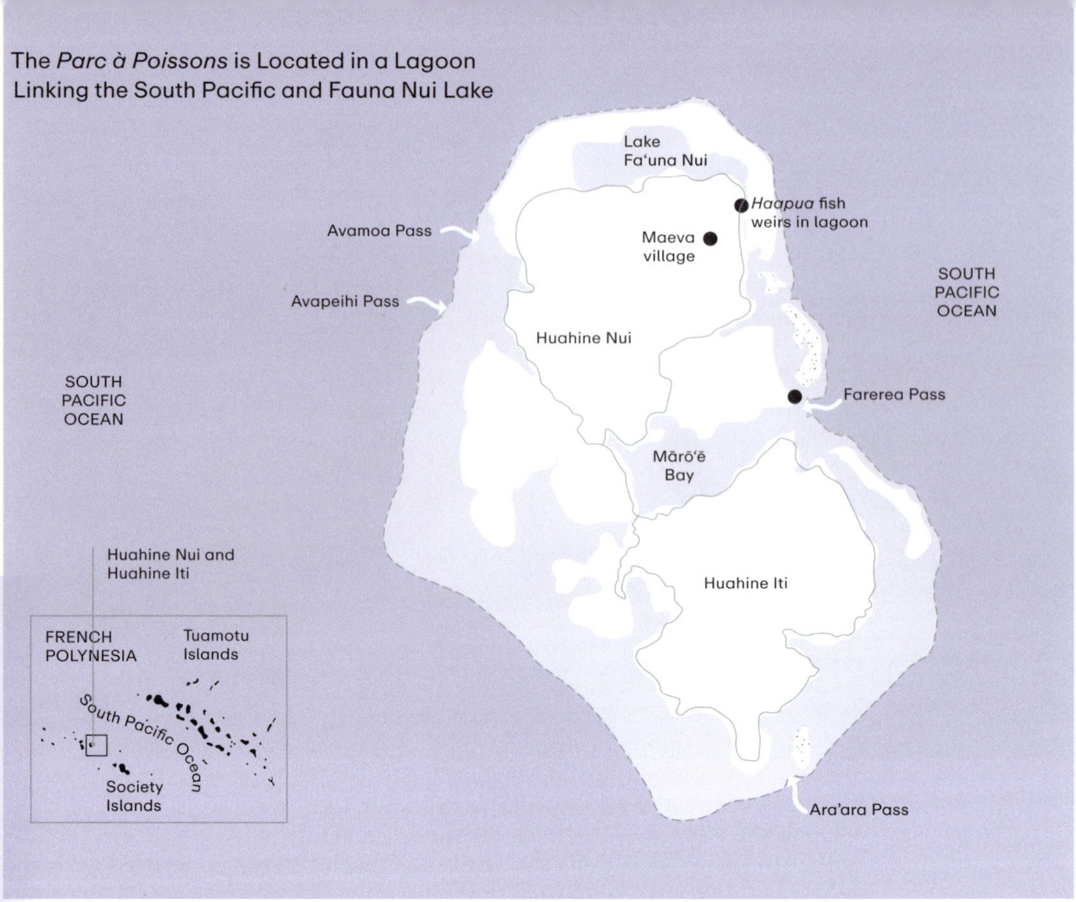

The *Parc à Poissons* is Located in a Lagoon Linking the South Pacific and Fauna Nui Lake

Lake Fa'una Nui
Haapua fish weirs in lagoon
Avamoa Pass
Maeva village
Avapeihi Pass
SOUTH PACIFIC OCEAN
Huahine Nui
SOUTH PACIFIC OCEAN
Farerea Pass
Mārō'ē Bay
Huahine Nui and Huahine Iti
Huahine Iti
FRENCH POLYNESIA
Tuamotu Islands
South Pacific Ocean
Society Islands
Ara'ara Pass

of all Mā'ohi. At times, specific rules were imposed on a particular species or trap, which posed threats to the ecosystem or the community.[10]

Two of Maeva's seven *horo i'a* are known to have belonged to the *ari'i*.[11] The remaining five were family owned and passed down from generation to generation. The name given to its *āv'a*, a term specifically meaning "enclosure," served as an indicator of ownership for each *horo i'a*. For instance, on Huanine, weirs are referred to by names such as *āv'a tahiverevere, āv'a wahamoa, āv'a momona, āv'a tepua, and āv'a puaaovir*.[12] The successful management of resources

3

and establishment of food security through *horo i'a* played a crucial role in the prosperity of the Maeva community.

The seven successive *horo i'a* found in the lagoon opposite Maeva village vary in size, length, and arrangement. These stone-built weirs are designed to harness tidal movement and capture fish as they enter or exit the lake. The engineering of these structures involves a thoughtful consideration of the natural movements of the water. Once the tide begins to recede, Mā'ohi collect fish isolated within each stony basin with nets, or occasionally spears.[13] Fish that are not captured are released into the sea when high tide returns by midday.

The fish weirs themselves, known by the technical native *haapua*, are circular enclosures that reach four and a half to six meters in diameter, with walls that are approximately a meter wide.[14] Each *haapua* has a meter-wide opening, from which two walls known as arero, directly translating to "tongue," extend.[15] The *arero* walls are generally slimmer than those of the *haapua*, measuring only half a meter in width. The height of *haapua* and *arero* vary according to the depth of the lagoon, which gradually slopes downward to two and a half meters at its lowest point. At high tide, the *haapua* enclosure and *arero* walls rise half a meter above the water level.[16]

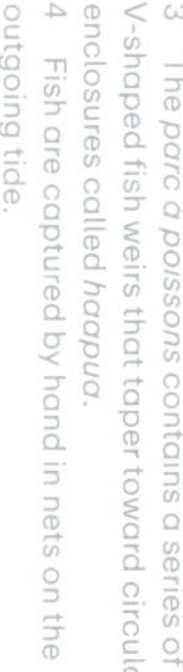

3 The *parc à poissons* contains a series of V-shaped fish weirs that taper toward circular enclosures called *haapua*.
4 Fish are captured by hand in nets on the outgoing tide.

4

Haapua openings are partially blocked with loose stones piled up from the lagoon floor. During low tide, the water level in the enclosure drops to less than a meter high.[17] The arrangement of stone barriers and entrances, along with the influence of tidal movement, serves to redirect fish away from openings in the weir, successfully ensnaring them for capture. For example, if the entrance to a *haapua* is left open overnight, the enclosure will teem with fish, lured into its stony, moonlit entrance in search of prey. Traditionally, a young boy assigned to monitor the haapua will report its yield each morning to the trap owner.[18] Fishermen arrive at the enclosure

Haapua Circular Enclosure where Species Are Funneled into Openings

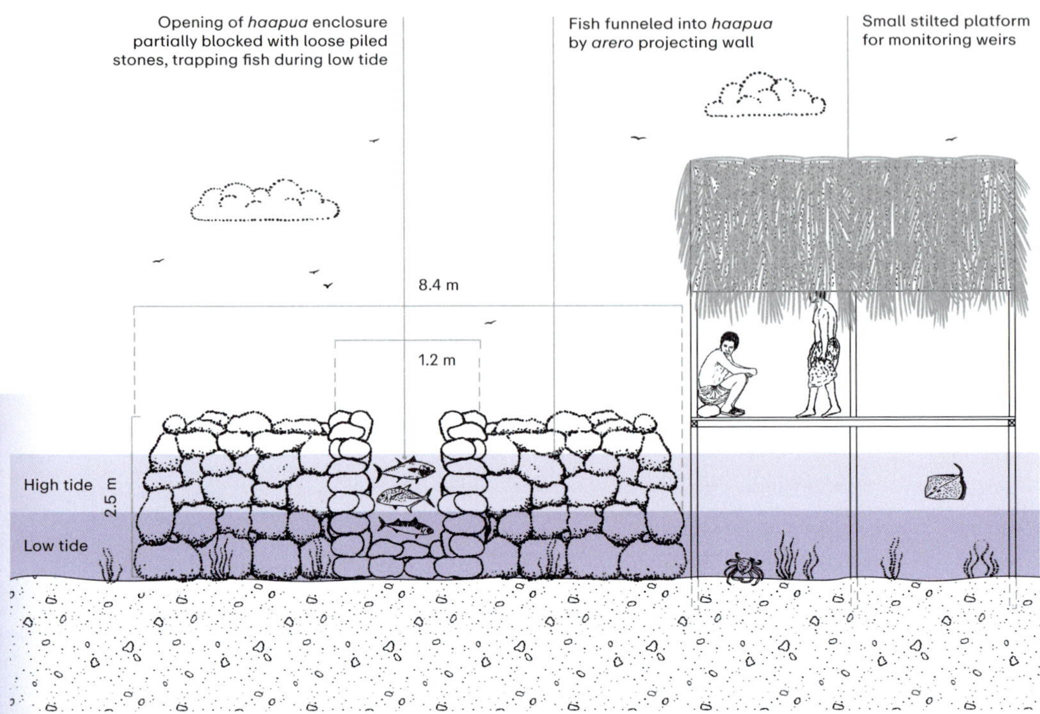

walls by canoe, standing as they use dip nets called *toto haipu* to scoop up the day's catch.[19] To secure additional fish in the same net, the bag can be twisted several times to secure already-caught fish before being dipped back into the water.[20]

The seven fish weirs interspersed throughout the neck of the lagoon can be categorized as three types: an A-shaped trap with one wide opening, a V-shaped trap with one narrow opening, and a W-shaped trap with two narrow openings. Four of the seven weirs are A-shaped—a typology characterized by two *arero* that flare outward, forming a wedge-like configuration that tapers toward the *haapua's* opening. The V-shaped and W-shaped weirs are more intricate in design. The two *arero* extending outward from the V-shaped trap create a sharper angle than that of the A-shape. One of these *arero* extends past the other, until it bends around its shorter counterpart. This curvature forms a secondary enclosure within the *arero* walls, effectively preventing fish from escaping. The sole V-shaped trap in Maeva is *aua pua'a-oviri*, with *pua'a-oviri* translating to "wild pig."[21]

The W-shaped weirs are the most structurally complex, as two *haapuas* mirror each other on each side of the stream. From there, two parallel *arero* exit each enclosure, extending outward until they bend and intersect each other. This point of connection is known as *mata hoto*.[22] Here, fish enter the trap through two gaps in the arero wall called the *uputa*.[23] Upon entry, the current and tight walls propel the fish deeper into the enclosure, where they are either caught with a scoop net or released. The seven fish weirs located in the neck of the lagoon were

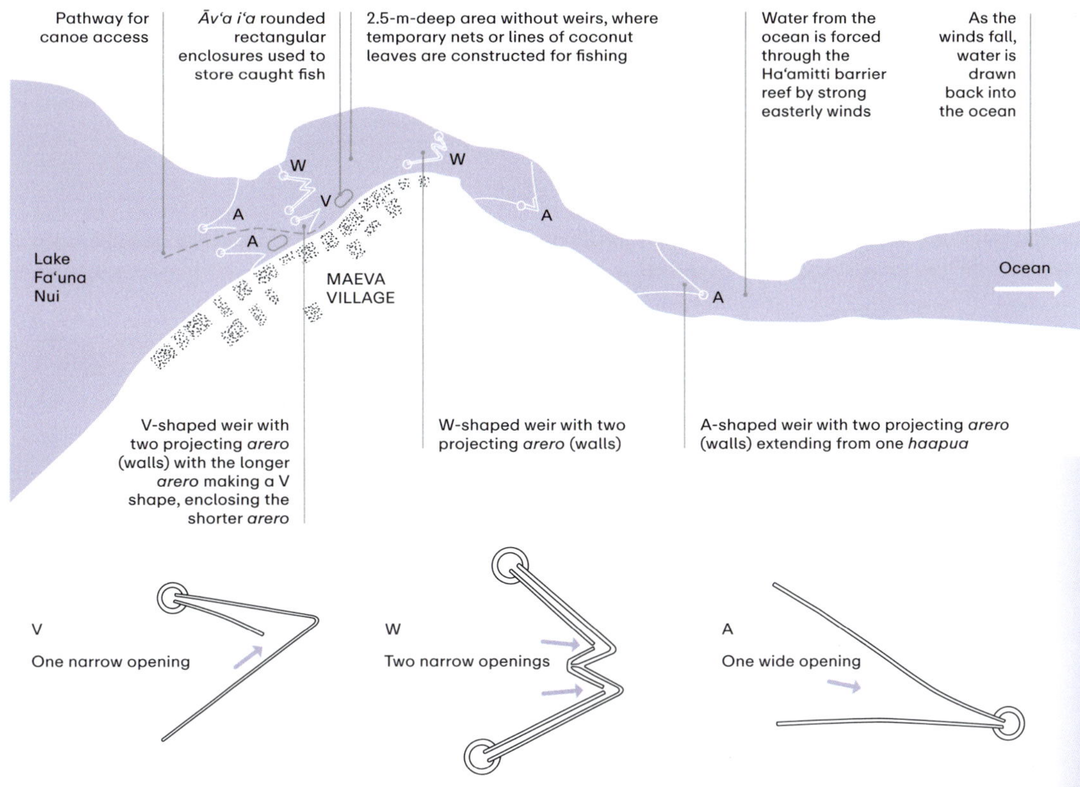

constructed to enable the smooth passage of a canoe from the saltwater lake of Fauna Nui to the Pacific Ocean.

Running between the mainland of Maeva and an elevated barrier reef along the east coast, the bottom of the lagoon gradually lowers to two and a half meters deep at the middle of the channel, leaving a gap without weirs.[24] These passes are sometimes temporarily blocked with nets or long lines of coconut leaves called *rau ere* to facilitate fishing.[25, 26] Strong easterly winds force the sea in through the pass at the Ha'amitti barrier reef. As the winds fall, the opposite occurs and seawater is drawn back into the ocean. Conditions are most ideal for fishing when easterly winds occur in conjunction with a full moon, as the reflection of the moonlight on the lagoon floor attracts larger fish seeking prey, and the movement of the seawater draws the fish into the lake.[27] When caught in large numbers, the fishermen from each family store them in small rectangular enclosures called *āv'a i'a* (fishponds).[28] Located in front of houses along the shore of the lagoon and constructed with stones, coral, wood, leaves, nets, or a combination of these materials, the *āv'a i'a* are strategically built temporary enclosures, intended to retain fish.[29]

Beyond food security for the Mā'ohi community, *horo i'a* provide a multitude of services to the surrounding ecosystem. On a micro scale, this infrastructure serves as a habitat for marine species like algae and zooplankton—a primary food source for the herbaceous fish that inhabit the lagoon. Of these fish species, those that are caught and consumed include *ava* (milkfish) and *paaihere* (giant

Āv'a Momona and *Āv'a Puaaovir* Weirs
Have Double Wall Bends Called *Mata Hoto*

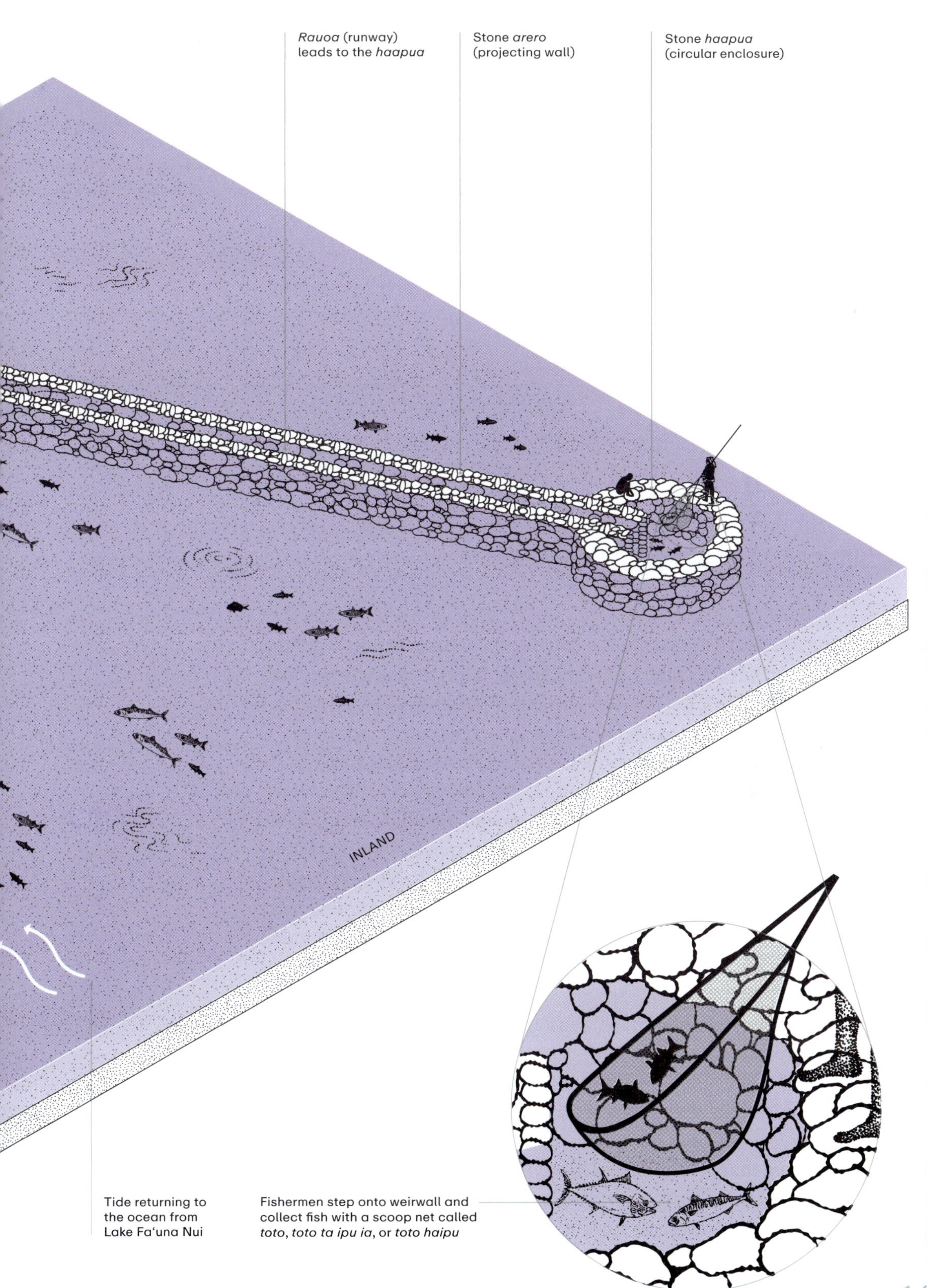
Rauoa (runway)
leads to the *haapua*
Stone *arero*
(projecting wall)
Stone *haapua*
(circular enclosure)
INLAND
Tide returning to
the ocean from
Lake Fa'una Nui
Fishermen step onto weirwall and
collect fish with a scoop net called
toto, *toto ta ipu ia*, or *toto haipu*

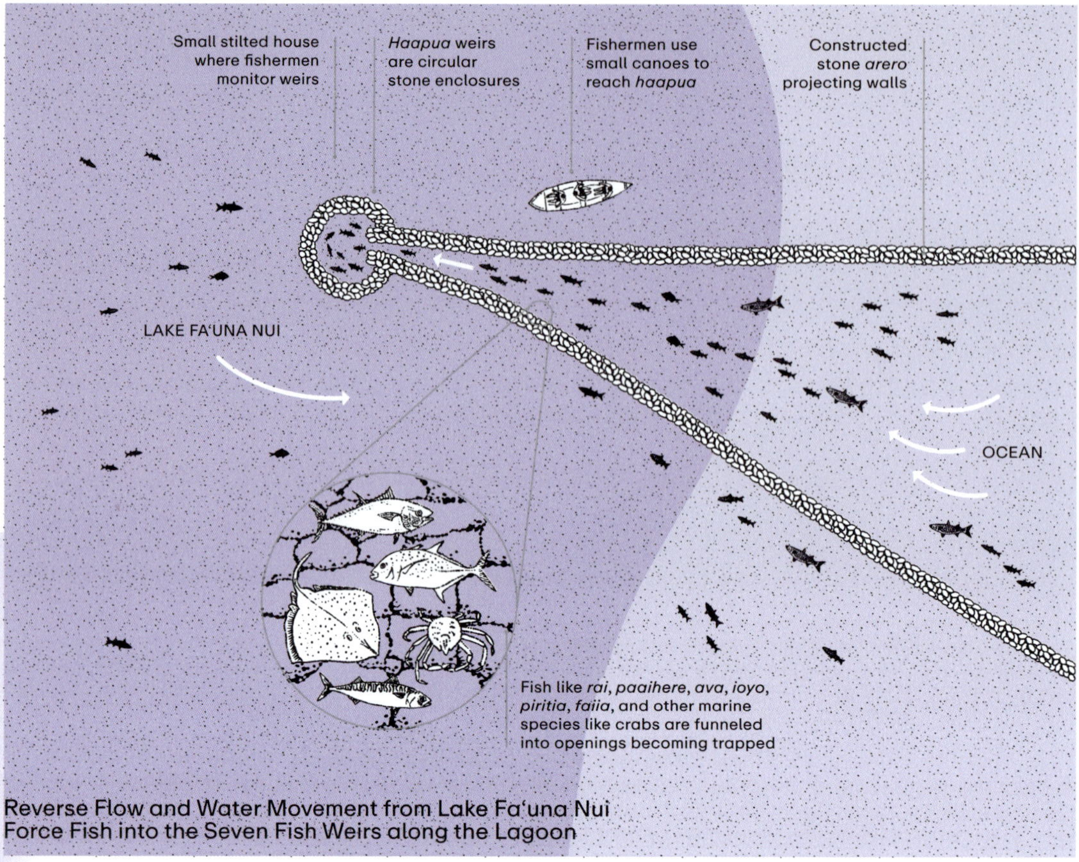

Small stilted house where fishermen monitor weirs

Haapua weirs are circular stone enclosures

Fishermen use small canoes to reach *haapua*

Constructed stone *arero* projecting walls

LAKE FA'UNA NUI

OCEAN

Fish like *rai*, *paaihere*, *ava*, *ioyo*, *piritia*, *faiia*, and other marine species like crabs are funneled into openings becoming trapped

Reverse Flow and Water Movement from Lake Fa'una Nui Force Fish into the Seven Fish Weirs along the Lagoon

trevally).[30] Crustaceans such as crabs—a Polynesian culinary staple—can also be found dwelling in the rocky interior of the *horo iʻa*. Migrating past these seven fish weirs, the center of the lagoon boasts impressive biodiversity, with reef outcrops and coral growths serving as a home to a variety of parrotfish and tangs.[31]

Meanwhile, clusters of dense brown algae in the outer lagoon provide a habitat to sea snail species like *Turbo setosus* and *Trochus niloticus*.[32] The *horo iʻa* in Huahine not only regulate this ecosystem by providing habitat services and managing fish populations but also act as a tidal barrier, capable of safeguarding the lagoon and lake ecosystem from storm surge during extreme weather events.

Horo iʻa fish weirs constitute just one part of the extensive resource management system implemented by Māʻohii chiefdoms. *Ariʻi* modified *rahui* in a way that not only met the community's needs and upheld customary practices but also established a balance among species, ensuring the preservation and sustainable use of the local ecosystem without causing disruption or overexploitation.

Accounts from the 19th and 20th centuries indicate that *rahui* could be enforced by *ariʻi*, other leaders, and landholders alike, despite the absence of "property rights," in the Western sense, throughout Polynesia.[33] The scale of a *rahui* could vary greatly, from a particular species to the trespassing of an entire reef, as could the intention of the restriction. In some cases, imposing *rahui* on an area of the ecosystem, marine or land, had ceremonial implications, such as mourning periods or the observance of rituals.[34] One 1970 testimony recounts

5 Located in the neck of the lagoon, the seven fish weirs were constructed to enable the smooth passage of a canoe.

5

the prohibition of fishing bonito and albacore until several significant ceremonies were concluded across the island.[35] In other instances, *rahui* could be prompted by something as straightforward as coastal landholders wanting to prevent overfishing in the nearby sea. In such scenarios, landholders themselves would enact *rahui* by placing a pole, adorned with bamboo leaves, along the shoreline they wished to restrict.[36] A *rahui* imposed on the reef—encompassing all of its resources rather than a particular species—was indicated by cordoning off the prohibited area with shrubs and tied cloth.[37] This adaptive enforcement of *rahui*, around *horo iʻa* and across the archipelago ecosystem as a whole, embodies the nuanced approach to sustainable resource management that remains ingrained in Māʻohi culture to this day.

BONITO A medium-sized, ray-finned predatory fish.

ALBACORE A species of tuna.

The French colonization and annexation of French Polynesia brought forth profound disruption to the Māʻohi people—particularly through the introduction of disease and the forcible erasure of Indigenous practices. Missionaries in the 19th century established legal codes aimed at dismantling *ariʻi* chiefdoms and suppressing the *rahui*, resulting in the erosion of the resource management practices so deeply intertwined with traditional social structures.[38] By 1925, only two among the seven *horo iʻa* near Maeva remained operational; the remaining five had fallen into disrepair after a century of cultural suppression.[39]

In the mid-20th century, Maeva's sacred sites underwent a revival as Japanese American anthropologist Yosihiko H. Sinoto led the recovery of ancestral locations that had deteriorated during colonial rule.[40] This initiative led to the restoration of the lagoon's remaining *horo iʻa*, which are still maintained and operated by the Māʻohi of Huahine today.[41] In recent years, Māʻohi communities, such as the Tahitian community of Teahupoʻo, have spearheaded the reintroduction of *rahui* in hybrid resource management plans.[42]

As ancient technologies are reinstituted in populations and shared with other island communities, the potential for resource production of these reefs comes into question. Like the weirs, which are powered by the natural rise and fall of tides, the gravitational interaction between the earth, the sun, and the moon also drives the production of tidal energy. In the coming era of renewables, when coal power will disappear in the wake of clean energy, a retrofit to form a hybrid system for both fishing and fuel could emerge. With the collocation of a tidal barrage, lagoon, or kite, energy sovereignty could become a key motivation for the reinvigoration of the traditional system.

The Māʻohi's *horo iʻa* fish weirs represent a strategic use of solar and lunar tidal fluctuations, and wind on seawater movements to produce a passive form of aquaculture. Structures can be adapted to block the exit of fish but high tides allow remaining fish to return to sea and continue their life cycles, avoiding over-exploitation. The traditional system of resource management through Māʻohii chiefdoms informed this intentional technology, adapting *rahui* according to environmental demands and community needs.[43] Responsive to time and space, the weirs have intelligently balanced the communities' needs for both resource protection and food production for a thousand years. As the climate changes and communities adapt, could this technology also evolve to accommodate energy production, using the passive tidal currents that have powered it for generations?

6 The height of weir walls varies according to the depth of the lagoon, with rounded *haapua* walls constructed wider than the straight *arero* walls.
7 The *haapua* are often accompanied by small stilted houses for fishermen to monitor their weirs.
8 These formations are strategically designed to channel fish through stone-walled labyrinths and into circular basins.

6

7, 8 ↓

ENDNOTES

1. Edward Smith Craighill Handy, *Houses, Boats, and Fishing in the Society Islands* (Honolulu: Bernice P. Bishop Museum, 1932), 94.
2. Paul Wallin, "Three Special Sites in Polynesia," in *Essays in Honour of Arne Skjølsvold 75 Years*, ed. Paul Wallin and Helene Martinsson-Wallin, vol. 5 of *The Kon Tiki Museum Occasional Papers 5* (2000): 111.
3. Handy, *Houses, Boats, and Fishing in the Society Islands*, 95.
4. Robert F. Kay, "Polynesian Isle of Huahine Out to Re-Create Past," *Los Angeles Times*, February 9, 1986, https://www.latimes.com/archives/la-xpm-1986-02-09-tr-6326-story.html.
5. "Huahine," DBpedia, accessed April 17, 2024, https://dbpedia.org/page/Huahine.
6. Daniella LoScerbo et al., "Fish Traps of the Society Islands," Sea Gardens across the Pacific, https://www.seagardens.net/society-islands.
7. Wallin, "Three Special Sites in Polynesia," 109.
8. Wallin, "Three Special Sites in Polynesia," 108–11.
9. LoScerbo et al., "Fish Traps of the Society Islands."
10. LoScerbo et al., "Fish Traps of the Society Islands."
11. Handy, *Houses, Boats, and Fishing in the Society Islands*, 95.
12. Handy, *Houses, Boats, and Fishing in the Society Islands*, 95.
13. Handy, *Houses, Boats, and Fishing in the Society Islands*, 96–97.
14. Handy, *Houses, Boats, and Fishing in the Society Islands*, 95.
15. Handy, *Houses, Boats, and Fishing in the Society Islands*, 96.
16. Handy, *Houses, Boats, and Fishing in the Society Islands*, 95.
17. Handy, *Houses, Boats, and Fishing in the Society Islands*, 96.
18. Handy, *Houses, Boats, and Fishing in the Society Islands*, 96.
19. Handy, *Houses, Boats, and Fishing in the Society Islands*, 96.
20. Handy, *Houses, Boats, and Fishing in the Society Islands*, 96.
21. Handy, *Houses, Boats, and Fishing in the Society Islands*, 95.
22. Handy, *Houses, Boats, and Fishing in the Society Islands*, 96.
23. Handy, *Houses, Boats, and Fishing in the Society Islands*, 96.
24. Handy, *Houses, Boats, and Fishing in the Society Islands*, 95.
25. Handy, *Houses, Boats, and Fishing in the Society Islands*, 95–96.
26. Handy, *Houses, Boats, and Fishing in the Society Islands*, 106.
27. Handy, *Houses, Boats, and Fishing in the Society Islands*, 94.
28. Handy, *Houses, Boats, and Fishing in the Society Islands*, 93.
29. Handy, *Houses, Boats, and Fishing in the Society Islands*, 93–94.
30. Handy, *Houses, Boats, and Fishing in the Society Islands*, 97.
31. Janet Davidson et al., "Prehistoric Fishing at Fa'ahia, Huahine, Society Islands, French Polynesia," *Journal de la Société des océanistes* 107 (1998): 149, https://doi.org/10.3406/jso.1998.2054.
32. Davidson et al., "Prehistoric Fishing at Fa'ahia, Huahine, Society Islands, French Polynesia," 149.
33. Tamatoa Bambridge, "The Law of Rahui in the Society Islands," in *The Rahui: Legal Pluralism in Polynesian Traditional Management of Resources and Territories*, ed. Tamatoa Bambridge (Canberra: ANU Press, 2016), 129.
34. Bambridge, "The Law of Rahui in the Society Islands," 129.
35. Bambridge, "The Law of Rahui in the Society Islands," 129–30.
36. Bambridge, "The Law of Rahui in the Society Islands," 128.
37. Bambridge, "The Law of Rahui in the Society Islands," 128–29.
38. Tamatoa Bambridge et al., "Integrated Indigenous Management of Land and Marine Protected Areas in Teahupo'o (Tahiti, French Polynesia): A Way to Enhance Ecological and Cultural Resilience," in *Islands of Hope: Indigenous Resource Management in a Changing Pacific*, ed. Paul D'Arcy and Daya Dakasi Da-Wei Kuan (Canberra: ANU Press, 2023), 150.
39. Handy, *Houses, Boats, and Fishing in the Society Islands*, 95.
40. Kay, "Polynesian Isle of Huahine Out to Re-Create Past."
41. Kay, "Polynesian Isle of Huahine Out to Re-Create Past."
42. Bambridge et al., "Integrated Indigenous Management of Land and Marine Protected Areas in Teahupo'o (Tahiti, French Polynesia): A Way to Enhance Ecological and Cultural Resilience," 157–60.
43. LoScerbo et al., "Fish Traps of the Society Islands."

COAUTHOR

DOROTHY PEGGY LUBIN-LÉVY (1949–2023)

Cultural Preservationist and President of Ōpu Nui Association

Dorothy Peggy Lubin-Lévy (1949–2023), known as "Mamado" by those close to her, was a Tahitian American cultural advocate and longtime resident of the French Polynesian islands Tahiti and Huahine. Born to a Polynesian father and American mother in California, Lubin-Lévy spent her early years in the United States. Her great-grandfather Émile Lévy, a Parisian merchant, sailed from France to Tahiti in search of black pearl, where he met her great-grandmother, a descendant of the local Polynesian royal family. Her father, Alfred Lévy, was born to an American mother and moved to Los Angeles in 1936 to deliver screenplays for The *Hurricane* and a remake of *Mutiny on the Bounty* to Metro-Goldwyn-Mayer. During her youth in Laguna Beach, California, Lubin-Lévy visited Tahiti with her family, before eventually emigrating at the age of 28.

Lubin-Lévy led a fulfilling life in Tahiti and Huahine for decades. She raised her daughter, Sabrina, on these islands, where she was a beloved friend to many neighbors and countless passersby. She would often recount stories of her adventures to such visitors, including her voyage to the Tahitian island of Moruroa on *Free*, the Dutch schooner, with her two-year-old and French activist Brice Lalonde to protest French nuclear testing in French Polynesia. Lubin-Lévy was a fierce advocate for environmental protection in the South Pacific, focusing on climate issues, including marine conservation, sustainable resource management, and the protection of fragile ecosystems.

Alongside her environmental activism, she was deeply committed to cultural preservation as the president of the Ōpu Nui Association. Lubin-Lévy worked closely with Indigenous communities and local organizations to raise awareness about the importance of preserving traditional practices, languages, and cultural knowledge. She is remembered for her efforts to bridge the gap between Indigenous wisdom and modern conservation practices, recognizing the inherent value of Indigenous knowledge in protecting the environment. Her deep connection to her Polynesian roots and her unwavering commitment to these causes made her a respected and influential figure in her community.

Outside of her advocacy work, Lubin-Lévy was well known for her friendship with cherished Hawaiian singer and cultural icon Bobby Holcomb. It was Holcomb who encouraged Lubin-Lévy to relocate to the ancient village of Maeva on Huahine. She was once quoted saying, "[Bobby] called me and said, 'Why don't you and Sabrina move here with me?' He said to be sure to bring the geese, guinea pigs, and the horse. We did!" Lubin-Lévy and Holcomb shared a home on the island until his death from cancer in 1991.

Lubin-Lévy spent her later years continuing her work as a devoted champion of Polynesian cultural preservation. She was active in the restoration and maintenance of Fare Pōte'e, a Polynesian heritage site and art museum, situated next to the Maeva Lagoon; she also spearheaded movements to recover the traditional art of kite-flying and to revive the Tahitian language in the local public school system. In these efforts, she frequently collaborated with academics around the South Pacific in an effort to expand scholarship and representation of these communities.

Lubin-Lévy passed away peacefully in March 2023. Though Dorothy is no longer with us, her spirit lives on in the continued efforts of those she inspired.

KAYALNILAM
DIKES, PONDS, *and* CANALS *of* THE MALAYALIS
India

Along the southern coast of India, in a low-lying, intertidal basin known as "the rice bowl of Kerala," clusters of palm-fringed islands occupy an intricately woven network of channels, surrounded by vast stretches of open water. Known as Kuttanad, this water-rich geography lies adjacent to the Arabian Sea, at an astonishing two meters below sea level. Crossed by five major rivers and connected to the Vembanad backwaters, India's second largest wetland ecosystem, Kuttanad is known as the only place in the country where paddy farming is practiced below sea level. Early Malayalis developed a unique method of reclaiming land from the backwaters by constructing artificial landforms called *kayalnilam*, in which *kayal* means "backwaters" and *nilam* means "ground." Often referred to as the "Holland of the East," the *kayalnilam* resemble the traditional Dutch polder landscape, whereby a polder or pond is constructed lower than sea level and protected by a raised barrier, called a dike.[1] However, in contrast to the Netherlands, the dikes in Kuttanad are constructed from local organic materials and produce a range of food. They are designed to synchronize with seasonally shifting salinity levels, as well as to prepare, adapt, and recover from climate extremes.

INTERTIDAL
An area of the shore covered by water at high tide and exposed to air at low tide.

1

In this waterlogged land—more than half of which is submerged for most of the year—the local Malayalis community has grown rice and coconut and fruit trees alongside saltwater and freshwater aquaculture for centuries. This highly productive system adapts to the seasons and the change in fresh and salt water, making it rich with local biodiversity endemic to wetland ecosystems. *Kayalnilam* also mitigate the impact of perennial flooding and saltwater intrusion, offer foreshore protection, enhance water quality, and sequester carbon. With the lack of freshwater resources for agriculture, the encroachment of the saltwater front, and the imminent threat of sea level rise becoming worldwide concerns for coastal environments, the Kuttanad *kayalnilam* offer a solution for flexible, biodiverse, and productive land reclamation in an intertidal landscape.

1 Kuttanad is a below-sea-level farming system that favors rice cultivation.
2 Kuttanad was once believed to be a wild forest with dense tree growth that was destroyed by a wild fire, and until recently burned black wooden logs were regularly mined from paddy fields.

PRE-HOLOCENE
The period on earth that occurred before the current geological epoch called the Holocene.

The dynamic nature of this landscape can be traced to the pre-Holocene period, when Kuttanad was a shallow bay in the Arabian Sea. It eventually silted up, forming a delta and a confluence point for five rivers, which would then release into the Vembanad backwaters.[2] Land reclamation in these backwaters was initiated by Malayalis during the 19th century under British rule, as a means of addressing food scarcity imposed on the region by colonial forces.[3] The primary goal behind land reclamation was to increase food production and expand paddy cultivation. A process known as *kayal kuthu* (backwater reclamation) was carried out by landless communities. However, these communities did not have ownership rights over the newly reclaimed land, as these rights were held by upper-caste groups. This situation perpetuated caste-based discrimination, leading to the exploitation of labor; highly productive reclaimed *kayal* benefited the landlords, widening the socioeconomic gap between the upper-caste elite landlords and the marginalized lower-caste population.[4]

Kayal reclamation in the Kuttanad wetland occurred in three distinct phases spanning the late 19th to mid-20th century.[5] From 1880 to 1945, the total area of *kayal* reclamation increased from nearly 1,765 hectares to about 4,406 hectares, indicating a growth rate of almost 150 percent over the course of 55 years.[6] Following independence from British rule, the Indian government emphasized better management of the reclaimed *kayalnilam*; large *kayalnilam* were divided by canals and embankments, reducing the total area to approximately 4,364 hectares.[7] Since the mid-20th century, settlements have emerged on the embankments, separating the reclaimed *kayal* to accommodate the region's growing population.

2

3

3 Kuttanad is a deltaic formation of four rivers—namely, Meenachil, Pamba, Manimala, and Achenkovil—and comprises primarily marshes, a vast network of water channels, and Vembanad Lake.

4 After rice harvesting, thousands of ducks occupy the fields for their feed, which replaces the use of pesticides. The ducklings are constantly on the move, for up to six months, from one field to another, until they are sold for food.

Today, daily life in Kuttanad is deeply tied to water, which is regarded as a symbol of prosperity. Vast stretches of the backwater banks of *kayalnilam* are community spaces for daily activities like bathing, washing, and fishing; canals are arteries for travel and trade; and in the evenings paddy fields become cricket pitches and playgrounds. This fluctuating, waterlogged landscape—inspiring both awe and trepidation among community members and outsiders alike—requires an extra degree of vigilance. Leading up to the harvest, Malayim fear the call, *"Achaaya! Paadam madaveene!"* ("Lord! The dike has been breached!"), as it would signal the destruction of crops for the coming year.[8] According to local folklore, bodies were stacked in the earthen dikes of the *kayalnilam* system to appease the seas and prevent water from entering the paddy fields—a sacrifice rooted in the belief that death gives way to life.[9]

4

The living intertidal agricultural landscape of the *kayalnilam* ingeniously adapts to freshwater and saltwater conditions while supporting food production, sustaining livelihoods, preventing flooding and salt intrusion, and protecting a thriving ecosystem. The construction, maintenance, and operation of this agricultural infrastructure occurs harmoniously with the water cycles of the sea, rivers, and monsoon. At the scale of the watershed and extending over 1,600 square kilometers, *kayalnilam* also act as a seasonal retention basin protecting inland communities.[10]

The construction of *kayalnilam* begins with the identification of shallow areas in the Vembanad backwaters.[11] These locations are marked by bamboo poles, upon which *kuttiyum chirayum* (earthen embankments) are constructed. Excess water is then pumped from the dikes into the surrounding backwaters. The inner reclaimed land is then divided into smaller fragments by constructing a network of *edavarambu* (inner dikes) and *vachaal* (minor canals). Dikes are built from local, natural, and unprocessed materials like sand, coconut by-products, and twigs. These materials are mixed with high-quality clay dug from the lakebed at a depth of 20 to 25 meters.[12] This low-embodied energy and low-carbon structure is further stabilized by planting local species of wild grass, including *karakam* and *kora pullu* (*Sheoneplectus*).[13]

Constructed Elements of *Kayalnilam* Land Reclamation

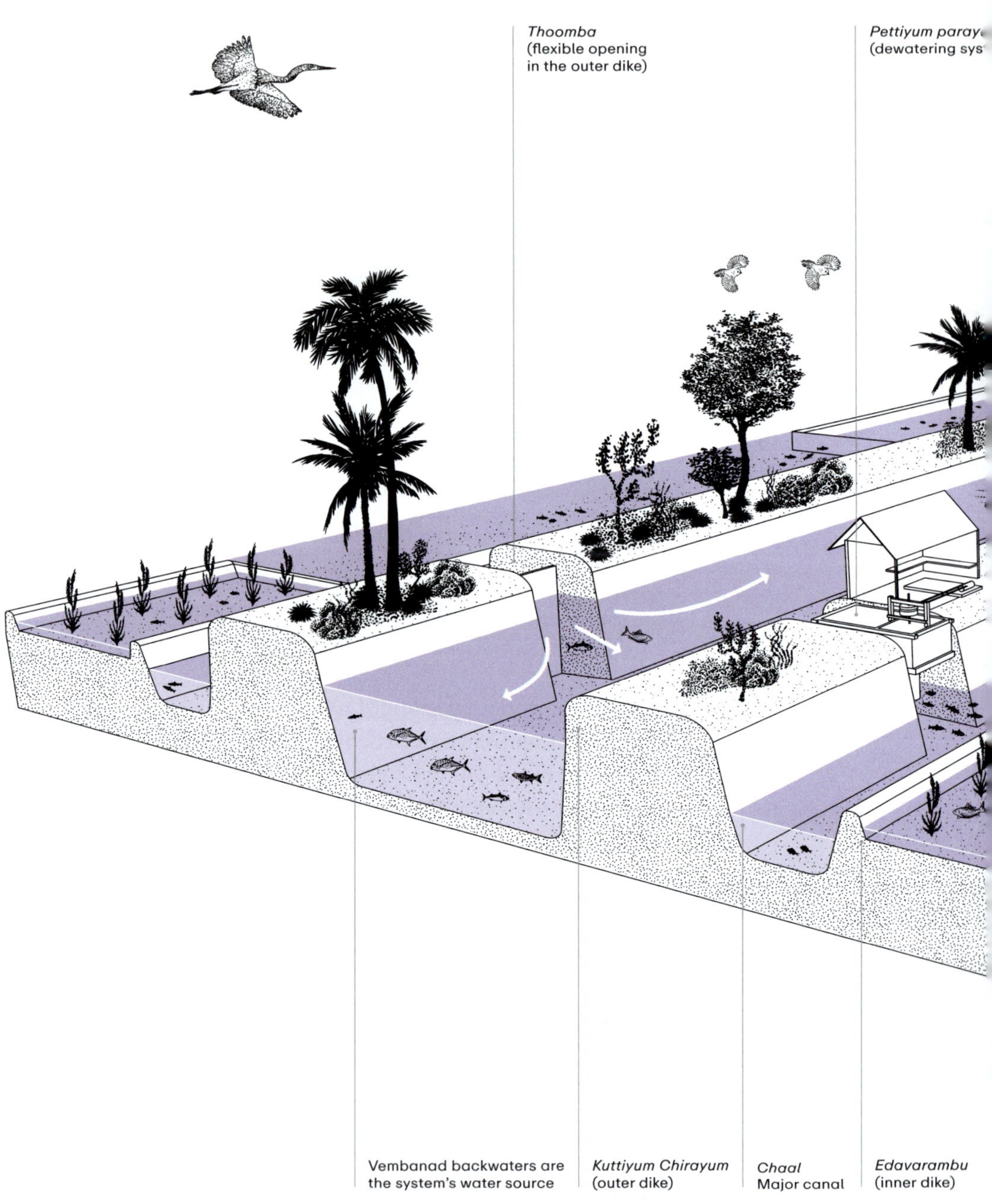

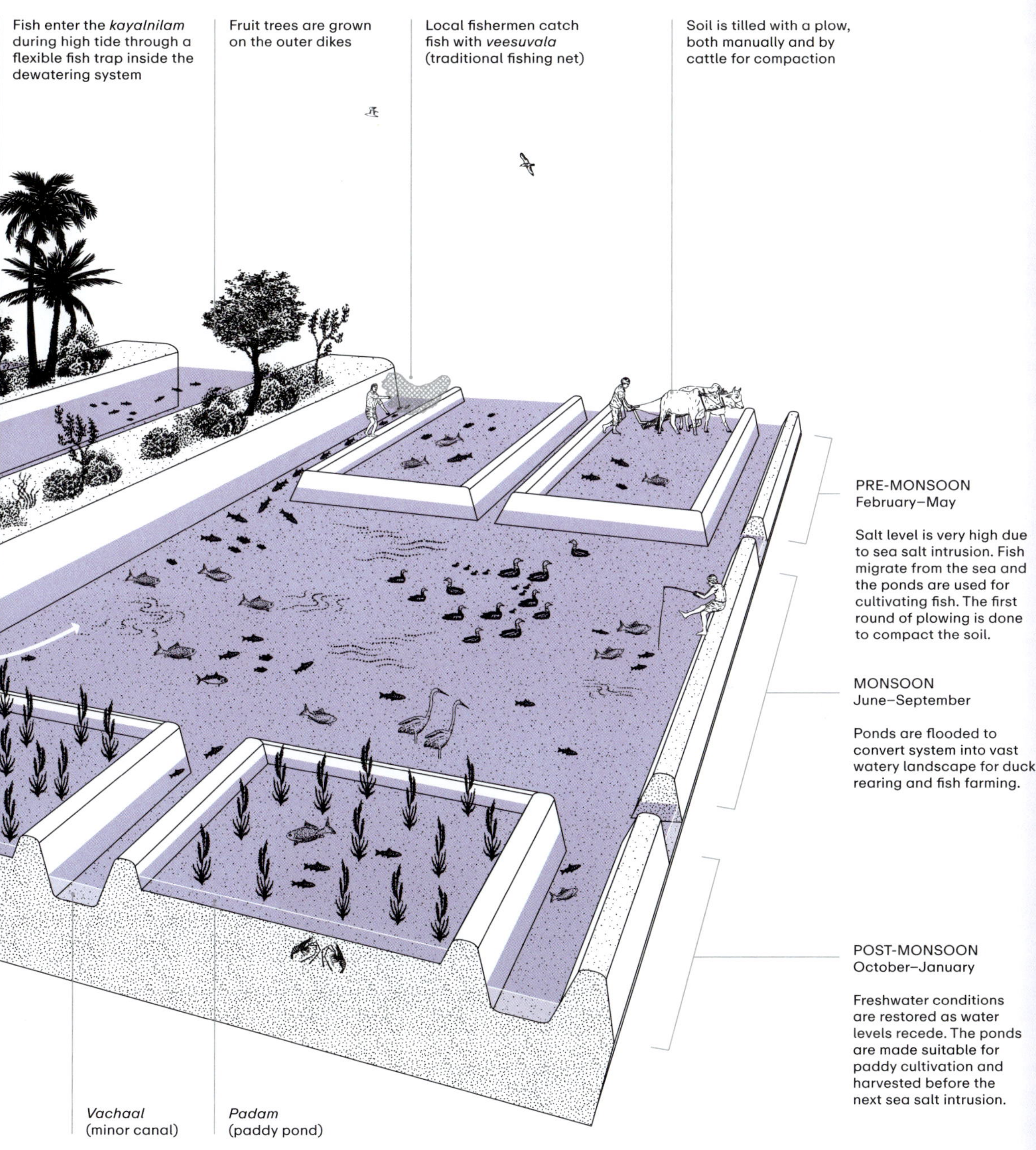

Fish enter the *kayalnilam* during high tide through a flexible fish trap inside the dewatering system
Fruit trees are grown on the outer dikes
Local fishermen catch fish with *veesuvala* (traditional fishing net)
Soil is tilled with a plow, both manually and by cattle for compaction
PRE-MONSOON
February–May
Salt level is very high due to sea salt intrusion. Fish migrate from the sea and the ponds are used for cultivating fish. The first round of plowing is done to compact the soil.
MONSOON
June–September
Ponds are flooded to convert system into vast watery landscape for duck rearing and fish farming.
POST-MONSOON
October–January
Freshwater conditions are restored as water levels recede. The ponds are made suitable for paddy cultivation and harvested before the next sea salt intrusion.
Vachaal
(minor canal)
Padam
(paddy pond)

Erected between half a meter and two and a half meters above sea level, dikes are designed to withhold water and prevent flooding.[14, 15] The surface water, which sheds off the slopes of these dikes on either side, flows directly into the lower areas. Irrigation water is channeled into the system through canals, which enter the paddy fields through an opening in the dike called a *thoomba*.[16] To avoid overwatering, a technology known as *pettiyum parayum* is placed at a strategic juncture between a dike and a canal, where it periodically removes excess water from the paddy fields.[17] Temporary barriers called *orumuttu* are also constructed, which block the seasonal entry of salt. These structures, made of sandbags and twigs, prevent saltwater intrusion and allow only fresh water to make its way to the fields.[18]

Beyond offering protection and producing food, *kayalnilam* dikes and canals structure a complex and biodiverse ecosystem. At high tide, fish swimming upstream enter the *kayalnilam* and are caught through a detachable net placed inside the *pettiyum parayum* dewatering technology, transforming it into a fish weir.[19] Made of bamboo or cane, the net captures both freshwater and brackish-water species such as milkfish, mullet, pearlspot, marine prawns, freshwater prawns, and mollusks like clams and mussels.[20] As filter feeders, clams and mussels remove pollutants like excess nitrogen from the water, incorporating it into their shells and tissues as they grow.

5

5 Farmers work with traditional water turbines to manually draw water to their rice fields.
6 Fish enter the *kayalnilam* during high tide through a flexible fish trap inside the dewatering system.

6

Kayalnilam Process of Construction

Coconut poles fenced by bamboo mats are hammered into the lake bed in two rows
High-quality clay is dug from deeper parts of the lake bed for dike construction
3 m
1–2 m above water level
Mud
1.5–2.5 m in width

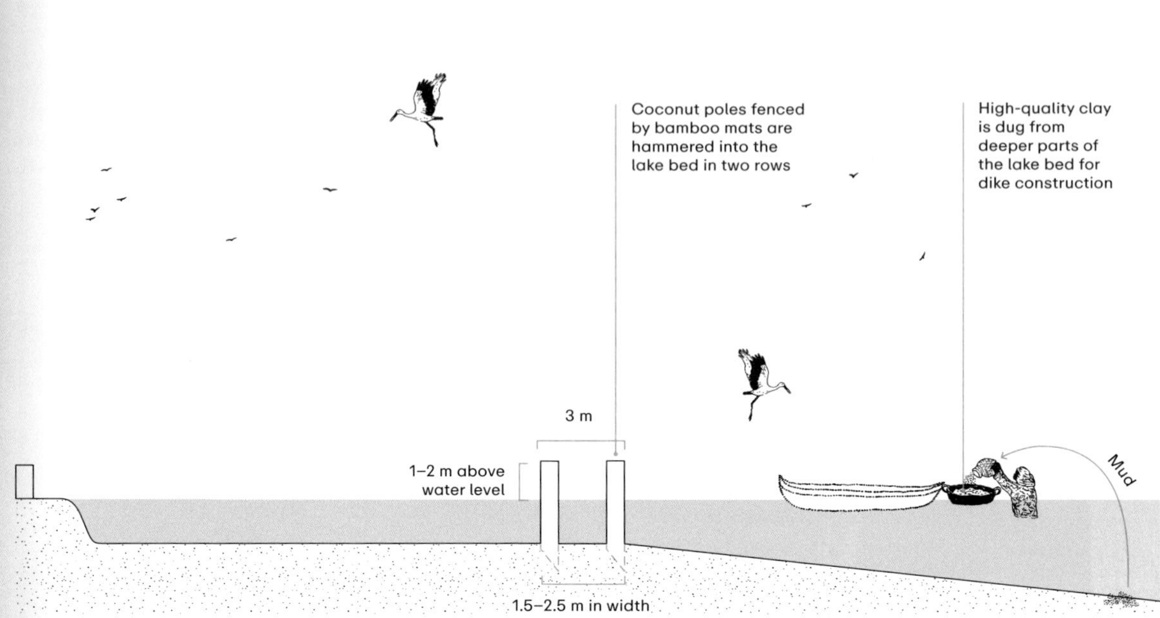

1. A skeleton of a dike is erected using coconut poles and bamboo mats along the periphery of shallow parts of the lake bed

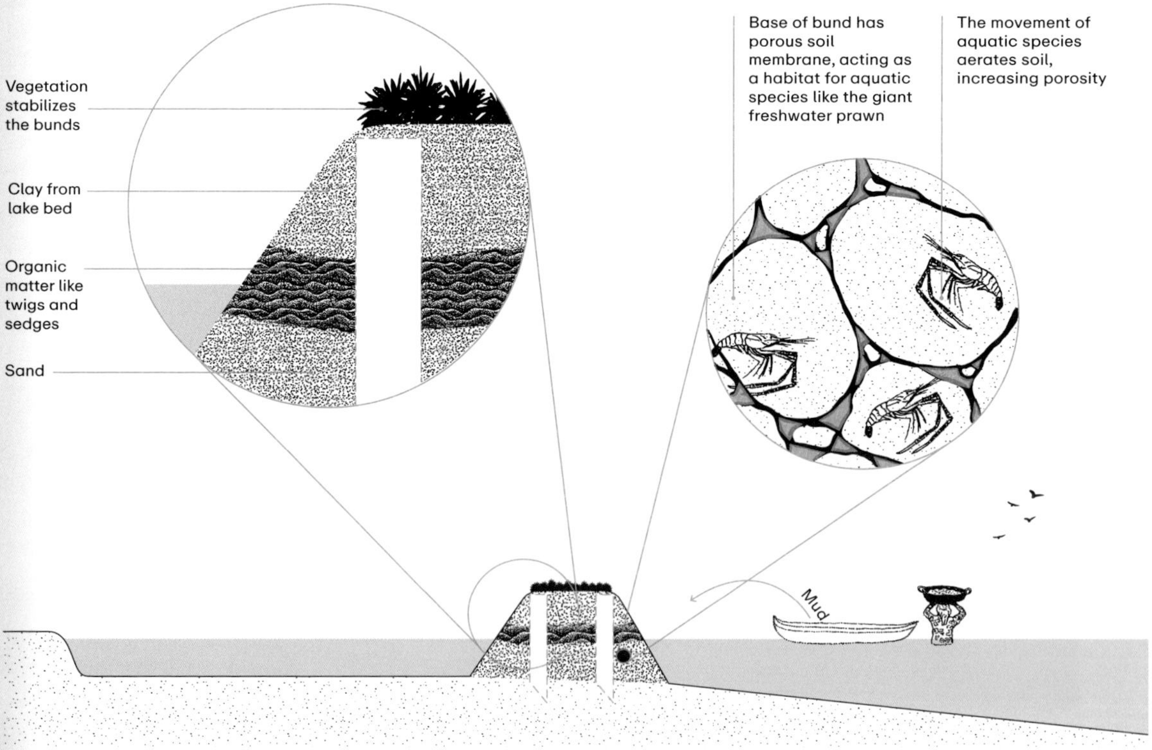

Vegetation stabilizes the bunds
Clay from lake bed
Organic matter like twigs and sedges
Sand
Base of bund has porous soil membrane, acting as a habitat for aquatic species like the giant freshwater prawn
The movement of aquatic species aerates soil, increasing porosity
Mud

2. The center of the dike is filled with locally available materials

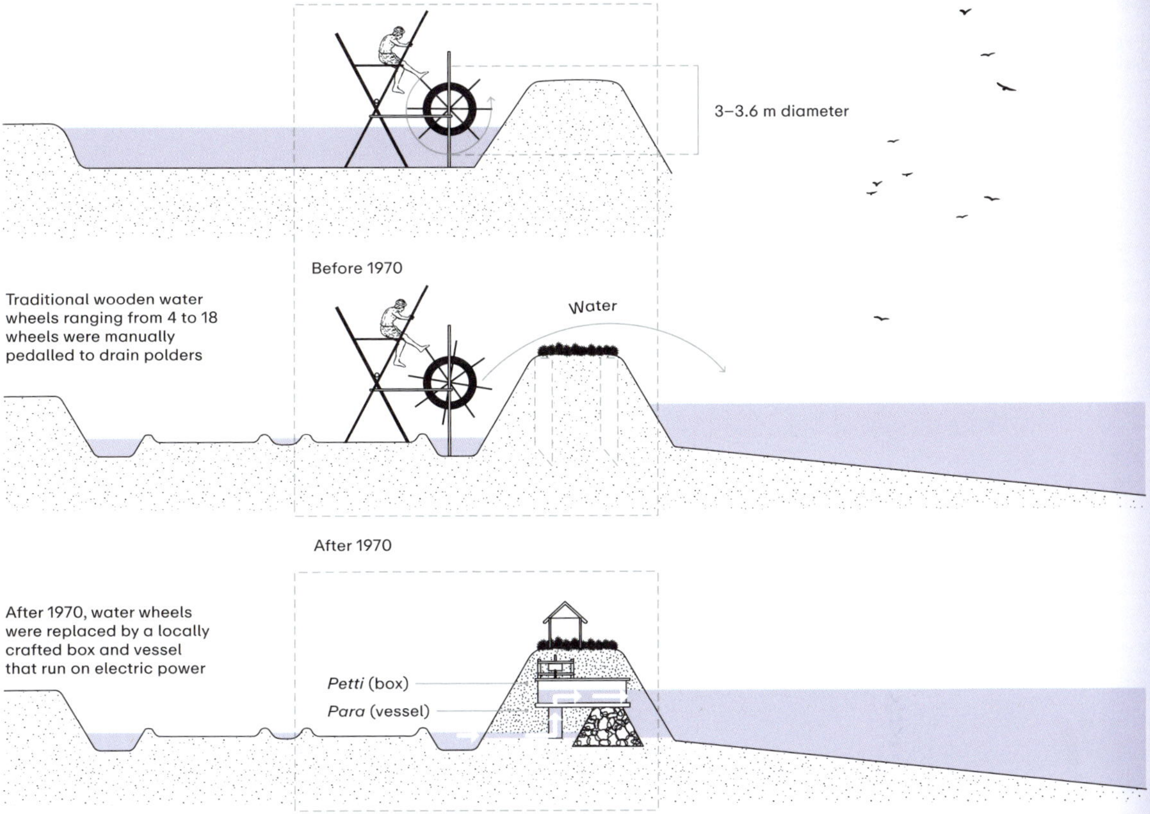

3–3.6 m diameter

Before 1970

Traditional wooden water wheels ranging from 4 to 18 wheels were manually pedalled to drain polders

Water

After 1970

After 1970, water wheels were replaced by a locally crafted box and vessel that run on electric power

Petti (box)

Para (vessel)

3. Precise water levels inside the *kayalnilam* are maintained by periodically removing excess water through dewatering techniques

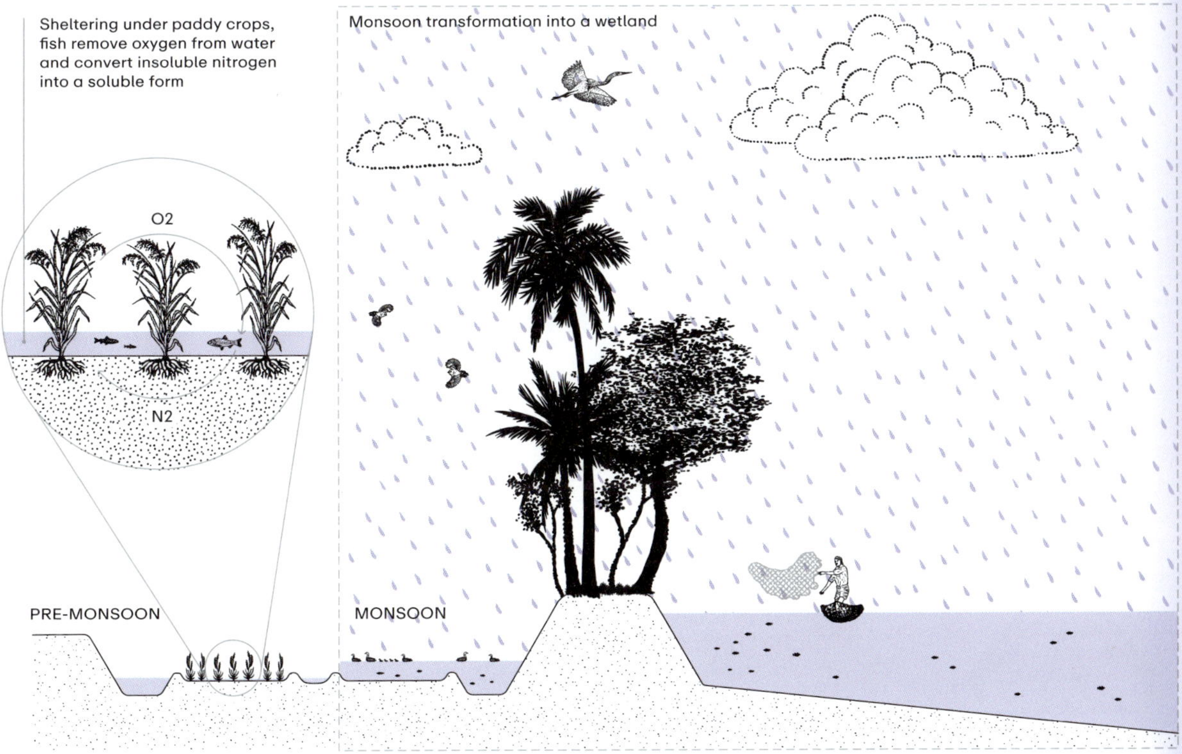

Sheltering under paddy crops, fish remove oxygen from water and convert insoluble nitrogen into a soluble form

Monsoon transformation into a wetland

O2

N2

PRE-MONSOON

MONSOON

4. Used for cultivating paddy crops, during the monsoon, *kayalnilams* are converted into a seasonal wetland for aquaculture and duck rearing

Freshwater Prawns Life Cycle Corresponds to Seasonal Saltwater Fluctuations

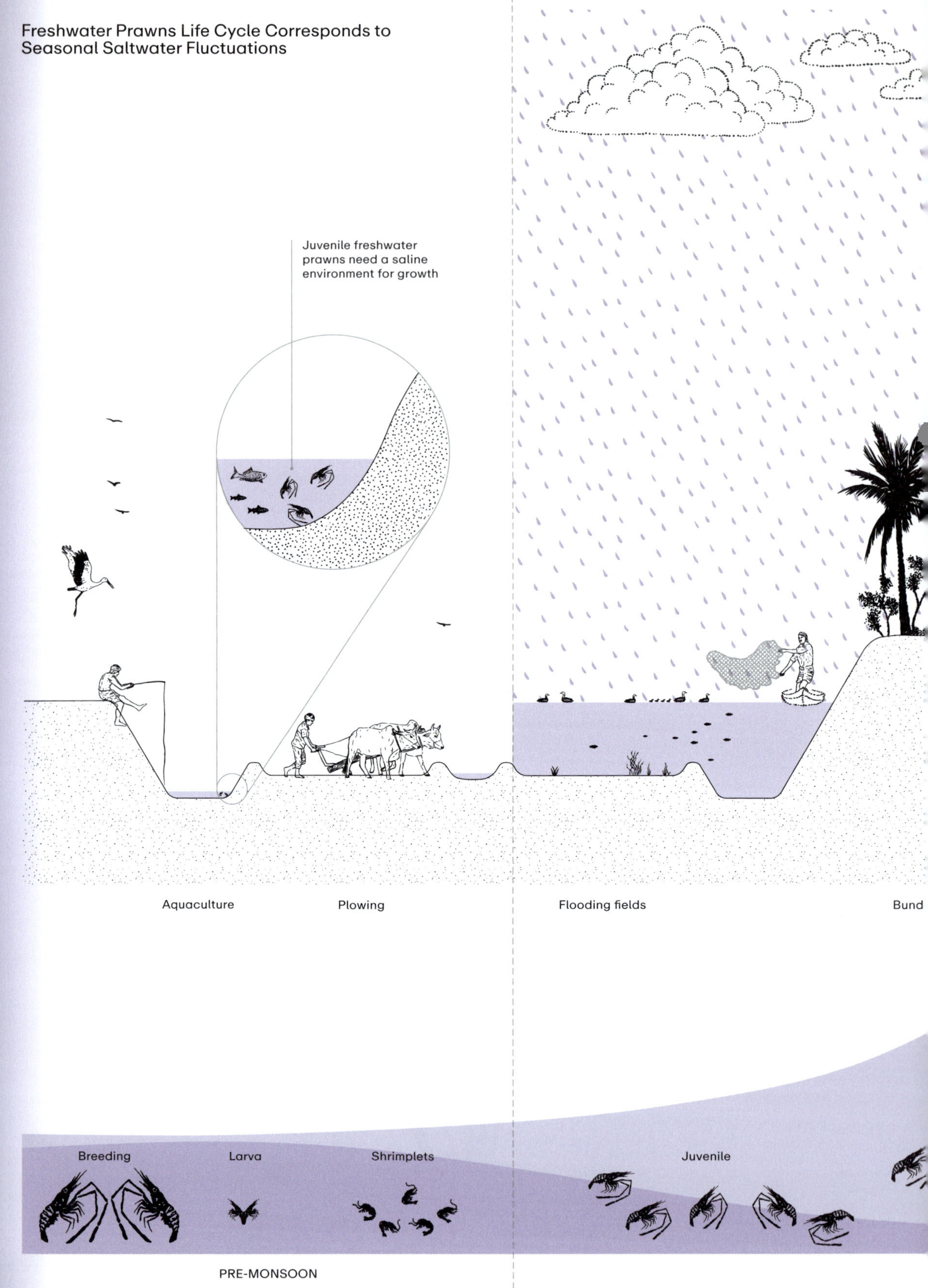

← Open this fold to reveal full illustration.

Rotating between agriculture and aquaculture throughout a three-season year composed of premonsoon, monsoon, and postmonsoon, the people of Kuttanad live in harmony with the seasonal mixing of fresh water from the rivers and salt water from the sea. For most of the year, water flows from rivers into the sea. During the premonsoon season, the water level of rivers drops below sea level, reversing seawater to flow inland.[21] This saltwater intrusion poses many challenges for local farmers. Increased salinity isn't suitable for postmonsoon rice paddy cultivation and freshwater fish aquaculture, so *kayalnilam* are deliberately flooded with salt water to begin the seasonal transition to saltwater shrimp and fish farming, accompanied by duck rearing.[22] The fresh water needed for rice paddy cultivation, which begins in the postmonsoon, is restored with the onset of the monsoon. Paddy fields then remain flooded during this period of heavy rainfall, while the soil enriches itself with silt carried down by the rivers, duck droppings, and waste from other aquatic species. In the meantime, farmers prepare the submerged ground by tilling soil using tools and buffalo in a process called wet plowing, as the rest of the village celebrates the monsoonal flooding with boat races called *vallamkali*. During the postmonsoon, water levels recede and paddy fields begin growing crops once again, which are harvested before the next saltwater intrusion.[23]

7

7 This unique geography makes conventional road transportation impractical in many areas. As a result, small boats and government service boats have become the primary means of travel.

As the monsoon waters subside, giving way to the postmonsoon period, the *kayalnilam* support the growth of rice, ducks, freshwater fish, and shrimp. As a permeable structure, earthen dikes are a favorable habitat for nesting among freshwater shrimp. Within the body of the submerged dike, shrimp construct nests in the cavities of the soil while breeding in the shallow, marginal waters of the irrigation ditches and canals, which spontaneously become fish nurseries and hunting grounds.

8

9

8 Small germinated paddy seeds are sown by hand in the paddy fields.
9 Differences in soil and terrain mean that machinery has to be improvised to suit specific conditions; for example, in the inundated paddy fields of Kuttanad, tillage is carried out by means of tractors with cage wheels.

The introduction of river fish into the system fosters a symbiotic relationship with the rice plant, as some fish seek refuge under the shade of crops.[24] Their stirring movements aerate the planting bed, increasing soil porosity, improving surface soil conditions for rice growing and accelerating the growth of paddy crops, while in turn providing oxygen and food for fish, as their roots favor the growth of edible microorganisms. With this diet, fish remove pests and weeds from the system naturally and fertilize the ponds with their waste, increasing crop yields.

The symbiosis between the crop cycle of rice and the migration of fish from the sea to the rivers is coordinated with the natural cycle of water, where salt enters the system before the monsoon. This favors species like the great freshwater prawn and some varieties of crabs that need a saline environment for breeding until hatched eggs reach their juvenile stage. By maturity, they are no longer salt tolerant and migrate inland to the paddy fields where the freshwater conditions are restored.[25]

10

10 Kuttanad is a biodiversity paradise, home to several rare mangrove species as well as migratory fish species and birds, which in turn support its different ecosystem services.

11 Even though houseboat tourism generates income, there is an environmental cost, which has led to pollution and degradation of water bodies by the dumping of waste, engine fuel, and plastics, along with other harmful materials.

Today, parts of the "rice bowl of Kerala" are slowly disappearing. Production has shifted away from the traditional system, which rotated between paddy farming and aquaculture in line with the seasonal mixing of fresh water in the rivers and salt water from the sea. During the latter half of the 20th century, India's Green Revolution introduced new forms of intensified crop production across the subcontinent. In 1975, the Thanneermukkom Salt Water Barrier was constructed across the Vembanad backwaters to control the amount of salt water entering the paddy fields during premonsoon.[26] With this addition, farmers were able to add a second crop to their harvest cycle, which resulted in an immediate agricultural boom.

In the 1970s, farmers started to strengthen earthen dikes and canals, using granite lining.[27] These new interventions were implemented to reduce dike breaching and repair during the monsoon season. Until then, waterways were the only means of transportation through this landscape. However, aquatic infrastructures spurred terrestrial transformation, resulting in road construction that cut off natural drainage and water systems. Four decades later, these interventions have proven unsustainable, causing social, ecological, and economic disruptions for the Kuttanad community. Today, many paddy fields lie fallow, as aquatic life is diminished and fewer fish are caught. As the impacts of climate extremes intensify, local governments are being persuaded to reconsider the construction of permanent infrastructure and return to more adaptive, flexible, and natural systems characteristic of Indigenous sub-sea-level farming systems. Discussions on deconstructing the permanent salt barrier and replacing hard infrastructures with living systems are taking place.

11

While the restoration of the *kayalnilam* offers a means to promote ecotourism alongside sustainable farming practices, they could also offer local Kuttanad communities a source of renewable energy. As paddy fields are left fallow, rather than restoring their soils for seasonal cultivation, they could remain flooded and instead be fitted with floating photovoltaics or floatovoltaics. Adapted fields would create a transitional landscape, retrofitted for renewable energy generation that combines fish and solar farming, surrounded by fruit trees grown on the higher grounds of bunds. Putting these functions on top of the water will give parts of the *kayalnilam* back to the Vembanad backwaters as sea levels rise, while protecting food production alongside renewable energy generation.

Accompanying this shift toward the sea, another technology that uses salinity gradients becomes available. Where fresh meets salt water, an ideal environment for osmotic energy production is created. By modifying the Thanneermukkom Salt Water Barrier to create a series of semipermeable membranes allowing fresh water and salt water to mix, a salinity gradient for energy generation could be produced. Combining renewable energy technologies with existing intertidal farming techniques could offer an innovative initiative that is complementary to existing food production and flood protection.

The expansion of land into the sea by polder dike system is a universally recognized response to sea level rise, with a complicated history of working against ecosystems. Though many coastal cities have adopted this response, the singular goal of controlling water can negatively affect people and places, ultimately just moving problems downstream. In contrast, the *kayalnilam* create multispecies habitats while supporting the natural cycles of water and salt. These cycles are synthesized with agriculture and aquaculture, making this complex, adaptable, and resilient system an ongoing success. This relationship with water is further accentuated by the lifestyle of the people and their unique cultural practices that revolve around and celebrate water, like the annual snake boat race festivals. In the wake of global food insecurity and salt intrusion in coastal agricultural lands—both further aggravated by climate change—this traditional intertidal freshwater to saltwater aquaculture and agriculture system can be a model for the direction of intertidal agricultural landscapes, forming a foreshore protection system for communities.

12 Once well known for its rich and traditional Indigenous farming practices and the associated high aquatic biodiversity, the future of Kuttanad is uncertain.

12

ENDNOTES

1. Sarath Chandran and Subrata Purkayastha, "History of Reclaimed Kayals in Kuttanad Wetland and Associated Social Divide in Alappuzha District, Kerala," *International Journal of Research and Analytical Reviews 5*, no. 3 (2018): 70.
2. D. Padmalal et al., "Consequences of Sea Level and Climate Changes on the Morphodynamics of a Tropical Coastal Lagoon during Holocene: An Evolutionary Model," *Quaternary International* 333 (2014): 170, https://doi.org/10.1016/j.quaint.2013.12.018.
3. Chandran and Purkayastha, "History of Reclaimed Kayals in Kuttanad Wetland and Associated Social Divide in Alappuzha District, Kerala," 70.
4. Chandran and Purkayastha, "History of Reclaimed Kayals in Kuttanad Wetland and Associated Social Divide in Alappuzha District, Kerala," 73.
5. Chandran and Purkayastha, "History of Reclaimed Kayals in Kuttanad Wetland and Associated Social Divide in Alappuzha District, Kerala," 72–76.
6. Chandran and Purkayastha, "History of Reclaimed Kayals in Kuttanad Wetland and Associated Social Divide in Alappuzha District, Kerala," 79.
7. Chandran and Purkayastha, "History of Reclaimed Kayals in Kuttanad Wetland and Associated Social Divide in Alappuzha District, Kerala," 79.
8. Kamal K. (local politician, Democratic Youth Federation of India), in discussion with the author, December 2019.
9. Shri RupeshKumar K (*kayalnilam* expert and project coordinator, State Responsible Tourism Mission), in discussion with the author, January 2023.
10. M Ajith Kumar, "Kuttanad: A Case in Point," DownToEarth, December 31, 1996, https://www.downtoearth.org.in/coverage/kuttanad-a-case-in-point-27265.
11. M S Swaminathan Research Foundation, *Kuttanad Below Sea Level Farming System: A Candidate System for Globally Important Agricultural Heritage Systems (GIAHS) Programme* (Rome: FAO, n.d.), 6.
12. M S Swaminathan Research Foundation, *Kuttanad Below Sea Level Farming System,* 6.
13. RupeshKumar, discussion.
14. Jacob (local farmer), in discussion with the author, January 2023.
15. 15 M S Swaminathan Research Foundation, *Kuttanad Below Sea Level Farming System,* 5.
16. Rahul Sukumaran (landscape architect), in discussion with the author, July 2019.
17. Dewatering is the process of pumping water out from the low-lying paddy fields to the major canals or backwaters. Traditionally, wheels 10–12 feet in diameter with a blade width of one to 15 feet were used. They were pedaled manually by men to remove water. The water wheel ranged from four-leaf to 18-leaf. Owing to the extensive labor needed to operate them, these wheels were later replaced by a technology crafted by local blacksmiths, which runs on electric power.
18. RupeshKumar, discussion.
19. Indiavideodotorg, "Pettiyum Parayum—Indigenous Technology for Irrigation, Kerala," YouTube, December 30, 2013, 1:54, https://www.youtube.com/watch?v=9Zp53nk2vf8.
20. RupeshKumar, discussion.
21. Mankombu Sambasivan Swaminathan, *Measures to Mitigate Agrarian Distress in Alappuzha and Kuttanad Wetland Ecosystem* (Chennai: M. S. Swaminathan Research Foundation, 2007), 61.
22. RupeshKumar, discussion.
23. Sukumaran, discussion.
24. RupeshKumar, discussion.
25. RupeshKumar, discussion.
26. Swaminathan, *Measures to Mitigate Agrarian Distress in Alappuzha and Kuttanad Wetland Ecosystem,* 75.
27. Swaminathan, *Measures to Mitigate Agrarian Distress in Alappuzha and Kuttanad Wetland Ecosystem,* 98.

COAUTHOR

SHRI RUPESHKUMAR K

Project Coordinator, State Responsible Tourism Mission

ctivist and columnist Shri RupeshKumar K has een instrumental in elevating India's state of Kerala ɔ a global hub for sustainable tourism. Coming from ɪe local community in Kuttanad, he also possesses xtensive knowledge of the *kayalnilam* system.

In the early stages of his career, RupeshKumar ctively opposed the unethical development of regional ɔurism, notably in Kumarakom, a village renowned ɔr its appeal to visitors to the Vembanad backwaters. Ie participated in a growing discourse advocating ɔr alternative tourism models that diverged from lobalization-driven approaches in Kumarakom. ligned with the vision of the Respon- ible Tourism Mission, his current fforts are dedicated to spearheading ɔurism projects that offer supplemen- ary income and improved livelihoods ɔ farmers, traditional artisans, and ɪarginalized communities, while prior- :izing the holistic establishment of ocial and environmental equilibrium in hese initiatives.

RupeshKumar has developed ɪany community-based tourism proj- cts, like Village Life Experience, which engages with everal communities across Kuttanad. This initiative ɔmmunicates traditional livelihood activities like arming, fishing, and coir craftsmanship to tourists; he Indian government has recognized the project s the best Rural Tourism Initiative. Drawing on this xperience, he developed People's Participation for 'ourism Planning and Empowerment through :esponsible Tourism, a project aimed at fostering fur- her community involvement and tourism advance- ɪent. He is also a part of the award-winning group ustainable Tangible Responsible Experiential Ethnic 'ourism, which aims to facilitate rural development, nhance traditional nature-based livelihoods, and pro- ect natural habitats through tourism-related activities.

During his career, RupeshKumar has received numerous national and international awards recognizing his efforts and dedication to developing the responsible tourism sector in his country. He was selected as a World Travel Market Responsible Tourism jury member in 2021 and has presented papers at various international and national conferences and venues.

VALLI DA PESCA
DIKES, PONDS, *and* CANALS *of* THE VENETIANS
Italy

VALLI DA PESCA DIKES, PONDS, *and* CANALS *of* THE VENETIANS *Italy*

Coauthored by
Michele Zanetti

PEOPLE Venetians
LOCATION Venice Lagoon, Italy TECHNOLOGY valliculture
ORIGIN 11th century ELEVATION 0 m
DISTANCE ABOVE OR BELOW WATERLINE −6 to +2.5 m
WATER LEVEL FLUCTUATION, TIDAL OR SEASONAL 0 to +1 m

FAO Nexus
WATER brackish ENERGY tidal FOOD fish

IPCC Adaptation Pathway
protect

World Bank NBS
CATEGORY salt marshes, bioretention areas, constructed inland wetlands, natural inland wetlands
FUNCTIONS biodiversity, coastal erosion regulation, salt intrusion regulation, water pollution regulation, coastal flood regulation
BENEFITS resource production, biodiversity, stimulate local economies and job creation, coastal flood risk reduction, carbon storage and sequestration, cultural, social interaction

1

1 As the largest Mediterranean coastal lagoon, the Venice Lagoon is characterized by the presence of 22 *valli da pesca*.

Sailing through the *colaùro* fishing canal and into the *chiari di valle* pastoral clearings, earthen embankments cluster around partially submerged ponds, blending with the wild backdrop of the Venice Lagoon. Here, humans have subtly shaped the landscape to take advantage of seasonal water pulses since the first millennium BCE, creating a vast system of enclosed waters known as the *valli da pesca*.[1,2] According to rare sources, even before the first buildings were erected around the fifth century CE, the *valli da pesca* existed on Isole Realtine, where Venice now stands.[3] Today, these brackish aquaculture ponds are separated from the lagoon's open waters by artificially constructed earthen embankments.[4] These embankments have successfully preserved the wetlands of the Venice Lagoon, protecting and conserving the *baréne* brackish marshes and the *vèlme* shallow mudflats.[5]

In this landscape of long deep canals; steep, narrow, bushy embankments; and reedbeds, fish farmed in medium- to large-sized ponds are naturally fed by lagoon resources as water is carefully regulated.[6] Since the 11th century, this aquaculture practice has formalized and spread along the lagoon shores of the Upper Adriatic Sea. With calm, shallow waters protected by sand dunes, the Marano and Grado, Bibione, Caorle, and Venice Lagoons; the Po River Delta; and the Valli di Comacchio were prime locations for the system. Today, 22 *valli da pesca* are found in the Venice Lagoon, spreading over one hundred square kilometers and converting almost 20 percent of the lagoon's surface.[7,8]

Valli da Pesca Are Located in the Deltaic Landscapes of Friuli-Venezia Giulia, Veneto, and Emilia-Romagna

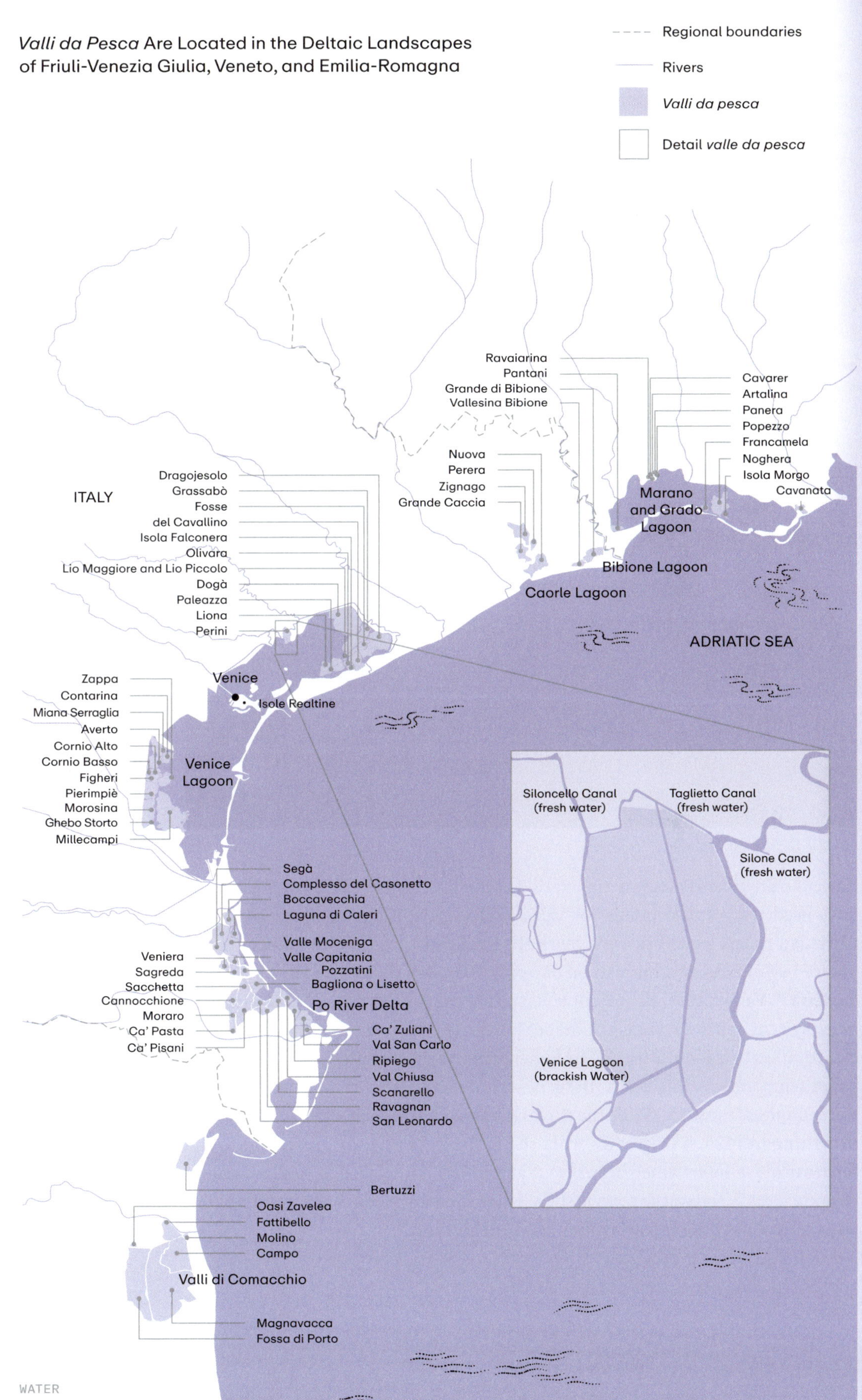

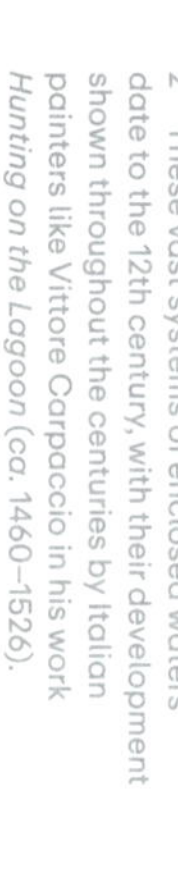

2 These vast systems of enclosed waters date to the 12th century, with their development shown throughout the centuries by Italian painters like Vittore Carpaccio in his work *Hunting on the Lagoon* (ca. 1460–1526).

3 Lio Piccolo, which reached a peak of about 500 inhabitants during its flourishing salt-industry era, is an ancient village, one of the many settlements scattered around the northern part of the Venice Lagoon.

2

Since the Etruscan-Paleovenetian period of the 12th century BCE, the Venetians have used reed-fenced ponds for valliculture in the Lagoon.[9] Dating to early Christian times, legend says St. Mark the Evangelist, caught by a storm in the Venice Lagoon, docked his boat on one of the wooden poles surrounding a *valle da pesca*.[10] Valliculture, an ancient aquaculture practice employed in the *valli da pesca* system, takes advantage of the seasonal reproductive migration of fish species from sea to lagoon, attracted by high nutrient concentration and comfortable water temperature. Venetians, in turn, secluded and bred these species within the confines of the *valli*. While the singular form of the Italian valle first appeared in writing in 1425, it originates from the Latin *vallum* (wall), referring to the fences made of intertwined branches that are built and placed in shallow waters as enclosures.[11] Today, the term is still used to identify parts of the wetlands and coastal lagoons used for fish farming and bird hunting.

There are three original types of *valli da pesca*, differentiated by perimeter material and the flow of water: the reed-fenced *valli a serraglia semplice*; the semiembanked *valli semi-arginate*; and the fully embanked *valli arginate*. Constructed using a common reed (*Phragmites australis*), *valli a serraglia semplice* were enclosed by weirs of *grisiole* (reed trellises), which are continuously relocated and partially removed in the spring to allow juvenile fish to feed in the *valli*, then closed in autumn to prevent fish escaping.[12] However, the fragility of the structures has historically caused many Venetian anglers to reinforce their *valli* with earthen dikes. The second type, known as *valli semi-arginate*, is contained by *grisiole* on the downwind side and earthen embankments on the upwind side, as a means of withstanding strong winter gusts. The third type, *valli arginate*, shifted from relying solely on the natural migration of fish and relied on *pescenovellanti* (fingerlings fishermen), specialized in the capture and rearing of juvenile fish, who caught and sold young marine species to be sown in the *valli*.[13, 14, 15] In both the *valli a serraglia semplice* and *semi-arginate*, water level depends on the lagoon's natural fluctuations, while in the *valli arginate* water level operates independently, entirely enclosed within elevated embankments.

3

Warmer Brackish Water from the Venice Lagoon Flows Inside the *Valle Da Pesca* and Induce Fish to Migrate toward *Lavorièri*

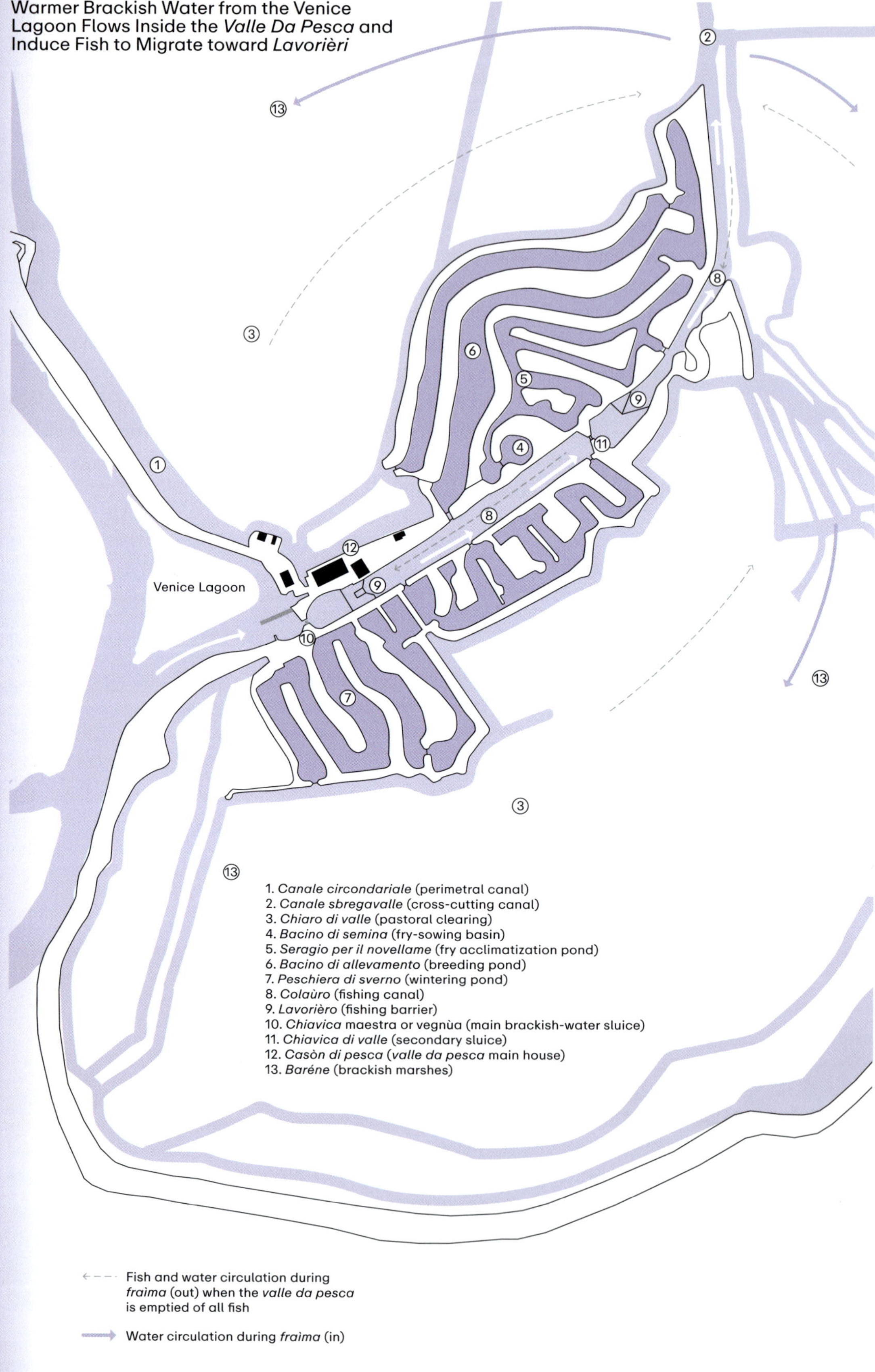

Through these three typologies, the *valli da pesca* emerged as a structured, managed form of valliculture. However, the evolution of the *valli da pesca* has not been linear, historically countered by government bans and limitations, with a primary concern being the unimpeded tidal fluctuation of the lagoon.[16] After the fall of the Serenissima Republic of Venice in 1797, Venetian anglers—taking advantage of the power vacuum—continued to transform the reed-fenced *valli* into semiembanked and embanked *valli*, shaping their forms as we know them today.[17]

4

4 This fish farming makes use of lagoon currents and fresh water to favor the ascent of the fry and the descent of the adult fish for capture.

Today, in the Venice Lagoon, the *valli da pesca* require traditional expertise, shared between the fishermen's families of the lagoon.[18] Until the 1980s, *capivalle* (fishing valley masters) of *valli da pesca* and *vallisani* (seasonal workers) came from Chioggia in the southern Venice Lagoon to be employed in the northern *valli da pesca* of the Venice Lagoon, while *pescenovellanti* sailed to the open Venice Lagoon mainly from Burano and Pellestrina.[19, 20] Mussel and oyster farmers, lagoon and sea fishermen, clam anglers, gillnet fishermen, and fishermen who capture molting crabs collectively make up the complex group practicing aquaculture in the Venice Lagoon.[21, 22]

5

5 For over a decade, flamingos have been settling in the area, with more than 8,000 wintering in the lagoon today.

Located on the outer edges of the lagoon and managed as state land under private concession, the limited accessibility of the *valli da pesca* has preserved and proliferated the biodiversity of the lagoon's flora and fauna.[23, 24, 25, 26] The one hundred square kilometers of the *valli da pesca's* brackish-water environment is composed of dikes, ponds, canals, reedbeds, marshes, and mudflats, all supporting a rich ecosystem of breeding fish and wintering and nesting birds.[27] Many waterbirds, including species of high hunting value, migrate to the undisturbed marshes and reedbeds from Northern Europe in search of food during the winter.[28, 29, 30] The aquaculture ponds are separated from the lagoon's open waters by artificially constructed two- to three-meter-high embankments. These embankments are made of earthen dikes reinforced by trachyte stone, which is resistant to salinity and brackish water.

TRACHYTE STONE
A volcanic rock with a light gray to brown color, used in construction for its durability.

6

The *valli* connect to surrounding fresh and brackish-water bodies through *chiaviche* (sluice gates) that are operated hydraulically or by hand. The *capovalle* controls and directs all the activities, operating the system with the *vallisani* and guardians who monitor the *valli* daily.[31] They allow brackish water from the lagoon and fresh water from streams to enter the system, regulating salinity gradients that range from 10 to 15 per mile and 40 to 50 per mile.[32] Water is circulated through a double-canal system, reaching even the furthest points from the sluice gates. The first canal, two to four meters deep, runs parallel to the main embankment, while the second splits the *valle* in two, letting water flow through the shallow ponds where fish are bred in spring and summer.[33]

6 The fishing valley master, *capovalle*, the fishing valley workers, and the guardian are the three principal figures managing the fishing valley.
7 The *capovalle* regulates the water regime and employs seasonal workers. While the workers manage different activities, the guardian is responsible for the daily monitoring of the valley.

This seasonal cycle in a valliculture system is influenced by water temperature, nutrient richness, salinity gradient, and natural fish migration also known as *smontàta* (movement of fish from the lagoon to the sea). The stage known as *fraìma* (at the gates of winter) occurs when temperatures drop between mid-October and the end of December. Derived from the Latin term *infra hieme* (below winter), activities such as water flushing, fish migration, fishing, and wintering all take place during *fraìma*.[34] Once occurring naturally, today it is carried out by means of a dual action of draining the whole *valle da pesca*, whereby water levels are lowered, and by attracting fish with the introduction of warmer, saltier lagoon waters, taking advantage of the abundant winter high tides.[35] This procedure stimulates a natural impulse for fish to migrate to the sea and reproduce.

7

During *fraìma*, fish swim toward V-shaped *lavorièri* fishing barriers inside the *valli da pesca*, where they are caught until late winter.[36] Traditionally, the *lavorièri*—constructed of reed lattices and wooden poles up to three hundred meters long—were positioned with the apex toward the lagoon and the sides against the banks of the *colaùro* canal, connecting the *valli* with the lagoon. Around the 1950s, reed *lavorièri* were transformed into concrete structures, requiring less maintenance.

Brackish Water from Venice Lagoon Enters the *Valle Da Pesca*, Attracting Fish

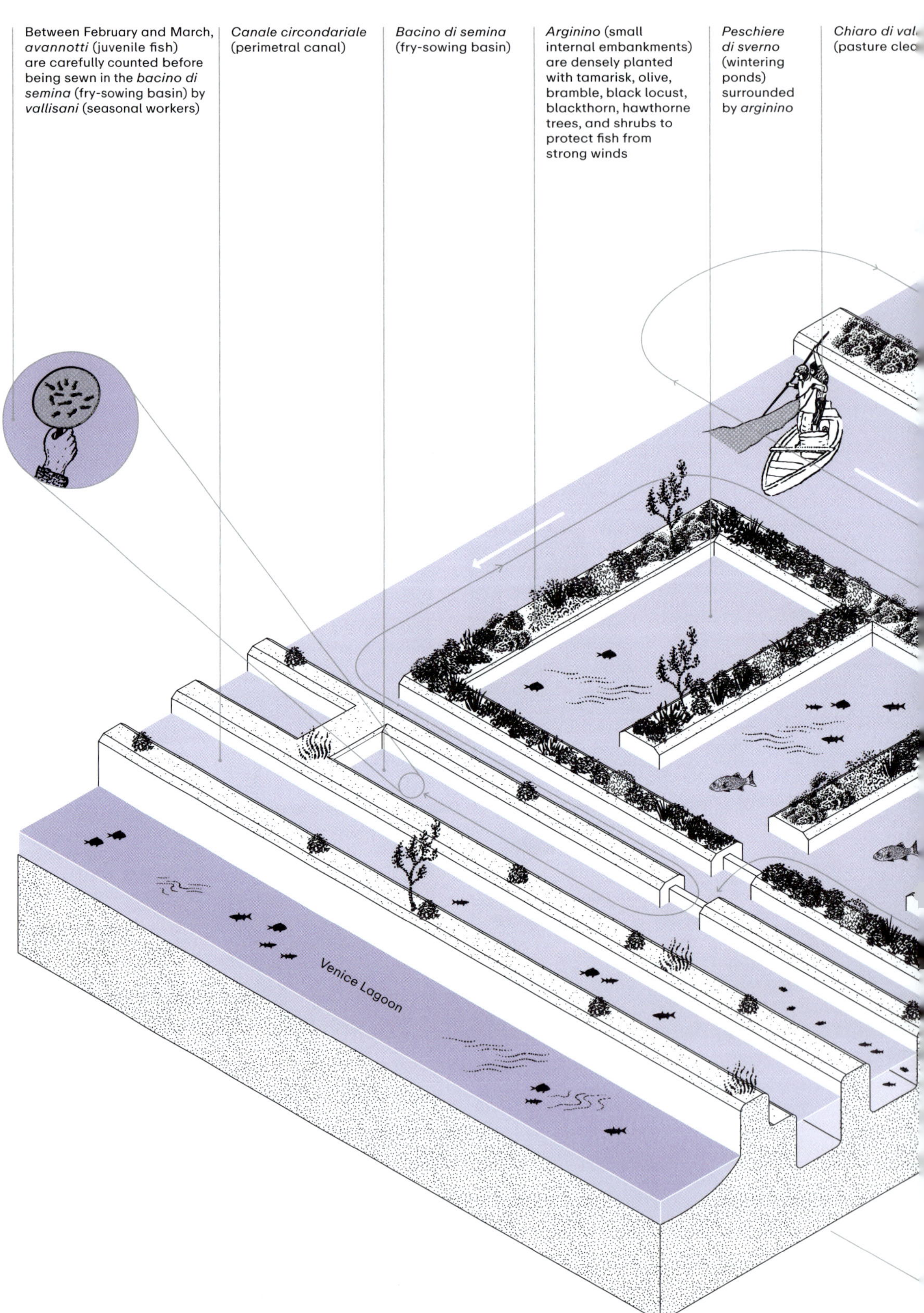

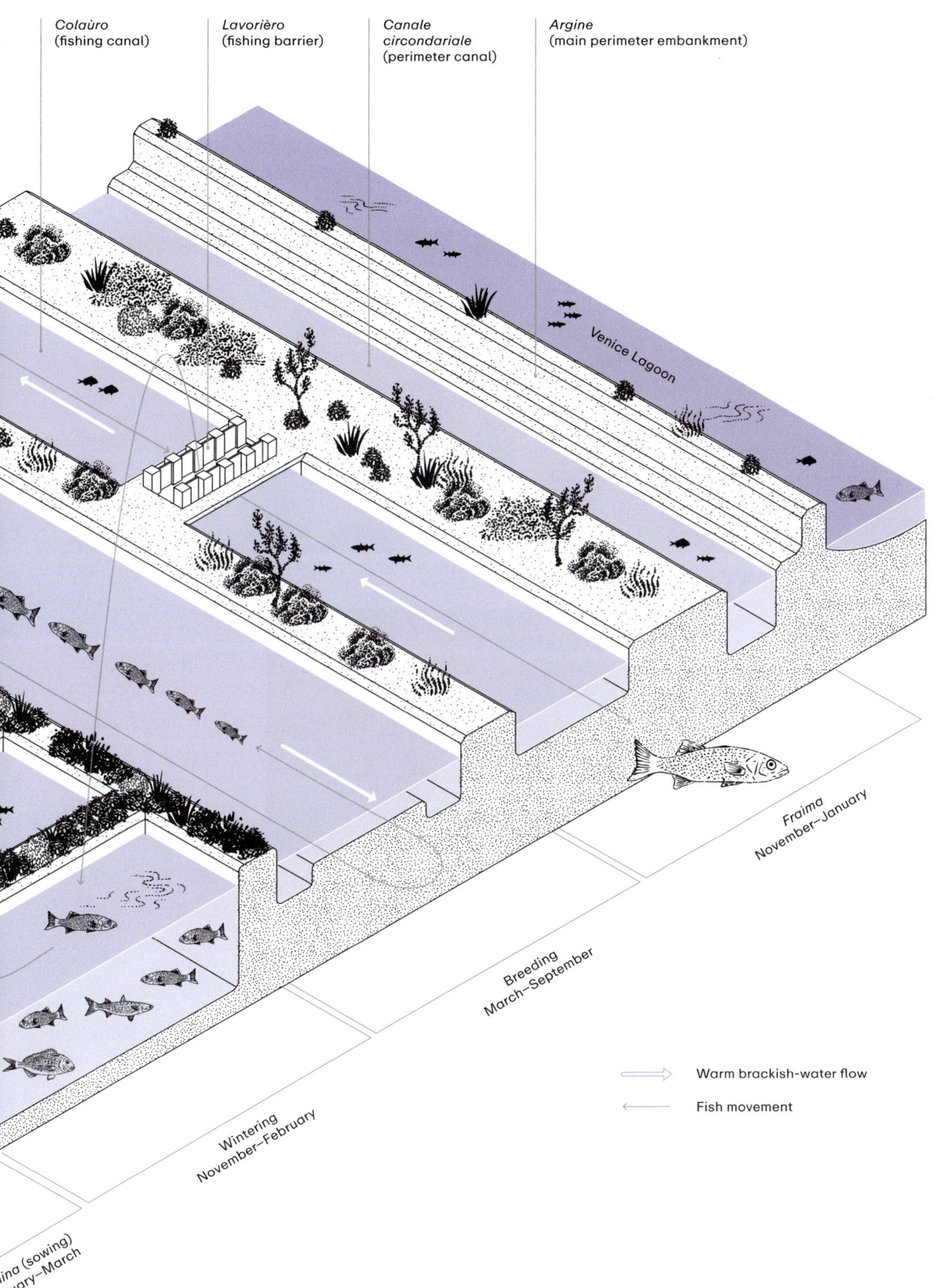
Colaùro
(fishing canal)
Lavorièro
(fishing barrier)
Canale circondariale
(perimeter canal)
Argine
(main perimeter embankment)
Venice Lagoon
Fraima
November–January
Breeding
March–September
Wintering
November–February
mina (sowing)
bruary–March
Warm brackish-water flow
Fish movement

Once caught in the *lavorièri*, fish are selected for market by species and size, with small and medium sizes placed in *peschiere* di sverno (wintering fishponds). These wintering fishponds, measuring three to five meters wide and five to six meters deep, are oriented windward to better protect fish from northeastern bora and southeastern sirocco winds. They are separated by earth embankments where dense bushes of tamarisk (*Tamarix gallica*) are planted, serving as windbreaks

8

9

8 *Peschiere di sverno*, or wintering ponds, are surrounded by *arginino*, where fish stay compact and still on the bottom during winter.
9 The counting and sowing of juvenile sea bream into the *bacino di allevamento*, or breeding basin.

while their roots stabilize the soil.[37] From January to the beginning of March, the *capivalle* and *vallisani* work to control valle conditions and protect fish from predatory birds, such as cormorants (*Phalacrocorax carbo*), yellow-legged gulls (*Larus michahellis*), and pygmy cormorants (*Microcarbo pygmaeus*).[38]

When spring arrives, fresh brackish water from the lagoon flows into the *bacini di allevamento* (breeding basins). Traditionally, during the *montàta* (return) stage, *avannotti* (juvenile fish) naturally migrating from the sea into the lagoon were attracted by the high nutrient concentration and comfortable water temperature. To welcome this migration, *valli da pesca* brackish-water sluices opened from St. John's Day on February 4th until St. Mark's Day on April 25th.[39] The origin of valliculture can be traced to the "nursery" role that coastal lagoons play in the biological life cycle of fish.[40]

10

11

10 Measuring three to five meters wide and five to six meters deep, wintering ponds are oriented windward to better protect fish from northeastern bora and southeastern sirocco winds.
11 *Peschiera di sverno* with protective nets to ward against cormorants.

One-Year Cycle of Fish Growth Related to Monthly Oscillation of Water Temperatures in the Lagoon and *Valle*

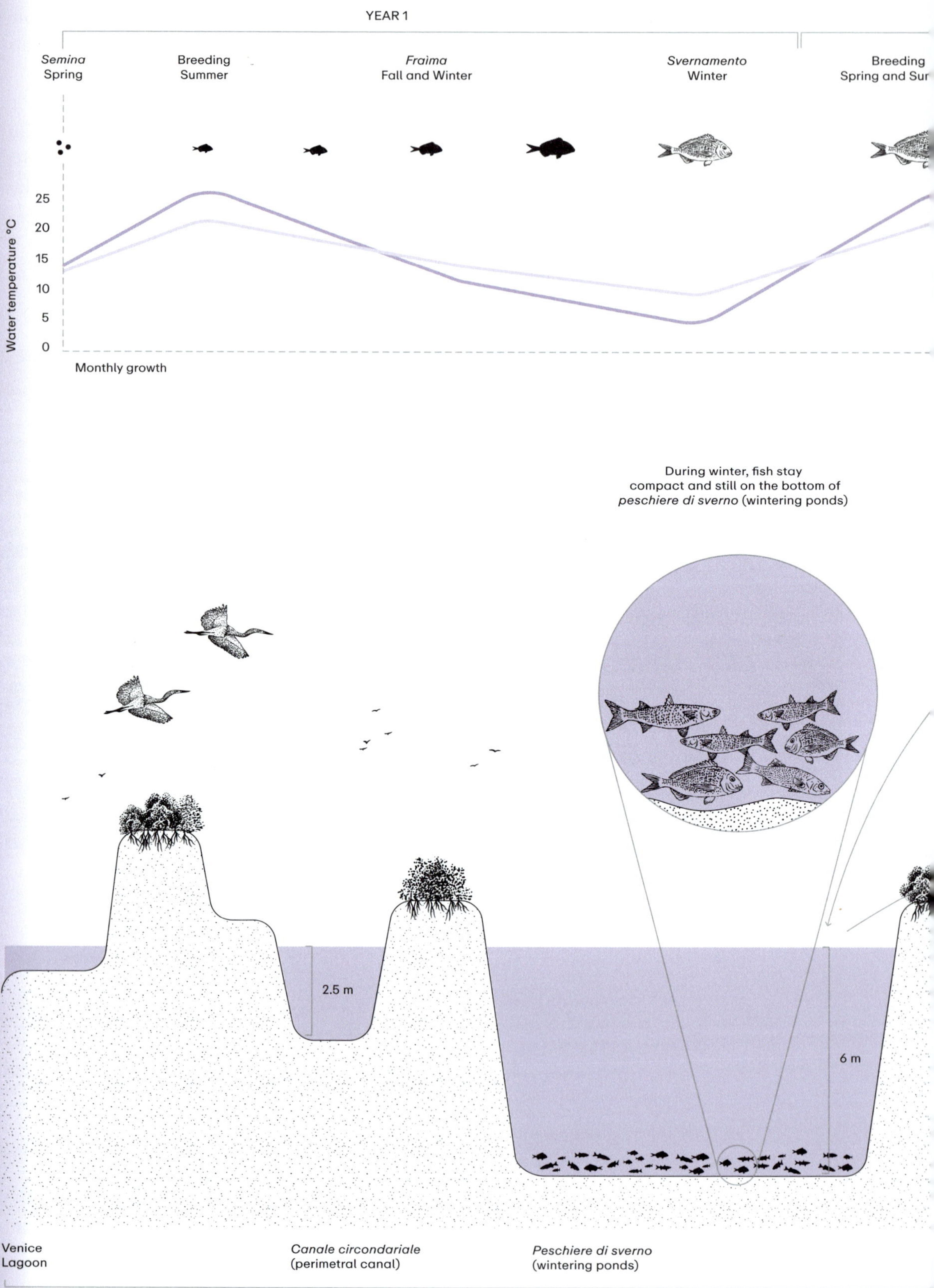

Historically, eels, crabs, and green crabs were widespread in the *valli* system, while 90 percent of today's farmed biomass is represented by flathead gray mullet (*Mugil cephalus*), European seabass (*Dicentrarchus labrax*), and gilthead sea bream (*Sparus aurata*).[41, 42] This historic aquatic biodiversity, which included over 25 different farmed species, is now gone, along with many traditional natural processes, as the majority of *valli da pesca* solely rely on juvenile fish sowing.[43, 44, 45] *Avannotti* are bred in the *bacino di semina* (fry-sowing basin) and in *seragio per il novellame* (enclosure for juveniles)—an impervious labyrinth where the fish acclimatize with the *valle* conditions. The main fish species sown in *valli* are those that tolerate salinity.

During the summer season, lasting from June to the end of September, maintenance, management, adjustment, and repair ensure the *valle*'s ongoing performance. The *capovalle* and *vallisani* fix damaged embankments, sluices, and devices; drain and clean canals; and monitor water quality and salinity, which increases rapidly in the summer heat due to evaporation.[46]

12

Over time, the *valli*'s embankments have protected the lagoon's *baréne*—its most distinctive landscape—from erosion caused by boat traffic.[47] These marshes support an abundance of life, while performing many supportive roles, including filtering and purifying water, regulating salinity, retaining sediment, absorbing carbon, limiting tidal impact, reducing wave impact, and mitigating strong winds.[48, 49] Designed to support human and more-than-human species alike, the *valli* technology is profitable and benefits the entire Venice Lagoon.[50, 51, 52] However, in the last decades of the 1900s, a crisis resulted in a change in ownership and a decline in the remaining *valli da pesca*.[53] This crisis was caused by an increase in migratory cormorants from the Netherlands, whose presence in the Venice Lagoon increased by 268 percent as they searched for fish.[54, 55] Additionally, commercial competition from the intensive mariculture of sea bream and sea bass in Croatia and Greece furthered the system's deterioration.[56, 57]

← Open this fold to reveal full illustration.

Today, fishing is minimal, with the system mostly remaining for its cultural significance and for bird hunting.[58] Many *valli da pesca* now integrate a mixture of activities such as animal breeding, tourist accommodations, crop cultivation, carbon compensation, and biomass production, which are juxtaposed with fish farming and bird hunting.[59] Recent transformations of the *valli da pesca* involve the system's hybridization in response to climate change and are creating localized energy futures. These new approaches toward *valli da pesca* are seen in Valle Miana Serraglia's biofuel and green energy production facility, and Valle Dogà's carbon-capture production project.[60, 61, 62] Valle Miana Serraglia, located in the central Venice Lagoon, is the only *valle da pesca* with agriculture surrounding fishponds. In recent years, Agricola Sant'Ilario's biodigester, located in Valle Miana Serraglia, has been producing biomethane for trucking. Adjacent to the biodigester is a power-generation plant, where biomass is used to produce energy from the farm's agricultural and forestry activities, such as cultivated corn, fallen leaves, pine needles, and marcs (leftovers of wine production).[63] Valle Dogà, located in the northern Venice Lagoon, is the largest *valle da pesca*, covering almost 17 square kilometers. Naturally, carbon-capture storage happens in the lagoon through the photosynthesis of algae and phytoplankton. Società Agricola Blue Valley is a company in the *valle* that sells blue carbon credits to offset companies' carbon dioxide emissions.

13

12 Artichokes blooming in summer in Isola Falconera, northern Venice Lagoon.
13 View of Valle Miana Serraglia toward *peschiere di sverno* and *colauro* (fishing canal).

Valli da pesca dikes and ponds in the Venice Lagoon are a millennia-old fish-farming system that contributes to the production of organic local resources and to the protection of wetland biodiversity and ecology of inestimable value, while fighting coastal erosion and supporting carbon storage and sequestration through the preservation of *baréne*. Centuries of usage and trial and error have designed and attuned their functioning to rely on the lagoon tidal dynamics and seasonal cycles, making them the most accurate environmental monitor. Rather than erasing the original system upon which it was cited, had the city of Venice been relocated to conserve the *valli* system, perhaps rising sea levels that seasonally submerge the city would have been mitigated. Given their unparalleled environmental, cultural, and social importance, and their potential for coevolution with local energy production, the remaining *valli da pesca* of the Venice Lagoon offer a glimpse into the future, through a light shone from the past. The ongoing protection of *valli da pesca* must be ensured, allowing them to continue supporting the whole lagoon ecosystem, while encouraging their continued transformation toward a new energy landscape.

1. Alessandra Aspes, *Il Veneto nell'antichità: preistoria e protostoria* (Milan: Mondadori, 1984).
2. Loredana Capuis, *I Veneti: società e cultura di un popolo dell'Italia preromana* (Milan: Longanesi, 1993).
3. Giustiniano Bullo, *Le Valli Salse da Pesca e la Vallicultura* (Venice: Officine Grafiche Carlo Ferrari, 1940), 6. Isole Realtine (Realtine Islands) represented an archipelago of emerged and buildable land in the tangle of salt marshes and mudflats. The islands were located around a narrow bend of the Rivus Altus ("deep channel"), which served as its port canal. Today, Rivus Altus corresponds to the Grand Canal, and Isole Realtine to the Rialto, a central area of Venice, Italy, in the *sestiere* of San Polo.
4. Michele Zanetti, "La Valle da Pesca Lagunare: Caratteri Strutturali e Funzionali," in *La Laguna di Venezia*, ed. G. Caniato, Eugenio Turri, and Michele Zanetti (Verona: Cierre, 1995), 299.
5. A. Granzotto et al., *La Pesca nella Laguna di Venezia* (Milan: Fondazione Eni Enrico Mattei, 2001) 46.
6. Associazione Piscicoltori Italiani, "Acquacoltura nelle Lagune e Foce Marine—Vallicoltura," Aquacoltura, accessed April 17, 2024, https://www.acquacoltura.org/acquacoltura-nelle-lagune-e-foce-marine-vallicoltura/.
7. Michele Zanetti (environmental conservation officer, Associazione Naturalistica Sandonatese), in discussion with the author, October 2022.
8. The effective number of *valli da pesca* of the Venice Lagoon is debated. Atlante della Laguna reports 17 *valli da pesca*; the official hydrographic chart of the Venice Lagoon *(Carta Idrografica della Laguna di Venezia)* in 1983 reported 29 *valli*; in 2023, 36
9. Giampaolo Rallo, "Paesaggio, Morfologia ed Economia delle Acque: Le Valli da Pesca" (lecture, Workshop Nazionale degli Ecomusei, Argenta and Bagnacavallo, Italy, November 14, 2015).
10. The legend of Saint Mark the Evangelist is reported in Bullo, *Le Valli Salse da Pesca*, 6: quoting "Breve notizia della fondazione dell'Isola di S. Nicolò dei Mendicoli e di molte altre cose a quella appartenenti. Descritta dal molto Rev. Don Francesco Braccolani. Dedicata all'Ill.mo Signor Zanetto Minotto" from 1664.
11. Bullo, *Le Valli Salse da Pesca*, 8: "Terminazione del 5 luglio 1425 in Rogadis (Consiglio dei Pregadi) conservata nel museo Correr nella raccolta di leggi venete sulla pesca, del Priuli, T. 1." The etymology of the term *valle da pesca* is still debated.
12. Giacomo Zolezzi, "La Pesca nella Provincia di Venezia," *Bollettino di Pesca, Piscicoltura e Idrobiologia* 22, no. 2 (1946): 155–231, cited in Tomaso Fortibuoni, Otello Giovanardi, and Saša Raicevich, *Un Altro Mare* (Chioggia: Associazione "Tegnue di Chioggia" Onlus, 2009), 143.
13. G.B. Voltolina, *Sulla pesca del pesce novello a Burano* (n. p.: Neptunia, 1894), cited in Fortibuoni, Giovanardi, and Raicevich, *Un Altro Mare*, 144.
14. G.S. Bullo, *Piscicultura marina. Stima delle coltivazioni in acqua salsa* (Padova: Stab. Prosperini, 1891), cited in Fortibuoni, Giovanardi, and Raicevich, *Un Altro Mare*, 144.
15. Bullo, *Le Valli Salse da Pesca*, 8.
16. Fortibuoni, Giovanardi, and Raicevich, *Un Altro Mare*, 147.
17. Michele Zanetti (environmental conservation officer, Associazione Naturalistica Sandonatese), in discussion with the author, March 2023.
18. Amina Chouairi, "Valli da Pesca of the Venice Lagoon," Circular Water Stories, 2020, https://circularwaterstories.org/analysis/fishing-valleys-in-the-venetian-lagoon/.
19. Zanetti, discussion, October 2022.
20. Granzotto et al., *La Pesca nella Laguna di Venezia*, 37.
21. Paolo Tagliapietra, *Serajante* (self-pub., 2020).
22. Zanetti, discussion, October 2022.
23. Fabrizio Ferrari, "Le Valli da Pesca Sono Demaniali," Edizioni Pubblicità Italia, 2008, https://www.pubblicitaitalia.com/pesce/prodotti/il-pesce/2008/5/8459.
24. Elvi Longhin, *Le Valli della Laguna di Venezia: da Pubblico Demanio a Privato Dominio?* (Venice: Provincia di Venezia Settore Politiche Ambientali, 2004).
25. Zanetti, discussion, October 2022.
26. "Valli da pesca," Banca Dati Ambientale sulla Laguna di Venezia.
27. *Valli da pesca* are Sites of Community Importance and Special Areas of Conservation as part of the Habitat Directive, composing the intricate network of the European protected sites called "Natura 2000."
28. "Valli da pesca."
29. Zanetti, discussion, October 2022.
30. Efrem Destro, former countryside manager employee at Società Agricola Sant'Ilario (Valle Miana Serraglia, Mira, Venice, Italy), in discussion with the author, November 2022.
31. Zanetti, discussion, October 2022.
32. Granzotto et al., *La Pesca nella Laguna di Venezia*, 33.
33. Fortibuoni, Giovanardi, and Raicevich, *Un Altro Mare*, 144.
34. Zanetti, discussion, October 2022.
35. Variante al P.R.G. per la Laguna e le Isole Minori. Sistema delle Valli da Pesca (Venice: Comune di Venezia, 2004), https://www.comune.venezia.it/it/content/vprg-la-laguna-e-le-isole-minori
36. Zanetti, discussion, October 2022.
37. Zanetti, discussion, October 2022.
38. Zanetti, discussion, March 2023.
39. A. Targioni Tozzetti, *La pesca in Italia* (Genoa: Ministero di Agricoltura, Industria e Commercio, 1872), cited in Fortibuoni, Giovanardi, and Raicevich, *Un Altro Mare*, 145.
40. Granzotto et al., *La Pesca nella Laguna di Venezia*, 29.
41. Zanetti, discussion, March 2023.
42. "Valli da pesca."
43. Valle Dogà in the northern Venice Lagoon still relies partly on the natural migration of fish.
44. Antonio Zacchello, owner of Società Agricola Blue Valley, and Silvia Bertaggia, employee at Società Agricola Blue Valley (Valle Dogà, Caposile, Venice, Italy), in discussion with the author, November 2023.
45. L. Sormani Moretti, *La pesca, la pescicoltura e la caccia nella Provincia di Venezia* (Venice: Tipografia della Società di Mutuo Soccorso tra Compositori-Tipgografi, 1884), cited in Fortibuoni, Giovanardi, and Raicevich, *Un Altro Mare*, 145.
46. Zanetti, discussion, October 2022.
47. Amina Chouairi, "The Operating Venetian Lagoon: The Agency of Barene" (master's thesis, Delft University of Technology, 2020).
48. Luigi D'Alpaos, *Fatti e Misfatti di Idraulica Lagunare. La Laguna di Venezia dalla Diversione dei Fiumi alle Nuove Opere alle Bocche di Porto* (Venice: Istituto Veneto di Scienze, Lettere ed Arti, 2010), 23–24.
49. Lorenzo Bonometto, *Il respiro della Laguna: Origini, Caratteri e Funzioni delle Barene* (Venice: Corte del Fontego Editore, 2015), 6–7.
50. Chouairi, "Valli da Pesca of the Venice Lagoon."
51. Zanetti, discussion, October 2022.
52. Destro, discussion.
53. Zanetti, discussion, October 2022.
54. Zanetti, discussion, October 2022.
55. Massimo Spampano, "Venezia: boom di uccelli in laguna, +800% in 20 anni," Corriere della Sera Ambiente, June 18, 2013, https://www.corriere.it/ambiente/13_giugno_19/laguna-venezia-boom-uccelli_f09f5760-d832-11e2-98e6-97ca5b2e4e27.shtml.
56. Zanetti, discussion, October 2022.
57. Granzotto et al., *La Pesca nella Laguna di Venezia*, 43.
58. For an extensive report of the current state of *valli da pesca* in the upper Adriatic Sea, see Alessandro Destro, "Tracce di Futuro Lagunare. Le valli da Pesca come Nuova Tipologia di Sostegno Economico" (master's thesis, Università Iuav di Venezia, 2018).
59. Granzotto et al., *La Pesca nella Laguna di Venezia*, 36.
60. Anna Sarzetto (Isola Falconera), in discussion with the author, June 2022.
61. Destro, discussion.
62. Società Agricola Blue Valley, "Blue Valley. Bio Fish & Carbon Credits," Bluev, accessed April 17, 2024, https://www.bluev.it/.
63. "Sant'Ilario Bioenergia BUR n. 77 del 5 luglio 2022," Bollettino Ufficiale della Regione Veneto, July 5, 2022, https://bur.regione.veneto.it/BurvServices/Pubblica/DettaglioDecreto.aspx?id=479612.

COAUTHOR

MICHELE ZANETTI

Environmental Conservation Officer

For over 22 years, Michele Zanetti has dedicated his career to his local environment as a fishing and hunting conservation officer for the Province of Venice. In this role, he oversees the delicate ecosystem of the lagoon and *valli da pesca* while also educating stakeholders on conservation laws. His principle duty is to enforce environmental regulations that govern lagoon activities, including fishing, hunting, and other practices that have an impact on the local environment.

Zanetti's parents, both agricultural workers, fostered his deep appreciation for nature and its beauty through their connection to the surrounding agrarian landscape. His formative years were spent at a specialized school in Portomaggiore, where he was immersed in the gardens and countryside. This unique school, led by Rina and Ida Nigrisoli—Jewish sisters who survived the Holocaust—offered innovative and engaging pedagogy. This childhood experience profoundly influenced Zanetti's commitment to the environment, evident in his early civil service work in conservation and natural sciences, and later in his professional career dedicated to protecting the lagoon.

As a conservation officer, Zanetti has developed a deep understanding of the Venice Lagoon's landscape—particularly during his early-morning shifts. He regularly monitors crucial areas like the *valli da pesca*, which host a diversity of wildlife, including thousands of migratory birds. Alongside combating fishing and poaching crimes, he conducts surveys in sensitive zones, compiling technical reports to establish protective measures. Outside of his professional life, he has authored several publications and fiction books set in the lagoon and *valli da pesca*, complemented by his passion for drawing and nature photography, which often feature in his works.

Today, Zanetti serves as the active leader of the Associazione Naturalistica Sandonatese, which is nearing its 50th year of operation. Over the course of his tenure, he has organized many conferences and cultural gatherings. Zanetti remains active in publishing nature-focused literature, alongside his role as a lecturer at the local Università della Terza Età.

SALTY
BRACKISH
3 FRESH

YAKHCHĀL ICE HOUSES *of* THE PERSIANS
Iran

YAKHCHĀL ICE HOUSES *of* THE PERSIANS *Iran*

(PEOPLE) Persians (LOCATION) Iranian Plateau
(TECHNOLOGY) passive ice storage
(ELEVATION) 830–1,800 m (ORIGIN) 400 BCE; documented 17th century
(DISTANCE ABOVE OR BELOW WATERLINE) –6 to 0 m

FAO Nexus
(WATER) fresh (ENERGY) radiative cooling
(FOOD) food preservation

IPCC Adaptation Pathway
accommodate

World Bank NBS
(CATEGORY) river floodplains
(FUNCTIONS) drought regulation, pluvial flood regulation, subsidence regulation, heat regulation
(BENEFITS) resource production, pluvial flood risk reduction, cultural, social interaction, education

1

Finding their origins on the alluvial plains of the Iranian Plateau—a vast and arid landscape of unforgiving temperatures—*yakhchāls* are monuments of utilitarian desert architecture.[1] Derived from Persian, where *yakh* means "ice," and *chāl* refers to a hollow or pit in the ground, these freestanding domed mud brick structures constructed where clay soils prevail are unrivaled in making the best use of water in a hostile desert environment—for making ice.[2] Similar ice houses existed as far back as the Middle Bronze Age along the Euphrates River.[3] Generally, *yakhchāls* would be located on the outskirts of a village near cultivation areas, where water was supplied from a *qanat* during the winter months, when demand for irrigation was at its minimum.[4] Although *yakhchāls* share many similarities with other types of vernacular ice houses found across the world, their cultural value, architectural elements, and community relevance truly set them apart.[5]

1 The *yakhchāl* ice house is unique because of the way the ice was made in the desert at temperatures above freezing.

2 Even though winter nights can be very cold in the deserts of Iran, temperatures rarely drop below freezing, but ice could be made even at temperatures just above freezing, due to a phenomenon known as night sky radiation or radiative cooling.

2

3

3 The ice house has a domed roof so that the hottest air would rise to the top, while the coolest air remained at the bottom, where the ice was stored.

Yakhchāls represent a fusion of two unique skills—the design and execution of domes and vaults in mud brick, and the innovative use of water in desert environments.[6] Although very few still exist, those that have been documented are located between 830 to 1,800 meters above sea level on the Iranian Plateau in areas where alluvial deposits feature clay-surface soils.[7] Characterized by extreme heat and cold winters, the desert climate of central Iran had specific environmental conditions in which *yakhchāls* became essential and flourished. These vernacular monuments, sometimes measuring up to 18 meters high, were often the tallest buildings in the village.[8] While thought to have existed earlier, documentation of these structures in Iran dates to the 17th century CE. At their peak in construction, *yakhchāls* could be found in urban centers, remote desert villages, and caravansaries.

Though *yakhchāls* vary in size, from smaller community-based structures to larger buildings serving entire villages, three main types have been recorded: freestanding constructions with domed roofs in the northeast and central desert, underground structures in the northwest (around Tehran), and open-air *yakhchāls* in the southwest, where the climate was cooler.[9] The system takes advantage of the

4

dark, clear desert sky's radiation-absorbing properties, which significantly decrease the ambient temperature by absorbing the energy of the surrounding environment. This allowed *yakhchāls* to make ice passively, even in situations where the overall temperature was above freezing.[10] The quantity of ice that was made was dependent on the temperature and amount of clouds in the sky. Cold cloudless nights increased the rate at which water froze, resulting in more water being poured into the ice pond. In contrast, during warmer or cloudy nights, since the rate of freezing was much slower, less water would be poured into the ice pond.[11]

Historically, *yakhchāls* were constructed by the local people using readily available sun-dried mud bricks and mud paste, using no mechanical gear or support.[12] A typical *yakhchāls* consists of four main components: an ice pond, shading walls, an ice pit, and a freestanding dome roof above the structure. To begin, an initial pit would be dug and excavated material would be reserved for the structure's bricks, mortar, or plaster. Built without the use of scaffolding or supports, construction began with a mud brick ring. Subsequent rings were constructed above—each inset by a few centimeters—until the desired height was reached. Both shading walls and domed roofs were built thicker at the bottom, tapering at the top to reduce the volume of material but increase the structural integrity. One example of a domed roof in Meibod began with a thickness of 240 centimeters at the base, and gradually shrank to 20 centimeters at the top.[13]

The ice ponds, which allow for production of ice on-site, are the most ingenious aspects of the *yakhchāls*. Located on the northernmost side, these

5

6

4 Outside the ice house were shallow pools or channels, and these were shaded with walls during the day so that they remained as cool as possible.

5 Once the ice was harvested, it was stored in a deep pit in alternating layers of ice and insulating straw.

6 On clear winter nights the shallow pools were filled with water. The depth of water varied, depending on how cold it was.

East to West Shading Walls Cast Shadows on the Ice Pond to Assist with Freezing

Entrance
Chal (pit) filled with layers of *yakh* (ice) and straw
Air vent
Main entrance below shade walll
Ice pond
Water entry
Cultivation area
15 m
6 m

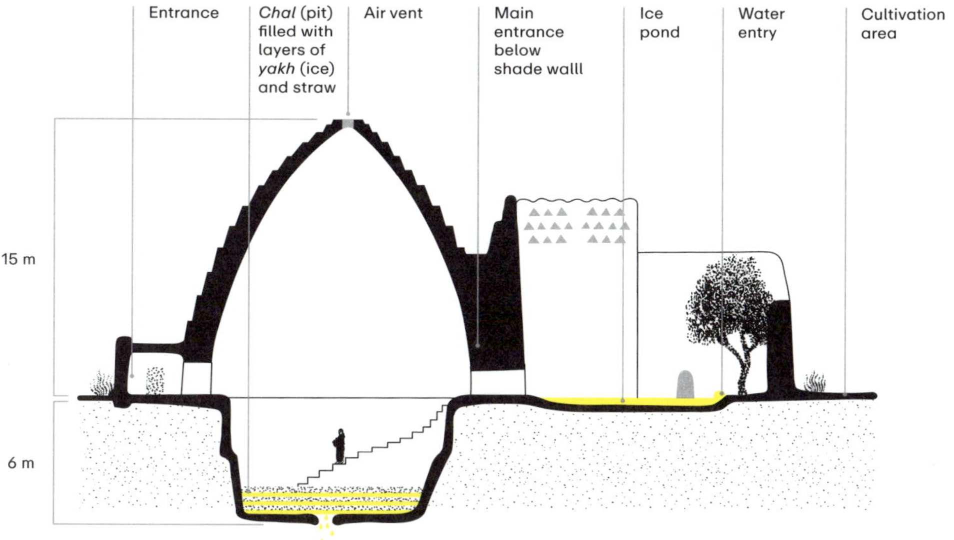

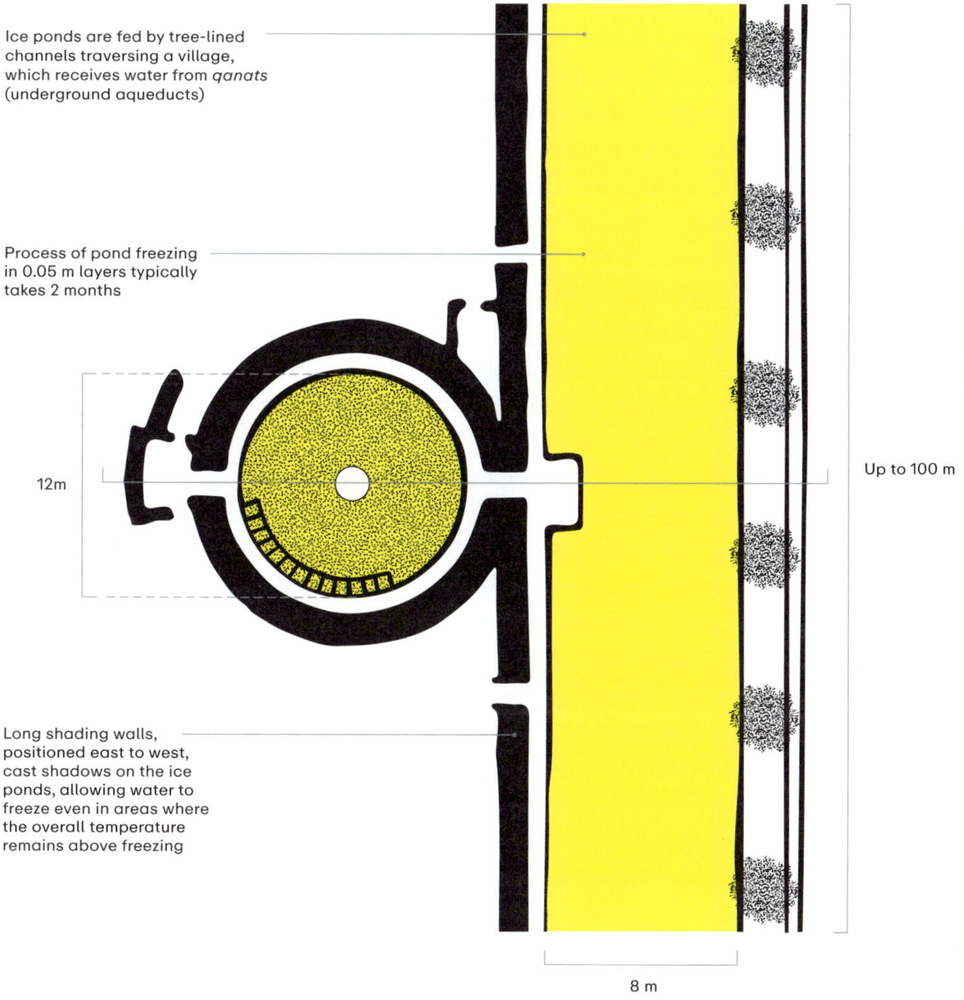

Ice ponds are fed by tree-lined channels traversing a village, which receives water from *qanats* (underground aqueducts)
Process of pond freezing in 0.05 m layers typically takes 2 months
12m
Up to 100 m
Long shading walls, positioned east to west, cast shadows on the ice ponds, allowing water to freeze even in areas where the overall temperature remains above freezing
8 m

7

7 The purpose of the hole is to let in daylight, eliminating the need for other light sources that would heat up the space and melt the ice. A piece of marble was placed on top of the hole, to block the cool air from escaping but let enough light pass through.

ice ponds set these ice houses apart from others found across the globe.[14] In areas where ice couldn't be brought in from nearby mountains, long shallow ponds—ranging from 40 to 50 centimeters deep, up to one hundred meters in length, and 10 meters wide—were excavated and fed by another ingenious invention known as the *qanat*—a type of subterranean irrigation canal—which was used to transfer water over long distances. Water was brought into the pond to be frozen in successive layers of around five centimeters, a figure calculated by the optimal freezing rate of ice produced per night.[15, 16] This process of incrementally filling the *yakhchāl* generally took about two months, though, depending on the climate and size, filling time would vary.[17, 18] Before storing the ice, the *yakhchāli* (ice house manager) would crush the individual ice pieces and pour water over them, turning them into a solid block of ice to optimize space and overall thermal efficiency.[19]

Long straight shading walls, stretching east to west and up to 10 meters tall, were located to the south and used to cast a shadow on the ice ponds.[20] In rare cases, they were curved and had perpendicular walls going northward to further decrease the sun's radiation. The temperature difference between the sunlit and the shaded areas in the Iranian Plateau could be about 15–20 degrees. This allowed for water to freeze even in areas where the overall temperature was still above freezing.[21] The addition of these shading walls increased the ice-making potential of *yakhchāls* exponentially.

The ice pits were excavated up to six meters deep and located in the center of the dome, where the collected ice was stored until it was used in the summer.[22] The purpose of these ice pits was to create the conditions for the greatest volume of ice to survive until after the following summer. A drainage hole connected to a well would sometimes be added beneath the ice pit to collect the melted ice, as this water would make the ice melt faster. To further prevent the ice from

8

9

8. The structure of the ice house is very thick, which helps keep it cool in the hot climate, due to the large thermal mass that regulates heat.
9. Once the ice house had been filled, the building was sealed and only opened in the summer when the ice was used to make iced drinks.

melting, several straw layers were added, with the topmost layer between one and two meters thick. The layers of straw kept the ice separated, making it easier to remove as needed, and, as a good insulator of heat, straw helped keep the ice cold enough to survive until the following year. In some instances, wicker or wood layers were used in conjunction with or instead of straw.[23]

Domes ranged five to 18 meters tall and seven to 23 meters in diameter, with an ice pit depth of six meters.[24] Regularly the tallest structure in the village, the higher the freestanding pointed domed roof was built over the ice pit, the greater distance the hot air would rise, thereby improving the structure's cooling efficiency.[25] The dome shape was preferential as a form that was self-bearing during construction, needing no wood for support and minimizing surface exposure to the sun. The shape, however, varied across a spectrum—from pure cones to paraboloids—and had a limited height of 18 meters.[26, 27] This dome would have a small opening at the top that served as ventilation, helping the hot air escape and promoting efficient air circulation.[28] The vent could be accessed by steps shaped across the domed surface, or by an external spiral staircase that would also accommodate the placement of fabric protection during a rainstorm.[29]

To further insulate the ice pit, a layer of thatch would sometimes be added to the exterior of the dome.[30] The dome had one main opening—generally located on the north side, being the most shaded side that was closest to the ice pond—used during the winter. In some instances, there would be another opening located on the east or west side, which was used in the

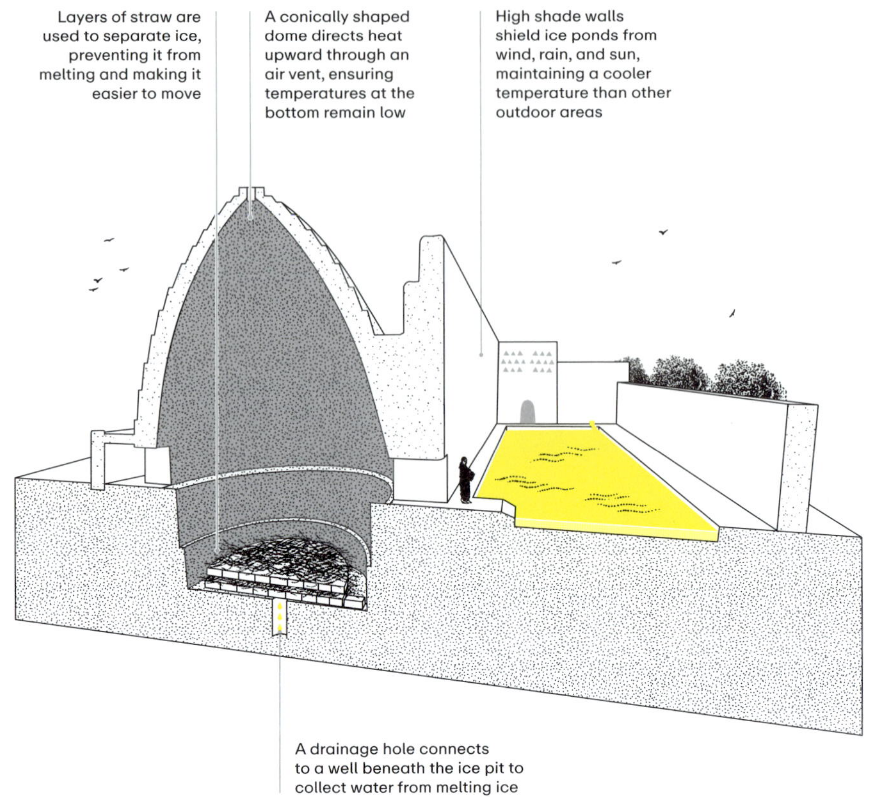

summer and was closest to the area where ice would be sold.[31] A simple foundation for the dome and shading walls began the construction process. A 50-centimeter-deep trench was excavated slightly wider than the planned thickness of the wall, while the excavated earth was gathered nearby, where it was mixed with burned lime and water to form a soft paste known as *sefteh*. A 15-centimeter-thick layer of paste was then placed in the trench, followed by a coarse stone temper. Subsequent layers of paste and stone temper were repeated until the foundation trench was filled.[32] Following a few weeks of setting, the construction of the walls would begin.

For the walls of *pisé* (rammed earth), clay was moistened and mixed with chaff (dried plant matter such as husk), which helped reduce shrinkage and the formation of cracks in dry periods, to create a straw-mud mix known as *kâh-gel*.[33] This was trodden on by barefoot laborers, kneaded into a plastic mass, and then thrown into lumps and placed to construct a course, reaching up to one meter high. This course was left to harden for several days, before the next was laid. A *kâh-gel* paste of similar composition was used for the mortar of the mud brick masonry, used to form the outer shape over the dome shells, and for surface plastering of domes and walls. The *khest* (mud bricks), typically 25 × 25 × 5 centimeters, were also made of *kâh-gel*, kneaded into a soft paste that was placed in wooden molds on the ground and covered with a thin layer of chaff to absorb moisture. Left in the sun to dry, the bricks were used after a couple of days.[34] Finally, *sarooj*, a mortar and plastering material, was used to render surfaces impermeable. *Sarooj* is a unique composition of mud paste made with lime, ash, egg white, and fine plant fibers or goat hair, which is added for strength and water impermeability.[35] Sacking would be wrapped around the top of the dome before a rainstorm to keep the water out, while constant evaporation through the mud brick dome shell would decrease both humidity and the temperature inside the dome.[36]

Yakhchāls were often owned by a *vaqf*—a type of Islamic charitable institution that also functioned as a public utility.[37] The ice produced in these places was sold but also given to the poor or anyone else that needed it free of charge. In some instances, *yakhchāls* were owned by the entire community, with ice that they produced divided accordingly. In the Kermān region, the majority of *yakhchāls* belonged to traders, who, until the beginning of the 1960s, sold ice directly to the people or in the bazaar. The manager of the *yakhchāl*, who had a unifying role in the community, was known as a *yakhchāli*.[38] They hosted village parties during the winter, when the building was sealed, and in the summer, when it was opened.[39]

While *yakhchāls* went out of use in the 1960s with modern refrigeration, in the 1970s Iranian authorities began once again taking an interest in them, though many had already fallen into disrepair.[40, 41] Their disappearance has been attributed to erosion, extreme climate conditions, and the impact of modern construction materials, with the majority of surviving *yakhchāls* found in the Semnan province.[42] Between 2007 and 2010, the most comprehensive survey was conducted by Hemming Jorgensen, who located, registered, codified, and mapped 129 *yakhchāls*, though many of them were barely recognizable.[43]

Yakhchāls stand as a testament to the ingenuity of desert civilizations in understanding the climate and potential of their region. They are a timeless example that proves passive energy and sustainable infrastructure can be evolved in the most formidable environments, by imagining technology tied to the characteristics of the seasons. The Persian people have not only given us a regenerative model for ice harvesting in the summer, they have also showed us what architecture can become when it evolves beyond an artificially controlled and isolated box, to embrace its surroundings by responding to them bioclimatically.

10

10 The disappearance of ice houses has been attributed to erosion, climate change, and the impact of modern construction materials.

ENDNOTES

1. Hemming Jorgensen, *Ice Houses of Iran* (Costa Mesa: Mazda Publishers, 2012), 1.
2. Jorgensen, *Ice Houses of Iran*, 30.
3. Jorgensen, *Ice Houses of Iran*, 2.
4. Jorgensen, *Ice Houses of Iran*, 25–38.
5. M. Mohammadjavad and Kavan Javanrudi, "Assessment of Ancient Fridges: A Sustainable Method to Storage Ice in Hot-Arid Climates," *Asian Culture and History* 4, no. 2 (2012): 133–43, https://doi.org/10.5539/ach.v4n2p133.
6. Elisabeth Beazley, "Some Vernacular Buildings of the Iranian Plateau," *Iran* 15 (1977): 89–102, https://doi.org/10.2307/4300566.
7. Jorgensen, *Ice Houses of Iran*, 70.
8. Jorgensen, *Ice Houses of Iran*, 163.
9. Bahareh Hosseini and Ali Namazian, "An Overview of Iranian Ice Repositories, an Example of Traditional Indigenous Architecture," *METU Journal of the Faculty of Architecture* 29, no. 2 (2012): 225–31.
10. Moslem Zare, Seyed Davoodmoosavian, and Hamid Eskandari, "A Scientific Study on the Performance of Iranian Ice Pits," *Research Journal of Recent Sciences* 4, no. 6 (2015): 14.
11. Armin Mehdipour and Ali Namazian, "Yakhchal; Climate Responsive Persian Traditional Architecture," *IPCBEE* 48 (2012): 175.
12. Jorgensen, *Ice Houses of Iran*, 5.
13. Hosseini and Namazian, "Overview of Iranian Ice Repositories," 228.
14. Hosseini and Namazian, "Overview of Iranian Ice Repositories," 225.
15. Jorgensen, *Ice Houses of Iran*, 25.
16. Jorgensen, *Ice Houses of Iran*, 184.
17. Jorgensen, *Ice Houses of Iran*, 25.
18. Jorgensen, *Ice Houses of Iran*, 187.
19. Hosseini and Namazian, "Overview of Iranian Ice Repositories," 224.
20. Hosseini and Namazian, "Overview of Iranian Ice Repositories," 227.
21. Hosseini and Namazian, "Overview of Iranian Ice Repositories," 227.
22. Hosseini and Namazian, "Overview of Iranian Ice Repositories," 228.
23. Hosseini and Namazian, "Overview of Iranian Ice Repositories," 225.
24. Jorgensen, *Ice Houses of Iran*, 163–67.
25. Mohammadjavad and Javanrudi, "Assessment of Ancient Fridges," 133–43.
26. Jorgensen, *Ice Houses of Iran*, 161.
27. Jorgensen, *Ice Houses of Iran*, 158.
28. Hosseini and Namazian, "Overview of Iranian Ice Repositories," 229.
29. Jorgensen, *Ice Houses of Iran*, 161.
30. Hosseini and Namazian, "Overview of Iranian Ice Repositories," 228.
31. Hosseini and Namazian, "Overview of Iranian Ice Repositories," 229.
32. Jorgensen, *Ice Houses of Iran*, 168.
33. Jorgensen, *Ice Houses of Iran*, 169.
34. Jorgensen, *Ice Houses of Iran*, 169.
35. Jorgensen, *Ice Houses of Iran*, 170.
36. Jorgensen, *Ice Houses of Iran*, 158.
37. Jorgensen, *Ice Houses of Iran*, 24.
38. Jorgensen, *Ice Houses of Iran*, 22.
39. Jorgensen, *Ice Houses of Iran*, 25.
40. Jorgensen, *Ice Houses of Iran*, 2.
41. Jorgensen, *Ice Houses of Iran*, 10.
42. Jorgensen, *Ice Houses of Iran*, 65.
43. Jorgensen, *Ice Houses of Iran*, 54.

NGÚMĀ FISH WEIRS *of* THE BAKA *Cameroon*

NGÚMĀ FISH WEIRS *of* THE BAKA *Cameroon*

Coauthored by
Venant Messe and Joseph Johnson Bibi

PEOPLE Baka LOCATION Cameroon, Congo, and Gabon
TECHNOLOGY weir fishing
ELEVATION 300–1,000 m ORIGIN unknown
DISTANCE ABOVE OR BELOW WATERLINE −0.6 to +0.4 m
WATER LEVEL FLUCTUATION, TIDAL OR SEASONAL +0.08 to +0.6 m

FAO Nexus
WATER fresh ENERGY tidal
FOOD fish

IPCC Adaptation Pathway
protect

World Bank NBS
CATEGORY bioretention areas, river and stream renaturation, river floodplains
FUNCTIONS biodiversity, water pollution regulation, pluvial flood regulation, riverine flood regulation
BENEFITS resource production, biodiversity, riverine flood risk reduction, carbon storage and sequestration, cultural, social interaction, education

1

During the major dry season, the sun rising to the middle of the sky signals the start of a Baka fishing expedition in the central African rainforest of southeastern Cameroon's Congo Basin. Once the dew in the densely wooded tropical forest has evaporated, women and children with pots, baskets, and machetes begin their three-kilometer journey from their *molongo* base camp to the closest river. As the oldest inhabitants of Cameroon's equatorial forest, the Baka practice a subsistence hunting-and-gathering lifestyle.[1] This seminomadic group has traditionally fished without the use of bait, rod, or line, with hook-and-line fishing only introduced after the 1950s.[2] Instead, they practice *ngúmā*, a systematic weir fishing technique involving dam-and-weir fishing, using local materials from the tree-lined riverbanks of rich clay soil.[3] As one of several types of weir construction strategies practiced by the Baka, this ingenious temporary construction, which is sited and built to maintain hydrology and habitat, could inspire changes in our "clean-energy" damming practices.

The Congo Basin contains nearly two million square kilometers of tropical rainforest, ranging from three hundred to one thousand meters above sea level.[4, 5] This region is home to the Baka people, who live across Central Africa's Trinational Dja-Odzala-Minkébé (TRIDOM) area, in southeastern Cameroon, northwestern Congo, and northeastern Gabon. They are the largest group of hunter-gatherers in this lowland region, with Cameroon having the greatest

1 The Baka are Indigenous hunter-gatherers who have lived in, protected, and shaped the Congo Basin rainforest for generations.

2

Baka population.[6] Here, Baka people live in small communities, often composed of 30 to 60 people, consisting of a single family or *yé* (clan).[7] Leadership is determined by experience and abilities, and includes *ngàngà* (healers) and male and female elders called *kobo* and *kobowossè*, who are responsible for decision-making and overseeing life within villages.[8] Baka people believe in a god called Komba; he takes the form of the spirit of the forest, Ejengui, who protects life, in addition to other smaller ghost spirits.

The Baka tend to the *ngúmā* fishing structures over the course of four annual seasons: two rainy and two dry. The year begins in *yaka*, the major dry season, which lasts from November to February—this is when *ngúmā* dam-and-bail fishing happens.[9] Each Baka community participates in a *molongo*, where they venture 20 to 50 kilometers south of their permanent settlements for two to three months to live in a constructed campsite in the forest.[10] Following this period, the minor rainy season lasts from March to June. During *langà*, the subsequent minor dry season from July and August, the Baka live and work on agricultural lands in villages of up to 29 households, where they continue to hunt, fish, and gather until dusk.[11, 12, 13] During *Sɔkɔ ma*, the major rainy season that occurs from September to November, the Baka return to the forest for hunting expeditions, in sites 10 to 20 kilometers away from their permanent settlements.[14, 15]

Up to 90 individuals venture on *molongo* trips, while the remaining families in the village continue to cultivate crops.[16] The *molongo* group moves five kilometers at a time down a river, changing camp every few days.[17] While a lack

3

2 Fishing is very important in Baka culture: Young boys are taught to fish using rods at a young age, while men fish using chemicals obtained from crushed plant material.
3 The Baka are a seminomadic people, but due to intensive deforestation are gradually becoming more sedentary.

Large Pieces of Wood and Local Materials Are Used to Dewater Sections of the Riverbed

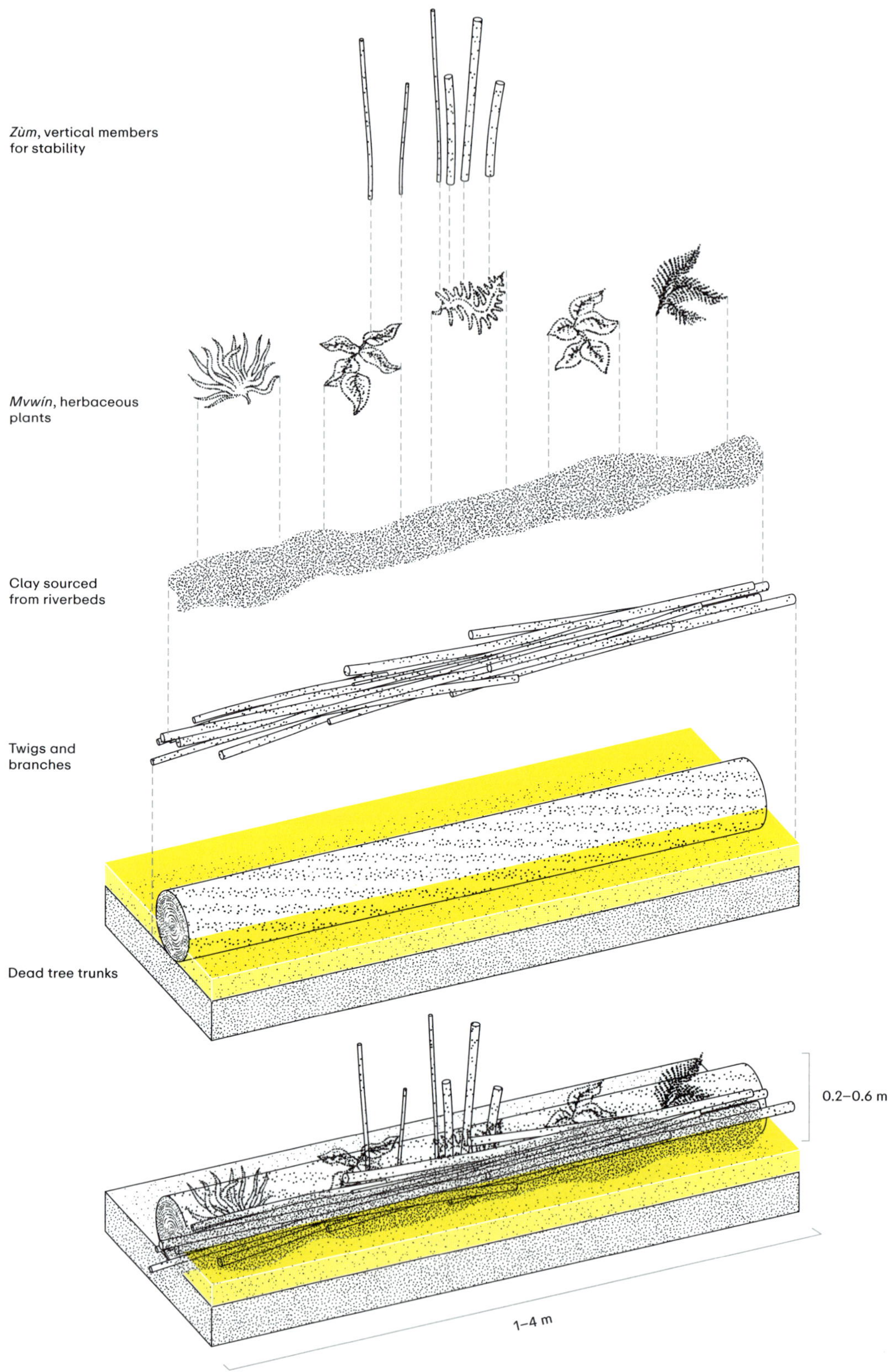

4 This fishing structure, which is used continuously, daytime and nighttime throughout the season of high water level, is installed by a group of several fishermen before the end of the dry season when the stream is dried up. The structure is composed of a solid dam, a platform oriented downstream installed in the middle of the dams during the rainy season. The water that is dammed bypasses into the funnel, where large fish are projected on the emerging end of the platform by the current.

of rainfall during the major dry season makes it harder to track animal footprints, dryer conditions and lower water levels are optimal for capturing fish at their fattest.[18] Regarded as skilled healers and botanists, the Baka are also able to determine which plants are suitable for eating and medicine, and which to avoid during *molongo*.[19]

The weir fishing technology created by Baka communities—primarily constructed and maintained by women—is a relatively straightforward technique that temporarily blocks a river using large pieces of wood and other locally available materials, in turn dewatering the dammed sections of the riverbed.[20] The Baka—as well as the Mvae and Ntumu communities—practice daytime fishing, which involves building two weirs—one at a stream branch and another upstream—using wood, *mvwín* leaves, aquatic herbaceous plants, and àdzíà (sludge).[21] Passive fishing infrastructure and temporary weir techniques similar to *ngúmā* are present throughout the Congo Basin. For example, the Mvae and Ntumu people also construct complex structures designed to passively trap fish with a river's natural current.[22, 23]

5 Dam fishing, in which water is removed from a dammed area and fish are taken from the exposed ground, is generally performed by women.

Groups of women from the Mvae and Ntumu communities—often a mother and her daughters—build these temporary shelter-fishing technologies, which are constructions of piled-up wooden sticks, sludge, and plant debris, all covered in shading palms. These are called *fís*, meaning "stick," by the Mvae, or *sàmà* by the Ntumu—a reference to the most regularly caught fish species. Occupying a 10- to 20-square-meter area, fish are attracted to these weir sites while traveling upstream in search of spawning areas.[24]

The Ntumu have developed an additional fence-fishing technology, referred to as *ndzíp* and *ndzíp nkɔ́t*. This system incorporates a watertight fence made of a solid wood frame, clay-soil aquatic vegetation, and heavy pebbles, with openings for woven basket traps to access the catch. Installed in the evenings, *ndzíp* are used at the beginning of the rainy season, when fish travel upstream, and are kept until the low-flood periods of the dry season, when the fish have finished spawning.[25]

The traditional practice of *ngúmā* fishing is carried out along waterways that are carefully identified by Baka communities. Women in particular play a crucial role in controlling the hydrography of each locality where weir fishing is practiced.[26] The *ngúmā* fishing technique, which is practiced during low water periods, involves the construction of one principal weir along an upstream portion of a river, with smaller weirs constructed further downstream near shallow dips in the riverbed where water collects.[27] Once the *myɛk* (weirs) are complete, Baka fishers drain pools by bailing out the water.[28] Women and children are the main actors in this fishing expedition; each dam-and-bail period, requiring up to 10 women, lasts anywhere between 45 minutes to an hour.[29]

6 While walking through the forest, women collect different plants, bark, and fruits.

6

Weirs Are Predominately Built during the Major Dry Season

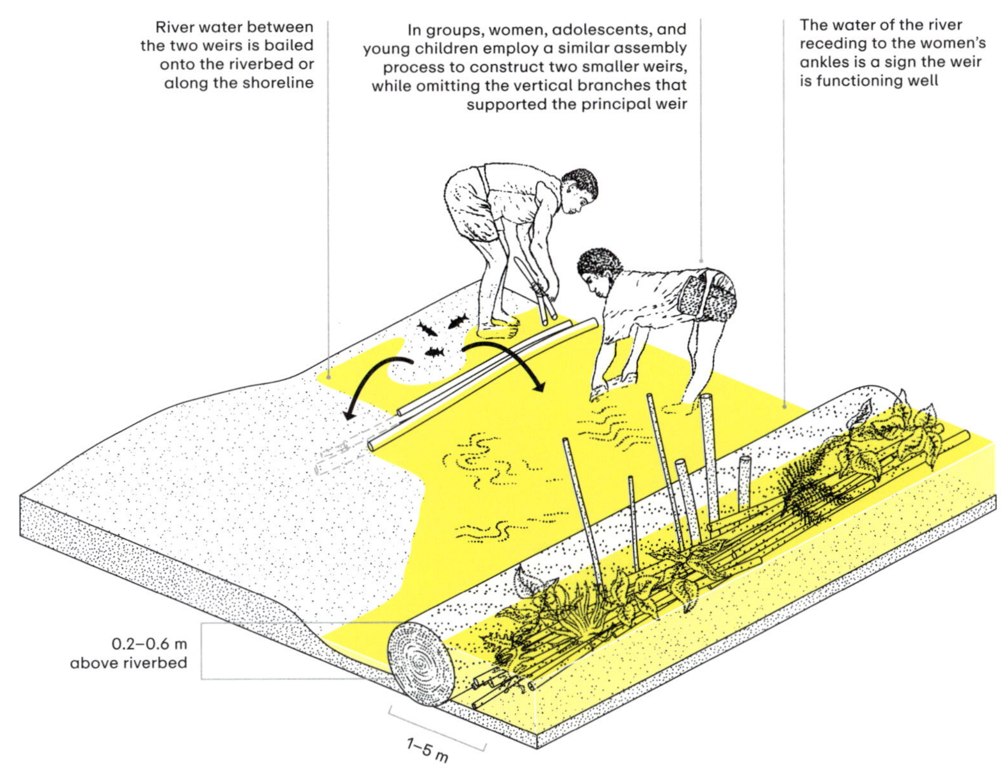

Ngúmā is a social activity that's full of energy, with women's and children's songs usually accompanying the physically demanding tasks required to fish and build.[30] On the day of the excursion, a mixed-age group ventures to a main river located near their campsite.[31] In the morning, the women form a line and head to the stream together, each with their own purpose: to provide for their families or to secure provisions for the days ahead. Before starting their work, they light a large *moutali* fire. Some gather dead wood, others collect leaves, and some start building a weir using branches, tree trunks, and mud to seal the water. Some search for fish, shrimp, and crabs in the cavities, cooking them in leaves over the fire for breakfast, gaining energy for the day. The oldest woman then announces the start of fishing, during which she invites the presence of ancestors for the fishing excursion.[32]

Nyi-ngúmā (the principal weir) is constructed at a location upstream, often where the river forks in multiple directions. Damming one of these tributaries allows water to enter the other side of the fork, preventing the weir from toppling too suddenly as the river's force is directed to the split stream. This approach also ensures the flow of the rivers are never permanently obstructed by human intervention.[33] The weirs span one to five meters in length, and range in height from 20 to 60 centimeters from the riverbed, depending on the size

7

8

9

7 *Ngúmā* is a social activity that's full of energy, with women's and children's songs usually accompanying the physically demanding tasks.
8 Women, adolescents, and young children bail water using pots alongside the fishers, who also remove water using the broad leaf of the Marantaceae plant.
9 The weirs span one to five meters in length, and range in height from 20 to 60 centimeters from the riverbed, depending on the size of the river.

of the river.[34] The structure of this principal weir consists of dead and fresh tree trunks that the women and children have gathered.[35] A few stakes called *zùm* are inserted vertically for stability, while smaller branches and *mvwín* (herbaceous leaves) are then stacked and interspersed throughout the system.[36] Finally, an assembly line is formed to transport sludge from the riverbed and its *mapolo* (embankment). Large pots filled with sludge are passed from person to person and applied to the structure, rendering the weir watertight.[37]

Once the principal weir is stable, multigenerational groups consisting of two to six people relocate to other downstream spots called éliba. Here, they construct *ngá aɲo* (secondary weirs) to form successive pools in the river.[38, 39] Soon, river water begins to recede around the women's ankles—a sign that the principal weir is a success. New weirs are then constructed along the riverbed where water is pooled, with further bailing to follow. In groups, women, adolescents, and young children use a similar method of construction to build two smaller weirs, but without the vertical branches that support the principal weir. Water is bailed between the two weirs using pots alongside the fishers, who also remove water using the broad leaf of the Marantaceae plant (*Megaphrynium macrostachyum*). When the pocket of the river between the two weirs is dry, the fish and shellfish that remain on the riverbed are either gathered by hand or captured using a machete.[40] The most frequently collected species are *ndéngē* (*Brycinus kingsleyae*), káànjì or shrimp, *ngbáàkà* or panchax (*Haplochilus sexfasciatus*), *ntia* or catfish (*Siluridae*), and *mbɔ̀sɛ̀* (*Momyrus macrodon*).[41] Baka women also capture reptile species such as pygmy crocodiles, turtles, and aquatic snakes.[42] During the weir fishing period, larger species of fish hide among small gaps in the riverbank, as well as behind rocks and branches.[43] Digging new banks in the riverbed serves an ecological function, as these cavities eventually host new nests for the next generation of fish and mollusks, which will be captured during the subsequent fishing season.[44]

Collection of fish requires weir deconstruction through the removal of the branches and trunks to locate fish buried in cavities referred to as *bìbàn*. This is a risky process, as a hand can easily be met by a venomous aquatic cobra, the sting of an electric catfish, the bite of an otter shrew, or the jaws of a dwarf crocodile. Among Baka women, this practice is considered to be a source of energy and courage.[45] After an exhaustive search, the group will head downstream to a different spot and repeat the hunt.

Constructing the weir, bailing water, and gathering fish are roles that are evenly shared among the group. The adults perform the more physically challenging acts of bailing, while younger children gather fish, staying in close range and

Between the *Nyi-ngumā* (principal weir) and the *Ngá aɲo* (secondary weirs) Successive Pools of Water Form

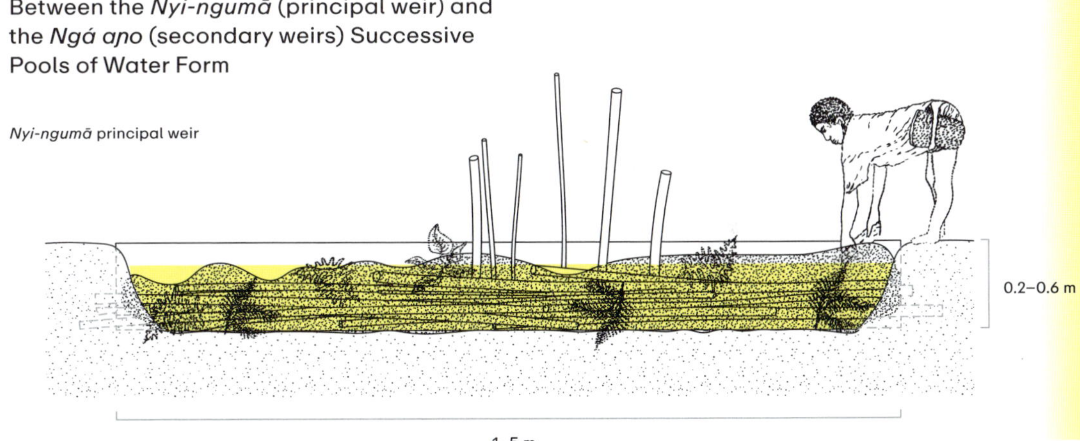

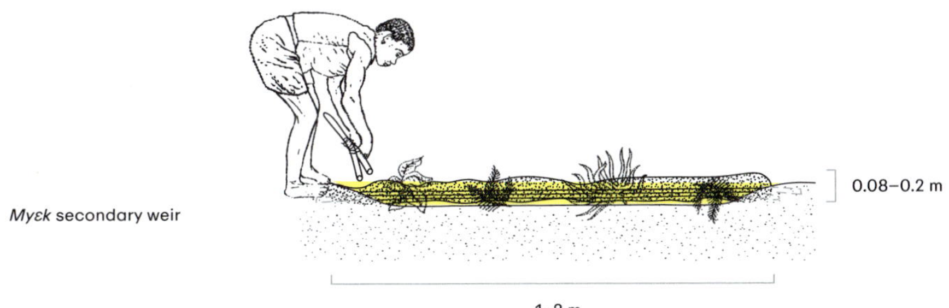

learning by mimicking in smaller streams.[46] Once the upstream water overpowers and topples the principal weir, the water level returns signaling the end of the fishing expedition.[47] Fish from each yield are divided evenly by size and distributed across households—a sharing process known as àkàp.[48] Even when weir fishing is performed solitarily, a single person can achieve a catch sizable enough to feed her family.[49] Not all fishing expeditions are successful; if this is the case, Baka women collect worms from decomposing bamboo found alongside previous weirs. Depending on the season, mushrooms are also foraged along the riverbed.[50]

Smaller and shorter expeditions led by adolescents can last between one and four hours; in these scenarios, they construct a single upstream dam-and-bail system in a shallower riverbed.[51, 52] Older children cut down branches from surrounding trees using a machete, while younger children bring the branches and loosened dirt for the construction.[53] These expeditions are performed in groups, ranging from four to eight children.[54] After the weir is made, the group breaks into smaller units that forage along the riverbank overturning rocks to capture fish, shrimp, or crabs. The older children bail water while the younger wait with collection baskets.[55] After they have finished gathering, they regroup to descale the fish.

Though both women and men participate in weir fishing, women bring in nearly double the catch, as men participate mainly in hunting.[56] Baka women achieve a higher yield per fishing expedition in the major rainy season; however,

10

10 The children's expeditions are performed in groups of four to eight children.
11 Small expeditions can be led by children, who construct a single dam-and-bail system in a shallow riverbed.
12 Fish are carefully selected, and only collected if their age and size are suitable, while the remaining fish are released back into the river.

11

12

Baka men achieve a higher overall yield of fish in the major dry season, when the fish are at their fattest. Low water levels during the dry season make it so that it's much less strenuous to bail the water. The one season that the Baka fish with the least regularity is the minor rainy season, as it interferes with the fish reproduction cycle.[57]

The location scouting of the weirs shows the symbiosis between the Baka and the forest and rivers they steward. Constructed through natural, local, biodegradable materials, these systems do not rely on exploiting or transporting building materials, making them energy efficient and producing little to no waste. By operating as a temporary weir, this technology is also designed for a specific season and its tidal fluctuations, avoiding overexploitation and reducing disturbance to the river's natural course. Fish are carefully selected, and only collected if their age and size are suitable, while the remaining fish are released back into the river. Catches are always practiced at a small scale, with Baka women and children only gathering enough to serve the needs of a family or clan.[58]

The bounty from fishing trips represents more than just a source of sustenance; it embodies essential values that underpin life in the forest. Concepts such as sharing, solidarity, coexistence, intergenerational harmony, and teamwork are vividly demonstrated through this activity. The practice of *ngúmā*, regardless of the season, serves as a cornerstone, ensuring the continuation of forest peoples' cultural heritage. Fishing catches are particularly significant during initiation rites like Edjengui, Béka, and Yéyi, symbolizing women's vital contribution to these ceremonies. It is also during these rites that knowledge is profoundly shared within the group. The younger members especially benefit from this occasion, learning the names of plants, leaves, fish species, and even the hydrography of the group's surroundings.[59]

The forest expeditions that have characterized the nomadic traditions of the Baka have slowly decreased in frequency and area in recent years. Following a colonial policy for sedentary settlement, Baka communities began semipermanent villages and increased agricultural practices as a means of sustenance.[60] Relatedly, Bantu ethnic groups now live alongside the Baka in permanent agricultural settlements centered around the Dja, Boumba, and Bek Rivers of southeastern Cameroon, connected by two main roads that were constructed for logging operations.[61] In the 1960s, the area covered by Baka fishing expeditions could reach over three thousand kilometers, but, by the onset of the 21st century, the area covered became gradually more localized, covering one thousand square kilometers to the southeast of the permanent settlements.[62] Twenty four percent of the TRIDOM Landscape, accounting for 35,968 square kilometers, has become protected, including through the establishment of Odzala-Kokoua National Park, Minkébé National Park, Ivindo National Park, Mwagna National Park, Boumba Bek National Park, Nki National Park, and the Dja and Ngoyla Faunal Reserves.[63]

Though many Baka women still cherish the tradition of *ngúmā* today, their practice is increasingly disrupted by climate change—particularly the erratic water levels crucial for this activity. The changing seasons have led to early rains, forcing women to leave the forest prematurely and destroying their weirs, resulting in sudden floods. These unpredictable conditions hinder certain populations, leading to scarcity and imbalances in aquatic resource distribution.[64]

New extractive activities such as logging, mining, bushmeat trade, and the establishment of national parks have greatly reduced the area that the Baka can access—as well as the species they can access, the species richness of the region, and the land's natural resources.[65] The seasonal needs of the Baka's own

13 Women in particular play a crucial role in controlling the hydrography of each locality where weir fishing is practiced.

13

agricultural lands conflict with the *molongo*, as the dry seasons are crucial for wild-plant gathering and for tending crops.[66]

As for the future of the system, though dam-and-bail fishing is not regarded as the main source of food for the Baka people, the disappearance of large game may contribute to its increasing popularity in coming decades. Fishing has also become a source of revenue for some, rather than a traditional sustenance-oriented *ngúmā* practice.[67] Increasingly, dwindling territory and economically rooted extractive demands are threatening the Baka community and the ecosystems they steward, emphasizing the need to recognize and protect the Baka people's roles as forest stewards.

Ngúmā weir fishing is an innovative practice, defined by subsistence fishing and damming without destruction of the ecosystem. Against the backdrop of clean-energy dam projects, which cause irreparable destruction to both communities and ecosystems, the Baka have evolved a system exemplary of sustainable thinking—adaptable, seasonal, deconstructable, and transient. Developed by the Baka and other forest communities in Central Africa, this type of technology could redefine how damming is practiced. As temporarily constructed systems, they avoid the permanent alteration of natural environments. *Ngúmā* systems reflect a conscientious way of sourcing food for sustenance and materials for construction that avoids exploitation. This system can be seen as an extension of the Baka people's deep relationship to the forests they inhabit. Informed by the riverine water fluctuations, *ngúmā* and other similar weir fishing technologies can be exemplary of how hydropower should perform, inspiring innovation for hybridized hydro-based energy systems.

1. Belmond Tchoumba and John Nelson, *Protecting and Encouraging Customary Use of Biological Resources by the Baka in the West of the Dja Biosphere Reserve: Contribution to the Implementation of Article 10(c) of the Convention on Biological Diversity* (n.p.: Forest Peoples Programme, 2006), 13.
2. Sandrine Gallois and Romain Duda, "Beyond Productivity: The Socio-Cultural Role of Fishing among the Baka of Southeastern Cameroon," *Revue d'Ethnoécologie*, no. 10 (2016): 13.
3. Gallois and Duda, "Beyond Productivity," 13.
4. Didier Devers et al., "Dja-Odzala-Minkébé (Tridom) Landscape," in *The Forests of the Congo Basin: State of the Forest 2006*, ed. Observatory for the Forests of Central Africa and Congo Basin Forest Partnership (n.p.: Central African Regional Program for the Environment, 2006), 148.
5. Jesús Olivero et al., "Distribution and Numbers of Pygmies in Central African Forests," *PLoS ONE* 11, no. 1 (2016): 3, https://doi.org/10.1371/journal.pone.0144499.
6. Hirokazu Yasuoka, "Long-Term Foraging Expeditions (Molongo) among the Bake Hunter-Gatherers in the Northwestern Congo Basin, with Special Reference to the 'Wild Yam Question,'" Human Ecology 34 (2006): 277.
7. Tchoumba and Nelson, *Protecting and Encouraging Customary Use*, 13.
8. Tchoumba and Nelson, *Protecting and Encouraging Customary Use*, 13.
9. Tchoumba and Nelson, *Protecting and Encouraging Customary Use*, 17.
10. Yasuoka, "Long-Term Foraging Expeditions," 277.
11. Venant Messe (coordinator of OKANI), in discussion with the author, October 2023.
12. Yasuoka, "Long-Term Foraging Expeditions," 279.
13. Shiho Hattori, "Current Issues Facing the Forest People in Southeastern Cameroon: The Dynamics of Baka Life and Their Ethnic Relationship with Farmers," *African Study Monographs* 47 (2014): 105–6.
14. Gallois and Duda, "Beyond Productivity," 3.
15. Yasuoka, "Long-Term Foraging Expeditions," 277.
16. Yasuoka, "Long-Term Foraging Expeditions," 281.
17. Yasuoka, "Long-Term Foraging Expeditions," 282.
18. Gallois and Duda, "Beyond Productivity," 6–9.
19. Jean Betti, "An Ethnobotanical and Floristical Study of Medicinal Plants among the Baka Pygmies in the Periphery of the IPASSA-Biosphere Reserve, Gabon," *European Journal of Medicinal Plants* 3, no. 2, (2013): 2.
20. Edmond Dounias et al., "The Safety Net Role of Inland Fishing in the Subsistence Strategy of Multi-Active Forest Dwellers in Southern Cameroon," *Revue d'Ethnoécologie*, no. 10 (2016): 14.
21. Dounias et al., "The Safety Net Role of Inland Fishing," 14.
22. Dounias et al., "The Safety Net Role of Inland Fishing," 18.
23. Dounias et al., "The Safety Net Role of Inland Fishing," 20.
24. Dounias et al., "The Safety Net Role of Inland Fishing," 15.
25. Dounias et al., "The Safety Net Role of Inland Fishing," 18.
26. Messe, discussion.
27. Gallois and Duda, "Beyond Productivity," 13–15.
28. Dounias et al., "The Safety Net Role of Inland Fishing," 14.
29. Gallois and Duda, "Beyond Productivity," 15.
30. Tchoumba and Nelson, *Protecting and Encouraging Customary Use*, 22.
31. Gallois and Duda, "Beyond Productivity," 13.
32. Messe, discussion.
33. Dounias et al., "The Safety Net Role of Inland Fishing," 14.
34. Izumi Hagino and Taro Yamauchi, "High Motivation and Low Gain: Food Procurement from Rainforest Foraging by Baka Hunter-Gatherer Children," in *Social Learning and Innovation in Contemporary Hunter-Gatherers*, ed. H. Terashima and B. S. Hewlett (Tokyo: Springer, 2016), 141.
35. Messe, discussion.
36. Dounias et al., "The Safety Net Role of Inland Fishing," 14.
37. Dounias et al., "The Safety Net Role of Inland Fishing," 18.
38. Gallois and Duda, "Beyond Productivity," 15.
39. Dounias et al., "The Safety Net Role of Inland Fishing," 14.
40. Gallois and Duda, "Beyond Productivity," 15.
41. Gallois and Duda, "Beyond Productivity," 9.
42. Messe, discussion.
43. Gallois and Duda, "Beyond Productivity," 15.
44. Messe, discussion.
45. Dounias et al., "The Safety Net Role of Inland Fishing," 14.
46. Gallois and Duda, "Beyond Productivity," 17.
47. Hagino and Yamauchi, "High Motivation and Low Gain," 141.
48. Dounias et al., "The Safety Net Role of Inland Fishing," 15.
49. Hiroaki Sato, "Foraging Lifestyle in the African Tropical Rainforest," in *Hunter-Gatherers of the Congo Basin: Cultures, Histories, and Biology of African Pygmies*, ed. Barry S. Hewlett (New Brunswick, NJ: Routledge, 2014), 178.
50. Messe, discussion.
51. Hagino and Yamauchi, "High Motivation and Low Gain," 138.
52. Hagino and Yamauchi, "High Motivation and Low Gain," 140–41.
53. Hagino and Yamauchi, "High Motivation and Low Gain," 141.
54. Hagino and Yamauchi, "High Motivation and Low Gain," 140.
55. Hagino and Yamauchi, "High Motivation and Low Gain," 141.
56. Gallois and Duda, "Beyond Productivity," 7–8.
57. Gallois and Duda, "Beyond Productivity," 6.
58. Tchoumba and Nelson, *Protecting and Encouraging Customary Use*, 22.
59. Messe, discussion.
60. Tchoumba and Nelson, *Protecting and Encouraging Customary Use*, 13.
61. Yasuoka, "Long-Term Foraging Expeditions," 278.
62. Yasuoka, "Long-Term Foraging Expeditions," 290.
63. Devers et al., "Dja-Odzala-Minkébé (Tridom) Landscape," 148.
64. Messe, discussion.
65. Gallois and Duda, "Beyond Productivity," 2.
66. Yasuoka, "Long-Term Foraging Expeditions," 292.
67. Tchoumba and Nelson, *Protecting and Encouraging Customary Use*, 22.

COAUTHOR

VENANT MESSE

Coordinator of the OKANI Association

Venant Messe is a prominent Baka community activist and the coordinator of the OKANI Association, a Baka-run advocacy group working to secure the rights and promote sustainable livelihoods of Indigenous communities in Cameroon's forests. ince 1992, he has played a pivotal role in the OKANI ssociation's efforts, collaborating closely with their ollective bodies known as the Council of Elders.

Messe was born in the forest near the village f Andom in eastern Cameroon. Growing up, hunt- ng, fishing, and subsistence farming were his fami- 's only sources of income. His family settled so that e and his siblings could attend primary school n the town of Minkolong. Messe eventually moved Bertoua, the region's capital city, to pursue his sec- ndary education at the Lycée Classique de Bertoua. fter graduating, Messe enrolled in the Pan-African nstitute for Central African Development in Douala continue his studies, aspiring to build a career dvocating for Baka rights. After graduating, e started the OKANI Association in collaboration ith young Baka community members. Their goal to promote and protect the rights of Indigenous rest peoples like the Baka. This includes ensuring neir right to citizenship, education, and improved ving conditions. It also involves addressing the hallenges faced by nomadic populations transition- ng to settled life and ensuring fair access to resources. hrough OKANI, Messe advocates for these rights ith a unified voice, engaging with local and national uthorities daily.

In his free time, Messe enjoys spending time ith his family. He is an avid reader—a pastime that e says allows him to connect to the spirits of his gen- ration, near and far.

JOSEPH JOHNSON BIBI

President of the Association Sanguia Baka Buma'a Kpodé

Joseph Johnson Bibi, born in 1992 in Yenga Tengue, is the president of the Association Sanguia Baka Buma'a Kpodé (ASBABUK) in Cameroon—a community-led coalition defending the rights of the Indigenous Baka peoples. Bibi's childhood was spent learning traditional activities with his family like fishing, gathering, hunting, and some agriculture. His primary school education, then French secondary school in Moloundou, were followed by diploma studies in Bertoua, the eastern capital of Cameroon, and the training school for *Agents Technique Medico Sanitaire*. His early career in healthcare included advanced training and work as a laboratory staff member at the Catholic health center in Moloundou. Due to age restrictions preventing him from taking the civil service entrance examination, he returned to his village to care for his family.

Since returning, Bibi has assumed the role of the second president of ASBABUK. In 2023, he played a pivotal role in securing an updated memorandum of understanding between the government of Cameroon and Baka communities in the country's southeast, which represented a significant milestone in the acknowledgment of Indigenous rights to forest resources. Expanding on a 2019 agreement granting Baka communities access to the Lobéké and Boumba Bek National Parks, the new deal offers access to the Nki National Park and the Ngoyla Faunal Reserve—crucial for maintaining traditional hunter-gatherer activities.

While Bibi is deeply passionate about defending Indigenous rights and securing funding for his community's education and health care needs, he is also a father of two children who still spends time doing traditional forest activities.

BAIRA FLOATING ISLANDS *of* THE BHUMIHIN KRISHOK

Bangladesh

BAIRA FLOATING ISLANDS *of* THE BHUMIHIN KRISHOK
Bangladesh

Coauthored by
Mohammed Rezwan

PEOPLE Bhumihin Krishok of Southern Bangladesh
LOCATION southern wetlands, Bangladesh
TECHNOLOGY floating vegetable gardens
ELEVATION 0 m ORIGIN 1600–1700s
DISTANCE ABOVE OR BELOW WATERLINE −0.5 to +0.5 m
WATER LEVEL FLUCTUATION, TIDAL OR SEASONAL +1 to +6 m

FAO Nexus
WATER fresh ENERGY bioenergy + cleansing
FOOD crops

IPCC Adaptation Pathway
accommodate

World Bank NBS
CATEGORY bioretention areas, constructed inland wetlands, natural inland wetlands, urban farming, river and stream renaturation
FUNCTIONS biodiversity, water pollution regulation, pluvial flood regulation, heat regulation, air pollution regulation, sea level rise adaptation, coastal flood regulation, riverine flood regulation
BENEFITS resource production, biodiversity, riverine flood risk reduction, pluvial flood risk reduction, carbon storage and sequestration, cultural, social interaction, stimulate local economies and job creation

1

Thousands of floating vegetable gardens sprawl across the low-lying alluvial plains of Nazirpur, Bangladesh. Birds like *bok* (great egrets) and *machranga* (kingfishers) fly close to the vast water surface.[1] From the top, these green islands look like the traditional Bengali quilt design known as *nakshi kantha*.[2] Nearly four hundred years ago, *bhumihin krishok* (landless farmers) developed this ingenious approach to subsistence agriculture, enabling a year-round cultivation of crops in a country where two-thirds of the territory is prone to flooding.[3, 4] This practice—referred to as *dhap* or *baira* farming depending on the region—uses floating beds of *kochuripana* (water hyacinth) secured to bamboo to form buoyant landlike surfaces. *Baira* farmers grow 41 varieties of vegetables and spices across 2,500 hectares of floating earth, in a landscape that is underwater for

ALLUVIAL A characteristic of fertile floodplains, riverbeds, or deltas caused by sediment deposits carried by flowing water.

2

1 A typical *baira* is usually two meters wide, with a length that can range from six to 55 meters.
2 Due to long-term waterlogging, farmland has historically been scarce, leading to the development of *dhap* or *baira* farming.

almost eight months of the year.[5] Found throughout the Pirojpur, Barisal, and Gopalganj regions of Bangladesh, which are increasingly inundated with flooding by monsoons, *baira* floating islands offer a viable, climate-adaptive agricultural solution amid a lack of arable dry land.

Historically, farmland has been scarce in Nazirpur, a subdistrict of Pirojpur, due to long-term waterlogging—a by-product of melting snow from the Himalayas and yearly monsoons, which flood the rivers and canals surrounding the district's nearly 230 square kilometers.[6] Vast swaths of low-lying land remain submerged in water, rendering conventional agriculture impossible. Despite difficulties tending to Nazirpur's existing soil, the main source of income for over 70 percent of its population is agriculture.[7] This can in part be attributed to floating garden innovations that have supported local communities for centuries.

Locals in Pirojpur traditionally referred to floating beds as *dhap*; the practice has spread to the neighboring southern communities of Barisal and Gopalganj, where the term *baira* was adopted instead. In Bengali, *dhap* refers to the unit of measurement covered by a step, while the word *baira* means "outside." These words are used synonymously to describe each floating bed.[8]

Today, this floating garden technology exists across the lowest riparian region of the Ganges-Brahmaputra-Meghna Basin, known as the Barisal Region locally. *Baira* farming is most suitable in coastal areas adjacent to sea banks that remain submerged for long periods of time—specifically, large bodies of still water, like *beels* (wetlands), *khaals* (canals), and *nodi* (rivers)

BEEL
A shallow, natural wetland serving as a vital habitat for aquatic flora and fauna and often used for fishing and agriculture.

3

3 Farmers harvesting with a canoe in a traditional floating vegetable garden in Banaripara.

4

5

in Bengal.[9] These are optimal sites for *baira* cultivation as they lack strong currents; floating beds cannot withstand waves and tides. Floating islands are also at risk of disintegrating if there is heavy rain.[10] *Baira* farming is suitable in areas not affected by frequent flooding, as repeated flooding can reduce the rate of water hyacinth growth, leaving landless farmers with little material to construct their rafts.[11, 12, 13, 14]

Baira have been instrumental in providing food security and self-reliance among landless farmers—one-fourth of the farmers are landless or lease other people's land for cultivation—and spurring the creation of floating markets across the river basin.[15, 16, 17] Today, *baira* are grown for domestic and commercial needs; farmer households often profit from a surplus after each crop cycle.[18] Every Tuesday and Saturday, farmers from 25 villages around Pirojpur travel along the Belua River by boat to the floating market in Baithakata, which opens at sunrise and closes by noon.[19] Wholesale buyers visit Baithakata and other

4 *Aus*, *amon*, *boro*, water hyacinth, and other invasive aquatic plants were introduced into *baira* construction, traditionally made from coconut husks, in the mid-20th century.

5 Over 2,500 hectares of inundated land are cultivated with 41 varieties of floating fruits, vegetables, and spices.

6 Farmer Mohammad Selim hangs a gourd with rope to a floating bed's ceiling, at his farm in Pirojpur.

6

floating markets to purchase the vegetables, seedlings, and aquatic plants grown on *baira*, reselling products to a network of growers and suppliers.

Baira cultivation is an ancestral practice that has been revived in response to severe flooding caused by climate change. As the sea level rises, saltwater intrusion makes coastal land unsuitable for growing crops and slows the flow of the river.[20, 21] These decomposing artificial islands, resilient to salt water and fluctuations in water level, are reconstructed as floating vegetable gardens that rise and fall with the swelling waters.[22] *Baira* were traditionally made from locally available resources like coconut husks and *aus*, *amon*, and *boro* (traditional paddy stub varieties that produce long straw); however, water hyacinth (*Eichhornia crassipes*) and other invasive aquatic plants were introduced into their construction in the mid-20th century.[23]

Introduced to Bengal in the late 19th century, water hyacinth, an aquatic plant native to South America, had reached all the region's bodies of water by the 1920s. This fast-growing species quickly obstructed river navigation and farmers' ability to cultivate crops in the wetlands. Continuous crop failure is considered to have contributed to the great Bengal famine, which led to the deaths of about three million people.[24] Before the monsoon, water hyacinth from upstream would wash down to the low-lying flooded lands in Nazirpur, leaving limited space for the landless farmers to build floating *dhap* or *baira* beds, traditionally made from coconut husks and paddy straw. Farmers had no other option but to reuse the artificial surface to grow vegetables; thus, they included water hyacinth in their island construction.[25]

Characteristics like size, shape, construction materials, and crop selection vary by region; however, nearly all farmers use water hyacinth to form the basis of *baira* due to the unique composition of the plant.[26] Today, the water hyacinth has

7

7 Farmers selling their *baira*-grown produce at a floating market.

invaded the warm, slow-flowing, and stagnant waterways across Bangladesh, where it grows into thick buoyant mats, making one plant indistinguishable from another. The buoyancy of *baira* can be attributed to air pockets in the tissue of these aquatic plant species, combined with the gasses produced by decaying layers of vegetation and peat. The base of a *baira* makes use of the large air pockets found in the bulbous swelling of the aerenchyma tissue of the petiole—the area of the plant that connects the leaf to the stem—allowing it to float. Though water hyacinth is considered

8

9

8 A guava farmer collecting from his garden to sell in a local retail market in Adamkathi, Pirojpur—a district famous for guava cultivation and a renowned Floating Guava Market during monsoon season.
9 The aquatic environment reduces vulnerability to pests and the risk of soil-borne disease, with minimal weeding required.

10

10. A man holds a rope as people transport floating beds toward a farm on Belua River.

an invasive species, it has been embraced as a valuable resource, enabling the traditional *baira* farming technique to flourish once again in recent decades.[27]

Both men and women take part in the construction of *baira* in May or July; in some areas, they start the preparation in September, depending on the type of vegetables to be grown. However, it entirely depends on the availability and maturity of water hyacinth, which takes 60 days to mature and become suitable for the creation of floating beds.[28, 29] To form an island, a farmer will stand atop a naturally occurring mat of hyacinth, while pulling in, weaving, and compressing surrounding plant matter to form a mat. Aquatic species like *durali* (watergrass, *Hygroryza aristata*), *topapana* (water lettuce, *Pistia stratiotes*), *khudipana* (duckweed, *Lemna minor*), and *kanta shaola* (water thyme, *Hydrilla verticillata*) are also woven into the mass of floating vegetation.[30]

Bamboo is then laid lengthwise across this layer of hyacinth to provide the structural reinforcement for the mat. The process of layering hyacinth is repeated until an island is formed into a desired size and shape—usually one to two meters above water level. A typical *baira* is six meters long, though a bed can reach 55 meters depending on the body of water it inhabits and the needs of the farmer.[31] However, the width of a bed is typically a standard one and a half to two meters, restricted by the length of a farmer's reach for planting, weeding, and harvesting.[32] Once built, farmers will anchor the island to its desired location using vertical bamboo poles, connecting the center of the *baira* to the lake bed below. This way, many *baira* are joined to form small island-shaped floating vegetable fields.[33] Each floating island is separated by increments of three meters—enough space for a farmer to navigate the water between the beds in a canoe. In the final stage of construction prior to crop cultivation, farmers will let islands decompose for 20 to 35 days, during which time the bed shrinks. Once the layers of hyacinth have degraded into

Constructing and Cultivating a Floating *Baira* Agricultural Island

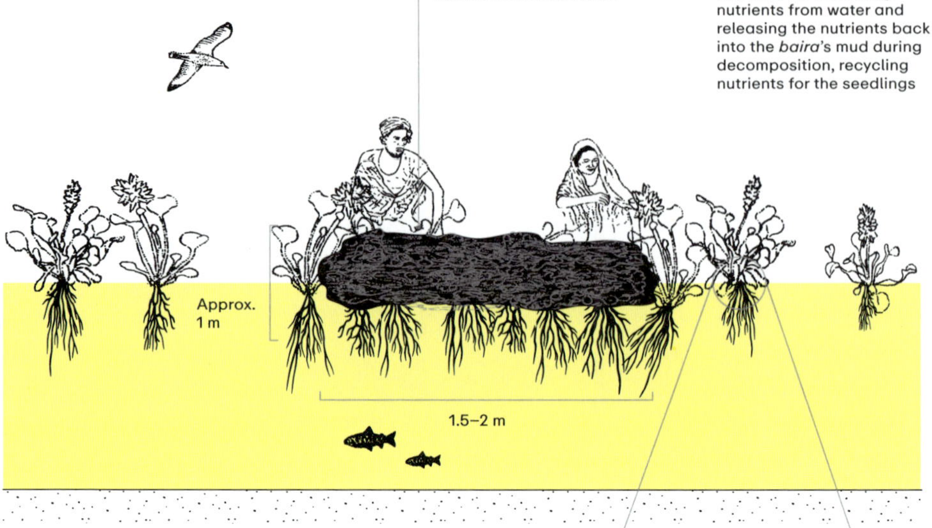

Farmers compress the layers of water hyacinth
Water hyacinth has a high capacity for absorbing nutrients from water and releasing the nutrients back into the *baira*'s mud during decomposition, recycling nutrients for the seedlings
Approx. 1 m
1.5–2 m

1. The first layer of a *baira* is a naturally matted mass of water hyacinth. More water hyacinth is then pulled in from both sides and piled onto the *baira*. The lower layers support buoyancy, while the upper layers become low-density compost.

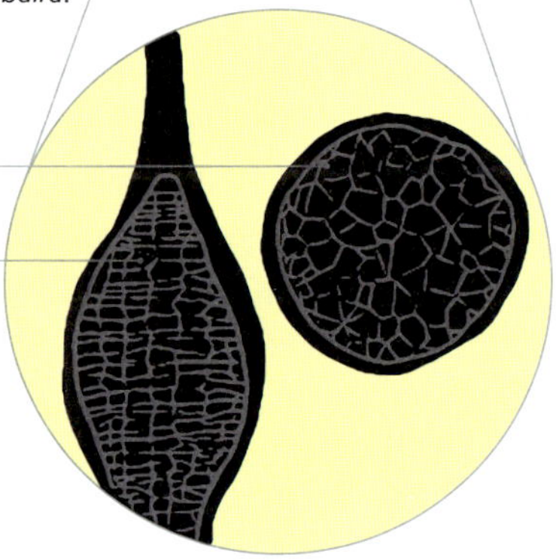

Water hyacinth is buoyant due to its bulbous *petiole* (leaf stem)
Internal spaces within leaves, called *lacunae*, help with flotation and gas exchange

The island gets lighter as it decomposes
Bamboo poles anchor the *baira* in place
Layers of bamboo are added to the structure

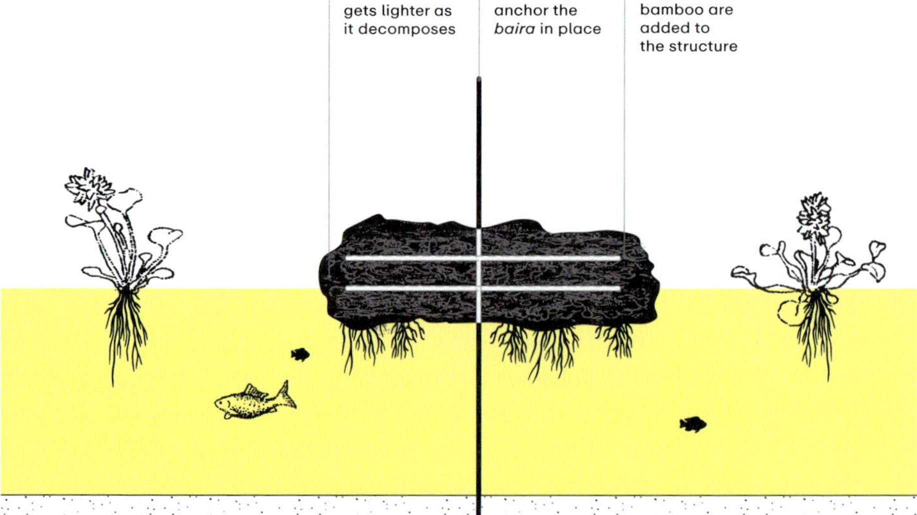

2. The *baira* is left for weeks to decompose, with a bamboo stick anchoring it. During construction, bamboo is placed horizontally within the layers of water hyacinth for structure and to define the shape.

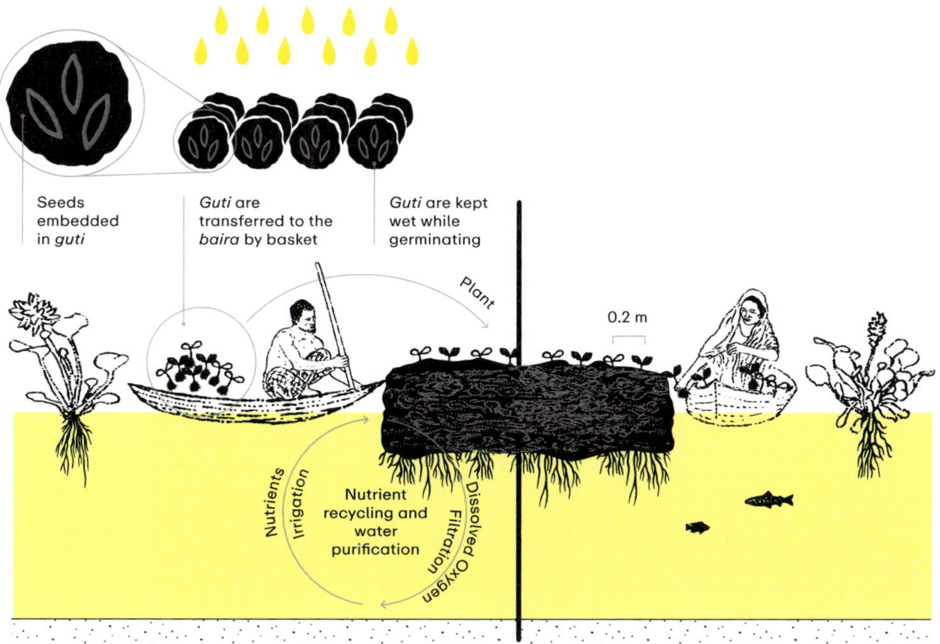

3. *Guti* are made from decomposing water hyacinth and other aquatic plants. They are embedded with seeds and left to germinate. When sprouted, *guti* are planted into the *baira* 20 cm apart.

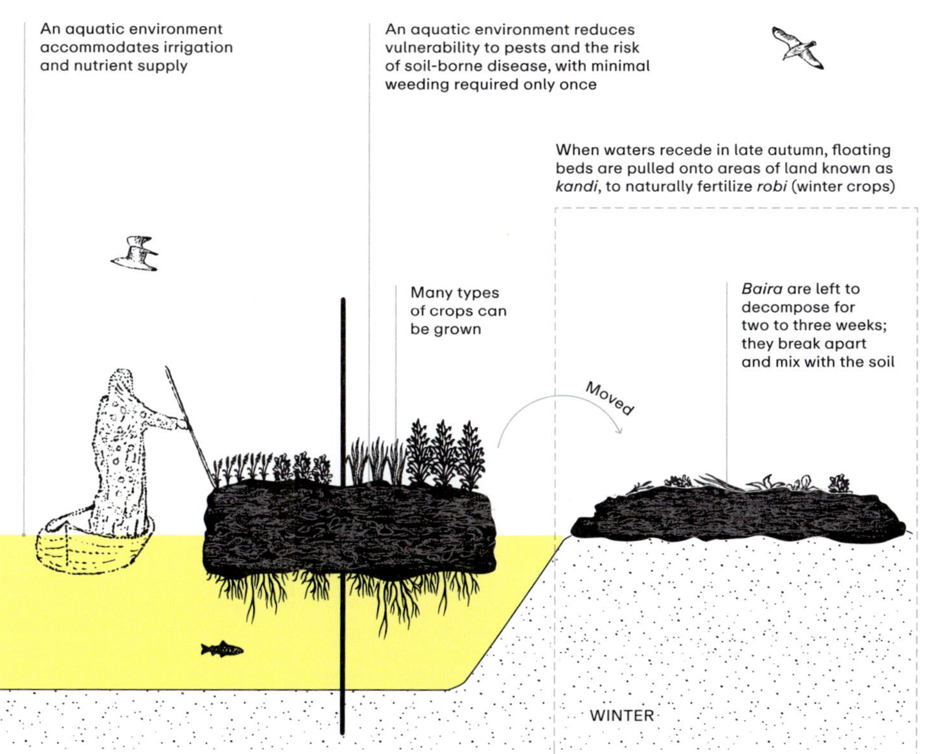

4. Summer vegetables are cultivated, then harvested. In the winter, the *baira* are planted on nearby higher ground, then broken down and used to grow winter vegetables.

a dense soil-like mud, a mixture of more decomposed plant matter, cow manure, and silt is added to the surface of the *baira*, preparing the bed for germinated seeds.

The seeds of some leafy vegetables such as *lal shak* (Chinese amaranth) and *pui shak* (malabar spinach) can be sown directly to the *baira*.[34] However, other seeds are soaked and then germinated in specially prepared palm-sized pods called *guti*, which are encased in peat and decaying aquatic plant matter that promote rapid seed germination.[35] Farmers will add multiple seeds to a pod, accounting for those that might not germinate; however, the exact quantity varies per crop.

11

12

11 Seeds of some leafy vegetables can be sown directly into the *baira*, while other seeds are soaked and then germinated in specially prepared palm-sized pods called *guti*.
12 Murshida Begum and Mohammad Ibrahim load seedling balls onto a boat to be planted on their floating farm in Pirojpur.

13

13 Small balls of seedlings, which are germinated before being installed in floating garden beds.

Guti are initially left in a shed for three to four days, then spread across open ground to allow for germination; once seedlings reach about 12 to 15 centimeters, they are transferred to *baira*. Crops are harvested within 15 to 25 days; it is common for *baira* to undergo two or three crop-rotation cycles during a single monsoon season.[36, 37, 38]

One *baira* may be used for five to eight months. When the water recedes in late autumn, floating beds are pulled from the water to higher ground known as *kandi*, where they are broken apart and left to decompose for several weeks.[39, 40, 41] Once these beds have been dismantled and watered, they are used on land as nutrient-rich gardening beds for *robi* (winter crops).[42, 43] *Robi* include *badhakopi* (cabbage), *barbati* (yard-long bean), and rice crops that are grown from mid-November to April.[44, 45]

Baira farming relies on the fertilizing nutrients, such as nitrogen, potassium, and phosphorus, found abundant in the flora of the floating infestation of water hyacinth flourishing across Bangladesh, removing the need for artificial treatments.[46] While land-based farming encourages fertilizer-heavy agricultural practices, *baira* provides an opportunistic example of chemical-free agriculture amid invasive species infestation.[47] Water hyacinth has a high capacity for nutrient absorption from the water, which is why they grow so quickly. During decomposition, the plants release and recycle those nutrients back into the *baira*'s mud for the new seedlings. As a result, crops grown on *baira* require less time to mature and more crops can be grown in a season. Fortuitously, the aquatic plant species that make up *baira* also assist in the natural cleansing of their surrounding aquatic ecosystem, ridding the water of contaminants, reducing the need for formal wastewater treatment for agricultural and domestic use while minimizing the need for municipal energy consumption.[48]

These agricultural islands also offer miniature paddocks for poultry and the pasturage of cattle during the monsoon season.[49] *Baira* crops are passively irrigated by surrounding bodies of water, employing little to no artificial infrastructure and requiring minimal maintenance; this also makes them less vulnerable to pests and soil-borne diseases.[50] These qualities are a testament to the nonextractive, regenerative potential of floating agriculture beds in Bangladesh's wetland ecosystems. *Baira* can be scaled and constructed from different organic materials, and are capable of adapting to and providing services for a myriad of environments.

14

14 Dulal Miah prepares a new raft, made from decomposed water hyacinth plants and straw, which are woven together to create a buoyant strip for planting.

Stages of *Baira* Decomposition, which Lasts 20 to 30 Days

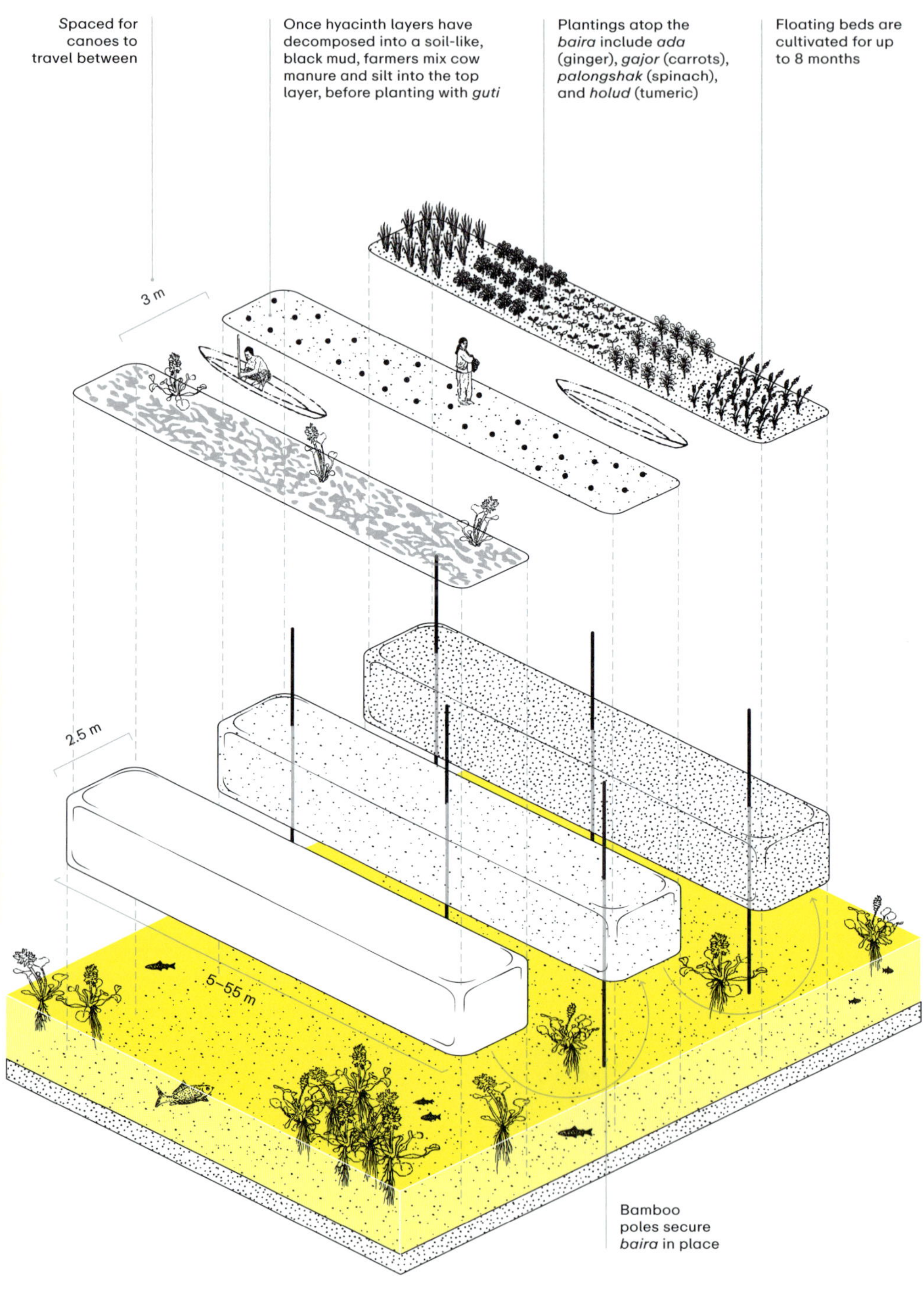

15

15 Farmers grow food for themselve, and sell produce to local markets.

A resurgence of *baira* agriculture since the mid-20th century can be attributed to the integration of buoyant invasive plant species, in addition to increasing support through government-funded initiatives in recent years.[51] The technology has also inspired the testing of these flood-resilient infrastructures in the northeastern wetlands of Bangladesh known as *haors*—swamp-like bowl depressions used to retain water between the levees of rivers—by the International Union for Conservation of Nature and the agency CARE International.[52] Saiful Islam, the director of the Institute of Water and Flood Management, forecasts that even a modest rise in average global temperatures, such as two degrees Celsius above preindustrial levels, will lead to a 24 percent surge in flooding in the Brahmaputra River basin, affecting northeastern India and Bangladesh.[53] If global temperatures were to rise four degrees Celsius, flooding in this region would increase by over 60 percent.[54] Considering their agricultural biodiversity, resilience to inundation, and cultural heritage, Bangladesh's floating gardens were acknowledged by the UN's FAO as a globally important agricultural heritage system in 2015.[55]

In the northern region, a local architect, Mohammed Rezwan, has drawn inspiration from the *baira* to create economic opportunities for landless people through the Farmer's Floating Farming initiative of his organization, Shidhulai Swanirvar Sangstha. Taking the initial concept for the floating farm garden, but in an area with a scarcity of water hyacinth, his floating farms include a duck

16

16 Architect Mohammed Rezwan has drawn inspiration from the *baira* to create infrastructures through the Farmer's Floating Farming initiative.
17 A farmer checks his crops of beans, bitter gourd, papaya, beets, pumpkins, tomatoes, and chilli.

17

coop, fish enclosures, and vegetable gardens moored by rope to the riverbank, accompanied by a small room equipped with solar panels.

Used to grow vegetables from seedlings in the rainy summer months for over four centuries, the *baira* floating agricultural islands are an efficient technology, which has been adapted to make use of the invasive water hyacinth to sustain cultivation in a water-prone environment, while supporting the health of the ecosystem through its cleansing and fertilizing properties.[56] Existing as an agricultural platform during monsoon season, which is then repurposed as fertilizer for the cultivation of winter crops, the *baira* operates through a circular system of reuse while providing a source of food and income for vulnerable populations that live in these flood-prone areas. Within and beyond Bangladesh, particularly in monsoon or flood-prone regions, the *baira* technology represents an opportunity for innovative cultivation that is fertile, financially viable, resilient, and constructed through locally abundant materials. This architecture encourages a reunderstanding of how nature-based resources can simultaneously solve problems of pollution, food security, flooding, habitat loss, and much more.

18

19

18–19 Taking the initial concept for the floating farm garden, but in an area with a scarcity of water hyacinth, Rezwan's floating farms include a duck coop, fish enclosures, and vegetable gardens moored by rope to the riverbank.

1. Mohammed Rezwan (executive director, Shidhulai Swanirvar Sangstha) in discussion with the author, March 2024.
2. Rezwan, discussion.
3. Kalpana Sunder, "The Remarkable Floating Gardens of Bangladesh," BBC, September 10, 2020, https://www.bbc.com/future/article/20200910-the-remarkable-floating-gardens-of-bangladesh.
4. "বাংলাদশেরে অসাধারণ ভাসমান সবজি বাগান," The Business Standard, September 15, 2020, https://shorturl.at/qJKZ5.
5. Sunder, "The Remarkable Floating Gardens of Bangladesh."
6. Banglapedia: National Encyclopedia of Bangladesh, s.v. "Nazirpur Upazila," accessed February 9, 2024, https://en.banglapedia.org/index.php/Nazirpur_Upazila.
7. Banglapedia: National Encyclopedia of Bangladesh, s.v. "Nazirpur Upazila."
8. "বাংলাদশেরে অসাধারণ ভাসমান সবজি বাগান."
9. Rezwan, discussion.
10. Rezwan, discussion.
11. Ministry of Agriculture, People's Republic of Bangladesh, Floating Garden Agricultural Practices in Bangladesh: A Proposal for Globally Important Agricultural Heritage Systems (GIAHS) (Rome: FAO, 2017), https://www.fao.org/3/bp777e/bp777e.pdf.
12. Sunder, "The Remarkable Floating Gardens of Bangladesh."
13. Archana Yadav, "Resort to Heritage," Down to Earth, April 15, 2016, https://www.downtoearth.org.in/news/agriculture/resort-to-heritage-53346.
14. "বাংলাদশেরে অসাধারণ ভাসমান সবজি বাগান."
15. Rezwan, discussion.
16. Sunder, "The Remarkable Floating Gardens of Bangladesh."
17. "বাংলাদশেরে অসাধারণ ভাসমান সবজি বাগান."
18. Haseeb Md. Irfanullah, Baira: The Floating Gardens for Sustainable Livelihood (Dhaka: IUCN Bangladesh Country Office, 2005), 25.
19. "প্রতনিধিি, জলো "শীতে জমে উঠছে ভাসমান সবজরি হাট," Dhaka Mail, January 24, 2023, https://dhakamail.com/country/66002.
20. "বাংলাদশেরে অসাধারণ ভাসমান সবজি বাগান."
21. Rezwan, discussion.
22. Sunder, "The Remarkable Floating Gardens of Bangladesh."
23. Irfanullah, Baira, 17.
24. Iftekhar Iqbal, "How the Deadly Water Hyacinth Invaded Bengal," The Daily Star, December 24, 2018, https://www.thedailystar.net/in-focus/news/how-the-deadly-water-hyacinth-invaded-bengal-1677862.
25. "কচুরিপানার ওপর দিয়ে হেঁটে নদী পারাপার," Prothom Alo, June 22, 2023, https://www.prothomalo.com/bangladesh/district/v6k6useam6.
26. Haseeb Irfanullah, "Floating Gardening in Bangladesh: Already Affected by Climate Variability?," in Biodiversity Conservation and Response to Climate Variability at Community Level, ed. Haseeb Irfanullah, Raquibul Amin, and Ainun Nishat (Dhaka: International Union for Conservation of Nature, United Nations Environment Programme, and United Nations University, 2009), 7.
27. Ministry of Agriculture, People's Republic of Bangladesh, Floating Garden Agricultural Practices in Bangladesh.
28. Sunder, "The Remarkable Floating Gardens of Bangladesh."
29. Irfanullah, Baira, 18.
30. Irfanullah, Baira, 18.
31. Sunder, "The Remarkable Floating Gardens of Bangladesh."
32. "নাজিরপুরে ভাসমান সবজি চাষে বিশ্ব স্বীকৃতি অর্জন," Protidiner Sangbad, September 7, 2020, https://www.protidinersangbad.com/todays-newspaper/news/231926/protidinersangbad.com/crime/241151.
33. "বাংলাদশেরে অসাধারণ ভাসমান সবজি বাগান."
34. "বাংলাদশেরে অসাধারণ ভাসমান সবজি বাগান."
35. Irfanullah, Baira, 22–23.
36. Ministry of Agriculture, People's Republic of Bangladesh, Floating Garden Agricultural Practices in Bangladesh.
37. Sunder, "The Remarkable Floating Gardens of Bangladesh."
38. Irfanullah, Baira, 26.
39. Irfanullah, Baira, 25.
40. "বাংলাদশেরে অসাধারণ ভাসমান সবজি বাগান."
41. Irfanullah, "Floating Gardening in Bangladesh," 8.
42. Ministry of Agriculture, People's Republic of Bangladesh, Floating Garden Agricultural Practices in Bangladesh.
43. Irfanullah, Baira, 6.
44. Irfanullah, Baira, 44.
45. "রবি মৌসুমে ফসলের যত্ন নেবেন যেভাবে," Jago News, February 14, 2021. https://www.jagonews24.com/agriculture-and-nature/article/643419
46. Sunder, "The Remarkable Floating Gardens of Bangladesh."
47. Irfanullah, *Baira*, 6.
48. Saurabh Mishra and Abhijit Maiti, "The Efficiency of Eichhornia Crassipes in the Removal of Organic and Inorganic Pollutants from Wastewater: A Review," *Environmental Science and Pollution Research* 24, no. 9 (2017): 7934–35, https://doi:10.1007/s11356-016-8357-7.
49. Sunder, "The Remarkable Floating Gardens of Bangladesh."
50. Sunder, "The Remarkable Floating Gardens of Bangladesh."
51. Sunder, "The Remarkable Floating Gardens of Bangladesh."
52. Sunder, "The Remarkable Floating Gardens of Bangladesh."
53. Faisal Mahmud, "Bangladesh Floods: Experts Say Climate Crisis Worsening Situation," Al Jazeera, June 22, 2022, https://www.aljazeera.com/news/2022/6/22/bangladesh-floods-experts-say-climate-crisis-worsening-situation.
54. Somini Sengupta and Julfikar Ali Manik, "A Quarter of Bangladesh Is Flooded. Millions Have Lost Everything," New York Times, July 30, 2020, https://www.nytimes.com/2020/07/30/climate/bangladesh-floods.html.
55. Ministry of Agriculture, People's Republic of Bangladesh, *Floating Garden Agricultural Practices in Bangladesh.*
56. Sunder, "The Remarkable Floating Gardens of Bangladesh."

COAUTHOR

MOHAMMED REZWAN

Architect of Floating Community for Climate Adaptation

Growing up in a flood-prone village, Mohammed Rezwan witnessed the devastating consequences of extreme weather events. In the monsoon season, homes and towns become isolated as earthen roads disappeared underwater in flood-prone regions, with many children unable to attend school. The floating schools Rezwan has designed provide school access year-round: if children cannot get to the classroom, the classroom comes to them. Drawing on his architectural training, Rezwan designs communal spaces on boats that accommodate several community needs, including a library, training, health care, and a playground. His work has served a community of nearly five hundred thousand people in Bangladesh over the past 22 years. Rezwan is the founding executive director of Shidhulai Swanirvar Sangstha, a nonprofit organization in Bangladesh. He has developed, expanded, and sustained floating schools since 2002. Today, this educational model operates in eight countries worldwide and is a recognized innovation by the United Nations Funds and Programmes. In 2007, Rezwan designed an integrated floating farm system, drawing inspiration from the traditional *baira*.

His designs have been showcased at prestigious exhibitions such as *Design with the Other 90%*, organized by Cooper-Hewitt, Smithsonian Design Museum, in collaboration with the Bill & Melinda Gates Foundation in the United States. Additionally, his work has been featured in the *Bengal Stream* architectural exhibition across Switzerland, France, Germany, and Bangladesh. Rezwan's achievements have garnered international attention, with coverage in newspapers like *The New York Times*, and his story was captured in the film *Easy Like Water*, produced by the Sundance Institute Documentary Film Program. The innovative nature of this work has led Shidhulai Swanirvar Sangstha to garner over 15 international awards, alongside notable national and international recognitions, such as the RTV SMC Monimix Inspirational Award 2019, the Curry Stone Design Prize 2017, and the Sri Sathya Sai Awards for Human Excellence 2016. His contributions have been documented in renowned publications like *Earth Heroes* and *Climate Rebels*, where he is recognized as a leading figure in environmental activism. This dedication has earned him titles including "Eco-Hero" in the *Cambridge Primary World English Learner's Book* and "Green Fighter" in *Sotokoto Magazine*'s esteemed list of the one hundred most influential individuals worldwide.

He is an honorary fellow of the Commonwealth of Learning and a fellow of the Royal Society of Arts. In 2023, he was selected as one of the three Child Rights Heroes in the running to receive the World's Children's Prize. In addition to these achievements, Rezwan has served on international advisory committees and regularly presents at global conferences.

Floating schools have significantly increased girls' access to education and delayed early marriage. Through education, empowerment, and resilience building, Rezwan has provided hope and opportunities to people living in the most vulnerable conditions and created a flexible, thoughtful, and sustainable model for addressing ongoing challenges exacerbated by climate change. As we contemplate a changing relationship with water worldwide, his vision provides a leading example.

MAA and MU'UT
ISLANDS
of THE POLUWATESE
and YAPESE
Micronesia

MAA and *MU'UT* ISLANDS of THE POLUWATESE and YAPESE *Micronesia*

PEOPLE Poluwatese and Yapese LOCATION Micronesia
TECHNOLOGY *maa* and *mu'ut* islands
ELEVATION 15–175 m ORIGIN 900–1700 CE
DISTANCE ABOVE OR BELOW WATERLINE −0.5 to +0.6 m
WATER LEVEL FLUCTUATION, TIDAL OR SEASONAL +0.5 to +0.65 m

FAO Nexus
WATER fresh ENERGY bioenergy + cleansing
FOOD taro

IPCC Adaptation Pathway
accommodate

World Bank NBS
CATEGORY bioretention areas, constructed inland wetlands, natural inland wetlands, urban farming, river and stream renaturation
FUNCTIONS biodiversity, water pollution regulation, pluvial flood regulation, heat regulation, air pollution regulation, landslide regulation, salt intrusion regulation, sea level rise adaptation, coastal flood regulation, riverine flood regulation
BENEFITS resource production, biodiversity, riverine flood risk reduction, pluvial flood risk reduction, carbon storage and sequestration, cultural, social interaction

1

1 The taro patch is the main form of agriculture on the island of Palau and said to be the pride of every Palauan woman who has one.
2 The atolls of Micronesia are coral reefs with groups of islands that sit on top and enclose a lagoon.

From the ring-shaped atolls to the mountainous coastal watersheds of Micronesia, taro is omnipresent, thought to have been originally planted by ghosts and spirits.[1] On the island of Palau, it is believed that the taro swamp is the mother of life.[2] Sweet taro (*Colocasia*) is a unique, primary crop, holding different meanings for different communities. On Pohnpei Island, parents might advise young children to visit a taro patch early in the morning and drink the water held in its upright leaves—this is believed to make someone *lolokong* (intelligent) and *marara* (a fast runner).[3] Taro patches are frequently assigned specific names and interacted with through a set of rules and rituals that determine who can use them, when, and how. The lush leaves of this crop grow easily in almost every ecosystem, from natural shallow bodies of water to human-made agroforestry systems, including shallow soils, dry depressions, mangrove swamps, marshes, raised gardens, excavated patches, house gardens, polyculture gardens, and floating patches found in saline water.[4] Taro crops are remarkably adaptable to water scarcity, limited physical space, and saline water and soils, which are widespread environmental constraints for communities not only on small islands but across the planet as a whole.

TARO
A tropical plant native to Southeast Asia that produces a starchy root vegetable.

Lying north of Australia and spreading across the central and western Pacific Ocean, the Federated States of Micronesia are a collection of over six hundred islands, including Yap, a cluster of small islands, and Poluwat, a coral atoll and municipality of the Chuuk state.[5] Though Micronesia contains both low-lying and high-altitude islands, the area's tropical climate produces year-round humidity, with less than 1 percent of dry land and limited fresh water.[6] This scarcity—along with frequent drought, salinity, and poor soil—inspired the creation of a number of nature-based taro technologies.

Suited to warmer climates, taro is a versatile, hardy root vegetable with an edible, starchy bulb and leaves that grow over half a meter high. Taro can withstand monsoonal rains, tolerate waterlogged soil, and is slightly tolerant of salt water. The primary species grown on these islands are giant swamp taro (*Cyrtosperma chamissonis*) and the smaller less salt-tolerant true taro (*Colocasia esculenta*). Giant swamp taro, the hardier shade-tolerant variety, is suited to agroforestry and marsh cultivation.[7] True taro quickly produces large yields

2

and is commonly grown on homesteads; this fast-growing species can be interplanted with giant swamp taro, as true taro provides shade that hinders weeds, while giant swamp taro grows for longer, remaining after the true taro is harvested.[8]

Taro is grown by creating stone-lined canals and pools, hanging baskets, floating gardens, raised beds, and patches in managed forests. Traditionally, cultivation is free from chemicals, fertilizers, and machinery. The Yapese have adapted to their environment through taro cultivation, mainly practiced by women, providing a basis for subsistence over the course of centuries.[9] In the Yapese language, taro patches are referred to as *mu'ut*.[10] *Mu'ut* can range significantly in size, from a small-scale plot to a field spanning over one hundred meters.[11] Extensive coastal taro patches are often adaptations of natural marshlands where a stream meets the ocean. Within deeper marshes in Yap, a unique *mu'ut* typology can be found—taro flourishes hydroponically in floating beds composed of vegetative material and algae-rich mulch.[12] This adaptation in Yap's wetlands is known to date back at least five generations.[13] Outside of these marshes, taro populates settlements and blankets of forest across Yap through a variety of agroforestry techniques; agroforests comprise 26 percent of the vegetation in Yap.[14] Meanwhile, in inundated areas of Poluwat Atoll, oval-shaped, elevated garden beds known as *maa* are constructed in freshwater pools to support the cultivation of taro, known locally as *woot*.[15] Without the use of artificial fertilizer, these various methods of cultivation produce yields higher than commercial farms.[16]

Among the many styles of *mu'ut* cultivation present in Yap, the floating beds located in the island's wetland interior are especially productive; taro grows hydroponically atop these buoyant gardens, with roots dangling below each island's mat-like bed.[17] Floating *mu'ut* are built on slow-moving, high-altitude water bodies, and are integrated into the various elevations of this mountainous island's watersheds.[18, 19] Women of all ages use surrounding marsh vegetation to compose the beds, relying on rigid plant species like common reed (*Phragmites*) to form the structure.[20, 21] A ditch is dug around the bed's perimeter with a stick, and any roots are cut to disconnect them from surrounding vegetation.[22] Yapese women will use their hands and feet to remove soil and silt from beneath the mat, layering it over the top of the floating *mu'ut* to cover the cut vegetation.[23] Giant swamp taro and true taro are both planted on floating *mu'ut*, where their roots thrive in algae-rich mulch. Starchy taro corm—the edible part of the crop—grows, as the plant's roots expand across the mat, absorbing nutrients from flowing water.[24]

3

4

5

6

3 Traditional taro patches in Yap located in the island's wetland interior are especially productive.
4 Extensive coastal taro patches are often adaptations of natural marshlands where a stream meets the ocean.
5 Floating mu'ut are beds are constructed for taro cultivation in freshwater pools of interior marshlands.
6 Raising taro for food is one of the most important traditional responsibilities for women in Yap.

Three Types of Taro Cultivation in Yap

7

7 Women cultivate taro in the swampy interior gardens by hauling out leaves to enrich the soil, mounding up those leaves and mud to mulch and fertilize their gardens, and nurturing each plant in the hope of producing large, strong, tasty plants.
8 Backward taro patches are commonly grown in the villages.
9 The distinct spidery veined leaf of the taro plant is rich in minerals and vitamins.

8

9

The Yapese developed other cultivation technologies adapted to the inundated conditions of the island. An alternative method employed for cultivating taro in deeper regions includes the creation of hanging baskets made of coconut fronds, which are then filled with nutrient-rich soil and mulch.[25, 26] In certain areas, these baskets are elevated and secured in position with sticks, to be planted with taro. This approach allows taro roots to penetrate the bottom of the basket and access water and nutrients below.[27] Similarly, a range of elevated beds are built in depressions during the dry season in preparation for wet months; these can be made from organic material like woven coconut fronds, coconut husks, and golden leather fern (*Achrosticum aureum*) leaves, piled with organic fertilizer, covered in soil, and held by supportive sticks.[28, 29]

Traveling underneath the dense forested canopy on Yap, paths paved with shells, coral, and sand follow a system of canals and ditches that connect raised cropland in low-lying areas and cleared patches for taro cultivation. Skylight breaks in the canopy assist the growth of yams and other subsistence crops.[30, 31] These highly productive gardens provide food and resources, while filtering air and water, preventing erosion, and enhancing biodiversity.

TREE GARDEN
A collection composed exclusively of trees of a variety of species.

Before planting taro and other crops, preparation of an agroforestry site begins with the clearing of small areas throughout the forest using shifting cultivation. This subsistence practice, used by communities across the world to clear land, involves cool or low-temperature burning to revitalize soils, while also working as an insecticide and herbicide. The canopy of the tree gardens surrounding these patches of crops protects soil from rain-induced erosion, while decomposing fallen leaves release nutrients that enhance crop cultivation.

10

10 The traditional forms of agroforestry practiced in tropical dry forests are integrated with the natural ecosystems and considered to be the most stable food-production systems on Yap.
11 Oval-shaped islet-like beds known as *maa* are initially constructed of coconut and screw palm trunks.
12 The beds are elevated using woven coconut fronds stabilized with sticks to form a low retaining wall.

Over 1,200 kilometers away, on the Poluwat Atoll, oval-shaped, islet-like beds known as *maa* are designed in response to the abundance of still fresh water in the interior swamplands of the archipelago.[32] To begin construction, a depression is either found or excavated. Coconut and screw palm (*Pandanus*) trunks are then vertically inserted into the depression to form pillars that are surrounded by decomposing vegetation. The sides of these elevated beds are constructed using woven coconut fronds, stabilized with sticks to form a retaining wall. The bottom is filled with organic leaf litter, trunks, and rotting vegetation, which the taro is finally planted into.[33] These islets—used to cultivate both true taro and giant swamp taro—are one meter high, with soil sitting half a meter above the water table.[34] One-and-a-half-meter-wide drainage canals separate the islands, which sit in the depression's center, where water is deeper and less saline. Surrounding vegetation also protects taro crops from salt spray and storm waves.[35] The Micronesian atoll of Ulithi constructs a similar style of taro islet; however, they take the shape of a triangle, as opposed to the oval *maa* shape.[36]

11

12

Floating *Mu'ut* (Taro Patch) in Yap

Maa (Taro Islet) in Poluwat

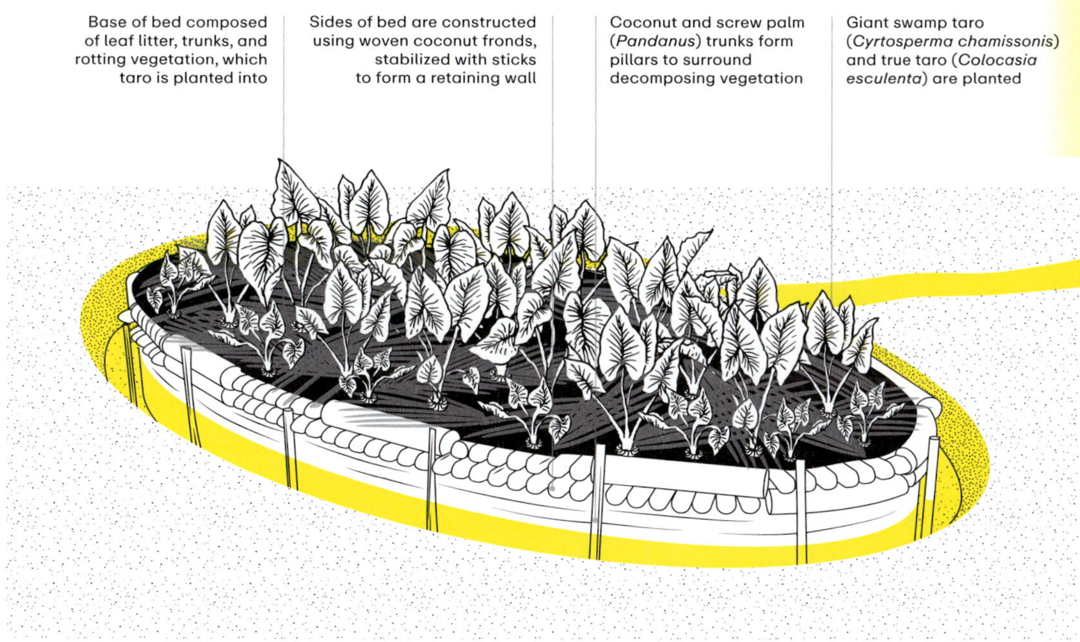

13

The diverse approaches to taro cultivation across Micronesia show successful adaptive agricultural practices in the face of limited geography, saline conditions, and inundated land. Yapese floating *mu'ut* and Poluwatese *maa* beds are highly productive, water-efficient, and disease-free methods for cultivating high-quality taro.[37] Their energy-efficient constructions responsibly use natural, local materials, in turn encouraging biodiversity and a habitat for the nesting of endemic avian species like the rail. Similar to mangroves and fishing areas, these water-based cultivation technologies trap silt, filtering water and regulating its flow into the surrounding marine environment.[38]

The ability of taro islets and floating beds to thrive in challenging environments exemplifies the innovation embedded in traditional wisdom, ultimately

RAIL A large family of small- to medium-sized terrestrial and semiamphibious birds.

14

13 Taro grown in upland conditions requires irrigation and reliable rainfall.
14 Taro patches are also grown on islands in flooded conditions, making the technology uniquely adapted to both dry to wet conditions.

15 The large, starchy, spherical underground stems or corms are commonly known as taro root.
16 The corms are consumed as a cooked vegetable, made into puddings and breads, and also made into *poi*, a thin, pasty, highly digestible mass of fresh or fermented taro starch.
17 Cultivating taro is not done using machines, but traditionally done by hand, with techniques passed down by elders to new generations of farmers.

15

highlighting how Indigenous knowledge holds the solutions to many of the issues faced by vulnerable coastal communities. Typhoons and tropical storms are common across Micronesia, affecting low-lying atolls only three to four meters above sea level. Higher-altitude Micronesian islands face increasing sea level rise, sea-surface temperatures, intensity and frequency of extreme weather events, storm surge, and erosion—all of which threaten inhabitants and infrastructures.[39] Restoring patches affected by sea level rise—which often leads to saltwater intrusion—and addressing the impact of typhoons with storm surges require both expertise and labor. Not all taro patches can withstand these challenges, underscoring the complexity of the renovation process.[40]

While taro patches remain a vital food source for communities throughout Micronesia, traditional cultivation methods such as the floating *mu'ut* beds and *maa* islets have become less common.[41] Global investment companies have taken on long-term leases in Yap to clear forests, causing widespread siltation, erosion, and roadbuilding, which disrupts ecosystems and water flow, affecting traditional management systems.[42] However, floating-island taro cultivation

16

17

can be revitalized and even integrated into roadbuilding, which often runs perpendicular to the natural water flow.[43] Local innovations to support this have already been developed, and, in some cases, are ready for implementation.[44] While some women are still well acquainted with this practice, they must pass on their knowledge to the next generation of taro growers to ensure the continued existence of this technique.[45]

Floating *mu'ut* beds and *maa* islets are just two of the many water-based methods for taro cultivation found throughout Micronesia, exemplifying how successful agricultural practices can thrive in challenging conditions like saline aquatic environments and limited land in mountainous terrain. These systems are resilient coastal agricultural infrastructures, varying in design and plant selection according to the ecosystems they inhabit, as seen in the marshland, agroforestry, and atoll environments. Floating taro islands adapt to saline water intrusion as a result of sea level rise, adopt versatile, local plants as construction materials, and use soil excavation to create systems of subirrigation. Beyond taro being a major and long-standing means of sustenance for much of the Micronesian population, this practice also reflects cultural intelligence and a deep connection to the natural ecosystems the Micronesians inhabit. Current climate conditions and cultural shifts in the area reiterate the importance of protecting, rebuilding, and expanding these practices.

ENDNOTES

1. Augustine Primo, "Colocasia Taro on Pohnpei Island," in *Proceedings of the Sustainable Taro Culture for the Pacific Conference*, ed. L. Ferentinos (Honolulu: University of Hawai'i, 1992), 6.
2. Trace V. Tipton, John W. Browni, and Pingsun Leungz, "Taro Trade and Cost of Production in Selected Areas of the American Affiliated Pacific," in *Proceedings of the Sustainable Taro Culture for the Pacific Conference*, ed. L. Ferentinos (Honolulu: University of Hawai'i, 1992), 112.
3. Primo, "Colocasia Taro on Pohnpei Island," 6.
4. Boyd Dixon et al., "Two Probable *Latte* Period Agricultural Sites in Northern Guam: Their Plants, Soils, and Interpretations," *Micronesica* 42, no. 1/2 (2012): 209–30.
5. Harley Manner, "Taro (Colocasia Esculenta (L.) Schott) in the Atolls and Low Islands of Micronesia," in *Proceedings of the Sustainable Taro Culture for the Pacific Conference*, ed. L. Ferentinos (Honolulu: University of Hawai'i, 1992), 88–100.
6. *Encyclopædia Britannica Online*, s.v. "Micronesia," accessed April 17, 2024, https://www.britannica.com/place/Micronesia-republic-Pacific-Ocean/Land.
7. Marjorie V.C. Falanruw, "Canaries of Civilization: Small Island Vulnerability, Past Adaptations and Sea-Level Rise," in *Indigenous Knowledge for Climate Change Assessment and Adaptation*, ed. Douglas Nakashima, Igor Krupnik, and Jennifer T. Rubis (Cambridge: Cambridge University Press, 2018), 250, https://doi.org/10.1017/9781316481066.018.
8. Marjorie Falanruw, "Taro Growing on Yap," in *Proceedings of the Sustainable Taro Culture for the Pacific Conference*, ed. L. Ferentinos (Honolulu: University of Hawai'i, 1992), 106.
9. Marjorie Falanruw (director, Yap Institute of Natural Science), in discussion with the author, November 2022.
10. Rosalind L. Hunter-Anderson, "A Review of Traditional Micronesian High Island Horticulture in Belau, Yap, Chuuk, Pohnpei, and Kosrae," *Micronesia* 24, no. 1 (1991): 37.
11. Hunter-Anderson, "A Review of Traditional Micronesian *High Island Horticulture in Belau, Yap, Chuuk, Pohnpei, and Kosrae*," 37.
12. Falanruw, "Canaries of Civilization," 249.
13. Falanruw, discussion.
14. Marjorie Falanruw et al., *Vegetation Survey of Yap, Federated States of Micronesia, Resource Bulletin PSW-RB-21* (Berkeley: U.S. Department of Agriculture, Forest Service, Pacific Southwest Forest and Range Experiment Station, 1987), 2, https://doi.org/10.2737/psw-rb-21.
15. Manner, "Taro (Colocasia Esculenta (L.) Schott," 94–95.
16. Falanruw, "Canaries of Civilization," 249.
17. Falanruw, "Canaries of Civilization," 249.
18. Falanruw, "Taro Growing on Yap," 108.
19. Falanruw, discussion.
20. Marjorie Falanruw, "Taro Growing on Yap," 108.
21. Falanruw, discussion.
22. Falanruw, "Taro Growing on Yap," 108.
23. Falanruw, "Taro Growing on Yap," 108.
24. Falanruw, "Taro Growing on Yap," 108.
25. Marjorie V.C. Falanruw and Francis Ruegorong, "Dynamics of an Island Agroecosystem: Where to Now?," in *Shifting Cultivation and Environmental Change*, ed. Malcom F. Cairns (London: Routledge, 2015), 376.
26. Falanruw, "Canaries of Civilization," 249.
27. Marjorie V. Cushing Falanruw, Reed M. Perkins, and Francis Ruegorong, "Integrating Traditional Knowledge and Geospatial Science to Address Food Security and Sustaining Biodiversity in Yap Islands, Micronesia," in *Societal Dimensions of Environmental Science: Global Case Studies of Collaboration and Transformation*, ed. Ricardo D. Lopez (Boca Raton: CRC Press Inc, 2019), 108.
28. Falanruw, "Taro Growing on Yap," 107.
29. Falanruw, Perkins, and Ruegorong, "Integrating Traditional Knowledge," 108.
30. Falanruw and Ruegorong, "Dynamics of an Island Agroecosystem," 370.
31. Falanruw et al., *Vegetation Survey of Yap*, 7.
32. Manner, "Taro (Colocasia Esculenta (L.) Schott," 94.
33. Manner, "Taro (Colocasia Esculenta (L.) Schott," 94
34. Manner, "Taro (Colocasia Esculenta (L.) Schott," 94.
35. Boyd Dixon et al., "Two Probable *Latte* Period Agricultural Sites," 229.
36. Boyd Dixon et al., "Two Probable *Latte* Period Agricultural Sites," 229.
37. Falanruw, "Taro Growing on Yap," 108.
38. Falanruw, discussion.
39. Falanruw, "Canaries of Civilization," 151.
40. Falanruw, discussion.
41. Falanruw, discussion.
42. Falanruw, discussion.
43. Falanruw, discussion.
44. Falanruw, discussion.
45. Falanruw, discussion.

NGAIS PASIR TERRACING SYSTEM *of* THE SUNDANESE *Indonesia*

NGAIS PASIR TERRACING SYSTEM *of* THE SUNDANESE *Indonesia*

Coauthored by
Ucu Suherlan

PEOPLE Sundanese LOCATION Neglasari Village, Tasikmalaya, West Java, Indonesia
TECHNOLOGY terracing ELEVATION 600–670 m
ORIGIN between 7th century and 12th century CE (the village's historical records were lost in an arson incident by DI/TII rebellion in 1956)
DISTANCE ABOVE OR BELOW WATERLINE −1 to +3 m
WATER LEVEL FLUCTUATION, TIDAL OR SEASONAL 0 to +1 m

FAO Nexus
WATER fresh ENERGY cleansing FOOD fish + rice

IPCC Adaptation Pathway
accommodate

World Bank NBS
CATEGORY terraces and slopes, bioretention areas, river and stream renaturation
FUNCTIONS water pollution regulation, biodiversity, cultural, riverine flood risk reduction, soil pollution regulation, drought regulation, landslide regulation, coastal flood risk reduction
BENEFITS resource production, biodiversity, carbon storage and sequestration, riverine flood risk reduction

Midway along the snaking highway between Garut and Tasikmalaya on the island of Java, a descent of 439 stone steps leads to the eastern-facing hamlet of Kampung Naga. Nestled in the village of Neglasari—between the bases of two forested mountains and encircled by an oxbow of the Ciwulan River—the hamlet lies in the lands of a Sundanese community known as the Tiyang Gunung (Mountain People).[1] With a history dating over nine hundred years, the Kampung Naga community—with *kampung* meaning "village," derived from the term *dina gawir*, the place where a *gawir* (cliff) meets its edge—has evolved a highly sophisticated and sustainable gravity-fed terracing system, known as *ngais pasir*.[2] This system is composed of the *dawuan* irrigation system, *petakan* rice terraces, and *balong* fishponds. In Sundanese, *balong* refers to an area where fish are raised in stagnant water, while *dawuan* signifies a place to divert river water,[3] which also has the potential for micro hydropower production. This symbiotic system—in a steep volcanic landscape prone to heavy rainfall and built on *taneuh bahe ngetan* (land slightly tilted to the east) to receive morning sunlight—provides food and clean water while preventing landslides by altering the slope and slowing runoff.[4]

In 1914, Dutch archaeologist Nicolaas Johannes Krom recorded Gunung Padang—*gunung* meaning "mountain," and *padang*, place of the great ancestors—a second-century BCE megalithic site located a mere 180 kilometers from Kampung Naga.[5] This evidenced that the *ngais pasir* terracing technology have

1 A descent of 439 stone stairs leads to the hamlet of Kampung Naga.
2 The island of Java is composed of a steep volcanic landscape prone to heavy rainfall and landslides, which rice terraces help prevent.
3 An oxbow of the Ciwulan River encircles half of the hamlet of Kampung Naga.

1

2

monopolized the mountainous regions of Tasikmalaya, Sukabumi, and Majalengka for over two thousand years.[6] The term for this ancient system speaks to the process of carrying away *pasir* (hill) for terrace agriculture, as if it were a child wrapped in a woman's *sinjang pangais* (sarong).[7] For the Sundanese, rice fields symbolize the prosperity of a landowner, while rice is considered to be the incarnation of the fertility goddess Nyi Pohaci—also known as Dewi Sri and Shridevi in Javanese and Balinese cultures.

OXBOW
A U-shaped curve in a river formed when a meander is cut off from the main channel, leaving a crescent-shaped body of water.

In the millennia-old philosophy of *Sunda Buhun* (Ancient Sunda), the cosmological concept of *tritangtu* offers a guide to a harmonious life, and translates into the spatial organization of communities.[8] This principle says that the universe is divided into three parts: *Buana Nyungcung* (Upper World), *Buana Panca Tengah* (Middle World), and *Buana Larang* (Under World).[9] This framework manifests in the physical layout of Kampung Naga, which is divided into three zoned programs. *Buana Nyungcung* is a sacred area for ancestors and holy spirits that contains protected *leuweung* (forests) such as Leuweung Karamat and Leuweung Biuk. The inner zone—*Buana Panca Tengah*—is a place for living, with housing and public buildings like the Bale Petemon community hall, the Bale Ageung (Great Pavilion), the Mosque, and *leuit* rice barns. This central region is enclosed by a bamboo fence called *kandang jaga*. The outermost zone, known as *Buana Larang*, is where the *ngais pasir* terracing and *balong* fishpond systems are sited.[10]

3

The oxbow of Ciwulan River that encircles half of Kampung Naga is diverted through piled river stones, enabling water

Water Levels and Rice-Planting Cycles

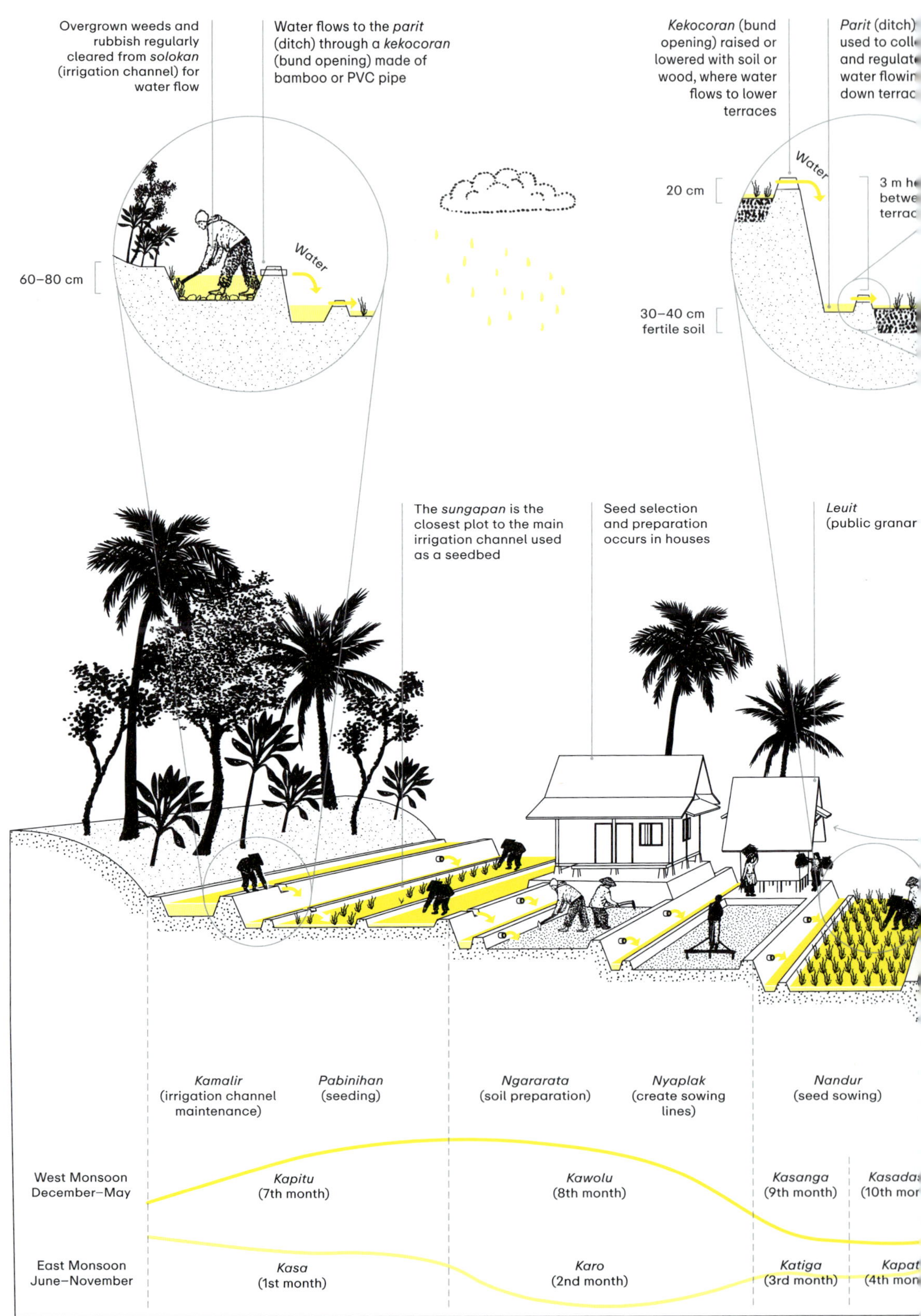

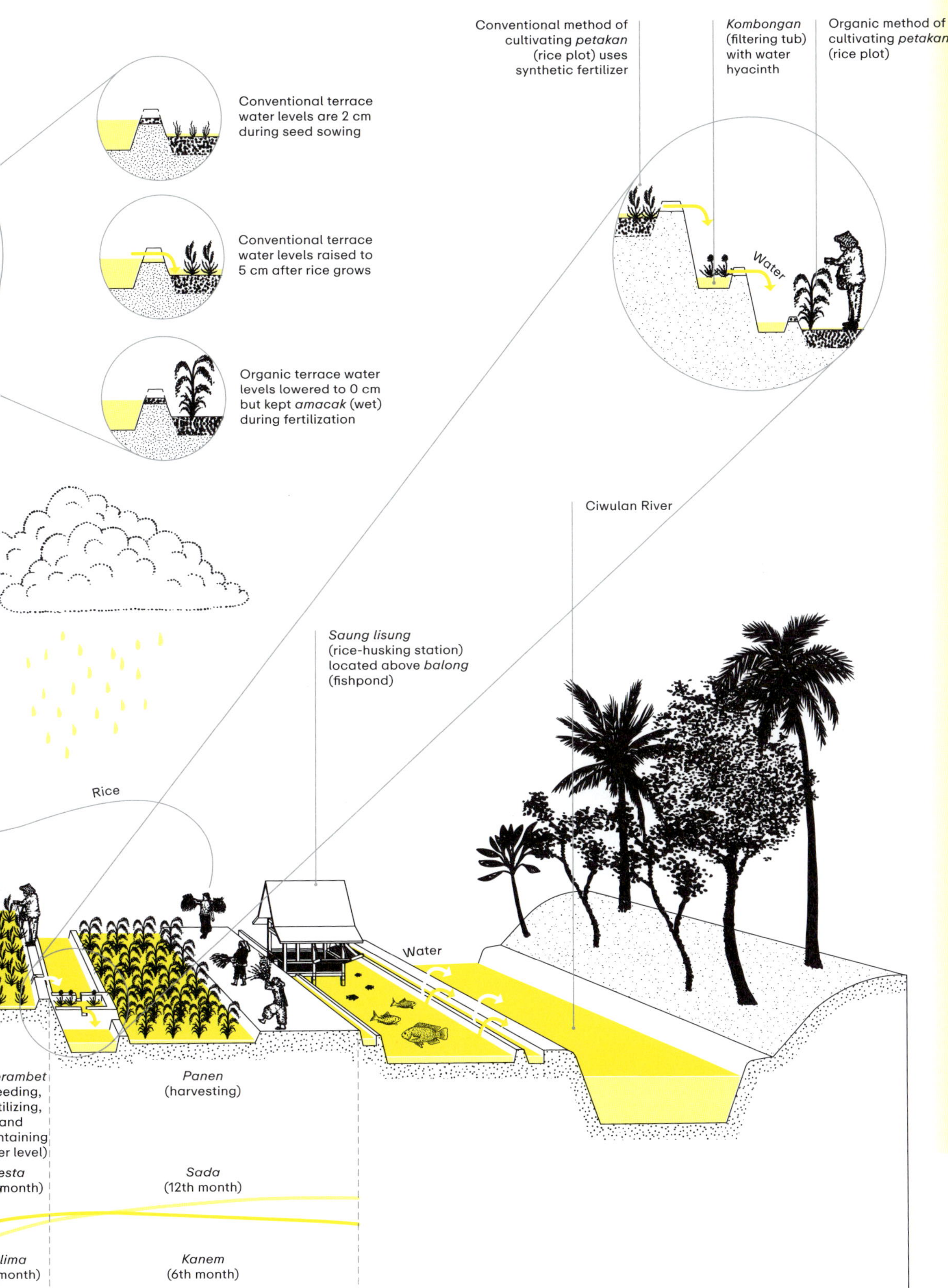
Conventional terrace water levels are 2 cm during seed sowing
Conventional terrace water levels raised to 5 cm after rice grows
Organic terrace water levels lowered to 0 cm but kept *amacak* (wet) during fertilization
Conventional method of cultivating *petakan* (rice plot) uses synthetic fertilizer
Kombongan (filtering tub) with water hyacinth
Organic method of cultivating *petakan* (rice plot)
Water
Ciwulan River
Saung lisung (rice-husking station) located above *balong* (fishpond)
Rice
Water
rambet
eeding,
tilizing,
and
ntaining
er level)
Panen (harvesting)
esta
month)
Sada (12th month)
lima
month)
Kanem (6th month)

4

5

to circulate to canals—the *ngais pasir* system's main water source—and trickle down terraces. The Sundanese *ngais pasir* method, also known as *nyabuk gunung* (belting the mountain) in Javanese, is an Indigenous innovation in water distribution widely practiced across the island of Java. The system encompasses the *dawuan* irrigation system, *petakan* rice terraces, and wastewater filtration and purification of the *balong* fishponds, where fish are raised in an interconnected pond system.[11]

Dawuan is an irrigation process that operates by draining water from high to low terraces through openings in the terrace walls or bunds called *kekocoran*. This process begins through two main *solokan* (irrigation canals) upstream: the southern *solokan garunggang* and the northern *solokan bongas*. Rice plots are then connected to the ditches known as *parit*, which regulate water flow. To maintain the soil stability of bunds without reinforcement, water must flow continuously to prevent the soil from drying out and cracking.[12] Bund heights are adjusted with soil or wood to manage water during the two planting seasons where two varieties of rice, *padi bulu* and *padi lepas*, are sown depending on their response to the water level. Methods of irrigating the rice terraces include organic, conventional, and semiconventional. These methods differ because of the different types of fertilizer and management of plot water levels throughout the growing season.

Petakan, the terraced rice plots of the *ngais pasir* system, are constructed parallel to the contours of the valley. Placed three meters apart, *petakan* terraces are bordered by 20-centimeter-high bunds of compacted soils, filled with 30 to 40 centimeters of fertile soil reaching down to an underground layer of clay. While

4 The *petakan* terraced rice plots are constructed parallel to the contours ofthe valley.
5 Residents of the hamlet prefer the use of local resources.
6 The traditional calendar is divided into 12 months following the course of the sun, in which there are two planting seasons.

the size of higher plots are usually smaller due to the steeper slopes, on average plots are 98 to 140 square meters, or seven to 10 *bata*, the Sundanese measuring equivalent. The largest recorded *petekan* is 210 square meters, or 15 *bata*, while the smallest is 28 square meters, or two *bata*. *Kombongans*—one- to two-square-meter tubs filled with water hyacinth (*Eichhornia crassipes*)—are located among *petakan* in order to filter water before flowing to further terraces.[13]

For the Sundanese, cultivation is guided by the *Pranata Mangsa*—a traditional calendar that divides the year into 12 *mangsa* (months) following the course of the sun.[14] There are two planting seasons in Kampung Naga. Beginning in January, the first is called *Porekatan* or *Musim Kecil* (Little Season).

6

The second season, which starts in July, is called *Musing Gede* (Big Season). Each season begins with *kamalir*—the maintenance of all waterways, trenches, and ditches between fields. *Kamalir* occurs after a traditional feast and ceremony called *slametan*, a custom practiced by the Sundanese, Javanese, and Maduranese, which is followed by the seeding of the plots.[15]

Seeds are readied for planting in a basket covered in banana leaves, where they soak overnight until shoots emerge. The process of seeding, known as *pabinihan*, is carried out in the *sungapan*—the closest plot to the main irrigation channel.[16] Rice fields are prepared through *ngabaladah* (rough hoeing) and *macul mindo* (second hoeing), *ngangler* (stamping), cleaning, *ngacak* (leveling), and *nyaplak*, which manually make lines on level ground using a wooden harrow.[17] Thirty days after *nandur*, when rice seeds are sowed, farmers begin a process of weeding, fertilization, and water level maintenance called *ngerambet*.[18] *Nyarian* is a custom practiced several days prior to harvest. During this ritual, farmers sprinkle seven types of food around the boundaries of the field, believing it enhances the flavor of the rice. After five months of cultivation, *panen* (harvesting) with an *ani-ani* (sickle tool) occurs in May and November.[19] Cultivation and land preparation in between planting seasons occurs in June and December, when rice straws left over from harvests are used as a natural composting fertilizer.[20]

Balong are fishponds found throughout traditional Sundanese villages in West Java. In Kampung Naga, *balong* are located with *ngais pasir* terraces in the outer area of the village, forming interconnected ponds. Each *balong* is filled with water from the northern irrigation canal *solokan bongas*, as well as excess water from the *petakan*. These terraced fishponds are built from excavated clay soil that has been compacted and supported using bamboo slats. The *balong* are interconnected through a bamboo pipe, which carries water from the highest to the lowest *balong*.[21] The average size of a *balong* is 168 square meters, or 12 *bata*.[22] The lowest pond is one meter deep, while the higher ponds are shallower, varying between 60 and 80 centimeters in depth.

The *balong* function as a treatment system for wastewater produced during rice cultivation, livestock rearing, rainwater runoff, and human activities. Strategically built above the fishponds are the agricultural terraces in the higher zones, *pacilingans* (lavatories), washing stations, and *saung lisung* (rice-husking houses). The fish that feed the community eat the waste and cleanse the water before it enters the lowest fishpond and flows into the main drainage channel of the river to the east.

The Sundanese raise freshwater fish like *mas* (common carp) and *gurame* (giant gourami) in private ponds. Fish are harvested for family events, such as weddings and circumcision celebrations, or sold to community members who don't own *balong*.[23] In the communal pond, *nilem* (bonylip barb), *nila* (tilapia), and other small fish are bred to be shared during traditional events, such as Hajat Sasih, a ceremony for blessing and safety. Fish are harvested through a process called *ngabedahkeun*, in which all water flows into the deepest pond, where someone will dive to open a drainage pipe, draining the ponds.[24]

7 *Balong* are the fishponds that form interconnected ponds and function as a treatment system for wastewater produced during rice cultivation.
8 Built above the fishponds are *saung lisung*, or rice-husking houses.

7

The logic of the *ngais pasir* system is grounded in its relationship to the broader ecosystem. Built on *taneuh bahe ngetan*, the system receives more sunlight in the morning, benefiting the health of both residents and crops. By adapting the steep slope into parallel terraces that support rice growth and increase the potential for water absorption into the soil, the risk of landslides is significantly reduced. Similar strategies are applied to the construction of homes downhill, typically supported by stilts on stone podiums with a base made of compacted soil and river stone. This building system reduces termites and allows water to seep into the soil.

Water from several sources is also strategically sourced for daily use from the Ciwulan River and two springs near Kampung Naga. One spring, located behind a hill on the west side of the village, is channeled to the outer area of the village, where it is used for washing and bathing during the rainy season, when the river water is murky.[25] Cai Nyusu, located on the south side of the village under the forbidden forest of Leuweung Karamat, is another spring that is accessed for drinking water. The forest, restricted from human use, consists of a vast network of roots that serve as pathways for rainwater to recharge the aquifers.

8

Today, the *ngais pasir* system occupies a limited area, affecting a small population of Sundanese people living in Kampung Naga. In recent decades, some Sundanese have moved outside of the village to retain the system's carrying capacity.[26] To maintain traditional ties between *warga naga* (residents still living in Kampung Naga) and *warga sanaga* (residents that have moved away), community activities such as religious rituals and

Balong Fishpond Construction and Colocation of Symbiotic Rice, Fish, and Human Waste

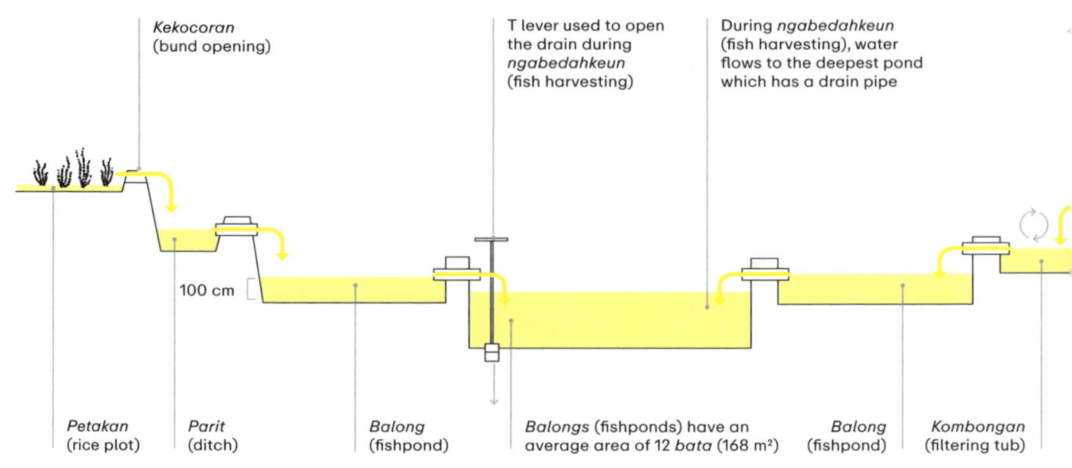

Rainwater from the settlement flows through the main drainage

Saung lisung
(rice-husking station)

Filtered water flows to the river through the main drainage

← Open this fold to reveal full illustration.

9

9 Washing stations are also located above the *balong* fishponds, along with toilets.
10 After rice is pounded manually using traditional tools at the rice-husking station, the husks are thrown into the fishpond to feed the fish.

village maintenance are held in the hamlet.[27] Maintenance, known as *bersih kampung* or *ngaruat lembur*, is periodic, voluntary, and cooperative work, and local materials are used to fix housing and infrastructure. Recently, artificial materials have been introduced to *balong*, such as concrete and PVC pipes, to reinforce the durability of the structure and the system.

The Ciwulan River surrounding the hamlet has also changed. As a result of forest degradation and transformation to agricultural land in the Ciwulan watershed, many years ago the river's water level dropped and stopped feeding the banks, causing the riparian zone to become overgrown with wild plants.[28] Many riverbanks have since been reinforced and transformed to expand the adjacent rice fields. Though this approach narrows the river and reduces its capacity, it ultimately produces higher yields during harvest. In July 2022, extreme rainfall flooded the river, reaching homes in the village's inner zone.[29] While houses built on stilts survived, the *balong* and two hectares of rice fields were submerged in water. Several rice-husking stations were also swept away in the flood. Currently,

10

11

12

the riverbank rice fields are not cultivated, once again merging with the Ciwulan River.

The river also encounters other challenges such as pollution from household and plastic waste that originates upstream.[30] An organization called Mitra Cai coordinates river maintenance with the local communities, monitoring rice terraces, rice-field expansion, irrigation canals, and water distribution between villages.[31] The community still adheres to the philosophy of *alam jeung jaman kawulaan, saur elingkeun*: "To keep up with the changing times, while still holding on to what was given by the ancestors, to sort out what is allowed and what is not."[32]

From its southern site in the morning sun to its terracing to prevent landslides, the *ngais pasir* system offers the Sundanese of Kampung Naga an intelligently designed subsistence, passive energy landscape, while cleansing water and encouraging symbiotic living. The *dawuan* irrigation system enables river water to flow through terraced *petakan*, facilitating rice growth, with the traditional calendar informing agricultural processes for optimal productivity. Through the strategic vertical division of the village landscape into three zones, *ngais pasir* becomes a water management system for potable water, a gravitational-distribution irrigation system, and a wastewater management system. In line with the philosophy of *alam jeung jaman kawulaan, saur elingkeun*, the introduction of micro hydropower could offer reliable local energy production for one of the

11 Rice grown in Kampung Naga is still milled in the traditional way: by hand, pounding, with a mortar and pestle.
12 During the two planting seasons, two varieties of rice can be sown, depending on their response to the water level.
13 By adapting the steep slope into terraces to grow rice, the risk of landslides is reduced.

13

most holistic and sophisticated examples of localized community self-sufficiency. Despite challenges, including land use change in the watershed, preserving this system is crucial for the local community and all the more-than-human inhabitants they steward. While the scale and natural carrying capacity of this system is unique to Kampung Naga, the deep understanding of landscape, climate, and topography that shape this technology should be consciously applied to other parts of the world. The challenges posed by climate change on communities are an example of where *ngais pasir* can be hybridized and scaled to produce integrated holistic systems of habitation—particularly in urban areas.

14

14 Kampung Naga is designed to be energy efficient and responsive to the local climate and cultural context.

ENDNOTES

1. Iwan Hermawan, "Sengkedan: Bentuk Rekayasa Lingkungan untuk Permukiman dan Pertanian," *Patanjala* 7, no. 2 (2015): 202.
2. Syavana Fairuzahira, Wara Indira Rukmi, and Kartika Eka Sari Rukmi, "Elemen Pembentuk Permukiman Tradisional Kampung Naga," *Jurnal Tata Kota dan Daerah* 12, no. 1 (2020): 33.
3. Ucu Suherlan (*punduh adat* and caretaker of Kampung Naga), in discussion with the author, November 2022.
4. Sekretaris Daerah Pemerintah Kabupaten Tasikmalaya, "Profil Kampung Naga: Warisan Sistem Pertanian dan Pangan," *Tasikmalaya: Pemerintah Daerah Kabupaten Tasikmalaya* (2016): 7.
5. Sutarman, Haryono Edi Hermawan, and Cecep Hilman, "Gunung Padang Cianjur: Pelestarian Situs Megalitikum terbesar Warisan Dunia," *Jurnal Surya: Seri Pengabdian kepada Masyarakat* 2, no. 1 (2016): 61.
6. Kiki Kurnia, "Terasering Ternyata Teknologi Masyarakat Sunda Sejak Ratusan Tahun Lalu," GalaMediaNews.com, June 15, 2022, https://galamedia.pikiran-rakyat.com/news/pr-354744844/terasering-ternyata-teknologi-masyarakat-sunda-sejak-ratusan-tahun-lalu?page=2.
7. Kosuke Mizuno et al., "Talun-Huma, Swidden Agriculture, and Rural Economy in West Java, Indonesia." *Southeast Asian Studies* 2, no. 2 (2013): 362.
8. Tessa Eka Darmayanti, "Sundanese Traditional Houses in Kampung Naga, West Java as Part of Indonesian Cultural Tourism," *Journal of Tourism* 3, no. 8 (2018): 60.
9. Darmayanti, "Sundanese Traditional Houses," 60.
10. Darmayanti, "Sundanese Traditional Houses," 60.
11. Shirley Wahadamaputera et al., "Pengolahan dan Pemanfaatan Elemen Air Sebagai Kearifan Lokal pada Arsitektur Kampung Naga," *Jurnal Reka Karsa* 2, no. 3 (2014): 10.
12. Suherlan, discussion.
13. Suherlan, discussion.
14. Sekretaris Daerah Pemerintah Kabupaten Tasikmalaya, "Profil Kampung Naga," 30.
15. Sekretaris Daerah Pemerintah Kabupaten Tasikmalaya, "Profil Kampung Naga," 33.
16. Sekretaris Daerah Pemerintah Kabupaten Tasikmalaya, "Profil Kampung Naga," 33.
17. Sekretaris Daerah Pemerintah Kabupaten Tasikmalaya, "Profil Kampung Naga," 38.
18. Sekretaris Daerah Pemerintah Kabupaten Tasikmalaya, "Profil Kampung Naga," 40.
19. Suherlan, discussion.
20. Suherlan, discussion.
21. Ayu Prestasia and Boomi Kim, "Living with Nature: Water Stories of Kampung Naga, Indonesia," *SPOOL* 7, no. 2 (2020): 69.
22. Suherlan, discussion.
23. Suherlan, discussion.
24. Suherlan, discussion.
25. Prestasia and Kim, "Living with Nature," 66.
26. Prestasia and Kim, "Living with Nature," 72.
27. Prestasia and Kim, "Living with Nature," 71.
28. Suroso, A. Putudewi, and Ardiansyah, "Impact of Land Use Changes on the Water Availability in Ciwulan Watershed, West Java," *IOP Conference Series: Earth and Environmental Science* 653 (2021): 1–2, http://doi.org/10.1088/1755-1315/653/1/012031.
29. Muhamad Fauzi and Adi Kristiadi, "Banjir Bandang di Kampung Naga Hanyutkan 2 Ton Ikan dari 30 Kolam," Media Indonesia, July 16, 2022, https://mediaindonesia.com/nusantara/507254/banjir-bandang-di-kampung-naga-hanyutkan-2-ton-ikan-dari-30-kolam.
30. Arfi Bambani, "River in Tasikmalaya Polluted by Plastic Waste," TheIndonesia.id, April 4, 2022, https://www.theindonesia.id/news/2022/04/04/073000/river-in-tasikmalaya-polluted-by-plastic-waste.
31. Suherlan, discussion.
32. Suherlan, discussion.

COAUTHOR

UCU SUHERLAN

Punduh Adat and Caretaker of Kampung Naga

'cu Suherlan was born in 1966 in a Sundanese village › the leader of Kampung Naga, where he has lived is entire life. From a young age, he has followed mandate to lead and protect the customs and alues of Kampung Naga. Historically, the residents f Kampung Naga discouraged outsiders by tending › spiritual barriers that ward off unwanted visitors. s regional tourism introduced increasing numbers f foreigners, Suherlan sought to uplift the values ıstilled in him at a young age to maintain and pro- ›ct local traditions.

While Sundanese cultural preservation ›mains a primary focus of his current work, Suherlan ites several significant experiences eyond Kampung Naga—particularly is time in Japan and Jakarta—as influ- ntial in his career trajectory. These xperiences abroad ultimately moti- ated him to return home, where he ›ould dedicate himself to community- riented work. Today, his family's man- ate and ancestral legacy guide his rofessional and personal life.

In 1987, Suherlan formed the ›cal cultural and education organization olidaritas Anak Pemangku Adat Naga, translating › Solidarity of Children of Naga's Traditional Rulers.)ne goal of the initiative was English-language nmersion among Kampung Naga's youth to give the ext generation the tools to communicate their culture nd history to outsiders accurately. In 1991, the organi- ation transformed into Himpunan Pramuwisata ıdonesia, the Association of Indonesian Tour Guides. 'his project aimed to encourage the participation f young individuals who joined without carrying the urden of the previous name. As chair, Suherlan envi- ions future programming that involves further nowledge exchange alongside craft and agriculture pportunities for residents.

Today, Suherlan serves many roles in Kampung Naga. As a member of the Institute for Preservation of Cultural Heritage Serang, he is the caretaker of protected sites around the village. Suherlan is also chair of Koperasi Warga Sauyunan (Sauyunan Residents' Cooperative), which aims to grow the village's economic potential. Within the traditional leadership structure of the village, he is a punduh adat—a role whose responsibilities include overseeing community members' behavior in accordance with customs and leading communal works.

Suherlan is also a farmer; outside of his professional life, he oversees water regulation in rice fields, checking for pests, maintaining bunds to prevent leaks, and caring for the fish in the fishponds. Under his leadership, Kampung Naga received the Indonesia Sustainable Tourism Award in September 2019 and the Asian Sustainable Tourism Award in November 2019. These awards have shed light on the critical value of maintaining tradition in the face of a growing tourism industry.

Suherlan continues to adhere to traditional principles in Kampung Naga, one of which is *saur elingken jaman kawulaan*. This concept signifies the importance of adapting to contemporary times while preserving ancestral teachings.

TATAMI-ISHI TERRACING SYSTEM *of* THE JAPANESE

Japan

TATAMI-ISHI TERRACING SYSTEM *of* THE JAPANESE *Japan*

PEOPLE Japanese LOCATION Shizuoka and Izu regions, Shizuoka Prefecture, Japan
TECHNOLOGY terracing
ELEVATION 1,340–1,720 m ORIGIN 1892 CE
DISTANCE ABOVE OR BELOW WATERLINE −1.22 to +0.02 m
WATER LEVEL FLUCTUATION, TIDAL OR SEASONAL +0.01 to +0.02 m

FAO Nexus
WATER fresh ENERGY tidal + bioenergy + cleansing
FOOD wasabi

IPCC Adaptation Pathway
accommodate

World Bank NBS
CATEGORY river and stream renaturation, terraces and slopes, bioretention areas, urban forests, river floodplains
FUNCTIONS biodiversity, drought regulation, pluvial flood regulation, subsidence regulation, air pollution regulation, landslide regulation, water pollution regulation, heat regulation, soil pollution regulation
BENEFITS resource production, biodiversity, stimulate local economies and job creation, carbon storage and sequestration, cultural, pluvial flood risk reduction, human health, heat-stress reduction

Along the southern coast of Japan's Honshu island, heavy rains that fall over the steep mountainsides feed dense forests, diverse croplands, and deep springs. From March to April, small white flowers carpet the river courses of the forest, while a sea of green vines hang over the stepped stone walls of *tatami-ishi* (rock matting) terraces. Constructed to grow *Eutrema japonicum*, a variety of wasabi Indigenous to the streambeds of Japanese river valleys, *tatami-ishi* is a style of terracing that mimics natural stream habitats.[1, 2, 3] The cultivation of wasabi dates to the late 16th century, when farmers began to cultivate this sharp-tasting, aromatic delicacy.[4] Today, wasabi is consumed as a condiment when its stem is grated, while its leaves, petioles, and floral axes are used for pickles, tempura, and other dishes. Receiving over three thousand millimeters of annual rainfall, which is concentrated and stored in the mountains, the *tatami-ishi* terracing systems that enable wasabi cultivation thrive among the headsprings and terrain that border mountain streams, where the potential to produce local energy coexists with the growth of high-quality crops that support life in mountain districts.[5]

Spreading across a region of 1,978 square kilometers, *tatami-ishi* wasabi cultivation is found in three distinct locations: the Izu region of the Mount Amagi range, the Shizuoka region of the Japanese Southern Alps, and the Kamo District towns of Higashiizu, Kawazu, Matsuzaki, and Nishiizu.[6] The practice of wasabi cultivation originated four hundred hundred years ago in the Keichō era; from 1596 to 1615, wasabi was cultivated around the village of Utogi, near Shizuoka

1 Wasabi, sometimes called Japanese horseradish (*Eutrema japonicum*), is a plant that grows naturally along mountain streams in Japan. Izu Peninsula in Shizuoka Prefecture is one of the main producers of wasabi in Japan.
2 Wasabi stems—which come from the wasabi plant of the Brassicaceae family—are used as a condiment with a strong pungent flavor.
3 *Tatami-ishi*, a style of terracing that mimics natural stream habitats, is constructed to grow *Eutrema japonicum*, a variety of wasabi indigenous to the streambeds of Japanese river valleys.

1

2

3

City, using the *jizawa* method.[7] The *tatami-ishi* style was introduced later in 1892, when stonemason engineers used the region's abundant water supply for wasabi cultivation by allocating fields along mountains.[8] This was followed by digging a deep foundation, laying large stones, then pebbles, and then finally fine sand, so that the cool, oxygen-rich stream water would spread underground and nourish the wasabi roots, helping them avoid common diseases of the time like soft rot.[9] The style of cultivation spread while being passed down through generations, resulting in each family's method varying slightly.[10]

Wasabi Cultivation Is Found in Three Locations, Spreading Across 1,978 Square Kilometers

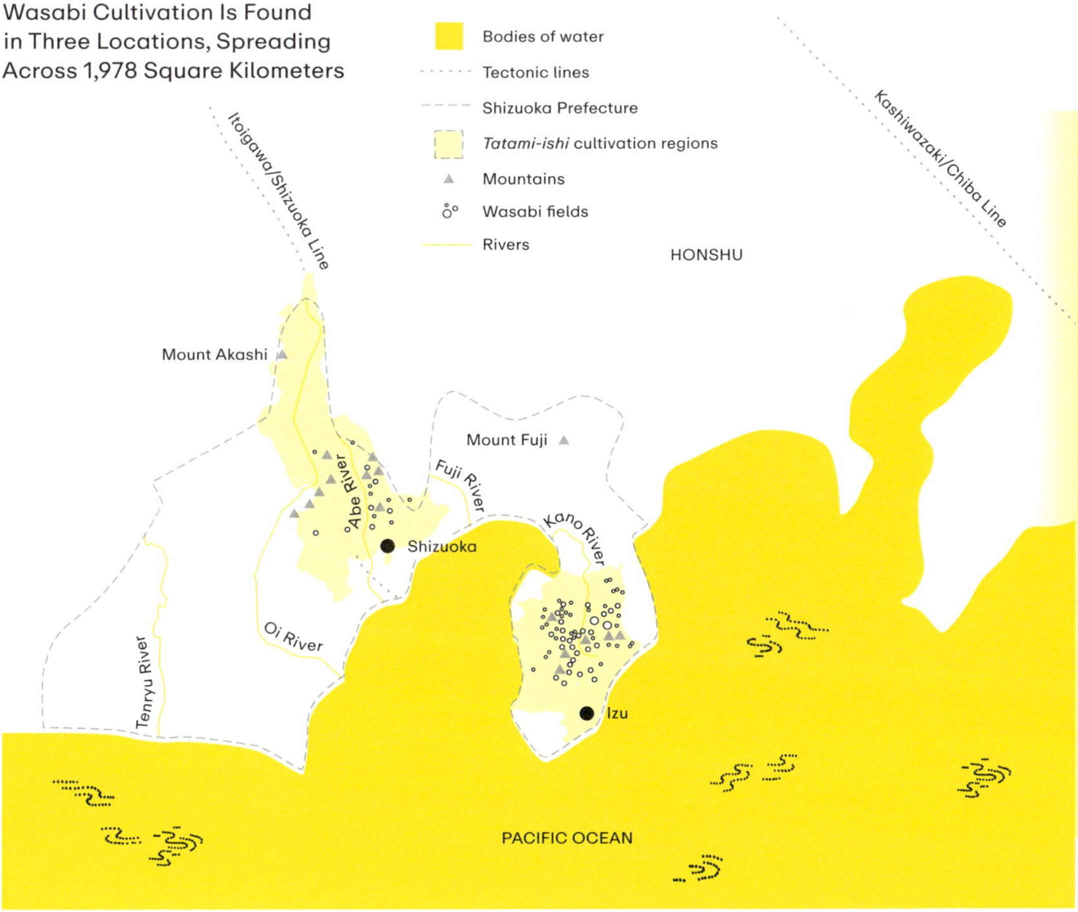

4

In the Shizuoka region, the wasabi fields are constructed to take advantage of fissures found along the surface of the dolerite bedrock, which store rainwater, arising from the tectonic movements of the Itoigawa-Shizuoka Tectonic Line.[11] Here, forests of coniferous trees, like Japanese cedars and Japanese cypress, surround *tatami-ishi* terraces, while honyama tea (*Camellia sinensis*) is grown just outside the forest, where there is direct access to sunlight.[12] In the Izu region, wasabi cultivation relies on the natural fertilization that occurs in the water system as nutrients leech from the volcanic soil and are washed into the terraces, which contain not only wasabi but also a variety of tree species and mushrooms.[13]

DOLERITE
Dolerite is a dark-colored igneous rock with a medium grain size, formed from the solidification of magma deep underground, often found in areas where ancient volcanic activity occurred.

Wasabi, a member of the *Brassicaceae* family, has been culturally significant in Japan for centuries. Its pungent flavor, which comes from isothiocyanate, not only defines its taste but is also purported to provide medicinal benefits, including the suppression of bacteria causing food poisoning, prevention of cancer and blood clots, support for bone health, and treatment of fungal infections.[14] The plant became a widespread component of Japanese cuisine tradition by the 19th century.[15]

Another vital element in *tatami-ishi* terracing—water—carries profound spiritual meaning for the local community in this region. Many shrines and religious rituals in the area are specifically linked to water.[16] Shizuoka City alone boasts 56 Shirahige shrines, with Utogi contributing to 20 percent of Japan's overall count, all dedicated to water deities and farming gods.[17] These shrines are located on high ground at the entrance or center of villages, with their main buildings and torii gates facing rivers or swamps, signifying their protection against food disasters in this water-abundant region.[18]

4 Spring water, originating from the uppermost level of the terrace system, descends into each successive terrace, soaking the roots of the wasabi plants.

5

5 Following harvest, discolored stems and leaves are removed from the roots and any areas eaten by worms are trimmed.
6 People sort wasabi roots at a farm in Ikadaba in the city of Izu, Shizuoka Prefecture.

Wasabi itself is frequently used as an offering at harvest festivals in the spring and autumn, alongside *shinto kagura* folk dancing.[19] Originating in ancient Japan, *shinto kagura* is performed in shrines to express gratitude to water deities for generous harvests.[20] Every August, the Bon Festival, a Japanese Buddhist event honoring the deceased, takes place at Tounji Temple's wasabi field, featuring altars decorated with wasabi as a protective measure for good fortune.[21] These traditions reflect a communal recognition of water's dual role—vital for sustenance and cultivation, yet potentially threatening through natural disasters.

The two traditional methods of wasabi cultivation, *tatami-ishi* and *jizawa*, are both reliant on ample spring water. The *jizawa* method of cultivating wasabi yields smaller quantities and is implemented in fields situated on a slight incline, where mud has been washed away, leaving a layer of 25 to 30 centimeters of sand and stones.[22] *Tatami-ishi* cultivation, an adapted version of *jizawa*, is carried out on sloped land, with significant fluctuations in water volume.[23] Today, *jizawa* cultivation is still practiced where the *tatami-ishi* method is not feasible.

6

Derived from the shallow *jizawa* method, the *tatami-ishi* technique uses terraces that are five to 10 meters in length, sloping downward at a gradient of 1 to 4 percent, with each terrace separated by vertical drops of approximately 60 centimeters.[24] Each terrace consists of three layers: first, a 40- to 100-centimeter-deep base of large rocks; next, a seven-centimeter-deep layer of final pebbles; and, lastly, a 15-centimeter-deep layer of soil on which plants are cultivated.[25, 26] Spring water, originating from the uppermost level of the terrace system, descends, gently trickling into each successive terrace and soaking the roots of the wasabi plants.

Channels used to divert stream water into terraces are located two to four meters apart, delivering one to two centimeters of irrigation water, which then travels through wasabi fields.[27] The water that permeates the surface soil maintains the stems at a stable temperature—between 11 and 19 degrees Celsius—and provides plants with oxygen and nutrients.[28] East Asian alder (*Alnus hirsuta*) is planted in and around terraces to provide shade and stabilize the ground with their roots.[29] The channels continue downward, returning naturally cleansed water to mountain streams to be reticulated and used for freshwater aquaculture and farming.[30]
Various cultivars and strains of wasabi are used to support stable year-round production. In this system, two wasabi stems can be cultivated per square foot and harvested within 16 to 20 months.[31] Changes in atmospheric temperature,

Tatami-ishi Terraces and Channels

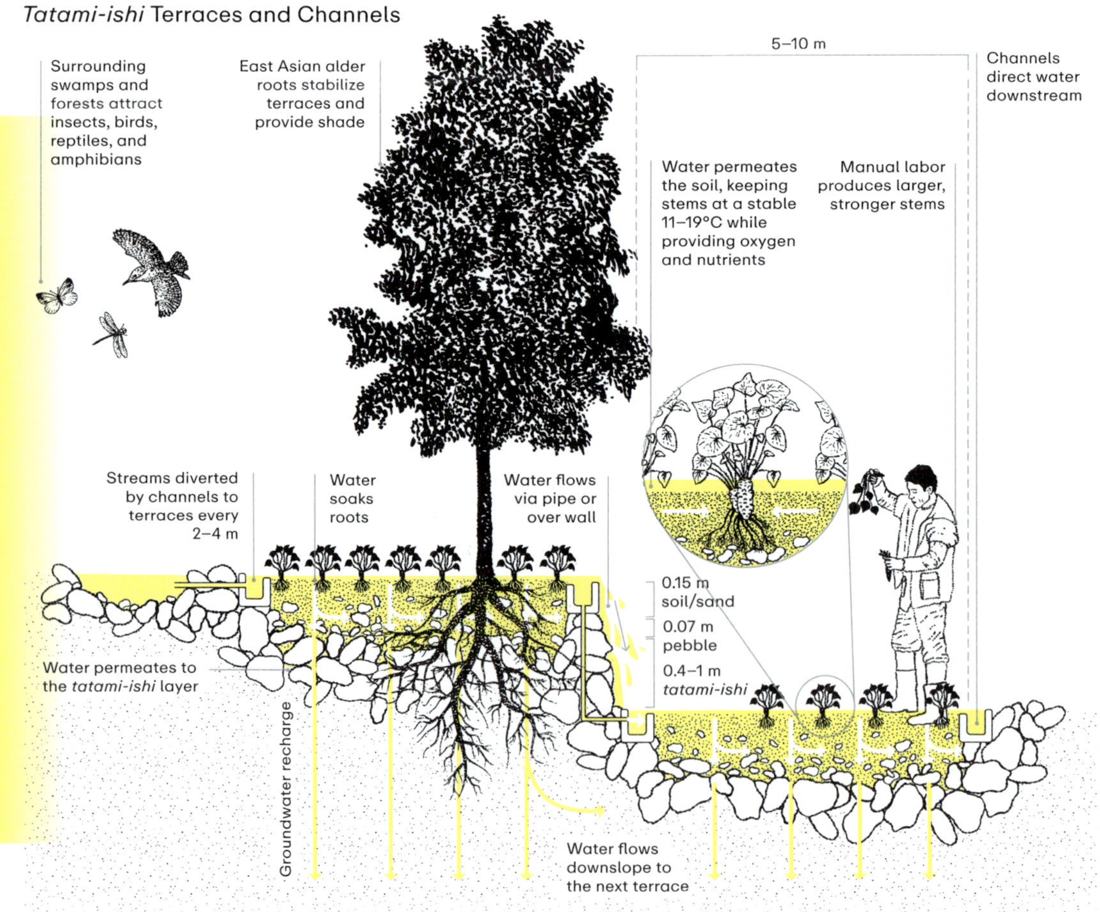

7

8

7 The practice of wasabi cultivation originated four hundred years ago, but the *tatami-ishi* style was introduced later, in 1892. It has since spread by being passed down through generations, resulting in each family's method varying slightly.

8 The *tatami-ishi* style, which allocates fields along mountains, allows cool, oxygen-rich stream water to spread underground and nourish the wasabi roots.

sunlight, weather, water quality, and the surrounding environment inform varietal innovation by producers to suit the state of particular fields.[32] For example, seedling production must be stable to uphold the system, so producers continually grow branching shoots of wasabi stems grown from seeds gathered in the spring. This continuous propagation strategy allows for replication of a parent plant's form, character, and yield, thereby contributing to stability in the production cycles.[33]

Between March and April, small white flowers bloom on wasabi plants and vines hang down the stone walls of the *tatami-ishi* to be harvested for seeds.[34] Seeds are stored in a humid environment and are grown in greenhouses for two to three months, before being replanted into wasabi fields and grown for another 11 months to two years.[35] Following harvest, discolored stems and leaves are removed from the roots and any areas eaten by worms are trimmed; clay, dead insects, decayed leaves, and other organic matter are also removed from the surface soil, which is then washed to avoid water blockage and risk of disease.[36]

The wasabi fields and their surrounding swamps and forests are biodiverse ecosystems with high populations of insects, birds, amphibians, and reptiles that form the foundation of the food chain in these mountain-stream areas. This includes aquatic insects that play an important role in the pollination of wasabi flowers, such as dragonfly species like *Epiophlebia superstes* and the broad-winged damselfly (*Calopterygidae*), the Hirata mayfly (*Heptageniidae*), Japanese firefly (*Luciola cruciata*), and Yotsume caddisfly (*Perissoneura paradoxa*). Other semiaquatic animal species inhabit the terraces as well, including snails and the Japanese clawed salamander (*Onychodactylus japonicus*).[37] Onashi stoneflies (*Nemoura fulva*), caddisflies (*Lepidostomatidae*), and freshwater snails (*Semisulcospira libertina*) eat and damage wasabi plants; however, dragonfly nymphs and Japanese freshwater crabs prey on these harmful animals.[38] The *Pieris melete* butterfly, found in wasabi fields and mountain streams, is a food source for the forest's many frogs, spiders, snakes, and birds.[39] In nearby streams, *amago* (red-spotted masu trout), Japanese sculpin, and freshwater salmon are eaten by forest birds like the crested kingfisher (*Megaceryle lugubris*) and the brown dipper (*Cinclus pallasii*).[40] The stable climate and few invasive species make *tatami-ishi* systems important species-preservation areas.

The *tatami-ishi* cultivation method plays a crucial role in mitigating downstream flooding by absorbing water through the terraces and layered rocks in each bed. These sloping, staggered terraces slow the rate of water moving downhill by providing more surface area, thereby reducing soil erosion.[41] In addition, the forested mountainous areas upstream of wasabi fields act as barriers, functioning as natural dams. Here, rainwater is stored and purified in the soil, where it is eventually used to irrigate terraces downhill. By channeling the

9

9 Wasabi terraces channel clean, cool, fast-flowing spring water continuously over the plant roots at a controlled depth and speed, which maintains the precise temperature, oxygenation, and moisture levels essential for wasabi cultivation.

10

10 Between March and April, small white flowers bloom on wasabi plants.

11

12

11 Wasabi contains special compounds called isothiocyanates (ITCs), which are referred to as nutraceuticals, compounds present in foods that have health benefits above basic nutritional value. These compounds are what give wasabi its unique spicy flavor, with the aquatic-grown wasabi containing higher ITCs than the field-grown plants.
12 The leaves and stems of the plant are also edible, and the entire plant is used in both food and health applications.

abundant rainfall of the Shizuoka and Izu regions into productive farming plots, *tatami-ishi* wasabi farming serves as a strategic adaptation for climate resilience.[42]

The spring water used for traditional wasabi cultivation produces larger stems, minimizes crop damage, reduces likelihood of disease, and prevents nutrient depletion, as often seen with repeated cultivation.[43] Rich in nutrients and dissolved oxygen, the percolation also contributes to a water-cleansing process, and the resulting water can then be reused in the fields below.[44] Toward the lower terraces, freshwater aquaculture is practiced in conjunction with *tatami-ishi*-style cultivation, where fish species are farmed.[45] Further downstream, regional farmers cultivate shiitake mushrooms under forest shade, as well as teas like *honyama* and matcha, and wetland rice in farmland outside the forest with direct access to sunlight.[46] Eventually, the water used to irrigate terraces flows into natural rivers, then drains into the Pacific Ocean.[47]

Prior to the introduction of *tatami-ishi* terracing, settling and cultivating these mountainous districts posed threats due to frequent flooding. Landslides following typhoons and severe rainfall are among the greatest threats to the regions of Shizuoka and Izu. In 1876, a flood washed away over 10 hectares of wasabi fields in Utogi, while a 1958 typhoon washed away nearly all the fields in the Nakaizu district of Izu City.[48] Despite the devastation of wasabi fields during these severe weather events, the *tatami-ishi* terraces integrated into steep slopes play a crucial role as a protective barrier, safeguarding towns and farms situated at the lower reaches of mountains from the potential catastrophic flooding of headwaters.

Processed wasabi goods have represented a major source of income for farmers, and have led to the development of industries for wasabi processing in the neighboring areas, resulting in further financial opportunities.[49] The production of traditional foods derived from *tatami-ishi* harvests, including wasabi pickles, wasabi miso paste, and wasabi seaweed, along with medicinal products, has emerged as a crucial source of income in the region.[50] Farmers and manufacturers have creatively repurposed once discarded wasabi leaves and petioles for dishes like wasabi croquettes and wasabi *konnyaku* jelly.[51]

Traditional methods of wasabi cultivation in Shizuoka have been recognized as a GIAHS and a Japanese Nationally Important Agricultural Heritage

Water Cycle of Wasabi Cultivation

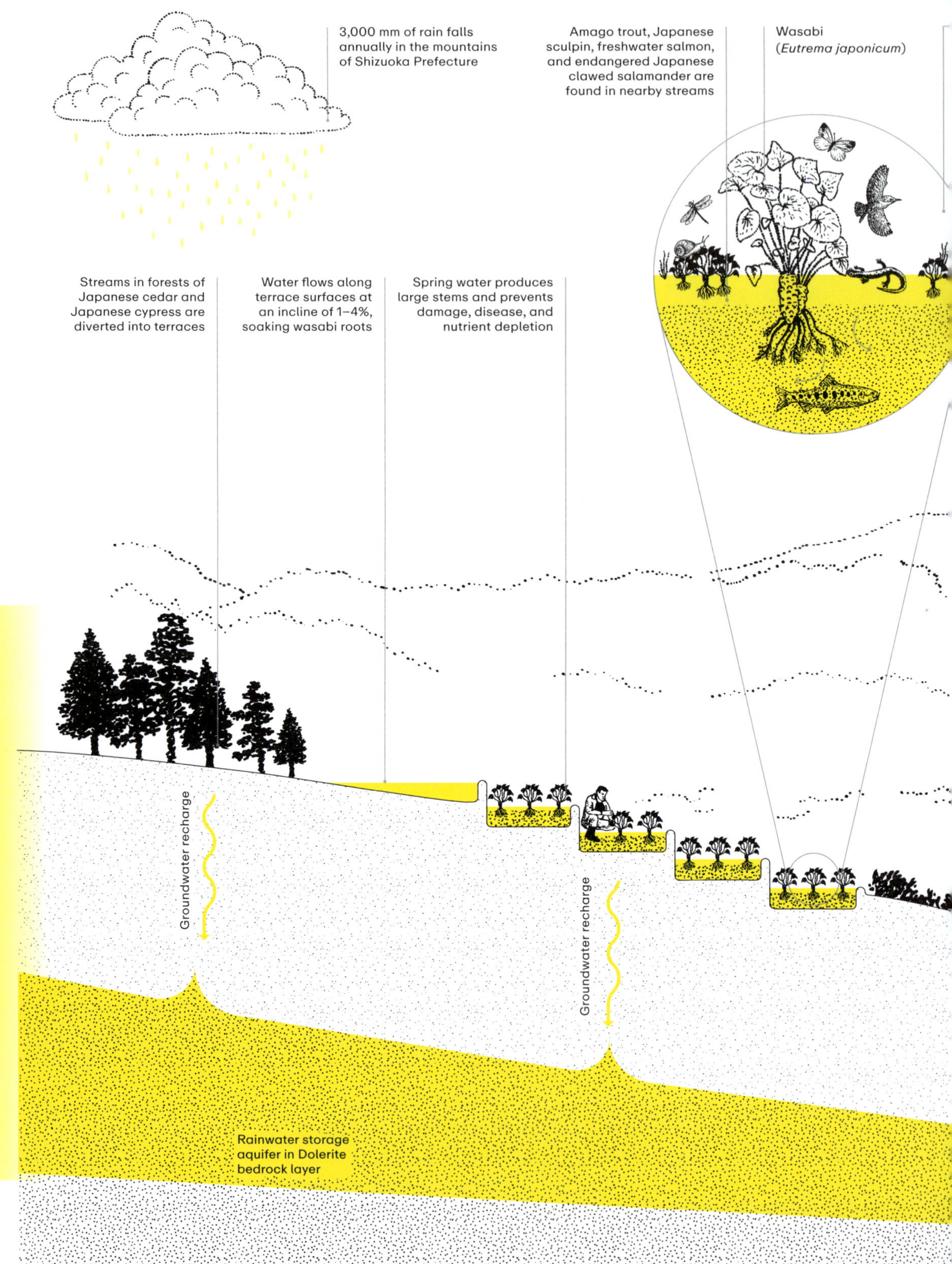

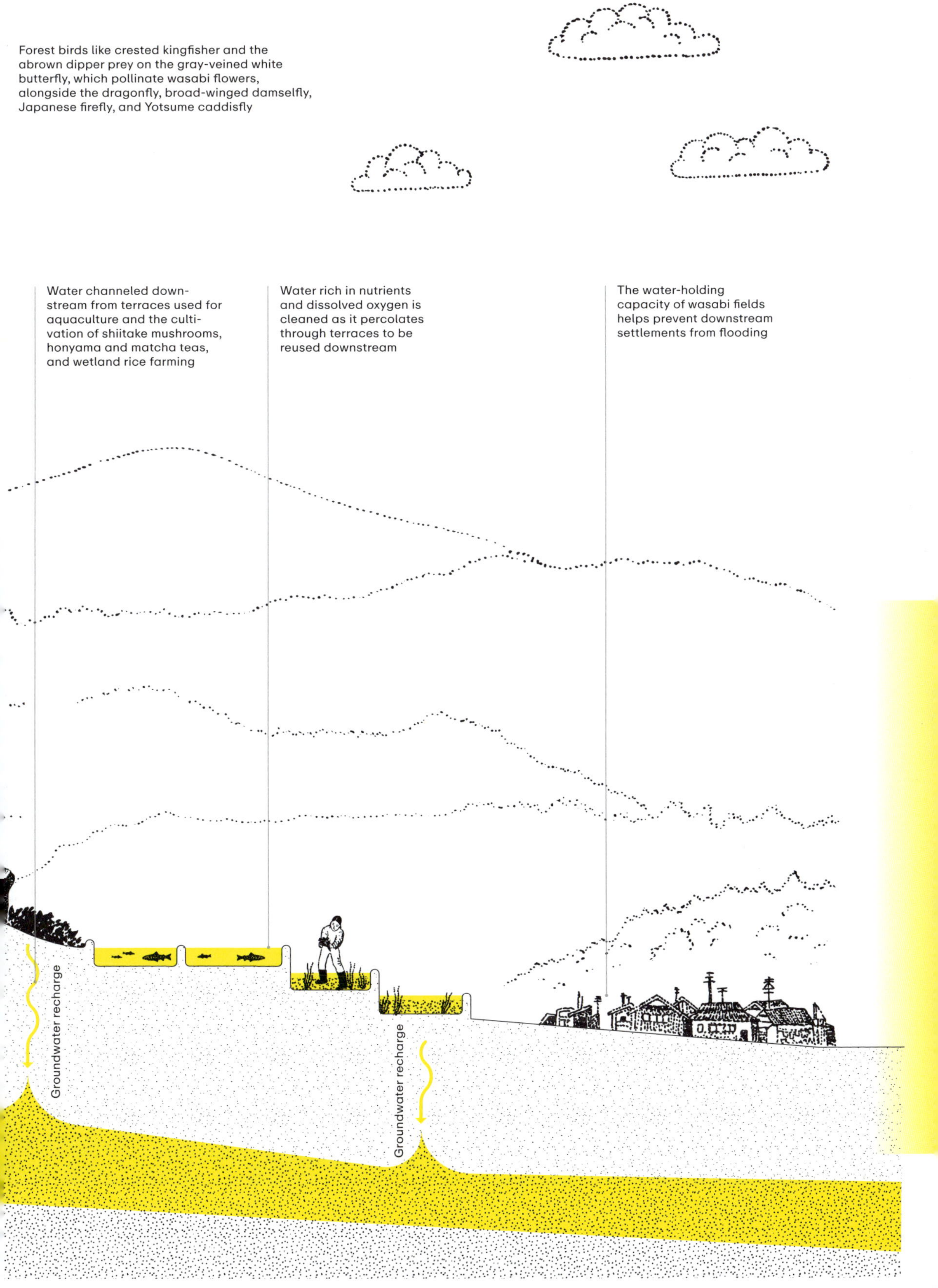

Forest birds like crested kingfisher and the abrown dipper prey on the gray-veined white butterfly, which pollinate wasabi flowers, alongside the dragonfly, broad-winged damselfly, Japanese firefly, and Yotsume caddisfly

Water channeled downstream from terraces used for aquaculture and the cultivation of shiitake mushrooms, honyama and matcha teas, and wetland rice farming

Water rich in nutrients and dissolved oxygen is cleaned as it percolates through terraces to be reused downstream

The water-holding capacity of wasabi fields helps prevent downstream settlements from flooding

Groundwater recharge

Groundwater recharge

System since 2018.[52] With nearly six hundred wasabi producers and 118, 383 beneficiaries of the system in the Shizuoka Prefecture in 2015, the wasabi industry supports life in mountain districts.[53] Today, the areas where *tatami-ishi* cultivation is practiced are experiencing a boost in tourism, attracted by their abundant forests, bubbling hot springs, and scenic mountains. Recognizing the crucial role of the ecosystem in *tatami-ishi* conservation, efforts, including weeding waterways and repairing drainage channels, have been made to enhance both the agricultural practice and the surrounding environment.[54]

These heritage designations are also aimed at attracting new businesses, providing financial incentives for younger workers to stay in the area.[55] One possible avenue could be the retrofit of the system to incorporate micro hydropower, providing clean energy to the farming communities. However, *tatami-ishi* cultivation is losing traction due to a lack of suitable land and the physical demands of field maintenance, often passed down through generations. Hence, initiatives aimed at revitalizing and expanding traditional ecological knowledge among the next generation have significant value in these regions—particularly as the practice of *tatami-ishi* growth poses significant potential for climate adaptation amid heavier annual rainfall and extreme weather events.[56]

13 Forests of coniferous trees, like Japanese cedars and Japanese cypress, surround *tatami-ishi* terraces.
14 A woman removes leaves from a wasabi root at a farm in Ikadaba in the city of Izu, Shizuoka Prefecture.
15 Mitsuyasu Asada, a third-generation farmer in Shizuoka Prefecture, is worried that climate change is threatening the future of wasabi.

13

14

15

Fed by abundant spring water and mountain streams, *tatami-ishi* wasabi cultivation benefits from its unique natural ecosystem while supporting broader environmental stability. Beyond agricultural production, wasabi fields slow the movement of water and enhance biodiversity. As a key industry in these mountainous regions, these traditional systems also represent the opportunity to support financial livelihood among farmers while sustaining the natural environment as a resource-producing, stabilizing infrastructure. Arable land in mountainous regions is typically scarce and susceptible to natural disasters. However, the clever use of water movement as a natural energy source, coupled with the cultivation methods and strains refined over many years by wasabi farmers, has led to the high-quality, year-round production of this crop.[57] While there are few global examples of this technology, its diverse capabilities highlight the need to preserve such existing examples and use them as inspiration for other mountainous regions.

16

16 This traditional system supports the financial livelihood of farmers while sustaining the natural environment as a resource-producing, stabilizing infrastructure.

ENDNOTES

1. "Highlighted Japanese Ingredient: Wasabi," Japanese External Trade Organization, accessed July 6, 2023, https://www.jetro.go.jp/en/trends/foods/ingredients/wasabi.html.
2. Shizuoka WASABI Association for Important Agricultural Heritage Systems Promotion, *Traditional Wasabi Cultivation in Shizuoka: Action Plan for the Proposed GIAHS Site* (Rome: FAO), 36, http://www.fao.org/3/CA3182EN/ca3182en.pdf.
3. Julia Watson, Avery Robertson, and Felix de Rosen, "Designing by Radical Indigenism," *Landscape Architecture Frontiers* 8, no. 3 (2020): 155, https://doi.org/10.15302/J-LAF-1-050019.
4. Shizuoka WASABI Association for Important Agricultural Heritage Systems Promotion, *Traditional Wasabi Cultivation*, 4.
5. Shizuoka WASABI Association for Important Agricultural Heritage Systems Promotion, *Traditional Wasabi Cultivation*, 1.
6. Shizuoka WASABI Association for Important Agricultural Heritage Systems Promotion, *Traditional Wasabi Cultivation*, 4.
7. Shizuoka WASABI Association for Important Agricultural Heritage Systems Promotion, *Traditional Wasabi Cultivation*, 15.
8. Shizuoka WASABI Association for Important Agricultural Heritage Systems Promotion, *Traditional Wasabi Cultivation*, 42.
9. Shizuoka WASABI Association for Important Agricultural Heritage Systems Promotion, *Traditional Wasabi Cultivation*, 10.
10. Natsu Shimamura, "Wasabi," Tokyo Foundation for Policy Research, June 2, 2009, https://www.tokyofoundation.org/research/detail.php?id=251.
11. Shizuoka WASABI Association for Important Agricultural Heritage Systems Promotion, *Traditional Wasabi Cultivation*, 6–7.
12. Shizuoka WASABI Association for Important Agricultural Heritage Systems Promotion, *Traditional Wasabi Cultivation*, 7.
13. Shizuoka WASABI Association for Important Agricultural Heritage Systems Promotion, *Traditional Wasabi Cultivation*, 1.
14. Shizuoka WASABI Association for Important Agricultural Heritage Systems Promotion, *Traditional Wasabi Cultivation*, 17.
15. Shizuoka WASABI Association for Important Agricultural Heritage Systems Promotion, *Traditional Wasabi Cultivation*, Executive Summary.
16. Shizuoka WASABI Association for Important Agricultural Heritage Systems Promotion, *Traditional Wasabi Cultivation*, 48–49.
17. Shizuoka WASABI Association for Important Agricultural Heritage Systems Promotion, *Traditional Wasabi Cultivation*, 48–49.
18. Shizuoka WASABI Association for Important Agricultural Heritage Systems Promotion, *Traditional Wasabi Cultivation*, 48.
19. Shizuoka WASABI Association for Important Agricultural Heritage Systems Promotion, *Traditional Wasabi Cultivation*, 48.
20. Shizuoka WASABI Association for Important Agricultural Heritage Systems Promotion, *Traditional Wasabi Cultivation*, 48.
21. Shizuoka WASABI Association for Important Agricultural Heritage Systems Promotion, *Traditional Wasabi Cultivation*, 48.
22. Shizuoka WASABI Association for Important Agricultural Heritage Systems Promotion, *Traditional Wasabi Cultivation*, 36.
23. Shimamura, "Wasabi."
24. Carol Miles and Catherine Daniels, *Growing Wasabi in the Pacific Northwest* (Pullman: Pacific Northwest Extension, 2020), 7.
25. Miles and Daniels, *Growing Wasabi in the Pacific Northwest*, 7.
26. Shizuoka WASABI Association for Important Agricultural Heritage Systems Promotion, *Traditional Wasabi Cultivation*, 36–37.
27. Shizuoka WASABI Association for Important Agricultural Heritage Systems Promotion, *Traditional Wasabi Cultivation*, 36–37.
28. Shimamura, "Wasabi."
29. Shizuoka WASABI Association for Important Agricultural Heritage Systems Promotion, *Traditional Wasabi Cultivation*, 13.
30. Shizuoka WASABI Association for Important Agricultural Heritage Systems Promotion, *Traditional Wasabi Cultivation*, 59.
31. Miles and Daniels, *Growing Wasabi in the Pacific Northwest*, 7.
32. Shizuoka WASABI Association for Important Agricultural Heritage Systems Promotion, *Traditional Wasabi Cultivation*, Executive Summary.
33. Shizuoka WASABI Association for Important Agricultural Heritage Systems Promotion, *Traditional Wasabi Cultivation*, 37–38.
34. Shimamura, "Wasabi."
35. Shimamura, "Wasabi."
36. Shimamura, "Wasabi."
37. Shizuoka WASABI Association for Important Agricultural Heritage Systems Promotion, *Traditional Wasabi Cultivation*, 29.
38. Shizuoka WASABI Association for Important Agricultural Heritage Systems Promotion, *Traditional Wasabi Cultivation*, 26–27
39. Shizuoka WASABI Association for Important Agricultural Heritage Systems Promotion, *Traditional Wasabi Cultivation in Shizuoka*, 27.
40. Shizuoka WASABI Association for Important Agricultural Heritage Systems Promotion, *Traditional Wasabi Cultivation*, 29.
41. Watson, Robertson, and de Rosen, "Designing by Radical Indigenism," 155.
42. Shizuoka WASABI Association for Important Agricultural Heritage Systems Promotion, *Traditional Wasabi Cultivation*, Executive Summary.
43. Shizuoka WASABI Association for Important Agricultural Heritage Systems Promotion, *Traditional Wasabi Cultivation*, Executive Summary.
44. Shizuoka WASABI Association for Important Agricultural Heritage Systems Promotion, *Traditional Wasabi Cultivation*, 1.
45. Shizuoka WASABI Association for Important Agricultural Heritage Systems Promotion, *Traditional Wasabi Cultivation*, 1.
46. Shizuoka WASABI Association for Important Agricultural Heritage Systems Promotion, *Traditional Wasabi Cultivation*, 59.
47. Shizuoka WASABI Association for Important Agricultural Heritage Systems Promotion, *Traditional Wasabi Cultivation*, 59.
48. Shizuoka WASABI Association for Important Agricultural Heritage Systems Promotion, *Traditional Wasabi Cultivation*, 44.
49. Shizuoka WASABI Association for Important Agricultural Heritage Systems Promotion, *Traditional Wasabi Cultivation*, Executive Summary.
50. Shizuoka WASABI Association for Important Agricultural Heritage Systems Promotion, *Traditional Wasabi Cultivation*, 21.
51. Shizuoka WASABI Association for Important Agricultural Heritage Systems Promotion, *Traditional Wasabi Cultivation*, 21.
52. "Traditional Wasabi Cultivation in Shizuoka," Shizuoka WASABI Association for Important Agricultural Heritage Systems Promotion, accessed October 29, 2024, https://www.shizuoka-wasabi.jp/en/.
53. Shizuoka WASABI Association for Important Agricultural Heritage Systems Promotion, *Traditional Wasabi Cultivation*, Summary Information.
54. Shizuoka WASABI Association for Important Agricultural Heritage Systems Promotion, *Traditional Wasabi Cultivation*, 16.
55. Shizuoka WASABI Association for Important Agricultural Heritage Systems Promotion, *Traditional Wasabi Cultivation*, 16.
56. Shizuoka WASABI Association for Important Agricultural Heritage Systems Promotion, *Traditional Wasabi Cultivation*, 59.
57. Shizuoka WASABI Association for Important Agricultural Heritage Systems Promotion, *Traditional Wasabi Cultivation*, 37–38.

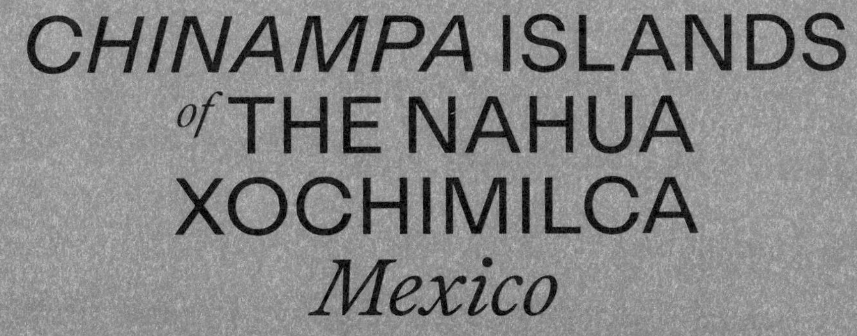

CHINAMPA ISLANDS *of* THE NAHUA XOCHIMILCA

Mexico

CHINAMPA ISLANDS *of* THE NAHUA XOCHIMILCA *Mexico*

Coauthored by
Pedro Mendez Rosas and
Rodrigo Alberto Lañado Cruz

PEOPLE Nahua Xochimilca
LOCATION Xochimilco Canals, Mexico City, Mexico
TECHNOLOGY agricultural floating islands
ELEVATION 2,240 m **ORIGIN** 1100 CE
DISTANCE ABOVE OR BELOW WATERLINE −1.5 to +0.88 m
WATER LEVEL FLUCTUATION, TIDAL OR SEASONAL +1.25 to +2 m

FAO Nexus
WATER fresh ENERGY bioenergy + cleansing
FOOD crops + fish + animals

IPCC Adaptation Pathway
protect

World Bank NBS
CATEGORY bioretention areas, constructed inland wetlands, natural inland wetlands, urban farming, river and stream renaturation
FUNCTIONS biodiversity, water pollution regulation, pluvial flood regulation, heat regulation, air pollution regulation
BENEFITS resource production, biodiversity, stimulate local economies and job creation, pluvial flood risk reduction, carbon storage and sequestration, cultural, social interaction, tourism and recreation

1

2

Rowing through the Xochimilco Canals in the darkness before dawn, blue flames believed to be spirits residing in the lake briefly flicker on the surface of the water. They embody the spirituality of the site and its microbial water-cleansing system, which has evolved over thousands of years.[1] The Xochimilco Canals have a surface area of 55,000 square meters and a maximum depth of two meters.[2,3] The canals are formed around raised fields known as *chinampas,* creating a ladder and checkerboard-like arrangement.[4] A species of willow tree known as *ahuejotes* (*Salix bonplandiana*) lining the *chinampa* frame one's line of vision when traveling through the Xochimilco Canals. These fields were a foundation of the Aztec Empire, who built this agricultural territory for food and water cleansing in the Valley of Mexico lakes, but the technology pre-dates them, having begun with the Nahua people.[5] Having been classified as a hotspot vulnerable to climate change in the wake of climate predictions like decreasing rainfall, increasing temperatures, and a soaring population, the expansion of the *chinampa* technology will critically improve the habitability of the Valley of Mexico lakes ecosystem.

The word *chinampa* comes from the Nahuatl word *chinamitl*, meaning "hedge close to the reed."[6] Located in Mexico City, the intensive agricultural raised-field system is surrounded by shallow canals and marshes; although these fields are often referred to as "floating gardens," they do not actually float.[7] Built up with organic material and soil rising past the surrounding water level, they are enclosed by wooden posts, woven organic materials, and living willow trees.[8] Naturally irrigated by canal water and fertilized by mud from the lake bed, *chinampas* are a highly productive agricultural technology capable of producing crops continuously for several years, while remaining fertile for centuries.[9] Mexico City informally relies on these islands in Xochimilco to cleanse its wastewater, acting as a biological treatment plant.[10, 11] In their combination of decaying and living organic matter, the *chinampas* are an agriculturally productive infrastructure with a deep spiritual connection to life and death for the Xochimilca Nahua.

The Nahua, who form over 20 percent of the country's Indigenous population, have influenced the culture, language, religion, societies, and technologies of many groups.[12, 13] As one of the earliest ancestors of the tribes of Mesoamerica, the Nahua migrated south from the High Central Plateau of Mexico to the central Mexican highlands during the 13th and 14th centuries.[14] Though mostly living around the peripheries of the Aztec Empire, they are now the largest Indigenous group of Mexico. For the ancient Nahua, nature was an integral part of life, determining crops, health, migratory patterns of animals, and natural events. Most religious ceremonies revolved around pagan deities that controlled the seasons, sun, moon, and other aspects of nature.[15]

The first *chinampas*—thousands of years before the Aztecs—were actually floating burial structures. The technology was then evolved for agriculture, becoming a form of territorial expansion. First made as a grid system on land in Teotihuacán by the Olmecs—thought to be a mother culture to those that emerged later in Mesoamerica—the Nahua adapted this system to the water.[16]

3

1 The patchwork of *chinampas* on the lake area of Xochimilco in Mexico are composed of raised fields surrounded by canals and ditches.

2 In the darkness before dawn, blue flames believed to be spirits residing in the lake briefly flicker on the surface of the water.

3 A species of willow tree known as *ahuejotes* (*Salix bonplandiana*) line the canals of Xochomilico.

4 A traditional *trajinera* boat passes the organic farm of Arca Tierra in the island gardens of Xochimilco.

The first *chinampa* floating islands were built in the Nahua settlement of Culhuacan, on the south side of the Iztapalapa Peninsula dividing Lake Texcoco from Lake Xochimilco.[17] Xochimilcas, the Nahua people living there, passed their knowledge orally over generations, keeping this technology alive to this day.[18] The Xochimilca community is protective of their traditional knowledge, as Pedro and Antonio Mendez Rosas, who come from a family of *chinampa* farmers dedicated to preserving wisdom and techniques of their heritage, explain: "to draw upon the architecture of the technology is different than to experience the rituals and magic behind them." For example, there is a longstanding belief that *chinampas* have the ability to regenerate bodies; once the broader system is comprehended, it's easy to see why.[19]

In the 1300s, the Aztecs were a small group that settled in the midst of Lake Texcoco in the Valley of Mexico, where present-day Mexico City now thrives. Upon arrival, conflicts with their new neighbors forced them to retreat to two small islands on Lake Xochimilco. There, the Aztecs adopted the *chinampa* system, which had been practiced for years along the margins of the lake. With its dual purpose as one of the most productive farming methods of the time and as a purification system, it provided Aztecs with land to live on, a surplus of food, and water cleansing in the densely populated capital city of Tenochtitlan.[20] They adopted and expanded this system for Tenochtitlan, reducing the salinity in the water.[21] For these reasons, *chinampas* were critical in the expansion of the Aztec Empire.[22]

Located at the southern edge of present-day Mexico City, this shallow body of water was known as the "Lake of the Moon" by the Aztecs. Historically, Xochimilco covered one-fourth of the Valley of Mexico during the rainy summer season, but reduced to five separate lakes in the dry winter: Zumpango in the

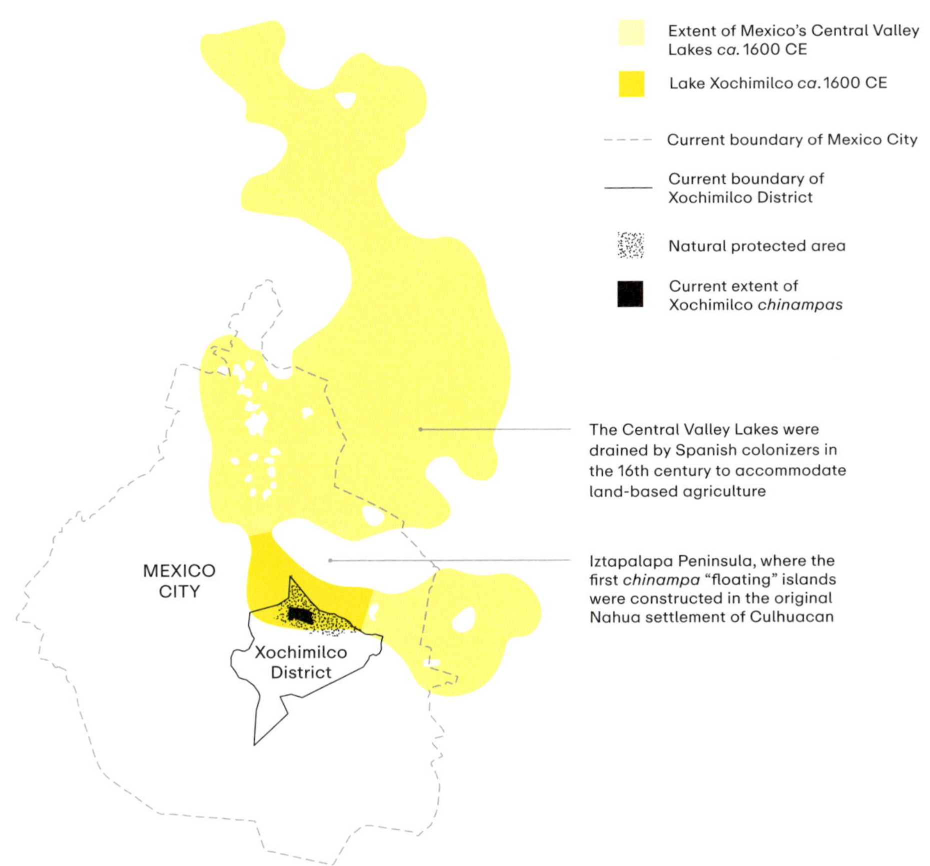

north, Xaltocún and Texcoco in the center, and Xochimilco and Chalco, separated by a causeway, in the south. In the second millennium BCE, villages spread throughout the valley, which is a landlocked basin surrounded by volcanic mountains approximately two and half kilometers above sea level. From these villages emerged the *chinampa* farmers.

Beginning in 1521, the Spanish colonial forces drained the Central Valley Lakes to make way for agriculture.[23] Tapping springs, digging wells, and building infrastructure like tunnels for the eventual development of Mexico City increased the valley's low water supply, leading to a reliance on treated sewage water for these floating island systems.[24, 25, 26] Today, all that remains of Lake Xochimilco are the Xochimilco Canals, which are now a nationally protected area, a UNESCO World Heritage Site, and a GIAHS site.[27, 28, 29]

Surrounded by water on at least three sides, a *chinampa* consists of a long narrow strip of fertile land that can be harvested up to eight times a year.[30, 31] These raised fields vary from eight to one hundred meters in length, and two to 25 meters in width, usually rectangular but occasionally triangular.[32] Traditionally, their proportions follow a one-to-three ratio: If a bed were three meters wide, then it would be nine meters long.[33] A complex drainage system of ditches and dams is built alongside the *chinampas* to control flooding.[34] Ditches of one to

Cut-and-Fill Construction of the *Chinampa* Raised Agricultural Fields and Xochimilco Canals

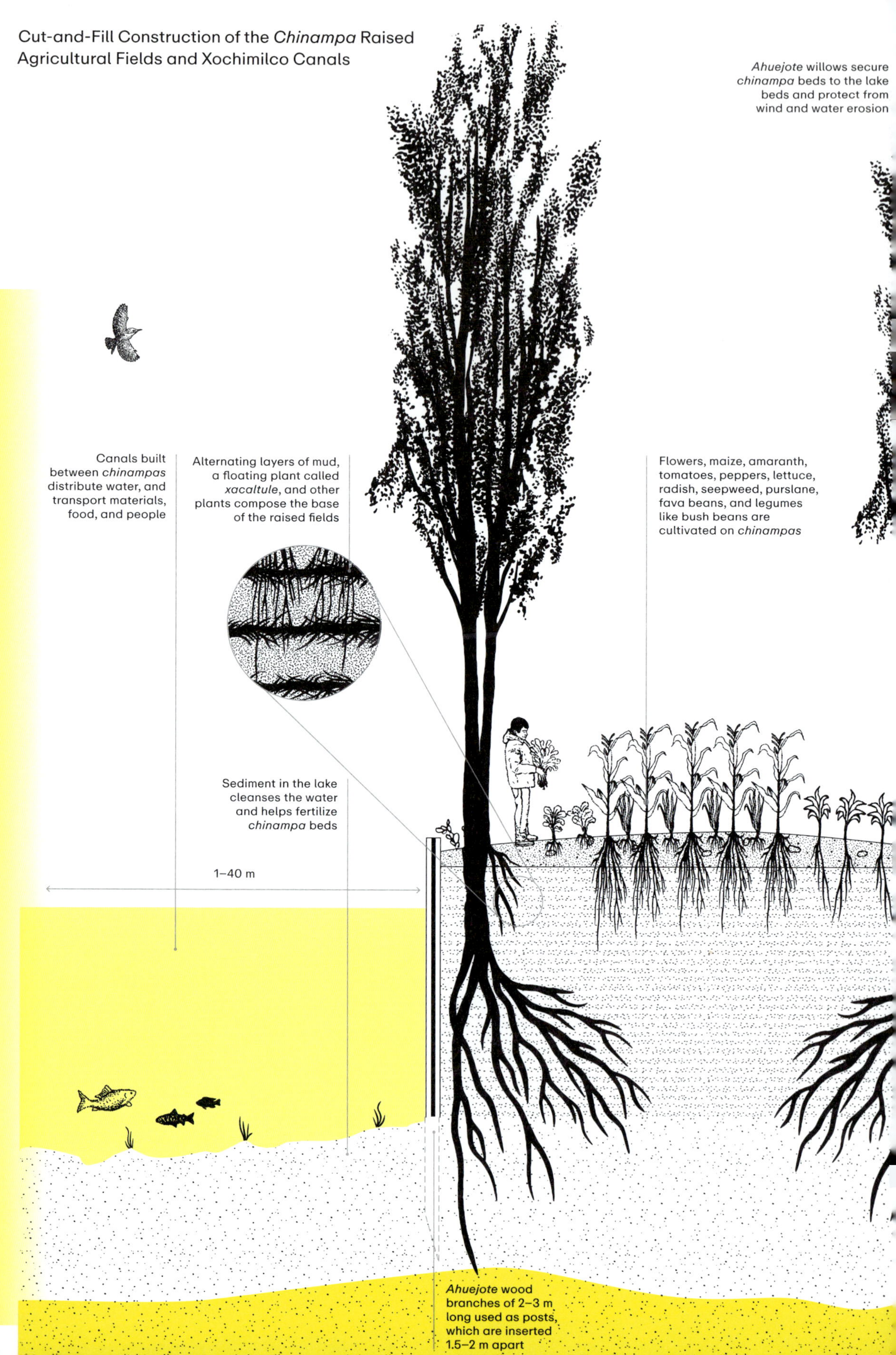

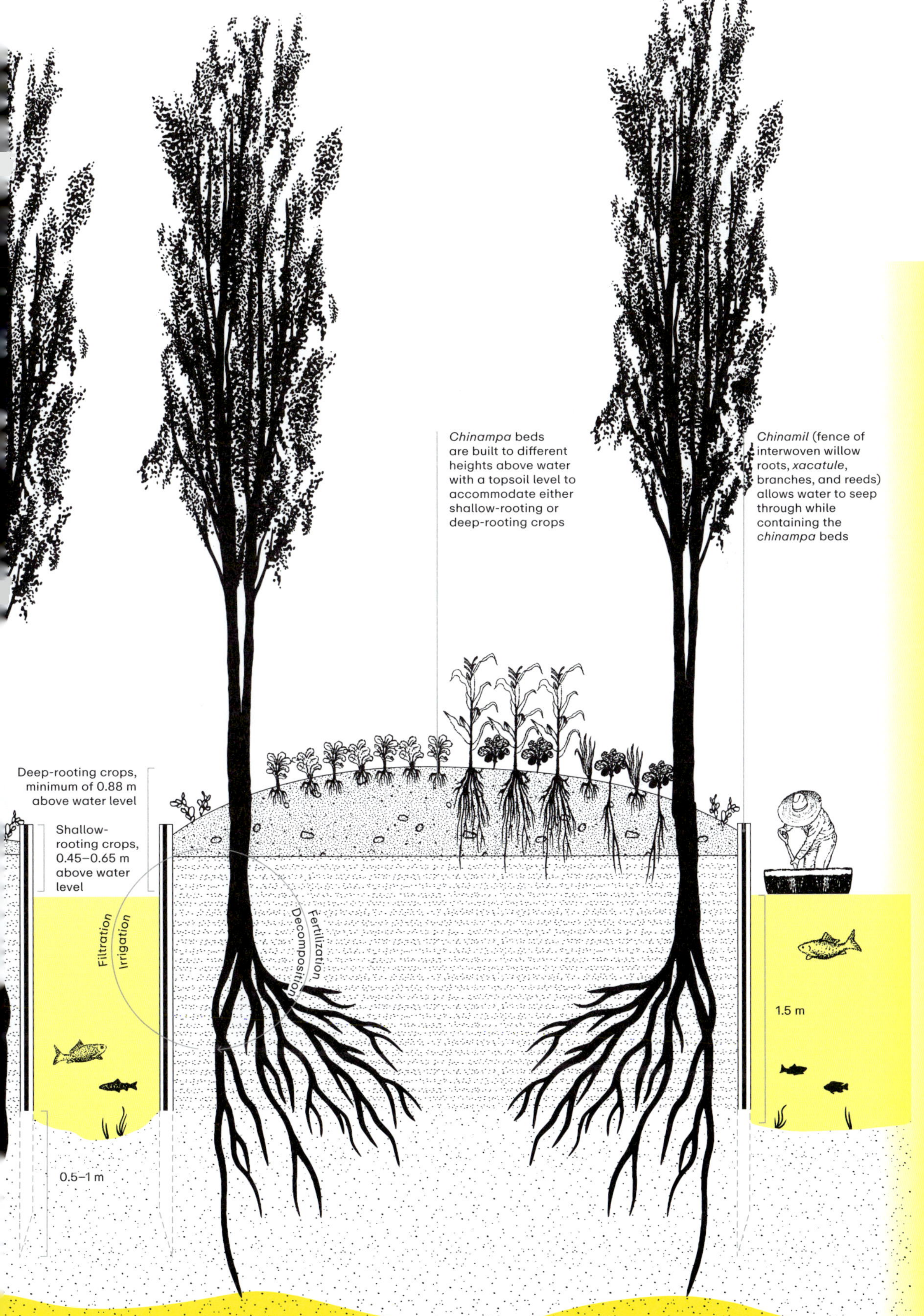
Chinampa beds are built to different heights above water with a topsoil level to accommodate either shallow-rooting or deep-rooting crops
Chinamil (fence of interwoven willow roots, *xacatule*, branches, and reeds) allows water to seep through while containing the *chinampa* beds
Deep-rooting crops, minimum of 0.88 m above water level
Shallow-rooting crops, 0.45–0.65 m above water level
Filtration
Irrigation
Fertilization
Decomposition
1.5 m
0.5–1 m

5 *Chinampa* farmers continually work to build up the soil, using the nutrient-rich mud dredged from the canal beds.

40 meters in width are built between each *chinampa* field, connecting them through canals navigated by canoe.[35, 36] The *chinampa* system has two different types of canals: the larger *acalotes*, an early urban hydrologic system designed to transport food and people faster than roads, and smaller *apantales* distribution channels for water, used by *chinampa* farmers.[37, 38] *Chinampas* encourage biodiverse agriculture, are kept in almost continuous cultivation, have renewable soils, and create a microenvironment that protects from frost, as temperatures range from 12 to 20 degrees Celsius.[39, 40]

6 *Chinampas* are a highly productive agricultural technology capable of producing crops continuously for several years, while remaining fertile for centuries.

The dimensions of each *chinampa* are guided by the desired capillary effect for a field: For example, if water is deficient during certain periods, then fields may be narrower. The height of the *chinampas* suits the body of water where they are situated, and must be high enough to allow for root growth and subirrigation for crops. If the surface of the bed rises above the water by 45 to 65 centimeters, it is suitable for shallow-rooting crops, whereas a minimum of 88 centimeters is needed for deeper-rooting crops, or soils with a higher capillary rise. While subirrigation reduces the need for irrigation, it does not replace it. During the dry season, from November to May, channel water is scooped from the canal and splashed on the *chinampas* using a *zoquimatl*—a ladle-like tool with a long handle. Today, farmers produce flowers, maize, legumes like bush beans and fava beans, amaranth, tomatoes, peppers, lettuce, radish, seepweed, and purslane, in addition to many other vegetables.

7 Surrounded by water on at least three sides, a *chinampa* consists of a long narrow strip of fertile land that can be harvested up to eight times a year.

8 Farmers produce flowers, maize, legumes, amaranth, tomatoes, peppers, lettuce, radish, seepweed, purslane, and many other vegetables.

8

Sometimes free-range animals, like chickens, ducks, swine, cattle, and sheep, are kept in corrals between the *chinampa* crops, as animals feed on excess produce and provide fertilizer with their manure.[41]

To begin construction, farmers locate an area of shallow canal where the lake bed is firm. Live branches of *ahuejote*, or Bonpland willows, are posted to mark the perimeter of the agricultural field. As a form of propagation, each living post, measuring two to three meters long, is placed into the ground in increments of one and a half to two meters apart and 50 centimeters to one meter deep.[42] *Chinampa* beds are aligned east to west, facing south to maximize sun exposure.[43, 44] The *ahuejotes* are first planted to form a fence surrounding the field, reinforcing the border of the agricultural islands. The *ahuejote* posts also secure the *chinampa* to the ground, provide shade, and serve as a trellis for vine crops, making the willow species an important structural element.[45] In moist or wet soil, *ahuejotes* grow to 10 meters in height and restore riparian systems affected by wind or water

RIPARIAN
The areas adjacent to water bodies characterized by specific ecological and environmental features influenced by the presence of water.

erosion by compacting soil and maintaining moisture. The *esqueje*, or *ahuejote* roots, expand horizontally, weaving together the wooden posts to form a protective barrier from sun, wind, and pests. Though the Bonpland willow is popular, other species in the willow family, as well as bamboo, are also used. The roots of the willow are then interwoven with an aquatic plant called *xacaltule*, reeds, and other branches to form the *chinamil*—a solid fence used to contain soil. The *chinamil* is filled with subaquatic organic material, including alternating layers of fertile mud, floating *xacaltule*, and other living and decaying aquatic vegetation from surrounding swamps and lakes. These are all added to the demarcated beds, creating an active composting system in the soil.[46]

9

The Xochimilca use a tool called *xoquimique* to place mud from the lake bottom.[47] The layering process continues until the bed is raised 50 centimeters above water level and can be stood upon, after which it is left to dry for several weeks.[48, 49] Later, more mud and organic matter is added to the bed; *chinampa* soils are of anthropogenic origin—commonly clay textures—and take on darker colors with increased moisture.[50] Hands are mainly used to care for agricultural beds because of the muddy, loose soil.

ANTHROPOGENIC
Environmental changes or processes that are caused by human activities.

Macro- and micronutrients in the Xochimilco Canals, generated from animals, plants, decaying organic matter, and more, contribute to soil fertility. Fish weirs and fences are strategically used to cultivate fish near *chinampas*.[51, 52] Carp (*Cyprinus carpio*) and tilapia (*Oreocrhomis niloticus*) are the main species present in Xochimilco, though aquatic salamander, axolotl (*Ambystoma mexicanum*), and crayfish (*Cambarellus montezumae*) are also found.[53] The system provides many habitats for terrestrial and aquatic animals and plants, including *tulares*, which are floating islands of cattail (*Typha latifolia*), bulrush (*Schoenoplectus americanus*), yellow water lily (*Nymphaea mexicana*), Xochimilco frog (*Rana tlaloci*), and 11 other wildlife species that are part of a special protection category.[54]

10

9 To begin construction, live branches of *ahuejote*, or Bonpland willows, are posted to mark the perimeter of the agricultural field.
10 The Xochimilca place mud from the lake bottom in a layering process that continues until the bed is raised 50 centimeters above water level and can be stood upon, after which it is left to dry for several weeks.

Like *chinampa* beds, the broader system in Xochimilco filters water, acting as a biological sewage and waste treatment plant.[55, 56, 57] Most of the water in the 22 square kilometers of the Xochimilco Canals comes from a water treatment plant located in Cerro de la Estrella, with output water that contains high levels of fecal coliform; the plant receives 80 percent of Mexico City's sewage from its 22 million residents.[58, 59, 60] Two thousand liters of water per second are discharged into the Xochimilco Canals from Estrella, as well as three smaller treatment plants and informal runoff, containing heavy metals, organic waste, synthetic materials, and dissolved salts.[61, 62, 63, 64, 65, 66] Xochimilco's *chinampas* actively cleanse the Mexico City wastewater discharged into wetland canals through bacteria present in its sediment, which has evolved for thousands of years, and the phytoextraction permitted by *ahuejote* roots. The submerged roots that help compose the agricultural beds create an ideal habitat for millions of microorganisms that feed off algae, carbon, and excess nutrients found in the water, and, in doing so, purify the water. The abundance of nutrients—primarily nitrates and phosphates—in this eutrophic body of water also supports life within the ecosystem.[67] However, excess contamination and waste still threaten the system.[68]

PHYTOEXTRACTION
A subprocess of phytoremediation in which plants remove dangerous elements or compounds from soil or water.

EUTROPHIC
Overly enriched with nutrients causing excessive harmful growth of algae and plants.

11

12

11 Incredibly efficient and self-sustaining, the *chinampas* of Xochimilco located in the south end of Mexico City, are planted with a vast array of agricultural produce.
12 If the surface of a bed rises above the water level by 45 to 65 centimeters, it is suitable for shallow-rooting crops, whereas a minimum of 88 centimeters is needed for deeper-rooting crops.

Chinampas Act as an Informal Wastewater Treatment Plant for 40–45 percent of Mexico City's Sewage

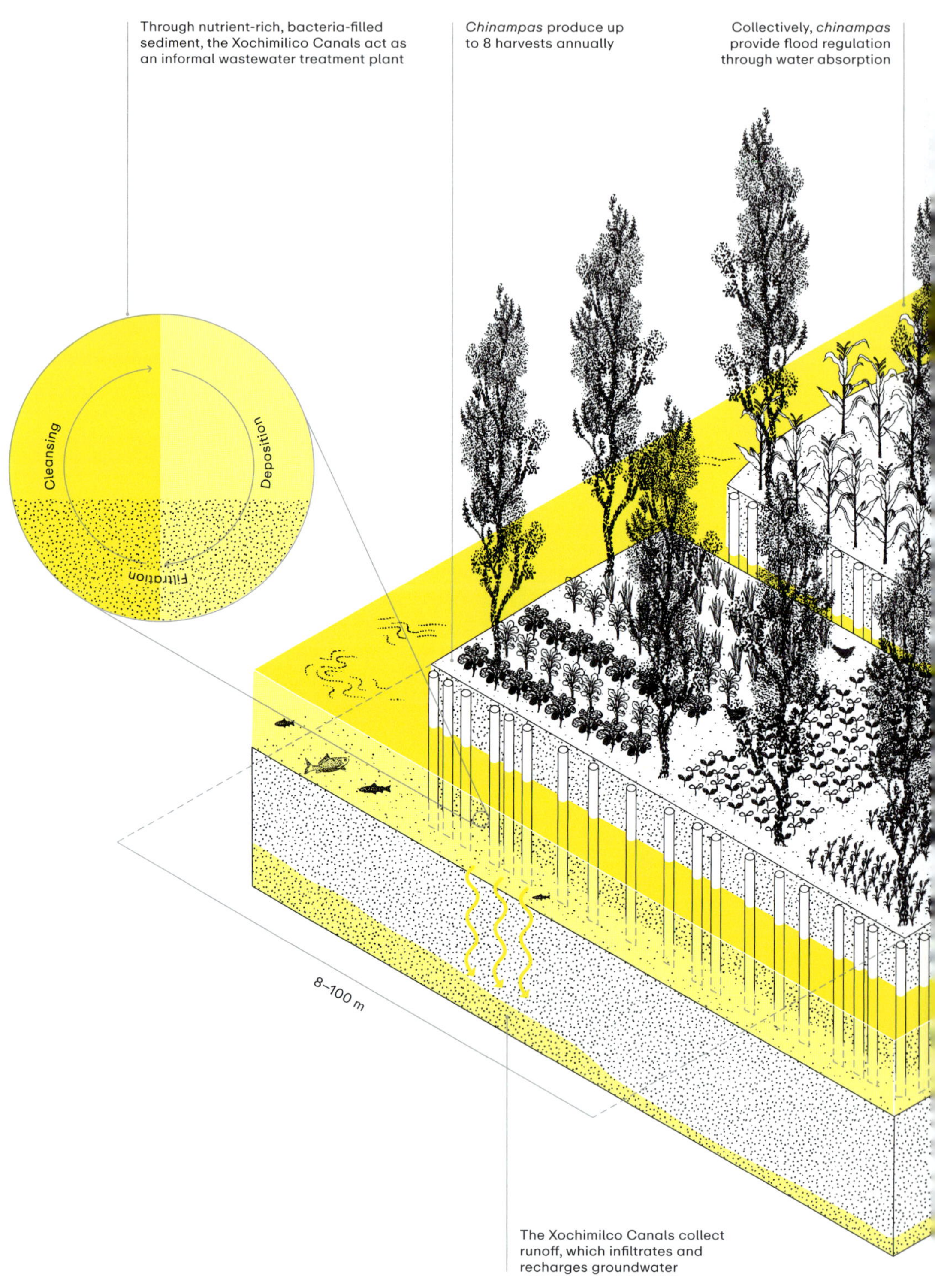

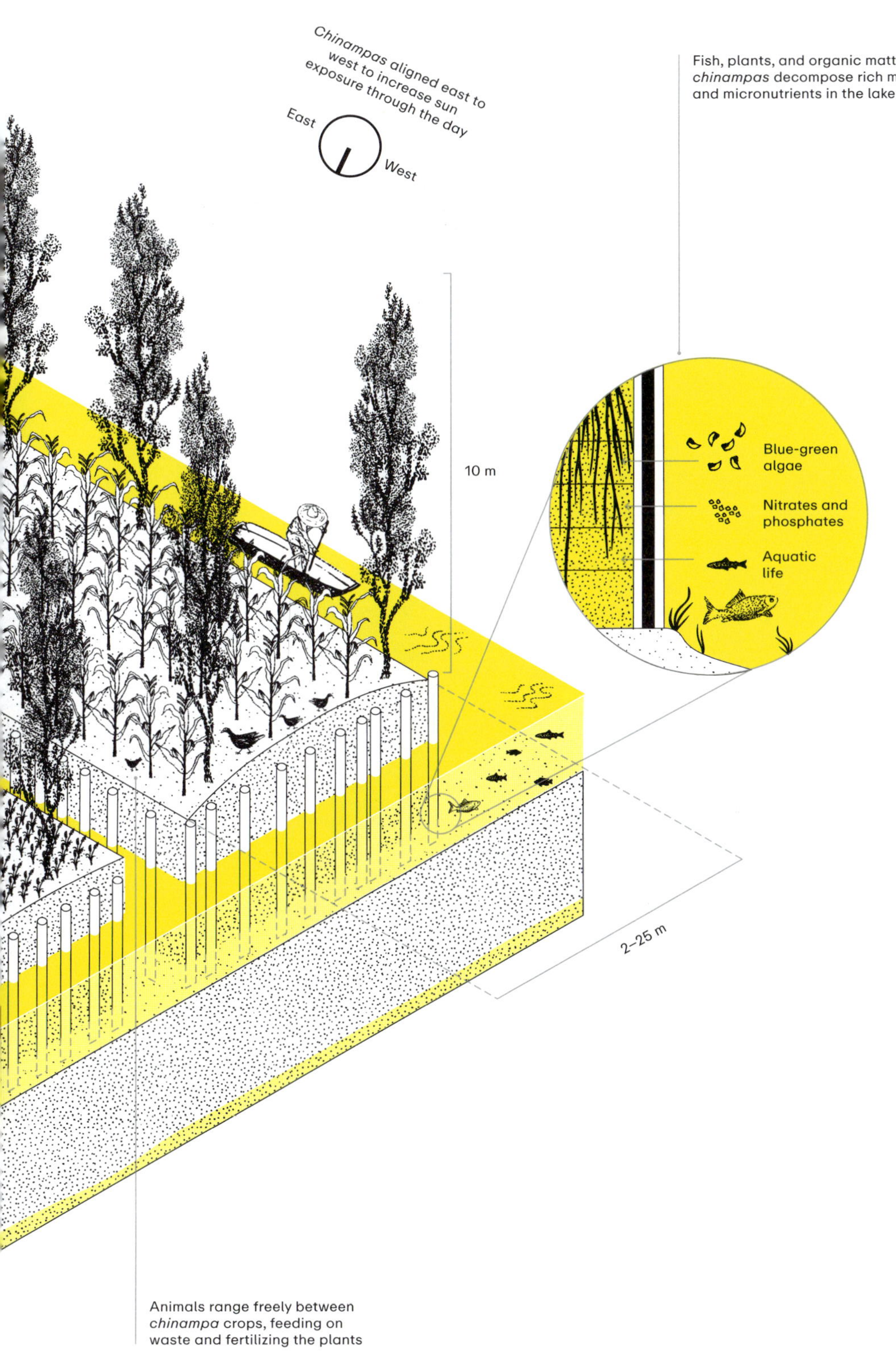
Chinampas aligned east to west to increase sun exposure through the day
East
West
Fish, plants, and organic matter help *chinampas* decompose rich macro- and micronutrients in the lake
10 m
Blue-green algae
Nitrates and phosphates
Aquatic life
2–25 m
Animals range freely between *chinampa* crops, feeding on waste and fertilizing the plants

13

14

13 The *trajineras*, flat boats that take tourists through the canals, at Cuemanco Pier are essential to the economy of the system.
14 *Chinampa* beds are aligned east to west, facing south to maximize sun exposure.
15 Incredibly efficient and self-sustaining, *chinampas* are productive year-round and continue to be used to grow food.

By retaining excess water, the system controls flooding in Mexico City and generates humidity, altering the climate, compacting soil, and reducing wind erosion.[69,70] People living in the Xochimilco District utilize the runoff from the Valley of Mexico and treated wastewater to recharge groundwater.[71,72,73] The *chinampas* naturally function as a system that harvests and treats water, produces food, provides cultivable land, captures carbon, and prevents flooding and erosion: a multifaceted climate change–adaptation tool.[74]

Rapid urbanization in the 1900s decreased land available for farming, and an earthquake in 1985 led to the abandonment of many *chinampas* when people lost homes in nearby towns.[75] However, an estimated five thousand acres of *chinampas* are still in use. While diverse vegetable production for subsistence

MONOCROPPING The agricultural practice of growing a single crop species over a large area of land, typically for multiple consecutive seasons or years.

or commercial purposes still occurs, commercial monocropping of floriculture has dominated this system, providing the highest financial returns, even though many flowers grow in salty, infertile soils.[76] Today, many associate the site with flowers, and the name Xochimilco itself derives from the Nahuatl words *xochitl* and *milli*, meaning "where the flowers grow."[77] *Chinampas* have also become central to tourism in the region, with decorated Mexican gondolas ferrying visitors through the canals.[78]

Following pandemic-related disruptions to industrial supply chains, a number of abandoned *chinampas* were restored to grow fresh local food.[79] New approaches to grow native plants on smaller, simplified structures, including stone or polypropylene borders in small ponds or lakes, are also being explored.[80] Some *chinampa* farmers now use mechanized irrigation systems with buckets and hoses as an alternative to subirrigation, which causes complications in the bed heights with excess water.[81] Small tunneled greenhouse structures are also commonly used to protect crops from frost and sun, while gasoline pumps carry mud from the canal bottom.[82]

The intelligence of the *chinampas* water-cleansing and food-producing technology, which once transformed the Central Valley from a series of lakes to the epicenter of the Aztec Empire, could become catalytic to the future habitability of this region. With limited application in the food production and cleansing of the complex contamination mix of Mexico City's urban waters, the *chinampa* technology could provide critical filtration, fertilization,

15

biofuel, bioenergy, food production, and microclimate mitigation for its future peri-urban communities.

Chinampas are a constructed food-growing and wastewater-cleansing system, which originated in the aquatic ecosystem of Lake Xochimilco and became a method of territorial expansion for the Aztecs. This ancestral technology, which has thrived for centuries, regenerates waste into food and water, driving a system of biological fertility that showcases how nature-based technology can address flooding, sequester greenhouse gasses, grow an abundance of food, support biodiversity, and create a more comfortable microclimate.[83] Rather than extracting energy, the *chinampa* system contains and functions through a powerful combination of natural passive energy systems.

16

17

16 Small tunneled greenhouse structures are also commonly used to protect crops from frost and sun.
17 The intelligence of the water-cleansing and food-producing technology of *chinampas* could become catalytic to the future habitability of this region.

1. Rodrigo Lañado Cruz (permaculture expert), in discussion with the author, September 2022.
2. Cecilia Enríquez García, S. Nandini, and S.S.S. Sarma, "Seasonal Dynamics of Zooplankton in Lake Huetzalin, Xochimilco (Mexico City, Mexico)," *Limnologica* 39, no. 4 (2009): 283, https://doi.org/10.1016/j.limno.2009.06.010.
3. Rodrigo Lañado Cruz (permaculture expert), in discussion with the author, May 2023.
4. Roland Ebel, "Chinampas: An Urban Farming Model of the Aztecs and a Potential Solution for Modern Megalopolis," *HortTechnology* 30, no. 1 (2020): 14, https://doi.org/10.21273/HORTTECH04310-19.
5. Erika Atalo, "Chinampas, the Floating Gardens of a Sinking City," *Field Study of the World*, January 14, 2018, https://www.fieldstudyoftheworld.com/chinampas-floating-gardens-sinking-city/.
6. Ebel, "Chinampas," 14.
7. Ebel, "Chinampas," 13.
8. Ebel, "Chinampas," 13–14.
9. Michael D. Coe, "The Chinampas of Mexico," *Scientific American* 211, no. 1 (1964): 90, https://doi.org/10.1038/scientificamerican0764-90.
10. Ebel, "Chinampas," 14.
11. Cruz, discussion, May 2023.
12. Encyclopedia.com, s.v. "Nahua Peoples," accessed March 21, 2023, https://www.encyclopedia.com/humanities/encyclopedias-almanacs-transcripts-and-maps/nahua-peoples.
13. "Nahua People | History, Culture & Religion," Study.com, June 10, 2021, https://study.com/academy/lesson/nahua-peoples-culture-religion-language.html.
14. Internet Encyclopedia of Philosophy, s.v. "Aztec Philosophy," accessed September 14, 2022, https://iep.utm.edu/aztec-philosophy/.
15. "Nahua People | History, Culture & Religion."
16. Cruz, discussion, May 2023.
17. Dimosthenis Vasiloudis, "'Chinampas': The Ancient Aztec Floating Gardens That Hold Promise For Future Urban Agriculture," *The Archaeologist*, December 17, 2021, https://www.thearchaeologist.org/blog/chinampas-the-ancient-aztec-floating-gardens-that-hold-promise-for-future-urban-agriculture.
18. "Chinampas of Mexico City Were Recognized as an Agricultural Heritage System of Global Importance," FAO, August 12, 2022, https://www.fao.org/giahs/giahsaroundtheworld/designated-sites/latinskaja-amerika-i-karibskii-bassein/chinampa-system-mexico/ru/.
19. Cruz, discussion, May 2023.
20. Coe, "The Chinampas of Mexico," 90.
21. Cruz, discussion, May 2023.
22. Coe, "The Chinampas of Mexico," 90.
23. Coe, "The Chinampas of Mexico," 90.
24. Ebel, "Chinampas," 14.
25. Coe, "The Chinampas of Mexico," 90.
26. Ximena Aide Mendoza Correa, "Las Chinampas Del Humedal de Xochimilco: Sistemas de Biorremediación Para La Sostenibilidad," (master's thesis, El Colegio de la Frontera Norte, 2018), 4, 54–57.
27. Ebel, "Chinampas," 13.
28. "Historic Centre of Mexico City and Xochimilco," UNESCO World Heritage Convention, February 8, 2024, https://whc.unesco.org/en/list/412.
29. "Chinampas Agricultural System in Mexico City," FAO, February 8, 2024, https://www.fao.org/giahs/giahsaroundtheworld/designated-sites/latin-america-and-the-caribbean/chinampa-system-mexico/partners/en.
30. Cruz, discussion, September 2022.
31. Coe, "The Chinampas of Mexico," 90.
32. Ebel, "Chinampas," 14.
33. Cruz, discussion, September 2022.
34. Ebel, "Chinampas," 15.
35. Cruz, discussion, September 2022.
36. Ebel, "Chinampas," 15.
37. Correa, "Las Chinampas Del Humedal de Xochimilco," 50.
38. Cruz, discussion, September 2022.
39. Ebel, "Chinampas," 13.
40. Enriquez García, Nandini, and Sarma, "Seasonal Dynamics of Zooplankton," 284.
41. Ebel, "Chinampas," 13–16.
42. Ebel, "Chinampas," 14.
43. Cruz, discussion, September 2022.
44. Coe, "The Chinampas of Mexico City," 90–99.
45. Cruz, discussion, September 2022.
46. Ebel, "Chinampas," 13–16.
47. Cruz, discussion, September 2022.
48. Ebel, "Chinampas," 14.
49. Atalo, "Chinampas, the Floating Gardens of a Sinking City."
50. Claudia Chávez-López et al., "Removal of Methyl Parathion from a Chinampa Agricultural Soil of Xochimilco Mexico: A Laboratory Study," *European Journal of Soil Biology* 47 (2011): 264–65, https://doi.org/10.1016/j.ejsobi.2011.06.001.
51. Ebel, "Chinampas," 14–16.
52. Cruz, discussion.
53. Luis Zambrano, Elsa Valiente, and Jake Vander Zanden, "Stable Isotope Variation of a Highly Heterogeneous Shallow Freshwater System," *Hydrobiologia* 646 (2010): 327, https://doi.org/10.1007/s10750-010-0182-2.
54. Government of Mexico City, *Chinampa Agricultural System of Mexico City, Mexico: A Proposal for Designation as Globally Important Agricultural Heritage System (GIAHS)* (n.p.: n.p., 2017): 30–31.
55. Ebel, "Chinampas," 14–15.
56. Cruz, discussion, September 2022.
57. Correa, "Las Chinampas Del Humedal de Xochimilco," 92.
58. Lisa Martine Jenkins and Mark Stevenson, "Sewage System Failures Plague Mexican Tourist Destinations," *The Seattle Times*, July 28, 2017, https://www.seattletimes.com/business/sewage-system-failures-plague-mexican-tourist-destinations/.
59. "Axolotls in Crisis: The Fight to Save the 'Water Monster' of Mexico City," The Guardian, December 4, 2018, https://www.theguardian.com/cities/2018/dec/04/axolotls-in-crisis-the-fight-to-save-the-water-monster-of-mexico-city.
60. Correa, "Las Chinampas Del Humedal de Xochimilco," 90.
61. Sarah Freeman, "This Fragile Wetland Is Dying: Tour Boats Could Be Its Unlikely Savior," National Geographic, January 31, 2022, https://www.nationalgeographic.com/travel/article/nanobubbles-tour-boats-could-rescue-endangered-mexican-wetland.
62. Patricia Martínez-Cruz et al., "Use of Constructed Wetlands for the Treatment of Water From an Experimental Channel at Xochimilco, Mexico," *Hidrobiológica* 16, no. 3 (2006): 212.
63. Hans Gehrels et al., *A Water Resilience Plan for the Heritage Zone of Xochimilco, Tlahuac and Milpa Alta* (n.p.: Resilience Agency of Mexico City, 2019): 19.
64. "Axolotls in Crisis."
65. Cruz, discussion, May 2023.
66. Ebel, "Chinampas," 15.
67. Correa, "Las Chinampas Del Humedal de Xochimilco," Abstract, 53, 58, 92–113.
68. Cruz, discussion, May 2023.
69. Government of Mexico City, *Chinampa Agricultural System*.
70. Correa, "Las Chinampas Del Humedal de Xochimilco," Abstract, 104.
71. Government of Mexico City, *Chinampa Agricultural System*.
72. Adrian Guillermo Aguilar et al., "7. The Basin of Mexico," United Nations University Archive, https://archive.unu.edu/unupress/unupbooks/uu14re/uu14re0s.htm.
73. Adriana Palma Nava, Timothy K. Parker, and Rafael B Carmona Paredes, "Challenges and Experiences of Managed Aquifer Recharge in the Mexico City Metropolitan Area," *Ground Water* 60, no. 5 (2022): 675, https://doi.org/10.1111/gwat.13237.
74. Cruz, discussion, May 2023.
75. Amanda Gokee, "In Mexico City, the Coronavirus Is Bringing Back Aztec-Era 'Floating Gardens,'" Atlas Obscura, June 25, 2020, https://www.atlasobscura.com/articles/mexico-city-chinampas-coronavirus.
76. Ebel, "Chinampas," 16.
77. *Encyclopædia Britannica Online*, s.v. "Xochimilco," accessed April 17, 2024, https://www.britannica.com/place/Xochimilco.
78. Ebel, "Chinampas," 13.
79. Gokee, "In Mexico City, the Coronavirus."
80. Cruz, discussion.
81. Ebel, "Chinampas," 16–17.
82. Cruz, discussion, May 2023.
83. Cruz, discussion, May 2023.

COAUTHOR

PEDRO MENDEZ ROSAS

Chinampa Farmer

Pedro Mendez Rosas is a *chinampero* who manages several *chinampas* in the Xochimilco area of Mexico City. His practice stems from his family tradition of working a system handed down for over eight hundred years, giving him invaluable xpertise in sustainable farming and agricultural nd expansion.

Rosas's expertise and extensive experience ith *chinampas* position him as one of the foremost uthorities on the subject. He has devoted his life) conserving and advocating for this ancient rming system. Through his teachings and work, e hopes to inspire others to adopt sustainable farmıg practices that are environmentally friendly, highly roductive, and biodiverse.

Rosas has created several educational prorams to teach children and adults about sustainable rming and *chinampa* preservation. He also collaboates closely with local farmers, equipping them with ıe necessary tools and knowledge to enhance their rming practices. Rosas's efforts have garnered interational recognition, leading to invitations to address onferences and events worldwide, where he shares is knowledge with diverse global audiences.

Rosas's commitment to sustainability and preerving his family's tradition is crucial for his commuity and resonates globally. Contact with Rosas was cilitated by non-Indigenous collaborator Rodrigo lberto Lañado Cruz, who has spent years learning :om Rosas's practices.

COAUTHOR

RODRIGO ALBERTO LAÑADO CRUZ

Permaculturist and Natural-Construction Expert

Rodrigo Alberto Lañado Cruz is a natural-construction and permaculture expert who has been involved in sustainable living for over 15 years. His expertise largely developed through immersion in Indigenous communities, where he learned firsthand about sustainable systems and practices. He has led courses, presented lectures, and held workshops in more than 10 countries. Cruz teaches students about sustainable approaches to homes, land restoration, food production, hydrologic design, water management, energy harvesting, and *chinampa* practices. With his background in soil and land restoration, he specializes in biomaterials like mycelium. He has trained more than 20,000 people around the world and completed more than one hundred projects in permaculture, bioconstruction, and self-sustaining systems in Mexico, South America, and Europe. Cruz has also produced three documentaries on the subject. He's currently exploring the fusion of artificial intelligence technology with ancestral practices and sustainable land management knowledge to pioneer a novel model for climate resilience and social development.

YE-CHAN

FLOATING ISLANDS *of* THE INTHA

Myanmar

YE-CHAN FLOATING ISLANDS *of* THE INTHA *Myanmar*

Coauthored by
Khaing Khaing Soe

PEOPLE Intha **LOCATION** Inle Lake, Myanmar
TECHNOLOGY floating islands
ELEVATION 900 m **ORIGIN** end of the 19th century
DISTANCE ABOVE OR BELOW WATERLINE −1.5 to +2 m
WATER LEVEL FLUCTUATION, TIDAL OR SEASONAL +2 to +5.5 m

FAO Nexus
WATER fresh ENERGY bioenergy + cleansing
FOOD crops

IPCC Adaptation Pathway
accommodate

World Bank NBS
CATEGORY bioretention areas, constructed inland wetlands, natural inland wetlands, urban farming, river and stream renaturation
FUNCTIONS biodiversity, water pollution regulation, pluvial flood regulation, heat regulation, air pollution regulation
BENEFITS resource production, biodiversity, stimulate local economies and job creation, pluvial flood risk reduction, carbon storage and sequestration, cultural, social interaction, tourism and recreation

A low pedal boat snakes through the sinuous *ye-chan* (water farm) islands and stilted bamboo houses of Inle Lake, which lies nestled in the hills between the forest-covered Shan Hills.[1] Shaped more than one and a half million years ago, Inle is the remnant of a series of lakes formed as water dissolved limestone in the landscape.[2] The Intha, meaning "people of the lake," first came here following a command from the king of Myanmar. As the country's second largest lake, Inle rests nine hundred meters above sea level on the Shan Plateau. The king was impressed by the location and size of this lacustrine landscape amid the mountains, measuring 22 kilometers in length and 20 kilometers in width.[3] Since then, *ye-chen* technology has spread across the lake's surface, blurring the line between water and land.[4, 5]

Known for their agriculture and fishing practices, 170,000 Intha—a subgroup of the Shan people—live in 20 villages along the lake's shoreline.[6, 7, 8, 9] Using teak boats known as *hlay*, the Intha glide to tend their floating agricultural *ye-chan* gardens, fish with conical nets, and trade at floating markets.[10, 11] Passed down through generations, their unique, one-legged rowing technique powers small timber canoes and large flat boats that transport aquatic plants and black silt for their *ye-chan*.[12] Made from wild floating masses known as *kyun mhyaw*, *ye-chan* cultivation presently covers 45 square kilometers of the surface by using a natural cycle of capillary action to passively irrigate crops with lake water.

The Intha's unique understanding of the cycle of life is reflected in their folklore as much as in their technologies. A traditional proverb says that when *nga-phein*, or Inle carp (*Cyprinus intha*)—a staple of the Intha diet—die, they become Intha, and that the Intha become carp. Following this cycle of reciprocity and reincarnation, the wild, uncut *kyun mhyaw* beds that form the base of the *ye-chan* are also used for Intha water burials, after which they are consumed by carp.[13]

Every year, a festival draws people from around the country to Inle Lake to celebrate the Phaung Daw Oo Paya Pagoda.[14, 15, 16] Inside is an illustrated origin

1

1 *Ye-chan*, meaning "water farm," islands cover 45 square kilometers of Inle Lake's surface.
2 Bamboo huts surrounded by incredibly fertile floating agricultural islands are supported by the lake's nutrient-laden water.
3 Floating gardens anchored by bamboo poles rise and fall with changing water levels, making them resistant to flooding.

2

3

story of the Intha, in which the king of Myanmar, Along-Si Thu, sent two of his boatmen to inhabit the lake. The boatmen called 36 families, who built four villages and named the lake Innlay Ywar, from the words *inn* (water surface), *lay* (four), and *ywar* (village).[17] Worshipping deities, known as *nats*, is deeply rooted in Intha culture; a *nat* known as Daw Gyig (big royal guard) is thought to protect Inle Lake. It is common for passersby to leave offerings, in the hopes of appeasing the *nat* and protecting the lake community.[18]

Ye-chan are a highly productive hydroponic system of buoyant agricultural beds, where crops are naturally irrigated with lake water.[19] Naturally occurring compact, floating masses known as *kyun mhyaw* are the basis of *ye-chan* construction, consisting of interwoven roots, stems, leaves, sediment, and debris.[20, 21, 22]

Ye-chan Floating Islands, Villages, and Markets

Open water
Ye-chan cultivation
Wetland
Main villages

Nyaungshwe
Ai Htaunt Gyi
Khaung Dine
Maing Thauk
LAKE INLE
Kyay Sar Khone
Nga Hpe Kyaung
Tha Le Oo
Kayla
Ywama
Phaung Daw Oo Pagoda
Pauk Par
Indien
Nampan
In Paw Khone

Together, these materials—afloat due to the gasses released during decomposition—are capable of not only growing crops but also sustaining the weight of a person. High grasses and swamp vegetation surround the lake, informing the material compositions of the beds and their agricultural cycles in accordance with the wet and dry seasons.[23] *Kyun mhyaw* form naturally over 10 to 15 years, as coarse grasses, reeds, sedges, duckweed, and other vegetation gather in shallow lake water near the shore edge. In this location, decomposing aquatic and marsh plants become entangled and bound together by moss and algae, creating a partially submerged floating structure.[24]

These soil-less beds primarily consist of local grasses like *kyu-phyu* (*Phragmites karka*) and *kyu-ni* (*Phragmites communis*),

4

4 The unique one-legged rowing technique of the Intha farmers allows them to navigate vegetation-laden waters.
5 Once they able to bear weight, the mats are sawn into narrow strips 1.5 meters wide and 100–200 meters long, and then these *ye-chan* are towed to lake villages.
6 Mud is taken from the algae-rich lake bottom and added to *kyun mhyaw* as fertilizer.

5

flowering plants like *taw-ngwe-pan* (*Hedychium coronarium*), and several local sedge species known as *sha-lone* and *sha-pya*.[25] According to some Intha farmers, the latter two are typically pioneer plants, after which grasses begin to grow. Farmers know the floating patch is ready for cultivation when species like *taw-ngwe-pan* (white garland lily) sprout and flower atop the beds. At this stage, the portion of the floating bed submerged under water has reached one to one and a half meters deep.[26] If herbaceous plants like elephant grass (*Saccharum spontaneum*), known locally as *kaing*, have grown on the beds, they are burned to form mulch for crop cultivation.[27]

Traditionally, floating islands are measured in units known as *alan*; one *alan* equals approximately two meters.[28] Farmers sew *kyun mhyaw* into rectangular mats that are one to two meters wide, ranging anywhere from 40 to 180 meters long.[29, 30] Sold for 200,000 Myanmar *kyats* ($95.15), the strips are then towed toward the middle of the lake, where designated *ye-chan* farming areas are assigned for different villages.[31] The strips are separated by two-meter-wide circulation channels and anchored to the bottom of the lake by bamboo poles, enabling them to slide up and down as the water fluctuates.[32] Typically, a 10-meter-long floating garden will require about eight boatloads of additional mud and weeds to increase fertility during the first round of crop cultivation; in subsequent rounds, less needs to be added.[33, 34] The islands' structure and fertility is enhanced with added silt and clay alluvium extracted from the lake bed, along with the integration of aquatic plants like water hyacinth.[35] Newly formed *ye-chan* beds are then sown with seeds, before being fertilized

6

Seasonal Timeline of *Ye-chan* Construction

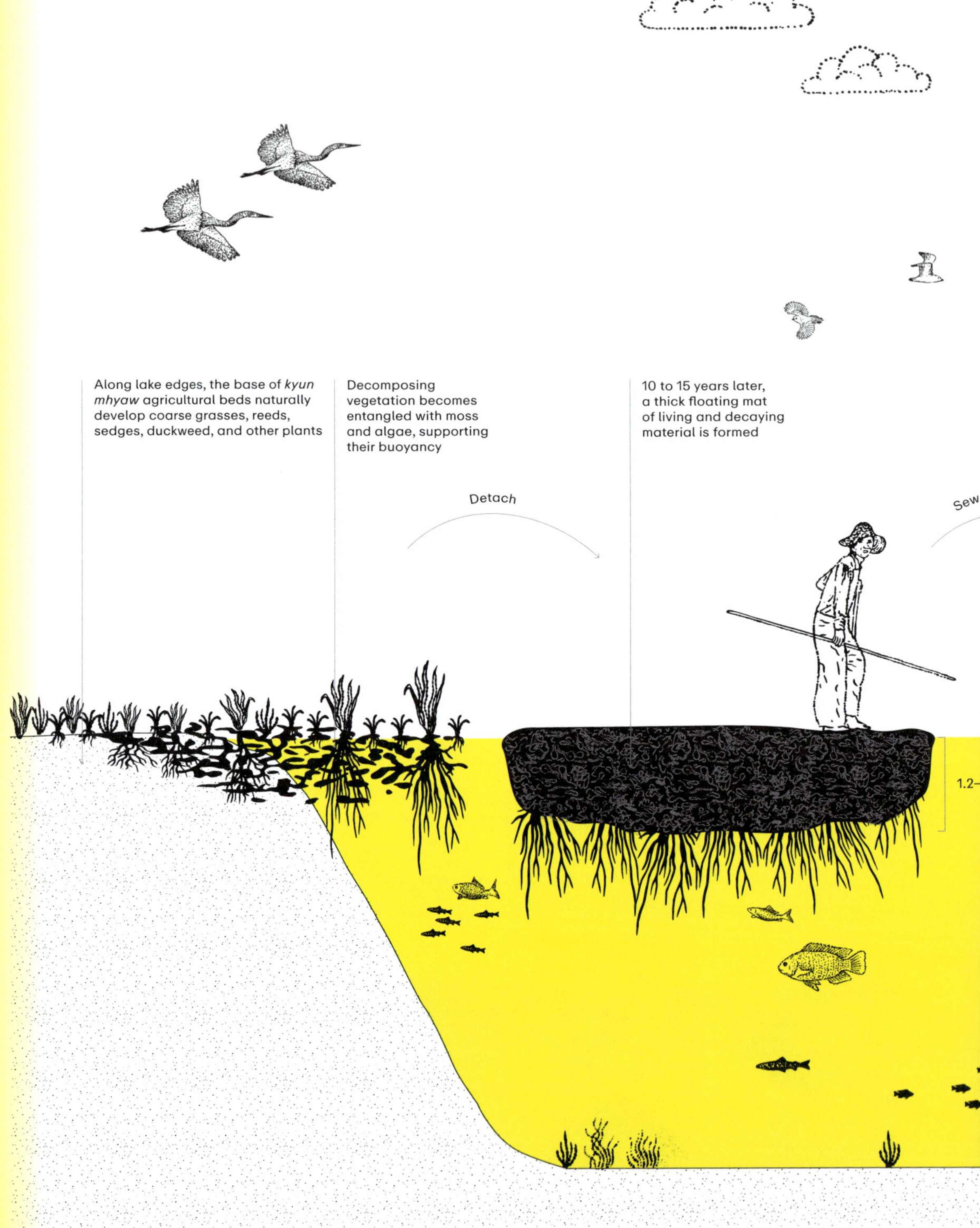

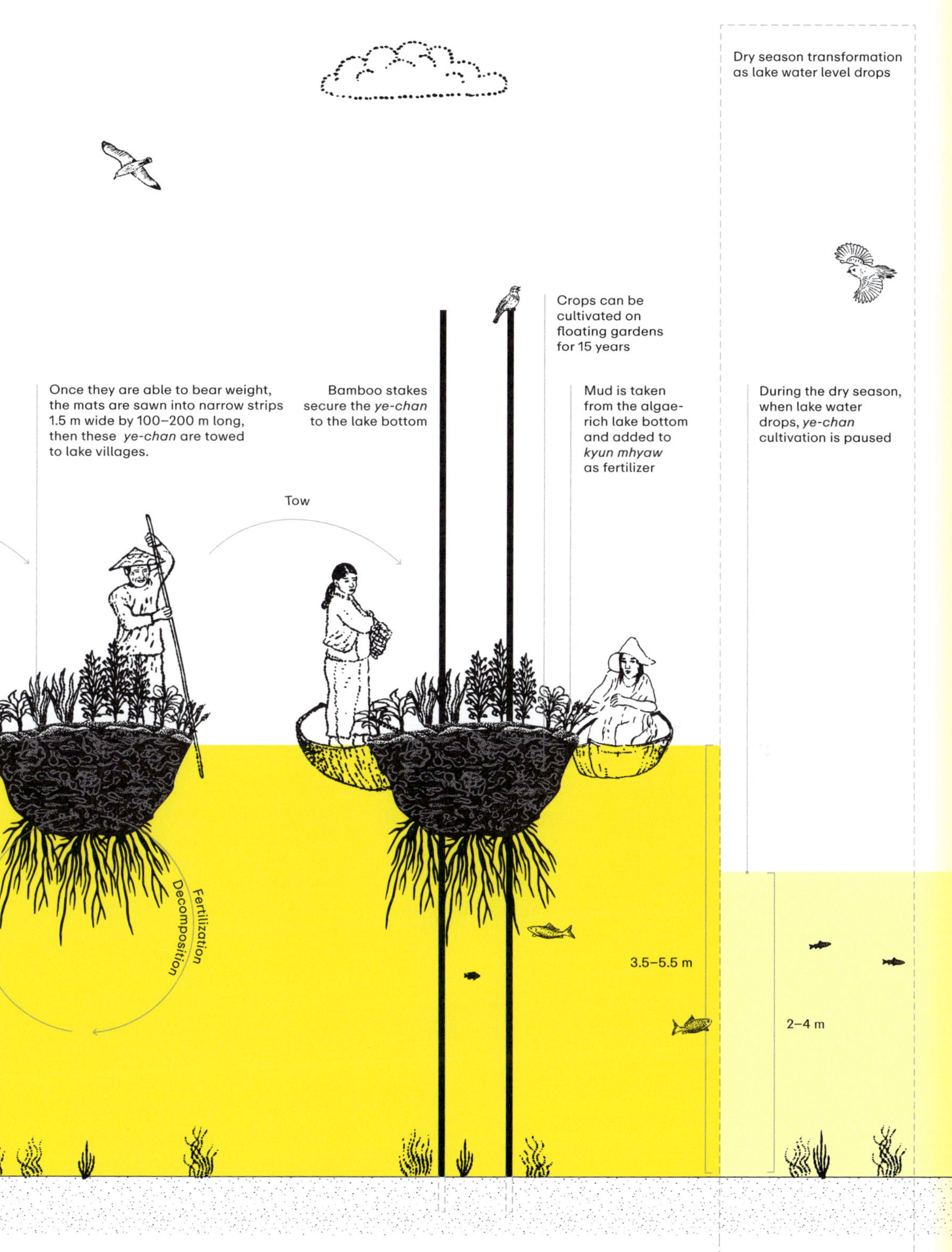
Dry season transformation as lake water level drops
Crops can be cultivated on floating gardens for 15 years
Once they are able to bear weight, the mats are sawn into narrow strips 1.5 m wide by 100–200 m long, then these *ye-chan* are towed to lake villages.
Bamboo stakes secure the *ye-chan* to the lake bottom
Mud is taken from the algae-rich lake bottom and added to *kyun mhyaw* as fertilizer
During the dry season, when lake water drops, *ye-chan* cultivation is paused
Tow
Irrigation
Fertilization
Decomposition
3.5–5.5 m
2–4 m

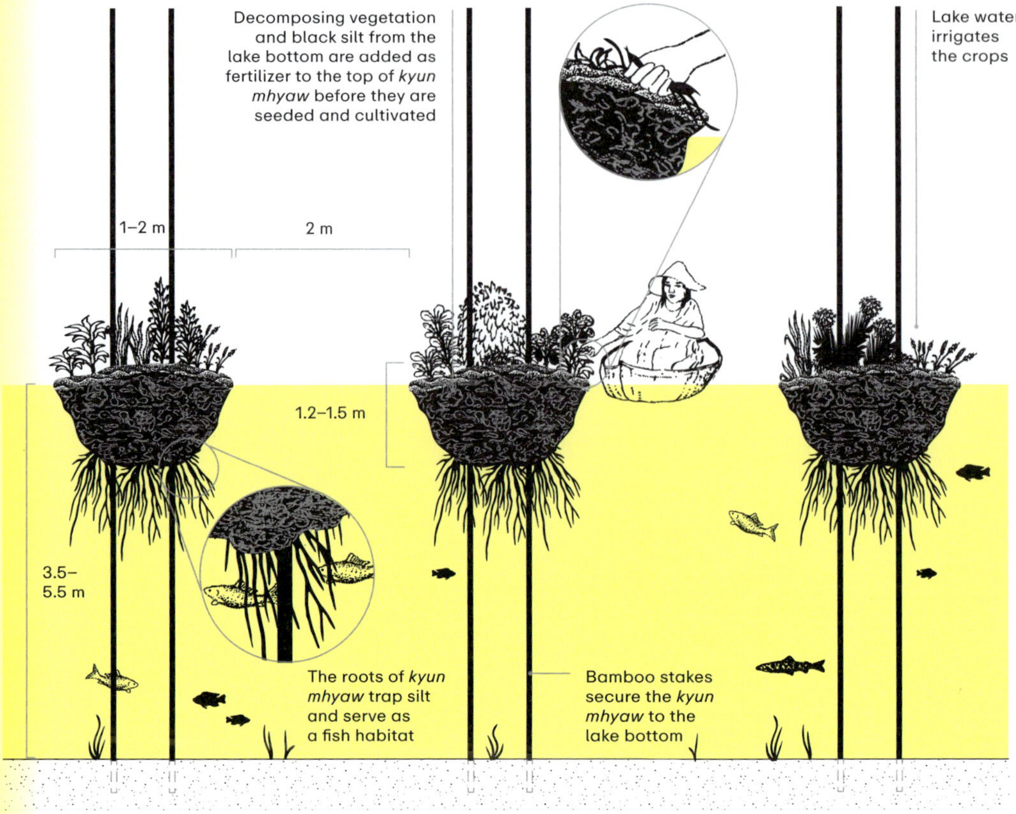

The Cultivation of *Ye-chan* Crops

Decomposing vegetation and black silt from the lake bottom are added as fertilizer to the top of *kyun mhyaw* before they are seeded and cultivated

Lake water irrigates the crops

1–2 m

2 m

1.2–1.5 m

3.5–5.5 m

The roots of *kyun mhyaw* trap silt and serve as a fish habitat

Bamboo stakes secure the *kyun mhyaw* to the lake bottom

once more by the lake's algae.[36] During the rainy season, when *ye-chan* cultivation takes place between May to October, the average lake depth ranges from three and a half to five and a half meters, while in the dry season, when cultivation is paused, it ranges from two to four meters.[37, 38, 39, 40] *Ye-chan* beds can remain productive for over 15 years—as long as gardens are trimmed annually and remain buoyant.[41] The emergence of taro (*Colocasia antiquorum*) on a bed indicates that the *ye-chan* has reached the end of its life cycle; at this point, the floating gardens become soft, dark masses that gradually sink to the bottom of the lake.[42]

Every year, the Intha clear out the previous year's crop to prepare and fertilize the *ye-chan* with mud and new seeds—a process that requires five people for five days.[43] The organic materials of the *ye-chan* biodegrade at the end of their life cycle, reentering the lake's ecosystem and contributing to the ongoing fertility of the lake, which in turn sustains the next generation of *ye-chan* as well as lowland and upland cultivation practiced around Inle Lake.[44]

7

7 A floating garden nearby Ywama, with tomato plants growing on both sides.
8 The traditional, distinctive fishing technique of the lake's fishermen uses a seven-foot-tall frame with a conically shaped net, which is held with both hands and plunged to the bottom of the shallow lake.

Home to 267 species of birds, 43 species of freshwater fish, 75 species of butterflies, and three species of turtles, Inle Lake was designated the Inle Wetland Wildlife Sanctuary in 1985, a Ramsar site in 2018, and an Important Bird Area; it became the first Myanmar site for UNESCO's MAB in 2017.[45] However, traditional *ye-chan* cultivation has not been protected, resulting in issues for hydrological processes, and other threats to the system.[46, 47, 48]

Originally intended for local, small-scale consumption, commercialization processes neglect the traditional balance between agriculture, biodiversity, the lake environment, and Intha life.[49, 50] Local *ye-chan* farmers usually cultivate one floating island per year, earning them a few hundred dollars. A portion of what is grown is used for subsistence and offerings, but the majority is used to grow cash crops sold for export at local floating markets.[51]

Beginning in the 1960s, a major boom in *ye-chan* production occurred as Myanmar transitioned from a socialist to a market-based economy, defined by the increased use of artificial and chemical practices.[52, 53] Today, 90 percent of *ye-chan* production consists of *inn khayanchin thee* (Inle tomato), grown from high-yielding, disease-resistant, hybrid tomato seeds intended for commercial markets. Cultivated year-round rather than seasonally, millions

8

9

10

9 Local *ye-chan* farmers cultivate one floating island per year, with a portion grown used for subsistence and offerings, while most is sold for export at local floating markets.
10 Almost grown as a monoculture, *ye-chan* farmers harvest tomatoes year-round.

of kilograms of tomatoes are distributed yearly throughout Myanmar, with an annual yield of 18 tons per hectare.[54] Traditional use of cow and poultry manure has been replaced by NPK compound fertilizer, and the use of neem and tobacco extracts for pest control have been superseded by imported harsh agro-chemicals that pollute the water, decreasing food safety and quality.[55] This has put local tomato varieties at risk, while replacing traditional fertilization and pest control practices.[56] A tourism industry has also risen around the lake, accounting for a jump from 26,000 to 850,000 foreign visitors between 1992 and 2013.[57] A result has been an increase in waste, the introduction of polluting

11 Green, yellow, and red tomatos are produced in the floating gardens.
12 The proliferation of cash crops like tomatoes has led to a huge increase in the number of floating gardens covering Inle Lake.

11

diesel-powered longboats, and the clearing of 250 hectares of land in anticipation of new hotels.[58]

The proliferation of cash crops like tomatoes has resulted in a major jump in floating gardens around Inle Lake. From 1992 to 2009, *ye-chan* increased by 500 percent, consequently diminishing water surface and seeping chemical fertilizers into the lake.[59] The maximum depth of the lake has also shifted from six to three meters over the course of the last century—the result of sediment accumulation and water level decline.[60, 61] As rapidly expanding *ye-chan* adversely affect the Inle Lake ecosystem, local fishermen compete with floating plantations for room to access open water.[62]

Bae-dar (water hyacinth) also poses a considerable threat to the *ye-chan* system, covering the lake and its tributaries, blocking roadways, contributing to a decline in Inle carp populations, and decreasing necessary sunlight and nutrients for native plants.[63, 64, 65] Fifteen years ago, the government attempted to mitigate issues associated with this invasive species, requiring boats exiting the village of Nyaung Shwe to leave with a specific quantity of water hyacinth. Large-scale use of dredges and pumps, public education efforts, and handmade baskets and bags have also been introduced to control the invasive species.[66] Today, water hyacinth has been adopted as a material to construct *ye-chan* beds, mainly mixed with animal manure to form an organic fertilizer.[67] The species poses some benefits, as it is capable of growing in wastewater, purifying water through absorption, and acting as a natural source of biofertilizer.[68] Thoughtfully integrating water hyacinth into *ye-chan* systems could present the opportunity to inexpensively cleanse water systems,

12

reducing the need to formally treat wastewater, which reduces energy consumption while supporting local agricultural practices.

Ye-chan are a unique, high-yielding form of hydroponic agriculture, embedded in the distinct culture of the Intha people and the mountainous ecosystem of Inle Lake. This technology represents an opportunity for other aquatic environments with limited arable land to grow plants symbiotically in a body of water. Unfortunately, the *ye-chan*'s recent shifts toward monoculture cropping, chemical pesticides, and fertilizers as a result of unsustainable globalization trends have had a negative impact on the lake's symbiosis. These shifts threaten the future of the ecosystem and life within it. The *ye-chan* and its recent industrial adaptations only emphasize the importance of traditional nature-based practices, highlighting the potential for careful use of invasive species like water hyacinth to address contemporary environmental issues and assist in restoring balance,

13 Today, 90 percent of *ye-chan* production consists of Inle tomato, grown from high-yielding, disease-resistant, hybrid tomato seeds intended for commercial markets.

14 Using teak boats known as *hlay*, the Intha glide to tend their floating agricultural *ye-chan* gardens, fish with conical nets, and trade at floating markets.

13

14

15 Sunrise on Inle Lake, with Buddhist temple, floating garden, and stilted house.
16 Cultivation uses a natural cycle of capillary action to passively irrigate crops with lake water.

15

16

its people, and its more-than-human inhabitants. As we see in many Indigenous knowledge systems, the Intha understand that they become the carp and the carp becomes them somewhere in the cycle of nutrient reuse, which is memorialized in the act of mythical storytelling.

ENDNOTES

1. "Inlay Lake Biosphere Reserve, Myanmar," UNESCO, July 28, 2022, https://en.unesco.org/biosphere/aspac/inlay-lake.
2. "Inlay Lake Biosphere Reserve, Myanmar."
3. Khaing Khaing Soe (agronomist), in discussion with the author, November 2022.
4. Voiland, "Floating Farms," NASA Earth Observatory, January 15, 2025, https://earthobservatory.nasa.gov/images/85606/floating-farms.
5. Myint Su and Alan D. Jassby, "Inle: A Large Myanmar Lake in Transition," *Lakes & Reservoirs: Science, Policy and Management for Sustainable Use* 5, no. 1 (2000): 49, https://doi.org/10.1046/j.1440-1770.2000.00090.x.
6. Zaw Lwin and M.P. Sharma, "Environmental Management of the Inle Lake in Myanmar," *Hydro Nepal: Journal of Water, Energy and Environment*, no. 11 (2012): 57.
7. Ray Waddington, "The Indigenous Intha People," The Peoples of the World Foundation, July 27, 2022, https://www.peoplesoftheworld.org/text?people=Intha.
8. Soe, discussion.
9. Soe, discussion.
10. Soe, discussion.
11. Erika Alatalo, "Floating Villages of Inle Lake," Field Study of the World, January 14, 2018, https://www.fieldstudyoftheworld.com/floating-villages-inle-lake/.
12. Soe, discussion.
13. Soe, discussion.
14. Soe, discussion.
15. "Lake Inle," Google Earth, accessed January 3, 2023, https://earth.google.com/web/searchInle+Lake,+Myanmar+(Burma)/@20.55113809,96.94320194,899.19061732a,37892.36223615d,35y,0h,0t,0r/data=CigiJgokCbqVMhdQcDVAEbmVMhdQcDXAGWoSTu2X-skIAIU5nREE3DkrAOgMKATA.
16. Thu Thu Aung, "Traditional Maritime Skills and Knowledge of Social and Economic Development in Lake Inle," (speech, 2020 Expert Meeting for Building Network on Maritime ICH, ICH Webinar Series on Maritime ICH, October 2020), https://webinar.unesco-ichcap.org/wp-content/uploads/2021/06/1-3_Thu-Thu-Aung.pdf, 39.
17. Soe, discussion.
18. Jeffrey Hays, "Intha Leg Rowers and the Floating Farms of Inle Lake," Facts and Details, July 22, 2022, https://factsanddetails.com/southeast-asia/Myanmar/sub5_5d/entry-3064.html.
19. Soe, discussion.
20. Soe, discussion.
21. Voiland, "Floating Farms."
22. Martin Michalon, "The Gardener and the Fisherman in Globalization: The Inle Lake (Myanmar), a Region under Transition" (master's thesis, University Lyon 2 Lumière, 2016), 22, https://doi.org/10.13140/2.1.4600.6083.
23. Hays, "Intha Leg Rowers and the Floating Farms."
24. Soe, discussion.
25. Daw Khin Win Myint and U Kyaw Win Maung, "Study on the Formation of Floating Islands in the Inle-Lake from Botanical Point of View" (Preliminary Survey, Forest Research Institute, 1996), 3.
26. Win Myint and Win Maung, "Study on the Formation of Floating Islands," 3.
27. Voiland, "Floating Farms."
28. Soe, discussion.
29. Soe, discussion.
30. Thin Nwe Htwe, "Changes of Traditional Farming Systems and Their Effects on Land Degradation and Socio-Economic Conditions in the Inle Lake Region, Myanmar" (PhD dissertation, University of Kassel, 2015), 3.
31. Soe, discussion.
32. Voiland, "Floating Farms."
33. Soe, discussion.
34. Michalon, "The Gardener and the Fisherman," 22–23.
35. Htwe, "Changes of Traditional Farming Systems," 3.
36. Hays, "Intha Leg Rowers and the Floating Farms."
37. Martin Michalon et al., "Accelerated Degradation of Lake Inle (Myanmar): A Baseline Study for Environmentalists and Developers," *Land Degradation and Development* 3 (2019): 2, https://doi.org/10.1002/ldr.3279.
38. Soe, discussion.
39. Aung, "Traditional Maritime Skills and Knowledge," 39.
40. Soe, discussion.
41. Htwe, "Changes of Traditional Farming Systems," 3.
42. Soe, discussion.
43. Hays, "Intha Leg Rowers and the Floating Farms."
44. Soe, discussion.
45. Moe Thae Oo, Zin Wai Aung, and Clelia Puzzo, "The Floating Garden Agricultural System of the Inle lake (Myanmar) as an Example of Equilibrium between Food Production and Biodiversity Maintenance," *Biodiversity and Conservation* 31, no. 1 (2022): 2435, https://doi.org/10.1007/s10531-021-02347-9.
46. Oo, Aung, and Puzzo, "The Floating Garden Agricultural System," 2435.
47. Myat Mon Thin, Elisa Sacchi, and Massimo Setti, "Hydrological Processes at Inle Lake (Southern Shan State, Myanmar) Inferred from Hydrochemical, Mineralogical and Isotopic Data," *Isotopes in Environmental and Health Studies* 52 (2016): 455, https://doi.org/10.1080/10256016.2015.1130038.
48. Voiland, "Floating Farms."
49. Oo, Aung, and Puzzo, "The Floating Garden Agricultural System," 2435.
50. Su and Jassby, "Inle," 49.
51. Su and Jassby, "Inle," 49.
52. Voiland, "Floating Farms."
53. Soe, discussion.
54. Michalon, "The Gardener and the Fisherman," 36.
55. Soe, discussion.
56. Soe, discussion.
57. Michalon, "The Gardener and the Fisherman," 75–76.
58. Hays, "Intha Leg Rowers and the Floating Farms."
59. Michalon, "The Gardener and the Fisherman," 31.
60. Voiland, "Floating Farms."
61. Michalon, "The Gardener and the Fisherman," 13–17.
62. "Myanmar's Famed Inle Lake Chokes on Floating Farms," Al Jazeera, November 16, 2023, https://www.aljazeera.com/gallery/2023/11/16/myanmars-famed-inle-lake-chokes-on-floating-farms.
63. Soe, discussion.
64. Hays, "Intha Leg Rowers and the Floating Farms."
65. Fadoua Karouach et al., "A Comprehensive Evaluation of the Existing Approaches for Controlling and Managing the Proliferation of Water Hyacinth (Eichhornia crassipes): Review," *Frontiers in Environmental Science* 9, no. 1 (2022): 1, https://doi.org/10.3389/fenvs.2021.767871.
66. Soe, discussion.
67. Soe, discussion.
68. Karouach et al., "A Comprehensive Evaluation of the Existing Approaches," 3.

COAUTHOR

KHAING KHAING SOE

Agricultural Specialist

Growing up among subsistence farmers, Khaing Khaing Soe inherited the tradition of *ye-chan* floating island agriculture, which she passed down through several generations of her family. Soe is an agricultural specialist from Nga Phe Chaung village track in the southern region of Shan State, Myanmar; like many other *ye-chan* farmers, Soe's family specializes in tomato cultivation. Attending schools around Inle Lake, she completed both her primary and secondary education in the region, with aspirations of pursuing formal studies in agriculture.

In 2008, Soe left her hometown near Inle Lake to enroll in Yezin Agricultural University (YAU)—the only institution in Myanmar dedicated to the field. She received her bachelor's degree in agricultural science in 2011. Her undergraduate studies included agronomy, soil chemistry, plant pathology, agri-economics, entomology, plant breeding, farm machinery, and animal science. Soe was also an active member of the university volleyball team.

Upon graduating, she returned home hoping to apply her formal training to support her family's *ye-chan* farm. Before long, she returned to YAU to pursue her master's degree, joining the Department of Plant Pathology with funding from the Mitsubishi Scholarship. Her academic excellence was recognized in 2014, as she was selected for the prestigious ASEAN Youth Student Exchange Program, allowing her to further her studies at Chiba University in Japan. During her graduate studies, Soe participated in several notable projects, including an organic horticulture training course organized by YAU in collaboration with Mokpo National University in Korea. In 2016, she earned her master's degree in agricultural science, specializing in researching bacterial wilt disease, a common affliction of tomatoes.

Soe launched her career at Capital Diamond Star Group (CDSG), where she received the Best Newcomer Employee Award in 2017. She was first hired as an assistant manager; in this position, her primary responsibilities included conducting research for productivity and quality evaluation of japonica paddy in Myanmar's Shan, Sagaing, and Kayin. After three years, she was promoted to agricultural project manager. As a CDSG manager, Soe managed large-scale potato-seed and chip production in Shan State, supervised a team of agronomists, and partially managed a coffee plantation farm in Ywarngan, Shan State.

In 2021, a military coup plunged Myanmar into a period of profound upheaval, disrupting the lives of countless people and instigating a cycle of political unrest. This ongoing crisis has precipitated a humanitarian emergency marked by widespread detentions and displacements. Due to these conditions, Soe left CDSG to return to Inle Lake, where she could support her family with farming activities. After living in her hometown and working on her family's farm for a year, she joined a five-month project funded by the United Nations Development Programme: Environmental Goods and Services (EGS) – Promoting Eco-Innovation and Local Sourcing through AgTech in Shan State. Even in the vicinity of Inle Lake, the repercussions of the 2021 coup's political upheaval persist, evidenced by sporadic skirmishes, the destruction of homes, and disruptions to internet connectivity.

ATHAPHUM
FLOATING ISLANDS
of THE PAAT-MI
India

ATHAPHUM FLOATING ISLANDS *of* THE PAAT-MI
India

Coauthored by
Manimala Chanu Asem

PEOPLE Paat-mi LOCATION Loktak Lake, Manipur, Northeast India TECHNOLOGY floating islands ELEVATION 168–768.5 m ORIGIN 1800s DISTANCE ABOVE OR BELOW WATERLINE −2 to +0.5 m WATER LEVEL FLUCTUATION, TIDAL OR SEASONAL +0.5 to +4.58 m

FAO Nexus
WATER fresh ENERGY bioenergy + cleansing
FOOD herbs +fish

IPCC Adaptation Pathway
accommodate

World Bank NBS
CATEGORY bioretention areas, constructed inland wetlands, natural inland wetlands, urban farming, river and stream renaturation
FUNCTIONS biodiversity, water pollution regulation, pluvial flood regulation, heat regulation, air pollution regulation
BENEFITS resource production, biodiversity, stimulate local economies and job creation, pluvial flood risk reduction, carbon storage and sequestration, cultural, social interaction

1

Speckled across Northeast India's largest body of fresh water, thousands of circular, floating meadows give the appearance of a lunar, lacustrine landscape. Nine kilometers wide and 11 kilometers long, almost 50 percent of Loktak Lake's surface is covered by several thousand natural and constructed floating meadows.[1] The site is home to the Paat-mi (lake people) of Manipur, who construct flood-resistant floating rings to live on and fish from. Referred to as the "lifeline of Manipur," the lake is ordained as a mother goddess, named Loktak Lairembee, by the Paat-mi people.[2] It is a unique biodiversity hotspot, with islands supporting important ecological processes, including nutrient recycling, water purification, groundwater recharging, and runoff control.[3] On the surface of the lake, these floating meadows, known as *phumdi*, are composed of buoyant mats of soil and vegetation. These suspended grasslands can then be topped by huts, which are locally known as *phumshang*, or they can be configured into ringlike floating formations, called *athaphum*, for traditional aquaculture practices.[4]

The *phumdi* play an important role in the history and identity of the Paat-mi people. Where *paat* translates to "lake" and *mi* means "people," the Paat-mi are a subgroup of the Meitei ethnic group Indigenous to the region; they live on the lake and identify themselves as much a part of its ecosystem as the water itself. Folklore tells of the symbiosis between the *phumdi* and the community since they left the mainland. According to the story, Khuyol Haoba and Nura Yaithing Konu were two lovers in a secret affair that was discovered by their warring families. Konu pleaded with Haoba to escape refuge on the lake while he waited for her.

1 Loktak Lake, a freshwater lake in the Shan Mountains in eastern Myanmar, has been recognized as a UNESCO World Heritage Site for its outstanding biodiversity and rich cultural heritage.

2

As days, months, and eventually seasons passed, he built a hut on the floating *phumdi*, which became the first *phumshang*. There are two versions to the end of this legend, which speak to the origin of the Paat-mi community. One version tells how Konu finally escaped her family and found Haoba; together, they made the lake their home. In the other, Haoba waits for many years, during which time people eventually join him by building huts on the floating meadows.[5]

As the legend tells, *phumdi* are naturally occurring floating meadows that play a vital role for the one hundred thousand people who depend on the lake for their livelihood. They maintain the ecology of the lake, and with it the economy of the state. Taking on a form akin to a giant mud cake topped by a lush meadow, the *phumdi* are land mass mixed with vegetation, decomposing organic matter, and black soil that have thickened into a solid and spongy soil known as peat. The top root layer is 15 centimeters deep, the middle mat layer is 25 to 65 centimeters thick, and the bottom layer, made of organic matter, is 25 centimeters deep.[6]

Phumdi naturally form when a dense mass of floating water hyacinth accumulates silt suspended on the water's surface. Grasses and other plants spontaneously follow, building up layers that begin to decompose to form peat—fertile soil composed of carbon, nitrogen, and organic mineral matter at varying stages of decomposition—making it uniquely buoyant.[7] Measuring up to two and a half meters deep, a *phumdi* forms like an iceberg, with one-fifth above water and four-fifths below.[8]

2 *Phumdi* are the naturally occuring floating meadows formed into the circular *athaphum* by the Paat-mi people of Loktak Lake for fishing.
3 People of Loktak Lake live in four cities bordering the lake, in numerous small villages along the lake's shores, and on the lake itself.

3

4

Phumdi act as both a biofilter and aquatic habitat that support productive fisheries, provide plants used for fencing and fuel, maintain the water quality, and create a source of high-quality compost, which helps decrease their proliferation across the lake. During the dry season, when water levels are low, the living roots of the islands reach the lake bed and absorb essential nutrients, naturally fertilizing the spring. During this period, the floating meadows are used for agriculture to grow *taothabi* (rice).[9]

Locals construct circular islands from the *phumdi* for fish farming known as *athaphum*.[10] The unique method of *athaphum* fish farming, which appears to pockmark the surface of the lake, is actually thousands of artificial circular enclosures. At approximately 20 to 50 meters in diameter, these rings are individually composed of multiple floating *phumdi*. This process begins with a large *phumdi* being selected from the lake. It is cut by two people into smaller pieces with a long knife, called a *thangol*, that resembles a billhook. Once cut, the pieces are tied together with rope, composing a circular shape.[11] Having formed

5

6

an *athaphum*, the structure is anchored by rope for stability to a long fixed bamboo stick.[12]

The *athaphums* allow fishermen to haul, on average, 1,500 tons of fish annually.[13] The fish are trapped by nylon netting draped from the interior perimeter of the *athaphum*, reaching down to the lake bed. Food thrown in the ring's center attracts fish, which enter through the netting to inhabit the ring. After a few months, these fish are caught by families, typically during a three day event called *phum-namba*.[14, 15] A minimum of five to six people are required to catch fish; however, there are always more than 10, as family and friends join. Later, food is arranged for everyone by the owner of the *athaphum*.[16] To ensure the success of the catch, silt from the lake bed is stirred up with bamboo poles to reduce oxygen levels in the water, bringing fish to the surface, where they are easily caught.[17] The *athaphum* are also used as fish nurseries, where fish are grown before they are caught.

The *phumshang* huts sit atop the *phumdi*, which are layered and bound together with strong bamboo skin thread to expand the *phumdi* area and increase thickness. *Phumdi* are anchored in place with strings tied to rocks, which are placed beneath the existing *phumshang* by community members.[18] Light bulbs on smaller pieces of *phumdi* are tied to bamboo stakes for night fishing.[19] Every three to four years, new *phumdi* are pushed under the existing *phumshang* to strengthen the base.[20]

A myriad of around 90 aquatic and *phum*-based plants are also found on and around *phumdi*, where they are used by local communities for diverse purposes, such as for livelihood, ritual purposes, and building material for the *phumshang*.[21] Common reed (*Phragmites karka*) and para grass (*Brachiaria mutica*) are the most common species found on *phumdi*. Manchurian wild rice (*Zizanialatifolia*), knotgrass (*Polygonum barbatum*), and rice paddy herb (*Limnophila aromatica*) also grow atop *phumdi*, to be later used as fodder. Galangal (*Alpinia galanga*), gotu kola (*Centella asiatica*), Benghal dayflower (*Commelina benghalensis*), water spinach (*Ipomoea aquatica*), Nepal dock (*Rumex nepalensis*), and white garland lily (*Hedychium coronarium*) are consumed as food, while butterfly ginger (*Hedychium coronarium*), sweet flag (*Acorus calamus*), whiteweed (*Ageratum conyzoides*), elephant creeper (*Argyreia nervosa*), pink blumea (*Blumea mollis*), greater pond sedge (*Carex riparia*), false daisy (*Eclipta alba*), water primrose (*Ludwigia adscendens*), shame plant (*Mimosa pudica*), and water chestnut (*Trapa natans*) are used for medicinal purposes: commonly as tonics and skin infection treatments as well as to fight gastric problems.[22]

4 Floating islands can be topped by huts, which are locally known as *phumshang*, or they can be configured into ringlike floating formations, called *athaphum*, for traditional aquaculture practices.
5 With the average depth of the lake only seven feet, over the centuries the fishermen have developed a unique way of casting their nets so that they can spread out in full size.
6 Another form of fishing used by fishermen is moving an arched swing net above the water.

The largest single mass of *phumdi* lies in the southeastern area of the lake, covering 40 square kilometers.[23] It is home to Manipur's state animal, an endangered deer known as *sangai* once thought to be extinct, which is protected here—on the planet's only free-floating national park. This *phumdi* island ecosystem supports over six hundred Indigenous plant and animal species, including the rare Indian python (*Python molurus*), grass, sedges, ferns, and herbs.[24] The high level of biodiversity supported by the *phumdi* and the deteriorating condition of Loktak Lake led to its 1990 designation as a Wetland of International Importance under the Ramsar Convention.[25, 26]

The 2006 establishment of the Loktak Development Authority (LDA), a state-run agency charged with the conservation of Loktak wetlands, has had a devastating impact on the local Paat-mi community. Under the guise of conservation, a 2011 state-led LDA campaign burned down 777 of the 1,110 *phumshang* floating hut islands. This act of terrorism, which destroyed the homes and livelihood of hundreds of Paat-mi, is annually memorialized by the community; it was a direct blow to the greatest human protectors of this ecosystem.[27] Since this incident, the considerable time and effort traditionally taken to construct permanent *phumshang*s has been abandoned and replaced by temporary huts, out of fear that they will be destroyed again. Once made solely of bamboo, these

Floating Circular Islands Composed of *Phumdi* Strung Together

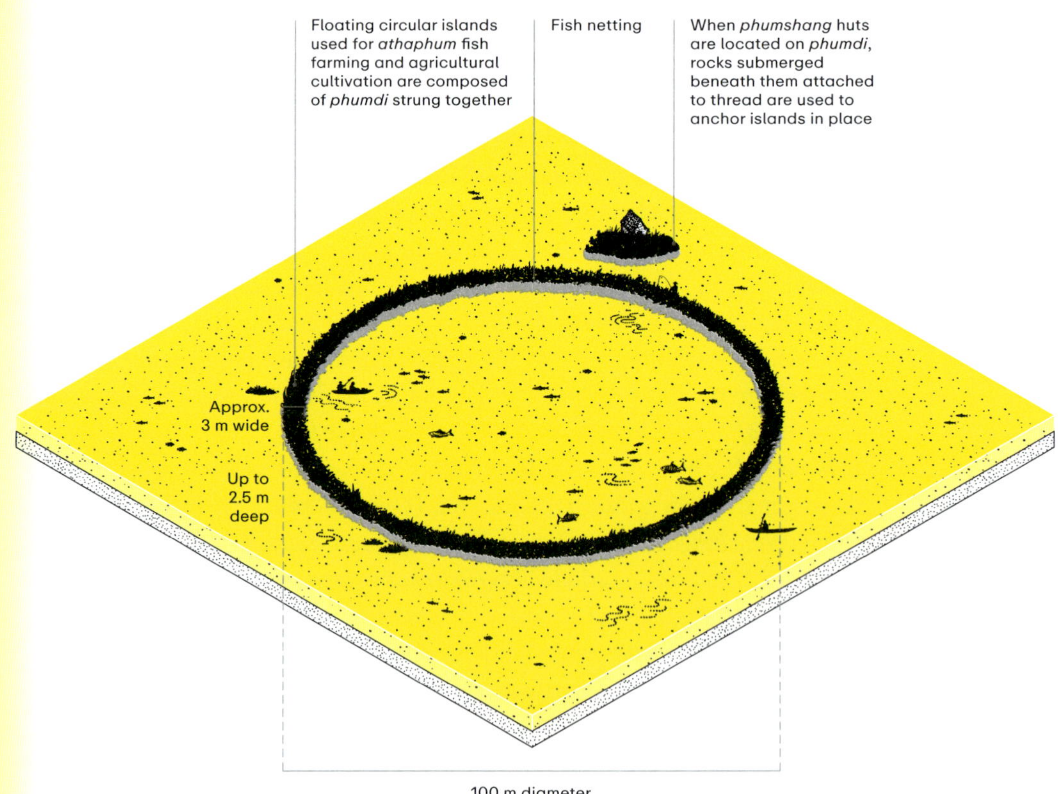

7 Draped from the interior perimeter of the *athaphum*, reaching down to the lake bed, the fish are trapped by nylon netting.
8 To ensure the success of a catch, silt from the lake bed is stirred up with bamboo poles to reduce oxygen levels in the water, bringing fish to the surface, where they are easily caught.

7

8

biodegradable traditional materials have now been replaced by plastic ropes, heavy rocks, wood, zinc plates, and iron rods, disrupting the delicate balance of the lake and reducing the services this constructed ecosystem provides.[28, 29] While, 20 years ago, two hundred kilograms of fish were caught per *athaphum*, over the past decade the Paat-mi have struggled to catch just 10 kilograms.[30]

The LDA asserts that uninterrupted human interaction with the lake has led to severe pollution. According to the LDA, to preserve the lake from further deterioration, human settlement must be prohibited, resulting in forceful eviction and arson in 2011. While prohibiting the community from living on the lake, the LDA has been developing a mega-tourism project, giving unhindered access

One-Fifth of a *Phumdi* Sits Above Water

Fish netting draped along the inside perimeter of the *athaphum*, reaching down to the lake bed

Food thrown in the ring's center to attract fish

Bamboo poles are used to stir silt to reduce oxygen levels in the water and bring the fish to the surface to be easily caught

3 m

Nutrients

Irrigation

Nutrient recycling and water purification are provided by *phumdi*

Dissolved Oxygen

Filtration

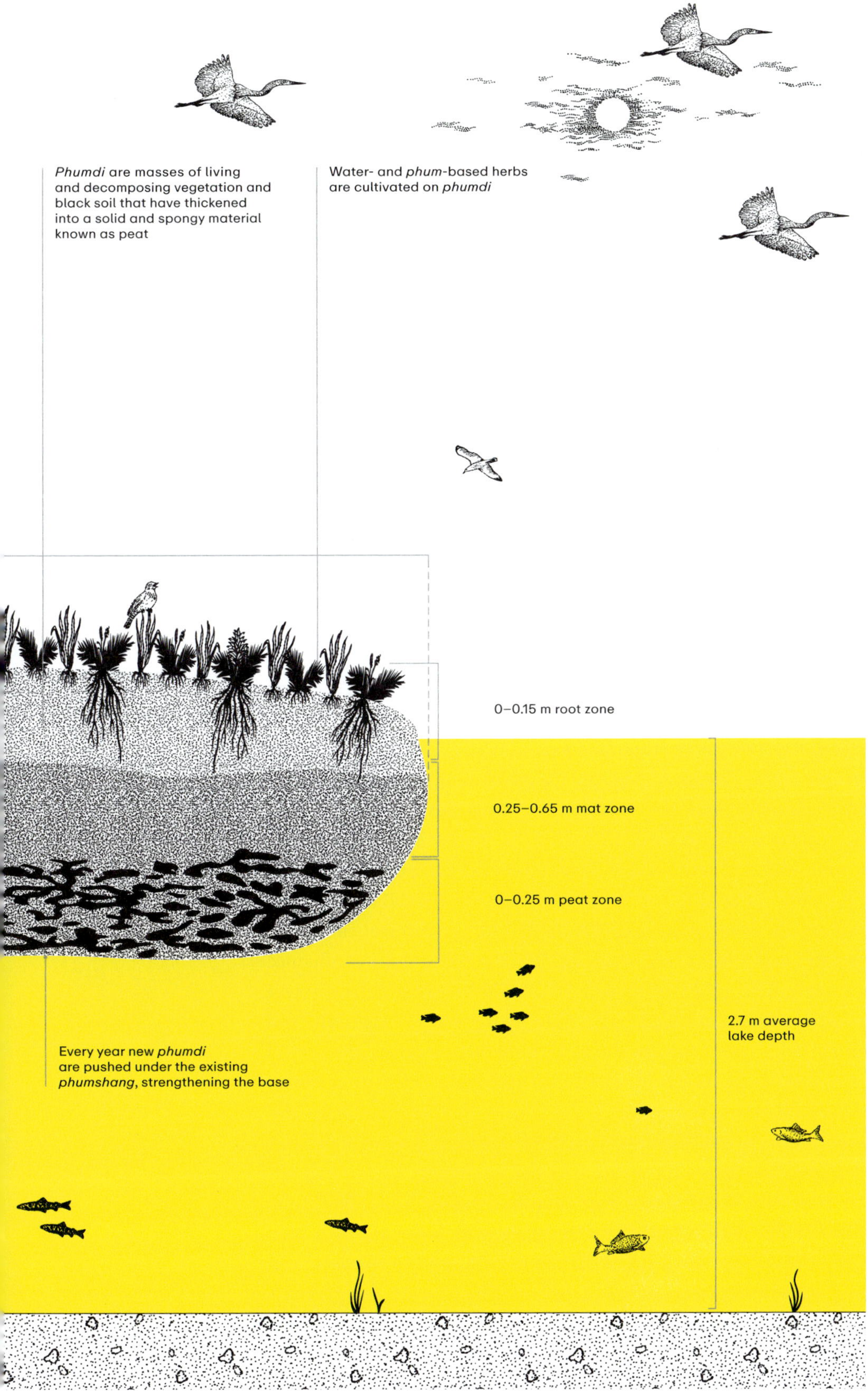

Phumdi are masses of living and decomposing vegetation and black soil that have thickened into a solid and spongy material known as peat

Water- and *phum*-based herbs are cultivated on *phumdi*

0–0.15 m root zone

0.25–0.65 m mat zone

0–0.25 m peat zone

2.7 m average lake depth

Every year new *phumdi* are pushed under the existing *phumshang*, strengthening the base

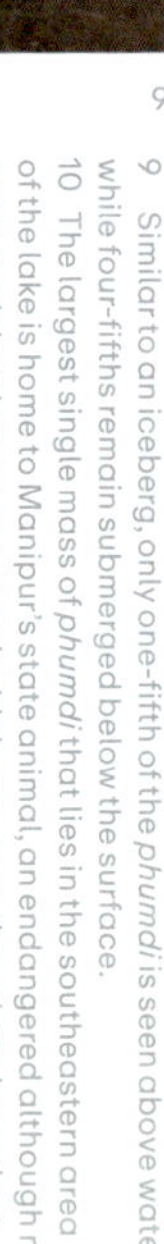

9

9 Similar to an iceberg, only one-fifth of the *phumdi* is seen above water, while four-fifths remain submerged below the surface.
10 The largest single mass of *phumdi* that lies in the southeastern area of the lake is home to Manipur's state animal, an endangered although now protected deer known as *sangai*, which was once thought to be extinct.

to tourist motorboats. Meanwhile, the Paat-mi believe that Loktak can be saved from further deterioration through collaboration, traditional knowledge, and state intervention. Some initiatives that the Paat-mi are fighting for include the prohibition of night fishing, bird catching, and the use of motorboats.

Phumdi technology and the surrounding ecosystem are threatened by a complex constellation of stressors, including the encroachment of humans and livestock, state-imposed arson and violence under the guise of conservation, the inflow of polluted water, and, on a regional scale, the Ithai Barrage.[31] Fed by almost 30 rivers, the lake inflow is contaminated by agricultural chemicals, domestic waste, and high levels of sediment. Built in the 1980s at the confluence of the Imphal River and Khuga River as part of the Loktak Hydroelectric Project, the Ithai Barrage is a dam intended to provide hydropower, irrigation, and drinking water for India's northeastern states. Despite these services, the project has altered water levels to generate electricity, disrupting the ability to cultivate rice and therefore threatening the life of the lake.[32, 33] Releasing an excess of water has contributed to environmental problems such as siltation, a proliferation of *phumdi*, eutrophication, prevention of fish spawning, loss of fish biomass and diversity, and, ironically, a loss of water available for hydraulic power generation.[34] The dam increases water levels, which remain high year-round, creating a permanent flood situation and preventing the *phumdi* from sinking to the lake bed for annual nutrient retrieval. The barrage also prevents the natural removal of old *phumdi*, which were typically washed away in monsoon season, while the fertilizer entering the lake from the rivers causes

10

an accelerated growth and proliferation of *phumdi*, which is proving harmful to the ecology of the lake. The increasing number of *phumdi* slows the flow of water, which contributes to siltation and blocks fishing routes, and rotting *phumdi* reduce water quality. While currently a problem, in the future these *phumdi* could provide a solution for local biomass energy generation, which would negate the energy produced by the dam and clear the waterways of detritus.

With a life cycle that enables them to transition seasonally between aquatic and terrestrial habitats, allowing for natural fertilization, *phumdi* are a technology well adapted to the monsoonal fluctuations. In addition to their role as aquatic agricultural systems, *phumdi* also clean water, reducing the need to formally treat agricultural and domestic wastewater, in turn reducing municipal energy consumption. Today, the major threats to the *phumdi* and their broader ecosystem can be linked to the Ithai Barrage, an upriver mega-dam hydropower project. This dam has removed the seasonal pulses of flooding and erased the natural flushing of the lake, leading to a proliferation of *phumdi* clogging the body

11

12

11 *Phumdi* technology and the surrounding ecosystem are threatened by a complex constellation of stressors, including state-imposed arson and violence under the guise of conservation by the LDA.
12 According to the LDA, to preserve the lake from further deterioration, human settlement must be prohibited, resulting in forceful eviction and arson in 2011, while they develop a megatourism project.

of water. However, inspired by the opportunistic integration of an invasive species into the construction of the *phumdi* architecture, a new form of low-impact, localized bioenergy production could take advantage of rotting *phumdi*—turning a waste into a resource—rather than ruinous, regional energy generation. Naturally buoyant, *phumdi* are able to support local communities during seasonal changes by accommodating water level fluctuations. They house

13

14

13 The *athaphums* allow fishermen to haul, on average, 1,500 tons of fish annually.
14 *Phumdis* used for fish farming cover a large portion of the Loktak Lake.
15 The Paat-mi believe that Loktak can be saved from further deterioration through collaboration, traditional knowledge, and state intervention.

15

productive fisheries, provide important plant species used for fencing and fuel, and are critical to the maintenance of water quality in the lake, providing passive energy generation in the production of clean water without the use of chemical or burning of fossil fuels, as well as being a great source of high-quality compost, which assists in controlling their proliferation in the lake. This system is part of a unique biodiversity hotspot, providing many environmental and cultural services such as nutrient recycling, nutrient absorption, water purification, groundwater recharging, runoff control, flood control, carbon sequestration, ritual importance, and daily consumption.[35, 36, 37] The Paat-mi's floating islands on Loktak Lake should inspire the construction of similar nature-based infrastructures on urban water bodies to enhance natural biodiversity, purify water, address climate-related issues, and sustainably support large-scale local aquaculture and energy systems.

ENDNOTES

1. Abha Lakshmi Singh and Moirang Leima Khundrakpam, "Phumdi Proliferation: A Case Study of Loktak Lake, Manipur," *Water and Environment Journal* 25, no. 1 (2011): 99.
2. Jaya Thakur, "The Ithai Barrage of Manipur: To Decommission or Not," Observer Research Foundation, May 6, 2020, https://www.orfonline.org/research/the-ithai-barrage-of-manipur-to-decommission-or-not-66917.
3. Prabhat Kumar Rai and Mayanglambam Muni Singh, "Wetland Resources of Loktak Lake in Bishenpur District of Manipur, India: A Review," *Science and Technology Journal* 2, no. 1 (2014): 98.
4. Ritu Bhardwaj, "Understanding the Seasonal Flows of Water," Survival Media, February 19, 2020, http://www.projectsurvivalmedia.org/757-2/.
5. Pang Sau, "People of the Lake: A Conversation with Asem Chanu Manimala on the Occasion of International Day of the World's Indigenous Peoples 2020," Pangsau, October 10, 2020, https://pangsau.wordpress.com/2020/08/09/people-of-the-lake-a-conversation-with-asem-chanu-manimala-on-the-occasion-of-international-day-of-the-worlds-indigenous-people-2020/.
6. Kiranbala Takhelmayum and Susmita Gupta, "Distribution of Aquatic Insects in Phumdis (Floating Island) of Loktak Lake, Manipur, Northeastern India," *Journal of Threatened Taxa* 3, no. 6 (2011): 1856.
7. Singh and Khundrakpam, "Phumdi Proliferation," 99.
8. Singh and Khundrakpam, "Phumdi Proliferation," 99.
9. Manimala Chanu Asem (ethnographer), in discussion with the author, May 2023.
10. Singh and Khundrakpam, "Phumdi Proliferation," 102.
11. Asem, discussion.
12. Asem, discussion.
13. Kasha Patel, "The Floating Islands of India," NASA, February 19, 2020, https://earthobservatory.nasa.gov/images/92090/the-floating-islands-of-india.
14. Asem, discussion.
15. Upasana Kakati, "Loktak Lake—Lives of the Fishermen Inhabiting the Phumdis," Unconventional and Vivid, November 16, 2018, https://unconventionalandvivid.com/loktak-lake-phumdis/.
16. Asem, discussion.
17. Richard J. Heggen, *Floating Islands: An Activity Book* (self-pub., 2018), 482.
18. Asem Chanu Manimala,"Wind, 'Phum' and Life on the Loktak Lake: A Photo Essay," Economic and Political Weekly, December 2, 2019, https://www.epw.in/engage/article/wind-phum-and-life-loktak-lake-photo-essay.
19. Asem, discussion.
20. Kakati, "Loktak Lake—Lives of the Fishermen."
21. "Keibul Lamjao Conservation Area."
22. Rajkumari Supriya Devi, Kunja Bihari Satapathy, and Sanjeet Kumar, "Ethnobotanical Plants of Phumdi, Loktak Lake, Manipur, India," *Asian Pacific Journal of Health Sciences* 9, no. 4 (2022): 78.
23. S. Singsit, "The Dancing Deer of Manipur," *Wildlife Institute of India Newsletter* 10, no. 3 (2003), archived from the original on February 19, 2012, https://web.archive.org/web/20120219231812/http://oldwww.wii.gov.in/publications/newsletter/autumn2003/fromthewild.htm.
24. Chongpi Tuboi, Mattonbiyil Mani Babu, and Syed Ainul Hussain, "Plant Species Composition of the Floating Meadows of Keibul Lamjao National Park, Manipur," *NeBIO* 3, no. 4 (2012).
25. "Keibul Lamjao Conservation Area," UNESCO World Heritage Centre, February 21, 2020, https://whc.unesco.org/en/tentativelists/6086/.
26. Manimala Chanu Asem (ethnographer), in discussion with the author, March 2023.
27. "9th Loktak Arson Commemoration Day Observed," All Loktak Lake Area Fishermen's Union, Manipur, November 24, 2020, https://ourmotherloktak.wordpress.com/2020/11/24/9th-loktak-arson-commemoration-day-observed-2/.
28. Khwairakpam Gajananda and Thokchom Sundari Chanu, "The Fate of Loktak Lake, India," Ramsar: The Convention on Wetlands, September 25, 2001, https://www.ramsar.org/news/feature-article-fate-loktak-lake-india.
29. Manimala Chanu Asem, "Wind, 'Phum' and Life on the Loktak Lake: A Photo Essay," Economic and Political Weekly, December 2, 2019, https://www.epw.in/engage/article/wind-phum-and-life-loktak-lake-photo-essay.
30. Asem, discussion.
31. Heggen, *Floating Islands*, 482.
32. Thakur, "The Ithai Barrage of Manipur."
33. Asem, discussion.
34. Rajiv D Kangabam, Sarojini D Boominathan, and Munisamy Govindaraju, "Ecology, Disturbance and Restoration of Loktak Lake in Indo-Burma Biodiversity Hotspot—An Overview," *NeBIO* 6, no. 2 (2015): 9–12.
35. "Keibul Lamjao Conservation Area."
36. Rai and Singh, "Wetland Resources of Loktak Lake," 98.
37. Neeta Satam, "Manipur: Ithai Dam Threatens the Loktak Wetland," Pulitzer Center, December 1, 2017, https://pulitzercenter.org/stories/manipur-ithai-dam-threatens-loktak-wetland.

COAUTHOR

MANIMALA CHANU ASEM

Ethnographer

Manimala Chanu Asem is an anthropologist from Ningthoukhong, a village in the northeastern Indian state of Manipur, who resides just a 10-minute walk from Loktak Lake—an ecosystem known for year-round food cultivation and its unique floating biomasses called phumdis, some of which support entire homes. Growing up, Asem was told stories of lake deities who supposedly abducted children, making Loktak, adorned with its lotuses and lilies, a place of mystery and beauty. As an adult, she has understood that the lake is home not only to these mythical beings but also to humans, plants, and animals.

Asem completed schooling in her village before continuing her studies in the northern parts of India. She moved to Norway in 2020 to pursue her PhD through the Fredrik Barth Scholarship at the University of Bergen. In 2018, she started a project funded by the Firebird Foundation for Anthropological Research; through her research, she began interviewing the community residing on the lake. This interest led her to embark on a PhD project focused on collaborating with the Paat-mi, a subgroup of the Meitei community known as "the lake people." As an ethnographer, she's immersed herself in their lifestyle; today, this endeavor has evolved into a long-term commitment.

As Asem spent more time with the Paat-mi community and listened to their stories, she became aware of the precariousness of their way of life—especially since their displacement began in 2011. Through her research, she's learned about environmental stewardship, realizing the interconnectedness of life forms within every ecosystem. Asem believes that this journey has transformed her into a more patient, environmentally conscientious, and attentive listener.

Asem's work aims to document the lifeworld of the Paat-mi, whose history has been overlooked in the state-sanctioned narrative, while also highlighting the significance of Loktak Lake. Immersed in ethnographic fieldwork around this ecosystem, she recognizes that this work is just the beginning, prompting her commitment to further engagement with the community. After her graduate program, Asem hopes to share her insights through media like newspapers, academic journals, and a book, shedding light on Paat-mi culture.

SANGJIYUTANG DIKES, PONDS, *and* CANALS *of* THE HAN *China*

SANGJIYUTANG DIKES, PONDS, *and* CANALS *of* THE HAN *China*

PEOPLE Han Chinese **LOCATION** Huzhou, China
TECHNOLOGY mulberry dikes, fishponds, and canals
ELEVATION 0–3 m **ORIGIN** approx. 900 CE
DISTANCE ABOVE OR BELOW WATERLINE −2.5 to 0 m
WATER LEVEL FLUCTUATION, TIDAL OR SEASONAL +1.5 to +4 m

FAO Nexus
WATER fresh ENERGY bioenergy + cleansing
FOOD fish + silk + sheep

IPCC Adaptation Pathway
protect

World Bank NBS
CATEGORY bioretention areas, constructed inland wetlands, urban farming, river and stream renaturation, river floodplains
FUNCTIONS biodiversity, water pollution regulation, pluvial flood regulation, riverine flood regulation, heat regulation, air pollution regulation, subsidence regulation
BENEFITS resource production, biodiversity, pluvial flood risk reduction, riverine flood risk reduction, carbon storage and sequestration, cultural, social interaction, stimulate local economies and job creation

For over five thousand years, the vulnerable lowlands of the Yangtze River Delta have been honeycombed by a network of polders and mulberry tree–lined dikes that form a sprawling mosaic dotted with dense settlements. *Sangjiyutang*, meaning "mulberry fishpond," is an intricate system of ponds and dikes that enables the otherwise waterlogged landscape that surrounds the delta to flourish. Among the individual *tanglu* (dikes) of the *sangjiyutang* system, plants and animals, including silkworms, fish, and livestock live in a self-sustaining loop of resource exchange reliant upon the feces of silkworms that inhabit mulberry trees planted along the dikes.[1, 2] The system, sited within a larger regional reservoir, the Lougangweitian, stores water, regulates floods, and mitigates drought.[3] Spanning 40 square kilometers in mulberry groves and one hundred square kilometers in fishponds, this complex system integrates renewable energy, water management, nutrient recycling, and food production through crop cultivation, silkworm rearing, animal husbandry, and aquaculture on the south bank of Taihu Lake in the district of Huzhou.[4]

POLDER

A tract of lowland reclaimed from abody of water by the construction of dikes parallel to the shoreline.

Historically, the annual monsoon rains that flooded the Dongdiao River led to waterlogging along the lower reaches of the Yangtze River Delta in Huzhou. Canalization projects under the Han, Tang, and Song Dynasties reshaped the regional landscape to retain heavy summer rainfall, while connecting cities across the delta. This canal system laid the foundation for the development of *tang*s—small channels lined with dikes on each side.[5] As *tang*s proliferated under the Song period to account for land loss, farmers used this expanding infrastructure to sustain an agroforestry system: mulberry trees were planted along dikes, while rice paddies were cultivated in polders. It wasn't until the Ming Dynasty of the 14th century that landowners adopted the highly integrated system of mulberry cultivation and fish rearing that exists today; farmers shifted from rice cultivation to aquaculture, as polders were prone to flooding

1

1 The honeycomb morphology of the mulberry dikes, fishpond, and canal system in Huzhou, China.
2 The *sangjiyutang* system is connected to a macro water management network of canals developed under the Han, Tang, and Song Dynasties.

2

when drainage channels were obstructed.[6] This transition gave way to the deliberate inundation and seasonal dredging of polders as a means of flood mitigation, while still supporting a growing demand for food. By the 17th century, the region was characterized by a thriving local economy built on aquaculture and silk production.

The *sangjiyutang* mulberry dikes and fishponds are a closed-loop system, enabling a year-round cyclical cultivation of crops, fish, and silkworms. Situated amid a larger marsh ecosystem, each dike-lined pond is the smallest module of a much larger water management system of the delta region.[7] The elevated banks that line each pond are created once flooded grooves in the earth have been dredged. After draining waterlogged depressions, farmers excavate mud deposits to transform the natural embankments surrounding each fishpond into high, stable dikes, which serve as raised beds for the cultivation of mulberry trees. Pond mud and humus—the fine, decomposing organic matter in soil—are the sole materials used in the creation of these round retaining walls and a vital source of nutrients for the mulberry trees that are planted around each pond.

Hydrologic Features of the Mulberry Dike–Fishpond Complex

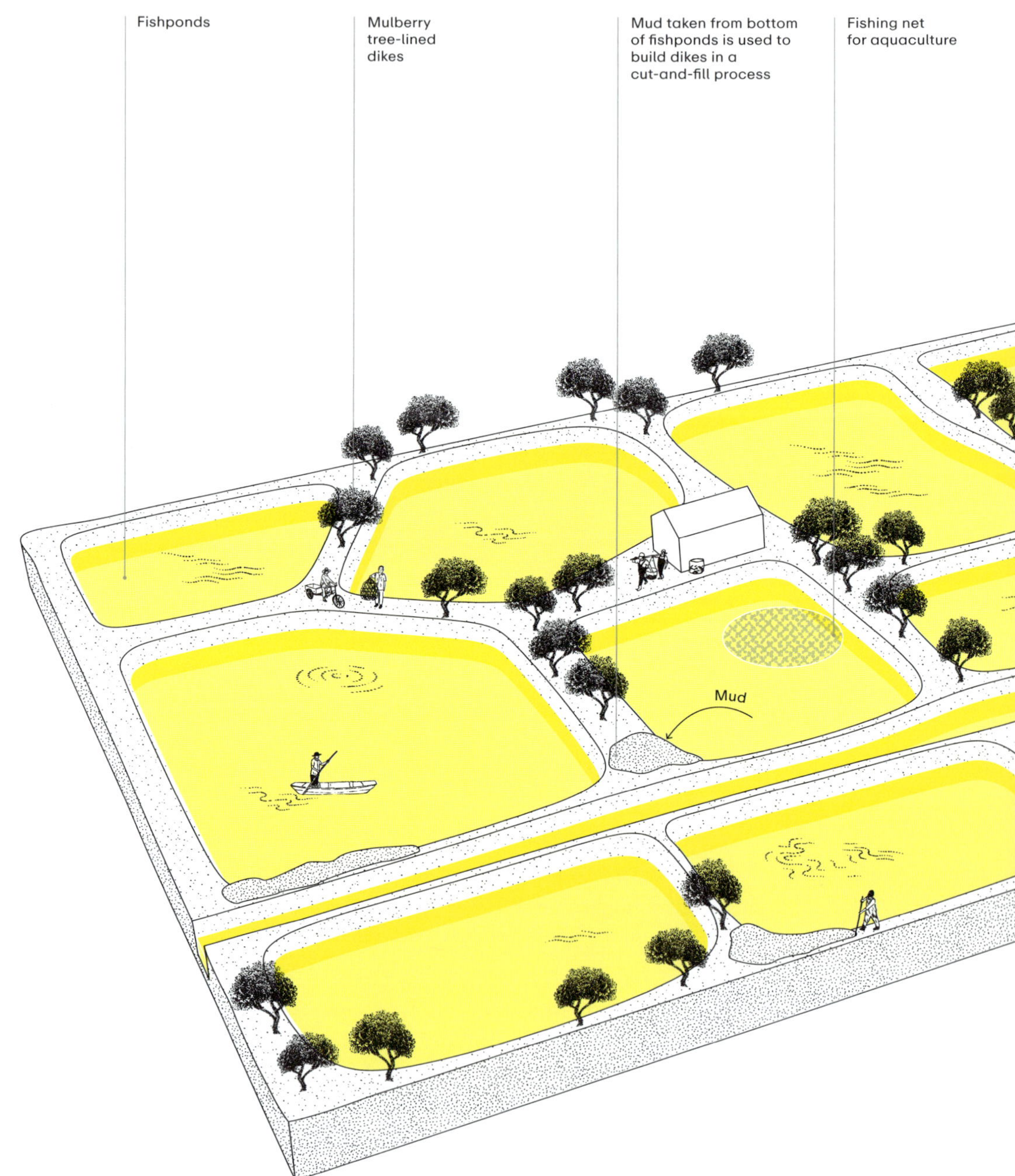

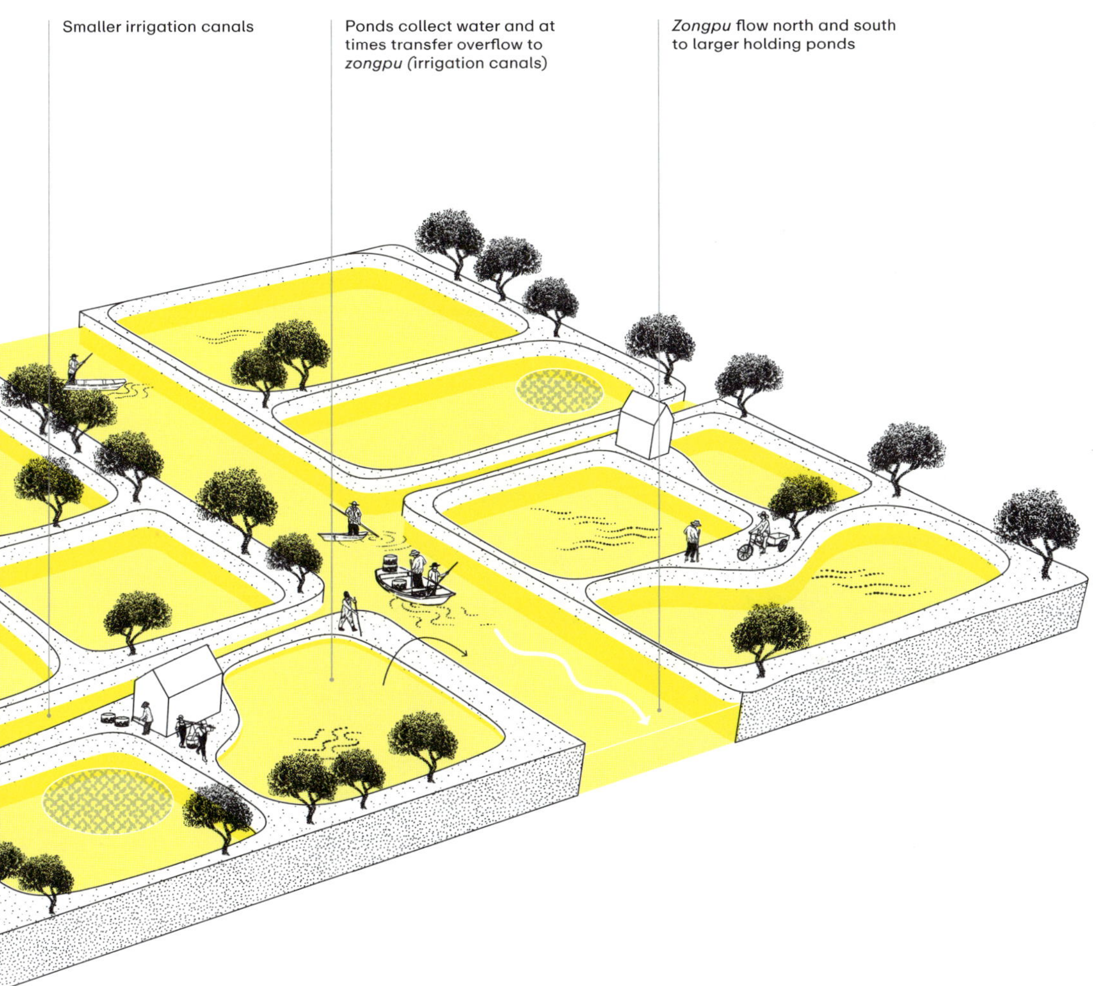
Smaller irrigation canals
Ponds collect water and at times transfer overflow to *zongpu* (irrigation canals)
Zongpu flow north and south to larger holding ponds

3

3 After harvesting and draining, farmers collect snails from the rich mud before dredging it to use as a chemical-free fertilizer for the mulberry trees.

4 By growing several species of fish in the same ponds, farmers rely on their different roles to manage threats from pests in the surrounding fields.

5 Every winter the fish are harvested and the ponds drained.

The process of building on the embankment and cultivating the species relations of a *sangjiyutang* ecosystem takes place in numerous stages over several seasons. The seasonal cycle begins in January, when mature fish are harvested from each pond, yielding 15,000 kilograms per hectare. Once harvested, mud is extracted from the bottom and added to embankments as fertilizer for mulberry trees. Farmers then add a layer of solid, dry soil—known as *tani* in the Kwatang Province and *baini* in the Zhejiang Province—across the embankments.[8] As early spring arrives, the budding of mulberry trees signals to farmers that the ponds are ready for fish farming. Starting in May, farmers start to rear silkworms, while using sericulture waste and mulberry foliage as fodder for fish. Throughout the

SERICULTURE The rearing of silkworms for the production of silk.

4

5

summer and autumn, liquid humus, referred to as *nihua* or *hsianoi*, is applied around trees two to three times to increase nutrients after the original fertilizer has aged. At the end of this season-to-season process, the base soil along the mulberry tree embankments will have risen by five to six centimeters.[9]

Mulberry trees are the basis of this complex multiscalar system: Their foliage is a source of fodder for silkworms, whose feces and sloughs fall into the surrounding pond, becoming feed for fish. The fish feces, along with the unconsumed silkworm and mulberry waste, are then decomposed by aquatic microorganisms, which produce nitrogen, phosphorus, and potassium; these nutrients are then returned to the mulberry trees as nutrient-rich fertilizer scooped from the bottom of the ponds, which feed the trees and begin the cycle once again.[10] Different tree species suited to these semiaquatic conditions,

Species Symbiosis of *Sangjiyutang* System

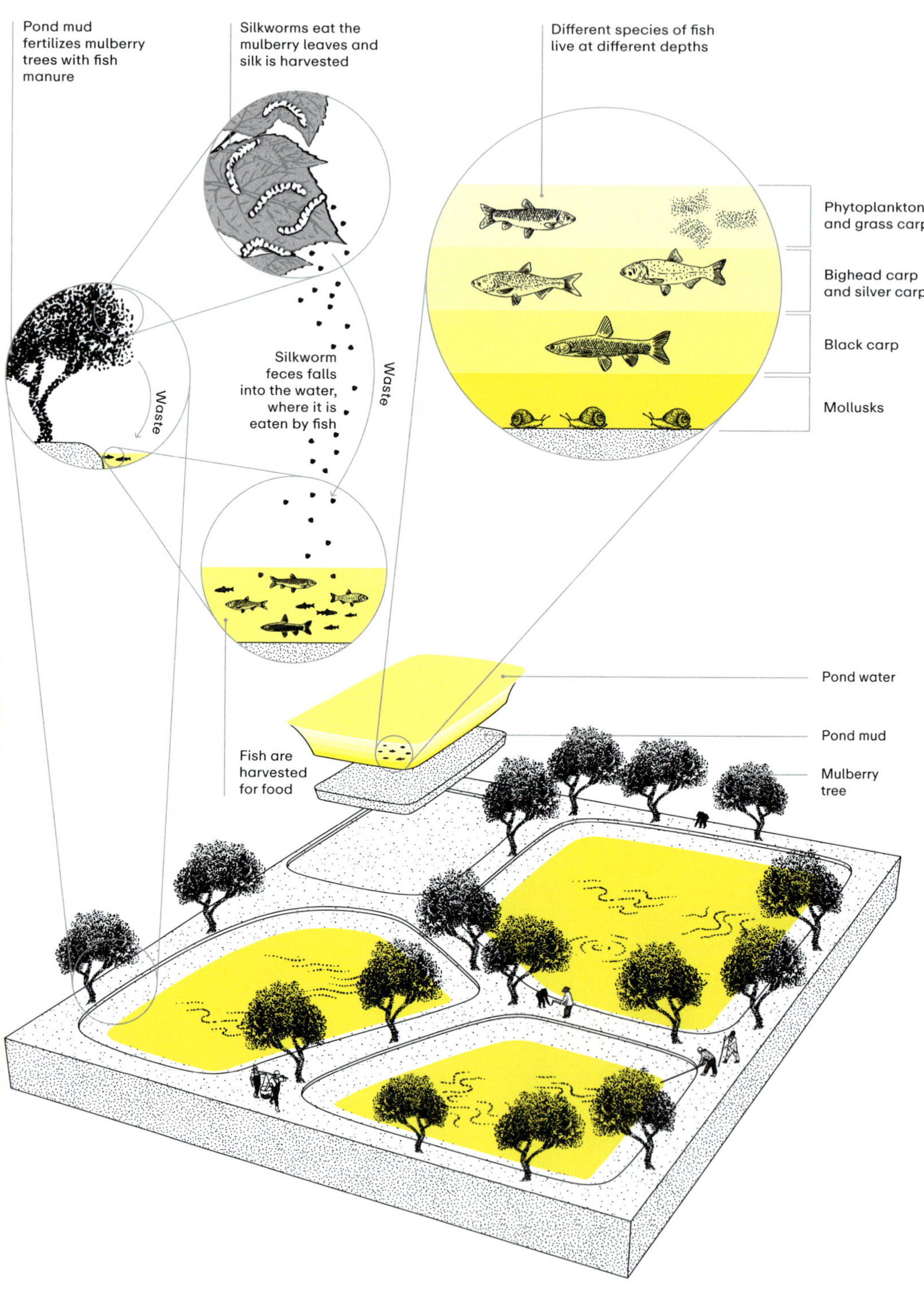

6

6 In January, when mature fish are harvested from each pond, farmers yield 15,000 kilograms per hectare.

such as willows and poplars, are also grown along these embankments. Their canopies provide shade for fishponds, while their roots offer nesting habitats for fish. The various fish species that inhabit these ponds do so as they occupy different depth zones. For example, silver carp inhabit the upper water, feeding on phytoplankton; bighead carp live in the middle water, consuming zooplankton; black carp reside in the deepest zone, feeding on snails and mollusks; and grass carp move between the middle and lower zones in search of algae and aquatic plants such as water hyacinth (*Eichhornia crassipes*).[11] These plants generate oxygen and glucose, supplying nutrition advantages for the fish in *sangjiyutang* ponds and triggering a cascade of benefits to the ecosystem.[12] Even though these fish species rely on various food sources, ranging from phytoplankton to snails, they all eat silkworm waste, which drops into the ponds from the mulberry cultivation. With a two-to-one feed conversion ratio—every two kilograms of silkworm pupae produces one kilogram of fish—the abundant presence of silkworm waste facilitates *sangjiyutang*'s flourishing proliferation of fish.[13]

PHYTOPLANKTON
Microscopic plantlike organisms at the base of the marine food web that remove carbon dioxide from the air.

ZOOPLANKTON
Zooplankton are floating or weakly swimming animals that rely on water currents to move.

Fishponds are integral to the Zong Pu Heng Tang system—with *zong pu* meaning "vertical rivers" and *heng tang* meaning "horizontal ponds"—which combines existing rivers and artificially created waterways into a grid formation.[14] In this ancient irrigation and drainage system, dating back thousands of years, rows of horizontal ponds are excavated perpendicular to rivers. By creating a protective zone between vulnerable farmland and natural water level fluctuations along riverbeds, the artificially constructed ponds act as reservoirs to contain excess water during flooding. It also establishes a network of water channels used for transport and communication throughout the region.[15] This checkerboard-like water management system, providing continuous storage for irrigation water throughout the year, feeds into Taihu Lake—the largest freshwater lake in the delta—mitigating the effects of flooding during the rainy season.[16] During the dry season, water is led into the fishponds to hydrate the channels and dikes.

7

7 At the beginning of spring, when mulberry trees begin budding, farmers prepare their ponds for fish farming.

8 In May, farmers start to raise the spring silkworms using leftover mulberry leaves.

Historically, the *sangjiyutang* mulberry dike–fishpond complex has supported the local and regional landscape—from reducing erosion to treating water—while yielding resources like fish and silk, generating income, and ensuring livelihoods. Nutrient-rich mud added to the embankments around each pond acts as a cheap, organic alternative to chemical fertilizers, pesticides, herbicides, and concrete flood barriers. The variety of plant species in ponds and along embankments sequester carbon, with mulberry trees in particular contributing to air purification and soil remediation through the absorption of heavy metals. The system's surrounding seasonal practices coexist with the mulberry dike-fishpond complex; a specific sheep breed, tailored to the sericulture cycle, is bred in Huzhou. Sheep are nourished with mulberry leaves as fodder, and their manure, combined with human waste, fertilizes the soil for mulberry cultivation, supporting the symbiosis in the system.

Today, the mulberry dike–fishpond complex of Huzhou is recognized as a GIAHS by the United Nation's FAO. However, the acknowledgment has its shortcomings, as it overlooks the evolving nature of *sangjiyutang*, current threats to the system, and its considerable potential for climate resilience. For example, urban sprawl presents a number of challenges, including air and water pollution—fluoride contamination, in particular,

8

9 Sited within a dense urban settlement and surrounded by industries, the system serves multiple functions.
10 A recent threat to the system is the establishment of large-scale solar farms on agricultural land and ponds.

9

10

has affected the yield of silkworm cocoons—fragmentation of a historically interconnected ecological network by urban and industrial development, and recent state-led incentives to "modernize" rural agriculture.[17] This has transformed the function and appearance of many ponds, with intensive fisheries expanding while the fishponds decline.[18]

Perhaps the most unexpected threat to the protection of *sangjiyutang* today is the establishment of large-scale solar farms on agricultural land and ponds in the northeastern area of the GIAHS-designated site. As of 2021, records indicate that nearly half (47 percent) of local land equipped with solar panels had supported mulberry dike–fishponds only 12 years prior.[19] While NGO recognition has raised awareness about this cultural landscape, it has not effectively mitigated the stressors, many of which are in the hands of the state, contributing to the system's decline.

As evidenced by the earliest iteration of this landscape—transitioning from rice cultivation to pond aquaculture during the Ming Dynasty—the *sangjiyutang* system has always evolved to meet the needs of the local populations. In the traditional practice, all labor required to support the system was produced by farmers, whereas in recent decades the practice has hybridized to include new materials and technologies in the face of contemporary challenges. One such case of hybridization is seen on the Nanxun Yunhao family farm, where large-scale mechanized mulberry sericulture is practiced. Here, traditional recycling of plant matter and animal waste in a closed-loop system is maintained, while economic potential is expanded through contemporary techniques. Although still in an experimental phase, the mechanized nature of this approach has accelerated the processing and production of mulberry leaves, expanding the potential for cultivating other types of agriculture.[20]

From an ecological perspective, the integrated processes of mulberry cultivation, aquaculture, and sericulture create a symbiotic relationship where growth and waste generation are intricately connected. The potential of this system could be enhanced by incorporating silk-reeling factories in the *sangjiyutang* complexes. Silk reeling—the practice of unwinding silk filaments from cocoons to create thread—typically occurs off-site. However, the integration of these production facilities into the very ecosystems where silkworms are reared would not only reduce transportation-related costs and emissions but also allow for the efficient channeling of organic by-products and wastewater back into the pond system, resulting in elevated nutrient levels and, consequently, a greater overall fish yield, with the potential to enhance both economic returns and ecosystem productivity for local farmers.[21]

The symbiotic ability for the *sangjiyutang* system to naturally cleanse wastewater remains an unrealized and scalable filtering system delivered by a chemical-free, renewable energy source. Already a feature of the infrastructure,

11

11 Women typically care for the silkworms in their homes, where they keep the trays clean, remain vigilant for signs of sickness, and make sure that there are always fresh leaves to eat.

12

12 Festivals occur every spring to bless the forthcoming harvest.

this ability stands in stark contrast to the inappropriate pairing of the abiotic solar panels. While a welcome transition to the production of clean energy, the placement of solar panels above traditional ponds has a negative impact on the multitude of organic processes this nature-based technology produces. Through the well-meaning colocation of high-tech, this thriving closed-loop system will inevitably be disrupted, sacrificing the ancestral for the industrial.

The integrated system of water and land resources constitutes a resilient and efficient closed-loop, hybrid-landscape solution. It has the potential to guide practices in water and land management, agriculture, sericulture, and aquaculture, particularly in regions prone to frequent flooding. *Sangjiyutang* optimizes local resources while producing commodities such as fish and silk. Historically, this has stimulated the local economy and provided job security for farmers in the Yangtze River Delta. Amid climate-related stressors, the mulberry trees that surround fishponds offer more ecosystemic benefits than typical agricultural plants because of their capacity for air purification and carbon sequestration.

The mulberry dike–fishpond complexes in Huzhou can inspire strategies for managing highly urbanized intertidal zones or frequently flooded urban areas, adding a living infrastructure to support sustainable cities. This multiscalar system exemplifies how to build infrastructures that are both ecologically and economically resilient. *Sangjiyutang* serves as a living example of how Lo—TEK solutions intertwine the threads of a city's past with technologies of the present.

13

13 Since ancient times, Huzhou has been known as "the Home of Silk in China," due to being the origin of the world-famous "Silk Road."

ENDNOTES

1. Xie Shi, "Water Management, Transport, and the Development of Market Towns in the Lake Tai Region, Eleventh–Sixteenth Centuries," *Global Environment* 9, no. 1 (2016): 42, http://dx.doi.org/10.3197/ge.2016.090103/.
2. Xingguo Gu et al., "Energy-Based Sustainability Evaluation of the Mulberry-Dyke and Fish-Pond System on the South Bank of Taihu Lake, China," *Sustainability* 14, no. 17 (2022): 2, https://doi.org/10.3390/su141710463.
3. Gu et al., "Energy-Based Sustainability Evaluation," 3–4.
4. Gu et al., "Energy-Based Sustainability Evaluation," 4.
5. Antonio Santoro et al., "From Flood Control System to Agroforestry Heritage System: Past, Present and Future of the Mulberry-Dikes and Fishponds System of Huzhou City, China," *Land* 11, no. 11 (2022): 5, https://doi.org/10.3390/land11111920.
6. Santoro et al., "From Flood Control System," 5–6.
7. "Zhejiang Huzhou Mulberry-Dyke & Fish-Pond System, China," FAO, https://www.fao.org/giahs/giahsaroundtheworld/designated-sites/asia-and-the-pacific/huzhou-mulberry/.
8. Hu Bao-tong and Yang Hua-zhu, "The Integration of Mulberry Cultivation, Sericulture and Fish Farming," trans. Min Kuan-hong (paper presented at the establishment of the Network of Aquaculture Centres in Asia, Bangkok, Thailand, December 1984), https://www.fao.org/fishery/docs/CDrom/aquaculture/a0845t/volume2/docrep/field/003/ac241e/AC241E00.htm.
9. Hu Bao-tong and Yang Hua-zhu, "The Integration of Mulberry Cultivation."
10. Zhong Gongfu, "The Mulberry Dike-Fish Pond Complex: A Chinese Ecosystem of Land-Water Interaction on the Pearl River Delta," *Human Ecology* 10, no. 2 (1982): 196.
11. Gongfu, "The Mulberry Dike-Fish Pond Complex," 199–200.
12. Gongfu, "The Mulberry Dike-Fish Pond Complex," 198–99.
13. Kuanhong Min and Baotong Hu, "Chinese Embankment Fish Culture," in *Integrated Agriculture-Aquaculture*, ed. FAO (Rome: FAO, 2001).
14. "Zhejiang Huzhou Mulberry-Dyke & Fish-Pond System, China," FAO, https://www.fao.org/giahs/giahsaroundtheworld/designated-sites/asia-and-the-pacific/huzhou-mulberry/.
15. Santoro et al., "From Flood Control System," 2.
16. Yijie Zhuang, "Rice Fields, Water Management and Agricultural Development in the Prehistoric Lake Taihu Region and the Ningshao Plain," in *Water Societies and Technologies from the Past and Present*, ed. Mark Altaweel and Yijie Zhuang (London: University College London, 2018): 88, muse.jhu.edu/book/81912.
17. Santoro et al., "From Flood Control System to Agroforestry Heritage System," 15–16.
18. Santoro et al., "From Flood Control System," 8.
19. Santoro et al., "From Flood Control System," 10.
20. Gu et al., "Emergy-Based Sustainability Evaluation," 8.
21. Kuanhong and Baotong, "Chinese Embankment Fish Culture."

JESSOUR TERRACING SYSTEM *of* THE AMAZIGH *Tunisia*

JESSOUR TERRACING SYSTEM *of* THE AMAZIGH *Tunisia*

Coauthored by
Mohamed Ouessar and Abdelhakim (Hakim) Issaoui,
supported by contributors Omar Wanas and Tasnime El Arbi

(PEOPLE) Amazigh (LOCATION) Tunisia
(TECHNOLOGY) terracing system (ELEVATION) 394–650 m
(ORIGIN) 900s–1000s
(DISTANCE ABOVE OR BELOW WATERLINE) –5 to +5 m
(WATER LEVEL FLUCTUATION, TIDAL OR SEASONAL) 0 to +0.5 m

FAO Nexus
(WATER) fresh (ENERGY) tidal + bioenergy + cleansing
(FOOD) olives

IPCC Adaptation Pathway
accommodate

World Bank NBS
(CATEGORY) river and stream renaturation, terraces and slopes, bioretention areas, river floodplains
(FUNCTIONS) biodiversity, drought regulation, pluvial flood regulation, subsidence regulation, air pollution regulation, landslide regulation, water pollution regulation, heat regulation
(BENEFITS) resource production, biodiversity, stimulate local economies and job creation, carbon storage and sequestration, cultural, pluvial flood risk reduction, human health, heat-stress reduction

The traditional rainwater-harvesting systems of Tunisia vary widely, reflecting the diverse topographies, climates, and cultures that have shaped this territory over centuries.[1] Constructed of locally available materials such as stone, soil, and palm residues, among these systems are the *al-maskat, al-mgoud, at-tawabi, al-mawajil, jessour,* and *al-fusquiyat.* In the water-scarce region of the Matmata Mountains in southern Tunisia, scattered stands of lush olive trees grow along streaked riverbeds that remain dry for most of the year. These trees thrive when planted in the area of an ingenious rainwater-harvesting technique known as *jessour*—an irrigation technology developed by the Amazigh people Indigenous to the Maghreb.[2,3] For the Amazigh communities that have lived in this region for millennia, olive trees—and the practices that support their growth—have profound significance, informing religious beliefs, cuisine, habits, and livelihoods. Designed as a communal division of water resources in an arid landscape, the *jessour* terracing system requires collaboration through fieldwork, maintenance, and harvest.[4,5,6]

The system is composed of terraced dams that stretch across the riverbed, placed successively one after the other downstream.[7] These terraces retain surface water and sediment for plants to grow, attracting flora and fauna while reducing climate-related risk.[8,9] Though the precise origin of this ancient system remains uncertain, it has existed for as long as the Amazigh people have inhabited the region, with written records describing *jessour* dating to the 10th and 11th centuries.[10,11] A landscape infrastructure associated with one of the oldest recorded legal systems for sharing water, known as water law, the *jessour* stands as a model for sustainable water usage and resource management in desert climates.[12,13] The innovative elements of the *jessour* are derived from not only its adaptability to complex site-specific conditions but also its effective management, development, and resolution of conflicts among its various stakeholders in the natural landscape or water basin of the system. The fundamental principles of water law revolve around the communal sharing of benefits derived from water without ownership.

1

1 In the Matmata Mountains of southeast Tunisia, vast stony plains open onto scenic landscapes of mountains, desert plateaus, crags, and rocky ridges.

2 Berber communities live in underground dwellings known as troglodyte houses, which are designed according to the classic layout of Tunisian houses, with a large central courtyard overlooked by the entrances to the various rooms, arranged on two levels.

2

This region is distinguished by its rugged topography, reaching up to seven hundred meters high, crossed by valleys with narrow and steep slopes. As an adaptation to the water-scarce environment, the strategy behind the *jessour* system takes advantage of ephemeral streams to cultivate cultural keystone species. Bordering the hot, dry, subtropical climate of the Western Sahara and the warm, humid Gulf of Gabes, the rocky landscape of the Matmata Mountains typically experiences a dry climate, with low and irregular rainfall averaging 22 days annually, accounting for an average of 200 millimeters between the months of October

EPHEMERAL Lasting for a very short time.

3

and May. While the region experiences a high evaporation period during this time, there is an almost absolute drought from May to September.[14]

Historically, Amazigh communities have lived alongside *jessour* dams—especially near terraces that receive more runoff, where it is optimal to live off and tend to olive groves.[15] These groves can produce an abundance of resources, with olive oil in particular serving as an indispensable commodity. Considered a symbol of purity, olive oil serves as a culinary essential enriched with medicinal benefits, along with numerous other everyday uses.[16] Today, Tunisia is one of the world's largest olive oil producers, cultivating two million hectares of olive groves, with 82 million trees, occupying 30 percent of the country's arable land.[17]

In Arabic, an individual terrace dam is referred to as a singular *jesr* (bridge), while the plural is *jessour*.[18, 19] These dams are built in a watercourse or positioned at the foot of a slope, where they operate as a microcatchment—collecting water in small areas and retaining sediment-rich runoff to enhance cultivation. They vary in their size, construction components, and preparation elements, depending on their location in relation to the main watercourse or one of its branches, resulting in two different types: slope *jessour and* watercourse *jessour*, with the latter being the most frequently used.[20] Slope *jessour* have a higher density of trees planted in a wider field at lower altitude and feature a single dike, spanning approximately 120 meters, that surrounds the field for water collection.[21] Watercourse *jessour* have a low density of trees and several shorter dikes, which measure 15 to 50 meters as they intercept the water source. Both *jessour* typologies are designed to take advantage of brief, infrequent rainfall events by gathering and slowing runoff from watershed systems, encouraging infiltration, and enhancing soil water storage through the aquifers under each *jesr*.[22] Beyond this, a *jesr* retains soil moisture for cropping, conserves groundwater, and controls flooding, thereby protecting downstream infrastructure.

3 In arid regions such as southern Tunisia, water harvesting techniques like the *jessour* have a long history.

4 These traditional water harvesting techniques are widely used for growing crops and fruit trees, allowing the cultivation of almond, fig, and olive trees beyond their climatic zone.

4

Jessour Collect Surface Water, Conserve Soil Moisture, and Control Flood Water

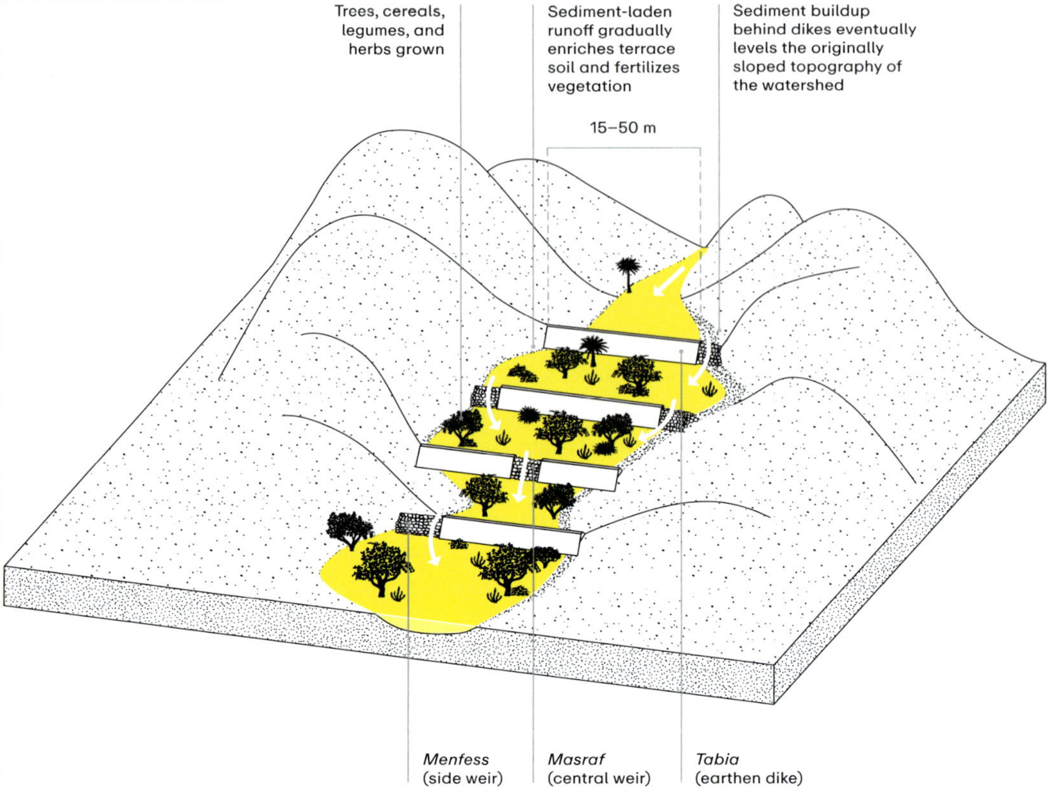

Trees, cereals, legumes, and herbs grown

Sediment-laden runoff gradually enriches terrace soil and fertilizes vegetation

Sediment buildup behind dikes eventually levels the originally sloped topography of the watershed

15–50 m

Menfess (side weir)

Masraf (central weir)

Tabia (earthen dike)

5 Fertile sediments accumulate behind the stone and earthen dikes, allowing the planting of trees and annual crops.

Each *jessour* system is composed of three sections: a sloping ground with an *impluvium*; one or more terraces; and an earthen dike called a *tabia*, or *katra* in the local dialect of Arabic.[23, 24] Dikes are built from stone-reinforced earthen embankments that are two meters wide and two to five meters high.[25, 26, 27] At the extent of the system, the *impluvium* informs where dikes are located.[28] This occurs across thalwegs—the line following the lowest part the wadi (dry riverbed that floods during the rainy season)—or gullies, which are landforms created by running water.[29, 30] They can have a single outlet (water supply point) on one side or in the middle, or outlets on both sides.[31]

Over time, the passage of water builds up sediment, forming a layer of soil behind the dikes that naturally levels the original sloped condition of the watershed.[32] Runoff accumulates on terraces as it rains, and the sediment gradually enriches the soil by adding minerals and organic matter that fertilize flora.[33] Excess water flows down to the next terrace through a central spillway called a *masraf*, or through a single or double lateral spillway called a *menfess*.[34] These weirs are located 30 to 80 centimeters below the *jesr* level.[35, 36] The type of weir used depends on the geology of the system's waterway; *masraf* are more secure and versatile, but *menfess* are preferred as more water can be stored.[37] Weirs are constructed using local drystones—each about the size of a brick—which are sometimes bound with

Watercourse and Slope are Two *Jessour* Types

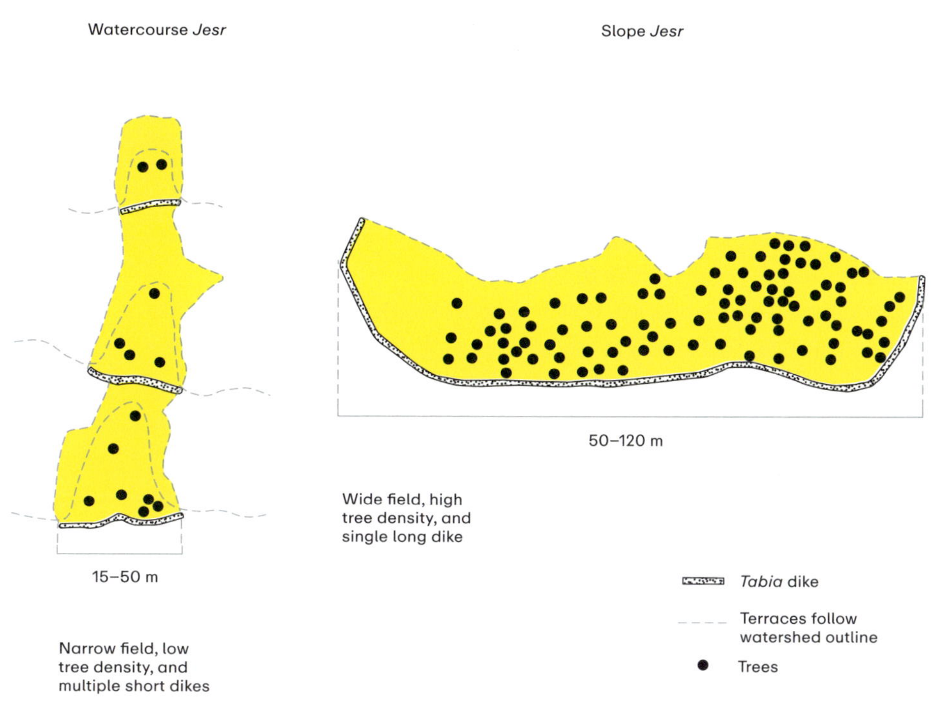

gypsum or vegetation, but are typically able to stand on their own. These spillways are also used to reinforce and protect other parts of the *jessour*.[38]

The *jessour* system is primarily used for growing olive trees; however, it can also support the cultivation of plants, such as figs, date palms, peaches, grapes, almonds, and pistachio trees.[39, 40, 41] During rainy years, cereals like barley and wheat, as well as legumes like peas, lentils, and fava beans, can be cultivated along the base of olive trees.[42, 43, 44] Cropping areas are populated with livestock, which are continuously moved between trees to avoid overgrazing land.[45, 46] If annual crops are not cultivated between the trees, a diverse variety of plants grow spontaneously due to the water accessibility and soil fertility established by the *jessour* system.[47, 48] Herbaceous plants on which livestock graze, like alfa (*Stipa tenacissima*), *drian* (*Stipagrostis pungens*), and *rem't* (*Hammada scoparia*), sprout naturally between groves.[49] Other species like Roman

5

chamomile (*Chamaemelum nobile*), wild rocket (*Diplotaxis tenuifolia*), and lazole are collected by the community as a secondary source of food.[50] Communal harvesting occurs at different periods depending on crops: olives from the end of November to February, barley from May to July, and figs from July to August.[51] Once harvested, the waste from crops is used as fodder for a mix of livestock, including sheep, goats, chickens, and camels.[52, 53]

6

The *jessour* system slows down surface water, retains moisture, spreads nutrients, and introduces a variety of edible species, which support biodiversity as well as food and water security in this drought-prone region.[54] While intense periods of drought present challenges to the infrastructure and reduce water availability to olive and palm trees, the return of rainfall during winter months restores these resilient species and the system as a whole.[55]

Careful management and maintenance are required for the system's ongoing success.[56] Once accumulated soil has reached the height of the earthen embankment, it must be vertically extended to continue to operate as a dike.[57]

6 An individual terrace dam is referred to as a singular *jesr*, while the plural is *jessour*.
7 The system has the ability to slow down surface water, retain moisture, and spread nutrients.

Runoff Accumulates Above *Tabia* of a *Jesr* Terrace

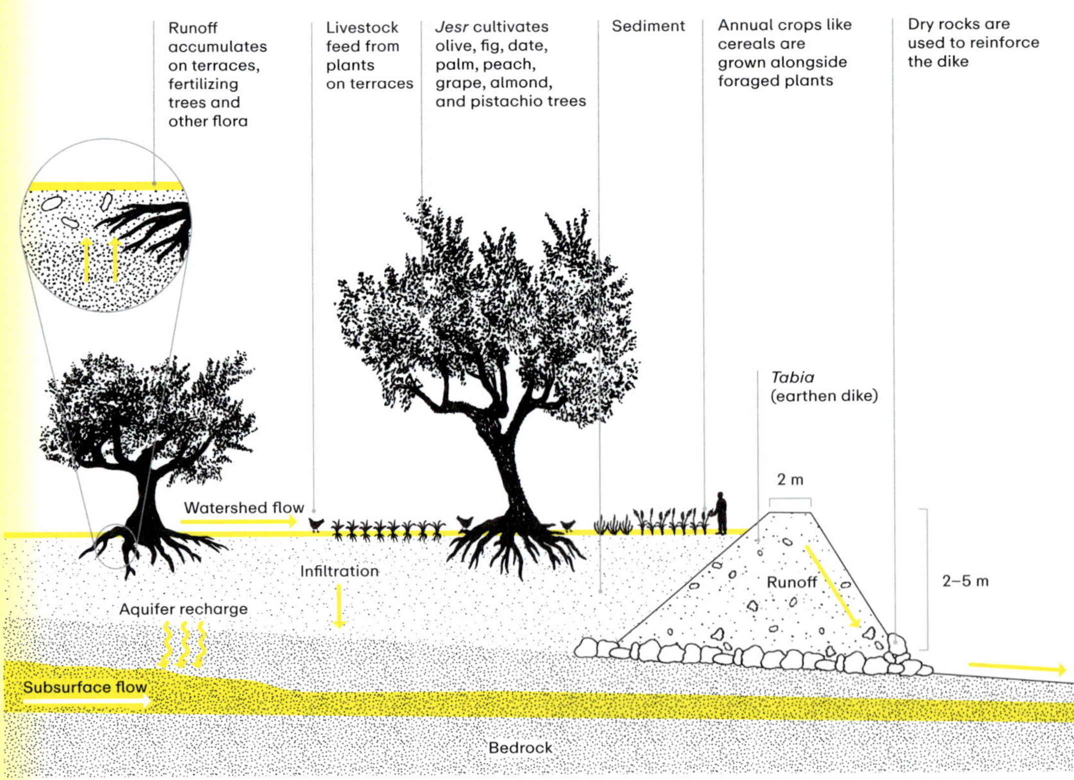

7

8

To prevent further damage, rodent burrows must be filled with stone or dirt to reduce leakage before the next runoff event.[58] Strategically situated along an ephemeral watercourse and built using local materials, *jessour* exemplifies a hydroagricultural system with a low carbon footprint and minimal resource demand capable of supporting livestock farming and ensuring access to water in arid regions.[59, 60] The system functions as an aquifer recharge, as well as a means for water cleansing as its terraced structure filters water flowing from level to level.[61] Wind erosion is controlled because sediment is prevented from reaching downstream plains, and soil moisture storage is increased, countering evapotranspiration, to extend crop-growing seasons and decrease the quantity of water needed to grow more water-intensive species, like fruit trees.[62] In light of changing global climatic conditions, the *jessour* system—an infrastructure that represents centuries of coadaptation between communities and the environment to counter water, food, and economic insecurity, while controlling the threat of flash flooding—offers a compelling example of a successful nature-based infrastructure for locations facing water insecurity.[63]

EVAPOTRANSPIRATION
The process by which water is transferred from the land to the atmosphere by evaporation from the soil and other surfaces and by transpiration from plants.

The majority of *jessour* systems remain in cultivation today, highlighting the technology's crucial role in local life and the economy; one study found that only 65 out of the 882 recorded *jessour* systems had ceased to be used.[64] However, several challenges threaten the sustainability of this practice. As knowledge of date palm cultivation—passed down among generations—dwindles, difficulties in sustaining small-scale date cultivation—a fruit grown in the system—have emerged.[65] Additionally, economic insecurity, challenges maintaining *jessour*, and the growing use of modern technologies have prompted a population migration to northern Tunisia, France, and Italy.[66, 67]

In recent years, dwindling access to land has posed a threat to the longevity of *jessour* systems. The southern region of Tunisia, where the *jessour* terraces have been stewarded for centuries, has been identified as a key site for renewable energy projects. The land-intensive wind and solar farms are intended for domestic domestic energy production and export to Europe.[68, 69] The acquisition of land for the siting of these large-scale renewable energy projects has created conflict surrounding the community relations and traditional land tenure systems that support the *jessour* technology.

Traditional communal land ownership is a topic of current debate related to renewable energy projects. Seeking to invest in regions occupied by traditional infrastructures, communal property rights currently form barriers to long-term, large-scale land leasing agreements proposed by international private companies.[70] However as relocation to urban areas increases, community resistance wanes. Traditionally constructed and managed by kin groups, the maintenance of existing *jessour* systems now extends beyond family to include acquaintances and neighbors. The longevity of these new relationships, sustained by social norms and a sense of mutual obligation, become vital to the continued operation of traditional water harvesting systems.

While FAO programs have worked to promote systems like *jessour* for cultural tourism, beyond preservation, the opportunity exists to restore these systems in rural locations and adapt them to urban contexts in Tunisia and beyond, with close consultation from Amazigh communities.[71] However, despite many Amazigh individuals retaining a strong connection to their lands and ancestral customs, there is a noticeable decline in the usage of the Amazigh language known as Tamazight among younger generations.[72] Accompanying the loss of Indigenous languages, colonial influences on the education system are contributing to the loss of traditional knowledge. Amongst local engineering schools, Indigenous technologies, like *jessour,* are deliberately excluded from Tunisian curricula.

As a low-cost, low-carbon, and non-resource-intensive practice that supports ecological systems while increasing agricultural yields, this system is a climate solution for resilience—particularly in the face of flooding and food scarcity—by passively redirecting and collecting runoff.[73, 74, 75] Simultaneously, it lengthens agricultural seasons, enhances soil quality, cleanses and restores water in aquifers, promotes biodiversity, reduces soil erosion, and lessens the risk of drought and flooding.[76] *Jessour* systems allow for regions that experience water scarcity—or water excess—to adapt to grow agriculture through a dam-based system, protecting the livelihood of the surrounding population and increasing the health of the ecosystems.

9

8 Historically, Amazigh communities have lived alongside *jessour.*
9 With the southern region of Tunisia identified as a keyzone for renewable energy projects, the *jessour* system is becoming increasingly threatened.

ENDNOTES

1. Francesco Pires et al., "The Role of the Jessour System for Agrobiodiversity Preservation in Southern Tunisia," *Biodiversity and Conservation* (2022): 2479, https://doi.org/10.1007/s10531-021-02286-5.
2. Pires et al., "The Role of the Jessour System," 2487.
3. Cain Burdeau, "Tunisia: Land of the Olive Tree," Olive Oil Times, February 8, 2018, https://oliveoiltimes.com/world/tunisia-land-olive-tree/62159.
4. Mohamed Ouessar (professor, Arid Regions Institute of Medenine) in discussion with the author, June 2023.
5. Ouessar, discussion.
6. Ouessar, discussion.
7. Pires et al., "The Role of the Jessour System," 2479.
8. Pires et al., "The Role of the Jessour System," 2479.
9. Martin Calianno et al. "Benefits of Water-Harvesting Systems (Jessour) on Soil Water Retention in Southeast Tunisia," *Water* 12, no. 1 (2020): 1, https://doi.org/10.3390/w12010295.
10. Ouessar, discussion.
11. Ouessar, discussion.
12. Pires et al., "The Role of the Jessour System," 2480.
13. Ouessar, discussion.
14. Pires et al., "The Role of the Jessour System," 2482.
15. Ouessar, discussion.
16. Ouessar, discussion.
17. Burdeau, "Tunisia."
18. Pires et al., "The Role of the Jessour System," 2480.
19. Ouessar, discussion.
20. Pires et al., "The Role of the Jessour System," 2485–2486.
21. Pires et al., "The Role of the Jessour System," 2485–2486.
22. Calianno et al., "Benefits of Water-Harvesting Systems," 4.
23. Mounir Louhaichi and Mouldi Gamoun, "Jessour for Diversified and Resilient Agroecological Systems to Ensure Food Security and Sustainable Livelihoods in Arid Ecosystems" (poster presented at the 5th World Congress on Agroforestry, Québec, Canada, November 2022).
24. Ouessar, discussion.
25. Pires et al., "The Role of the Jessour System," 2482.
26. Calianno et al., "Benefits of Water-Harvesting Systems," 3–4.
27. Ouessar, discussion.
28. Pires et al., "The Role of the Jessour System," 2484.
29. Pires et al., "The Role of the Jessour System," 2479.
30. Merriam-Webster.com, s.v. "wadi," accessed May 9, 2023, https://www.merriam-webster.com/dictionary/wadi.
31. Ammar Adham et al., "A Methodology to Assess and Evaluate Rainwater Harvesting Techniques in (Semi-) Arid Regions," *Water* 8 (2016): 3.
32. Pires et al., "The Role of the Jessour System," 2482.
33. Pires et al., "The Role of the Jessour System," 2480–83.
34. Pires et al., "The Role of the Jessour System," 2482.
35. Pires et al., "The Role of the Jessour System," 2482.
36. Ouessar, discussion.
37. Ouessar, discussion.
38. Ouessar, discussion.
39. Pires et al., "The Role of the Jessour System," 2487.
40. Louhaichi and Gamoun, "Jessour for Diversified and Resilient Agroecological Systems."
41. Giulio Castelli et al., "Effect of Traditional Check Dams (Jessour) on Soil and Olive Trees Water Status in Tunisia," *The Science of the Total Environment* (2019): 227, https://doi.org/10.1016/j.scitotenv.2019.06.514.
42. Pires et al., "The Role of the Jessour System," 2483.
43. Louhaichi and Gamoun, "Jessour for Diversified and Resilient Agroecological Systems."
44. Castelli et al., "Effect of Traditional Check Dams," 227.
45. Louhaichi and Gamoun, "Jessour for Diversified and Resilient Agroecological Systems."
46. Ouessar, discussion.
47. Louhaichi and Gamoun, "Jessour for Diversified and Resilient Agroecological Systems."
48. Pires et al., "The Role of the Jessour System," 2487.
49. Francesco Pires et al., "The Role of the Jessour System," 2487.
50. Francesco Pires et al., "The Role of the Jessour System," 2487.
51. Ouessar, discussion.
52. Pires et al., "The Role of the Jessour System," 2487.
53. Louhaichi and Gamoun, "Jessour for Diversified and Resilient Agroecological Systems."
54. Pires et al., "The Role of the Jessour System," 2491.
55. Ouessar, discussion.
56. Louhaichi and Gamoun, "Jessour for Diversified and Resilient Agroecological Systems."
57. Pires et al., "The Role of the Jessour System," 2482.
58. Ouessar, discussion.
59. Ouessar, discussion.
60. Pires et al., "The Role of the Jessour System," 2491.
61. Pires et al., "The Role of the Jessour System," 2492.
62. Pires et al., "The Role of the Jessour System," 2491.
63. Pires et al., "The Role of the Jessour System," 2491–92.
64. Pires et al., "The Role of the Jessour System," 2492.
65. Ouessar, discussion.
66. Pires et al., "The Role of the Jessour System," 2491.
67. Ouessar, discussion.
68. C. Ben Rouine and F. Roche, "Renewable Energy in Tunisia: An Unjust Transition," in *Dismantling Green Colonialism: Energy and Climate Justice in the Arab Region*, ed. Hamza Hamouchene and Katie Sandwell (n.p.: Pluto Press, 2023).
69. Aymen Chibani, "Europe's 'Green Battery': Extraction and Dispossession of Energy Infrastructure in Tunisia's South," The Tahrir Institute for Middle East Policy, May 21, 2024, https://timep.org/2024/04/04/europes-green-battery-extraction-and-dispossession-of-energy-infrastructure-in-tunisias-south/.
70. Chibani, "Europe's 'Green Battery.'"
71. Ouessar, discussion.
72. Ouessar, discussion.
73. Adham et al., "A Methodology to Assess and Evaluate," 3.
74. Adham et al., "A Methodology to Assess and Evaluate," 19–20.
75. Pires et al., "The Role of the Jessour System," 2479.
76. Pires et al., "The Role of the Jessour System," 2491.

COAUTHOR

MOHAMED OUESSAR

Arid Regions Institute Researcher

Mohamed Ouessar was born in the rural southeastern Tunisian city of Tataouine. Throughout his upbringing, he was actively engaged in dryland farming and often worked alongside his grandparents on school holidays. Ouessar pursued his education at the Institut National Agronomique de Tunisie, where he obtained his diploma in agricultural sciences in 1989, specializing in soil and water conservation.

After receiving an offer from the University of Ghent in Belgium, he joined the inaugural cohort of the MSc program in eremology (desert sciences). Graduating in 1991, he was honored with the prestigious De Boodt-Maselis Award for his outstanding studies in eremology. Subsequently, he earned a PhD fellowship as recognition of his academic excellence. Returning to Tunisia in 1994, he was appointed a researcher at the Arid Regions Institute (IRA) of Médenine, concurrently advancing his PhD thesis through a sandwich program.

Ouessar received his doctorate in pplied biological sciences, with a focus on land management, from the University of Ghent in 2007. He is currently a senior researcher and head of the Laboratory of Eremology nd Combating Desertification at the IRA, where he lso coordinates the institute's Remote Sensing and Geographic Information Systems (GIS) units.

Since he was appointed a researcher at the IRA in 1994, he has actively contributed to the realization of over 30 joint research projects funded or conducted by national and international agencies, including the UNDP, the United Nations Convention to Combat Desertification, the European Union, UNESCO, nd the United States Agency for International Development. His research programs have focused n water harvesting, resource mobilization and mangement, geospatial-based hydrological modeling nd decision support systems, impact assessment, watershed management, land degradation and rehabilitation, climate change impacts and adaptation, combating desertification, and drylands management. Ouessar has also taught part-time at universities, authored over 70 scientific papers, edited more than 15 books, and contributed to over 30 book chapters. As a reviewer for over 20 esteemed international journals, he has been sought after by national ministries, international organizations, and local development agencies for consultancy, and he has provided expertise for global projects in countries such as the UAE, Saudi Arabia, and Mauritania.

Abdelhakim "Hakim" Issaoui, an engineering expert in agroecology with a focus in biodiversity, desertification, and drought, who coauthored the Ramli chapter, additionally coauthored this chapter.

Additional contributors include Omar Wanas, an Irish-Egyptian landscape architect, researcher, participatory urban development consultant, and member of International Federation of Landscape Architects (IFLA), and Tasnime El Arbi, a Tunisian urban planner, graphic designer, and researcher at Oecumene Spaces for Dignity, where she researches the impact of climate change on public spaces.

RYBNÍK FISHPONDS *and* *PŘÍKOP* CANALS *of* THE SOUTHERN BOHEMIANS
Czechia

RYBNÍK FISHPONDS *and* *PŘÍKOP* CANALS *of* THE SOUTHERN BOHEMIANS *Czechia*

Coauthored by
Jan Pokorný

PEOPLE Southern Bohemians LOCATION Třeboňsko, Czechia TECHNOLOGY fishponds and canals ELEVATION 430 m ORIGIN 1300s DISTANCE ABOVE OR BELOW WATERLINE −10 to +2 m WATER LEVEL FLUCTUATION, TIDAL OR SEASONAL +1 to +10 m

FAO Nexus
WATER fresh ENERGY cleansing FOOD fish

IPCC Adaptation Pathway
protect

World Bank NBS
CATEGORY bioretention areas, constructed inland wetlands, river and stream renaturation, river floodplains
FUNCTIONS biodiversity, water pollution regulation, pluvial flood regulation, heat regulation, air pollution regulation, subsidence regulation, riverine flood regulation
BENEFITS resource production, biodiversity, stimulate local economies and job creation, pluvial flood risk reduction, riverine flood risk reduction, carbon storage and sequestration, cultural, social interaction, tourism and recreation, education

1

In the wetlands of South Bohemia, among the pastures, small villages, and wide rivers, hundreds of fishponds are contained by earthen dikes reinforced by ancient oaks.[1, 2] Over the last seven centuries, this tradition—originating in the cloisters of the nearby Kladruby monastery—has transformed the marshlands and forests of the seven-hundred-square-kilometer Třeboň Basin into one of the most unique Indigenous fish-farming infrastructures in Europe, which also produces clean energy and cleanses wastewater. Since the 15th century, the fishermen of the Třeboň Ponds have reared carp in an aquaculture system of *příkop* (long narrow ditches or canals), dams, and over five hundred *rybník* (fishponds). Fed by the Lužnice River and Nežárka tributary in the upper portion of the Lužnice watershed, the ponds cover 64 square kilometers of the basin. As the largest exporter of common carp in Central Europe, this system also provides a critical habitat for over 50 endangered species.[3, 4]

While most of the fishponds were constructed in the 16th century, they were begun in the region's monasteries and appeared in the 12th century at Rožmberk Castle. The nearby town of Třeboň houses the Svět and Rožmberk fishponds, along the Lužnice River and Zlatá stoka (golden canal). Today, the town's population of eight thousand is the center of the harvest ceremonies, culture, and knowledge sharing—as celebrated when the ponds are drained and the fishermen appear outfitted in traditional dress.[5] The fishponds of Třeboň and southern Bohemia are an innovation of water storage, flood prevention, food production, and habitat restoration for a landlocked territory, where water makes up only 1 to 2 percent of the country's total surface area. Whereas in southern Bohemia this jumps to 10 percent, owing to the system's ability to cycle water resources.

1 Fishermen pull nets during the traditional carp haul in the lake of Dvoriste near the south Bohemian town of Trebonon.
2 Today's Třeboň Region was created in medieval times, when fish farming was first being developed.

Originally covered in wetlands unsuitable for farming, the Třeboň Basin was transformed by this ancient practice of aquaculture. Archives from the 12th century mention fishponds that lined the cloisters at the Kladruby monastery, providing fish for religious feasts. Monks learned the practice of damming during their pilgrimages to Palestine, eventually bringing the technology to Třeboň, where they constructed fishponds that gradually altered the landscape from wetlands to waterways.[6,7] As wet marshes were drained to form fishponds, fertile soil for the cultivation of grain and potatoes remained.[8]

The fishponds constructed in the 12th century were slowly expanded, upon an edict from Emperor Charles IV outlining their use beyond fish cultivation, citing "hydrological, climate-modifying, sanitary, and aesthetic" advantages.[9] At the same time, fishponds were introduced into medieval villages with the establishment of fortifications.[10] These fishponds were essential for mill operation, power generation, and flood control.[11] By 1450, 20 individual fishponds populated the region.[12]

As Třeboň ushered in the 16th century and the pond operations scaled, fishing became profitable, spurring a construction boom of aquatic infrastructure that lasted for a century. It was during this period that the majority of fishponds were constructed alongside an intricate system of canals known as *příkop*, for the capture and release of water from the surrounding rivers. This interchange of water is orchestrated by a network of smaller canals connecting smaller basins, fishponds, and larger canals—namely, the Zlatá stoka to the west, providing water to the two hundred fishponds fed and drained by surrounding rivers, including the Lužnice. The Třeboň Basin's *rybník* include the Horusický, Bošilecký, Záblatský, Ponědražský, Koclířov, Velký Tisý, Rožmberk, Svět, Opatovický, and Humlenský.[13]

2

Fishponds and Canals of the Třeboň Basin in Czechia

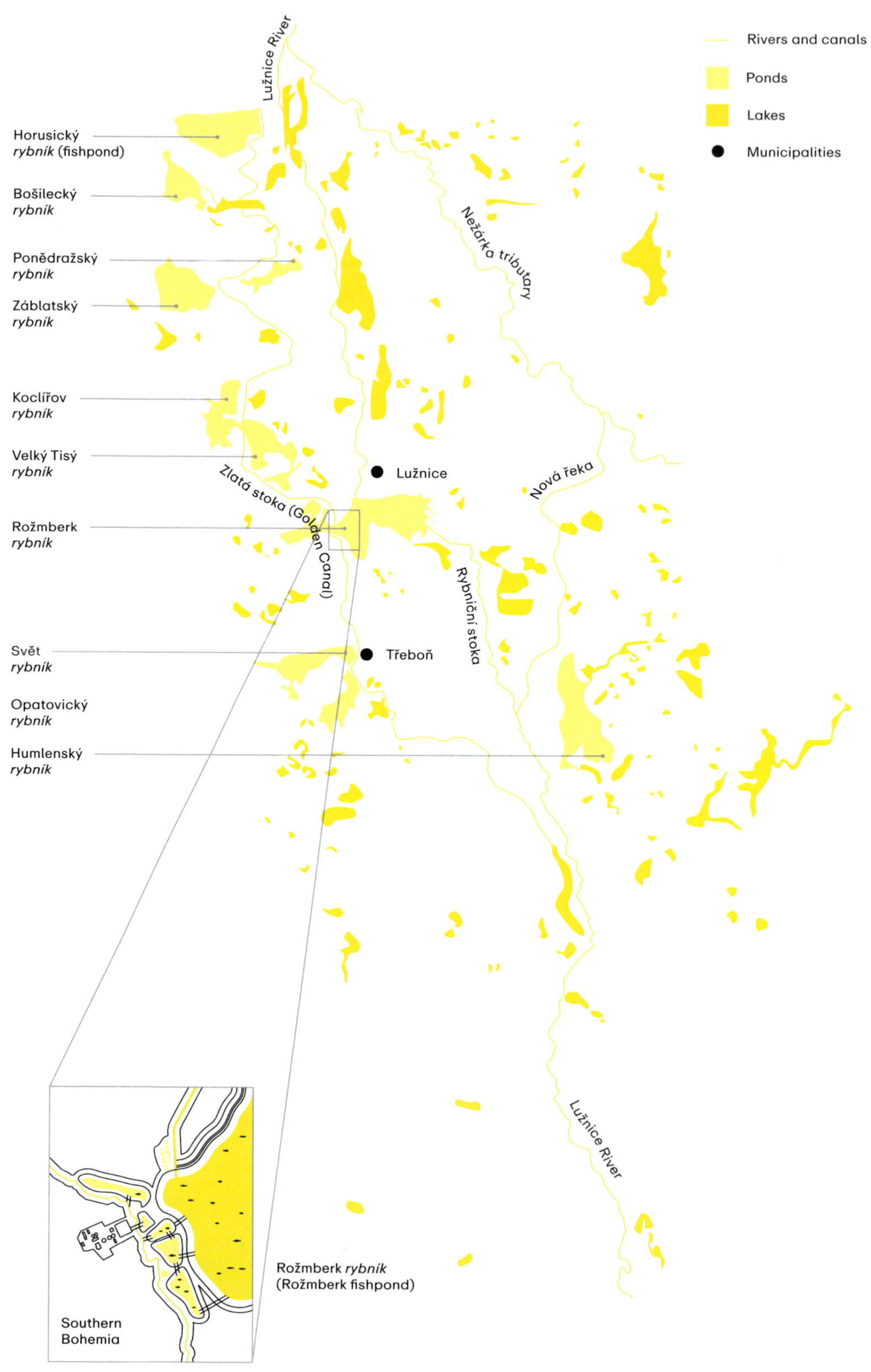

3

4

3 Founded at the end of the 16th century, the Rožmberk is the largest fishpond in the world.
4 Fisherman are assisted by poles when wading through mud during preparations for the fish harvest.

To provide passive inflow of water, many fishponds were originally constructed in the valleys parallel to the Lužnice River, which flows northward through the Třeboň lake region.[14] In the 16th century, the 45-kilometer-long channel of the Zlatá stoka was built in between two bends in the two-hundred-kilometer river. The base was constructed using mostly gravel, but, in areas that pass through peat bogs, timber of young willow and birch trees line the bottom for insulation, stopping the water flowing from one fishpond to another.[15] Today, it is the largest and most important canal in the region, as it plays a critical role alongside the Lužnice in the unique seasonal symbiosis of the fishponds. Water is drained from the fishponds through the canals during times of fish harvest; during times of intense rain, canal water fills the fishponds as a means of flood control.

Fishpond construction slowed in the 19th century, leading to the propagation of agricultural activities on newly reclaimed land. The fishponds that remained were located along sandy banks too fragile for agriculture.[16] Today, these fishponds are still used daily by fisheries and anglers. Fish culture is the only agricultural section in Czechia that has increased production since 1989, offering fishers viable employment opportunities.[17] Autumn and winter months bring harvest festivals with ceremonious music performances and fishing expeditions.[18]

5

5 Original water pipes made from hollowed tree trunks, reassembled using sea moss and clay as a natural sealant to prevent water seepage.

In traditional *příkop* construction, massive 10-meter-long tree trunks were used as outlet pipes to move water from one fishpond to another.[19] Oak, pine, and fir trunks were cut in two, hollowed out, and reassembled using sea moss and clay as a natural sealant to prevent water seepage.[20] These hollowed trunks were placed along the beds of the fishponds to funnel out water. The lack of oxygen in those depths prevented rotting, enabling the use of these timber pipes for

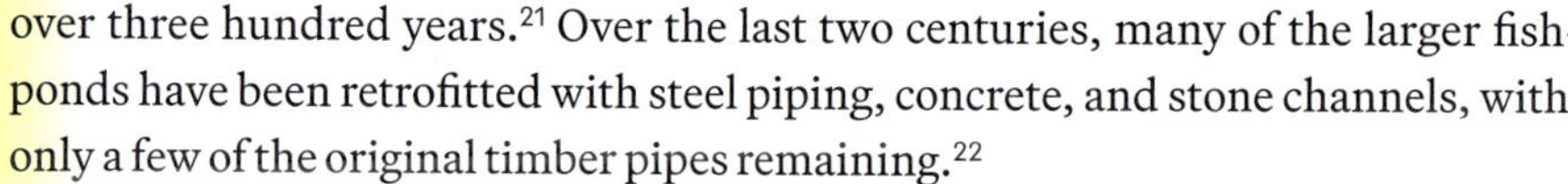

over three hundred years.[21] Over the last two centuries, many of the larger fishponds have been retrofitted with steel piping, concrete, and stone channels, with only a few of the original timber pipes remaining.[22]

The system of dams enveloping the fishponds was traditionally constructed from materials local to the wetlands. Soils were molded to form dikes 30 meters long, 12 meters high, and 60 to 80 meters wide at their base.[23] However, these soils were weak and prone to erosion. Oak trees were planted along the paths of the earthen dikes to stabilize the soil with their root systems.[24] The trees have cascading benefits for the ecosystem, with oak trees along with the forested area of the basin acting as carbon and nitrogen sinks for the region. The roots help remove excess water and replenish dry soils in the event of sparse rainfall, while providing habitat for a vast variety of aquatic and terrestrial species. The oak-lined dikes are now an iconic characteristic of the landscape, with these constructed landforms standing in contrast to the pine and spruce forests that cover half the territory.[25]

The dikes are fortified along their banks with riprap or retaining walls.[26] The riprap from the original construction consisted of wooden logs held in place by wooden stakes that suffered a similar fate to the wooden pipes, being replaced by stone.[27] The form of a dike responds directly to the water levels of its adjacent ponds. A dike in between a fishpond and a smaller basin must be built steeper along the side of the fishpond, while gradually tapering along a shallow slope on the other side until its edge touches the shallower water. This ensures the dike's stability, protecting against failure due to the force of the larger quantity of fishpond water.

The predominant fish species cultivated, harvested, and exported from this aquaculture system is the common carp (*Cyprinus carpio*), which thrives best

A System of Dams Envelops the Fish Ponds

The Flow of Water Beneath a Dike Between Fishponds

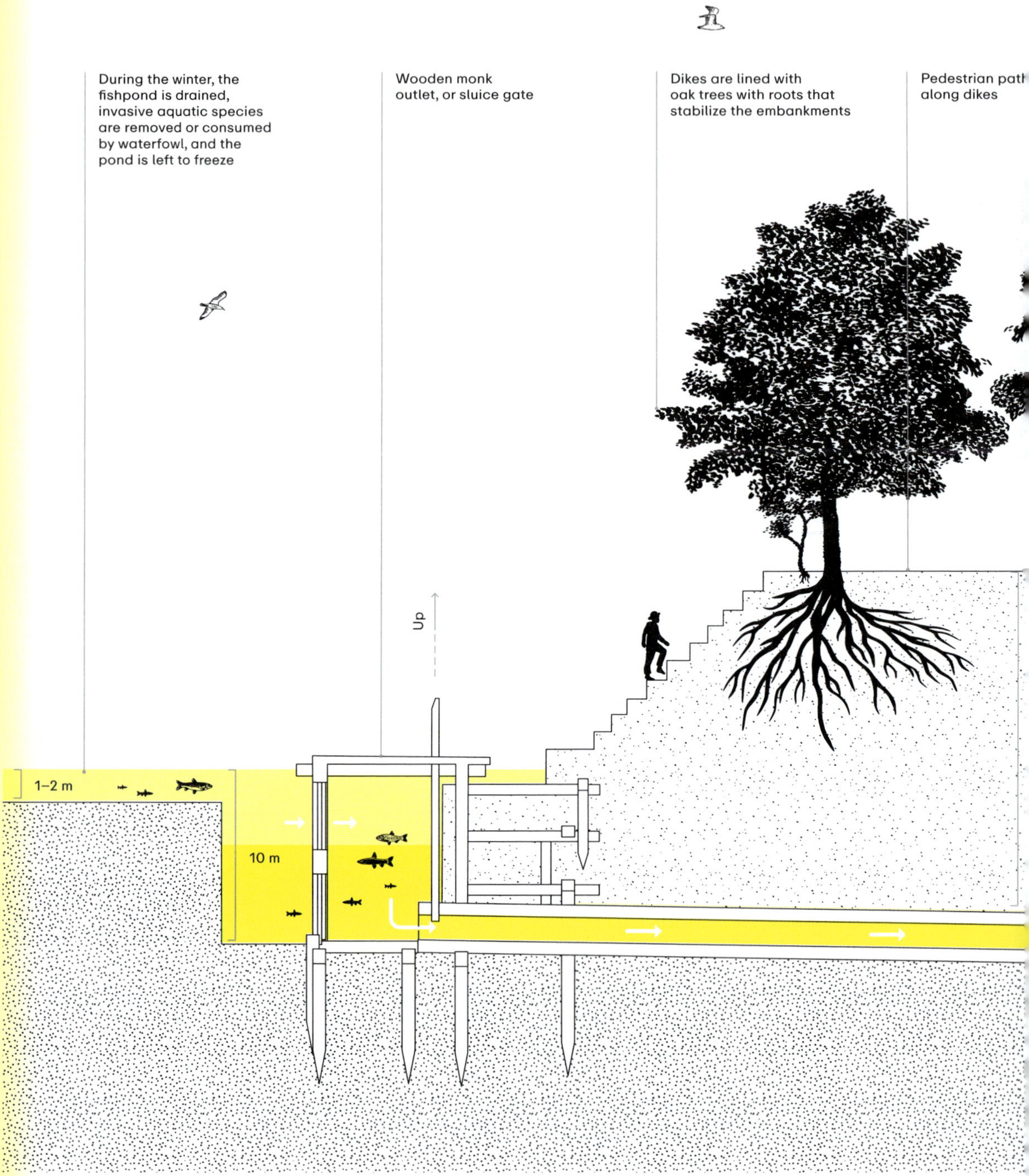

During the winter, the fishpond is drained, invasive aquatic species are removed or consumed by waterfowl, and the pond is left to freeze

Wooden monk outlet, or sluice gate

Dikes are lined with oak trees with roots that stabilize the embankments

Pedestrian path along dikes

Up

1–2 m

10 m

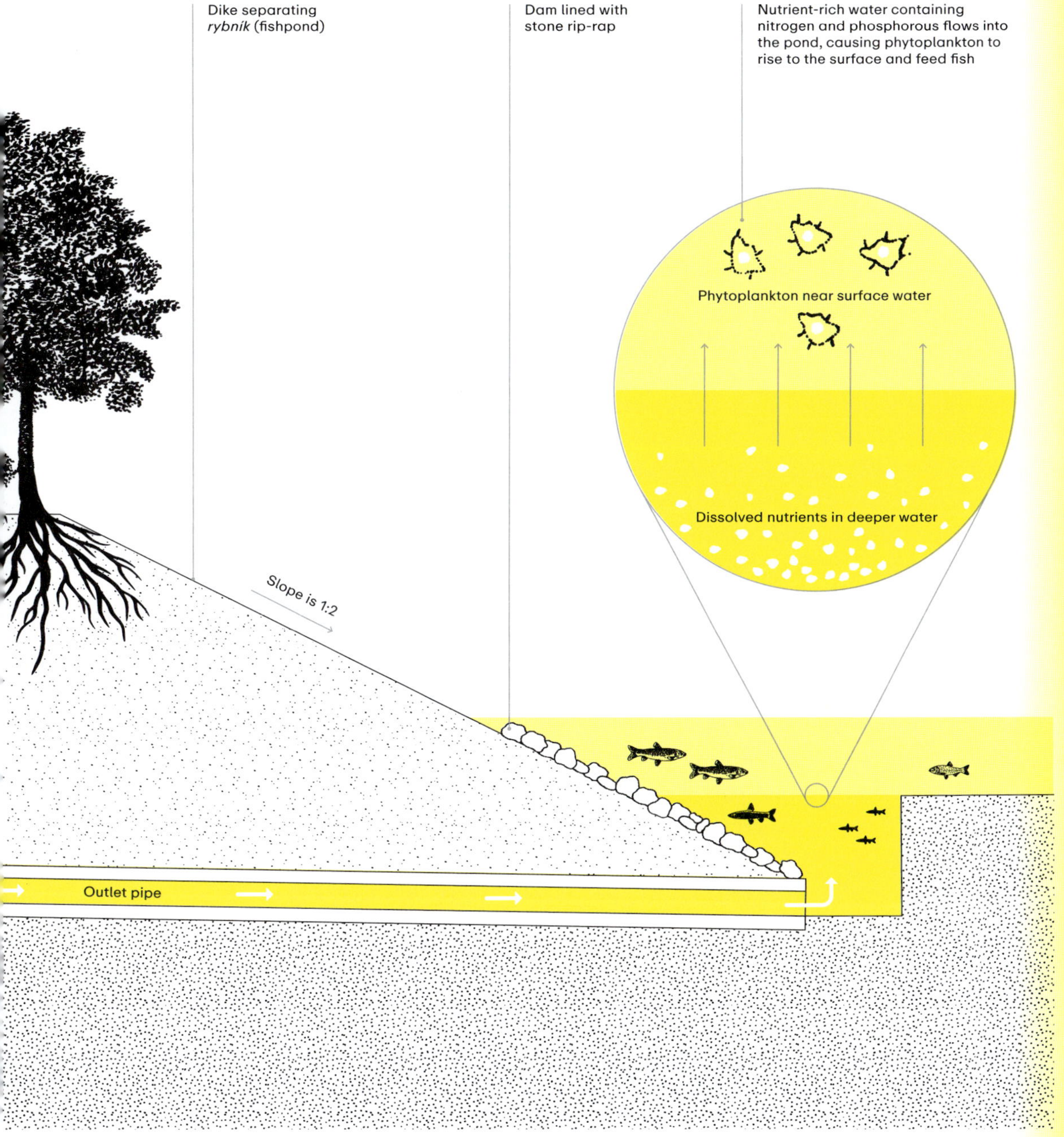
Dike separating
rybník (fishpond)
Dam lined with
stone rip-rap
Nutrient-rich water containing
nitrogen and phosphorous flows into
the pond, causing phytoplankton to
rise to the surface and feed fish
Phytoplankton near surface water
Dissolved nutrients in deeper water
Slope is 1:2
Outlet pipe

6

7

in shallow waters one meter in depth. While canals provide water and dams maintain water levels, sluice gates control the water level, allowing the interior waters of the ponds to be drained as needed. The type of gate varies depending on the size of the pond, with smaller ponds using a wooden monk outlet and larger ponds a steel-plated sluice gate.[28] The vertical position of the outlet also varies—with some located higher to take in oxygen-rich surface water, and others lining the bottom of the polder to take in less oxygen-rich water.[29] Some fishponds are even connected, passing water to one another through a series of outlet pipes.[30]

MONK OUTLET
An outlet built inside the bank at the deep end of the pond.

Today, the pre-17th-century infrastructure of the fishponds has been enveloped by the natural landscape.[31] The use of local building materials fostered many animals that now inhabit the oak trees, sand embankments, marshlands, and water reservoirs. Over 150 bird species nest in this area annually, with others stopping in Třeboň during their migration between Scandinavia and Africa.[32] The polders are home to plant life such as the bristleseed sandspurry (*Spergularia echinosperma*), coral necklace (*Illecebrum*), sandrush (*Juncus tenageia*), and pillwort (*Pilularia globulifera*).[33] Today, 159 ponds and habitats in the region are of international importance. In 1977, the basin was designated a biosphere reserve by UNESCO to protect a number of endangered species of insects (e.g., *Odonata*, *Plecoptera*, *Megaloptera*, and *Trichoptera*) and other invertebrates (e.g., *Mollusca*, *Crustacea*, and *Araneae*) from dying off, as they have in the surrounding regions.[34]

Though the 19th century marked the gradual end of fishpond construction, existing fisheries intensified their practices for higher quantities of fish.[35] Accompanying the carp is a fish polyculture that includes grass carp, silver carp, tench, and pike.[36] The carp-rearing cycle is a three to-four-year-long process.[37] Carp production begins in May, with a few embryos spawned in local hatcheries, while 70 million carp fry are imported from a hatchery in eastern Czechia before being transported to a fishpond on-site designed for their embryonic development.[38, 39] In the fall, the fry are moved to a very shallow pond with a water temperature of 20 degrees Celsius.[40, 41] After a few weeks, the pond water is drained and refilled, and then other small fish are introduced.[42] In the spring, the young carp feed on invertebrates and larger zooplankton until they grow to the length of a finger in the fall, when water levels are raised to a depth of one and a half meters to provide enough insulation for survival during the colder months.

6 Oak-lined earthen dikes, which surround the ponds and rivers, are reinforced by ancient root systems.
7 Carp, the traditional Czech Christmas Eve dinner, is fished primarily from southern Bohemian ponds, with fishermen using traditional methods to catch the local fish.
8 Fishermen sort fish during the traditional carp haul at Zablatsky pond.

In January, young carp are moved to a pond with other first-year carp and are fed a mix of zooplankton and grain.[43] In the autumn of the second or third year of cultivation, these gray-gold fish are ready for harvest, after the pond has been drained in the summer.[44, 45] This process reduces the risk from sudden and frequent changes to the environment and the loss of dissolved nutrients in the water, while minimizing the need for water manipulation.[46] Overall, Třeboň supplies a sizable portion of Europe's freshwater fish, producing nearly three thousand metric tons of common carp annually.[47]

The draining-and-harvest cycle initiates a ceremony at Rožmberk, the largest pond of the region, which spans five square kilometers and takes 14 days to drain.[48, 49] The festival brings locals and visitors to the small town, with crowds gathering in the town square to hear "fish rousing anthems," while fishers wearing traditional clothing conduct a live catch. Once harvested, fish are transported to small basins to be displayed and sold. The winter holidays are a special time for the Třeboň fish market, as farmed carp are sold alive, and families house them in their household bathtubs prior to serving them for Christmas Eve dinner.[50]

8

In May, embryos are spawned and remain as small eggs for 7–10 days

In autumn, fishermen move carp fry to a very shallow pond with a water temperature of 20°C, where they are fed small zooplankton

After a few weeks, the pond is drained and refilled with water, then smaller fish species are introdu
In the spring, the fish eat larger zooplankton and invertebrates.

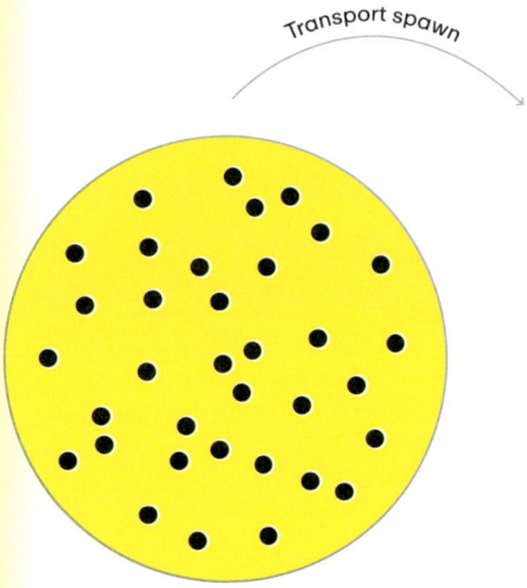

Transport spawn

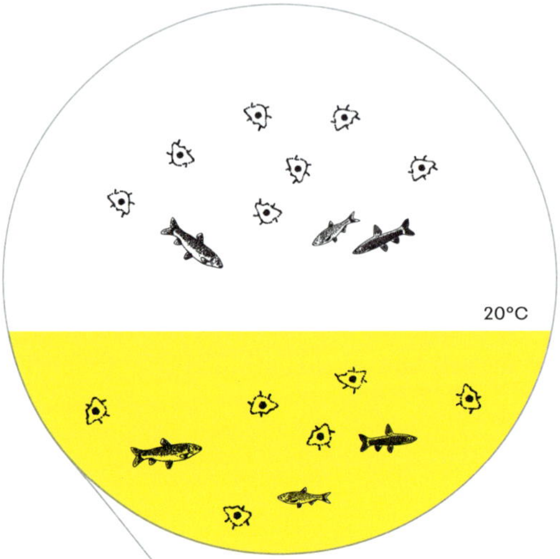

20°C

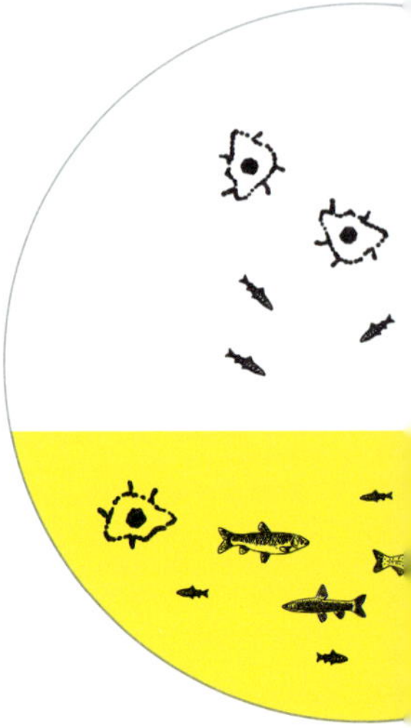

Hatcheries are located in eastern Czechia

Shallow water

Refilled wa

Biological p

Příkop (canal)

Inlet pipe

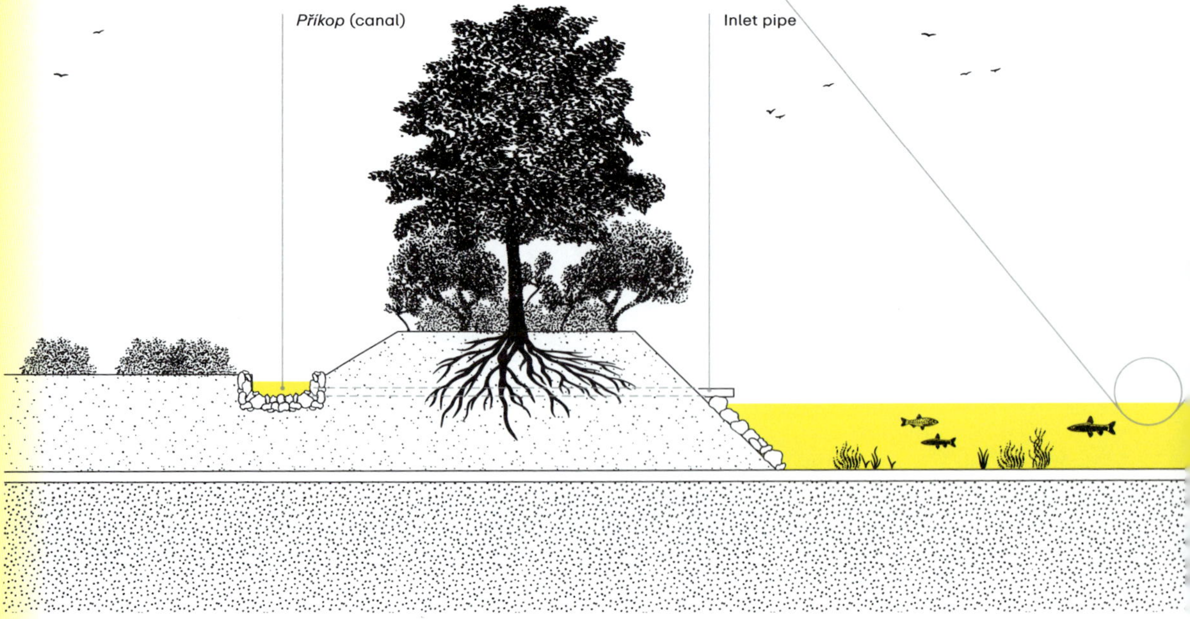

← Open this fold to reveal full illustration.

The fishponds play a paramount role in Třeboň, and their contribution to the region extends beyond economics. Farming fish requires a water depth far below the carrying capacity of the ponds; during events of heavy rainfall, the ponds can support tens of millions of additional cubic meters of water, which in turn keeps the surrounding town and villages safe from flooding.[51] The Svět fishpond, which lines the southwest edge of Třeboň, has been designated a site for critical flood control, acting as the town's main defense against downpours that would otherwise flood the streets.[52,53]

Another benefit of the fishpond system is its ability to control invasive species. When detected in a fishpond, invasive species are removed, or consumed by waterfowl, and the pond is left to frost over during the winter.[54] Unlike large-scale agricultural practices that pollute and deplete landscapes of their groundwater, the Třeboň fishponds are one of the only forms of high-yield, organized food production that conserve and cleanse water.[55]

Today, the carp production in Třeboň currently provides passive wastewater treatment. Flanking the Rožmberk pond system is a biogas plant that contains wastewater, which is primarily treated to remove pathogens, then secondarily treated during the summer in small biological ponds inhabited by young carp. Wastewater is often a catalyst for eutrophication and oxygen deficiency, but this is combated by the hungry mouths of young carp that have a high metabolism in the summer, and eagerly devour the high load of nutrients.[56]

As an ancient aquatic system covering seven square kilometers, reflecting old and new techniques of aquaculture construction combined with energy generation, the Třeboň landscape is also one of Europe's largest exporters of fish. Despite the success and scale of the *rybník* and *příkop* infrastructure, the system is experiencing anthropogenic demands that exceed its limits.[57] An influx of organic fertilizers, coinciding with recent intensive fish harvesting, has led to highly eutrophicated waters and the loss of plants that relied on the water's low turbidity.[58] Extreme floods, like the one in 2002, exceed the ponds' carrying capacity, causing significant damage.[59]

TURBIDITY
The quality of being cloudy, opaque, or thick with suspended matter.

While carp still comprises 80 percent of fish production, demand for other types of fish has led to the introduction of invasive species, like the stone moroko (*Pseudorasbora parva*) and brown bullhead (*Ameiurus nebulosus*), which devastate zooplankton, leading to algal blooms.[60] While there is interest in fixing these issues, experts disagree on the approach. One proposal recommends extending the number of fishponds protected by the biosphere reserve, and limiting these ponds to water retention and species propagation, rather than fish cultivation.[61] Another proposal by the Ministry of Agriculture suggests additional fishponds, or the restoration of existing ones. Centuries ago, these decisions rested in the hands of the nobility that owned the fishponds; however, contemporary pond operations are divided among hundreds of separate fisheries.[62] This decentralized ownership has resulted in a gridlock in decision-making on their future.

Beyond fish cultivation, the aquaculture system of the Třeboň Basin proves that a single system can support food production, flood control, energy

9

production, water cleansing, economic activity, wildlife protection, and more. Relying primarily on the natural seasonal systems within fishponds that nourish carp and reduce the need for fish feed, the *rybník* fishponds and *příkop* canals represent an environmentally intelligent system that uses minimal effort to produce food while supporting the ecosystem. In the face of increased flooding or resource depletion, adapted and hybridized versions of these canals and fishponds could continue to support this unique southern Bohemian system. Having originated hundreds of years ago in the cloisters of monks, this technology indicates the importance of learning from and retrofitting preexistent systems, to adapt them to contemporary needs.

10

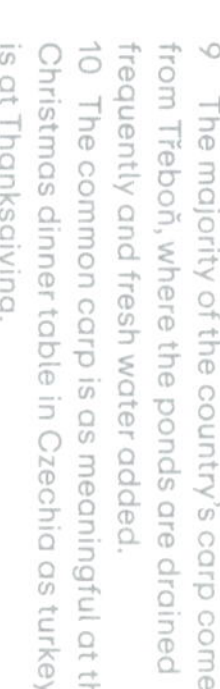

9 The majority of the country's carp come from Třeboň, where the ponds are drained frequently and fresh water added.
10 The common carp is as meaningful at the Christmas dinner table in Czechia as turkey is at Thanksgiving.

ENDNOTES

1. Richard Lhotský, "The Role of Historical Fishpond Systems during Recent Flood Events," *Journal of Water and Land Development* 14, no. 1 (2010): 54.
2. Michael Ezban, "Fishponds of the Třeboň Basin, Czech Republic," in *Aquaculture Landscapes: Fish Farms and the Public Realm* (New York: Routledge, 2019), 53.
3. Miroslav Hátle, "Information Sheet on Ramsar Wetlands" (n.p.: Administration of Třeboň Basin Protected Landscape Area and Biosphere Reserve, 2002), 4.
4. Zdeněk Adámek et al., "Aquaculture the Czech Republic in 2012: Modern European Prosperous Sector Based on Thousand-Year History of Pond Culture," *Aquaculture Europe* 37, no. 2 (2012): 9.
5. Ezban, "Fishponds of the Třeboň Basin," 53.
6. Lhotský, "The Role of Historical Fishpond Systems," 53.
7. Jan Pokorný (*rybník* expert), in discussion with the author, July 2022.
8. Pokorný, discussion.
9. Ezban, "Fishponds of the Třeboň Basin," 53.
10. Pokorný, discussion.
11. Lhotský, "The Role of Historical Fishpond Systems," 53.
12. "Fishpond Cultivation and Nature," Garni Hotel Třeboň, July 7, 2022, https://www.garnihoteltrebon.cz/en/trebon-and-its-surroundings/fishpond-cultivation-and-nature.
13. Miroslav Hátle and Eva Jelínková, "Třeboň Basin: A Wetland-Based Biosphere Reserve" (presentation for UNESCO MAB: Man and the Biosphere Programme, 2017), 2.
14. Encyclopædia Britannica Online, s.v. "Lužnice River," accessed April 17, 2024, https://www.britannica.com/place/Luznice-River.
15. Pokorný, discussion.
16. Jan Pokorný and Jan Květ, "Fishponds of the Czech Republic," in *The Wetland Book II: Distribution, Description, and Conservation*, ed. C. Max Finlayson et al. (Berlin: Springer Nature, 2018), 471.
17. Jan Plesník et al., "The Czech Republic," in *Fishing for a Living—The Ecology and Economics of Fishponds in Central Europe*, ed. IUCN (Gland, Switzerland and Cambridge: IUCN, 1997), 20.
18. Ezban, "Fishponds of the Třeboň Basin," 53.
19. Pokorný, discussion.
20. Pokorný, discussion.
21. Pokorný, discussion.
22. Lhotský, "The Role of Historical Fishpond Systems," 52.
23. "Fishpond Cultivation and Nature."
24. Ezban, "Fishponds of the Třeboň Basin," 53.
25. Plesník et al., "The Czech Republic," 4.
26. Ezban, "Fishponds of the Třeboň Basin," 59.
27. Lhotský, "The Role of Historical Fishpond Systems," 52.
28. Lhotský, "The Role of Historical Fishpond Systems," 52.
29. Pokorný, discussion.
30. Pokorný, discussion.
31. Lhotský, "The Role of Historical Fishpond Systems," 1.
32. Pokorný, discussion.
33. Plesník et al., "The Czech Republic," 6.
34. Plesník et al., "The Czech Republic," 6.
35. Plesník et al., "The Czech Republic," 12–13.
36. Ezban, "Fishponds of the Třeboň Basin," 56.
37. Plesník et al., "The Czech Republic," 18.
38. Pokorný, discussion.
39. Plesník et al., "The Czech Republic," 17.
40. Plesník et al., "The Czech Republic," 18.
41. Pokorný, discussion
42. Pokorný, discussion.
43. Pokorný, discussion.
44. Plesník et al., "The Czech Republic," 18.
45. Pokorný and Květ, "Fishponds of the Czech Republic," 478.
46. Plesník et al., "The Czech Republic," 18.
47. Ezban, "Fishponds of the Třeboň Basin," 53.
48. Plesník et al., "The Czech Republic," 17.
49. Pokorný, discussion.
50. Ezban, "Fishponds of the Třeboň Basin," 53.
51. Pokorný and Květ, "Fishponds of the Czech Republic," 473.
52. Ezban, "Fishponds of the Třeboň Basin," 60.
53. State Institute for the Preservation of Cultural Heritage, Prague, "Fishpond Network in the Trebon Basin," UNESCO World Heritage Convention, July 7, 2022, https://whc.unesco.org/en/tentativelists/1509/.
54. Pokorný, discussion.
55. Pokorný and Květ, "Fishponds of the Czech Republic," 476.
56. Pokorný, discussion.
57. Pokorný and Květ, "Fishponds of the Czech Republic," 483.
58. Plesník et al., "The Czech Republic," 23–25.
59. Lhotský, "The Role of Historical Fishpond Systems," 59.
60. Pokorný, discussion.
61. Pokorný, discussion.
62. Pokorný, discussion.

DRYCODE

SEAWEED THATCH REIMAGINED

PROJECT CREDIT Studio Kathryn Larsen: Kathryn Larsen, Monika Jakaityte, James Birkenshaw, Gabriel Pantoja, Andrejs Mocalov PROJECT DATE 2019 PROJECT CLIENT KEA Copenhagen School of Design and Technology LOCATION Copenhagen, Læsø, and Møn, Denmark TYPOLOGY material technology ELEVATION 3 m TEK eelgrass thatching COMMUNITY OF ORIGIN Læsø and Møn Islanders

Envision a nontoxic, insulating building material that is resistant to fire and rot—one that even has the potential to support carbon-negative construction. While recent trends in sustainable design are producing new visions and applications of nature-based material technology, designer Kathryn Larsen is embracing a modern approach to the centuries-old Danish tradition of eelgrass construction.

Fabled in Norse mythology with coastlines punctuated by shipwrecks, the islands of Læsø and Møn caught Larsen's eye for another reason—their clusters of seaweed-thatched homes dating to the 17th century. The use of this silvery seaweed as a roofing material was born out of a need to transition from timber construction amid the rapid deforestation of Denmark's islands three hundred years ago. While shipwreck-sourced wood provided foundations for new homes, island locals turned to dense piles of eelgrass as an insulated roofing alternative. The traditional wisdom embedded in this design has faded over the last century, after a fungal disease depleted much of Denmark's coastal eelgrass in the 1920s. With modern technology and Larsen's architectural innovation leading the charge, we are witnessing the reinvention of this critically regenerative material.

Before opening her design studio, Larsen laid the groundwork for her material exploration in eelgrass, formally titled Seaweed Thatch Reimagined, while conducting undergraduate research at the Copenhagen School of Design and Technology. During her studies, Denmark's construction sector experienced a costly controversy surrounding the use of magnesium oxide (MgO) board windbreak panels. In the face of skepticism toward material innovation that arose and upon discovering that her campus received a supply of eelgrass from local seaweed farmers, Larsen began to research and design a prefabricated seaweed-thatched panel.

Rooted in the vernacular tradition of Læsø, these modular panels offer a contemporary, scalable solution to the construction industry's material shortcomings. Consisting of wood frames, filled with malleable, hydrated eelgrass that molds to a desired shape once dried, they can be applied to roofs and facades. These seaweed-thatched panels can weather outdoor conditions for up to two hundred years, with insulation potential comparable to mineral wool. Eelgrass, being carbon neutral, also played a crucial role in creating a carbon-negative footprint—with a deficit of 8,500 kg—for the Modern Seaweed House, a similar project by Danish architects that employed the material. The salt impregnated in eelgrass contributes to its fire resistance. The strength of these premade panels lies not just in their remarkable durability and lack of toxicity but also in the broader implications of seaweed cultivation as a means of marine carbon sequestration, along with generating income for coastal communities.

Recently, the studio's work has helped connect researchers and stakeholders outside of Denmark to local TEK-centered businesses, such as Søuld. Søuld is a seagrass-centered acoustic design company, founded by architects Tobias Øhrstrøm and Pi Fabrin, sustainable design engineers Gunnar Agerskov and Kirsten Lynge, and eelgrass thatcher Henning Johansen. A Læsø native, Lynge has inherited the seagrass tradition through multiple generations of her family. Her stepfather, Johansen, is the master thatcher on the island of Læsø, who is responsible for preserving the tradition of seagrass roofs on the island. Alongside the community of Læsø, the Seaweed Bank was created to store bales of seagrass to preserve the seagrass roofs for future generations.

Up to this point, Larsen has conducted her research on a small scale, focusing on local construction projects. She has begun to channel her expertise in eelgrass construction into restoration initiatives protecting coastal ecosystems. With marine eelgrass populations significantly depleted in the last century—only to be further threatened by agricultural runoff in recent years—Larsen has partnered with the Fieldwork Company to replant eelgrass meadows off the shores of the Netherlands. She has also collaborated with marine biologist Shannon Hanson to produce ReefCircular—a project using shell waste to create 3D-printed artificial reefs that restore degraded marine ecosystems and enhance coastal biodiversity.

Alongside Seaweed Thatch Reimagined, these initiatives are truly emblematic of Larsen's primary goal as an innovator: to keep existing structures and materials in circulation as long as possible, and, above all, to place restoration at the forefront of her studio's design ethos. Studio Kathryn Larsen's continued research and fabrication has elevated eelgrass thatching from a nearly forgotten piece of Danish architectural history to an increasingly promising building material with applications in insulation, cladding, and sound insulation in coastal landscapes.

REF. PAGE 444

The use of aquatic plants as an organic material technology enables a single, endemic species to function in a multitude of ways, from reed housing atop floating islands that offer underwater habitat, fertilization, fencing, fuel and biofiltering, to fire and rot resistant roof thatching—all while offering the regenerative potential to support carbon-negative construction.

ANGSILA OYSTER SCAFFOLDING PAVILION

PROJECT CREDIT Chat Architects, Angsila Fishermen Community, International Program in Design and Architecture (INDA), Chulalongkorn University **PROJECT DATE** 2023 **PROJECT CLIENT** INDA, Chulalongkorn University Thailand. Thailand Office of Contemporary Art and Culture **LOCATION** Ang Sila City, Mueang Chonburi District of Chonburi Province in the eastern region of Central Thailand **TYPOLOGY** architecture **ELEVATION** 0–5 m **TEK** traditional bamboo oyster cultivation scaffolding pavilion **COMMUNITY OF ORIGIN** Angsila fishermen's community

Chatpong Chuenrudeemol has made a career from what he affectionately refers to as "Bangkok Bastards," adapting vernacular architecture with ingenuity and flair. Across the bustling capital, his studio Chat Architects has "bastardized" projects: staircases have been adapted to house elegant retail stalls; residential windows have been jerry-rigged to support drying racks for clothes. Sixty kilometers southeast of Bangkok, true to the Chat Architects ethos, the Angsila Oyster Scaffolding Pavilion reimagines a traditional oyster-fishing pavilion as a rural ecotourism destination. Located off the coast of the historic Angsila fishing village in Thailand, the pavilion is a bastard in its own right. Inspired by the bamboo scaffolds traditionally used for oyster cultivation, the simple design adapts the local vernacular into an eye-catching hospitality venue, accented by its dramatic pitched roofs and vivid red agricultural tarps, commonly used by nearby plant nurseries.

Once a thriving small-scale fishing town, the community has struggled in past decades to sustain its way of life. Over the past four years, nearby factories and new suburbs have released unfiltered waste into the rivers and canals, feeding directly into the Angsila Bay. The resulting diminished water quality, decreased aquatic life, and drop in seafood-cultivation profitability has forced the village to abandon traditional fisheries. This problem has particularly affected the village's youth, who migrate in search of employment in factories, offices, or retail businesses near Bangkok. In response, the pavilion seeks to revitalize the village's struggling fishing and seafood industry by seeding an industry resurgence through the design of a new oyster ecotourism bamboo prototype. Completed in 2023, the Angsila Oyster Scaffolding Pavilion has been awarded Best of the Best at the Seoul Design Award 2023, and the International Building Beauty, Special Prize category, at the World Architecture Festival 2023.

Rising above the shallow coastal waters, the structure is surrounded by hundreds of bamboo oyster and mussel cultivation structures. The pavilion itself infuses the same traditional bamboo-scaffolding methods and materials of the neighboring oyster-harvesting stations. The pavilion then hybridizes these traditional techniques by introducing reused and retrofitted everyday inexpensive materials, local labor, and sustainable construction techniques. Like these scaffoldings, the pavilion is built entirely by Angsila fishermen, using native shallow-ocean bamboo-construction techniques that require no power tools. The fishermen manually drive individual bamboo columns into the ocean floor, "pogo stick" style. Rejected car seatbelts, from local auto plants, acquired at a discount due to discoloration, are used to tie all of the bamboo members together. A graphic red (complimenting the greenish bay waters) light-filtering agricultural tarp, commonly used in nearby nurseries, shades visitors from the ocean sun yet allows for the passage of ocean breezes.

Named for the nearby village that once served as a hub for Thailand's formerly thriving oyster trade, the structure is designed to host workshops that combine an intimate and educational look at on-site shellfish cultivation and harvesting—led by local fishers—with a unique al fresco dining experience. When in use, local fishermen bring small groups of visitors from Angsila to the pavilion, where they can handpick oysters pulled from the ocean below, which are then prepared fresh to eat. This oyster-tasting experience opens up visitors to the fishermen's history and heritage through novelty and interactions. When not in use as a tasting pavilion for tourists, the covered platforms become recreational fishing piers for local fishermen, who bring their families to the platform with fishing poles, bait, and hooks to catch a variety of local fish naturally drawn to the clean shellfish-filtered waters surrounding the oyster and mussel bundles in the waters below.

In a landscape devastated by industrial pollution and degraded water quality, the pavilion's simple program fuses environmental awareness with civic and economic function. Aiming to revitalize Angsila's struggling mariculture industry through a new oyster ecotourism prototype, this infrastructure provides the opportunity for local fishermen to campaign for the protection of Angsila Bay's sensitive coastal ecology.

MARICULTURE A specialized branch of aquaculture cultivating marine organisms for food and other products.

REF. PAGE 446

As a foundation of coastal food systems, mariculture architecture uses molluscs as a building block. Using a gridded scaffolding of timber to structurally support an artificial habitat, these filter feeders can cleanse pollution from waters in support of surrounding ecosystems and local economies.

SHINNECOCK KELP FARM

(PROJECT CREDIT) Shinnecock Kelp Farmers, Green Wave, School of Marine & Atmospheric Sciences at Stony Brook University, and the Sisters of St. Joseph (PROJECT DATE) 2023
(LOCATION) Southampton, New York, USA (TYPOLOGY) restoration
(ELEVATION) 0 m (TEK) traditional aquaculture and mariculture
(COMMUNITY OF ORIGIN) Shinnecock Indian Nation

In 2019, Tela Troge, an attorney and member of the Shinnecock Nation, sought a way to create jobs and clean up Shinnecock Bay—a coastal body of water in Southampton, New York, that flows into the Atlantic through several inlets. Troge, who has represented the tribe in a number of federal land rights cases, envisioned a solution that would benefit both her community and the environment. For centuries, the Shinnecock stewarded this body of water—a major source of subsistence, rich with clams, striped bass, flounder, and bluefish. In recent decades, however, this once-thriving ecosystem has succumbed to ecological degradation due to overdevelopment in the Hamptons, the absence of a municipal sewer system, and fertilizer runoff spiking nitrogen levels and contaminating the water. Contamination, coupled with worsening climate conditions, has made the relocation of the tribal nation an impending reality. Leveraging a 13,000-year-old traditional relationship with the sea and seaweed, Troge and five other women from her community turned to kelp farming as the key to ecosystemic remediation, forming the Shinnecock Kelp Farm. This multi-generational collective is the first Indigenous-run farm of its kind on the East Coast.

Sugar kelp (*Saccharina latissima*) is a large, fast-growing brown seaweed found throughout the Northern Hemisphere, growing abundantly in the colder waters of the Atlantic, Arctic, and Pacific Oceans. It forms dense, subaquatic forest ecosystems and is cultivated globally as a food source. Sugar kelp has a powerful regenerative capability, absorbing excess carbon dioxide, nitrogen, and phosphorus from the water, acting as a natural, off-coast filtration system. Unlike land-based crops that also filter pollutants and sequester carbon, kelp farming requires fewer resources and less labor, making it an ideal solution for addressing ecosystem degradation under economic constraints.

In 2019, the Shinnecock community, comprising about 800 residents on their Long Island reservation, was approached by GreenWave, a nonprofit that promotes regenerative ocean farming. Troge and other Shinnecock locals recognized that the sustainable practices promoted by GreenWave were already deeply embedded in their culture. Their traditional ecological knowledge and expertise in regenerative ocean farming—which includes the integrated aquaculture of scallops, oysters, and clams—had been a core aspect of their community for generations, long before similar business models were introduced to Long Island.

That same year, six Shinnecock women established the intergenerational kelp farming collective. The team developed a partnership with the Sisters of St. Joseph, a local Catholic ministry that donated a cottage to the farmers where they could begin hatchery operations close to the shore. Within a few months, the cottage was transformed, equipped with fish tanks and warming lights.

The project is a collaborative effort, with the Sisters of St. Joseph assisting in operations, helping look after some Shinnecock farmers' young children, and even starting a "Kind Words Program," where they sing and recite poetry to the kelp seedlings—a practice that has become routine, based on research that plants respond well to high-frequency tones.

Early phases of the initiative required some trial and error; it took time to identify the most suited seaweed species and overcome outbreaks of an algae that inhibit kelp growth, Eventually sugar kelp was deemed the most appropriate option. In December 2021, after two years of preparation, the Shinnecock Kelp Farm was officially launched, with the women planting 20 spools of sugar kelp in the bay. Within a few months, they harvested 100 pounds of kelp, most of which was dried and sold as organic fertilizer. The following cultivation season, they expanded their efforts, planting 10 times the amount of kelp from the previous year, with 200 spools sown into the bay.

By June 2023—two farming seasons after the team launched their first planting in the bay—the group witnessed a remarkable increase in the presence of scallops, clams, sea horses, and other species that had been scarcely visible for years. This abundance of marine species was observed sheltering in the farmers' kelp lines. Though the water quality is not quite high enough to cultivate kelp for human consumption, the Shinnecock Kelp Farm team has started exploring future uses for kelp in food and cosmetics. For now, selling harvested and dried kelp as fertilizer has been a significant source of income for the group as they continue their efforts to remediate the bay's waters.

In just a few short years, the women of the Shinnecock Kelp Farm have embarked on a successful mission to revive the marine conditions of Shinnecock Bay. Their work to restore the bay's natural ecosystem highlights an approach deeply rooted in generations of traditional ecological knowledge—an effort that underscores the importance of sustainability beyond environmental remediation, extending to encompass cultural and economic resilience. The collective has solidified an economic lifeline for the tribal nation that promotes the preservation of Indigenous knowledge.

REF. PAGE 448

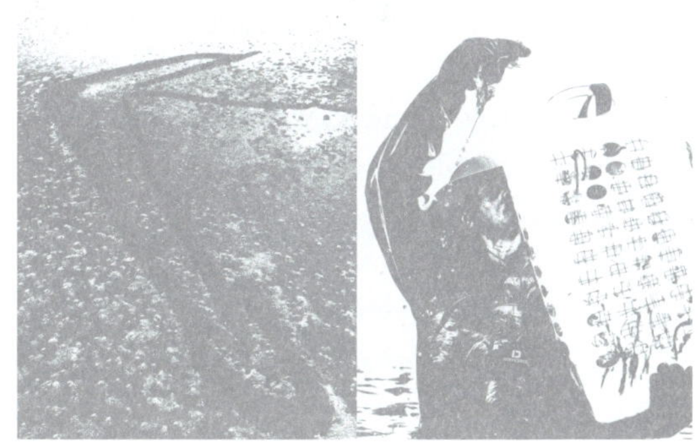

Occupying an intertidal zone, kinship collectives practice aquaculture to grow resources, while indirectly enhancing the biodiversity of underwater ecosystems by providing essential habitat and breeding grounds for aquatic species.

SWINOMISH CLAM GARDEN

PROJECT CREDIT Swinomish Indian Tribal Community PROJECT DATE 2022 PROJECT CLIENT Swinomish Indian Tribal Community LOCATION Kukutali Preserve, Kiket Island, Pacific Northwest, USA TYPOLOGY restoration ELEVATION 0 m TEK mariculture COMMUNITY OF ORIGIN Coast Salish

In August 2022, a group assembled under the summer sun at the Kukutali Preserve in Washington state, creating a chain as they passed rocks from hand to hand. This initiative—led by the Swinomish Indian Tribal Community (SITC)—culminated in the construction of a wall along the shore's intertidal zone, reaching two feet high and 200 feet long. The wall, forming the base of a seaside terrace, will transform into the first modern clam garden in the United States—marking the revival of an Indigenous mariculture technique that dates back 4,000 years.

Inhabiting the coastal regions of the Pacific Northwest, the Coast Salish people, of which the Swinomish are a part, have a rich history of clam garden formation. Clam gardens involve the construction of rock walls in the intertidal zone, where the ocean meets land between low and high tides. As the tide rises, sediment filters through holes in the rock walls, forming an extended soft sediment beach that is an ideal habitat for native clams. Clam gardens are also referred to as sea gardens as they are capable of supporting immense biodiversity. The practice of constructing and tending clam gardens increases shellfish production by expanding clam habitat and boosting species diversity. Historically, these mariculture systems were a crucial food source, providing a reliable and accessible resource for many First Nation communities throughout the year. Beyond sustenance, clam gardens rely on community cooperation and the preservation of traditional knowledge across generations.

The displacement of Indigenous communities over the past few centuries, colonization and shoreline development, has resulted in the erasure of this traditional knowledge and the overall deterioration of existing infrastructures. While the WSÁNEĆ and Hul'q'umi'num First Nations in British Columbia have partnered with Parks Canada to restore clam gardens in the Gulf Islands National Park Reserve, no functioning clam gardens had been identified in the United States until the Swinomish Indian Tribal Community built the new garden in 2022.

The ambition to revive a traditional clam garden in Washington State emerged from the Swinomish Climate Change Initiative's efforts to strengthen community resilience against intensifying weather and tidal events on the Swinomish Indian Reservation. In 2010, the initiative released a Climate Action Adaptation Plan, emphasizing Indigenous knowledge, cultural resilience, and community health in their climate action approach. A team of Tribal staff surveyed areas vulnerable to climate-related flooding, such as recreational spaces, archaeological sites, and burial grounds, discovering that natural shellfish beds were at high risk. They realized and documented that climate extremes, such as ocean acidification and sea level rise, could lead to the loss of native habitats and harvest sites. With adaptation preparedness goals including the preservation of treaty rights, cultural practices, and the reestablishment of natural diversity in harvestable clam populations, engineering a new clam garden became a clear solution for climate adaptation.

With funding from Washington Sea Grant (WSG), the Bureau of Indian Affairs (BIA), and the Environmental Protection Agency (EPA), the Tribe's Fisheries Department, Community Environmental Health Program, and Tribal leaders gathered guidance from Indigenous knowledge keepers and clam garden researchers to determine a site that would maximize the ecological and socio-cultural benefits of a clam garden. The Tribe's staff sought community input to evaluate three potential sites, with the most suitable choice approved by the SITC. With support from a WSG program development grant, researchers and Swinomish tribal members attended two clam garden restoration events in British Columbia, where they gained hands-on experience with these traditional mariculture techniques from the WSÁNEĆ and Hul'q'umi'num First Nations.

The Tribe's tidelands surrounding Kukutali Preserve was the location of the proposed site for the new clam garden. Acquired in 2010 after decades of private, nontribal ownership, today the uplands are owned by the United States in trust for the Tribe. When clam garden construction finally began in August 2022, a barge delivered 35 tons of rocks—all sourced from the Swinomish's ancestral territory— to the shores of the Kukutali Preserve. Over the course of two days, nearly 60 people from SITC, First Nations in B.C., and various organizations gathered to pass these rocks, one by one, to the shore's intertidal zone, where they built a knee-high, curving wall spanning 200 feet long and reaching two feet tall. Still in the early phases of development, the collective behind the clam garden expects to see the site transform over time into a biodiverse terrace brimming with clam growth, as sediment accumulates behind the wall.

The years-long effort that brought forth a new clam garden at Kukutali Preserve is a powerful example of how wisdom can address imminent environmental threats. In reviving this nature-based system, the Swinomish Indian Tribal Community is able to preserve cultural heritage while creating a sustainable and productive habitat that can withstand the impacts of climate change—a hopeful path forward for communities looking to mitigate climate challenges through culturally responsive, and site specific methods that have been deployed for thousands of years.

REF. PAGE 450

Intertidal rock walls, constructed to practice aquaculture, indirectly introduce protective barriers for storm events while serving as artificial reefs that support a diversity of waterborne species.

RIDGE-TO-REEF RESTORATION

PROJECT CREDIT Lomani Gau Network **PROJECT DATE** 2005– **LOCATION** Gau, Fiji **TYPOLOGY** restoration **ELEVATION** 0–715 m **TEK** mangrove cultivation and weir construction **COMMUNITY OF ORIGIN** iTaukei

"Prepare while there is still daylight": This is what is meant by the Fijan proverb *vakarau ni se siga toka*. On the island of Gau, it is customary to prepare for the inevitable well before it occurs. Today, this sentiment holds particular significance for Fijians and other Pacific Island communities that are situated on the front lines of the climate crisis. Since 2005, this proactive ethos has been put into practice through Lomani Gau—a dynamic community-led network initiated by local leaders to strategize an ecosystem management plan across Gau.

In Fijian, the word *lomani* means "care for." Lomani Gau's overarching goal is to create a thoughtful, resilient pathway for climate change adaptation throughout the island—one that is attuned to the specific needs of the island's three thousand residents and is as dynamic as the evolving conditions of the climate. The initiative aims to make Gau a model for climate change adaptation across Pacific Island countries where the people are empowered to do what they can to adapt to climate change impacts. In previous decades, Pacific Island governments focused on national-level actions, while international entities working in sustainable development developed generic courses of action. Lacking alignment with local culture, social relationships, and holistic ecosystems, these generic management plans had limited success. Lomani Gau's community-driven initiative seeks to rectify this by providing a framework for effective, place-based climate adaptation strategies rooted in the traditional knowledge of island communities.

The Lomani Gau initiative was first implemented in one of the island's three *tikina* (administrative units) as a means of creating a limited study that could later be assessed by the community. Throughout the three-year period of this trial, residents were so pleased by visible positive outcomes that the activities were extended to two further districts. These activities included the effective management of marine resources and waste, safeguarding watershed areas, and rehabilitating coastal habitats.

In the 20-year period since Lomani Gau was established, the network has continued to focus on an ever-evolving and iterative approach to restoration and adaptation. Amid the many accomplishments of Lomani Gau are the network's significant strides in the protection of the islands' water resources. The network has developed a comprehensive approach to watershed management that leverages the ancestral knowledge that ecosystems—from an island's highest ridge to its surrounding reefs—are all part of an interconnected continuum. On small islands such as Gau, the degradation of just one ecosystem can have a cascading effect on the protective services of another. This Ridge-to-Reef framework is one lens through which Lomani Gau's whole-system water management initiatives can be understood.

Gau's mountainous inland topography soars upward, culminating in two peaks that are blanketed by a lush montane cloud forest. Predating Lomani Gau, the Gau Island Council set forth an initiative in the 1990s that aimed to protect the biodiversity of this forest as development and impacts from the villagers' coastline activities encroached. Since 2005, Lomani Gau has undertaken a series of projects that advance this effort, declaring forest reserves in the catchment basins to ensure a continued supply of water.

Moving down the slopes of the island's interior, newly planted mangrove forests line rivers and shorelines. Lomani Gau spearheaded a number of successful mangrove-restoration projects as a means of reducing coastal erosion—particularly around the brackish ecosystems where freshwater streams feed into the sea. This landscape is where Lomani Gau has made some of its most impressive contributions to climate adaptation on the island.

With funding from the Global Environmental Facility and the UNDP, Gau residents planted hundreds of thousands of trees during a coastal vegetation-rehabilitation project from 2011 to 2013. The growth of a dense coastal canopy has created a protective perimeter around the island, not only managing shoreline erosion but also alleviating the impact of storm surges. In the barrier reef that encircles much of the island, Lomani Gau has implemented an additional protective measure—a newly constructed weir. Constructed with a hybrid of locally sourced materials and external engineering expertise, the weir serves as a critical defense against rising sea levels, while protecting shorelines from erosion. This function is designed to safeguard the reef resources that generations of Gau residents have traditionally depended on, preventing disruption and depletion by unauthorized people.

Through a combination of traditional wisdom and modern knowledge, Lomani Gau demonstrates the power of local involvement in safeguarding both natural resources and cultural heritage. As the network looks ahead, its dedication to nurturing Gau's ecosystem and community remains unwavering, reflecting the true essence of *lomani*—caring deeply for the well-being of the land and its people.

REF. PAGE 452

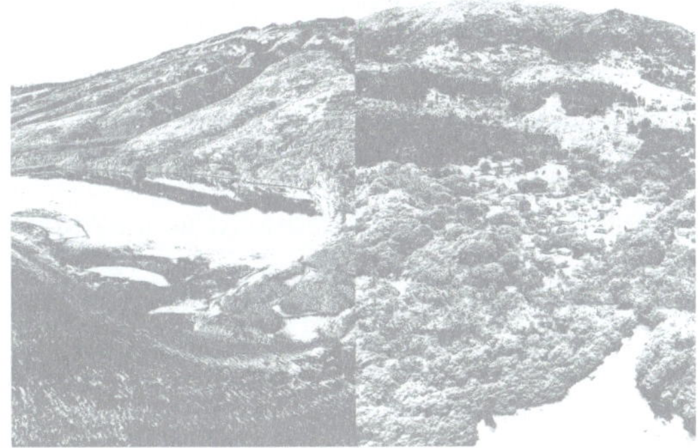

Underpinned by generations of collective knowledge, a proactive ethos towards community-led adaptive ecosystem management that functions across the scale of watersheds is typical of South Pacific island communities.

DUWAMISH FLOATING WETLANDS

(PROJECT CREDIT) Green Futures Lab (PROJECT DATE) 2018– (PROJECT CLIENT) City of Seattle (LOCATION) Seattle, USA (TYPOLOGY) material technology (ELEVATION) 53 m (TEK) salmon migration stewardship (COMMUNITY OF ORIGIN) Coast Salish

The Green River snakes westward through Washington State for 105 kilometers. Along its final leg before merging with the saltwater expanse of Puget Sound, the watershed's tributaries converge into the Duwamish River. Like many Pacific Northwestern watercourses, the Duwamish teems with salmon—a meandering route in which hatchlings, born in the river's freshwater reaches, set out for adulthood at sea, only to later return upstream and reproduce, thus fulfilling their life cycle. The survival of Chinook salmon depends on the migratory networks established by Washington's watercourses. Salmon, in turn, contribute to the health of these ecosystems, providing crucial energy and nutrients throughout the environment over the course of their migrations.

For the Coast Salish people, salmon represent more than just a food source; they are a keystone species intertwined with cultural identity. Across generations, salmon have been revered as gift-bearing relatives, with the annual salmon return celebrated as a symbol of renewal and the continuation of life. Traditional weirs, stone traps, and reef nets have been used by the Coast Salish to catch and preserve salmon for winter and trade. With tribal populations returning to pre-19th-century levels, the need for salmon today is more important than ever, according to the Columbia River Inter-Tribal Fish Commission.

Over the last century, Seattle's rapid transformation has fragmented its landscape, severely impacting wetland ecosystems. Heavily dredged and channelized, 97 percent of the Duwamish River's wetlands have been replaced by five thousand acres of urbanized shoreline. Despite historic sovereignty legislation, development has compromised the Coast Salish's ability to fish in their ancestral land—in particular the Chinook salmon.

In 2018, a team of researchers from the University of Washington's Green Futures Lab set out to address the ecosystem threat posed by the loss of regional estuaries using a hybrid, nature-based solution: constructed floating wetlands.

Located in the brackish transitional zone between Puget Sound and the Green River, the Duwamish Floating Wetlands were the initial version of several iterations aimed at bolstering juvenile salmon populations. The Green Futures Lab team intended to evaluate whether floating wetlands could offer refuge and food for out-migrating juvenile salmon while deterring predators, and, secondarily, whether the phytoremediation services of the wetlands could enhance water quality to support the needs of salmon and other native aquatic species. The team designed wetland platforms, or "biobarges," of rigid rectangular wood frames supported by tubular buoyancy cells, with overall dimensions of approximately three meters wide and six meters long. Each biobarge was equipped with four modular wetland plant baskets called "biofilters." These baskets, made of steel mesh, contained local wetland plants growing on layers of wood chips, MycoBoard, wood straw, and green brush—a design enabling the root systems of aquatic plants to extend downward into the river below, attracting salmon and the invertebrates that they feed on. Upon completion, floating wetlands were deployed, moored, and monitored in four estuarine sites in the Duwamish Waterway over the course of two years.

In the following years, freshwater wetlands were installed in Lake Union, while marine units designed with BioMatrix were attached to docks at Shilshole Bay Marina. The marine units contain a custom substrate mix, including biochar, and are planted with halophytic species. Two units are submerged and planted with eelgrass, providing fish refuge. Eelgrass, a culturally significant species for many First Nation communities in the Pacific Northwest, is traditionally harvested for food.

The team has actively incorporated community-science programs, involving residents from nearby neighborhoods and community groups in environmental monitoring activities. Community scientists worked alongside the monitoring team, participating in field data collection and other related opportunities—engagement that not only enhances data collection but also fosters a sense of ownership and connection to the Duwamish River among local residents. For its freshwater community initiative, in addition to sponsoring educational events with local Indigenous children, the Green Futures Lab hosted the Sweetgrass Community Eco Arts Event in 2021. The event, which showcased constructed floating wetlands, brought together local Indigenous and non-Indigenous creatives to design artwork and write poetry for informational signage and banners that were then positioned alongside the floating wetlands.

The Green Futures Lab's research demonstrates the critical role of floating wetlands in restoring the degraded ecosystems of Washington's urban estuaries and in supporting salmon populations. By mimicking natural marsh habitats, these floating wetlands potentially provide refuge and food for juvenile salmon during migration while enhancing water quality through phytoremediation. Through community-engagement programs, the project not only advances scientific knowledge but also revitalizes connections between communities and their local environment, highlighting the importance of collaborative efforts in ecological restoration.

MYCOBOARD
A building material that uses mycelium to bind loose agricultural plant particles into boards or molded shapes.

PHYTOREMEDIATION
The treatment of pollutants in soil or water with green plants.

BIOCHAR
A carbonized biomass from sustainable sources that is sequestered in soils to enhance agricultural and environmental value.

BAREFOOT SOCIAL ARCHITECTURE

PROJECT CREDIT Yasmeen Lari, Heritage Foundation of Pakistan
PROJECT DATE 2022 **PROJECT CLIENT** N/A **LOCATION** Pakistan
TYPOLOGY architecture **ELEVATION** 1,000–1,300 m, 2,000–3,000 m
TEK traditional *chaura* construction and *dhijji* technique
COMMUNITY OF ORIGIN Pakistan's southern regions

Crisis has inspired a design philosophy emphasizing Barefoot Social Architecture, which follows the principles of cocreation with community, the use of carbon-neutral materials, and design inspired by traditional and vernacular architecture for Pakistan's first female architect, Yasmeen Lari. Through the development of agile construction techniques using bamboo, mud, and lime, which adhere to sustainable low-cost, zero-carbon, and zero-waste principles, Lari's work has had a significant impact both in her home country and internationally. She is renowned for her innovative and socially conscious approach to architecture through her Karachi-based nonprofit organization Heritage Foundation of Pakistan, which works to conserve the nation's historic art and architecture while providing large-scale humanitarian aid to local communities. Cofounded with her husband, Suhail Zaheer Lari, in 1980, Heritage Foundation of Pakistan is pioneering the design of self-build sustainable shelters and housing for displaced populations.

Since 2005, while designing relief architecture in response to a sequence of earthquakes, floods, and conflicts, Lari devised various programs based on women-centered zero-carbon-footprint structures and sustainable building techniques. This has resulted in 40,000 green shelters, making Pakistan the world's largest zero-carbon shelter program. The largest provider of these shelters, Lari has also designed the self-build, zero-carbon Chulah Cookstove, which is a safer alternative to dangerous open flames and emits lower emissions than a traditional stove; over 80,000 of these stoves are in use today.

Following severe flooding in the Khyber Pakhtunkhwa and Sindh Provinces in 2010, the foundation developed a design for modular community centers raised on stilts, which safely survived more floods a couple of years later. When earthquakes hit the Balochistan Province in 2013 and Shangla in 2015, Lari designed shelters using a cross-braced bamboo framework, a structure borrowed from the vernacular *dhijji* technique. These shelters could be easily rebuilt using the same organic materials—unlike their concrete and steel counterparts.

In the aftermath of the devastating floods in Pakistan in 2022, hundreds of Lari's OctaGreen One Room Homes were constructed. These prefabricated bamboo shelters can be erected by a team of six or seven people in just a matter of hours. This self-build technique gives people in disaster-stricken areas a sense of agency by teaching them how to build their own homes. The octagonal shape of these emergency shelters is made of bamboo panels lined with date palm matting and topped with a conical roof. The design of the conical roof recalls the south's traditional *chaura* construction, while the bamboo framework echoes the north's cross-braced *dhijji* structure. The more permanent structures are coated in mud for insulation. Each shelter is disaster-resistant and can be constructed from locally sourced materials at a cost of 25,000 Pakistani rupees ($108) each.

The octagonal form is inherently strong, and, unlike concrete, the light bamboo frames pose no danger if they were to collapse. The mud exterior both provides ballast to prevent the shelter from overturning and acts as insulation. Bamboo, though lightweight, is a long-lasting material, and the structure, though intended as transitional, can be used quasi-permanently if needed. Each structure has enough room for five people to sleep on the floor or two *charpoys* (string beds) with some space to walk around. These structures can be expanded by clustering them together and leaving internal openings. The designers have devised tweaks to this basic technique for structures that can be used as bathrooms, kitchens, schools, and a host of other functions. A simpler bamboo shelter—constructed using an umbrella-like roof without walls, which can be covered with matting—is also being rolled out as an even faster, albeit temporary, solution. In the long run, the bamboo shelters can be turned into permanent structures. Once the floodwaters recede, the shelters can be moved from high ground back into villages, where they are built into foundations made of lime bricks.

Beyond providing shelters, the Heritage Foundation of Pakistan has also been teaching people how to make not only emergency toilets, aquifer trenches, and wells to absorb rainwater but also solar water stands and fish farms to ensure safer drinking water, improve food security, and generate income. Nearly 10 villages surrounding one of the main prefabrication sites are now being trained in making essential products such as the matting used to cover the shelters and mosquito nets to use and sell to each other.

Barefoot Social Architecture has become a sustainable grassroots model for the development of Pakistan's built environment and a development program for impoverished communities. In Sindh Province, training programs train rural villagers to make building components and products that they can sell to each other. Each village specializes in making a different item—from bamboo panels, glazed tiles, mud bricks, and ceramic goods to fuel briquettes and soap—minting a new class of "barefoot entrepreneurs." In the process, 80 percent of the communities have since been raised above the poverty line.

REF. PAGE 456

Earthen construction systems designed for inundation during the cycling of the monsoon seasons can either productively capture or prohibitively protect, for the benefit of vulnerable communities.

EDEN IN IRAQ WASTEWATER GARDEN PROJECT

(PROJECT CREDIT) Meridel Rubenstein, Davide Tocchetto, Jassim al-Asadi, Mark Nelson, Hydar Ali, and Joppe Cramwinckel
(PROJECT DATE) 2011– (PROJECT CLIENT) Al-Chibayish District
(LOCATION) Al-Chibayish, southern Iraq (TYPOLOGY) parkland
(ELEVATION) 9 m (TEK) floating wetlands and qasab reed construction
(COMMUNITY OF ORIGIN) Maʿdan

Situated beside the Euphrates River, a mosaic of date palms, reeds, and geraniums sprawls across an expanse of 34,000 square meters in the southern Iraqi town of Al-Chibayish. Featuring the classic reed-built structures of the Maʿdan people, the design of this public park replicates the intricate geometry found in ancient Mesopotamian textile art through its streams, pathways, and gardens. Beneath the surface, however, this garden serves a much deeper purpose than aesthetic charm.

The Eden in Iraq Wastewater Garden project—a joint initiative between academics, designers, engineers, and hydrologists—is an innovative solution to the contamination of drinking water in the wetlands of southern Iraq. In recent years, the Mesopotamian Marshes have borne the visible effects of drought, and the absence of sewage treatment has escalated into a growing public health crisis. In collaboration with the Iraqi Ministry of Water Resources, the interdisciplinary team behind Eden in Iraq has devised a strategy employing phytoremediation to treat water for approximately 10 thousand people. As a passive water-purification technology, this wastewater garden uses plant matter to cleanse pollutants from the surrounding soil and water, restoring once contaminated water to a safe and usable state.

Bordered by a perimeter of adobe bricks and ceramic tiles spanning 890 meters, the project site extends 375 meters, with a width of 70 meters. The first area of the constructed wetland, which is designed to reduce the odor emanating from untreated water, involves a seven-thousand-square-meter bed of reeds that reach a height of 1.8 meters. A series of switch stations then pump sewage into large septic tanks, where anaerobic bacteria converts sewage into mineral substances. After passing through the septic tanks, the sewage proceeds to vertical-flow wetlands and then moves on to horizontal-flow constructed wetlands. In the final phase, the treated wastewater is used for subsoil irrigation, which supports an array of both ecologically functional and ornamental grasses, shrubs, and fruit trees. Considering the daily sewage intake at each switch plant, the project site requires a total area ranging from 10,000 to 20,000 square meters for septic tanks, vertical and horizontal treatment wetlands, and the final subsurface irrigation garden.

Beyond its primary function as a passive wastewater-cleansing system, Eden in Iraq offers innumerable ecological services for the town of Al-Chibayish. The Mesopotamian Marshes, formerly the largest wetland in western Eurasia, have witnessed increasing environmental degradation in the past few decades.

This initiative aims to reconstruct a habitat for native flora and fauna while restoring a larger hydrological ecosystem. Nature Iraq, a local collaborator, is actively involved in animal conservation efforts, particularly focusing on the Basra reed warbler (*Acrocephalus griseldis*)—a migratory bird species that has traditionally used the marshes in its flyways. Incorporating one hundred thousand native plants will offer essential carbon-sequestration services, building to reinstate the natural wetland's role as the most effective carbon sink worldwide.

Beyond fulfilling these crucial environmental functions, the Eden in Iraq team envisions the park as a meaningful cultural space in Al-Chibayish. The park offers an array of shaded pavilions—built in the vernacular tradition of *qasab* reed architecture—to host gatherings, events, and markets. Three herb gardens line the site, growing a variety of medicinal and aromatic plants for local use. The team will involve local artisans in the design process, commissioning the construction of reed-built structures and ornamental details for pathways, bridges, and walls. Project director Meridel Rubenstein has partnered with Baghdadi artist and archaeological conservator Nawar Ihsan to design ceramic relief tiles for the main entrances of the park. The duo received a grant awarded by Anonymous Was a Woman and the New York Foundation for the Arts in August 2023.

Eden in Iraq stands as a pivotal response to the intersecting challenges of a public health crisis and environmental degradation, offering a nature-based and community-centered approach that addresses both the well-being of the local population and the restoration of a crucial ecosystem. The application of passive wastewater treatment systems in the Mesopotamian Marshes and beyond underscores the promise of sustainable, low-impact methods that can adapt to the evolving environmental challenges we face. A green infrastructure seamlessly intertwined with local Indigenous tradition, Eden in Iraq emerges as a solution ensuring a resilient future for the community of Al-Chibayish and the intricate wetland ecosystem that envelops it.

REF. PAGE 458

For aquatic communities, water quality is a critical and complex issue. Where communities once used endemic materials and ecosystem dynamics to construct amphibious settlements, those same materials and ecosystems are now needed to cleanse contaminated drinking water from high levels of salination and wastewater intrusion.

SANYA MANGROVE PARK AND NANCHANG FISH TAIL PARK

(PROJECT CREDIT) Turenscape (PROJECT DATE) 2016, 2017 (PROJECT CLIENT) Sanya Municipality, Nanchang Municipality (LOCATION) Sanya, Hainan Province, China; Nanchang, Jiangxi Province, China (TYPOLOGY) parkland (ELEVATION) 0–20 m, 121 m (TEK) cut-and-fill polder dikes (COMMUNITY OF ORIGIN) Han, Hani, and Huzhou communities

Along the coastal expanse of Sanya, Hainan Province—just off the southeastern mainland of China—a freshwater river meets the salty embrace of the surrounding ocean, giving way to an estuary that snakes through the urban fabric of the city. Here, freshwater currents and sea water flow into a series of meandering pools, enclosed by a maze of mangrove-lined embankments. These pools sprawl a distance of 10 hectares along the Sanya River, forming an artificial wetland system that absorbs, retains, and cleanses water. This site—Sanya Mangrove Park—is one of the many examples of the "sponge city" development pioneered by landscape architect Kongjian Yu and his firm Turenscape.

A leading expert in climate-resilient ecological infrastructure, Yu has spent the past two decades bringing his vision of "porous," nature-based cities to life—that is, systems capable of mitigating the mounting environmental challenges related to water in our increasingly wet, urbanized world. Water-related stressors are especially pertinent in Yu's home country: In a 2017 essay, he noted that over 75 percent of China's surface water is polluted; half of the country's cities are vulnerable to flooding; and over half of the county's wetland habitats have been lost in the last 50 years. This spectrum of problems, Yu states, is rooted in a singular cause—a century-old reliance on impervious flood management infrastructure that has done more to submerge cities than protect them.

Yu spent his childhood intimately observing the traditional ecological knowledge embedded in local agricultural practices. Generations of ancestral wisdom have sculpted the landscape of China's rural farmland, giving rise to a network of countless human-made ponds and earthen embankments. These structures serve as conduits, directing water into the natural flow of rivers, which fluctuate in size with the passing seasons. For Yu, the ancient techniques that maintained these landscapes between the wet and dry months serve as the very foundation for his modern sponge city development. He draws inspiration from—and, in many instances, directly integrates—a number of traditional agrarian principles to shape more resilient cities.

At Sanya Mangrove Park, drawing from ancient wisdom as a precedent takes form in several cost-effective and sustainable solutions. Three decades of industrial development have encased many of the tropical city's waterways in concrete, polluting and fragmenting the site located between two biological communities—waterways and riparian habitats. To remediate this contamination, Yu designed a series of new ecotones using a cut-and-fill strategy. A traditional landscape technique used by farmers in China and beyond, the cut-and-fill technique uses the earth excavated to form a depression such as a canal to fill or construct the embankments that will surround it. Transforming an uninhabitable or toxic landscape into a habitable or productive one, the cut-and-fill practice allows farmers to reshape terrain using materials readily available on-site, minimizing the need for added transportation and labor.

The embankments constructed from earth excavated along the Sanya River were shaped into series of interlocking fingers, which guide saline ocean currents from the bay into the park. Dotted with dense clusters of mangrove plantings, these undulating embankments serve as a habitat to rehabilitate this coastal tree species while also functioning as nature-based flood management. In the wake of mangroves' regional decline, embankments were deliberately designed to protect fledgling plants from tropical monsoon storms and urban runoff. In turn, the mature mangrove communities serve as a vital buffer between the natural and built landscape of the city as a resilient, long-term strategy that can effectively mitigate climate-related stressors while bolstering a sensitive local ecosystem. The park offers immense habitat diversity beyond the mangrove community, with over 25 palm and fruit tree species like *Licuala grandis* (ruffled fan palm) and *Cerbera manghas* (sea mango) planted on-site. Between interlocking embankments, water fluctuates from zero to one and a half meters deep—a dynamic aquatic environment where aquatic species thrive.

Further up the river, the Turenscape team has transformed a degraded former industrial landscape into Sanya Dong'an Wetland Park—another sponge city design that implements traditional agrarian wisdom. The park features a more comprehensive array of water-retentive typologies, replacing the site's existing concrete flood walls with a mosaic of greenways, rice paddies, and ponds. Cut and fill is used again over 66 hectares as a means of creating three traditional earthwork systems: ponds and dikes, terraces, and islands.

One edge of the park is speckled with ponds of varying sizes, depths, and plant communities—a web of small-scale retention basins, each enclosed by earthen dikes. These embankments are topped with paved pathways, allowing visitors to easily traverse the wetland that sprawls across the city's downtown. Another side of the park uses a traditional terracing technique to slow stormwater runoff where slopes are particularly steep—a climate-related challenge that would have previously been addressed through impervious gray infrastructure. Earthen islands planted with marsh-friendly banyan trees are also strategically placed across the park's largest body of water. Banyan tree root systems grow deep into the soil of this artificial archipelago, where they filter excess nutrients from the wetland's water. Altogether, the process of transforming the site into Sanya Dong'an Wetland Park reflects Yu's commitment to minimizing intervention while maximizing return. Employing proven climate-resilient, low-impact, and traditional methods, the development of the wetland incurred costs roughly one-third of those associated with a typical regional park.

Yu emphasizes that the success of the sponge city model, endorsed by the Chinese government for the past two decades, hinges on its ability to adapt as a site-specific response to the particular region in which it is implemented. In his own practice, he has sought to actualize hyperlocal flood management solutions that are reflective of geographic and urban conditions in regions beyond Hainan.

Over one thousand kilometers northwest of the island, the team embarked on a project in the mountainous province of Jiangxi to create Nanchang Fish Tail Park. In recent decades, the encroachment on wetlands and lakes by unchecked urban development has led to chronic flooding, affecting the city's 6.2 million residents. This expansion also significantly diminished these ecosystems natural water-regulating abilities, led to the deterioration of surface water quality due to increasing amounts of urban and industrial runoff, and severely impacted the habitats of resident and migratory birds, as well as other wildlife.

To address these pervasive environmental issues, Turenscape implemented a nature-based solution in a parkland situated as the cornerstone of a New District earmarked for dense urban development. At the time of conceptualization, almost 30 percent of the site—a former 51-hectare fish farm—was actively used as a dumping ground by nearby power plants. Coal ash, which is a fine-grained, powdery material that is produced from burning pulverized coal, had polluted the site's waterways, alongside fish feed, and urban runoff. In response, Turenscape designed a resilient, ecologically inspired urban sanctuary that embraces obstacles as opportunities.

The project innovatively repurposed coal ash, originally dumped on the site, by blending it with dirt from fishpond dikes, to construct islets. This sustainable construction technique showcases the potential of transforming waste into a valuable resource, setting a precedent for creating industrially symbiotic landscapes. Created using a traditional cut-and-fill technique, these islets rise above a newly formed lake, designed to accommodate water-level fluctuations and capable of capturing 1 million cubic meters of stormwater. This cut-and-fill strategy differs from the typical agrarian polder-dike landscape seen in China. Turenscape cites traditional floating island systems such as the *chinampas* of the Nahua Xochimilca in Mexico City as the inspiration for the park design.

The firm selected tree species that would not just withstand fluctuating water levels, but thrive in potentially waterlogged conditions. Bald cypress (*Taxodium distichum*), pond cypress (*Taxodium distichum var. imbricatum*), and dawn redwood (*Metasequoia glyptostroboides*) are all coniferous species that were carefully chosen by the team to create a forested park landscape that would flourish year round. Due to the fact that the rise and fall of water levels often reveals muddy shorelines, the firm also selected perennial and annual wetland plants to be planted along shores and island edges—both as an aesthetic tool but also as a means of reducing shoreline erosion as seasons change and water levels fluctuate. Meanwhile, lotus plants—essential biofilters and hosts of aquatic biodiversity—were installed across the entire vicinity of the park to provide lake cover.

This forest of cypresses and redwoods, situated above the water, becomes submerged during the annual monsoon floods. Turenscape's design, fluctuating across seasons, creates a unique opportunity for city residents and tourists alike to explore nature in an immersive marshland setting. Along the periphery of the park, beyond the central forest, the waterfront is designed to accommodate 20-year floods. Turenscape also designed terraced constructed wetlands in this area to filter urban runoff.

Notably, this buffer zone also meets the recreational needs of the local population, with natural playgrounds, beaches, and lawns extending across the park perimeter. A web of pedestrian paths and elevated platforms surround the lake, enabling visitors to access the forested islands and explore the lush wetland landscape. This extensive network of boardwalks is designed to be inundated during 20-year flood events, as well as annual monsoon floods.

The central part of the park is rendered inaccessible by these major flooding events for several days at a time—a factor that the firm took into consideration when fabricating man-made structures like benches and walkways. Circular paths for pedestrians and bikes are protected, as they are situated above the 20-year flood event line; however, the boardwalk and platforms in the central part of the lake are constructed of prefabricated concrete, which is detached from the ground below or floating above water. These features were designed to be resilient in the face of unpredictable flooding. They can be washed and reused after being submerged during flood events. Many of the structures across the park, like bridges, benches, and pavilions, are also made of a cost-efficient perforated aluminum—modern elements which juxtapose the idyllic, natural setting of the site.

Built in the span of three years with a modest budget of $4 per square foot, Nanchang Fish Tail Park has successfully transformed from a polluted, industrial dumping ground into a popular urban oasis speckled with manmade islets and flood-resistant flora, attracting birds and wildlife. Today, the park has become a prominent destination in Nanchang's New District. Widely covered by regional and national media, Nanchang Fish Tail Park now serves as a landmark on the city's subway system, spurring even further development in the area.

The landscape designs led by Yu and Turenscape exemplify a model for hybridizing ancient wisdom and modern ecological principles. Through projects like Sanya Mangrove Park and Nanchang Fish Tail Park, the team has demonstrated the successful implementation of sponge city development, addressing pressing environmental challenges in China's urbanized areas. Integrating traditional agrarian practices, such as terracing and cut and fill, and fostering biodiversity through strategic landscaping, these initiatives both mitigate climate-related stressors and contribute to the restoration of vital ecosystems. Yu's vision of porous, nature-based cities serves as a beacon for sustainable urban development, emphasizing adaptability and site-specific responses to create resilient environments.

REF. PAGE 460

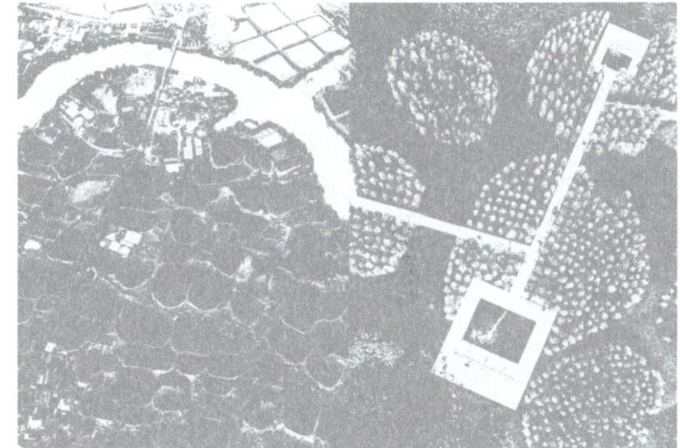

REF. PAGE 462

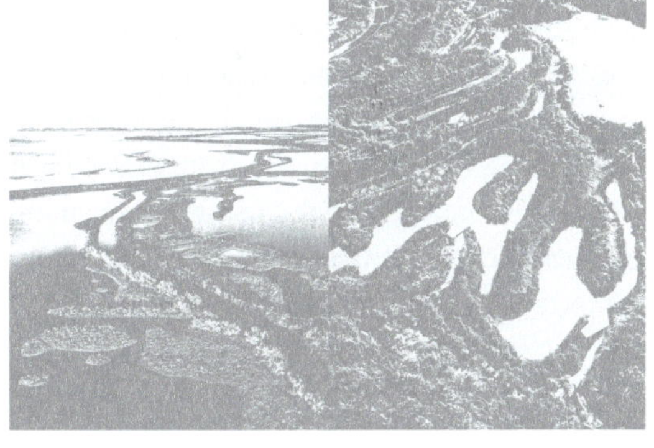

Cut-and-fill polder dike technologies allow farmers to reshape intertidal terrain to create closed-loop systems for fish rearing and crop cultivation, bringing cascading benefits such as enhanced biodiversity, flood prevention, stormwater management, coastal protection, and the regulation of salt intrusion, heat, land subsidence, and water and air pollution.

THE NEW WIERDE

PROJECT CREDIT Sanne Dijkstra PROJECT DATE 2022–
PROJECT CLIENT N/A LOCATION Leermens, Groningen, Netherlands
TYPOLOGY restoration ELEVATION 0–1 m TEK mounded earthworks
COMMUNITY OF ORIGIN Groningers

As early as 500 BCE, agrarian communities in the northern Netherlands adapted to frequent fluctuations in seawater without the use of the dike infrastructure that the region is known for today. Living along low-lying coasts, ancient Dutch communities like the Frisians and Groningers developed mounding systems that protected settlements from storm surge; the elevated land served as a passive way of rerouting flooding, while making use of land inundated by saltwater to cultivate saline crops, fish, and shrimp. Referred to by different names across the North European Plain, these mounds are known as *wierden* in the northeastern province of Groningen.

In the last two centuries, the advent of gray hydrologic infrastructure such as concrete-encased dikes and canals has not only marked a significant departure from the region's most traditional approach to stormwater management but can also be seen as a driving force behind pressing environmental issues facing the Dutch coastline today: land subsidence, freshwater shortage, sea level rise, and increasing soil salinity. Drawing from the ancient adaptations developed in this region—local designer Sanne Dijkstra is envisioning a solution that harks back to Groningen's past.

The New Wierde, proposed by Dijkstra in 2022 as a master's thesis while at the Academy of Architecture, Groningen, is a vision of a renewed relationship between humans and nature, spanning landscape remediation to the adaptive reuse of existing structures, thereby building resilience among rural Dutch communities along the Netherlands' coast. The project seeks to tackle the issues associated with modern land reclamation, reinstating a soft and dynamic transition between land and seawater that coastal communities maintained throughout the region's history.

The gradual reintegration of Groningen's sandbars, dunes, and islands offers a solution to a secondary problem: freshwater shortages and an economy centered around monoculture crop production. In Groningen, the historic cultivation of saline crops has been replaced by monoculture farming and extensive natural gas extraction. What were once small-scale communities in this area have evolved into large-scale production zones centered around the major cities and the global food market. By working with seawater rather than against it, Dijkstra suggests that transforming Leermens, a historic mound village, into a salt marsh could facilitate a return to the circular and site-specific techniques historically practiced there. Tractor paths, made from reused gas mining materials, delineate the boundaries between basins where various crops are cultivated, including seaweed, samphire, sea lavender, fish, crustaceans, and shellfish. Over time, this system can develop into a circular food system, where fish waste is used to nourish the plants. The water is cycled and pumped from one basin to another, transporting nutrients, similar to the *kayalnilam* of Kuttanad in India. Additionally, the design envisions freshwater and brackish zones where livestock farming and agriculture can be combined, allowing for hemp cultivation. Ultimately, this approach will lead to an incredibly diverse and productive landscape, blending age-old techniques with modern principles.

Within this 25-square-kilometer network, three buildings made of local materials are designed to blend into the site's surroundings, anchoring the site to Groningen's landscape history. The former gas plant is adapted into a community meeting space and a workshop centered around saline farming practices is erected in the newly formed salt marsh, built atop pillars of reused steel from the gas site, to protect the building from fluctuating water levels. In Leermens, where the ancient mound is already partly excavated, a restaurant made from rammed earth, hemp, and reeds, is erected.

As encroaching salt water threatens the dynamic landscape established in the New Wierde, fresh water will become more scarce and expensive, exacerbating an existing issue. Historically, fresh water was conserved in a structure known as a *dobbe*, an open pool on the mound, for drinking and irrigation. Today, Groningen is dotted with over 150 abandoned gas sites from the mining industry; these sites are marked by generic concrete slabs ranging from six to nine acres, slightly elevated above fields. These sites are contaminated with heavy metals like barium from years of gas drilling and polluted production water. Openings in this concrete will be used to plant reeds, rushes, and cattails, which can purify the soil within 10 to 20 years. Eventually lawns at these sites can be excavated to collect rainwater—providing purified water for over one thousand people per site.

The history of adapting to the challenges of the Dutch landscape, from ancient mound systems to modern infrastructure, highlights the need for sustainable solutions in the face of environmental changes. Dijkstra's New Wierde project embodies this ethos, proposing a coexistence with nature through innovative design and resource management that bolsters climate resilience and supports a self-sufficient, coastal community-oriented alternative to globalized monoculture production.

REF. PAGE 464

Found across the globe, the technique of reclaiming land from the sea along low-lying coasts by creating dikes and ponds has enabled traditional communities to live, cultivate, and prosper in these ever-changing and seasonally fluctuating intertidal landscapes.

MUD FRONTIERS

PROJECT CREDIT Emerging Objects (Ronald Rael and Virginia San Fratello) PROJECT DATE 2019–
LOCATION La Florida, Colorado TYPOLOGY material technology
ELEVATION 2,336 m TEK architecture
COMMUNITY OF ORIGIN Puebloan and Indo-Hispano communities

In the high-altitude desert of Colorado's San Luis Valley, where the Rio Grande begins its southward journey, a series of human-scale structures are crafted from sand, silt, clay, and water. Rooted in the adobe construction techniques of communities Indigenous to the American Southwest, these protoarchitectures showcase the cutting-edge work of Emerging Objects, a design and research firm led by architects Ronald Rael and Virginia San Fratello. What distinguishes this project from the region's vernacular practices, as well as the broader tradition of mud-built architecture and landscape technologies found worldwide, is the unique method used to aggregate earthen materials. Pioneering cost-effective and low-labor construction, Emerging Objects uses a large portable 3D printer to shape earthen material into intricate, functional structures, merging tradition with contemporary design.

The upper reaches of the Rio Grande watershed serve as a laboratory for this material innovation. This region has a history of using earth for construction, relying on river and stream water for malleability. The Puebloan people of northern New Mexico built multilevel complexes using a puddled mud technique, forming structures by hand-kneading an earth-and-water mixture. Spanish colonization introduced adobe brick construction, further shaping the architectural style of the area.

Rael, a designer Indigenous to the region and cofounder of Emerging Objects, has drawn inspiration from his upbringing in this landscape. In the summer of 2019, their team relocated to the San Luis Valley village of La Florida, where Rael grew up, producing the first Mud Frontiers series. They applied their 3D printing expertise to construct several mud-based structures, designed for southern Colorado's high desert terrain.

The team transported a robotic paste-extrusion technology called Potterbot XLS-1, which they codeveloped with the company 3D Potter, to the La Florida site. This portable machine stands at nine feet tall with a nine foot diameter, and it is capable of printing materials like clay, concrete, and mud in a 360-degree continuous rotation—a feature absent in most 3D printers. Meanwhile, the team turned to traditional methods of sifting, filtering, and mixing silt, clay, and sand with natural additives like straw and water to produce a material viscosity capable of moving through the printer's nozzle, all while holding shape once extruded, before being baked by the sun. These materials were sourced on-site, and further experiments were done with wild micaceous clay harvested with local experts in New Mexico to be printed into small vessels inspired by traditional ceramics.

At the end of the two-and-a-half-month development of Mud Frontiers, the Emerging

Objects team built four earth-based typologies: Hearth, Beacon, Lookout, and Kiln. Each structure followed a consistent model, using 3D printing to create undulating lines of mud that form concentric circles. These rings were layered vertically, resulting in silo structures with shell-like walls. Each typology focuses on a specific function, showcasing a scalable application. The Lookout features a durable adobe coil staircase that ascends to a platform, emphasizing the material's durability. The Hearth innovates by reinforcing thin mud walls with rot-resistant juniper wood—a technique that draws from local methods as well as Sudano-Sahelian earth-based innovations in West Africa. Its interior features a 3D-printed adobe tarima (bench) situated around a fogón (fireplace), which emits radiant heat contained by the structure's mud walls. The Beacon explores the thinnest possible structural solution for enclosure; the Kiln, on the other hand, employs thicker interlocking walls to form an insulative structure than can be used to fire clay.

The following year, Rael and San Fratello returned to the La Florida site to create the next iteration of their material exploration: Casa Covida. Inspired by the pandemic era when the project originated, "covida" also alludes to the Spanish term for cohabitation—the three conjoined silos feature enhanced doorways, windows, and lintels. This refined dwelling is better suited for habitation, equipped with a sleeping platform, hearth, and bathtub within one unified structure.

Since the group's early experiments in earthen printing, Rael has taken the work of Mud Frontiers to new levels. In 2022, he designed Skylos—an installation of eight 3D printed earthen silos arranged in an interconnected ring that frames a central courtyard. Not only is Skylos the largest 3D printed building in the world—it's the first of its kind to be permitted for construction. The next year, he completed construction on Terrano, the first earthen structure with a roof printed in-situ in the world.

The name Mud Frontiers aptly captures the essence of this project—a pioneering exploration of locally sourced, traditional materials translated through high-tech processes. Emerging Objects' work is a critical investigation into the possibilities of replicating and scaling age-old earthen construction with minimal cost and labor. The initiative breathes new life into a traditional practice that has lost traction over the course of the last century, while envisioning a promising future for sustainable construction solutions in the years ahead.

MICACEOUS
Consisting of or resembling mica.

REF. PAGE 466

In arid environments, earthen architecture reliant on water to render the materials malleable is built with innately insulative properties that can keep ice frozen and fire contained.

FLOATING TREATMENT WETLANDS

PROJECT CREDIT Dr. Muhammad Afzal, Dr. Muhammad Arslan, Dr. Jochen A. Müller, Dr. Samina Iqbal, Dr. Razia Tahseen, Engr. Muhammad Shoaib Hassan, Ghulam Shabir, Salman Younus, Dr. Mohamed Gamal el-Din (Scientific Personnel) National Institute for Biotechnology and Genetic Engineering, Faisalabad, Pakistan; Karlsruhe Institute of Technology; University of Alberta, Edmonton, Canada **PROJECT DATE** 2014– **PROJECT CLIENTS** Water and Sanitation Agency, Faisalabad, Pakistan; Rajian Oil Field, Chakwal; Dakhni Gas Plant, Jand, Attock; Akhuwat University, Kasur; Gulshan colony, Jauharabad; Manak village, Lahore; Hassanpur village, Multan; Chak No. 171, Khanewal; Sahianwali village, Sargodha; NED UET University, Karachi; Urban Forest Park, Clifton, Karachi; Sapphire Spinning Mill, Sheikhupura; Bagh Ibne Qasim, Clifton, Karachi; Soon Valley, Khushab; Two Star Mill, Kamalia; Jallo Park, Lahore; Laitan village, District Sheikhupura; Haripur; University of Engineering & Technology (UET)- KSK Campus, Sheikhupura; Interloop Limited, Khurrianwala, Faisalabad; Mari Petroleum, Gotki, Sindh; Toyota Lyallpur Motors, Faisalabad; Toyota Chenab Motors, Faisalabad; Logistics Momentum Khanewal, and village Buchoke-Manjha, Lahore **LOCATION** 22 sites across Pakistan **TYPOLOGY** material technology **ELEVATION** 2,336 m **TEK** nature-based waterborne construction techniques **COMMUNITY OF ORIGIN** Indo-Aryan People (Lohar and Arain)

Lush, green beds of aquatic plants float on the surface water bodies across Pakistan. Unlike ordinary islands, however, these are floating treatment wetlands (FTWs), supported by bamboo frames and adorned with a tapestry of native wetland plants. Vibrant hues of Typha, vetiver grass, and common reed sway in the breeze, casting reflections on the water below. These buoyant mats are much more than a habitat for aquatic flora—they serve as a powerful tool in the fight against Pakistan's pervasive water pollution. The first of these FTWs was created over a decade ago as part of an ongoing, nationwide wastewater-remediation project tackling water contamination challenges affecting Pakistan's urban and rural communities. These FTWs are at the forefront of wastewater treatment biotechnology, merging traditional ecological knowledge with modern engineering to develop cost-effective, sustainable solutions to one of the nation's most pressing environmental issues. As extreme weather events exacerbate contamination caused by unregulated industrial waste disposal and rapid population growth, the country of 230 million struggles with water management plagued by distribution inequity and infrastructure decay. If all of the country's eight primary wastewater treatment plants were in operation, less than 10 percent of the urban wastewater would be subject to primary treatment, and secondary treatment does not exist. In Faisalabad, a city with a strong industrial sector, wastewater is retained in so-called stabilization ponds, which have become overrun and odorous. Due to local water scarcity, their contents are used to irrigate over 70 percent of the surrounding agricultural land, posing a significant public health hazard.

Since 2014, FTWs, tailored to address specific contamination problems, have been deployed and assessed at 22 sites across Pakistan. Constructed using aquatic plants known as macrophytes to form buoyant mats, these hybrid floating islands use phytoremediation, mimicking the filtration and beneficial microbial processes occurring in natural wetlands. Their buoyancy is attributed to gasses produced by microbial biofilms on the root surfaces of the plants, as well as air spaces within the root tissue of some plant species. For example, Typha, vetiver grass, and common reed have been selected for their strong root systems, which can transport oxygen from the air into the surrounding water or soil, increasing buoyancy through bubbling. These plants have traditionally been used for a number of cultural practices: Typha leaves, for example, for weaving religious mats; Typha roots, for cleaning earthenware; and vetiver roots, for rope making. Each treatment island consists of a raft made from a polyethylene sheet—a material selected for its high buoyancy and accessibility. Some of these rafts are surrounded by a floating bamboo frame, following the traditional method for constructing waterborne structures in the area. Natural materials such as dried grass and coconut shavings are used to secure aquatic plants to the thin plastic pots that are inserted into the mats. Additional soil, such as chikni matti (clayey soil) traditionally used for plastering mud walls, and gravel are layered around their edges to protect the plants from sunlight and heat, and to provide resistance to erosion from rain and wind. An individual unit measures 1.2 meters by 1.8 meters; a treatment wetland typically comprises about one hundred of these floating beds. The systems effectively treated wastewater, eliminating hazardous contaminants and remedying the water safe for use. These efficient wastewater treatment systems are implemented at low capital since they are passive infrastructures built from available natural materials and have low operational costs, at least five hundred times less than conventional treatment systems. The treatment wetlands provide a multitude of ecosystem services, not unlike the traditional floating attaphum and ye-chan technologies also present in South and Southeast Asia.

The implementation of FTWs in Pakistan marks a significant advancement in addressing the nation's wastewater management challenges. The pollution in Pakistan's bodies of water is not merely an environmental problem but also a deeply rooted sociopolitical issue, particularly affecting vulnerable communities in rural and urban areas. These communities bear a disproportionate burden of the public health risks associated with water contamination, often necessitating relocation. By integrating traditional ecological knowledge with modern engineering, FTWs offer a sustainable and cost-effective approach to mitigating these ecological and social challenges, providing a necessary pathway toward water remediation amid intensifying climate extremes.

REF. PAGE 454

Clumps of aquatic floating plants which trap silt to form floating clusters of islands, offer refuge for terrestrial and aquatic animal, algae and insect species living both above and below the waterline.

BLANKET OF WARMTH

(PROJECT CREDIT) MacPherson Engineering, Star Blanket Cree Nation, University of Regina (PROJECT DATE) 2019
(PROJECT CLIENT) Star Blanket Cree Nation (LOCATION) Regina, Canada
(TYPOLOGY) material technology
(ELEVATION) 1,893 m (TEK) traditional radiant heating
(COMMUNITY OF ORIGIN) Star Blanket Cree Nation

In 2018, Wendell Starblanket met with the founders of Saskatchewan's MacPherson Engineering to tackle an invisible crisis affecting the homes and health of Canada's First Nation communities. Starblanket, a Star Blanket Cree Nation member, lived in a house with a conventional HVAC system, leading to inadequate heating and widespread mold growth in his basement. The pervasive issue of mold contamination, posing a significant public health risk across the homes of many First Nation communities, had prompted the country's parliament to consider a national task force earlier in the year. Despite this proposal, the combined grassroots initiative of the Star Blanket Cree Nation, MacPherson Engineering, and a University of Regina team brought to life a real cost-effective solution inspired by Indigenous knowledge, known as the Blanket of Warmth.

The Blanket of Warmth is a hybrid passive heating and cooling system designed to minimize energy consumption and costliness while improving residents' thermal comfort and health. The inspiration for this alternative to standard HVAC systems in modern homes is deeply rooted in the traditional tepee homes of the Star Blanket Cree Nation. These ancestral dwellings rely on radiant heat for consistent thermal conditions. In such traditional structures, radiant heat typically emanates from a central hearth, while the insulating properties of animal hides and wooden frames help regulate internal temperatures.

The Blanket of Warmth adapts this passive heating strategy to align with the contemporary construction practices used to build most homes today. Leveraging the infrastructure of these homes as a means of minimizing the project's footprint, the MacPherson team employed hybrid radiant heating panels that easily affix to walls. These panels use existing basement furnaces—many of which are not in use—as the main energy source for the entire system. However, what sets the Blanket of Warmth apart from both the ancestral homes of the Star Blanket Cree Nation and many modern applications of radiant heating is its unique use of water as the primary medium for heat transfer.

This technology functions as a hydronic system, circulating a mixture of water and glycol through cross-linked polyethylene piping embedded within panels attached to each wall. Instead of relying on a costly, high-maintenance boiler as an energy source, the system draws its heat from a combination of the existing furnace and a RadiantLink coil, engineered by MacPherson. The furnace's hot air heats the circulating glycol-water mixture in the coil, which then moves through a piping system installed on the basement walls, releasing heat into the space. Using the homes' existing concrete foundations as a means of conducting radiated heat, the system allows the surrounding floor and walls to absorb and store energy without embedded piping, effectively acting as a thermal mass. This is reflective of the use of rocks that traditionally surround the hearth of a tepee.

The Capstone Report carried out by University of Regina Industrial Systems Engineering students revealed that, on average, basements equipped with Blanket of Warmth technology were 3.5 degrees Celsius warmer compared to similar basements without this system. Because thermal mass has the ability to retain heat for longer periods than heated air alone, basements with the Blanket of Warmth technology see less fluctuation in internal temperature. Crucially, the study indicated that MacPherson's engineered radiant heating system reduced surface humidities by up to 10 percent, illustrating that homes with radiant heating are less susceptible to mold growth.

Beyond the public health strides represented by the Blanket of Warmth initiative, it provides a necessary transition from space heaters, commonly used to heat underinsulated homes on reserves. Space heaters are responsible for 79 percent of Canada's fatal fires, and only 56 percent of First Nation communities have adequate fire protection, putting them at particular risk. Additionally, a University of Regina study found that the MacPherson system produces heat equivalent to two standard space heaters. By replacing two space heaters, each operating eight hours daily, with hydronic radiant technology, occupants can save approximately $886.65 annually in electricity costs.

The Blanket of Warmth is a transformative solution, addressing not only the immediate challenges of inadequate heating and mold contamination in First Nation communities but also broader issues of public health, safety, and sustainability. The collaborative efforts of the Blanket of Warmth team have yielded a remarkable hydronic system that embraces Indigenous wisdom while adapting to contemporary construction practices. Beyond its impressive energy efficiency and cost-effectiveness, the Blanket of Warmth represents a departure from hazardous space heaters, fostering safer living conditions in underinsulated homes. This initiative underscores the importance of culturally thoughtful, community-driven approaches to address the unique challenges faced by First Nation communities.

HVAC Heating, ventilation, and air conditioning

TOTORA REED INSULATION

PROJECT CREDIT Cecilia Jimenez, Teresa Montoya, and Silvana Loayza (Centro Tierra, Centro de Investigación de la Arquitectura y la Ciudad, Pontificia Universidad Católica del Perú)
PROJECT DATE 2018– LOCATION Puno, Peru
TYPOLOGY material technology ELEVATION 4,000 m
TEK totora reed construction COMMUNITY OF ORIGIN Chimu

For centuries, the communities around southern Peru's Lake Titicaca have lived in homes built on floating wetlands, all constructed from the totora reed endemic to the lake's shores. South America's highest-altitude freshwater body, Titicaca rests between Andean Mountains formed by millennia of tectonic activity. The aquatic plant that populates the lake's shorelines—thriving at depths of two and a half to three meters—has become a cultural keystone species of great importance, characterizing the lake communities' way of life for generations, playing a vital role in practices tied to medicine, food, and textile design. In the face of the gradual decline of the traditional use of totora, a team of multidisciplinary researchers from Pontificia Universidad Católica del Perú has developed an ingenious method that upholds the tradition while addressing a pressing issue affecting the region's most vulnerable communities.

Puno, a western plateau along Lake Titicaca, stands over four thousand meters above sea level; its climate is characterized by intense daytime solar radiation and extreme temperatures dropping as low as negative 10 degrees Celsius. Concurrently, the region is prone to significant seismic activity. Seismic events have a profound impact, particularly in poor and rural areas, where government responses are often delayed. Harsh climatic conditions exacerbate these challenges, as emergency shelters, ill suited for the extreme cold, are quickly damaged by the strong winds and hailstorms that are common throughout the year. After a 6.3 Richter scale earthquake in 2016, most of the homes in the village of Orduna were destroyed; community members constructed makeshift homes out of tin walls and roofs supported by timber frames.

In response to the 2016 earthquake, a Centro Tierra (CT) research team from Pontificia Universidad Católica del Perú, set out to design a bioclimatic, cost-effective model for shelters that could be easily replicated and assembled for disaster relief. A material already so deeply embedded in local tradition, totora arose as the optimal source of insulation, outperforming alternatives such as hemp, sheep wool, and polyurethane foam. The outcome of this research was a full-scale prototype of a modular, prefabricated shelter that synthesizes traditional knowledge and materials with contemporary approaches to engineering, altogether improving thermal comfort for temporary residents.

The CT team actively collaborated with the Chimu community—the only Indigenous group around Lake Titicaca still practicing totora mat production—to learn how to best harvest the reed and craft it into mats known as *q'esanas*. These traditional *q'esana* mats served as the foundation for the modular insulation panels placed between the beams and columns of the temporary home's structure. However, the group modified the traditional mat-making process to better align with the insulation needs provided by totora. In most parts of the shelter, panels consisted of mats that were doubled and tightly bound together, following traditional Chimu craft techniques while using tighter seams. When shielded from humidity, sun, and rain, the totora panels could last up to 10 years. However, if exposed to the extreme high-altitude conditions of southern Peru, they would likely need to be replaced every one to two years.

The totora panels were inserted into the prefabricated timber framework of the prototype, raised 50 cm above the ground on foundation boxes to minimize heat transfer. This addressed the thermal discomfort due to bare earthen flooring common in the region. The prototype's floor was made of wood planks over totora mats, and the exterior walls were finished with wood to protect the vertical totora panels from rain and sun. The roof, covered with tin sheets over the totora panels, included two skylights for passive solar heating in an area known for intense solar radiation. This surface was also topped with a photovoltaic solar panel to power lighting and small appliances. The total cost for prefabrication and construction was $6,500; however, the research team maintains that mass production could reduce the cost. Upon completion, the 20-square-meter dwelling could house four to six family members, providing three rooms for sleeping, cooking, dining, cleaning, and storage. The lifespan of a single totora-insulated emergency home ranges from one to three years and can be assembled and dismantled by four people in as few as four days. The CT team's research has continued to expand as they reassemble and test the prototype at higher altitudes and locations to improve its construction and thermal performance.

Sustaining the traditional ecological knowledge embedded in using totora as a construction material goes beyond cultural preservation; it represents a pragmatic response to an urgent problem experienced by many in this region on a yearly basis. The innovative approach taken by the researchers from Pontificia Universidad Católica del Perú, combining Indigenous knowledge with modern engineering techniques, offers a necessary blueprint for addressing the lack of thermally comfortable emergency shelters in climatically extreme, earthquake-prone regions like Puno.

BIOCLIMATIC Concerned with the relations of climate and living matter.

REF. PAGE 468

Bioclimatic, cost-effective, biodegradable, and regeneratively sourced material technologies, deeply embedded in local tradition, offer pragmatic responses to urgent climate-related problems.

SHIDHULAI NOUKA SCHOOL

PROJECT CREDIT Mohammed Rezwan PROJECT DATE 2002– PROJECT CLIENT Shidhulai Swanirvar Sangstha LOCATION Natore, Pabna, and Sirajganj Districts, northwest Bangladesh TYPOLOGY architecture ELEVATION 11 m TEK vernacular aquatic architecture COMMUNITY OF ORIGIN Indo-Aryan Peoples (Lohar and Arain)

A *nouka* (boat) school travels along the winding river flowing around the mud-corrugated iron homes, markets, and rice fields located about 118 miles northwest of Dhaka, the capital city of Bangladesh. A group of students eagerly anticipate their slow journey home after hours of schooling aboard this boat. Embarking homeward requires patience beyond the familiar sound of a bell. Their classroom, swaying as it passes rows of floating fish enclosures, duck coops, and floating shops moors along the riverbed, where students disembark one by one before another group of children board the boat. This *nouka* school, plying through the river, is a school bus and schoolhouse in one, making multiple stops along the riverbank to pick up students and arrange onboard class.

In Bangladesh, approximately 2,340 children attend school in floating classrooms created by local architect Mohammed Rezwan. Serving as the executive director of Shidhulai Swanirvar Sangstha, a nonprofit committed to constructing climate-resilient facilities for education, new skills, agriculture, and health care, Rezwan has successfully built 26 fully equipped floating *nouka* schools that offer educational services across the country's vast network of waterways. These school boats operate year-round and offer a complete primary school education up to grade five.

Founded in 1998, Shidhulai arose in response to the persistent annual flooding that disrupts communities throughout Bangladesh. In the face of looming climate challenges, children are particularly at risk, facing heightened vulnerability due to the destruction of local schools by floods and riverbank erosion. Rezwan's visionary response, offering a climate-adaptive alternative to traditional education and reducing the demand on land-based school infrastructure in flood-prone areas and riverbanks, has come to life, illuminating a path for resilient and sustainable learning.

Rezwan designed the *nouka* school with sustainable alternative technologies grounded in a local vernacular tradition, focusing on making the school an integral part of the community. Local boat builders built the school boats following the wooden boat-building heritage of northwestern Bangladesh, using endemic timber from *shala* trees (*Shorea robusta*) as the main construction material. Measuring approximately 17 meters in length and 3.5 meters in width, these boats feature a single large cabin capable of accommodating 30 children and a teacher. The boats' multilayered weather-resistant roofs, designed to endure heavy monsoon rains, are upheld by arched metal beams, resulting in an open classroom space that is uninhibited by columns. A row of side windows ventilates the interior of the classroom, allowing cool air to pass through when the boat is docked underneath a tree canopy during a lesson. Observed from the riverbanks, an onlooker might remark that the boat bears a resemblance to a large river turtle.

Since the first school boat was built in 2002, Rezwan's concept for the floating classroom has evolved significantly. The organization has introduced a two-tiered model, with the upper deck featuring a playground equipped with slides, swings, and monkey bars, while the lower deck serves as a classroom. Solar panels have also been installed atop each boat, generating enough power to support computers and internet connectivity. Recognizing the diverse living conditions of the students, many of whom are children of landless farmers, Shidhulai ensures that each pupil receives a rechargeable Surya-Hurricane Solar Lantern. This low-cost solar lantern, made from recycled parts of the conventional and much-used kerosene lantern, was designed by Rezwan and is intended to offer sufficient light to complete homework in the evening in off-grid areas.

Bangladesh is a low-lying delta, and, as climate change advances, flooding and riverbank erosion are intensifying across the country. Rezwan's floating alternative to land-based schools is a symbol of resilience in the face of the country's environmental challenges. Adapting traditional vessels to create mobile schools, Rezwan has not only provided primary education to thousands of students but also laid the foundation for a climate-adaptive, sustainable, and community-focused future. The impact of Shidhulai Swanirvar Sangstha's floating schools extends beyond the boundaries of classrooms, fostering an awareness of the surrounding environment and uplifting the exchange of traditional wisdom.

REF. PAGE 470

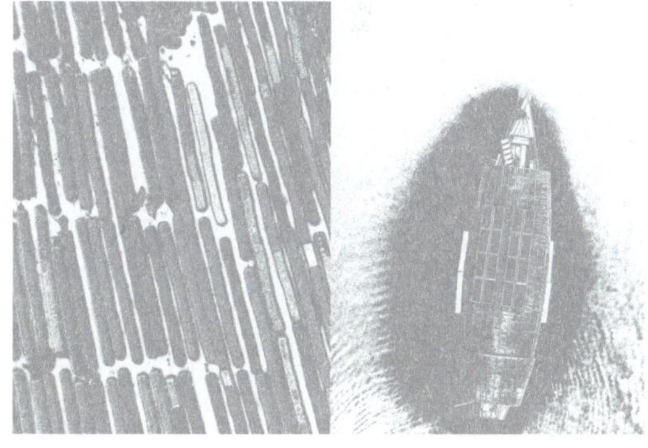

Across the globe, rising flood waters have challenged local communities to adapt by adopting buoyancy as a biological performance to support infrastructure, agriculture, transportation, education, economy, ecology, and energy.

THAMMASAT UNIVERSITY ROOFTOP FARM AND CHULALONGKORN CENTENARY PARK

(PROJECT CREDIT) LANDPROCESS (PROJECT DATE) 2019, 2017
(PROJECT CLIENT) Thammasat University, Chulalongkorn University
(LOCATION) Pathum Thani Province, Thailand; Bangkok, Thailand
(TYPOLOGY) parkland (ELEVATION) 12 m (TEK) agricultural terrace systems
(COMMUNITY OF ORIGIN) traditional architecture of Chao Phraya River basin

Throughout the last century, unregulated urban development has left its mark on the once prosperous agrarian landscapes of Southeast Asia. Sprawling cities, now encased in impermeable, human-made materials, are increasingly uninhabitable in a region well known for its annual rainy season. As the climate crisis unfolds, this challenge will only intensify, leading to more turbulent weather conditions, food insecurity, and water scarcity.

Confronted with these climate stressors and urban challenges, LANDPROCESS, a Bangkok landscape architecture firm led by Kotchakorn Voraakhom, has developed pioneering solutions inspired by Thailand's agrarian heritage. The ingenuity of the LANDPROCESS design methodology is twofold. Firstly, the studio converts otherwise neglected pieces of urban infrastructure into efficient, climate-adaptive sources of food production. Secondly, the firm highlights the potential of traditional ecological knowledge in widely embraced modern design concepts like green roofs.

One of these projects is Thammasat University Rooftop Farm (TURF) located atop an academic building on Thammasat University's Rangsit Campus in Pathum Thani, Thailand. Constructed in 2019, TURF is Asia's largest organic rooftop farm. It grows more than 40 edible species across a terraced green roof designed to harness storm runoff for the irrigation of a productive organic urban farm, yielding 20 tons of food each year and capable of generating 80,000 meals in the campus canteen. The integration of terracing in this design is essential to the building's functionality, providing a means to mitigate the impacts of progressively unpredictable climate conditions.

Spanning 22,000 square meters, TURF takes on the distinctive shape of an "H," in which two curved, parallel wings slope downward until they reach ground level. A hybrid between traditional earthwork terraces and modern green-roof technology, this cascading design can effectively decrease runoff speed up to 20 times more effectively than a standard concrete rooftop. As rainwater zigzags from the highest point of the building downward, unique clusters of microwatersheds emerge, which resemble a traditional rice terrace system in its ability to absorb, filter, and purify rainwater. Descending into four retention basins, the site is capable of containing up to 3,095,570 gallons of water.

Another seminal project, inspired by the Yakrong Indigenous agricultural gardening system, is Bangkok's first critical piece of green infrastructure: Chulalongkorn Centenary Park. Opening in 2017, the park mitigates ecological issues and reduces disaster risk by harnessing the power of gravity in a flat, previously amphibious city. By imposing a three-degree angle, the park is able to sustainably collect, treat, and hold water to reduce urban flood risks in its surrounding areas. This aquatic versatility was inspired by the sophisticated canals, channels, and irrigation system of local Indigenous fruit farming, which controlled, dispersed, and retained fluctuating flood conditions.

Featuring sustainable drainage systems, a green roof, wetlands, porous areas, ponds, an open swale, small pocket parks, detention lawns, and a retention pond—not a single drop of rain is wasted. The rain and runoff are pulled down through the park's topography to generate a complete water-circulation system. Taking into account a 50-year period of rainfall intensity and the frequently overwhelmed public sewage system, the park is able to hold up to a million gallons of water during heavy rainfall.

Excessive runoff from the green roof then flows down to four constructed wetlands, two on each side of the park. A series of cascading weirs and ponds slow the runoff and increase water aeration, aided by native water plants that filter and clean the water. The main lawn at the park's center is a vast inclined open space for recreational activities. On stormy days, the lawn absorbs rain and runoff, using gravity to send the water to the retention pond by the low end of the park. During severe flooding, this retention pond can double in size by expanding into the park's main lawn.

LANDPROCESS's projects represent more than a homage to Thailand's agricultural legacy; they are platforms for the restoration of traditional knowledge that has sustained local communities for millennia. Only a century ago, the region underwent irreversible changes when the Thai monarchy constructed an extensive network of canals, intended to irrigate industrial-scale rice plantations. This initiative paved over vast swathes of agrarian land, reshaping the dynamics through which local communities engaged with tradition, food, and, crucially, water. "Floods used to be a source of food, a source of fertilization," Voraakhom told Bloomberg in 2021. "Changing the way we have lived as a city these past 30 to 50 years, we have completely turned our back to natural change and called it disaster."

TURF and Chulalongkorn Centenary Park challenge this perspective, demonstrating how civic infrastructure can work with the surrounding environment rather than impose upon it. LANDPROCESS's work is a testament to the efficacy of permeable design and, above all, highlights the potential of traditional ecological knowledge as the cornerstone of our urban future.

REF. PAGE 472

REF. PAGE 474

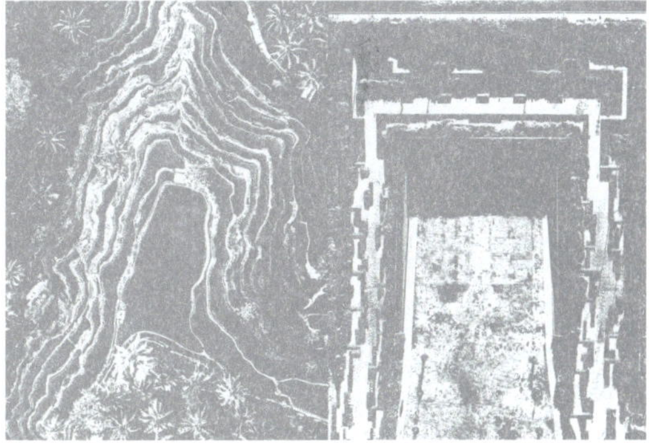

For thousands of years, terraced agriculture has transformed slopes into productive ponds, while pioneering innovative stormwater and wastewater management systems in regions subject to drastic seasonal monsoonal fluctuations. In an increasingly wetter world, these systems offer informal, scalable, and transportable technologies.

REC COMTAL MASTER PLAN

PROJECT CREDIT Carles Enrich Studio PROJECT DATE 2017–
PROJECT CLIENT City of Barcelona LOCATION Barcelona, Spain
TYPOLOGY restoration ELEVATION 22 m
TEK water canalization COMMUNITY OF ORIGIN Catalans

Today, residents of Barcelona's Vallbona neighborhood use water flowing through a small ditch to irrigate orchards that have been in their families for generations. Only exposed to daylight in the city's northern outskirts, this canal is the vestige of an ancient infrastructure that once served as one of Barcelona's primary sources of water. For nearly a millennium, the Rec Comtal was a vital artery for the city and surrounding rural areas, delivering water to vast swathes of farmland and powering local mills, including the textile mills of Sant Andreu. Spanning over 14 kilometers from its peak in the 10th century to the mid-20th century, today the remains of the Rec Comtal in Vallbona account for only 5 percent of the system's original expanse. While the Rec Comtal's historic roles in supporting farmland and mill activities have been supplanted by modern industrial alternatives, the site's cultural importance remains irreplaceable. The presence of an open-air irrigation channel was a catalyst for the development of public spaces and social life in Barcelona. Today, much of the Rec Comtal's natural environment and social activity have been lost, and the archaeological remains have suffered from neglect.

In 2017, Barcelona-based architecture and landscape firm Carles Enrich Studio set out to revive this ancient water system that once sustained the city. The studio's comprehensive plan for the restoration of the Rec Comtal hopes to restore the canal's historic function as a local water supply, while also responding to current needs like irrigation and recreation. The plan carefully distinguishes between the two main sections of the canal: the rural canal, which is primarily used for water transport, mainly for irrigation purposes; and the urban canal, which no longer fulfills this role. One of Carles Enrich Studio's primary objectives is to reclaim the functional heritage of the Rec Comtal by reintroducing water into Barcelona, particularly in uncovered sections of the canal.. The plan also emphasizes the importance of a long-term strategy to reduce nonrenewable energy consumption and prioritize sustainable resource management for the city's postindustrial future.

As the first pilot project within the framework of the Rec Comtal recovery plan, an environmental restoration and renaturing intervention is being implemented at two points in the Vallbona neighborhood. These areas had undergone a process of degradation and abandonment, turning the Rec Comtal into a neglected space at risk of disappearing. To restore this section's historical significance and reestablish its role as a green infrastructure, the proposal includes the planting of riverside vegetation and macrophyte species, including narrow-leaved ash (*Fraxinus angustifolia*), gray willow (*Salix atrocinerea*), intermediate periwinkle (*Vinca difformis*), chaste tree (*Vitex agnus-castus*), yellow iris (*Iris pseudacorus*), hanging sedge (*Carex pendula*), roundhead bulrush (*Scirpus holoschoenus*), and spiny rush (*Juncus acutus*). The integration of these species not only enhances water quality but also provides more shade to cool the river temperature, revitalizing habitat for newly reintroduced fish, birds, and amphibians.

MACROPHYTE
An aquatic plant growing in or near water.

The restoration of the Rec Comtal's historic biodiversity necessitates the planting of species that attract Indigenous fauna and ensure the biological cycles of growth, dispersion, and recycling, aiming for as much autonomy as possible. These interventions enhance the quality of surface water and aquifers, mitigate the negative effects of rainfall, improve drainage and soil quality, regulate urban microclimates, create climatic shelters, and enhance local ecosystems. This renaturation initiative creates a green corridor along the Rec Comtal.

Two lightweight structures have been constructed out of corrugated profiles supported on pre-existing elements like retaining walls to provide safe access to the water. These new biodiversity lookouts are landscape features that will be replicated at other points along the Rec Comtal route as the recovery project continues.

The restoration of the Rec Comtal in Barcelona's Vallbona neighborhood revitalizes ancient infrastructure and reconnectes the city's cultural heritage. While the canal's original functions have evolved, its significance as a historical and social landmark remains paramount. Carles Enrich Studio's efforts and implementation of new restoration strategies has restored the Rec Comtal to its historic state and transformed it into a vibrant hub for community engagement.

REF. PAGE 476

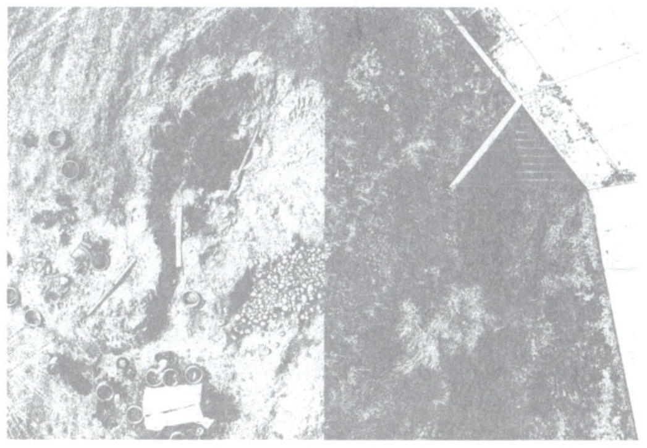

Gravity-fed water infrastructures, sustainably sourced from aquifers or harvested surface water, have supported the expansion of cities across Western Asia to the northwestern edge of Europe for thousands of years.

GREAT GREEN WALL

(PROJECT CREDIT) African Union (PROJECT DATE) 2007–
(PROJECT FUNDING) World Bank, Green Climate Fund, Global Environment Facility (LOCATION) Sahelian region, Africa
(TYPOLOGY) restoration (ELEVATION) 200–400 m
(TEK) agroforestry and drylands farming innovations
(COMMUNITY OF ORIGIN) Sahelian communities

Stretching 5,900 kilometers from Africa's Atlantic coast to the Red Sea, the Sahel stands as a transitional belt where the savanna meets the Sahara Desert. This expanse, characterized by vast grasslands and the broad canopies of acacia trees, has been home to hundreds of communities practicing nomadic herding and subsistence agriculture for generations, adapting their way of life to the diverse climatic conditions that vary across the region. In recent years, there has been a noticeable decline in the quality of land used for farming and grazing in this region of Africa, attributed to both climate change and inadequate land management practices.

In 2007, the GGWI was launched by the African Union as a response to intensifying land degradation and its associated socio-economic impacts—a project to revive land productivity in the face of desertification. The GGWI was originally conceived with the intention of creating a belt of trees, spanning 15 kilometers wide, from Senegal to Djibouti. However, land degradation in the Sahel is the result of a century's worth of mismanaged arable land—the direct consequence of European colonialism—rather than the spread of the Sahara Desert. As a result, in the years following the project's inception, it has experienced substantial changes in its approach to regeneration, now leading a plan to create a "mosaic of green and productive landscapes" by implementing Indigenous land management, agroforestry, and conservation farming techniques tailored to specific subregions across 22 countries in the Sahel. By 2020, 18 million hectares of degraded land had been restored using these interventions. The GGWI aims to revitalize one hundred million hectares of land, sequester 250 million tons of carbon, and create 10 million jobs by 2030.

The African Union team leading the initiative has adopted nuanced, site-specific strategies to regenerate arable land. In Senegal, afforestation efforts have included the planting of over 50,000 acres of trees. The majority of these trees belong to the acacia species *Senegalia* senegal, which is valued for its economic potential because of its production of gum arabic—a material primarily used as a food additive and for pharmaceutical purposes.

The GGWI supports traditional dryland farming methods to restore soil health. In Niger, farmers use *zai* pits and crescent-shaped ditches known as "half-moons" to capture and retain water for crops in areas with limited rainfall. Some add manure to *zai* pits to attract termites, which help decompose soil further, improving underground irrigation. These methods increase yields of crops like millet and sorghum while preserving soil quality. Farmers also allow *Faidherbia albida* trees to grow in moderate numbers in their fields. This species becomes dormant during the wet season, shedding its leaves and enriching the soil through leaf litter decomposition when it rains. Since these trees are leafless during the typical growing season, they do not shade crops when sunlight is crucial.

The GGWI is implementing and scaling Indigenous water-catchment technologies such as *fanya chini* and *fanya juu*, trench terracing methods from Kenya and Tanzania. These techniques involve building bunds and ditches along slopes, reducing runoff speed and nutrient leaching while increasing water availability for crops. Small runoff microbasins known as negarim, characterized by their diamond shape and enclosed by low earthen bunds, are also being used across the GGWI to cultivate trees and bushes and prevent soil erosion.

These approaches are combined with technologies like assisted natural regeneration, which involves protecting land to allow trees and vegetation to regenerate. The United Nations Convention to Combat Desertification and GLOBHE, a drone service company, are using innovative technology to assess tree populations along the GGWI. GLOBHE deploys drones to collect high-resolution data, helping researchers plan and implement actions effectively. Their joint project combines satellite and drone data to verify and accelerate baobab tree populations in northern Ghana, supporting the GGWI's goal of restoring degraded land.

The project is also committed to building economic resilience on a community level. Throughout the Sahel, the GGWI is training men and women in agroforestry and other practices that generate income. For instance, in Kollo, women have been able to secure land to cultivate moringa trees, whose nutritious leaves and seed pods can be consumed as vegetables, dried and ground into powder, used to extract oil, or used for water filtration. A cooperative has been established to manage these activities, with the women operating a small shop to prepare and sell various products.

The GGWI aims to restore one hundred million hectares of degraded soil across the Sahel before 2030, and, until then, the organizations involved are progressing in tailoring solutions to the specific, local conditions of sites from Senegal to Sudan. Such initiatives serve as a crucial model for nuanced, contextual approaches to large-scale landscape restoration, which will likely become more common as desertification intensifies alongside climate extremes.

REF. PAGE 478

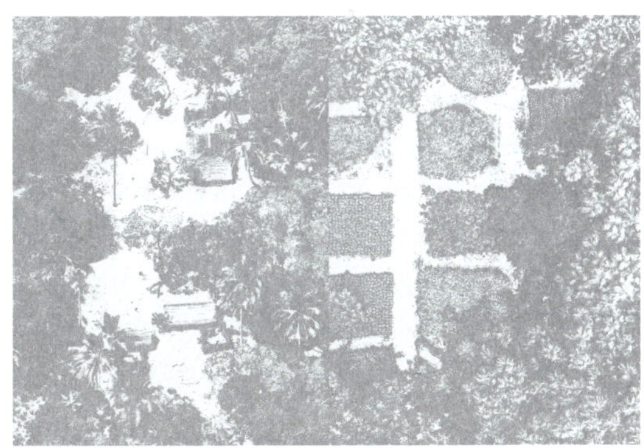

Adaptive small-scale Indigenous infrastructures and land management techniques, when replicated en masse, create large-scale systems that can reverse desertification while supporting local economies, communities, and ecologies.

REGENERATION WITH AGAVES

PROJECT CREDIT Fernando Laposse PROJECT DATE 2021–
LOCATION Santo Domingo Tonahuixtla, Mexico
TYPOLOGY restoration ELEVATION 1,327 m
TEK traditional terracing and anti-erosion agave reforestation
COMMUNITY OF ORIGIN Mixteco from Tonahuixtla in the Mixteca Baja region

For Miami Art Week 2019, the Miami Design District was transformed by pink beasts—a collection of 30 pink hairy sloths that hang from ropes, trees, and arches, as well as 10 hammocks and 25,000 hanging tassels. The installation, by Mexican product and material designer Fernando Laposse, an advocate for sustainable craft traditions, aims to connect natural materials and processes to artisan communities who practice this activity. For pink beasts, two different Indigenous groups and their technologies were collected as Laposse collaborated with fiber artist Angela Damman and artisans in Sacaban, Yucatán. The brightly colored pink creatures used sisal, an agave fiber—a resistant ecological substitute to plastic threads—colored using an amazing Indigenous technology.

The hue is achieved using a traditional Aztec dying technique from Oaxaca, which uses a natural dye called cochineal, a small bug that is a pest of the prickly pear cactus. When combined with the right amounts of lime juice and baking soda, it produces a vibrant pink. The pink sisal locks that hung down from the traditional Mayan designs were handmade by a community of Mayan weavers in Yucatán. This included the production, cleaning, and dying of the fiber, which comes from henequen (*Agave fourcroydes*), a species of agave from the Yucatán region that produces pale resilient twine. This utilitarian material was used by the Mayan people to make everything from hammocks and marine nets to hard-wearing carpets and cross-body bags.

Damman and the 45 Mayan women weavers from Yucatán worked together over a period of three months, dyeing, brushing, and knotting the fibers by hand. Both Laposse and Damman are motivated to find new markets for henequen craft products, noting two main factors—the increased price of labor and the plastic industry—that have contributed to the decline of the industry. Since WWII, synthetic fibers have gradually replaced henequen sisal in many of its industrial applications. Local communities now work with Laposse to produce his sisal design works, and the proceeds are reinvested to plant more agave.

In the Regeneration with Agaves project, Laposse uses agave to restore ecosystems and support Santo Domingo Tonahuixtla, a small village in Puebla. International trade agreements in the 1990s led to the rejection of traditional agriculture, with aggressive herbicide and pesticide use causing severe soil erosion. Since 2015, Laposse has worked with the community to regenerate the land and replenish groundwater by reviving Indigenous terracing traditions, planting agave along mountainsides—the only local plant that can withstand the arid conditions.

The village grows agave in bulk to fight soil erosion and provide fibers for design pieces.

However, these pieces are the final step in a series of actions to combat erosion. The focus has been on encouraging traditional agricultural methods, using agave and Indigenous terracing to slow water flow and foster floral diversity. Agave, growing in eroded mountains, retains soil and water, creating conditions for wild shrubs to return. Trenches are dug and leveled along contours, with agave planted downside, forming shallow pools that filter water, replenishing the water table. The long-term plan aims to retain soil and water, allowing wild plants to regenerate between terraces.

The agave, which must grow for seven years before being harvested, is planted in front of a hole that is one meter deep. When it rains, the water gets slowed down by these ditches, and the agave starts to hold the soil that it creates along with all the organic waste of the same plant. Once harvested, the fiber, which turns a blond color after washing and drying, is made through a simple process of beating and scraping the leaves.

So far, the team has planted 45,000 agaves across 120 hectares. Regeneration with Agaves emphasizes the importance of sustainable agricultural practices, celebrating design as a tool for renewal. Through a collaborative approach, this project aims to restore both the land and the community while innovating with native materials and craft techniques.

Whether working with rural communities in southern Mexico, lecturing at universities, or developing new prototypes at his studio, Laposse understands the impact that materiality and design can have in shaping and redefining current planetary dynamics. This project underscores the importance of raising awareness and fostering change, even if it starts on a local scale. Laposse's unconventional use of materials, such as agave fibers and avocado dyes, showcases the Indigenous knowledge and innovative approaches employed by the communities he collaborates with.

REF. PAGE 480

Dry-terracing ephemeral water catchment topographies for moisture capture, microclimate adaptation, and soil rebuilding supports indigenous plant ecologies, reverses desertification, and supplements local economies.

KYALASANAHALLI LAKE RESTORATION

(PROJECT CREDIT) Anand Malligavad (PROJECT DATE) 2017
(PROJECT CLIENT) Sansera Engineering Limited
(LOCATION) Anekal, a major town in the suburbs of Bengaluru city, India (TYPOLOGY) restoration (ELEVATION) 900 m
(TEK) Indigenous hydrological knowledge
(COMMUNITY OF ORIGIN) Chola dynasty

When it was built in the 16th century, Bangalore, "India's Silicon Valley"—or Bengaluru, as it is now known—was a city known for its abundance of water. An ancient human-made lake system of reservoirs provided water for agriculture and drinking to millions of residents. These reservoirs absorbed rainwater, kept groundwater levels high, and helped maintain the landlocked location's uniquely moderate microclimate. In the last 30 years, Bengaluru's lakes have degraded and shrunk as the city grew from four million people in the 1990s to about 13 million today, becoming India's high-tech hub. Villages turned into electronic cities, and lakes were filled in for bus terminals or cricket stadiums. As housing demand grew, high-rise apartments covered the canals leading to the remaining lakes. Consequently, urban area increased tenfold, transforming a rural landscape into India's fourth-largest city, now unable to absorb rainwater.

Sewage and water infrastructure have lagged behind this explosive growth, leading to both flooding and water scarcity. Today, fewer than 450 lakes remain, and just 10 percent of those have clean water. The rest are so polluted by sewage and industrial effluents that fires in the foamy waters of Bellandur, one of the city's largest lakes, were routine. Bengaluru is now facing a water shortage of about 172 million gallons per day, a figure likely to double by the end of 2030. The growing water crisis is a direct result of the loss of the ancient system of interconnected lakes, which are now dry or choked with pollution.

This self-sustaining network of irrigation lakes was constructed during the centuries-long rule of the medieval Chola dynasty, who ruled the surrounding Deccan Plateau for five centuries. This Indigenous knowledge, recorded for 1,500 years, turned low-lying areas into reservoirs for drinking and irrigation. In 2017, the restoration of the 36-acre Kyalasanahalli Lake near Bengaluru began when Anand Malligavad persuaded his company to contribute $120,000. The process starts by draining the lake and removing silt and weeds. Dams are strengthened, canals restored, and native trees and aquatic plants replanted. The goal is to reintroduce soil, water, plants, and canals, allowing rains to rebuild the ecosystem. Today, Kyalasanahalli's restoration is part of India's City of Lakes revival.

With three earthmovers and six trucks, a team of local volunteers removed almost four hundred thousand cubic meters of mud, waste, and plastic from Kyalasanahalli Lake. Drawing on ancient Chola techniques such as trapping silt and sludge using carved stones, which need no maintenance, and the Ridges-to-River method, teams unblocked channels and separated inputs from sewage lines with high embankments, so wastewater could be naturally treated and aerated. This area was created with separate lagoons alongside the lakes, where silt and garbage could be separated from sewage, with the human waste used later as fertilizer. Using the Ridges-to-River method, mud walls were constructed in a cascading shape to transport excess water during rainfalls to lakes in lower areas before ending up in the river. Along the way, the flow supports agriculture.

After dredging the lake bed, local grasses, native trees, and vegetation were planted. The team used the Miyawaki method, a Japanese technique enabling saplings to grow 10 times faster and denser, enhancing biodiversity and water-holding capacity. A wetland was developed to absorb pollutants, and lotuses and lilies were planted. In total, 18 thousand saplings were planted, including three thousand fruit trees and two thousand medicinal plants. Excavated mud created five islands for bird nesting, and native grasses reinforced the banks—all in 45 days, costing Rs 1.5 crore ($183,000). The next monsoon revived the lake, and within six months, residents were boating amid ducks and migratory birds.

Since the revival of Kyalasanahalli Lake, Malligavad has restored 35 lakes in Bengaluru, covering about eight hundred acres with a water-holding capacity of 106 million gallons. This increased the region's groundwater level by about eight feet. His success led nine Indian states to appoint him as an adviser for about three thousand projects. He has revived around 80 lakes across India, including in Odisha and Uttar Pradesh. The Karnataka state government has now asked him to devise a strategy to revive 5,600 lakes and water bodies in rural areas.

Malligavad has developed a replicable lake-revival model adaptable to different terrains. While cleaning and desilting are common initial steps, each lake's revival depends on its unique geology, groundwater depth, climate, and pollution levels. While each individual lake revival is itself a success, the underlying source of the problem remains: 60 percent of Bengaluru's sewage continues to flow into its lakes through the network of storm drains. Unless that changes, these initiatives will be short-lived. Further, these revived lakes will only have a significant impact on groundwater levels if the district reduces its groundwater extraction and undertakes more measures to recharge underground aquifers.

REF. PAGE 482

Urban wetlands are not only environmentally and socially beneficial landscapes, they also offer enormous financial incentives to cities.

PŌHAKU, KALO, WAI: STEWARDSHIP IN CONTEMPORARY HAWAIʻI

PROJECT CREDIT Joshua Diem (Principal Designer and Researcher, Biocultural Design); Lei Wann (Director, Limahuli Valley Garden and Preserve) PROJECT DATE 2024–
PROJECT CLIENT Limahuli Valley Garden and Preserve
LOCATION Hāʻena, Kauaʻi, USA TYPOLOGY restoration
ELEVATION 70 m–120 m TEK loʻi kalo terraces
COMMUNITY OF ORIGIN Native Hawaiians

In the heart of the forested slopes of Kauaʻi's Limahuli Valley sits a centuries-old agroecological site comprising over one hundred stone-built, interconnected terraces. This network of *ʻauwai* (freshwater irrigation ditches) and cascading wetland pools known as *loʻi kalo* (wetland taro) once sustained the families that lived and cared for this place. After decades of colonial land dispossession, the spread of invasive species, and the impacts of tourism, this *loʻi kalo* complex in the *ahupuaʻa* of Hāʻena has been left in disrepair—a phenomenon not unique to this site but emblematic of broader environmental and cultural challenges. Today, over 90 percent of the food and supplies needed to sustain Hawaiʻi's population arrives by sea or air, raising significant concerns about food security. This has prompted a collaborative effort between landscape architects and Indigenous practitioners to restore the ecological and cultural benefits of this historic *loʻi kalo* site in Limahuli Valley—an initiative underway to breathe new life into an ancestral technology. Pōhaku, Kalo, Wai: Stewardship in Contemporary Hawaiʻi represents a partnership between designer Joshua Diem, director of Limahuli Garden & Preserve Lei Wann, and a team of local knowledge keepers, blending contemporary tools with traditional wisdom to revitalize a critically important piece of agroecological infrastructure for future generations.

Beyond its agricultural value, the integral role of taro (*Colocasia esculenta*), a keystone in the *loʻi kalo* land system, holds immense importance in shaping Hawaiʻi's physical landscape and cultural identity, with roots dating to the initial settlement of Hawaiʻi. The earliest Polynesians adapted to diverse environments, constructing agricultural systems reflecting each ecosystem's characteristics. In river valleys like Limahuli, alluvial floodplains suited taro cultivation. By altering water flow, wetland *kalo* became a staple, symbolizing the deep cultural connection to the land. These irrigation systems evolved over generations, reflecting the cumulative knowledge and environmental adaptation of the *makaʻāinana* (people of the land).

This restoration honors traditional ecological knowledge passed down through generations to rebuild a 2.8 acre *loʻi kalo* complex in Hāʻena. The remnant landscape architecture of the site consists of over one hundred terraces that are fed by a single perennial spring and series of ephemeral drainages. These terraces are constructed of rough stone and hard pack clay—a style known as *uhau humu pōhaku*.

The project, which started in 2024 and is ongoing, consists of several phases; its overarching ambition is to clear invasive forest canopy, restore stone walls under the direction of *uhau humu pōhaku* practitioners, and, finally, to return water to open *loʻi* patches. The initial phase of the restoration will reopen the *puna wai* (freshwater spring), the system's primary water source. Concurrently, the structural revitalization of several features will take place: the *ʻauwai puhi* (main irrigation ditch) responsible for delivering water to the entire wetland complex, a small stone aqueduct and check dam, and the first tier of *loʻi* patches.

Using advanced mapping techniques and extensive fieldwork, the team has decoded the intricate water-flow system and uncovered the site's original architectural framework, paving the way for a full-scale restoration effort. This research process was carried out through extensive landscape fieldwork, including global navigation satellite system (GNSS) field data collection, LiDAR imagery data processing, existing archaeological reports, and extensive ground truthing. Recording the size, spacing, and elevation of each terrace and key landscape feature, set against topographical information, allowed for the deciphering of water flow, and thus how the system functions.

Positioned on land designated for conservation, the approach is novel, integrating this historical agricultural system into contemporary agricultural and conservation practices to both restore the architecture and create a haven for species of the surrounding ecosystem. This includes endangered *ʻoʻopu* (Hawaiian freshwater goby), *ʻōpae* (Hawaiian freshwater shrimp), *ʻamaʻama* (flathead gray mullet), and several endangered waterbird species. A reestablished *loʻi kalo* also nourishes forest plantings during periods of drought and uses natural drainage to improve soil fertility.

Today, the type and location of this *loʻi kalo* complex is unique and highly endangered. Other active *loʻi kalo* exist exclusively in marshy lowlands—nowhere else in Hawaiʻi can one be found *mauka* (mountain side). This restoration holds significance beyond the mere physical transformation of the Limahuli Valley site. It symbolizes the revival of ancestral farming practices and passive food production—a significant stride toward reestablishing the many self-sustaining agricultural systems that have deep roots in Hawaiʻi's history. Pōhaku, Kalo, Wai: Stewardship in Contemporary Hawaiʻi is a compelling example of the growing number of collaborative restoration initiatives that employ an integrated approach to stewarding Hawaiʻi's future, bridging traditional knowledge with contemporary technology to build community resilience for generations to come.

LiDAR
Light Detection and Ranging is an active remote sensing system that can be used to measure vegetation height across wide areas.

REF. PAGE 484

Stone terracing technologies constructed along watersheds cultivate endemic keystone species, while nourishing surrounding ecologies during drought and improving soil fertility.

CONCLUSION

THE INTELLIGENCE OF WATER

Water is not a passive element but a living intelligence. Water moves dynamically—swelling with the tides daily, rising with the moon monthly, replenishing the land through seasonal floods, withdrawing in times of drought, and, when displaced, returning to restore lost connections. Recognizing these patterns requires deep observation—a practice cultivated by Indigenous communities over generations.

Across time and territories, civilizations have worked in close commune with water. The Aztec capital of Tenochtitlán once flourished atop an intricate system of lakes, *chinampas*, and canals by evolving a blueprint for building with water. When colonial forces drained the capital's lakes and forced its rivers underground, they turned a thriving, water-adapted civilization into a city now sinking under its own infrastructural load. The story of once saturated settlements—like London, Jakarta, and Venice—now swollen into sinking cities has repeated across the globe. Water's absence has fostered urban instability, ecological collapse, and widespread water insecurity.

The climate crisis is amplifying these consequences, as rising sea levels threaten entire nations, droughts devastate food systems, and aging urban infrastructures fail under the impact of extreme weather. These conditions were not unforeseen. Long before climate science developed predictive models, Indigenous prophecies warned of this moment—the Hopi spoke of a time when water would turn against humanity, while the Anishinaabe's Seventh Fire Prophecy described a crossroads between renewal or destruction.

ANISHINAABE
A large group of Indigenous people that span from Quebec to the Rocky Mountains, down to Oklahoma and up to Ottawa.

Water has always carried these warnings. It does not die alone; when it is poisoned, obstructed, or exploited, it takes entire ecosystems and communities with it. The question is whether humanity will listen in time to restore its balance.

AN EPOCH OF ANCESTRAL INTELLIGENCE

Alongside big tech, the Age of TEKnology—synthesizing traditional ecological knowledge with contemporary design—is arriving, offering a critical yet missing alternative to industrialized approaches. This epoch will not reject contemporary innovation, but redefine technology as an entity that coexists with and enhances natural systems rather than destroying them. This volume serves as a field guide for this time of TEKnologists—practitioners who apply TEK to solve environmental, agricultural, architectural, and social challenges. It documents Indigenous water technologies that have sustained human settlements for thousands of years, explores contemporary architectural and ecological projects that integrate TEK into modern climate adaptation strategies, and provides structured frameworks for integrating TEK into policy, planning, and education.

Lo—TEK, Water begs the question—what if cities could remember? The principles that once shaped Tenochtitlán—its floating gardens, permeable landscapes, and water-woven design—offer more than a relic of the past; they present a blueprint for the future. Rooted in Lo—TEK, these ancestral technologies did not seek to control or conquer water but to exist in reciprocity with it. They embraced porosity over pavement, adaptation over rigidity, and regeneration over depletion. The *chinampas* of Tenochtitlán were not just agricultural fields; they were living infrastructures, filtering water, sequestering carbon, and sustaining entire ecosystems. Across the world, Indigenous settlements have been built on these same foundations—from the stilted homes of the Wale I Asi people of the Solomon Islands to the tidal rice terraces of Ifugao, Philippines—each a testament to an urbanism that thrives in sync with nature's rhythms. In reclaiming these principles, as exemplified in the contemporary TEK-infused projects presented in this book, a glimpse is offered to how cities today can evolve beyond extraction and crisis toward a model that is resilient, biocultural, and alive.

The ancestral technologies and contemporary TEK-infused projects profiled are deeply rooted in their local landscapes, yet they share fundamental patterns that define Indigenous nature-based technologies. As Tyson Yunkaporta highlights in *Sand Talk*, true understanding lies not just in individual elements but in the relational forces that connect them—patterns that exist beyond linear time and offer insight for sustainable design.[1] By recognizing these ancestral patterns as a set of industry specifications, designers can shift from extractive practices toward relationships of reciprocity and regeneration. The following specifications synthesize these underlying principles, framing them as living, coevolutionary, symbiotic, co-energetic, and cyclical ancestral renewables.

TEKnology Is Living

Technology is composed of complex, responsive, and emergent interactions between biological organisms and their environments, sustaining life through entire material cycles. This aligns closely with Indigenous perspectives, where technology is viewed not as a collection of tools but as a dynamic process deeply interconnected with the natural world. For Indigenous peoples, these systems are manifestations of a vital life force—a continuous flow of energy that shapes relationships and fosters balance between people, land, and ecosystems. This force, known by many names worldwide, is integral to how human societies interact with and adapt to their environments.

In Melanesia and Polynesia, this life force is called *mana*, a sacred energy that binds all aspects of existence, from the natural world to the human spirit.[2] *Mana* emphasizes the interconnectedness of all things, where power is not isolated but shared between individuals, communities, and the environment. Similarly, the Haudenosaunee (Iroquois) understand this force as *orenda*, a dynamic energy that exists in all living things and the world itself, requiring balance and respect to maintain harmony.[3] The Lakota refer to this energy as *wakan*, meaning sacred or imbued with power. *Wakan* is a vital force that exists in everything—from stones to skies—and is central to Lakota ceremonies and essential for maintaining harmony.[4] The Anishinaabe recognize this force as *manitou*, a pervasive presence that connects all aspects of the natural world. *Manitou* guides actions and decisions, with respect and reciprocity being fundamental to maintaining life's balance and ensuring sustainability.[5]

This understanding of technology as living, dynamic, and interconnected is fundamental to Indigenous ways of relating to the earth. Indigenous technologies are not static but living systems that evolve in response to environmental, social, and ecological changes. These technologies foster resilience by adapting to their surroundings, ensuring sustainability and long-term balance with the natural world. These technologies are living, breathing systems, flowing with the rhythms of place, weaving a continuous thread of connection that carries communities into a future rooted in wisdom.

TEKnology Is Coevolutionary

Indigenous water technologies are intentionally designed to persist across generations by adapting to environmental extremes. These systems are coevolutionary, developing in continuous relationship with both their ecosystems and communities, influencing ways of living, knowing, and adapting. In contrast, modern infrastructure and fossil fuel–based technologies resist adaptation, disrupt ecological balance, and become obsolete over time. While industrial systems degrade and contribute to environmental collapse, coevolutionary technologies foster resilience, guiding human evolution toward reciprocal and regenerative relationships with the earth.

A coevolutionary system is exemplified by the *chinampas* agricultural floating gardens, constructed on shallow lakes by the Nahua, and designed to adapt to fluctuating water levels, ensuring productive land during flood and drought. Over time, this technology evolved to meet these environmental challenges, continuously adjusting to the needs of the people and the land—playing a crucial role in the growth of the Aztec empire. As the empire expanded, these agricultural islands became vital for supporting large populations in cities like Tenochtitlán. The resilience of the *chinampas* was key to sustaining the food supply for this urban center, which relied on the continuous production of crops from these adaptive gardens. The relationship between the people, the technology, and the ecosystem was deeply integrated, with each influencing and shaping the other. The *chinampas* showcase the value of coevolutionary systems, which foster long-term sustainability through adaptability. The Nahua's Indigenous water technologies embody how human societies can work in harmony with their environments to ensure resilience.

TEKnology Is Symbiotic

Symbiotic systems optimize reciprocal relationships to sustain and regenerate ecosystems, leveraging biological interdependencies to create exponentially generative networks. For instance, wetland filtration systems integrate microbial, plant, and animal interactions to cleanse water while creating biodiverse habitats.

Floating agricultural islands harness symbiotic exchanges between crops, aquatic organisms, and microbial communities, forming self-sustaining nutrient cycles that increase fertility over time.

Indigenous knowledge systems encode these complex symbiotic relationships within myth, storytelling, and ritual, offering a framework for ecological sciences that extends beyond empirical observation into lived experience. These narratives function as ecological blueprints, guiding communities in their interactions with the environment. By embedding ecological science within mythology, Indigenous cultures ensure that symbiotic design principles are not just understood but revered as practices that harmonize human activity with the self-organizing intelligence of nature.

By designing with symbiosis, ancestral innovations demonstrate how architecture and infrastructure can move beyond extraction and depletion, instead cultivating regenerative, self-perpetuating ecologies that expand in productivity, resilience, and biodiversity. These systems are not built to dominate nature but to participate in its intricate web of relationships, allowing humans to function as cocreators within ecosystems that thrive through mutualism, adaptation, and balance.

TEKnology Is Coenergetic

Unlike industrial systems that extract, consume, and deplete, ancestral water technologies harness nonexploitative, reciprocal energy flows—working with, rather than against, natural forces. These systems are coenergetic, meaning they opportunistically integrate human ingenuity with ecological intelligence to create infrastructures that generate, rather than exhaust, resources. From the gravitational pull of the moon that maintains tidal rhythms to the metabolic cycles of microbial communities that purify water, Indigenous technologies are designed to work in close choreography with the earth's dynamic energy systems.

By aligning with natural energy flows, these infrastructures operate through passive hydrodynamics, biological filtration, and solar or geothermal interactions. Agricultural islands regulate nutrient cycles through the exchange of organic matter, fish, and crops. Tidal weirs synchronize with the lunar cycle, allowing water levels to replenish fish stocks without over extraction. Each of these processes mirrors the principles of coenergetic exchange found in ecosystems—where energy is cycled, transferred, and regenerated rather than lost.

Beyond the physical structures, Indigenous knowledge encodes these coenergetic principles within oral traditions, ceremonies, and place-based mythologies. Stories of water deities and ancestral spirits often correspond to precise hydrological and meteorological patterns, serving as reminders to guide sustainable water management. By embedding environmental energy cycles into cultural mythologies, Indigenous communities maintain a long-term, adaptive relationship with their ecosystems, ensuring that technologies work opportunistically with climatic changes. By designing with coenergetic principles, regenerative, self-sustaining systems can amplify the living landscapes they inhabit—where interconnected cycles fuel abundance rather than exhaustion.

Time in Indigenous systems is not linear but governed by the rhythms of nature. Seasonal flooding renews soils, tidal flows shape fishing and farming cycles, and intergenerational stewardship ensures longevity. These practices align with the cyclical patterns of the earth, where life is constantly renewed and replenished. In stark contrast, industrialized water management systems operate on a linear model of extraction, leading to overconsumption and eventual collapse. This linear approach disregards the natural cycles that sustain life, focusing instead on never-ending exploitation and depletion.

While modern societies view time as a linear progression from past to present to future, Indigenous knowledge systems recognize time as cyclical—a sequence of renewal, measured by celestial movements and ecological rhythms. Ancestral civilizations coevolved technologies with these cycles, attuned to the ebb and flow of oceanic tides, the daily shifts of solar rays, the seasonal pulses of monsoonal rains, and the metabolic rhythms of living organisms. These technologies do not seek to control nature but coexist in dynamic equilibrium, respecting the natural world's self-regulating forces.

SUMERIAN
A member of the Indigenous non-Semitic people of ancient Babylonia.

Linear time, a concept born with the Sumerians and further amplified through colonialism, shifted human progress away from cyclical regeneration toward unrelenting extraction.[6] This shift birthed industrial infrastructures that severed humanity's connection to nature's regenerative cycles. Yet Indigenous knowledge, passed down through myth and oral traditions, offers a different understanding—one where humans are not superior manipulators of nature but equal participants in an unfolding, interconnected creation. This view emphasizes balance and reciprocity, offering a holistic framework that aligns with the natural world's inherent rhythms.

Many Indigenous prophecies, such as the Anishinaabe Seventh Fire and the Hopi Fifth World, reflect this cyclical understanding of time. These narratives, born from millennia of careful observation, echo the predictions of modern climate science, recognizing that humanity stands at the crossroads of either renewal or destruction. Water, the carrier of memory, has witnessed past mass extinctions and planetary recoveries. It teaches that survival depends on aligning with its rhythms—listening, adapting, and ultimately returning to the role of protector rather than exploiter. Today's move toward renewable energy sources like solar, wind, and tidal power signals a shift toward hybrid-time technologies, where industrial systems begin to reconcile with nature's cycles. Indigenous infrastructures, already built on principles of regeneration, offer sustainable solutions for surviving and thriving in a warming world.

THE URGENCY OF PROTECTING INDIGENOUS INTELLECTUAL PROPERTY

If TEK is to inform contemporary climate solutions, its knowledge holders must be rightfully recognized and compensated. IIP cannot be safeguarded by Western legal systems alone, which prioritize written agreements over oral traditions and collective obligations.

1

2

The *Symbiocene* project, commissioned by the City of London for the Barbican's *Our Time on Earth* exhibition in 2022, introduced SOU as a legal and technical innovation to protect IIP. The SOU is a nine-part oral contract designed to replace traditional legal frameworks like memorandums of understanding (MOU) with a more culturally aligned, ethically grounded approach. It ensures that Indigenous cultural and intellectual property remains with its rightful owners, emphasizing consent, self-determined value, reparations, and collective obligation rooted in oral traditions.

Inspired by "smart contracts" stored on public blockchains, the SOU envisions a future where oral oaths are transformed into binding agreements through blockchain technology, ensuring security, transparency, and sustainability. By integrating policy-related provenance-tracing tools, it aims to create a new standard for ethical design collaborations with Indigenous communities and their TEK. The full transcript of the SOU, published in the section, titled "Future Directions," following the conclusion, as an open-source oral contract, serves as a template for designers and organizations seeking to engage with Indigenous communities in a just and reciprocal manner.

As we shift towards honoring IIP through models like the SOU, we begin to recognize that protecting this knowledge is not just a legal or ethical obligation but a call to reconnect with the earth's rhythms. This reconnection extends beyond intellectual property; it's a call to honor the wisdom that has sustained ecosystems and human societies for millennia. Integrating TEK into contemporary climate solutions protects not only the knowledge but also the life-giving relationships that sustain planetary systems. In doing so, the potential is unlocked for a future where technology, culture, and nature coevolve in harmony, and the survival of our cities and ecosystems becomes a testament to the power of collective, regenerative cocreation.

CUSTODIANS OF AN ANCESTRAL FUTURE

Water has always remembered. It recalls the buried waterways that once sustained cities, the farming of its fertile floodplains that nourished civilizations, and the ancient aquifers that have cradled communities for millennia. It also recollects a time when it was cared for, when it was respected, when it was understood.

Now, it is humanity that must remember.

We stand at a branch in the river of time—one stream runs blackened with the filth of extractive, short-term technological solutions, while the other channel flows toward a return to water's intelligence. The TEK-infused projects and ancestral technologies explored here are not merely examples; they are blueprints for survival, forged from the understanding that humanity's future depends on reconnecting with the earth's regenerative rhythms. Yet these technologies, often rooted in reciprocal care and mutual respect, are absent from the curricula of architecture, urbanism, and engineering schools around the world. Instead, the prevailing pedagogy more often disregards the wisdom that could guide designers toward a regenerative future—keeping ancestral technologies from shaping imaginations of world dreamers, shapers, and leaders. This is a call

1 *Symbiocene* is a multimedia artwork that explores ideas for how people can live in the future.

2 The exhibition features scaled models animated by projection mappings that suggest how non-Indigenous designers can work with Indigenous knowledge to cocreate future technologies.

to reawaken the knowledge that has always been present, protected by the practices and stewardship of Indigenous cultures.

There are profound lessons to be learned from the absence of a singular word for nature or the earth in many Indigenous languages—an absence that reflects a worldview in which humans are inseparable from the living systems that sustain them. Rather than an object to be owned or exploited, the earth is simply called *mother* or *home*, a source of life and renewal.

With the ocean as the mother's amniotic fluid, cradling generations within her currents, water is not merely a resource but a guiding force—one that calls for reconnection and reawakens custodianship. Indigenous cultures have long recognized water as a living entity, shaping landscapes, nourishing all beings, and flowing through the cycles of time as an ancestor rather than a commodity. Yet the dominant extractivist paradigm, which seeks to control and exploit water and land for short-term gain, disrupts this enduring balance, severing the relationships that have sustained life for millennia.

In contrast, the survival of cities, coastlines, and ecosystems will not be secured by concrete dams, steel seawalls, fortified barriers, and high-tech industrial systems alone. It will require a radical reengagement with ancestral wisdom—living, regenerative, and deeply embedded in place. Moving beyond the extractivist mindset, a model of custodianship emerges that recognizes the earth's intrinsic value, not as a commodity to be consumed but as a collaborator in coevolution.

The solutions have always flowed beneath our feet, murmuring in the tides and echoing through the currents. Water is not merely a resource, nor a force to be feared—it is living, calling for us to remember, to reclaim our role as its guardian and renew the bond once meant to be honored.

ENDNOTES

1. Tyson Yunkaporta, *Sand Talk* (San Francisco: HarperOne, 2020), 79–80.
2. Ty P. Kāwika Tengan and Matt Tomlinson, eds., *New Mana: Transformations of a Classic Concept in Pacific Languages and Cultures* (n.p.: ANU Press, 2019), https://library.oapen.org/handle/20.500.12657/32433.
3. J. N. B. Hewitt, "Orenda and a Definition of Religion," *American Anthropologist 4, no. 1* (1902): 1–10, https://doi.org/10.1525/aa.1902.4.1.02a00050
4. Stephen E. Feraca, Wakinyan: Lakota Religion in the Twentieth Century (Lincoln: University of Nebraska Press, 1992).
5. Basil H. Johnston, *The Manitous: The Spiritual World of the Ojibway* (St. Paul: Minnesota Historical Society Press, 2001).
6. Ulla Susanne Koch, "Concepts and Perception of Time in Mesopotamian Divination," in Time and *History in the Ancient Near East: Proceedings of the 56th Rencontre Assyriologique Internationale, Barcelona, July 26th-30th, 2010*, ed. Lluis Feliu et al. (University Park: Penn State University Press, 2013), 127–142.

ANCESTRAL BLUEPRINTS FOR A Lo—TEK CITY

As we navigate the rising currents of a world reshaped by climate uncertainty, the wisdom of Indigenous ecological traditions offers an ancestral blueprint for resilience. Beyond theory, beyond utopianization, lies the urgent call to action—to reframe, regenerate, and reimagine settlements through the ancestral intelligence that has guided Lo—TEK. This section elucidates on two transformative frameworks that serve as bridges between ancestral knowledge and the future of the planet. These frameworks are not merely concepts; they are pathways—actionable strategies for governance, ethical collaboration, and regenerative urban design. They chart a navigable course toward an ancestral future where ecological reciprocity is woven into policy, cultural continuity informs development, and ancestral wisdom shapes all inhabited landscapes.

The first is the Lo—TEK City, which offers a scalable, adaptable framework for water-led TEKnological urbanism that seamlessly integrates aquatic ancestral ecological knowledge, regenerative infrastructure, and collective governance. Challenging conventional city planning, it promotes hyperlocal, biocultural resilience—ensuring that urban environments exist in harmony with water-rich landscapes rather than disrupting them. The model reflects the regenerative practice of Indigenous-led urban frameworks that offer insights into how cities can be designed to uphold local sovereignty while fostering aqueous ecological stewardship. The second framework is the SOU, which establishes a guiding ethical protocol for engaging with Indigenous knowledge in design, planning, and policy. It ensures that traditional ecological practices are honored, safeguarded, and applied equitably, fostering reciprocal, just, and long-term collaborations between Indigenous communities and urban practitioners. Together, these frameworks offer a paradigm shift—from extractive urban development to coevolutionary, living cities that grow, adapt, and regenerate alongside the ecosystems that sustain them.

A GUIDE TO GROWING A LO—TEK CITY

Can a city learn to live again by remembering how to honor water? A Lo—TEK City flows from this question, offering an TEKnological vision of urbanism that revives ancestral intelligence and redefines resilience. Rather than perpetuating cycles of depletion and collapse, this model reawakens the knowledge that once allowed civilizations to thrive in water-rich landscapes. By integrating TEK with contemporary urbanism, cities can transition from rigid, hydrophobic, extractive systems to adaptive, hydrophilic, living environments that coevolve with their aqueous ecosystems. Instead of resisting water, a Lo—TEK City embraces it—adopting hyperlocal water management, material sustainability, and communal stewardship to ensure long-term regeneration.

Grounded in the place-based adaptability of TEKnological Urbanism, the Lo—TEK City confronts the climate crisis by designing regenerative systems that ensure the continuity of life for future generations. Shaped by people, place and time, TEKnolgoical urbanism regenerates ecosystems while sustaining cultural continuity. It does not separate nature from design; it uses nature as the architect and culture as the engineer—expanding urbanism beyond human constructs to embrace the complex interdependencies of all living systems. TEKnological urbanism provides a powerful counterpoint to dominant planning models—one rooted in reciprocity, sovereignty, and deep ecological intelligence. These frameworks don't just mitigate climate risk; they restore landscapes, revive waterways, and reestablish cultural connections to place.

In Australia, country-centered design embodies the deep relationality between land, water, and life.[1] The Murujuga Living Knowledge Centre restores ecosystems and reinforces Indigenous governance, while cultural burning revives fire as a regenerative tool, informing climate-responsive urban strategies.[2] In Canada, biocultural resilience is central to First Nation–led planning, where the Seńáḵw development reclaims urban space for the Squamish Nation, and the Thunder Bay Indigenous Friendship Centre interweaves Anishinaabe design with regenerative sustainability.[3, 4]

In Aotearoa (New Zealand), Māori urbanism follows the Te Aranga Māori Design Principles, embedding *kaitiakitanga* (guardianship) into city making.[5] The Auckland Waterfront Revitalization restores biodiversity while recentering Māori narratives, and the Whanganui River Settlement, which grants the river legal personhood, redefines governance beyond human law.[6] In the United States, land rematriation and self-determined urbanism reclaim space through projects like the Tamien Nation's Urban Land Back Initiative and the Thunder Valley Regenerative Community Plan, where water sovereignty, renewable energy, and self-sufficient housing establish new models for Indigenous-led futures.

These frameworks are beyond theoretical—they are blueprints for a Lo—TEK City, proving that urbanism can be reciprocal, regenerative, and deeply intelligent. By embracing these regenerative practices, cities can shift from extractive to symbiotic, imposed to adaptive, forging a future where human settlements thrive in deep alignment with nature. The following section explores the 10 principles that guide TEKnological urbanism for a Lo—TEK City. Organized thematically, these principles move from foundational cultural and governance frameworks to spatial design, material systems, and ecological technologies. Each principle builds on Indigenous knowledge systems and water-based logics, offering a layered and interconnected framework.

1. Spirituality, Mythology, and Cultural Continuity

Cultural and Spiritual Design: The city recognizes that human settlements are not only functional but also deeply cultural and spiritual, reflecting the interconnectedness of people, place, and the more-than-human world. Design honors the recognition of land and water as living entities, embedding spiritual and ecological relationships into urban form.

Sacred Geographies and Cultural Continuity: The city's design honors sacred landscapes, ritual spaces, and culturally significant waterways as central to its urban identity. Informed by ancestral geospatial systems and celestial alignments, the urban configuration reflects Indigenous worldviews that recognize land and water as living entities. Mythologies and storytelling traditions are interwoven into public spaces, fostering a deep connection to ancestral knowledge and promoting environmental stewardship. Economic and governance systems are designed to prioritize and protect these sacred relationships, ensuring their continued care and renewal for future generations.

Water as Foundation: Water is understood not only as a resource but as a guiding force in shaping the urban environment. Design acknowledges water's memory and movement, integrating hydrological patterns into the city's structure while upholding its cultural and spiritual significance.

2. Collective Governance and Indigenous Codesign

Collaborative Knowledge Systems: Urban planning is guided by a process of cocreation with Indigenous and local communities, ensuring long-term ecological health and intergenerational knowledge exchange. Governance models are distributed and commons-based, while respecting local self-determination and upholding local leadership in decision-making.

Ethical Protocols of Engagement: Design and planning processes are anchored in culturally appropriate, trust-based protocols that honor Indigenous sovereignty, protect knowledge integrity, and guarantee benefits for Indigenous communities. These frameworks prioritize transparency, reciprocity, and shared benefit, fostering relationships that are not extractive but regenerative and rooted in long-term accountability.

Holistic Water Management: Water stewardship is informed by traditional ecological knowledge, ensuring that water governance reflects both practical management and cultural responsibilities. Cities embed legal protections for water systems, ensuring their regeneration and ongoing stewardship.

3. Commons-Based Resource Management

Collective Stewardship: Land, water, and air are managed as shared responsibilities rather than privatized commodities. Stewardship-based governance structures ensure that ecological systems remain in balance, sustaining life for future generations.

Water as Sacred and Shared: Water is treated as a communal trust, safeguarded through principles of reciprocity and responsibility. Urban design ensures access to clean water as a fundamental right while restoring natural hydrological systems.

4. Ancestral Technologies as Innovation

Water Wisdom as Technology: Traditional water systems—such as flood-based farming, aquifer-fed irrigation, water-cleansing landscapes, and water-harvesting landscapes—are revitalized, adapting their principles and hybridizing their systems to blend with high-tech to address contemporary urban challenges.

Regenerative Infrastructure: Cities embrace water management systems that mirror natural hydrological cycles, allowing infrastructure to support rather than disrupt the ecological processes that sustain life.

5. Indigenous Multispecies Urbanism

Coexistence with Nature: Cities are designed to complement the natural abilities of all life forms, integrating natural corridors, pollinator-friendly habitats, and biodiverse landscapes that support ecological resilience.

Waterways as Living Corridors: Rivers, wetlands, and aquifers are restored as interconnected lifelines that support biodiversity, filter pollutants, and ensure ecological abundance.

Infrastructures Embed Indigenous Ecologies: Urban ecological restoration integrates Indigenous knowledge, food system, traditional water and land management, and stewardship.

Indigenous Foodways and Culinary Revitalization: By centering Indigenous ecological knowledge, cities can cultivate resilient food networks that support both environmental restoration and the revival of local food systems. This includes fostering the growth of Indigenous culinary spaces and prioritizing culturally significant plant species used in Indigenous cuisine and medicine—restoring native ecologies while nourishing cultural continuity.

6. Water-Centered Urban Planning

Aligning with Water and Cosmos: The city's layout is shaped by the rhythms of water and sky, aligning with celestial cycles and seasonal hydrological shifts to ensure resilience and balance.

Water-Responsive Organization: Cities are planned with water at their core, integrating rivers, wetlands, and aquifers into the built environment rather than forcing water into rigid containment.

Responsive Water Forms: The built environment reflects the seasonal flow of rivers, floodplains, and underground water channels, allowing natural hydrological systems to guide development.

Dynamic Urban Evolution: Infrastructure remains flexible, adapting over time as ecological conditions shift, ensuring that urban systems remain in harmony with land and water.

7. Living Systems over Concrete Structures

Nature-Based Solutions: Urban environments prioritize regenerative, land-based systems—such as polder dike wetlands and floating islands—over static, industrial infrastructure.

Indigenous Climate Infrastructures: Climate infrastructures built to protect cities are constructed from the DNA of the site, opportunistically scaling the systems and infrastructures that are native to place. They passively generate energy while being stewarded by local communities.

Sacred Waterways and Ecological Pathways: The city's mobility and movement systems are guided by its natural hydrology, treating rivers, lakes, and wetlands as sacred corridors that shape urban life. Rather than disrupting these flows, infrastructure is elevated or adaptive—working with the landscape to maintain ecological continuity. These pathways not only facilitate human movement but also sustain multispecies relationships, reinforcing the city's spiritual and environmental integration with water.

8. Water-Based Materials and Bioclimatic Architecture

Locally Sourced Materials: Construction prioritizes natural, regionally available materials that provide thermal efficiency and durability while reducing environmental impact and the threat from climate-induced catastrophic events.

Climate-Responsive Water Design: The built environment incorporates passive water management techniques, using architecture to capture, filter, and store water while naturally regulating temperature and humidity.

Water-Efficient Construction: The use of biodegradable and water-sensitive materials supports resource conservation, ensuring that buildings regenerate rather than deplete ecological systems.

9. Industrial Symbiosis and Regenerative Cycles of Production

Waste as Resource: Urban economies function as regenerative loops, ensuring that materials, energy, and nutrients continuously cycle rather than being extracted and discarded.

Circular Production Models: Industrial processes are restructured to integrate ecological wisdom, ensuring that urban production systems align with the regenerative cycles of the land and land management systems.

Decentralized Production Hubs: Cities transition away from centralized, high-impact industries, fostering hyperlocally scalable, low-impact production that supports local economies and ecosystem health.

10. Regenerative Water, Energy, and Waste Systems

Water as Energy: Water is understood as a force for regeneration, supporting sustainable energy systems that integrate hydrological, tidal, and solar cycles into urban infrastructure.

Circular Water Systems: Water continuously cycles through the landscape, with purification and reuse systems ensuring that urban environments remain hydrologically self-sufficient.

Waste-to-Energy: Organic waste is transformed into resources that nourish ecosystems, support food production, and generate clean energy, fostering a self-sustaining urban metabolism.

Indigenous Green Energy Sector: Indigenous climate infrastructures expand the green-energy job sector in combination with environmental stewardship, Indigenous food security, and the provision of municipal services.

As cities confront the cascading pressures of climate disruption, biodiversity loss, and cultural disconnection, the search for new urban paradigms has become not only urgent but existential. Over the past decades, Ecological Urbanism and Landscape Urbanism have emerged as thoughtful responses—offering frameworks that emphasize systems thinking, adaptive design, and the integration of natural processes into the built environment. These approaches have moved the field beyond static planning toward dynamic, performative, and resilient strategies that seek to align urban form with ecological function. They have expanded our vocabulary of sustainability, calling for landscapes that filter, cool, absorb, and adapt.

Yet while these paradigms have advanced critical progress, they often remain rooted in technocratic, human-centered logics that view nature as resource, infrastructure, or aesthetic. Their interventions, though ecologically informed, risk operating within colonial frameworks that extract from Indigenous knowledge without re-centering Indigenous presence. They speak of resilience, but often without relational reciprocity. They design with nature, but rarely with culture—especially the cultures of place-based peoples whose knowledge systems have shaped regenerative relationships for millennia.

TEKnological Urbanism arises as an evolution of these frameworks—carrying forward their commitments to ecological integration and systems thinking, but grounding them in deeper relational, spiritual, and cultural foundations. Rooted in Traditional Ecological Knowledge (TEK), TEKnological Urbanism reimagines the city as a living, sacred system where water governs form, land is rematriated, and design emerges from reciprocal relationships with place, rather than imposed onto it. It centers biocultural resilience, ancestral intelligence, and ethical co-design—offering not only climate adaptation strategies but pathways to cultural resurgence and collective healing.

Tenochtitlán offers a vivid ancestral blueprint for this evolution. Once a thriving water-based city built atop lakes and canals, its *chinampas* were not merely agricultural fields, but dynamic infrastructures—filtering water, supporting biodiversity, and adjusting with seasonal floods. The Nahua people's coevolutionary relationship with water gave rise to a metropolis designed to move with, rather than against, ecological rhythms. But when colonial powers drained the lakes and forced rivers underground, that harmony was broken—leaving a legacy of urban instability that echoes today in the sinking sprawl of modern Mexico City.

TEKnological Urbanism asks: what if cities could remember? What if urban design could once again be shaped by porousness, reciprocity, and reverence for the more-than-human world? This paradigm does not reject ecological or landscape urbanism, but matures them—rooting them in intercultural

1 A 3D reconstruction westward toward Chapultepec of Tenochtitlan in 1518—just before Spanish colonization—shows one of the world's largest cities at the time, with over 200,000 residents supported by a tribute system of five million people. The vibrant Aztec capital is a canal-based city woven with *chinampas* and waterways.

2 A 2023 aerial view west toward Chapultepec shows Mexico City sprawled over a drained lake system, where roads replaced canals and urban growth erased the island's edge—leaving a sinking city with chronic water shortages.

1

2

dialogue, biocultural restoration, and Indigenous futurity. It invites a return to relational infrastructures and sacred technologies that co-evolve with climate, culture, and kin. In this fusion lies the potential to co-create truly regenerative cities: places where ecology and culture are inseparable, where urbanism is not only sustainable, but symbiotic. By embracing this paradigm, cities can move beyond mitigation toward restoration—reweaving land, water, governance, and kinship into urban life, and realizing futures where cities do not merely sustain life, but actively regenerate it.

ENDNOTES

1. "International Indigenous Design Charter," Indigenous Design Charter, accessed March 20, 2025, https://indigenousdesigncharter.com.au/.
2. Mary T. P. McDonald et al., "Cultural Fire and Ecosystem Restoration: Integrating Indigenous Fire Management into Ecosystem Restoration and Governance," *Ecology and Society 28, no. 1* (2023): 17, https://doi.org/10.5751/ES-13701-280117.
3. Squamish Nation, "Seńáḵw Development," accessed March 21, 2025, https://senakw.com/.
4. Thunder Bay Indigenous Friendship Centre, "Home," accessed March 21, 2025, https://tbifc.ca/.
5. "Te Aranga Māori Design Principles," Auckland Design Manual, accessed March 20, 2025, https://www.aucklanddesignmanual.co.nz/en/places-and-spaces/m_ori-design/te-aranga-principles.html.
6. Miriama Cribb, Elizabeth Macpherson, and Axel Borchgrevink, "Beyond Legal Personhood for the Whanganui River," *Environmental Law Review 26, no. 2* (2024): 123–45, https://www.tandfonline.com/doi/full/10.1080/13642987.2024.2314532.

A SMART OATH OF UNDERSTANDING (SOU)

The following transcript introduces the SOU, a groundbreaking approach to safeguarding Indigenous Intellectual Property (IIP) in design, planning, and policy. Developed as part of the Symbiocene project for the Barbican's *Our Time on Earth* exhibition, the SOU reimagines legal agreements through an oral, blockchain-supported framework rooted in Indigenous traditions. By replacing conventional memorandums of understanding (MOUs) with a culturally aligned, ethically grounded alternative, the SOU ensures rightful ownership, consent, and equitable collaboration. This transcript serves as an open-source template for those seeking to engage with Indigenous knowledge holders in a way that prioritizes respect, reciprocity, and long-term stewardship.

Part 1: Introduction and Invocation

I, [insert name and role], who represents and has the authority to speak for and bind [insert name of entity], being [insert name of legal entity] and its associated entities, stand before you, [insert name of addressee], who represents the [insert name of community/people]. [Recognize any other individuals, entities, ancestors, and places customarily recognized.]

Part 2: Recognition of Valuable Technology

Your people and your ancestors have developed [insert name of traditional ecological technology]. Your sacred technology provides your people, the [insert name of community/people] with many amazing benefits, including [highlight key features and benefits].

Part 3: Realization of Opportunity to Learn

I believe that we can learn from your technology and that it can help us bring many benefits to other people around the world. Through my organization, which is a company of [insert company member's role], I would like to request your permission, on behalf of your people, for [insert name of entity] to learn from and use, for research and communication, your technology and ideas.

Part 4: Proposed Collaborative Manner of Working Together

If you permit us to do so, we will learn from you in a cooperative and collaborative manner in good faith, and in the spirit of trust and respect. We agree to resolve any difficulties, disputes, or disagreements by working together in good faith. Our hope is that our cooperation and collaboration will serve as a living example of the possibility for sustainable development of universally beneficial ecological technology. We pledge that our overriding goal in this collaboration is to benefit humanity and for the common good of our shared earth.

Part 5: Pledge to Equitably Share Profits and Created Value

If you permit us to learn from your technology, and we collaboratively develop helpful ideas, proposals, and documentation that generate profits directly from your technology, then we will equitably and proportionately share those profits (amounts we generate after accounting for the costs and expenses of developing the technology) with [insert name of community expert] and your people, the [insert name of community/people]. The value created from our collaborative engagement with your technology will be identified, defined, and tracked with the goal of equitably and proportionately sharing such created value and all associated short-term and long-term benefits.

Part 6: Use of Public Blockchain to Enforce Terms of Oath

To guarantee and assure you that we will continue to equitably share any profits derived directly arising from your technology with your people, we are happy for our agreement to be memorialized on a public blockchain. Where there is a profit arising from our use of your technology, a smart contract will be set up in a form that is reflective of this oath and supported by policy-related provenance-tracing technologies that are transparently encoded.

Part 7: Potential Formation of Decentralized Autonomous Organization Committee for In-Kind Distributions

Because we wish to give you the flexibility to accept our gratitude and your rightful share of the profits directly arising from your technology in a form that best and most authentically benefits your community, at the relevant time when there may be such profits, we may by mutual consultation establish an independent committee of experts, which we invite you to attend and participate in, to determine the needs and interests of your community. This committee may be governed through a decentralized autonomous organization, where possible, on the same public blockchain on which the oath is recorded. With your permission, and following the advice of the committee, we will distribute any profits and create value to you in a manner you specify.

Part 8: Request For Assent and a Meeting of Minds

Pursuant to these terms and in furtherance of our overriding principle of benefiting humanity and the common good of our shared earth, I, who represents and has the authority to speak for and bind [insert name of entity], ask that you, [insert name of addressee], who represents the [insert name of community/people] grant [insert name of entity] permission to cooperatively and collaboratively learn from and use your technology and ideas.

Part 9: Proposed Acknowledgment [Spoken in Indigenous Dialect]

[Cultural greeting]. I, [insert name] who represents the [insert name of community/people] from [place/location], understand your proposal to learn from and use, for research and communication, our technology and ideas, collaboratively develop solutions and equitably share profits, and I agree to work together on these terms in the interest of benefiting humanity and the common good of our shared earth.

IMAGE CREDITS

Lo—TEK WATER A FIELD GUIDE FOR TEKNOLOGY

Image Credit Name and Surname

Cover Image

Image Credit Name

Introduction

Image Credit Name

Introduction

Abdelhakim (Hakim) Issaoui 102 top, 106 top, 113; Abraham Jacob M/Picxy 192 top left; Adam Jones 228, 230 top; Adeng Bustomi 300 bottom,309, 310; Adobe Stock/Somnath 377 top; Adriana Zehbrauskas/NYT/Redux/laif348 top; AG-ChapelHill/iStock 466; Akhil Kulkarni 137, 138, 139, 140, 141, 149, 150, 153, 456; AL-Travelpicture/iStock 233 bottom; Aloysius Guchbuw 58 right top, 59 top, 65; Amelie Ferrier 73 right; Amina Chouairi 204, 213 bottom, 217, 218; Anders Ryman/Alamy Stock Photo 63; Andrew Klaver 442 bottom; Andy Maser 260 bottom; Ann Marie Kirk 120; Anna Sarzetto 212 top; Anoop Negi 135; Antoli Studio/Arca Tierra 344 bottom; Anton Ivanov/Alamy Stock Photo 229 bottom; Arayilpdas/Wikimedia 184; Arca Tierra 345 bottom; Arco/F. Schneider/Alamy Stock Photo 54; Ayu Prestasia 307 top; BackyardProduction/iStock 127; Bastian AS/Shutterstock 308; benedek/Getty Images 88; Bensliman Hassan/Shutterstock 76 left; Beryl Shereshewsky 471; Bill Jeffrey 55 top, 56, 58 right bottom, 59 bottom, 448; BlackBoxGuild 545 bottom; Blond Ninon 417; Bloomberg/Getty Images 325 top; Brandon Denina Pundamiera 38 top, 40, 44, 49, 451; Brett Cole 482; Cameron Judith Peters 449; Carl Court/Getty Images 320; Carles Enirch Studio, Adrià Goula 477; Cecilia Jimenez 469; César Hernández Hernández 337; CGH Earth Experience 178; Chao-Feng Lin/iStock 232, 233; Charly Triballeau/Getty Images 319 left, 321 bottom, 329 left; Christian Bickel 229 top; Chuanzhi Sun 403 top; Clotilde Audroing Philippe 77 top; CTK/Alamy Stock Photo 431 bottom; Cum Okolo/Alamy Stock Photo 436 right; Daniel James Clark 343, 349; Daniel Patlán 350 bottom; Danny Ye/Alamy Stock Photo 385 top; David Fleetham/Alamy Stock Photo 289 bottom right; David Hosana/Shutterstock 472, 475; Davide Tocchetto 459; Deshakal Yan Chowdhury/AFP/Getty Images 386 top; Development Workshop Digital Archive 230 bottom right; Dinodia Photos RM/Alamy Stock Photo 180, 181; Dorothy Lubin- Lévy 173; Douglas Peebles/Alamy Stock Photo 58 left, 118; dpa picture alliance/Alamy Stock Photo 280, 282 bottom right; Dr. Muhammad Afzal 455; Edmond Dounias 245 top; Elma Okic 398, 399 top, 401, 402 top , 404; Emerging Objects/Ronald Rael & Virginia San Fratello 467; Eric Lafforgue/Getty Images 328; Erika Alatalo 365, 368 top; Esme Allen 458; EW 289 bottom left; Fahmida Akter 269 top; FAO/Jianyi Dai/Photo-Library@fao.org 394; FAO/Shizuoka Wasabi Associaton for Important Agricultural Heritage System Promotion 318, 484; Gaël Kervarec 74; Gastone Dissette 208; Georg Berg/Alamy Stock Photo 319 right; George Steinmetz 454; GIAHS/Huzhou Mulberry-dyke and Fish Pond System 399 bottom, 402 bottom, 405; GIAHS/Shizuoka Wasabi Association for Important Agricultural Heritage Systems Promotion 321 top, 324 right, 330; Gideon Bouro 86 bottom left, 95 left; Google Earth 39, 386 bottom; Gregoire Le Bacon 159, 160, 167, 169 bottom; Gulfu Photography/Getty Images 179, 185, 464; Günter Flegar/Alamy Stock Photo 414; Hans Lucas 297, 300 top; Haobam Paban Kumar 385 bottom right; Harley I. Manner 286 bottom; Hemis/Alamy Stock Photo 76 right, 242, 248 top right, 248 bottom, 251 bottom, 358, 366, 367 top, 369 bottom; Heritage Foundation of Pakistan 457; Hi'ilei Kawelo 129 left; Holger Leu/Getty Images 92 bottom, 161; Ian Wood 81; ICARDA 421, 481; Idrees Mohammed/Getty Images 483; imageBROKER.com/Alamy Stock Photo 191; Imago/Alamy Stock Photo 403 bottom; Iman Hamikhah 235; Iniciativa Agroecológica Xochimilco A.C. 342 top; irumge 148; Ismi Fitri Hodijah/Dreamstime 296; Izanbar/Dreamstime 119 top; Jacopo Pasotti 262 top left; James B. Friday 286 top; Jamie Marshall – Tribaleye Images/Alamy Stock Photo 468; Jan Pokorný 432; Janine Tewid 284; Joaquín Enríquez 336 top, 342 center; John De Mello/Alamy Stock Photo 285 bottom; John Johnson 119 bottom; John S. Lander/Getty Images 324 left; Jordi Zaragozà Anglès 243; Joseph Johnson Bibi 255 right; Joshua Diem 485; Karel Tomicek/Shutterstock 436 left; Kathryn Larsen 445; Kerala Tourism 193; Khaing Khaing Soe 371; Kinohi Fukumitsu 129 right; leonovo/Alamy Stock Photo 359 bottom; Libor Sváček, 428, 429, 431 top; Lilia Blaise 106 bottom; Ludo Kuipers 5 bottom, 288 bottom; Manimala Chanu Asem 381, 384, 389; Mark Lee 121, 124 right; Marko Prešlenkov/Alamy Stock Photo, 46 top; Martin Michalon 361 top, 364; Matej Divizna/Getty Images 437 right, 442 top; Mauricio Ferrando 453; mauritius images/Alamy Stock Photo 248 top left, 412; Max Tala Nossin 465; Melanie Shook Dupre 169 top; Michael Bernhardt 285 top; Michael Stubblefield/Alamy Stock Photo 282 center right; Michele Zanetti 207 bottom, 221; Mickey Pauole 452; Mint Images Limited/Alamy Stock Photo 379; Mira Amira 303 bottom; Mohamed Oueasar 423; Mohammed Rezwan 272 top, 273, 275; Mountain Kingdoms Ltd 368 bottom; Myo Myint 361 bottom; Nathan Allen/Alamy Stock Photo, 45; Nicola Colonna 282 top, 282 bottom left; Nicolas Marino 250; Nicolas Marino/Alamy Stock Photo 246, 253; Nithin Thankappan/Alamy Stock Photo 192 top right; Northwest Indian Fisheries Commission 450; NurPhoto/Getty Images 264 top; Oleg Breslavtsev/Dreamstime.com 474; Omar Faruk/Alamy Stock Photo 271; Omar Wanas 418, 480; Panoramic Studio/Landprocess 473, 475; Pedro Mendez Rosas 353 left; Peter Adams/DanitaDelimont.com/Alamy Stock Photo 378 bottom; Peter Yeung 348 bottom; Philip Game/Alamy Stock Photo 90, 92 top, 93; Photo Beto 345 top; picture alliance/Associated Press/Ng Han Guan 461, 463; picture alliance/REUTER/Zohra Bensemra 415; picture alliance/Reuters/Carlos Jasso 342 bottom; picture alliance/Reuters/Jihed Abidellaoui 102 bottom, 103, 109 top right; picture alliance/Reuters/Mohammad Ponir Hossain 260 top, 262 bottom, 263, 264 bottom, 265, 268 bottom, 470; picture alliance/Reuters/Zoubeir Souissi 103 bottom; Pierre Antoine Muraccioli 158; pilesasmiles/Getty Images 378 top; Prisma by Dukas Presseagentur/Alamy Stock Photo 303 top; Queserasera99/iStock 325 bottom; Rameshchandra/Karnajit Maibam – Hueiyen Lanpao 385 bottom left; Riccardo Roiter Rigoni 213 top; Richard Sowersb /Alamy Stock Photo 195; Robert Klein 369 top; Robert Michael Poole 281; Rodrigo Alberto Lañado Cruz 353 right; Rodrigo Lañando Cruz 344 top; Roman Fohanno 77 bottom; S.H. Rashedi 476; Sam Youkilis 336 bottom; Sanand Karunakaran 192 bottom; Sandrine Gallois 245 bottom, 251 top; Sansara/iStock 301; Satoshi Tachibana 323 bottom; Saurabh Chatterjee/Picxy 387; Scott Kanda 124 left; Sergii Rudiuk/iStock 73 left; Shashank Srinivasan/iStock 136; Shiho Fukada/The New York Times/Redux/Redux/laif 323 top, 329 right; Shri RupeshKumar K 197; Simon Bourcier 71, 79; Skander Khlif 109 bottom; SkySat 444; solo84 91; Somnath Chatterjee/Alamy Stock Photo 376; Stefan Auth/Alamy Stock Photo 413; Symeon Ekizoglou 38 bottom; Taylor Luck 109 top left; Teresa Nalon 212 bottom; Thomas Kole 545 top; Thomas Schoch 360; Tim Whitby 536; Timbre/Alamy Stock Photo 289 top; Tina Manley/Alamy Stock Photo 230 bottom left; Tjetjep Rustandi/Alamy Stock Photo 307 bottom; Toby Harriman 359 top; Tonello Photography/Shutterstock 205; Travel Pix/Alamy Stock Photo 126; travelib environment/Alamy Stock Photo 377 bottom; Tsatsa Seimarlie 95 right; U.S. Department of Agriculture 288 top; Ucu Suherlan 313; Ulrich Doering/Alamy Stock Photo 478; Valentina Rocco 202, 207 top, 209; Venant Messe 255 left; volkerpreusser/Alamy Stock Photo 367 bottom; Wasim Muklashy 170/71; Westend61/Amazing Aerial 261, 262 top right; Wirestock, Inc./Alamy Stock Photo 86 top, 86 bottom right; Wison Tungthunya & W Workspace 447; WWF Tunisia 110; Xavier Bourgois/UNHCR 479; Xinhua/Alamy Stock Photo 395, 460; Yongyot Therdthai/Shutterstock, 46 botom; Zakir Hossain Chowdhury 268 top, 269 bottom, 272 bottom; Zoltan Bagosi/Alamy Stock Photo 419, 420; ZUMA Press/Alamy Stock Photo 350 top

BIOGRAPHIES

Hala Abukhodair

Abukhodair is a Saudi architect and urban designer born and raised in Riyadh, Saudi Arabia, which instilled in her a deep appreciation for the intricate balance between culture, urban landscapes, and city planning. She holds a bachelor's degree in architectural engineering, laying the foundation for her early professional experience, which included contributions to Riyadh's public transport infrastructure—a pivotal project for the region, as it is the region's largest public transport system. Later, she pursued a master's degree in urban design at Columbia University in New York City, expanding her interest in green infrastructure and sustainability. In Riyadh, her childhood was spent in air-conditioned homes. Now, Abukhodair's overarching objective is to explore innovative natural solutions that encourage and enhance people's time outdoors, aiming to bridge the gap between urban living and a harmonious connection with nature.

Naeema Ali

Ali pursued her master's degree in landscape architecture at the Delft University of Technology (TU Delft), with a focus on integrated water management. Since then, she has been working on the design, policy research, and advocacy of water-sensitive projects in Europe, Southeast Asia, and the Middle East for both the private and public sectors. Ali also works closely with international research groups and global think tanks, who look at designing a climate-proof future by applying the knowledge gained from Indigenous cultures and communities in different parts of the world. Her graduation project, *Land Can Sometimes Be Water*, exhibited at the London Design Biennale in 2021, was awarded a grant from the TU Delft Global Initiative for its contribution to sustainable development in flood zones.

Amina Chouairi

Chouairi is an Italian-Moroccan landscape architect and researcher born in Milan, currently living in Venice, Italy. She received her bachelor's degree in architecture at Politecnico di Milano and in 2020 earned her master's cum laude in landscape architecture at the TU Delft. She is currently pursuing a PhD in urbanism at Università Iuav di Venezia, where she is developing an in-depth study on the critical understanding of wet ecologies, nature-restoration projects in transitional territories, and landscape-based knowledge systems. At a young age, spending most of her childhood holidays between the coastal lagoons of Caorle and Bibione, along the coast of the Veneto region in northeastern Italy, spurred her fascination with these brackish landscapes.

Jennah Jones

Jones is a New York–based designer pursuing a master's in architecture at Columbia University's Graduate School of Architecture, Planning and Preservation (GSAPP). Her approach to architecture is deeply informed by her background in product design, where her curriculum stressed human-centered design and community partnerships rooted in reciprocity. In her academic and professional work, Jones investigates how we can change our relationship with waste and waste management through prioritizing environmental justice and the circular economy. She currently works as a waste consultant at the Center for Zero Waste Design. Previously, she has held design research positions at Julia Watson LLC, the Natural Materials Lab at Columbia GSAPP, BlocPower, and Tesla.

Boomi Kim

Kim is a South Korean landscape architect and researcher. She studied landscape architecture at Kyungpook National University in South Korea and received her master's degree from TU Delft in the Netherlands. Her research focuses on relationships between humans and nature, and how this manifests through traditional cultural wisdom. Kim is interested in building networks, especially among people who rely on natural bodies of water, whether for sustenance or more generally. Aside from her solo academic research, she manages the construction of ecologically friendly cities across Korea. Kim has lived in eight different cities over 10 years. Whenever she moves to a new city, her way of adapting is to jog. In fact, she completed a half-marathon and is currently training for a full marathon. In her free time, she enjoys surfing and free diving. One day, she hopes to apply the Lo—TEK lens to Korean traditional knowledge and contribute to passing down its invaluable legacies.

Itamar Lilienthal

Lilienthal is an interdisciplinary artist, architect, and biodesigner based between the borderlands of Southern California and northern Baja California in Mexico, also known as Las Californias. He was born in Mexico City and migrated to San Diego at an early age. He has a BFA in studio art from New York University and an MArch in Bio-Integrated Design from the Bartlett School of Architecture, University College London. He currently leads Casa Tamarindo, a vernacular research and design house that focuses on developing novel methods for combining bioclimatic and vernacular architecture with advanced fabrication and computational design tools. His research and obsession with *yakhchāls* began several years ago when researching passive, sustainable refrigeration solutions for hot, arid regions.

Despina Linaraki

Linaraki is a Greek-Australian architect, engineer, and researcher. She was born and raised on the Greek island of Crete, then later moved to New York to complete her master's in Advanced Architectural Design from Columbia

University. She currently works as a lecturer in Architecture, Design, and Technology on the Gold Coast in Australia, where she is completing her PhD dissertation, "Growing Living Islands, An Architectural Design Framework for the Growth of Living Islands in Atoll Environments." Her research, inspired by the concept of living architecture, explores methods to expand land in the water by incorporating corals as fundamental elements in the design of underwater structures, which stems from her upbringing on an island.

Luiza Marguerite Leiser Livingston

Livingston is a Brazilian-American designer and researcher born in São Paulo, focused on urban and landscape architecture. Growing up, she had the opportunity to experience life in many places due to her parents' work, including Brazil, Lebanon, Guatemala, and the United States, though she now lives in Italy and is pursuing a master's at the Politecnico di Milano. Livingston received a dual bachelor's degree from Parsons School of Design and the New School in Sustainable Cities (BFA) and Global Studies (BA), during which she lived in Copenhagen on exchange at arki_lab. Given the first Lo—TEK book by her father, Livingston became fascinated with it and referenced it in various projects.

Ayu Tri Prestasia

Prestasia is a landscape architect and researcher born and raised in Central Java; she now resides in Yogyakarta. After several years working as an architect in Bali, she moved to the Netherlands to study at TU Delft, where her thesis project was exhibited at the 11th Barcelona International Biennial of Landscape Architecture, in 2020, and in BK Africa: A Laboratory of the Future? in 2023. Her interest in traditional water systems led her to join the Circular Water Stories Lab at TU Delft, where she published articles about Kampung Naga, Indonesia. She is a landscape architect partner at DEKONA Studio and a research fellow at the Resilience Development Initiatives in Indonesia, where many traditional knowledge systems are in danger amid rapid development.

Brandon Denina Pundamiera

Pundamiera, originally from Las Vegas, Nevada, and raised in Carson, California, comes from a Filipino family whose roots trace back to the Philippines; his grandparents immigrated to the United States in 1963. Currently residing in Berkeley, CA, he is pursuing a master's degrees in landscape architecture and city planning at the University of California, Berkeley. Pundamiera is a first-generation college graduate: he graduated with a bachelor's in society and environment and ecosystem management and forestry, with a minor in sustainable design from University of California, Berkeley in 2020. Pundamiera's involvement with the *atob* fish weirs of the Visayans, Philippines chapter began as a personal journey to explore his Filipino-American identity, motivated by a desire to uncover his family's cultural heritage.

Sophia Swedback

Swedback is a designer and researcher from Southern California. As a Regents' and Chancellor's scholar, she attended UC Berkeley, where she received a bachelor's in landscape architecture and the history of the built environment in 2021. Upon graduating, she was awarded the university's Geraldine Knight Scott Traveling Fellowship to conduct research on the ongoing legacies of ecological disruption around the Aral and Salton Seas. She has worked at SFMOMA, ONE Lab, and Mariam Issoufou Architects. Her family is from Dushanbe, Tajikistan, and Fargo, North Dakota.

Graphic Design, Art Direction	Piera Wolf, W—E studio Stephanie Specht, Specht Studio
Illustrations	Lina Müller Illustration
Illustration Design	Julia Watson and Lina Müller Illustration
Copyeditor	Danielle N. Carter
Typesetting	Ina Halbfas
Editorial Coordination	Nora Dohrmann
Production	Rossella Castello
Project Assistants	Luiza Marguerite Leiser Livingston Sophia Swedback
Research Collaborators	Amaya (Mona) Abraham, Hala Abukhodair, Naeema Ali, Amina Chouairi, Jennah Jones, Boomi Kim, Itamar Lilienthal, Despina Linaraki, Luiza Marguerite Leiser Livingston, Ayu Tri Prestasia, Brandon Denina Pundamiera, Pilar Rivera, Nic Speed, Sophia Swedback, Natalia Trujillo, Avantika Velho, Clara Waldheim, Patricia Watson
Coauthors and Collaborators	Tasnime El Arbi, Manimala Chanu Asem, Gideon Bouro and Tsatsa Seimarlie, Joachim Cabral, Rodrigo Alberto Lañado Cruz and Pedro Mendez Rosas, Margie Francisco, Kinohi Fukumitsu and Hi'ilei Kawelo, Thomas Ganang and Aloysius Guchbuw, Hakim Issaouï, Shri Rupesh Kumar K, Dorothy Peggy Lubin-Lévy, Venant Messe and Joseph Johnson Bibi, Mohamed Ouessar, Mohammed Rezwan, Khaing Khaing Soe, Ucu Suherlan, Omar Wanas, Ian Wood, Michele Zanetti, Cynthia Neri Zayas
Symbiocene Collaborators	Azam Alwash, Fergus Anderson, Joshua Apperly, Jassim al-Asadi, Peter Bateman, Paul Eastell, Morningstar Khongthaw, Daniel Knott, Randolph Langstein, J. Steven Langstein, Despina Linaraki, Ferdinand Ludwig, Aparajita Majumdar, Edmund Metters, Wilfred Middleton, Mark Mollé, Rachel Monteith, Smith Mordak, Sally Pickard, Matthew Vaughan-Shaw, Kitty Walker, Julia Watson, Natasha Watson, Ir. I Wayan Alit Artha Wiguna, *Indigenous Academic Advisers from the Enrich Hub:* Keolu Fox (UCSD), Māui Hudson (Waikato), Jane Anderson (NYU), *Video Editors from the War Khasi Community:* Mukul Bhandori, Mewarshwa Nongrum, Morningstar Khongthaw, Chester Khongloh
Project Collaborators	Anand Malligavad, African Union, Biocultural Design and Limahuli Valley Garden and Preserve, Carles Enrich Studio, Cecilia Jimenez and Teresa Montoya (Centro de Investigación de la Arquitectura y la Ciudad, Pontificia Universidad Católica del Perú), Emerging Objects, Green Futures Lab (University of Washington), Heritage Foundation of Pakistan, LANDPROCESS, Lomani Gau Network, MacPherson Engineering and Star Blanket Cree Nation, Dr. Muhammad Arslan, Nature Iraq, Sanne Dijkstra, Shidhulai Swanirvar Sangstha, Shinnecock Kelp Farmers, Studio Kathryn Larsen, Swinomish Indian Tribal Community, Turenscape
Typefaces	Repro and Repro Mono by Dinamo Martina Plantijn by Klim Type Foundry
Printed in	Italy
ISBN	978-3-8365-9444-8
	EACH AND EVERY TASCHEN BOOK PLANTS A SEED! Each year, we offset our annual carbon emissions with carbon credits at the Instituto Terra, a reforestation program in Minas Gerais, Brazil, founded by Lélia and Sebastião Salgado. To find out more about this ecological partnership, please check: www.taschen.com/institutoterra. Inspiration: unlimited. Carbon footprint: (almost) zero.
	Want to see more? Visit taschen.com to view our current publications, browse our latest magazine, and subscribe to our newsletter.
	I'd like to acknowledge that I'm writing this book from the traditional land of the first people of Brooklyn, New York—the Lenape people past and present—and honor them and the land with gratitude.
	Lo—TEK, Water is supported by Independent Projects, a partnership program of the New York State Council on the Arts and the Architectural League of New York. Independent Projects grants are made possible with public funds from the New York State Council on the Arts, with the support of the Office of the Governor and the New York State legislature

JULIA WATSON

Landscape Designer, award-winning educator, and best-selling author, Julia Watson is a leading expert on Indigenous, nature-based technologies for climate-resilient design. Watson has traveled the earth over to understand these technologies and respectfully share the messages of their makers with the world. She grew up in Australia, where aboriginal science and knowledge is not only acknowledged in the school system but systematically integrated into university curricula. She is thus driven to steer other nations towards properly respecting and integrating Indigenous knowledge into the "mainstream."

In 2008, Watson graduated from Harvard's Landscape Architecture program with the most distinguished prize of the program, the Charles Eliot Fellowship, a nomination for the national Olmsted Award, and an American Institute of Landscape Architecture Design Honors Award. With an unconventional approach to the field, inspired by pilgrimages to sacred sites like Mt. Kailash and Machu Picchu, she spent the next 12 years traveling and teaching as a professor of architecture, landscape, urban design, and ecotechnology at Harvard, Columbia, Rhode Island School of Design, and Rensselaer. In publishing her first book with TASCHEN in 2019, titled *Lo—TEK, Design by Radical Indigenism*, Watson coined a new term and a design movement, which looks to the past to envision an inclusive planetary future.

Watson's groundbreaking work has been featured in *The New York Times, The Guardian, Monocle, Emirates Magazine, The Financial Times, Architectural Digest, Dezeen, VICE, Wallpaper*, Purple magazine, the BBC, CNN, DER SPIEGEL, Vogue, El País, Dazed Magazine, Politiken, The Washington Post*, and many more publications. She has published work in journals such as *DOMUS, Venice Architecture Biennale 2025 Catalogue, Topos Magazine, and the Indigenous Peoples and Climate Technologies Guidebook* by the International Work Group for Indigenous Affairs.

Watson is a Long Now and a TED speaker; she has held fellowships with Summit REALITY and Pop!tech, and she was a Disruptive By Design Ambassador for *WIRED*; she has received a Christensen Fund grant for her conservation work, and she has won an Arnold W. Brunner award for Architectural Research and two New York State Council of the Arts Architecture + Design awards. *Wallpaper** named her as one of the people defining creative America in 2023 and 2024, she is the 2024 recipient of the Institute of Classical Architecture and Art's Arthur Ross Award for lifetime achievement in education and the 2025 recipient of the American Institute of Landscape Architects New York Chapter's President's Award for Climate Advocacy.

Watson co-leads the Lo—TEK Office for Intercultural Urbanism, with Indigenous and non-Indigenous designers and scientists. Together, they approach urbanism through a lens of reciprocity, drawing on ancestral knowledge systems to envision culturally rooted, climate-resilient futures. The Office is supported by an Advisory Circle of knowledge holders, allies, and cultural guides. Watson also co-leads the Lo—TEK Institute to champion generational wisdom through Living Earth, a curriculum and digital database which embeds traditional ecological knowledge within STEM learning. She is on the advisory board of the Eden in Iraq Wastewater Treatment Garden in the Mesopotamia Marshes, the Advisory Cirlce of ISPAD's PILAT Project, and for the Futures Reframed Foundation.